Standard

LESSON COMMENTARY®

2006–2007

edited by

RONALD L. NICKELSON

published by
Standard Publishing

Jonathan Underwood, Senior Editor

Mark A. Taylor,
Director of Church Resources

Thirteenth Annual Volume

Standard®

PUBLISHING

Bringing The Word to Life

Cincinnati, Ohio

CD-ROM AVAILABLE

The *Standard Lesson Commentary*® is available separately in an electronic format. This compact disk contains the full text of the King James *Standard Lesson Commentary*® and *The NIV Standard Lesson Commentary*®, a variety of preparation resources powered by the Libronix Digital Library System, and a collection of presentation helps that can be projected or reproduced as handouts. Ask for the *Standard Lesson eCommentary* (#06007) at your local Christian bookstore or directly from Standard Publishing.

System Requirements: Windows XP/2000/ME/98/95; Pentium 133 MHz processor (300MHz recommended), 64 Meg RAM (128 recommended); 60 Meg Available Hard Drive Space; 2x or better CD-ROM drive.

If you have any questions regarding the installation, registration, or activation of this CD-ROM, please contact Logos **Customer Service** at **(800) 875-6467.**

If you have problems with the CD, *Technical Support* is available by telephone at *(360) 679-4496,* by e-mail at *tech@logos.com,* or online at *www.logos.com/support.*

Lessons based on International Sunday School Lessons. © 2004 by the Lesson Committee.
Used by permission of the Lesson Committee.
Cover design by DesignTeam.

© 2006
STANDARD PUBLISHING
a division of STANDEX INTERNATIONAL Corporation
8121 Hamilton Avenue, Cincinnati, Ohio 45231
Printed in U.S.A.

In This Volume

Fall Quarter 2006
God's Living Covenant
Writers

Lesson Development.................................Lloyd Pelfrey (1-4), Mark Krause (5-9), Doug Redford (10-13)
Verbal Illustrations ....Charles Boatman
Discovery Learning and Reproducible Activities.......................Ronald G. Davis (1-9), Alan Weber (10-13)
What Do You Think?..........................A. Eugene Andrews (1-4), Mark Moore (5-9), David Marvin (10-13)
Why Teach This Lesson?..Vicki Edwards

Winter Quarter 2006-2007
Jesus Christ: A Portrait of God
Writers

Lesson Development ....Mark Krause (1-5), Tom Thatcher (6-13)
Verbal Illustrations ....James B. North
Discovery Learning and Reproducible Activities.........................Alan Weber (1-5), Ronald G. Davis (6-9),
....Richard A. Koffarnus (10-13)
What Do You Think?...Ken Beck (1-5), Jeff Snell (6-9), Ken Beck (10-13)
Why Teach This Lesson?..Joseph Parker (1-5), A. Eugene Andrews (6-13)

Spring Quarter 2007
Our Community Now and in God's Future
Writers

Lesson Development.................................Kenny Boles (1-4), Mark Krause (5-9), James A. Smith (10-13)
Verbal Illustrations ....Charles Boatman
Discovery Learning and Reproducible Activities...........Ronald G. Davis (1-4), Richard A. Koffarnus (5-13)
What Do You Think?..............................Ted Simonson (1, 2), Vicki Edwards (3, 4), Kenneth Goble (5-9),
....A. Eugene Andrews (10-13)
Why Teach This Lesson?..Alan Weber (1-4); A. Eugene Andrews (5-13)

Summer Quarter 2007
Committed to Doing Right
Writers

Lesson Development..........................J. Michael Shannon (1, 2), Lee M. Fields (3, 4), Mark Krause (5-9),
....Lloyd Pelfrey (10, 11), Doug Redford (12, 13)
Verbal Illustrations ....James B. North (1-9), A. Eugene Andrews (10-13)
Discovery Learning and Reproducible Activities...........Ronald G. Davis (1-4), Richard A. Koffarnus (5-13)
What Do You Think? ....A. Eugene Andrews (1-4), Kenneth Goble (5-9), A. Eugene Andrews (10-13)
Why Teach This Lesson? ....Joseph Parker (1-4); A. Eugene Andrews (5-9); David Marvin (10-13)

Index of Printed Texts, 2006–2007

The printed texts for 2006-2007 are arranged here in the order in which they appear in the Bible. Opposite each reference is the page number on which the lesson that treats the passage begins in this volume.

Cumulative Index of Printed Texts

A cumulative index for the Scripture passages used in *The NIV Standard Lesson Commentary*® for September 2004–August 2007 is presented here for your convenience.

How to Say It

The following pages list some of the names and other hard-to-pronounce words used in the lessons of this edition of *The NIV Standard Lesson Commentary*® along with a phonetic pronunciation guide for each. In each lesson is an abridged version of this list that includes only the words used in that lesson.

Abiathar. Ah-BYE-uh-thar.
Abinoam. Uh-BIN-o-am.
ad hominem. add HAH-muh-nem.
Adonijah. Ad-o-NYE-juh.
Ai. AY-eye.
Amalekites. AM-uh-leh-kites or Uh-MAL-ih-kites.
Amorites. AM-uh-rites.
Apocalypse. Ah-POCK-uh-lips.
Arc de Triomphe. Ark du treh-ONF.
Arianism. AIR-ee-uh-nih-zim.
Arimathea. AIR-uh-muh-*THEE*-uh.
Artaxerxes. Are-tuh-ZERK-seez.
Asherah. Uh-SHE-ruh.
Ashkelon. ASH-ke-lon or AS-ke-lon.
Ashtoreths. ASH-toe-reths.

Baalim. BAY-uh-leem.
Babel. BAY-bul.
Bedouin. BED-uh-wun.
Berechiah. Bair-uh-KYE-uh.
Beth-aven. BETH-*AY*-ven.
Bethphage. BETH-fuh-gee.
Boanerges. BO-uh-*NUR*-geez.
Byzantine. BIH-zen-teen.

Caesar Augustus. SEE-zer Aw-GUS-tus.
Caiaphas. KAY-uh-fus or KYE-uh-fus.
Capernaum. Kuh-PER-nay-um.
Caphtor. KAF-tor.
carnelian. kar-NEEL-yun.
Chaldeans. Kal-DEE-unz.
Chios. KI-ahs (I as in EYE).
Cicero. SIH-suh-row.
Constantinople. KAHN-stan-ten-oh-puhl.
Cornelius. Cor-NEEL-yus.

Dagon. DAY-gon.
Darius Hystaspes. Duh-RYE-us Hiss-TAS-pus.
Docetism. Doe-SET-iz-um.
Domitian. Duh-MISH-un.

Ebal. EE-bull.
Ebenezer. EB-en-EE-zer.

Epaphroditus. Ee-PAF-ro-*DYE*-tus.
Esdraelon. ES-druh-*EE*-lon.

Gerizim. GAIR-ih-zeem or Guh-RYE-zim.
Gibeon. GIB-e-un
gnosticism. *NAHSS*-tih-SIZZ-um

Hades. HAY-deez.
Hagia Sophia. HAG-ee-uh So-FEE-uh.
Harosheth. Huh-ROE-sheth.
Hernando de Soto. Er-NAN-do da SO-tow.
Hezekiah. Hez-ih-KYE-uh.
Hilkiah. Hill-KYE-uh.
Huldah. HUL-duh.

Ishmael. ISH-may-el.
Issachar. IZZ-uh-kar.
Istanbul. IS-tun-bull.

Jael. JAY-ul.
Jedidiah. Jed-ih-DIE-uh.
Jehoahaz. Jeh-HO-uh-haz.
Jehoiachin. Jeh-HOY-uh-kin.
Jehoiakim. Jeh-HOY-uh-kim.
Jeroboam. Jair-uh-BOE-um.
Jochebed. JOCK-eh-bed.
Jotham. JO-thum.

Kedesh. KEE-desh.
Kerith. KEY-rith.
Keturah. Keh-TOO-ruh.
koinonia (Greek). koy-no-NEE-uh.
Krzyzewski. Sha-SHEF-ski.

Laban. LAY-bun.
Laodicea. Lay-ODD-uh-*SEE*-uh.
Lappidoth. LAP-pih-doth.
logos (Greek). LAW-goss.

Maccabees. MACK-uh-bees.
Macedonia. Mass-eh-DOE-nee-uh.
Machir. MAY-ker.
Manasseh. Muh-NASS-uh.
Marduk. MAR-duke.
Micaiah. My-KAY-uh.

Naphtali. NAF-tuh-lye.
Nebuchadnezzar. NEB-yuh-kud-*NEZ*-er
Nineveh. NIN-uh-vuh.
Nisan. NYE-san.

Origen. OR-uh-jen.

Padan-aram. PAY-dan-A-ram.
Patmos. PAT-muss.
Pentateuch. PEN-ta-teuk.
Plato. PLAY-tow.
propitiation. pro-PIH-she-*AY*-shun
Punic. PYU-nik.

Rabbinic. ruh-BIN-ik.
Rabboni. Rab-O-nye.
Rehoboam. Ree-huh-BOE-um.
Rephidim. REF-ih-dim.

Septuagint. Sep-TOO-ih-jent.
seraph. SAIR-uhf.
seraphim. SAIR-uh-fim.
shalom (Hebrew). shah-LOME.
Shaphan. SHAY-fan.
Shechem. SHEE-kem or SHEK-em.
sheol. SHE-ol.
Siloam. SIGH-LO-um.
Sisera. SIS-er-uh.

Tekoa. Tih-KO-uh.
Theophanos (Greek). The-AH-fan-us.
Timnath Heres. TIM-nath *HEE*-reez.
tsunami. sue-NAH-me.

Uriah. Yu-RYE-uh.
Uzziah. Uh-ZYE-uh.

Wittenberg. WIH-ten-berg or VIH-ten-berk.

Zacchaeus. Zack-KEY-us.
Zadok. ZAY-dok.
Zarephath. ZAIR-uh-fath.
Zedekiah. Zed-uh-KYE-uh.
Zerubbabel. Zeh-RUB-uh-bul.
Zipporah. Zi-PO-ruh.

Fall Quarter 2006

God's Living Covenant

Special Features

Lessons

About These Lessons

Marriage vows. Mortgages. Credit card agreements. We don't use the word *covenant* much in everyday speech, but covenants are all around us nonetheless. They are part of the very fabric of our lives. Nowhere is this more important than in the spiritual sense. Learning about God's covenants makes us more attuned to his will. May we be more pleasing to him as we do so.

Sep 3

Sep 10

Sep 17

Sep 24

Oct 1

Oct 8

Oct 15

Oct 22

Oct 29

Nov 5

Nov 12

Nov 19

Nov 26

Three Times Two!

In our 2004–2005 edition we noted that the six-year cycle of the past had become a three-year cycle. That change has now been enhanced: the six-year cycle is back, but it is divided into two three-year segments.

Each three-year segment features six themes: *Creation, Call, Covenant, Christ, Community,* and *Commitment.* You can see those themes reflected in the quarter titles below. This new arrangement means that each of the six themes will be covered four times in the course of the six-year cycle. But each of the four treatments is distinctive. The studies draw on different texts; each study stands on its own.

May these changes serve to lift our eyes ever upward to Jesus. To him be the glory forever.
—R. L. N.

International Sunday School Lesson Cycle
September 2004—August 2010

YEAR	FALL QUARTER (Sept., Oct., Nov.)	WINTER QUARTER (Dec., Jan., Feb.)	SPRING QUARTER (Mar., Apr., May)	SUMMER QUARTER (June, July, Aug.)
2004-2005	The God of Continuing Creation (Bible Survey)	Called to Be God's People (Bible Survey)	God's Project: Effective Christians (Romans, Galatians)	Jesus' Life, Ministry, and Teaching (Matthew, Mark, Luke)
2005-2006	"You Will Be My Witnesses" (Acts)	God's Commitment— Our Response (Isaiah; 1 & 2 Timothy)	Living in and as God's Creation (Psalms, Job, Ecclesiastes, Proverbs)	Called to Be a Christian Community (1 & 2 Corinthians)
2006-2007	God's Living Covenant (Old Testamant Survey)	Jesus Christ: A Portrait of God (John, Philippians, Colossians, Hebrews, 1 John)	Our Community Now and in God's Future (1 John, Revelation)	Committed to Doing Right (Various Prophets, 2 Kings, 2 Chronicles)
2007-2008	Creation (Genesis)	God's Call to the Christian Community (Luke)	God, the People, and the Covenant (1 & 2 Chronicles, Daniel, Haggai, Nehemiah)	Images of Christ (Hebrews, Gospels)
2008-2009	The New Testament Community (New Testament Survey)	Human Commitment (Old Testament; Luke)	New Creation in Christ (Ezekiel, Luke, Acts, Ephesians)	Call Sealed with Promise (Exodus, Leviticus, Numbers, Deuteronomy)
2009-2010	Covenant Communities (Joshua, Judges, Ezra, Nehemiah, Mark, 1 & 2 Peter)	Christ the Fulfillment (Matthew)	Teachings on Community (Johannine, Ruth, New Testament)	Christian Commitment in Today's World (1 & 2 Thessalonians, Philippians)

| "Creation" | "Call" | "Covenant" | "Christ" | "Community" | "Commitment" |

A Living, Loving Covenant

by Douglas Redford

Many are familiar with the concept of a "living will." This is a document in which a person can stipulate that no extraordinary measures are to be used to prolong his or her life in the event of a terminal illness. Although the lessons for the upcoming quarter develop the theme of "God's Living Covenant," we can pause to consider how different the definition of God's living covenant is from that of a living will.

With his living covenant God chooses to take extraordinary measures in revealing his will to individuals. Instead of avoiding the prolonging of life as a living will potentially does, God's desire is that all humanity experience the fullness of life and blessing. The problem God seeks to address is the terminal spiritual illness that no human remedy can cope with: sin.

The lessons we will study this quarter provide a survey of the Old Testament. A primary focus is on how God used both individuals and groups in the unfolding of his covenant program.

Unit 1: God's Covenant with the Patriarchs

September

Lesson 1 and *Lesson 2* of this unit call attention to God's special relationship with two men: Noah and Abraham. Both were commanded by God to do something that seemed utterly absurd at the time. Noah was instructed to build an ark in preparation for a coming flood (in an area that was predominantly dry); Abraham was commanded to leave his homeland for a place with an address known only to God.

Both men obeyed the Lord. As a result, they received very special promises from God. To Noah God promised that he would never again destroy the earth by means of flood. Abraham was informed that he and his wife Sarah would become proud parents in spite of their advanced age. The experiences of Noah and Abraham illustrate a key principle: the blessings of a covenant relationship with God come only to those who are willing to obey him, even when his directives appear to defy human logic.

Lesson 3 deals with a very special covenant of God. This one concerns not an individual but an entire nation: Old Testament Israel, which became his "treasured possession" (Exodus 19:5). What a sacred privilege and responsibility!

The people apparently understood God's expectations of them when they responded to Moses at Sinai, "Everything the Lord has said we will do" (Exodus 24:3). The people said much the same thing to Joshua during a time of covenant renewal (Joshua 24:24). That occasion of renewal at Shechem is the focus of *Lesson 4.*

Unit 2: God's Covenant with Judges and Kings

October

Sadly, the book of Judges portrays the abject failure of God's people to live up to the good intentions that they had voiced at the close of the book of Joshua. *Lesson 5* describes what might be termed the *sui-cycle* (playing on the word *suicide*) that characterized their behavior during this distressing segment of Old Testament history.

The cycle could be labeled in the following alliterative manner: Sin, Slavery (to foreign peoples whom God raised up to oppress his people), Supplication (crying out to God to "supply" help), and *Salvation* (deliverance through judges such as Deborah, who is the subject of *Lesson 6*). The period of the judges illustrates a sobering truth: the greatest threat to the Israelites was not to be found in any outside threat. Rather, it was they who were their own worst enemies!

Lesson 7 highlights the ministry of Samuel. He served as a kind of transition figure as Israel moved from life under judges to life under kings.

Among Samuel's many roles was that of intercessor, praying for God's people in times of crisis (1 Samuel 12:23). Intercessory prayer remains one of the most meaningful privileges of God's people. Whenever someone says to us, "Pray for me," we may agree rather flippantly to do so without really intending to follow through on our promise. In reality we should consider such a request a sacred trust.

The theme of *Lesson 8* is God's covenant with David, as described in 2 Samuel 7. This chapter begins with David expressing his concern that the ark of the covenant be placed in more suitable surroundings; thus he desired to build an appropriate house for the ark.

God's response to David was, in effect, "No, David, let *me* build a house for *you*. I can build a much better house for you than you could ever build for me." God proceeded to give David this promise: "Your house and your kingdom will endure forever before me" (2 Samuel 7:16). It is a stunning promise indeed, with messianic foreshadowings.

Lesson 9, the final lesson in this second unit, covers Solomon's request to God for wisdom. Solomon asked for this so that as king of Israel he might carry out the Lord's desires as faithfully as did David, his father. For Christians the passion for living by God's wisdom should lead us to further devotion to the one "greater than Solomon" (Matthew 12:42), "in whom are hidden all the treasures of wisdom and knowledge" (Colossians 2:3). That wisdom is still "supreme" (Proverbs 4:7). It can provide reliable counsel for anyone, whether king or commoner.

NOVEMBER

UNIT 3: LIVING UNDER GOD'S COVENANT

This section of our study confronts us with the sobering reminder that living under God's covenant is not just a matter of receiving blessing after blessing. Rather, his covenant also makes certain requirements of those who receive these blessings. He calls these recipients to account if they fail to live up to those requirements.

Lesson 10 draws our attention to the contest on Mount Carmel between Elijah and the prophets of Baal. The Lord's victory there came at a time when Baal worship had made serious inroads into the northern kingdom of Israel, thanks mostly to the aggressive and ruthless efforts of Jezebel.

Elijah's construction of an altar made of 12 stones reflected his conviction that the covenant God—the God of all of Israel's 12 divided tribes—was still on his throne. This was true despite Jezebel's best efforts to remove him.

Lesson 11 examines one of Judah's most godly kings, namely Josiah. This lesson calls special attention to Josiah's leadership in spearheading a ceremony of covenant renewal, climaxed by a celebration of the Passover.

How such leadership is needed in today's world, both in the church and in society! The presence of godly kings such as Josiah in Judah's history is a primary reason why Judah lasted approximately 130 years longer than did the northern kingdom, Israel. Those ten tribes had no kings who were considered godly.

Lesson 12 covers the tragic, bitter consequences of refusing to honor the Lord and keep his covenant. One of the printed texts for this lesson, Psalm 137:1-6, captures quite vividly the anguish of a people who longed to be back home in their beloved city of Jerusalem. Yet they had no one to blame for their plight of exile except themselves. God had tried time and time again to get their attention by means of his prophets, but they had stubbornly rejected these messengers' pleas (2 Chronicles 36:15, 16).

Nebuchadnezzar, king of the Babylonians, led the onslaught against God's city and temple. But the Scriptures make it quite clear that he did not act alone. God "brought up against them" the Babylonians or Chaldeans (2 Chronicles 36:17); Nebuchadnezzar was simply his tool.

Thankfully, our studies do not end with the somber message of Lesson 12. *Lesson 13* concludes the quarter with a study entitled, "God Offers Return and Restoration."

Just as God had used one foreign ruler to punish his people, he used another foreign ruler to issue the decree that allowed them to go back to Judah. The God of the living covenant has never been limited by any earthly ruler in fulfilling the promises of his covenants. In the New Testament, this is illustrated in the way God used the decree of Caesar Augustus to bring Joseph and Mary to Bethlehem so that Jesus could be born there in fulfillment of prophecy (Micah 5:2).

OUR FAITHFUL GOD

Throughout the course of this Old Testament survey, we see God as faithful and committed to keeping his side of the covenants. He is just as faithful to those who live under his new covenant today in Jesus Christ.

Yet the competition for our allegiance is fierce! We know all too well of the constant and intense pressures to listen to other voices beside the Lord's. Thus Joshua's challenge uttered at Shechem rings across the centuries to confront us in our time: "Choose for yourselves this day whom you will serve. . . . But as for me and my household, we will serve the Lord" (Joshua 24:15).

Lesson Planning Page

List the aims here, either directly from the lesson or revised to suit your individual needs.

LESSON AIMS

Begin with an opening activity like the illustration from the beginning of the lesson, "Into the Lesson" from the Discovery Learning page, a discussion question, or some other appropriate opener.

GETTING STARTED

LESSON DEVELOPMENT

List in order the activities you will use. These include discussion questions, activities from the discovery learning page and the reproducible page—as well as key points from the commentary section.

    I.

    II.

    III.

How will you bring the lesson to a climax, stressing the key point and desired action steps?

CONCLUSION & APPLICATION

Dismiss the class with an activity that reinforces the Bible lesson.

CLOSING ACTIVITY

Mt. Carmel •

Haroush •

Kishon River

Mt. Tabor •

Yarmuk River

Mt. Ararat •

Jerusalem •
• Babylon
• SINAI
EGYPT

Jordan River

• Shechem

Jabbok River

Bethel •

Mizpeh •
• Ramah

Jerusalem •

Bethlehem •

DEAD SEA

OLD TESTAMENT WORLD

Judges of Israel

Judge	Major Oppressor	Years as Judge
Othniel (Judges 3:8-11)	Mesopotamia (Cushan-Rishathaim)	1373–1334 B.C.
Ehud (Judges 3:12-30)	Moabites (Eglon)	1319–1239 B.C.
Shamgar (Judges 3:31)	Philistines	1300 B.C.
Deborah (Judges 4, 5)	Canaanites (Jabin)	1239–1199 B.C.
Gideon (Judges 6-8)	Midianites	1192–1152 B.C.
Abimelech (Judges 9)	Period of Civil War	1152–1150 B.C.
Tola (Judges10:1, 2)	Ammonites	1149–1126 B.C.
Jair (Judges 10:3-5)	Ammonites	1126–1104 B.C.
Jephthah (Judges 10:6-12:7)	Ammonites	1086–1080 B.C.
Ibzan (Judges 12:8-10)	Philistines	1080–1075 B.C.
Elon (Judges 12:11, 12)	Philistines	1075–1065 B.C.
Abdon (Judges 12:13-15)	Philistines	1065–1058 B.C.
Samson (Judges 13-16)	Philistines	1075–1055 B.C.
Eli (1 Samuel 1-4)	Philistines	1107–1067 B.C.
Samuel (1 Samuel 7-9)	Philistines	1067–1043 B.C.

GOD'S COVENANT WITH NOAH

LESSON 1

WHY TEACH THIS LESSON?

Is the glass half empty or half full? It's the classic question to determine if one tends to focus on the negative or the positive. After the cleansing of planet Earth by a flood, it would have been very easy for Noah's clan to focus on the loss.

It's true that God, grieving the immense evil of humanity, destroyed the world. But that's not all he did. He also preserved a remnant of his original creation. Stop to think about that original creation. With less than a week's work, a mere six days, he created the universe. That means that after the great flood he could have created everything all over again. Undoubtedly, he could have retooled people to be less trouble-prone. But a key character trait of our God is love . . . and love, he tells us, never gives up.

Today's lesson focuses on a new chapter in God's relationship with us—a new start, complete with fresh commands and a fresh promise sealed with a celestial sign. Today, God promises each willing person a new beginning. This promise is sealed with the blood of Jesus.

INTRODUCTION

A. "THE GOOD OF THE PEOPLE"

In about 360 BC the Greek philosopher Plato wrote, "Mankind must have laws and conform to them, or their life would be as bad as that of the most savage beast." This is simply another way of saying that laws are necessary for each person to know the mutual obligations that are expected in any social group.

Observing those expectations will ordinarily promote the general welfare of both the individual and the group. The Roman statesman and orator Cicero (106–43 BC) said, "The safety of the people shall be the highest law." The popular version of his statement is, "The good of the people is the highest law."

We humans seem to be in a constant state of give-and-take with our laws. The year 1957 saw the governor of the U.S. state of Arkansas defy a 1954 U.S. Supreme Court ruling concerning racial integration in schools. He used the Arkansas National Guard to prevent the ruling from taking effect in Little Rock, the state capital. President Eisenhower responded by federalizing the National Guard and sending a unit of the U.S. Army to Little Rock. The ruling of the court was enforced.

The fall of that same year saw the establishment of a new Bible college, and a social experiment was suggested. Would it be possible for the students in such an institution to function together with only the laws of the state and the Bible to guide them? The students expressed an eagerness to cooperate in such an endeavor. A plan to devise a complete set of rules by using student handbooks from other colleges thus was abandoned.

DEVOTIONAL READING:
PSALM 36:5-9
BACKGROUND SCRIPTURE:
GENESIS 9:1-17
PRINTED TEXT:
GENESIS 9:1-15

LESSON AIM

After participating in this lesson, each student will be able to:

1. Summarize the commands and promises that God gave to Noah immediately after the flood.

2. Explain the security that results from knowing God's expectations and promises.

3. Tell how he or she will use each observance of a rainbow as a reminder that God keeps his promises.

KEY VERSE

I establish my covenant with you: Never again will all life be cut off by the waters of a flood; never again will there be a flood to destroy the earth.

—Genesis 9:11

As time went on, however, rules were added as various liberties were abused. For example, a person could play a radio as loudly as desired, but that liberty would end where the ears of another were involved. This liberty had to be balanced with another person's right to quiet, especially if the hours for nighttime sleeping were involved! The list of rules slowly grew, and within a few years a handbook came into being.

People need to know what they should and should not do. Toddlers, for example, learn that parents have a favorite word: *No!* As children crawl, walk, or run, they must understand that there are boundaries and that there are consequences for bold adventures into prohibited areas. Children learn that the family's unwritten code of laws also increases. A child may have to tolerate the fact that older siblings have privileges that are not yet granted to those who are younger. Laws or rules—whether at the level of the government, Bible college, or family—are for the common good.

One frequent designation for the first five books of the Bible is "the Law." The main reason for this designation is that these books record the covenantal laws that the Lord put into place at various times. We have much to learn from God's Old Testament laws and covenants yet today.

B. LESSON BACKGROUND

The flood that occurred the year Noah was 600 had just ended. Noah, his family, and the animals emerged from the ark after spending many months within it.

The account of the flood is always fascinating to read. It is interesting that over 200 similar accounts have been found in legends around the world. These sagas have common threads of a god or gods who were displeased with humanity and thus destroyed just about everything except for one individual and his family. Over two-thirds of the stories indicate that animals also were saved. Over half of the stories have the vessel of safety landing on a mountain. There are many differences among the accounts, so the conclusion for the Christian is that the straightforward presentation as found in Genesis is the only one that is authentic.

The New Testament contains several references to the events of the great flood. Matthew 24:38, 39; Hebrews 11:7; 1 Peter 3:20; and 2 Peter 2:5; 3:6 confirm that Jesus and the inspired writers of the New Testament were confident that the flood was a historical event.

As the family of Noah departed from the ark, they found themselves alone in a world that had been cleansed. We can only wonder how the raging waters of the flood affected continents and climates, topography and temperatures. In his wisdom God does not reveal those things to us. Noah's first action upon leaving the ark was to offer sacrifices of the clean animals and birds (Genesis 8:20). As the aroma arose, the Lord spoke first to himself about the earth—its daily and annual cycles. He then spoke the words that are the printed text for today's lesson.

The word *covenant* is a very important word in God's expression of his will for humanity in every age. That word occurs nearly 300 times in the Bible. It is a vital part of today's lesson, "God's Covenant with Noah."

I. GOD'S COMMAND (GENESIS 9:1-7)

Noah needs assurance about the things that the Lord desires for him, his three sons, and the wives of each man. Their experiences convince them that God keeps his word and that he punishes sin. But they also need to know of the blessings that await them.

DAILY BIBLE READINGS

Monday, Aug. 28—God Is Gracious (Psalm 36:5-9)

Tuesday, Aug. 29—Noah Enters the Ark (Genesis 7:1-12)

Wednesday, Aug. 30—The Flood Rages (Genesis 7:13-24)

Thursday, Aug. 31—The Water Subsides (Genesis 8:1-12)

Friday, Sept. 1—God Makes a Promise (Genesis 8:13-22)

Saturday, Sept. 2—God Instructs Noah (Genesis 9:1-7)

Sunday, Sept. 3—God Covenants with Noah (Genesis 9:8-17)

VISUALS FOR THESE LESSONS

The visual pictured in each lesson (example: page 22) is a small reproduction of a large, full-color poster included in the Adult Resources packet for the Fall Quarter. The packet is available from your supplier. Order No. 192.

A. PROCREATION PRESCRIBED (v. 1)

1. Then God blessed Noah and his sons, saying to them, "Be fruitful and increase in number and fill the earth.

The phrase *God blessed Noah and his sons* means that God is granting the abilities for them to enjoy prosperity in the areas of life that are important. They will be successful in their endeavors. This assurance provides a confidence that they need in their changed situations. God had made a similar pronouncement at the creation of humans (Genesis 1:28). In that case the ensuing prosperity led to humanity's detriment as people used God's blessings to focus on evil (Genesis 6:5).

God sets forth his plan with three terse imperatives: *be fruitful and increase in number and fill the earth.* The last command notes that it is the earth that is to be filled. The ancients correctly viewed this command as God's authorization of marriage. That naturally involves a man and a woman.

Obeying the command to multiply is not considered an ideal in certain nations today. Children often are viewed as expensive (and they are!) and as interfering in the quest for life at its fullest. The gift of procreation with which God endowed humanity has deteriorated in many cases into a selfish, sensual sexuality. Many seek ever more perverse ways to find elusive fulfillment. But disobedience to God will result in emptiness.

B. PROTECTION PROMISED (v. 2)

2. "The fear and dread of you will fall upon all the beasts of the earth and all the birds of the air, upon every creature that moves along the ground, and upon all the fish of the sea; they are given into your hands.

The statement that animals of all types will *fear* or *dread* humans introduces a new concept. It produces speculation that the eight people in the ark originally experience fright as they watch the animals leave (perhaps from the size or appearance of some of the animals), but that fright is now on the part of the animals. All we can do is wonder if this indicates a change from the past.

The promise by God that the animals will fear humans is a general principle. It is normally true that wild animals do whatever they can to avoid humans, but we all know about the exceptions. The exceptions ordinarily have to do with the self-preservation instincts that God placed within the animals. In normal circumstances most animals run from encounters with us.

C. PROVISIONS CONCERNING FOOD (vv. 3, 4)

3. "Everything that lives and moves will be food for you. Just as I gave you the green plants, I now give you everything.

Humanity receives permission to eat the flesh of animals. This becomes a new source of protein. Immediately after the initial creation, God said that he was giving *plants* and fruit as *food* for humanity and plants for the animals (Genesis 1:29, 30). We would like to know more about this situation in the years before the flood, but in his wisdom God does not reveal it to us.

The law of Moses, which is to be given at Mount Sinai, will modify the acceptability of food sources for the Israelites. They are to distinguish between clean and unclean animals that they can eat (see Leviticus 11).

That restriction, however, is for Old Testament Israel only. In the Christian age the distinction is removed entirely. A person may eat whatever he or she wishes (Mark 7:19; 1 Timothy 4:4). If, however, an individual chooses not to eat a specific type of food, he or she should not attempt to enforce that choice on others

WHAT DO YOU THINK?

With blessings come responsibilities! What are some of the responsibilities that you and your church have received because of the blessings available in Christ? How well are you living up to these?

WHAT DO YOU THINK?

"Into your hands" reflects the earlier part of Genesis, where God gave humanity dominion over the world. What are some ways this responsibility has been misused? How can we do better?

HOW TO SAY IT

Cicero. SIH-suh-row.

Deuteronomy. Due-ter-AHN-
uh-me.

Festus. FES-tus.

Galatians. Guh-LAY-shunz.

Gentiles. JEN-tiles.

Hebrews. HEE-brews.

Moses. MO-zes or MO-zez.

Plato. PLAY-tow.

tsunami. sue-NAH-me.

(Romans 14:2, 6). Also, our freedom to eat certain foods is restricted when the faith of others may be at stake (1 Corinthians 8).

4. "But you must not eat meat that has its lifeblood still in it.

The eating of meat does have a restriction: the blood of the animal is not to be consumed. Moses will repeat this restriction for the nation of Israel (see Leviticus 17:12-14). The same limitation is found in Acts 15:20, 29 among the restrictions that Gentile Christians are encouraged to observe. Many scholars see parallels between Genesis 9 and Acts 15.

D. PUNISHMENT FOR TAKING LIFE (vv. 5, 6)

5, 6. "And for your lifeblood I will surely demand an accounting. I will demand an accounting from every animal. And from each man, too, I will demand an accounting for the life of his fellow man.

> **"Whoever sheds the blood of man,**
>   **by man shall his blood be shed;**
> **for in the image of God**
>   **has God made man.**

Clearly, God views the taking of human life to be a very serious thing. The sanctity of *blood* as the life principle puts it into God's domain to render such a judgment. It also becomes evident that the taking of human life is much different from taking the life of an animal; in the previous verses God approved the latter as a means of obtaining food.

No one should interpret the dramatic loss of life in the great flood to mean that human life is cheap. God can choose to take human life in any manner he chooses, because he is the one who gives the breath of life to all in the first place. Anyone who deliberately and with malice aforethought takes the life of someone else must understand that there can and should be severe consequences from earthly tribunals. There also will be *an accounting* in the final judgment of God.

The reason for the equal retribution *Whoever sheds the blood of man, by man shall his blood be shed* is very specific: *for in the image of God has God made man.* Since each person is made in the image of God, no individual should endanger the lives of the innocent.

In verse 6 God authorizes governments and those who are in places of authority to exercise capital punishment for murder. Romans 13:4 states that the person in authority, "God's servant," bears a sword "to bring punishment on the wrongdoer." The individual who is authorized to use deadly force is sometimes called a peace officer, for he or she is to restore peace. When Paul stood before Festus, he recognized the authority of the court to impose the death penalty (Acts 25:11).

The Mosaic law demonstrates the mind of God in that he recognizes exceptions in applying the death penalty. While the Mosaic law is no longer binding (see Galatians 3:24, 25), it is helpful to use it to show that accidental death is duly recognized (Deuteronomy 19:4, 5). God gave the Israelites a method to protect the individual who took life accidentally (without hatred or malice). Further, those who serve as executioners are never assigned any penalty. Certain traditional teachings cite verse 6 as disallowing abortion.

THE PURPOSE OF PAIN

Wouldn't it be wonderful if we didn't have any aches or pains? Parents wouldn't have to deal with a baby's cry because he or she could not tell Mom where it hurts. Middle-aged weekend athletes wouldn't wake up hurting on Monday because they

WHAT DO YOU THINK?

How can Christians take the lead in promoting the sanctity of innocent life?

had abused their aging muscles in Sunday afternoon church softball games. Aching, arthritic joints wouldn't plague senior citizens!

On second thought, maybe it wouldn't be so wonderful. Grade-school student Ashlyn Blocker is one of a very few people who suffers from congenital insensitivity to pain (CIPA) with anhidrosis (inability to sweat)—a rare genetic disorder. She can't tell if her food is too hot; if she falls on the playground and skins her knee, she won't know it until her teacher sees the blood; if she gets overheated, she won't perspire; if she gets too cold, she won't shiver. The way God has created us, pain is a blessing; it is a "wake-up call" to the fact that something is wrong with our bodies.

The nightly news is filled with tragic stories of murder and attempted murder. Do these reports alarm us or have we become numb to them? Nations agonize over the issue of capital punishment. Yet nations that allow grievous crimes to go without sure and serious punishment will see their moral fabric disintegrate. The pain that a God-fearing nation feels when serious crime occurs is God's way of saying, "Look at the danger you are in!" May we heed his warning.   —C. R. B.

E. PROCREATION EMPHASIZED (v. 7)

7. *"As for you, be fruitful and increase in number; multiply on the earth and increase upon it."*

The imperatives of the first verse of the chapter are repeated and therefore emphasized. God seems not to be concerned about overpopulation.

II. GOD'S COVENANT (GENESIS 9:8-15)

The first use of the word *covenant* in the Bible occurs in Genesis 6:18. That occurrence was before the flood as God promised Noah that he would make a covenant with him when the flood-judgment was complete. Now we see God ready to fulfill his promise.

A. COVENANT'S PARTIES (vv. 8-10)

8, 9. *Then God said to Noah and to his sons with him: "I now establish my covenant with you and with your descendants after you*

A *covenant* often serves to establish a relationship, and that is the case here. It is *God* who is presenting the covenant. The recipients first named are *Noah* and *his sons with him*. But they are not the only recipients!

This particular covenant and its preceding promises are to extend to future generations, for it is to Noah and his seed *after* him. The proper response is to serve obediently the one who is offering such a covenant with its attendant blessings.

10. *". . . and with every living creature that was with you—the birds, the livestock and all the wild animals, all those that came out of the ark with you—every living creature on earth.*

The covenant's scope also includes *every living creature* that goes *out of the ark*. It is universal in its reach and effect. During the creation week, God pronounced blessings on the *animals* and upon humanity (Genesis 1:22, 28). The establishment of this covenant relationship is now added to the blessings, and it includes both humanity and the animals.

B. COVENANT'S PROMISE (v. 11)

11. *"I establish my covenant with you: Never again will all life be cut off by the waters of a flood; never again will there be a flood to destroy the earth."*

Do You Remember Your Covenant With God?

Visual for Lesson 1. Pose this question to your class to open a discussion of our obligations under the new covenant.

The *covenant* affirms that *never again will* God destroy *all life* on the earth *by the waters of a flood.* The history of the earth demonstrates that God has been faithful to keep this promise. There have been local floods involving terrible loss of life. But there has not been another flood *to destroy* all life on *earth.*

C. COVENANT'S PERMANENCE (vv. 12-15)

12, 13. And God said, "This is the sign of the covenant I am making between me and you and every living creature with you, a covenant for all generations to come: I have set my rainbow in the clouds, and it will be the sign of the covenant between me and the earth.

The *rainbow* is the perpetual sign of the *covenant* being announced by God. Isn't it marvelous to see a rainbow yet today? When conditions are just right, we can even see two rainbows. No need to search for the mythical pot of gold at the end of the rainbow. God's promise is better than gold!

14, 15. "Whenever I bring clouds over the earth and the rainbow appears in the clouds, I will remember my covenant between me and you and all living creatures of every kind. Never again will the waters become a flood to destroy all life."

Some have conjectured that the appearance of a *rainbow* in the heavens was a new phenomenon. The conditions on the earth prior to the flood are not precisely understood, but it is very likely that the combination of light and moisture to form a spectrum was not new. God, however, gives it a new significance. He repeats that this is a perpetual reminder that he will *never again* destroy all living creatures on the face of the earth.

THE END WILL COME!

On December 26, 2004, the world was shocked by news of the massive earthquake and tsunami in the Indian Ocean. We can still remember the mind-numbing reruns of the destruction captured on video that day. Within a week the death toll had passed 150,000 in a dozen nations. More would die from disease in the weeks that followed. No one will ever know for sure how many died in the event. But it was one of the greatest losses of life by flood in modern history.

There is no end to natural disasters. In a rather macabre acknowledgement of this fact, some newspapers carry a regular "Earth Watch" column listing the previous week's earthquakes, floods, cyclones, and unusual weather phenomena such as extreme cold or heat. So, does this mean that God has not kept his covenantal promise? Not at all! Even the most extensive floods of the past thousand years have not come close to equaling the devastation of Noah's day.

In that day God destroyed almost the entire human race by supernatural disaster. God has promised that he will not do so again by means of floodwaters. Even so, "the end of all things is near" (1 Peter 4:7). The end of creation as we know it will come by fire (2 Peter 3:10). The time to prepare ourselves is now.

—C. R. B.

CONCLUSION

One lady stated that her first connection between the God of Scripture and the God of her own little world as a child came after being read this account of Noah and the flood in a Bible-story book and then being shown the rainbow after a particularly heavy rainstorm. Such an association is exactly what God intended. The beauty of the brilliant spectrum of light in the sky is to remind people of any age, in every age, that they have a connection to God. It is up to individuals to determine if they will be faithful or faithless in their responses to the God who makes covenants with us.

Discovery Learning

This page contains an alternative lesson plan emphasizing learning activities. Classes desiring such student involvement will find these suggestions helpful. The next page is a reproducible activity page to further enhance discovery learning.

LEARNING GOALS

After participating in this lesson, each student will be able to:

1. Summarize the commands and promises that God gave to Noah immediately after the flood.

2. Explain the security that results from knowing God's expectations and promises.

3. Tell how he or she will use each observance of a rainbow as a reminder that God keeps his promises.

INTO THE LESSON

Write THEGEYESRAOFCTHEELORD on the board so that students can see it as they arrive. Someone should quickly decipher it as "Finding grace in the eyes of the Lord."

INTO THE WORD

Right after the Into the Lesson puzzle is deciphered, have one of your good oral readers stand before the group and read Genesis 6:5, 7, 8, 13, 22; 7:1, 7-10, 21, 22; 8:1, 4, 15, 16, 20-22 consecutively. After the reading, ask the students to look for all the demonstrations of God's grace toward Noah as the study progresses.

Say to your class, "A covenant is a 'what-is' and 'what-is-not' document or statement. Such a statement, whether contract or license or will, says what is permitted and expected and what is not. Consider each of the following statements as you look at today's text in Genesis 9:1-15. Decide if the statement is accurate and then what verse or verses reveals the *yes* or *no* involved."

Read the following statements in random order. Allow your class to respond, both with verse numbers and relevant comments. Verse numbers are given here, but do not mention them before students respond.

(1) God says *yes* to marriage and sexual activity (v. 1). (2) God says *no* to filling the earth with people (v. 1). (3) God says *yes* to domestication of animals (v. 2). (4) God says *yes* to our dominion over creatures of the sea (v. 2). (5) God says *no* to humans eating animals (v. 3). (6) God says *no* to humans consuming blood (v. 4). (7) God says *yes* to capital punishment (vv. 5, 6). (8) God says *yes* to humans being made in his image (v. 6). (9) God says *no* to making covenants with people (v. 8). (10) God says *yes* to making a covenant with animals (v. 9). (11) God says *no* to a second universal flood (v. 11).

(12) God says *yes* to using a visual reminder of his will (vv. 12, 13). (13) God says *yes* to repeating his promises for emphasis (vv. 14, 15).

As students respond to each statement, take the opportunity to ask follow-up questions. Repeat Genesis 6:8 and comment, "We usually think of God showing grace to Noah in saving him from the death of the flood—and that is true—but God continued to show grace in a variety of ways. Let's look at today's text to see the continuous outpouring of grace on Noah and his family."

Ask the class to look at Genesis 8:22–9:15 and identify examples of God's grace. Accept reasonable answers. If responses are slow in coming, ask a few questions, such as, "How does God's dietary expansion, such as in Genesis 9:3, represent his grace?" (*Humans have more variety in tastes and dietary opportunity.*) "How does God's imposition of capital punishment in Genesis 9:5, 6 indicate grace?" (*The existence of every moral principle is a sign of God's concern for our welfare in spite of sinful choices; this one offers protection from the inclination to assume that "might makes right."*) "How is the rainbow an act of grace?" (*When rain is falling, thoughts might well hark back to the deluge of destruction. But at just such a time God says with his beautiful science of prismatic reflection, "Remember my grace!"*)

(The Doctrine and Noah activity from the reproducible page is an alternative exercise.)

INTO LIFE

Prior to class collect eight-inch pieces of yarn or thread in a variety of colors from some of the crafters in your class. Let each learner select a piece in the color of his or her choice. Then challenge students to complete this assignment sometime this week: "Have someone tie a simple bow around one of your fingers on a day in the week ahead. When someone asks about the significance of the bow, relate your confidence in the promises of God as studied in class today."

For those not quite so bold, suggest that they tie the bow somewhere they will see it often, perhaps near the bathroom mirror. This should serve as a reminder of today's study and of the assurance of God's many promises to those who find his grace. (Also use The Colors of God's Grace activity from the reproducible page as time allows.)

Doctrine and Noah

Noah "walked with God" (Genesis 6:9), so Noah's doctrine and practice were godly. How different this is from most people today! What does today's society, in general, erroneously think about each of the following elements of doctrine? After you identify the faulty view, affirm God's view, as seen in his dealings with Noah. Include references from today's text and other Bible texts that mention Noah. The first is done as a sample.

ISSUES	FAULTY VIEWS	GOD'S VIEW (as seen in his dealings with Noah—Genesis 6 and following)
Grace	God's love and "niceness" are so great that he will show grace and save everyone.	God's saving grace is available to all, but that grace is not operative for those who remain in rebellion.
Divine Justice		
Sexual Activity		
Nature of Humanity		
Capital Punishment		
Covenant		

The Colors of God's Grace

God shows his love after he shows his holiness, justice, and wrath.

On each of the bands of the rainbow image, write a truth gleaned from today's text for which a rainbow should serve to remind us. (Special challenge: start each successive statement with the letter of a color band: V—violet, I—indigo, B—blue, G—green, Y—yellow, O—orange, R—red.) One example is given to get you started.

GOD'S COVENANT WITH ABRAHAM

LESSON 2

WHY TEACH THIS LESSON?

A corporation will go to great lengths to make sure that its name and trademarks are not used improperly. The reputation of the firm is at stake! Yet this is nothing new. Thousands of years ago, God revealed something about himself to Abram: his name is God Almighty. No sooner did he reveal his name than he made Abram a promise that was impossible from a human standpoint. Why didn't God promise Abram a son 50 years earlier? It seems that it was God's purpose to *show* as well as *tell* Abram about his absolute might.

Then God gives both Abram and his wife new names. What an amazing way to assure of them of his promise and to forge an identity for his people! By renaming them, then fulfilling his promise to them, God shows how he transforms his faithful ones. Today's lesson will remind your learners that God Almighty overcomes our doubts too. We who have had our names changed to *Christian* have experienced this time and again. The God who transformed Abraham and Sarah transforms us as well.

INTRODUCTION

A. SINGING, EXERCISE, AND DOCTRINE

We used to call them action choruses. Young people of varying ages were encouraged to use their arms and hands to simulate motions for the fountain that flowed deep and wide, the little light that shined, or the rains that threatened the houses of the wise and foolish builders. The choruses taught spiritual truths, helped the youngsters expend pent-up energy, and enabled youth workers to fill prolonged periods of time.

In recent years another such chorus was very popular with young people. The opening phrase affirms that Abraham had many sons. That is biblically true, for Paul says the same thing—that Abraham is the father of all who believe (Romans 4:11, 16; compare Galatians 3:7). As the lyrics reach the refrain, the words prompt several physical exercises that require agility, balance, and much energy. Most youngsters love to sing this exhilarating chorus, but it is doubtful that they realize the doctrinal implications of the opening words. That initial affirmation is a part of the lesson today.

Abraham is the great example of faith for all who believe in Christ. Abraham is the first person in the Bible of whom it is said that his belief was reckoned for righteousness (Genesis 15:6). He has more verses about him in the Faith Chapter (Hebrews 11) than any other Old Testament saint. His name appears more than 200 times in the New Testament. So the next time you hear young people singing the chorus about Abraham having many sons, remember that that really is a profound truth (with or without the suggested athletic movements!).

DEVOTIONAL READING:
HEBREWS 6:13-20
BACKGROUND SCRIPTURE:
GENESIS 17
PRINTED TEXT:
GENESIS 17:1-8, 15-22

LESSON AIMS

After participating in this lesson, each student will be able to:

1. Retell the promises of God's covenant with Abraham.

2. Compare and contrast with his or her own life both the faith and the doubt expressed by Abraham.

3. Suggest a specific area in his or her life where applying a faith like Abraham's can make (or is making) a difference.

KEY VERSE

I will establish my covenant as an everlasting covenant between me and you and your descendants after you for the generations to come, to be your God and the God of your descendants after you. —Genesis 17:7

B. LESSON BACKGROUND

The lesson last week was about the covenant that God made with Noah. Using the Genesis chronology, there are hundreds of years between Noah and Abraham. The Bible is silent about any direct communication from God to humankind during that period of time.

After the flood the sons of Noah and their descendants did well in obeying the command to fill the earth (Genesis 9:1, 7). The "table of nations" in Genesis 10 gives the names of individuals who were the founders of nations or tribal groups. The incident at the tower of Babel (11:1-9) served to separate people by language, which God devised and assigned to the families of humankind. It is said that language, more than any other difference, serves to divide people yet today.

God's first message to Abraham occurred while he was still in Ur of the Chaldeans. There are several sites named Ur, with the traditional site of Abraham being in southern Mesopotamia (Acts 7:2). It was a city with sanitary sewers, schools, and the worship of a moon god and goddess. This was a very modern city in the twenty-first century BC when Abraham left to become a sojourner.

Abraham's obedient response to leave with his family is a positive example of faith, for he did not know where God was leading him (Hebrews 11:8). The family traveled toward northwestern Mesopotamia, finally stopping in Haran (Genesis 11:31).

It is interesting that both Ur and Haran are known as centers of worship for a moon god and goddess. Idolatry eventually was common after the flood, and it was even practiced by Abraham's father and brother (Joshua 24:2). Some, however, did maintain a genuine faith. (It is often assumed that Job lived during this time, and his faith is highly exemplary.) When God selected Abraham, he chose a man without children, land, or reputation. To such a person God is ready to promise a son, a land, and greatness!

I. PROMISES TO ABRAHAM (GENESIS 17:1-8, 15, 16)

Abraham, Isaac, and Jacob, patriarchs in the book of Genesis, receive promises by God on different occasions. God gives messages to Abraham several times in Genesis (12:1-3, 7; 13:14-17; 15:4, 5, 13-18; 17:1-22; 18:17-33; 22:15-18). Acts 7:2 indicates an earlier contact before the family leaves Ur.

Similar promises are given twice to Isaac (Genesis 26:4, 24) and Jacob (Genesis 28:14, 15; 35:9-12). As we open our lesson, we remember that Abraham's name originally was Abram (Genesis 17:5, below).

A. NAME FOR GOD (vv. 1, 2)

1. **When Abram was ninety-nine years old, the LORD appeared to him and said, "I am God Almighty; walk before me and be blameless.**

The factor of Abram's age is of interest. He was 75 when he, Lot (his nephew), and others departed from Haran to go to the land of Canaan (Genesis 12:4, 5). When Abraham was 85, his wife suggested that perhaps she could have children through Hagar, her maidservant (16:2, 3). Abraham accepted the proposal, which was a contemporary practice for a wife who was barren. Ishmael was born when Abraham was 86 (16:16).

Such statistics interest some people, but the message underneath them is very important: God keeps his promises, but the time of waiting may be a testing of the patience and faith of those who are the recipients of the promises. In this case Abram and his wife Sarai were "running ahead" of God instead of waiting for his time.

WHAT DO YOU THINK?

Just as God called Abraham to move out by faith, so he continues to desire that Christians walk by faith today. In what areas do you need to do a little more "faith-walking"? How do you know when you've crossed the line into foolishly walking by blind faith?

WHAT DO YOU THINK?

Our timing often is not God's timing, nor is God's timing ours. What was an occasion in your life when you tried to force your timing on God? How did things turn out?

The Lord identifies himself with his first words to Abram. He is not just God, but he is Almighty. This God is one who can accomplish things that are considered impossible. Over 1,400 years later Jeremiah will echo the same thought when he writes that nothing is too difficult for God (Jeremiah 32:17).

Two imperatives are used by the Lord to express his expectations. First, Abram is to *walk before* God. Second, his walk must be *blameless;* Abram is to do his best in meeting his obligations to God.

"WHAT'S IN A NAME?"

In the early 1960s General Motors tried unsuccessfully to sell its new, economical compact model the Nova in Latin America. The problem, it seems, was that the name *Nova* means "no go" in Spanish. After GM changed the car's name to *Caribe,* sales took off—at least so the story goes. Actually, this is one of those urban legends we hear from time to time. For one thing, sales weren't really that bad, and the Caribe was sold by Volkswagen (www.snopes.com). However, this story has gained lots of "mileage" (pardon the pun) by being repeated many times in marketing textbooks and business seminars.

Let's try another one. When Coca-Cola entered the Chinese market, it had to find Mandarin characters that sounded like "Coca-Cola." The characters they chose could mean "to allow the mouth to be able to rejoice" but could also be translated "bite the wax tadpole." Hmmm.

Whether or not either story is true, in the final analysis their very existence points to the fact that names are important. So it was with the name by which God revealed himself to Abram. Abram's culture believed in many gods, but the God who spoke to Abram was the Almighty God! He was significantly different from the fictitious gods that people worshiped. He was—and is—the God who has power and who makes covenants with those who believe him.   —C. R. B.

2. "I will confirm my covenant between me and you and will greatly increase your numbers."

This is the first of 13 uses of the word *covenant* in this chapter. It is used only once with Abram prior to this chapter, in Genesis 15:18. In that chapter God specifically promises that Abram will have a son and that his descendants will be as numerous as the stars (Genesis 15:5). The word *will* accompanies many of God's blessings as given in this chapter. This construction shows that the fulfillments are in the future, but God will keep his promises.

B. NATIONS TO RESULT (vv. 3, 4)

3, 4. Abram fell facedown, and God said to him, "As for me, this is my covenant with you: You will be the father of many nations.

Abram's immediate response is to fall and assume a position of utmost respect. The implications of what the Lord has just said are racing through his mind, and he is overwhelmed! God's next words reinforce the thought that *Abram* is to have many descendants.

An excellent commentary on Abram's thoughts can be found in Romans 4:19, 20. In these verses Paul states that Abraham was not weak in faith, even as he considered his own body and his wife's womb to be dead. The God who created life in the beginning could do the same again for this elderly couple!

In verse 4 God states that the covenant being made is with Abram, and one outcome is that *many nations* will result. The factor of nations (plural) is a new concept. The singular form of the word is used in Genesis 12:2, so this adds a dimension to the promises that God is making.

WHAT DO YOU THINK?

Five years ago tomorrow is a day etched in history. The September 11, 2001 terrorist attacks challenged the faith of many. How do you hold to the truth that God is the Almighty in the face of such atrocities?

HOW TO SAY IT
Abraham. AY-bruh-ham.
Abram. AY-brum.
Babel. BAY-bul.
Canaan. KAY-nun.
Chaldeans. Kal-DEE-unz.
Esau. EE-saw.
Hagar. HAY-gar.
Haran. HAIR-un.
Isaac. EYE-zuk.
Ishmael. ISH-may-el.
Jacob. JAY-kub.
Keturah. Keh-TOO-ruh.
Mesopotamia. MES-uh-puh-TAY-me-uh.
Messiah. Meh-SIGH-uh.

Of course, living in the twenty-first century AD means that we are aware of the historical fulfillment of this prophecy. But it must be a staggering thought for Abram in the twenty-first century BC! Some of the descendants of Abram who will produce many sons include Ishmael and the six sons that Abraham had by his second wife, Keturah (Genesis 25:1, 2).

C. NEW NAME FOR ABRAM (v. 5a)

5a. "No longer will you be called Abram; your name will be Abraham,

A new name is given to Abram, and it is very meaningful as a part of this covenant. Whereas Abram means "exalted father," the name Abraham means "father of a multitude." This new name itself is a challenging part of this expanded covenant.

The exact nature of this exchange between God and Abraham is not given; it may have been a personal, private event. One can only wonder at the responses of others when Abraham tells them that his name is now "father of a multitude." Abraham has a private army (Genesis 14:14); when those men think of Abraham as a childless, elderly man, how can they use his new name without a snicker?

D. NATIONS AND THE KINGS (vv. 5b, 6)

5b, 6. ". . . for I have made you a father of many nations. I will make you very fruitful; I will make nations of you, and kings will come from you.

The thought that Abraham will be *a father of many nations* is repeated from verse 4. This time the concept is amplified: Abraham's descendants will be *very fruitful.*

Abraham's offspring will also include *kings.* This is a new factor, not mentioned previously. Moses (the author of Genesis) will later record the names of several kings who are descendants of Abraham's grandson Esau (Genesis 36:31-39). Students of biblical history are aware of Saul, David, Solomon, and other kings who trace their lineage to Abraham (Matthew 1:2-11). God's promises do come to pass!

E. PEOPLE OF THE COVENANT (v. 7)

7. "I will establish my covenant as an everlasting covenant between me and you and your descendants after you for the generations to come, to be your God and the God of your descendants after you.

This special *covenant* relationship will continue into the future for the children of Abraham, for it is an *everlasting covenant.* It must first be noted that the applications of these phrases are restricted: in this same chapter the descendants of Ishmael are excluded, in spite of Abraham's expressed thought that the covenant could be fulfilled in him (vv. 18-21, below).

This verse also allows us to compare the use of the word *descendants* here in the *New International Version* with the word *seed* in the *King James Version.* The selection of the word *seed* seems to be better, for Paul uses the fact that it is singular to show that the ultimate fulfillment is a spiritual one in Christ, that he is the promised seed (Galatians 3:16; compare Acts 3:25). The beauty of the apostles' argument is that all people now have access to the spiritual blessings that the redemptive work of the Messiah makes available (compare Genesis 12:3; 22:18).

F. PLACE ASSIGNED (v. 8)

8. "The whole land of Canaan, where you are now an alien, I will give as an everlasting possession to you and your descendants after you; and I will be their God."

WHAT DO YOU THINK?

Covenants are based upon promises of commitment on the part of both parties entering into the covenant. What promises of God, revealed in both his old and new covenants, help you to face life daily?

[Be sure to consider Psalm 126:6; Isaiah 51:3; Matthew 6:33; John 10:10; and Hebrews 6:18, 19 in your answer.]

The *land of Canaan* had been promised to Abraham previously (Genesis 12:5, 7; 15:18). These words from God provide a further confirmation of that promise. There is a certain irony here: it has been 24 years since Abraham entered Canaan (compare Genesis 12:4, 5; 17:1), and so far Abraham does not possess any of it. God told Abraham previously that his *descendants* would be oppressed 400 years in another land, and in the fourth generation they would occupy Canaan when the sin of the inhabitants had "reached its full measure" (Genesis 15:13, 16).

G. POSITION FOR SARAI (vv. 15, 16)

15, 16. God also said to Abraham, "As for Sarai your wife, you are no longer to call her Sarai; her name will be Sarah. I will bless her and will surely give you a son by her. I will bless her so that she will be the mother of nations; kings of peoples will come from her."

The intervening verses record the establishment of circumcision as a sign of the covenant for Abraham's male descendants. Now the role of *Sarai* in the promises is expressed for the first time. God begins by changing her name for the role that she will have in redemptive history: to become the mother of nations and kings. This will have its beginning in her own son, Isaac.

The meanings of the names *Sarai* and *Sarah* seem to be the same, but there is the difference in spelling. Both names mean "princess."

II. PERPLEXITIES OF ABRAHAM (GENESIS 17:17-22)

Abraham finally has an opportunity to express his reactions. Those reactions concern two people: Sarah and Ishmael.

A. PROBLEMS STATED (vv. 17, 18)

17. Abraham fell facedown; he laughed and said to himself, "Will a son be born to a man a hundred years old? Will Sarah bear a child at the age of ninety?"

Abraham's emotional response is laughter. The fact that *Sarah* is to become a mother goes beyond what is humanly reasonable. If God is in it, however, then it becomes reasonable!

Abraham projects the promises a year into the future, the earliest time for a son to be born. Abraham will then be 100 and Sarah will be 90, and he inwardly wonders about what he has just heard. Could it possibly be true?

18. And Abraham said to God, "If only Ishmael might live under your blessing!"

At this time *Ishmael* is 13 years old (compare Abraham's age in Genesis 16:16 and 17:1). Abraham loves this young teenager and states that he is willing to accept him as the child of promise. In his humility he does not demand that God go to any special trouble.

B. PROBLEMS SOLVED (vv. 19-22)

19. Then God said, "Yes, but your wife Sarah will bear you a son, and you will call him Isaac. I will establish my covenant with him as an everlasting covenant for his descendants after him.

God assures Abraham that *Sarah* is the one who will *bear* the *son* who will fulfill the promise. In addition, God continues to provide names for the people involved: the son is to be called *Isaac*. The name *Isaac* means "laugh," and it will ever serve as a reminder of Abraham's reaction when he heard the prediction.

The *I will* statements of this section continue. God asserts that it is through Isaac that the everlasting covenant is to be established and that it will continue for generations *after him*.

WHAT DO YOU THINK?

We jokingly say, "God, give me patience and give it to me now!" When there is a delay in our receiving something, our faith and patience are put to the test. In what ways has your patience, and the patience of your church, been put to the test?

DAILY BIBLE READINGS

Monday, Sept. 4—*God's Promise Is Sure (Hebrews 6: 13-20)*

Tuesday, Sept. 5—*Abraham Had Heroic Faith (Hebrews 11: 8-16)*

Wednesday, Sept. 6—*God's Promise to Abram (Genesis 15: 1-6)*

Thursday, Sept. 7—*God Foretells Future Greatness (Genesis 15:12-21)*

Friday, Sept. 8—*God Blesses Hagar (Genesis 16:1-15)*

Saturday, Sept. 9—*God Covenants with Abraham (Genesis 17:1-8)*

Sunday, Sept. 10—*God Promises a Son (Genesis 17: 15-22)*

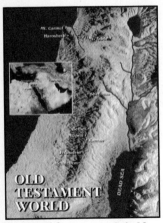

Visual for Lessons 2 & 12. *Keep this map posted throughout the quarter to help set the geographical context.*

20. "And as for Ishmael, I have heard you: I will surely bless him; I will make him fruitful and will greatly increase his numbers. He will be the father of twelve rulers, and I will make him into a great nation.

God assures Abraham that his concerns for *Ishmael* have been heard and that blessings are included for him. They are similar in nature to the promises of the covenant. But limitations are set concerning the number of future leaders among his descendants (*twelve rulers*). The final promise is that Ishmael's descendants will become *a great nation*.

21. "But my covenant I will establish with Isaac, whom Sarah will bear to you by this time next year."

The closing words of God in this account restate the factors that are to have imminent fulfillments: that the *covenant* is to be continued through *Isaac*, that *Sarah* is to be the mother, and that these things will occur the *next year*. One can only wonder concerning Abraham's final reflections and actions: will they be outwardly exuberant and joyful, silent and profound contemplation, or overwhelming gratitude? It will take time for the reality of the promises to be grasped fully.

UNINTENTIONAL FRAUD

Alceo Dossena (1878–1937) was a stonemason from northern Italy. He became skilled at carving reproductions of sculptures from ancient times, and his work was so good that others began selling his carvings as genuine antiques. Despite Dossena's best efforts to spread the truth of the matter, dealers in antiquities continued the fraud since they were reaping handsome profits. So many pieces of his work were in circulation as genuine that it became impossible to trace them all. It is said that some of Dossena's copies are accepted as genuine antiquities yet today.

With the best of motives, Abraham and Sarah also perpetrated an unintentional fraud. They had received God's promise of a son as a sign of God's covenant with them. Time went by, and still there was no pregnancy. Their solution was for Abraham to have a son by Sarah's servant girl, Hagar.

The consequences of their decision were far-reaching. We see the effects today in strife in the Middle East, as some elements of religious extremism claim covenantal blessings through Ishmael. Although the child Ishmael would be blessed by God, he was not the "genuine article"—the son of the covenantal promise. We always get into trouble when we try to push God's timetable!   —C. R. B.

22. When he had finished speaking with Abraham, God went up from him.

God departs from *Abraham,* and this brings to a conclusion this stage of Abraham's developing role in the covenant. There are more interactions to follow, but the new factors are overwhelming.

CONCLUSION

If it sounds too good to be true, it probably is—unless God is in it. The covenant that God made with Abraham offered promises that another human could not deliver. It is comforting to know that God did not hold the negative reactions of Abraham and Sarah against them. Their reservations did not thwart God's redemptive plan.

It is God's plan to provide Heaven for all the redeemed. That's something that sounds just too good to be true, but it is true. It sounds too good to be true that God forgives and forgets the sins of the redeemed, but God does that—even though we tend to burden ourselves with memories of our failures.

God offers Heaven to sinners who believe on his Son and follow his plan of salvation. That sounds too good to be true—but it is true!

Discovery Learning

This page contains an alternative lesson plan emphasizing learning activities. Classes desiring such student involvement will find these suggestions helpful. The next page is a reproducible activity page to further enhance discovery learning.

LEARNING GOALS

After participating in this lesson, each student will be able to:

1. Retell the promises concerning God's covenant with Abraham.

2. Compare and contrast with his or her own life both the faith and the doubt expressed by Abraham.

3. Suggest a specific area in his or her life where applying a faith like Abraham's can make (or is making) a difference.

INTO THE LESSON

Several years ago, a Christian singer made her song "El Shaddai" a top tune. The words recited many of the biblical names of God, and so the song has remained popular for devotional and worship occasions. Obtain a recording of that song (by any artist) and play it for the class as your study session begins.

Say, "When God comes to Abram in verse 1 of today's text in Genesis 17, El Shaddai is the way God identifies himself. 'Almighty God' or 'God Almighty' are the common ways that that name is translated into English." Highlight that concept by asking, "Why is this name that God chooses for himself especially appropriate on the occasion of Genesis 17?" (Use the commentary to enhance your students' responses.)

INTO THE WORD

Say, "Abram's given name reflects the optimism of his parents and perhaps the work of the Holy Spirit. Abram's name means 'exalted father,' yet for more than 80 years he fathered no children at all. For such a childless one to become a father, indeed an 'exalted father,' shows the grace and power of God the Father."

Give a half sheet of paper and a pencil to each student. Ask students to write "Exalted Father" at the top of their papers. Then instruct students to make a list indicating how Abram became "Father of _____," using today's text or their own general knowledge of Abraham, his life, and his physical and spiritual heritage.

Give students one example: "Father of Isaac," from verse 17 of today's text. Indicate to the class that they can coin their own labels if they can explain their reasoning. Here are other such designations, from the text and elsewhere: "Father of the Century" (v. 1 and Abram's age); "Father of the Covenant" (v. 2); "Father of Many Nations" (v. 4); "Father of a Multitude" (per lesson writer's note on Abram's new God-given name); "Father of Kings" (v. 6); "Father of the Everlasting Covenant" (v. 7); "Father of the Land" (v. 8); "Father of Laughter" (v. 17 and Isaac's name); "Father of the Faithful" (traditional); "Father of Division" (based on later animosity of the descendants of the two sons); "Father of Twenty-First-Century Conflict" (based on tensions and hatreds between various religious factions today).

Give students eight to ten minutes to compile their lists, then compare and contrast lists. Be sure to get explanation for any that are unclear to you or appear to be unclear to others. (For expanded Bible study, use the God and Abraham exercise from the reproducible page.)

INTO LIFE

Ask, "If you had a faith like Abraham's, what would you do for God?" Accept general answers, then give each student a printed sheet with these completion statements: (1) "By faith [student's name], when called to _____, obeyed and _____." (2) "By faith [student's name], when God tested him/her, offered _____." (3) "By faith [student's name], was looking forward to _____."

Read Hebrews 11:8-19 to the class and suggest that they use this passage as a pattern for their responses.

As an alternative activity, label Abraham's faith as a "countercultural faith." Read Hebrews 11:8-19 and ask, "What exactly did Abraham believe about God that is unlike the belief system of the twenty-first century?" Accept reasonable responses, but insert the following if they are not identified by the group: (1) Abraham believed God was capable of giving life to a dead body; (2) Abraham believed that no matter where he was that God would provide for his needs; (3) Abraham believed God was capable of overcoming the laws of nature; (4) Abraham believed he did not have to understand fully everything about God and his will.

Finish the discussion by asking, "How is your own belief system? Is it culturally biased, or is it culturally free?" (If your class uses the student books, consider using the Abraham's Child activity as a concluding experience; Faith and You from the reproducible page is also an option.)

God and Abraham

Today's text in Genesis 17 ends at verse 22: "When he [God] had finished speaking with Abraham, God went up from him." God spoke to Abraham friend to friend. Genesis records several specific occasions that God spoke to Abraham. Look up each of these references and briefly indicate what God said to him.

Genesis 12:1-3 _____

Genesis 12:7 _____

Genesis 13:14-18 _____

Genesis 15:4, 5, 13-18 _____

Genesis 17:1-22 _____

Genesis 18 _____

Genesis 22:15-18 _____

Faith and You

What if Hebrews 11:32 read, "And what more shall I say? I do not have time to tell about Gideon, Barak, Samson, Jephthah, David, Samuel, and the prophets" and then concluded with your name? What could the writer of Hebrews write about you and your faith? Fill in your name in each of the following, and then write some acts of faith you have taken or will take.

By faith _____ has (or will) _____.

By faith _____ has (or will) _____.

By faith _____ has (or will) _____.

GOD'S COVENANT WITH ISRAEL

LESSON 3

WHY TEACH THIS LESSON?

"Where are you from?" "What's your favorite restaurant?" "If you were a tree, what kind of tree would you be?" We often use simple, even silly questions to learn about each other.

The learning process, though, is essential to relationship building. Building a relationship with a holy God is a different process, yet also dependent upon knowing what God is like and what he will and will not allow from people who have a relationship with him. Today's lesson shows the birth of another covenant between God and people. This one spells out laws of behavior that Israel must keep in order to be God's cherished people, a kingdom of priests.

We as Christians are also called to be God's children, a royal priesthood. We too are called to behave in ways that often set us apart from others. Your learners should remember that the covenant-making God still has a covenant for us. It's not the old covenant with Israel, but the new covenant that comes through the blood of Christ. It requires that we die to our old way of life and live in a way that honors him.

INTRODUCTION

A. KEEPING YOUR WORD

Governor William Penn arrived in North America on October 27, 1682. One of his first actions was to confer with the leaders of nearby Indians. Penn and his men arrived unarmed, as did the Indians. Penn spoke through an interpreter and gave the principles that he intended to follow. Penn said that since they were all of one flesh and blood, and therefore brothers, they would settle any disputes in council, not with warfare. There would be openness and love. One account notes that the Indian chiefs said that as long as the rivers ran and the sun shone that they would live in peace with Penn's children.

For over 70 years there were no battle cries between the two groups. It is easy to conclude that the original participants kept the words that they had spoken as a treaty or covenant.

When an individual becomes a Christian, he or she becomes a part of the new covenant that is provided through Christ. It is evident that many people want the benefits of the covenant, but they do not desire to fulfill their covenantal obligations. To keep one's commitment to Christ seems to have an extremely low priority—unless there is a crisis, and then prayers and laments are expressed that implore God to hear and answer the prayers.

The conscientious person will always try to keep his or her word. Whether that word is simply spoken, involves a handshake, is a lengthy business contract, concerns marriage vows, or confessing Jesus as Lord: keep your word!

DEVOTIONAL READING:
PSALM 119:33-40
BACKGROUND SCRIPTURE:
EXODUS 19:1-6; 24:3-8
PRINTED TEXT:
EXODUS 19:1-6; 24:3-8

LESSON AIMS

After participating in this lesson, each student will be able to:

1. Describe the covenant relationship that God designed for Old Testament Israel.

2. Discuss the meaning and importance of God's covenant relationship with Old Testament Israel.

3. State one specific way he or she will demonstrate greater faithfulness to the new covenant.

KEY VERSES

"Out of all nations you will be my treasured possession. Although the whole earth is mine, you will be for me a kingdom of priests and a holy nation." These are the words you are to speak to the Israelites. —Exodus 19:5b, 6

LESSON 3 NOTES

B. LESSON BACKGROUND

The statistics given in Genesis and Exodus show that there are 621 years between the lesson of last week (Genesis 17, which states that Abraham was 99 years old) and the initial giving of the law through Moses at Mount Sinai. The first of the 621 years is the time between the promise of Isaac's birth and its fulfillment when Abraham was 100 years old.

Three references account for the other 620 years. Isaac's age is given as 60 when Jacob is born (Genesis 25:26). Jacob, upon the occasion of his family's entering Egypt, states that he is 130 years old (47:9). Finally, Exodus 12:40, 41 states that the Israelites spent 430 years in Egypt.

Many familiar events of biblical history are within that period of 620 years. With the help of his mother, Rebekah, Jacob deceived his father in order to receive the patriarchal blessing. Jacob was compelled to flee from the wrath of his brother, and he goes to Padan Aram to find a wife. (He never saw his mother again.) Jacob himself was deceived by his Uncle Laban: on Jacob's wedding night he received Leah as his wife instead of Rachel—the younger sister for whom he had worked seven years. After one week Rachel became his wife also. These two women plus their two maidservants became the mothers of the 12 sons of Jacob.

The providential work of God shows itself in the fascinating account of Joseph being sold into slavery by his brothers. Joseph rose to be second-in-command of Egypt. In a time of famine, Joseph was able to provide for his father, his 11 brothers, and their families.

The Israelites entered Egypt as a family, but 430 years later they left as a nation. The military census of men over age 20 totaled 603,550, and that did not include the tribe of Levi (Numbers 1:46, 47).

Moses became the leader of that nation. The events of his birth, exile at age 40, and his initial call by God at age 80 are thrilling to read. The 10 plagues credentialed Moses' leadership for the nation. They demonstrated to the Egyptians that the God of Israel was the only God. As a result, the pharaoh finally allowed this "nation of slaves" to begin its journey back to the land that had been promised to Abraham.

In Exodus 12 several things of importance are noted. First, instructions were given so that the Israelites could be spared the death of their firstborn in the tenth plague. Second, the departure from Egypt gave rise to the Passover and the Feast of Unleavened Bread (Exodus 12:14, 15, 43-49; 13:3-10). Third, the Lord announced that the nation of Israel was to have its own calendar, beginning with the month that they left Egypt (Exodus 12:2).

I. ARRIVAL AT SINAI (EXODUS 19:1, 2)

As our lesson opens, the year is about 1446 BC.

A. DEPARTURE REMEMBERED (v. 1)

1. In the third month after the Israelites left Egypt—on the very day—they came to the Desert of Sinai.

The experiences of the Israelites after leaving Egypt involved several miracles that should have developed trust in the Lord. These mighty works of God included the pillar of fire or cloud (Exodus 13:21; 40:36), the crossing of the Red Sea (Exodus 14), the making of bitter water into sweet water (15:25), the provisions of manna in the mornings and quail in the evenings (16:12), Moses' striking of a rock to produce water (17:6), and an unusual method of victory over enemies (17:11-13).

DAILY BIBLE READINGS

Monday, Sept. 11—*Our Pledge to God* (Psalm 119:33-40)

Tuesday, Sept. 12—*Moses Chooses Judges* (Exodus 18:13-27)

Wednesday, Sept. 13—*Moses Goes Up to God* (Exodus 19:1-9a)

Thursday, Sept. 14—*Preparing for God's Covenant* (Exodus 19:9b-15)

Friday, Sept. 15—*God Gives the Commands* (Exodus 20:1-17)

Saturday, Sept. 16—*The People Vow Loyalty* (Exodus 24:3-8)

Sunday, Sept. 17—*Moses Enters God's Presence* (Exodus 24:12-18)

The Israelites reach the area *Desert of Sinai* in the *third month*. The exact meaning of that phrase is uncertain. Does it mean the first day of the third month, or does it imply that it is exactly three months since leaving Egypt? The traditional view is that it is the first day of the third month.

B. DESTINATION REACHED (v. 2)
2. *After they set out from Rephidim, they entered the Desert of Sinai, and Israel camped there in the desert in front of the mountain.*

Three major events occur after the Israelites reach *Rephidim* (Exodus 17, 18). This is (1) where the Israelites receive water from a rock, (2) where they are victorious over the Amalekites, and (3) where Moses receives advice from his father-in-law on the importance of delegating leadership duties to others.

The arrival at *Sinai* fulfills the promise that was made to Moses. In this very place he had turned aside to see the burning bush (Exodus 3:2, 4). God had promised the sign that when Moses brought the people out of Egypt that he would serve God here. The exact location of Mount Sinai is uncertain. About 15 different sites are suggested! Recently a theory has been proposed that a certain *mountain* in Saudi Arabia (ancient Midian) could be Mount Sinai, but access to it is denied for any thorough investigation.

The Israelite nation spends almost a year at Sinai. It is interesting that archaeologists are not able to find evidence of such an encampment at the traditional site. The important fact is that the events recorded did take place, even if archaeology cannot accurately determine the location.

II. ANNOUNCEMENTS AT SINAI (EXODUS 19:3-6)
This new nation needs a constitution—a covenant to guide them in living before God and with their fellow humans. Sinai is the place where it is to be given.

A. ASCENT BY MOSES (v. 3)
3. *Then Moses went up to God, and the LORD called to him from the mountain and said, "This is what you are to say to the house of Jacob and what you are to tell the people of Israel:*

What a privilege it is to be addressed personally by *God* himself! But with great privilege comes great responsibility. God isn't just making small talk with Moses. God has a vital message to deliver *to the house of Jacob* and *the people of Israel.*

The expression *house of Jacob* is used only here in the writings of Moses. The phrase *the people of Israel* is probably just a parallel expression of the previous phrase. This is typical of Hebrew literature. If there is any significance in the difference, it may be a subtle reminder that to be able to change another person's name (as God changed Jacob's name to Israel in Genesis 32:28; 35:10) indicates that you are superior to that person. (See examples in 2 Kings 23:34; 24:17.) By using both terms, God may be asserting that he has the right to grant covenants. He is both God and *Lord!*

B. ASSERTIONS BY THE LORD (vv. 4-6)
4. *"'You yourselves have seen what I did to Egypt, and how I carried you on eagles' wings and brought you to myself.*

The opening phrase *You yourselves have seen what I did to Egypt* is a reminder that the Lord has the credentials to provide a covenant. The second assertion *how I carried you on eagles' wings* is a reminder of how God has provided for the Israelites' every need on the journey to Sinai (compare Deuteronomy 32:11). The

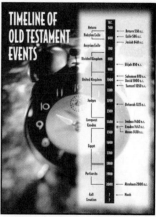

Visual for Lesson 3. *This timeline will remind your students of God's patient watchfulness through the centuries..*

WHAT DO YOU THINK?

History reveals that God is the provider, sustainer, and protector of his people. In what ways has God carried you and your church "on eagles' wings"?

WHAT DO YOU THINK?

From Genesis 4:7 to Revelation 22:19, Scripture is filled with the conditional word if. In what ways do people sometimes bypass the ifs of God's Word? Why?

WHAT DO YOU THINK?

What are some ways that you fulfill your priestly role as God intends? What will interfere with your priestly service?

implication usually given is that an eagle may force its young out of the nest to compel flight, but the older eagle is ready to catch the fledgling bird if necessary. In a similar way the Lord has provided care for his people.

5. "'Now if you obey me fully and keep my covenant, then out of all nations you will be my treasured possession. Although the whole earth is mine,

The little word *if* indicates that the Lord is ready to announce the stipulations of the *covenant.* The requirement is that Israel is to *obey* the Lord and *keep* the covenant's terms. Accepting and entering into a covenantal relationship is often rather simple. It is the keeping of a covenant over an extended period of time that becomes difficult!

The first stated blessing is that Israel will be elevated above *all nations.* God does not, however, surrender his control over the nations, for the final phrase is a reminder that God owns the entire *earth.* The expression *treasured possession* may refer to a valuable possession owned by a king. The concept shows the special relationship that God's people have. In the New Testament the concept is applied to Christians (Ephesians 1:14; Titus 2:14; 1 Peter 2:9).

6. "'. . . you will be for me a kingdom of priests and a holy nation.' These are the words you are to speak to the Israelites."

The second blessing of the pending covenant is that Israel will be a *kingdom of priests.* A priest has access to God in prayer. This concept is also applied to Christians in 1 Peter 2:9 and Revelation 5:10.

The final phrase that Moses delivers is a challenge for Israel to be *a holy nation.* God's holiness is foundational. Those who serve God are commanded to be holy as he is holy (Leviticus 11:44, 45; 1 Peter 1:16).

A TREASURED POSSESSION

If you ever stand in check-out lines, you know the name of Anna Nicole Smith from the tabloids. While working as an "exotic dancer" in 1991 at age 23, she met J. Howard Marshall II, age 86. They married in 1994; he died about a year later. Very quickly, the legal fight for the "treasured possession" of Marshall's $780 million estate began. Smith claimed her husband had promised her half of his estate.

After six years, a court awarded her $475 million. Another court subsequently ruled in favor of Marshall's son and left Smith with no money. Still another court later ruled in her favor and gave her $88.5 million. Then in 2004, that ruling was reversed and Smith was again without an inheritance. As they say at the end of some television programs, "To be continued"!

Israel was to become God's treasured possession, a concept that cannot be valued in monetary terms—not $88.5 million, not $475 million, not $780 million! But along with privilege came the responsibility to be a holy nation. Sadly, this was a duty that the people failed to perform. God's covenants contain both duty and privilege. Our covenant with God through Christ is no different from the others in this respect. "Be holy, because I am holy" (1 Peter 1:16). —C. R. B.

III. ACCEPTING THE COVENANT (EXODUS 24:3-8)

The material between the two segments of today's lesson contains the covenant's fundamentals, including the Ten Commandments. The Israelites may be free from their slavery in Egypt, but this new freedom must be accompanied by virtuous living. Otherwise, chaos and anarchy will be the result.

A. RESOLVE OF THE PEOPLE (v. 3)

3. When Moses went and told the people all the LORD's words and laws, they responded with one voice, "Everything the LORD has said we will do."

The first two verses of the chapter tell of yet another trip up the mountain by *Moses,* and this time he was accompanied by others. When Moses descends the mountain, his purpose is to tell *the people* all that God has prescribed. The people pledge their obedience *with one voice.* This is the second such affirmation by the people (see Exodus 19:8 for the first one).

Promises, Promises

If you plan to lie to someone, make sure you aren't near an MRI machine! Magnetic Resonance Imaging can show a difference in brain activity between liars and truth tellers.

A 2004 study at Temple University School of Medicine showed that different parts of the brain are used for lying and truth telling. Seven areas of the brain were activated in subjects who lied and only four were used in the brains of those who told the truth. One conclusion drawn from the study was that it takes more work to lie than to tell the truth. And that's not counting the work it takes telling more lies to cover up the first one!

We've all heard the phrase *promises, promises* spoken with sarcasm and disdain when someone has a history of not keeping his or her word. We don't know whether the Israelites were telling the truth when they gave multiple assurances to Moses that they would do whatever God commanded them to do. Probably they were sincere.

Yet we all know how easy it is to make promises under the influence of a moment's emotional pressure and then forsake the promise when the moment is gone or when other pressures are at work on us. God could well have responded, "Promises, promises!" Israel's example should be a caution to us about the need to speak the truth and then faithfully follow through with what we have vowed to do.

—C. R. B.

B. Responses by Moses (vv. 4-7a)

4. Moses then wrote down everything the Lord had said.

He got up early the next morning and built an altar at the foot of the mountain and set up twelve stone pillars representing the twelve tribes of Israel.

Three responses by Moses are given. First, he *wrote down* what the Lord had communicated through him. In the past it was sometimes taught that Moses may have used picture writing because at this time in history alphabetic writing is not yet developed. Such a theory is now proven to be invalid because examples of alphabetic writing have been found from the era in which Moses lived and even before his time. In 1999 the earliest alphabetic writing discovered to date was found in Upper Egypt. It is dated to around 1900 or 1800 BC, hundreds of years before the exodus (see www.jhu.edu and www.archaeology.org).

Since Moses was trained in all the learning of Egypt (Acts 7:22), his writing with an alphabet is not a problem. If you had lived a century ago, you would have been hard pressed to answer the critics on this issue. One lesson from this is that it is essential to maintain your faith against such attacks. You may not have the answers personally; however, in the places where God's Word can be tested against the evidence of archaeology, the integrity of the Bible is validated.

After writing, Moses begins work *early* the next day to construct *an altar.* He also erects *twelve stone pillars,* one for each of the *tribes of Israel.* These pillars not only represent the tribes, but they seem to become a part of the ratification of the new covenant (see v. 8, below).

5. Then he sent young Israelite men, and they offered burnt offerings and sacrificed young bulls as fellowship offerings to the Lord.

What Do You Think?

Telling the truth, the whole truth, and nothing but the truth is not always appreciated. In what ways do preachers and teachers fail to tell "all the words" of the Lord? In what ways do people close their ears to these words of truth?

How to Say It

Aaron. AIR-un.
Abraham. AY-bruh-ham.
Amalekites. AM-uh-leh-kites or Uh-MAL-ih-kites.
Isaac. EYE-zuk.
Jacob. JAY-kub.
Laban. LAY-bun.
Levi. LEE-vye.
Leviticus. Leh-VIT-ih-kus.
Midian. MID-ee-un.
Moses. MO-zes or MO-zez.
Padan Aram. PAY-dan A-ram.
Rebekah. Reh-BEK-uh.
Rephidim. REF-ih-dim.

Aaron (Moses' brother) and his sons are not yet functioning as priests; that won't come until Exodus 28. So Moses commissions *young Israelite men* to offer *burnt offerings* and *fellowship offerings.* Ordinarily, a burnt offering is completely burned (Leviticus 1). For the fellowship offering, however, only a portion is burned, and the remainder becomes something of a fellowship meal (Leviticus 3). This sharing is a part of the ceremony of commitment. The fact that blood is shed to confirm the covenant adds to the solemnity and seriousness of the event.

6. Moses took half of the blood and put it in bowls, and the other half he sprinkled on the altar.

The reason for taking *half of the blood* and putting *it in bowls* will be made clear in verse 8, below. For now, the other half of the blood is *sprinkled on the altar,* perhaps to sanctify it.

7. Then he took the Book of the Covenant and read it to the people.

The things that Moses had written are now *read* in the presence of *the people* (or at least before the leaders). The phrase *Book of the Covenant* is the designation for this early form of the covenant (compare 2 Kings 23:2).

C. RATIFICATION COMPLETED (vv. 7b, 8)

7b, 8. They responded, "We will do everything the LORD has said; we will obey." Moses then took the blood, sprinkled it on the people and said, "This is the blood of the covenant that the LORD has made with you in accordance with all these words."

This marks the third declaration by *the people* that they will keep the *covenant* (see comments on 9:3, above). They test the Lord's patience before Sinai with their constant complaining, but for now they express a determination to do what *the Lord has said.*

Moses completes the ceremony by taking the other half of *the blood* that was collected and sprinkling it *on the people.* Many have assumed that the blood is actually sprinkled on the leaders who are near or that it is sprinkled on the 12 pillars as representing the people (see v. 4). For New Testament references to the sprinkling of blood, see Hebrews 9:13-22; 11:28.

The final part of the ratification is Moses' declaration that *this is the blood of the covenant* for all the *words* that the Lord had spoken. The ratification of the new covenant is complete, and it is in effect for this new nation. God's ultimate purpose for the nation is that the promised Messiah will be an Israelite of the tribe of Judah. History records that these things are fulfilled just as God had promised. We have the blood of Jesus sprinkled on us (Hebrews 12:24; 1 Peter 1:2).

CONCLUSION

Almost 2000 years ago a young man in Galilee said something about seeking first the kingdom of God and the righteousness of God (Matthew 6:33). The current culture prefers not to be reminded of such claims by Jesus, so it has become preferred to avoid mentioning even his name.

That same young man also said something about the importance of confessing him before men (Matthew 10:32). Only then will he acknowledge such persons to the Father in Heaven.

As each Christian goes through life, he or she will be making decisions that involve loyalties to the Christ who gave the new covenant. It is possible, but often difficult, to maintain the proper priorities when others have no respect for Jesus. The consequences of faithfulness are not always pleasant, but to do otherwise is a violation of covenant. It is a serious thing to be ashamed of Jesus.

Discovery Learning

This page contains an alternative lesson plan emphasizing learning activities. Classes desiring such student involvement will find these suggestions helpful. The next page is a reproducible activity page to further enhance discovery learning.

LEARNING GOALS

After this lesson, each student will be able to:

1. Describe the covenant relationship that God designed for Old Testament Israel.

2. Discuss the meaning and importance of God's covenant relationship with Old Testament Israel.

3. State one specific way he or she will demonstrate greater faithfulness to the new covenant.

INTO THE LESSON

Recruit three class members to play the game "Pin the Mountain on the Sinai." Display an outline map of the exodus area. This can be either a simple hand drawn one or a commercial map. Tell your recruits you want them to close their eyes and let you turn them around once before they approach the map and put their token where they think the children of Israel encamped for a year.

Give each recruit a small (one-inch round) token with reusable adhesive applied to the back. Let each student adhere his or her "mountain" to the map. After all three are adhered, ask, "Which of these three tokens comes the closest to the real mountain where God gave the law to Moses?"

As noted by the lesson writer (see notes on verse 2), the true location remains disputed, but the traditional site is well known. Review the exodus from Egypt to the mount to establish the setting for today's texts. (Alternative: distribute either the Legal Papers or the Eagles' Wings exercise [or both] from the reproducible page for students to work on as they arrive.)

INTO THE WORD

Prepare copies of the text below. Call this, "Today's text as copied by a nearsighted, careless scribe." Ask the class to make corrections to the error-filled text with their Bibles closed.

In the third week after the Hebrews left captivity, on the very same day, they came to the Dessert of Sinai. After they set out from Seraphim, they entered the forests of Sinai, and Israel rested there in the dry place in the front of the volcano.

Then Moses went up to where God was, and God roared to him from the mountainside and said, "This is where you are to stay with the house of Israel and what you are to sell the people of Israel: 'You yourselves have seen what I did in Egypt, and how I carried you on angels' wings and brought you to my mountain. Now if you obey me carefully and keep my commandments, then out of all nationalities you will be my treacherous possession. Although the whole earth is special, you will be to me a country of priests and wholly a nation.' These are the words you are to preach to the Israelites."

When Moses went and told the people half the Lord's words and laws, they groaned with one voice, "Everything the Lord has said we will consider." Aaron then wrote down everything that Moses had said.

Moses woke up late the next morning and built and altered the foot of the mountain and set up stone pillows representing the twelve tributes of Israel. Then he sent young Israelite women, and they burned offerings and stacked up young bulls as fellowship offerings to the Lord. Moses took half of the bulls and put them in pens, and the other half he altered on the sprinkler. Then he took the Book of the Covenant and gave it to the people. They responded, "We will try to do everything the Lord has said; but we will disobey."

Moses then took the blood, showed it to the people and said, "This is the bond of the covenant that the Lord has made with you in agreement with all these works."

This can be a small-group activity, if desired. After students finish identifying errors, have them open their Bibles to verify their corrections. Share points from the commentary as appropriate.

INTO LIFE

Have students turn to Hebrews 8, a passage affirming the superiority of the new covenant in Christ. Read that short chapter responsively—you reading the odd-numbered verses and the class reading the even-numbered. After the reading, ask students how they will live up to the holy status that they hold in covenant with God in the week ahead.

Legal Papers

Compare God's offer of a covenant to Israel with each of the common "covenants" listed down the left.

COVENANT	Who decides the terms?	How are the terms recorded?	How may it be accepted or rejected?	What penalty if violated?	What protection to those involved?
A contract offered to a professional athlete					
A student handbook of a school or college					
A loan agency's expectation of repayment					
An appliance warranty given with the purchase					
A last will and testament					

How do the covenants listed above differ from God's covenants? Jot your ideas in the blocks. (If the boxes are too small, use a separate sheet of paper.)

Carried on Eagles' Wings

God tells the children of Israel that he carried them through their trials of the exodus "on eagles' wings." Do you sense that same soaring-but-protected care by God? On one of the wings below, describe a time you knew God was lifting you above dangers and fears. On the other wing, word a brief prayer of thanks for your ride on eagle wings.

COVENANT RENEWED

WHY TEACH THIS LESSON?

The morning worship service had been inspiring and uplifting. Afterward, two couples decided to go out to eat together, as was their usual practice. Sitting at their table in the restaurant, they proceeded to complain about every perceived fault: the service was too slow, the portion sizes were too small, there was a dead fly on the windowsill—nothing seemed to be quite to their liking. One wonders what others thought about them as Christians and about the Christian spirit as those four sat, dressed in their "Sunday best," complaining about everything in loud whispers!

While we'd like to think we wouldn't forget the truly important aspects of our lives so quickly after a worship service, the truth is we are all too easily distracted. In today's lesson the people of Israel recount God's faithfulness. Then they recommit to obey God. Yet most of us know how easily the Israelites were distracted afterward!

God allowed his chosen people to have the right to do just that. This is true for us as well. To be true to our relationship with Christ, we each need to remember God's goodness to us. We also benefit from periodically setting aside time for a brutally honest spiritual inventory, then recommitting our life to God and his purposes.

INTRODUCTION

A. SEEING THE POTENTIAL

A very ordinary, jagged piece of marble may seem as nothing in the eyes of the average person. It can, however, become an elaborate, detailed statue when shaped by the hands of an experienced sculptor. A rough-hewn block of wood may seem fit only to be burned. However, it can be carved into a thing of polished beauty by a master craftsman.

A conscientious teacher or youth worker cannot look at a group of students as immature and time-consuming. For there may be one or more in that group who, with careful teaching, can become great leaders for God and humankind. A slave people in a foreign land may appear to be nothing, but they may be chosen by the God of Heaven and earth to receive a special covenant. Despite their many failures in being faithful, in the fullness of time that nation can have the Son of God as one of its offspring—the long-awaited Messiah who offers salvation to all.

The potential within each person obviously is different. If, however, each person's resolve to fulfill his or her potential is combined with God's discipline and love, that potential can be realized.

B. LESSON BACKGROUND

The biblical accounts are usually interpreted to show that the Israelites spent 11 months and 20 days at Sinai, from the first day of the third month (Exodus 19:1) to the twentieth day of the second month of the second year (Numbers

DEVOTIONAL READING:
PSALM 51:1-12
BACKGROUND SCRIPTURE:
JOSHUA 24
PRINTED TEXT:
JOSHUA 24:1, 14-24

Sep
24

LESSON AIMS

After participating in this lesson, each student will be able to:

1. Describe the renewal of the covenant by Israel in the last days of Joshua's life.

2. Evaluate the benefits that come from regular reviews of commitments to God.

3. Make a plan for periodic reaffirmations of faithfulness to God.

KEY VERSE

The people said to Joshua, "We will serve the LORD our God and obey him." —Joshua 24:24

DAILY BIBLE READINGS

Monday, Sept. 18—*Pray for Renewal (Psalm 51:1-12)*

Tuesday, Sept. 19—*Be Strong and Bold (Deuteronomy 31:14-23)*

Wednesday, Sept. 20—*God Commands Joshua (Joshua 1: 1-9)*

Thursday, Sept. 21—*Recalling God's Mighty Acts (Joshua 24:1-7)*

Friday, Sept. 22—*God Gives a Land (Joshua 24:8-13)*

Saturday, Sept. 23—*Choose Whom You Will Serve (Joshua 24:14-18)*

Sunday, Sept. 24—*The People Renew Their Vows (Joshua 24:19-24)*

10:11). At that time the cloud lifted from the tabernacle, and the journey to Canaan continued.

While at Sinai, other details of the law were given. The Israelites were instructed how to build the tabernacle, and it was constructed according to the pattern given. The incident of the golden calf (Exodus 32) was a sobering event during Moses' 40 days on the mount. The intricacies of the sacrificial system and the priesthood are given in the book of Leviticus. Numbers 1:3 tells of a military census of all men who were age 20 and older. The total was 603,550 (2:32).

As the nation of Israel approached Canaan, 12 spies were sent into the land. Ten of the spies brought back a negative message of fear, and they prevailed over the minority report of Caleb and Joshua (Numbers 13). The punishment was announced by the Lord: the people were to spend a total of 40 years as shepherds in the desert (one year for each day the spies were gone; 14:33, 34); all the men of war except Caleb and Joshua were to perish in the wilderness (14:38). This means that 603,548 did not reach Canaan. That is an average of more than 40 deaths per day if we count only men age 20 and over!

The Israelites ultimately were successful in conquering the lands east of the Jordan. Two and one-half tribes were granted permission to settle on that side. Moses died at the age of 120, and the leadership fell to Joshua.

The miraculous crossing of the Jordan when it was in flood stage validated Joshua's role as the new leader (Joshua 3). The conquest of Jericho was offset in part by a temporary reversal at Ai (Joshua 7:3-5), the second city to be conquered. The victories continued in the central cities of Canaan (including the miracle of the long day as given in Joshua 10), southern Canaan, and then against the northern coalition. These primary battles consumed several years, ending in approximately 1400 BC. The land was divided among the remaining nine and one-half tribes. Cities were assigned for the Levites, with six of the cities designated as cities of refuge (Joshua 20).

Each of the last two chapters of the book of Joshua depicts national gatherings for covenant renewal. It is the second such event that is the background for today's lesson. There are no chronological references for these events. They are often assumed to be as early as 1390 BC but probably are later.

I. CONVOCATION (JOSHUA 24:1)

In one sense you cannot go back to where special events took place in the past and expect to find things as they were. Even so, there is value in returning—not to try to "live in the past," but just to reminisce and to walk among the monuments of memories. To visit again the place where a person was baptized or married, or other locations of special interest, can produce a nostalgia that is good for the soul. The last major event in the book of Joshua takes place in a special location. It has special meaning to those assembled, for it produces memories of their spiritual heritage.

1. Then Joshua assembled all the tribes of Israel at Shechem. He summoned the elders, leaders, judges and officials of Israel, and they presented themselves before God.

Two things prompt *Joshua* to gather the principal persons of *all the tribes of Israel.* First, as indicated in Joshua 23:1, his advanced age moves him to request that the nation again experience a formal covenant renewal. In this action he has the example set by Moses. Moses, just before his death, called the nation together to renew the covenant (Deuteronomy 29–34).

Second, Joshua is fully aware that this nation needs to be reminded again of its special relationship to *God*. Moses had commanded that the law be read to the nation every seven years (Deuteronomy 31:10-14). This occasion may be one of the fulfillments of Moses' command. A commitment on a national scope should be followed by continued and regular instruction in each community and home.

The first verse of the chapter specifies that *Shechem* is the location where Joshua chooses to have this ceremony. Since Joshua's hometown is Timnath Heres (also known as Timnath Serah; Joshua 19:49, 50; Judges 2:9), his selection requires him to make a full day's journey to the northwest.

Shechem is an appropriate site for several reasons. First, it is the first place in Canaan where Abraham built an altar to the Lord. It is here that the promise of this land was made for Abraham's descendants (Genesis 12:6, 7). It may be assumed that since Joshua had been commanded by God to meditate on the law (Joshua 1:8), that Joshua was fully aware of this historical background.

Second, a part of the heritage of Israel is that Jacob also built an altar at Shechem upon his return to the land with his family (Genesis 33:18-20). When Jacob left Shechem, he led his family in a spiritual housecleaning. This rededication involved burying all the accumulated household gods (Genesis 35:2, 4).

Third, this is the place where Joseph's bones are buried (Joshua 24:32). Joshua is of the tribe of Ephraim (1 Chronicles 7:20-27), so Joseph (Ephraim's father) is an ancestor. Joseph's exemplary life could be cited for anyone who comes to Shechem.

Fourth, Joshua had assembled the entire nation in this vicinity immediately after conquering Jericho and Ai. Joshua 8:30-35 records that the nation divided itself into two groups in accord with the command that Moses had given toward the end of his life (Deuteronomy 27:12, 13). One group stood on Mount Ebal and responded with "Amen" when the curses of the covenant were read, and the other group stood on Mount Gerizim and answered in the same way when the blessings were read.

The town of Shechem is immediately to the west of the pass between the two mountains. To be at this site again undoubtedly brings back many memories to the older leaders. It is very probable that the plastered stones, with the law written on them, are still visible as reminders of that earlier occasion (Deuteronomy 27:2, 3; Joshua 8:30-32). The large altar of uncut stones that Joshua had erected on Mount Ebal was a part of the earlier covenant renewal ceremony. It may be assumed that it is still in place at the occasion before us.

The Necessity of Godly Leaders

In the mid-nineteenth century, European Christians were awakening in their faith. The natural result was a desire to spread the gospel of Christ around the world. Dutch and German missionaries worked to gain access to the tribes of Indonesia. The first missionaries were rejected and many were killed. By the 1860s only 50 members of the Batak tribe had become Christians.

But then the missionaries, led by Ludwig Nommensen (1834–1918), turned their focus to reaching the tribal leaders in an attempt to create a church that was culturally Indonesian rather than European. The church mushroomed. By 1911 the number of converts had reached more than 100,000. Over the next half-century, ever-larger numbers of Western missionaries worked to create indigenous churches in Indonesia and other countries. The result is astounding: today there are more Christians in the developing nations than in the Western world.

When Joshua gave his final exhortation to Israel, he used this principle of focusing on the leaders. He challenged Israel's tribal leaders to be faithful to God.

What Do You Think?

If you were to go back to that "special place" to reaffirm your initial commitment to Christ, where would it be and why?

He knew that without godly leaders the nation would be lost. This principle would be proven true numerous times in Israel's history over the next few hundred years. The principle is still valid today. Seldom do people rise above their leaders.   —C. R. B.

II. CHOICES (JOSHUA 24:14-18)

There is a dramatic change in the emphasis between the first part of the book of Joshua and these final chapters. The early chapters of the book stress the faithfulness of God in helping Israel to conquer Canaan (Joshua 1:9; 3:10; 4:23, 24). In the last chapters the continued faithfulness of the people is emphasized (Joshua 23:6-8). To express faithfulness and thankfulness is one thing; to live it is much more demanding.

A. PROPOSALS BY JOSHUA (vv. 14, 15)

14. "Now fear the LORD and serve him with all faithfulness. Throw away the gods your forefathers worshiped beyond the River and in Egypt, and serve the LORD.

The historical review like the one in Joshua 24:2-13 (not in today's text) is a standard part of the covenants of the second millennium BC. Following that review, Joshua now begins to assert the foundational requirements that the Lord expects to receive from his covenant nation: the people are to *fear* and to *serve him*. Jesus makes a similar statement in Matthew 10:28. It is more logical to worship the creator instead of what he created (compare Romans 1:25). That is why the Israelites are to *throw away the gods your forefathers worshiped beyond the River and in Egypt.*

That second part of Joshua's statement is intriguing. After experiencing all the mighty miracles of God, does this covenant nation still have idols in its midst? The text makes it clear that they did—both in Egypt and also over the 700 years prior to that time when Abraham and his family crossed the Euphrates River.

This command by Joshua to give up their idolatry is similar to Jacob's command in Genesis 35:2. The people of Israel seem to maintain a fascination for idolatry until after the Babylonian exile in 586 BC. It will take a 70-year captivity before they are more or less cured of this spiritual weakness.

15. "But if serving the LORD seems undesirable to you, then choose for yourselves this day whom you will serve, whether the gods your forefathers served beyond the River, or the gods of the Amorites, in whose land you are living. But as for me and my household, we will serve the LORD."

This is considered one of the greatest verses in the entire book. It presents the choice in vivid language. The Israelites must choose whom they will serve: *the gods* that some of their ancestors worshiped before Abraham entered Canaan, or *the gods of the Amorites* where they now live, or *the Lord*!

Joshua boldly announces his own decision. As Joshua looks back over his life, this choice is the only one that makes sense. He is able to recall the many miracles that he has witnessed—from the plagues in Egypt to the battle of the long day. In Joshua 23:14 he states that not one promise of the Lord has failed. With these things in his mind, he can make what is now that famous declaration: *as for me and my household, we will serve the Lord.* Many Christian homes have this saying posted on a wall in the form of an embroidery, etc.

B. PREFERENCE OF THE PEOPLE (vv. 16-18)

16. Then the people answered, "Far be it from us to forsake the LORD to serve other gods!

WHAT DO YOU THINK?

What are some of the gods we hold on to? Why is it so hard to put away these gods?

Choose
you this day
whom ye
will serve

...but as
for me and
my house,
we will serve
the Lord.
—Joshua 24:15

Visual for Lesson 4. *Ask for a show of hands: Who among your students has this famous passage displayed somewhere in the house?*

Prompted by the power of Joshua's reason and example, the people are moved to make the same choice. At this moment it is preposterous to think of serving *other gods.*

17, 18. *"It was the LORD our God himself who brought us and our fathers up out of Egypt, from that land of slavery, and performed those great signs before our eyes. He protected us on our entire journey and among all the nations through which we traveled. And the LORD drove out before us all the nations, including the Amorites, who lived in the land. We too will serve the LORD, because he is our God."*

Sometimes the choices of the past are ignored when tough decisions are made. This time the vibrant review of the nation's history (vv. 2-13) moves the leaders to express their own account of days gone by. They are compelled to remember where they had been (in Egypt), where they are now, and what it took to get there. Faced with this evidence, they affirm again that they will *serve the Lord.*

III. CHALLENGE (JOSHUA 24:19-21)

Is the affirmation of verses 17, 18 enough for Joshua? Apparently not!

A. PRESENTATION BY JOSHUA (vv. 19, 20)

19, 20. *Joshua said to the people, "You are not able to serve the LORD. He is a holy God; he is a jealous God. He will not forgive your rebellion and your sins. If you forsake the LORD and serve foreign gods, he will turn and bring disaster on you and make an end of you, after he has been good to you."*

Joshua's reply seems to be out of place, for the affirmation by the people was certainly the desired result—or was it? Do his words *You are not able to serve the Lord* simply reflect Joshua's previous experiences of this fickle nation? Does he discern a hollow mockery in their affirmation?

Joshua's charge that they are unable to serve the Lord in the long run is based on two reasons. First, God *is a holy God,* and Joshua doubts that the Israelites are able to be faithful for an extended period. Second, God's jealousy demands absolute loyalty. There is to be no spiritual adultery, no going after other gods.

B. PRIORITY OF THE PEOPLE (v. 21)

21. *But the people said to Joshua, "No! We will serve the LORD."*

This reaffirmation by the people produces the result that Joshua's challenge desires. It also makes their priority even stronger in that they can be reminded in the future of what they have said so emphatically.

IV. COMMITMENT (JOSHUA 24:22-24)

Now we come to the climax. Things have reached a fever pitch!

A. PRONOUNCEMENT BY JOSHUA (v. 22a)

22a. *Then Joshua said, "You are witnesses against yourselves that you have chosen to serve the LORD."*

Joshua reminds the people that their commitment to *the Lord* is quite serious. What they have said cannot be taken lightly. They have become their own *witnesses* before God and people in their declaration.

B. PROCLAMATION OF THE PEOPLE (v. 22b)

22b. *"Yes, we are witnesses," they replied.*

In short, pithy statements the dialogue goes back and forth. The people testify to their commitment for the third time.

WHAT DO YOU THINK?

What blessings has God given your church that should lead to even deeper commitments to him? How can we make sure we count and recount these blessings?

WHAT DO YOU THINK?

Sometimes our actions belie our words. In what ways can the things that we do devalue our promise of allegiance to God? How can we do better?

PRAYER

Our God in Heaven, we resolve to study your Word in order to understand better our obligations to you and to others. In Jesus' name, amen.

HOW TO SAY IT

Ai. AY-eye.

Amorites. AM-uh-rites.

Babylonian. Bab-ih-LOW-nee-un.

Caleb. KAY-leb.

Canaan. KAY-nun.

Ebal. EE-bull.

Egypt. EE-jipt.

Euphrates. You-FRAY-teez.

Gerizim. GAIR-ih-zeem or Guh-RYE-zim.

Jericho. JAIR-ih-co.

Joshua. JOSH-yew-uh.

Levites. LEE-vites.

Leviticus. Leh-VIT-ih-kus.

Shechem. SHEE-kem or SHEK-em.

Sinai. SIGH-nye or SIGH-nay-eye.

Timnath Heres. TIM-nath HEE-reez.

WHAT DO YOU THINK?

In quick succession the people of God offered their allegiance to God four times. How can we follow their example in reaffirming our dedication to God?

C. DISTINCTIVE REMINDER (v. 23)

23. "Now then," said Joshua, "throw away the foreign gods that are among you and yield your hearts to the LORD, the God of Israel."

Joshua says that the first test of the covenant's renewal by the Israelites is to discard *the foreign gods*, which they still had. These gods could be items of value or located in special places of devotion. Sometimes it costs to serve the Lord, but it costs even more not to serve him.

IDOLATERS ANONYMOUS?

Alcoholics Anonymous (also known simply as A.A.) was founded in 1935 by a New York stockbroker and an Ohio surgeon. Both men admitted to having been hopeless drunks. Their goal was to stay sober themselves and help others to overcome their addiction to alcohol. Today there are over two million A.A. members in 150 countries.

The success of A.A. has led to the founding of other "anonymous" groups. These groups are for drugs addicts, compulsive shoppers, overeaters, and even for those who cannot seem to control their use of profanity! The literature of these "anonymous" groups often recognizes that the source of the cure is a Higher Power. That may be a little vague for those of us who think the reference should be specifically to God, yet therein lies the genius of the whole "anonymous" movement.

It would not be far off the mark to state that Joshua was, in effect, trying to start an "Idolaters Anonymous" movement. He knew the power idolatry had over Israel; the people seemed incapable of helping themselves. He also knew that trust in God was the only source of a cure. The same can be said for any sin that besets us. Without the intervention of the cross of Christ, our sin problem can never be finally solved.   —C. R. B.

D. DEFINITE REJOINDER (v. 24)

24. And the people said to Joshua, "We will serve the LORD our God and obey him."

For the fourth time the people affirm their intention to *serve* and *obey* the Lord. The entire scenario is almost a preview of Jesus' challenges to Peter after the resurrection (John 21:15-19). Joshua 24:25-27 is not part of the lesson text, but provides the close of the covenant's renewal.

Joshua is to be admired in calling this assembly as he tries to instill faith in the generation to follow. It is extremely important that this be done. If the second generation sees compromise in the first generation, then the second generation will deviate even more. And the third generation, with these examples, will essentially abandon the faith.

CONCLUSION

Until 1998 the phrase *Most Favored Nation Status* was used to designate nations that received equal treatment by the U.S. in trading relations. The term was discontinued because most nations were in this category, and it seemed deceptive. The newer term is *Normal Trade Relations*. The nation of Israel, however, definitely was a nation with a "most favored" status before God. Yet, as has been expressed many times, *there is peril in privilege.*

The teaching of the New Testament is similar. The individual who becomes a member of the body of Christ enjoys the privileges of sins forgiven, the gift of the Holy Spirit, and the promise of Heaven. Yet Hebrews 6:4-6 warns about those who have enjoyed the privileges of the gospel and then fall away. *There is peril in privilege.*

THOUGHT TO REMEMBER

To serve the Lord is costly. Not to serve him costs even more.

Discovery Learning

This page contains an alternative lesson plan emphasizing learning activities. Classes desiring such student involvement will find these suggestions helpful. The next page is a reproducible activity page to further enhance discovery learning.

LEARNING GOALS

After this lesson, each student will be able to:

1. Describe the renewal of the covenant by Israel in the last days of Joshua's life.

2. Evaluate the benefits that come from regular reviews of commitments to God.

3. Make a plan for periodic reaffirmations of faithfulness to God.

INTO THE LESSON

As students arrive, offer each a choice: either a pencil or a penny. After all have made choices, say, "I'm going to show you both sides of six cards. Pick one letter of the two from each card and write it down. When we're finished, we'll see if anyone has a key word from today's study." Before class prepare six large cards with the following pairs of letters front and back: A, C (card 1); K, H (card 2); O, S (card 3); D, O (card 4); S, T (card 5); E, Y (card 6). Show the cards in the order given. Make certain all students see both sides.

After you have revealed all six cards and each student has chosen six letters, ask, "Does anyone have the six letters that—taken in sequence—spell the key word?" (*The word is CHOOSE.*) If no one has the word, ask, "Does anyone think he or she knows what the word is?" After the word has been revealed, comment on the choice each student had at the beginning: one choice was critical to success while the other was inconsequential. (Alternative: distribute part 1 of the Covenant Renewal exercise from the reproducible page for students to work on as they arrive. Discuss. Save part 2 as an alternative exercise for the Into Life segment.)

INTO THE WORD

Read aloud Joshua 8:30-35 to remind your class of the appropriate location for the assembly described in Joshua 24. Emphasize the division of the Israelite people into two "amen choruses." (See the commentary for verse 1.) Divide your class into two sides. (This can be done without anyone physically moving.) Recruit two of your good oral readers to share in a reading of today's text in the manner that follows, with pauses for "amen" responses from the half of the class assigned to each reader.

Reader One (R1): "Now fear the Lord and serve him with all faithfulness."

Reader Two (R2): "Throw away the gods your forefathers worshiped beyond the River and in Egypt."

R1 & R2: "Serve the Lord."

R1: "But if serving the Lord seems undesirable to you, then choose for yourselves this day whom you will serve."

R2: "Whether the gods your forefathers served beyond the River, or the gods of the Amorites, in whose land you are living."

R1 & R2: "But as for me and my household, we will serve the Lord."

R1: Then the people answered, "Far be it from us to forsake the Lord to serve other gods!"

R2: "It was the Lord our God himself who brought us and our fathers up out of Egypt, from the land of slavery, and performed those great signs before our eyes. He protected us on our entire journey and among all the nations through which we traveled."

R1: "And the Lord drove out before us all the nations, including the Amorites, who lived in the land."

R1 & R2: "We too will serve the Lord, because he is our God."

R2: Joshua said to the people, "You are not able to serve the Lord. He is a holy God; he is a jealous God. He will not forgive your rebellion and your sins."

R1: "If you forsake the Lord and serve foreign gods, he will turn and bring disaster on you and make an end of you, after he has been good to you."

R1 & R2: But the people said to Joshua, "No! We will serve the Lord."

R2: Then Joshua said, "You are witnesses against yourselves that you have chosen to serve the Lord."

R1 & R2: "Yes, we are witnesses," they replied.

R1: "Now then," said Joshua "throw away your foreign gods that are among you and yield your hearts to the Lord, the God of Israel."

R1 & R2: And the people said to Joshua, "We will serve the Lord our God and obey him."

INTO LIFE

Prepare and distribute copies of the Say It Over and Over exercise from the reproducible page. Challenge class members to sign the affirmation, then carry or post it where they will see it often. Suggest that they read it aloud at least once a day.

Covenant Renewal

1. In what sense does each of the following occasions serve as a renewal of your covenant with Christ? Jot down your thoughts.

Attendance at a Sunday worship gathering

Observing a new believer being baptized into Christ

Participating in the observance of the Lord's Supper

Approaching God in prayer

Contributing financially to the Lord's church and its activities

2. What special way could you celebrate the anniversary date of the occasion when you first affirmed your faith in Christ and your initial submission to his lordship? Plan an annual event; describe it here.

Say It Over and Over

In today's text from Joshua 24, the people of God repeat over and over their choice to serve the Lord. Take a look at the affirmation below. Are you willing to sign this commitment between you and God? Are you willing to begin each day by repeating it?

> ## "Lord God, today I will serve you!"
>
> signed: _____

GOD SENDS JUDGES

WHY TEACH THIS LESSON?

When we think of the Great Commission that Jesus Christ gave his followers to make disciples of all nations, we may be tempted to look at a map and say, "done deal." But the truth is that the task is far from finished. I admit that I was shocked when, in a class on how to share your faith, one man in his late forties said he didn't know who Jesus was until he was an adult. Each new generation represents something of a new "nation"—a new group of people who need to hear the liberating words of God.

Today's lesson shows God sending judges to rescue his people in times of need. Our rescuer is Jesus. While we may or may not be called to leave our homeland to spread his gospel, we must be ready always to be his hands and feet. That is the only way that those around us will see the love of Christ. His love is lived out in his children.

INTRODUCTION

A. The Passing of Generations

In 2004 the Allies marked the sixtieth anniversary of the Normandy D-Day invasion. It was a reunion of the primary World War II partners: U.S., Canada, Russia, Britain, and France. The Germans were also invited for the first time, because there was some recognition that the German people suffered terribly in World War II.

Many noted that this was likely the last big hurrah for the World War II veterans. At the time the youngest of these veterans were in their late seventies. Quickly fading was what Tom Brokaw had labeled The Greatest Generation.

The World War II generation had dominated the national and international scene for 50 years, far beyond the normal cycle. Hard work, integrity, and a willingness to fight for freedom characterized that generation. What will the world be like when its influence becomes a legacy and then that legacy fades?

In the book of Judges, a surprisingly similar state of affairs is presented in the history of Israel. After the miraculous events of the exodus and the period of temporary residence in the wilderness, the people of Israel entered the promised land. There the armies of Israel fought many battles to liberate territory from the Canaanites. In this week's lesson Joshua and his warrior generation have died off. The next generation is in control, and its stories are told in the book of Judges.

B. Lesson Background

The book of Judges records the history of Israel from the time of Joshua's death until the time of Samuel, Israel's last judge (see 1 Samuel 7:15). This is roughly the time period 1400–1050 BC. During this time period, Israel had no king but was instead guided by judges. Judges were men and women who arose providentially in times of national crisis to deliver the nation. They seemed to be endowed with the Spirit of God in a special way (at least some of them). The

DEVOTIONAL READING:
DEUTERONOMY 6:4-9
BACKGROUND SCRIPTURE:
JUDGES 2:6-23
PRINTED TEXT:
JUDGES 2:11-14, 16-23

Oct
1

LESSON AIMS

After participating in this lesson, each student will be able to:

1. Describe the situation Israel repeatedly faced when the faith held by one generation was not passed on to the next.

2. Compare and contrast Israel's challenge of passing on its faith to the next generation with the twenty-first-century church's challenge to do the same.

3. Identify one way that he or she will help prepare the next generation of church leaders.

KEY VERSE

The LORD raised up judges, who saved them out of the hands of these raiders. —Judges 2:16

LESSON 5 NOTES

judges were a colorful cast of characters, including the woman-warrior Deborah, the fleece-man Gideon, the left-handed assassin Ehud, and the ancient "superman" Samson.

The judges of Israel served several functions. At times they were judicial arbiters. More often they were national deliverers, frequently as military leaders. Judges were not like kings in that there was no hereditary succession. The one son of a judge who tried to succeed his father in this manner failed (Abimelech, son of Gideon; Judges 9).

Furthermore, the judges of Israel did not function like kings by imposing taxes or negotiating treaties with other nations—functions expected of kings. Israel's judges had no standing army but relied on the tribal leaders of Israel to provide men when military action was necessary. The judges did not have grand palaces or courtiers. They were seen as regular citizens with extraordinary responsibilities.

The period of the judges is in many ways the record of Israel's "Dark Ages." The Israelites had become a settled nation, living in cities and villages. They were farmers, not nomadic shepherds like the patriarchs. Yet this is a time of crisis between faith and culture, between covenant loyalty and the enticing sins of the Canaanites.

Chapter 2 gives a preview of the book and outlines a cycle that is repeated many times in the period before Israel has a king. The cycle is tragically repetitive: apostasy leads to crisis, which leads to repentance, which leads to deliverance, which drifts back to apostasy. The verdict of the book of Judges is that this was a time of moral chaos. "In those days Israel had no king; everyone did as he saw fit" (Judges 21:25).

I. GENERATION VEERS OFF COURSE (JUDGES 2:11-14)

A. PEOPLE'S BETRAYAL (vv. 11-13)

11, 12. Then the Israelites did evil in the eyes of the LORD and served the Baals. They forsook the LORD, the God of their fathers, who had brought them out of Egypt. They followed and worshiped various gods of the peoples around them. They provoked the LORD to anger

The previous generations of Israelites had experienced many mighty things. They had seen the parting of the Red Sea and the destruction of the Egyptian army (Exodus 14). They had been the beneficiaries of miraculous food and water in the wilderness (16:11-15; 17:6). They had witnessed the supernatural on the mountain of Sinai (19:16-20). They had beheld the mighty presence of God in the tabernacle (40:34, 35).

Now the descendants of the exodus generation have settled in the land of Canaan and become infatuated with Canaanite religion. They have violated God's covenant and embraced idolatry. They have become conformed to the darkness of the world. From our vantage point it is easy to understand why God becomes angry with them. God has fulfilled every one of his promises to them, and they have rejected him.

THE PRICE OF "FUN"

J. L. Hunter "Red" Rountree was the oldest known bank robber in America. He was 92 when he died in prison on October 12, 2004.

Red got a late start in his profession. In his late eighties he pulled off his first robbery at a Mississippi bank. He was given three years' probation, a fine, and was told to get out of the state. A year later, in 1999, he robbed a Florida bank and re-

WHAT DO YOU THINK?

Where do you think our society is right now in this cycle? Or is it even appropriate to draw a parallel between then and now?

WHAT DO YOU THINK?

What false gods do you find today's generation chasing after that make God angry? Is it fair to say that we are all idolaters at some level? Explain.

ceived a three-year sentence. He was released in 2002. In 2003 he robbed a Kansas bank and was sentenced to nearly 13 years in prison.

Red Rountree had turned bitter many years earlier because of something about a bank loan that didn't go well. The bitter spirit festered for years before he acted upon it. In a prison interview he said, "You want to know why I rob banks? It's fun. I feel good, awful good. I feel good for sometimes days, for sometimes hours." No family member claimed his body upon his death. Apparently his bitterness had made him a lonely old man.

Israel's time-and-again pursuit of fictitious gods shows some of that same futility. Like Red Rountree, Israel persisted in doing what was "fun." But sinful "fun" is fleeting. In the long run the cost of sinful "fun" is always very steep. Both the experiences of Red Rountree and Israel should teach us a lesson. Will we learn?

—C. R. B.

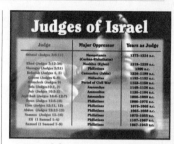

Visual for Lesson 5. *You may wish to post this chart alongside the* Old Testament World *map visual or the* Timeline of Old Testament Events.

13. . . . *because they forsook him and served Baal and the Ashtoreths.*

As we look at this from a vantage point of over 3,000 years after the event, it is puzzling as to why the people of Israel would abandon their God and turn to the Canaanite gods. What was so enticing there?

There are two deities mentioned as receiving worship from the Israelites. *Baal* is actually a title meaning "lord." Baalim (in Judges 2:11) is the plural form of Baal. The ancient Canaanites worship a chief male god whom they had given the title *lord.* He is seen as the weather god or storm god, and thus he is the god who controls the destiny of the people. If Baal withholds the rain, the crops do not grow and the people starve.

It also appears that the Canaanites believe that each field has a lesser god that controls its fertility. These gods are lords of the fields and have the power to give abundant or meager crops. Thus, the Canaanites serve the "big Baal" of the weather as well as the "little Baals" of each individual farm.

Ashtoreths is also a plural form and is feminine. In Canaanite religion she is the consort of Baal. She is a fertility deity who is thought to control the fertility of both women and of fields. See also Judges 10:6.

The agricultural society of the Canaanites venerates these gods by practices that included ritual prostitution (male and female), child sacrifice, and orgy-like worship. Some scholars believe that almost every woman living in a Canaanite village served a term as a temple prostitute before marriage. The Canaanite religions thus combine idolatry with forbidden sexuality. This is why it is common in the Old Testament to see the worship of false gods as prostitution (see Deuteronomy 31:16; Judges 2:17). To make sexual immorality an act of devotion is strictly opposed to the holy morality of the law that the Israelites had received from God.

The Canaanites have gods with no morality, and this makes it easy to see why the men of Israel are attracted to this religion. Yet it is also clear why there can be no accommodation here for those who are supposed to live according to the holy covenant that their nation has with the holy God of Israel.

B. LORD'S ANGER (v. 14)

14. In his anger against Israel the LORD handed them over to raiders who plundered them. He sold them to their enemies all around, whom they were no longer able to resist.

Are we surprised that this outrageous behavior provokes the hot anger of God? The result is the lifting of God's providential protection for *Israel*. The nation is powerless to fight off the *raiders* from surrounding peoples. A common strategy in those days is for an armed force to swoop down at harvesttime and steal the crops while killing all who *resist.* Thus, the tragedy of deaths and destruction is followed by grim times of famine and starvation.

II. STORY SADLY REPEATS (JUDGES 2:16-19)

A. GOD DELIVERS (v. 16)

16. Then the LORD raised up judges, who saved them out of the hands of these raiders.

The author is clear that the people of Israel stand powerless before these foreign marauders. Their deliverance comes only when God chooses and empowers leaders, called *judges,* to rescue them. This is a primary lesson found throughout the Bible. We can never hope to save ourselves. Salvation comes from God, who hears our cries, understands our helplessness, and comes to save us. "Say to those with fearful hearts, 'Be strong, do not fear; your God will come, he will come with vengeance; with divine retribution he will come to save you" (see Isaiah 35:4).

B. PEOPLE TURN AWAY (v. 17)

17. Yet they would not listen to their judges but prostituted themselves to other gods and worshiped them. Unlike their fathers, they quickly turned from the way in which their fathers had walked, the way of obedience to the LORD's commands.

We are drawn to share God's frustration in this cycle. The people suffer for their sin, so God delivers them. But then they sin again, bringing on another cycle of suffering. Why can't they figure out this pattern?

From a coolly analytical viewpoint, it is easy for us to see their folly. However, our life experiences are filled with similar cases. Sin leads to punishment and suffering (see Jeremiah 14:10). God notices our cries of suffering (see Exodus 3:7; Nehemiah 9:9). Repentance saves us from destruction (see Jonah 3:10), because God never stops loving us (see Psalm 89:32, 33, which applies these principles to the royal descendants of David).

The text draws a strong contrast to the faithfulness of "the Joshua generation" and the faithlessness of "the Judges generations." Their ancestors obeyed God's commandments, but they did not so. False worship and disobedience go hand in hand.

C. GOD STILL DELIVERS (v. 18)

18. Whenever the LORD raised up a judge for them, he was with the judge and saved them out of the hands of their enemies as long as the judge lived; for the LORD had compassion on them as they groaned under those who oppressed and afflicted them.

God is involved repeatedly in the deliverance of his people. He provides *a judge* to deliver them, and he is *with the judge.* The book of Judges tells the stories of the judges with all their human failings. For example, Samson is presented as a slow-witted show-off who can be tempted easily by an attractive woman (Judges 14–16). Although Samson is humiliated due to disobedience, God is with him until the end, empowering him to destroy many of the enemy Philistines through his own death (Judges 16:28-30).

The Lord's compassion causes him to relent from his fierce anger. God's wrath has given way to his mercy. God is never overwhelmed by anger (see Hosea 11:9).

D. PEOPLE STILL TURN AWAY (v. 19)

19. But when the judge died, the people returned to ways even more corrupt than those of their fathers, following other gods and serving and worshiping them. They refused to give up their evil practices and stubborn ways.

There is a great sadness in this verse. It is not just that the people lapse into disobedience, but that they return to their sin so energetically! Depravity can quickly become a downward spiral of destruction.

The root cause of this pattern is given to us: human stubbornness. This is sometimes celebrated as a virtue, but it should not be. Stubbornness is not the same as faithfulness and an uncompromising stand for righteousness. Stubborn people are usually prideful and unwilling to admit error. Stubbornness is equated with an unrepentant heart in Scripture; "because of your stubbornness and your unrepentant heart, you are storing up wrath against yourself" (Romans 2:5). God will not abide this type of human defiance.

SOME CALL IT STUBBORN

"Bullheaded," "set in their ways," or some just call it being "stubborn." That's how we describe other people when they are being inflexible. Examples of this trait might be a crotchety old person who refuses to take medications or the proverbial husband who rejects his wife's pleading to stop the car and ask directions.

On the other hand, when it is we who are being inflexible, we see ourselves to be acting with "dogged persistence," having "steadfast fidelity to a cause," or exhibiting "plain ol' stick-to-it-ive-ness." Perhaps we see ourselves in the mold of a detective who single-mindedly pursues a "cold case" for years and finally brings a criminal to justice. Or as a Thomas Edison, who may work diligently for years, performing hundreds of experiments to perfect the light bulb. We all like to believe that we act with motives that are more noble than the motives of others, don't we?

There is an important difference between the virulent trait of stubbornness and the virtuous trait of fidelity. During the time of the judges, Israel made no pretense of holding to righteousness. Instead, the people stubbornly resisted God's warnings and refused to see the plain evidence of what their sinfulness got them. What do you think: has human nature changed much since then? —C. R. B.

III. COVENANT BROKEN (JUDGES 2:20-23)

A. DELAYING PROMISES (vv. 20, 21)

20, 21. Therefore the LORD was very angry with Israel and said, "Because this nation has violated the covenant that I laid down for their forefathers and has not listened to me, I will no longer drive out before them any of the nations Joshua left when he died.

Before his death Joshua reminded the people of Israel that God had never failed to keep his promises to them (Joshua 23:14). God's promises are always true. The land of Canaan was referred to as the land promised to the fathers of Israel (see Exodus 13:11). But Joshua also warned the people that if they worshiped the false gods of the Canaanites, then God had promised to punish them and make the land an inhospitable and oppressive place (Joshua 23:12-16).

God's promises, then, are both absolute and contingent. God sets the terms of *the covenant.* God always upholds his end, absolutely keeping his promises. However, when the human participants fail to honor the covenant's terms, then God withholds the promised blessings. Instead, he delivers the curses or punishments also promised in the covenant. Thus the contingency element lies in God's promised response to human obedience or disobedience.

DAILY BIBLE READINGS

Monday, Sept. 25—Love the Lord (Deuteronomy 6:4-9)

Tuesday, Sept. 26—God and the Hebrew People (Psalm 78:1-8)

Wednesday, Sept. 27—Prayer for a Nation (Psalm 85: 4-13)

Thursday, Sept. 28—Israel Disobeys God (Judges 2:1-5)

Friday, Sept. 29—A New Generation (Judges 2:6-10)

Saturday, Sept. 30—Israel Abandons God (Judges 2:11-15)

Sunday, Oct. 1—Call to Repentance (Judges 2:16-23)

B. TESTING EACH GENERATION (vv. 22, 23)

22, 23. "I will use them to test Israel and see whether they will keep the way of the LORD and walk in it as their forefathers did." The LORD had allowed those nations to remain; he did not drive them out at once by giving them into the hands of Joshua.

I had the measles as a child and now have an immunity to this disease. My daughter is also immune to measles because she received a childhood immunization against them. She arrived at her immunity via a different path, but the result is the same. But if my daughter has a child, that baby will not be protected. Measles immunity cannot be inherited; it must be acquired by enduring either the disease or painful inoculations.

Each generation is tested. Because faith is a personal relationship, it cannot be inherited. Furthermore, the true nature of faith is unknown until it is tested. The tireless God knows that the faith of each generation of his people must be proved (see 1 Peter 1:7).

CONCLUSION

A. CHASING OTHER GODS

The Bible is an account of God's pursuit of his lost children. It is also the story of humanity's flight from God and continual quest of other gods.

Society embraces the worship of a surprising array of other gods. We see open worship of the gods of the pagan deities of nature. We see the worship of wealth and of power. We see the worship of sexuality and celebrity. We see the worship of sports and entertainment. We see the worship of technology and of materialism. Our generations are not pursuing a single false god but many!

The Bible labels such vain pursuit as idolatry. Today's lesson gives the inevitable results. First, we kindle the anger of God (Judges 2:12). Second, we suffer the withdrawal of God's blessings (2:14). Third, God begins to oppose us or may even fight against us (2:15). But, fourth, God sends a rescuer (2:16). As Christians, we realize that this gets to the core of the gospel. We have strayed in sin, incurred the wrath of God, and experienced the withdrawal of his blessings. Our deliverer, Jesus Christ the Savior, rescues us from much more than national peril. He wants to save us, individually, from sin and the curse of eternal death.

B. GENERATIONAL LEGACIES

There have been no world wars for over half a century, and we hope the twenty-first century will not see their return. The "greatest generation" with its many virtues and accomplishments has given way to its children and grandchildren. The transition has been difficult, and the church bears the scars of generational conflict. It is not easy to step aside when one has been in control for a long time. It is difficult to trust those who are younger, less experienced, and whom we have seen make serious mistakes growing up.

Yet we cannot stop the transition. It will take place whether we facilitate it or resist it. We must trust God to work patiently with the new crop of leaders, as he has for thousands of years.

So ask yourself: Have the leaders of my church allowed a place of influence for those younger, those in their twenties and thirties? Are the primary leaders of my church all 50 and older? What can I do to facilitate the transition? Do I have an attitude of encouragement or one of criticism for younger leaders? What can I do to support new and younger leaders in my church? Is there a particular young leader I can pray for this week?

WHAT DO YOU THINK?

In what ways can we help the next generation avoid the cycle of apostasy and repentance? What could happen to our church and nation if we neglect our duty in this regard?

WHAT DO YOU THINK?

Share a time in your life when you went through this cycle of apostasy and repentance. What caused your downward spiral, and what or whom did God use to pull you out of it?

PRAYER

Mighty God, we marvel at your eternal consistency. You always keep your promises. May we be faithful and receive promised blessings rather than curses. We pray this in the name of your mighty Son, Jesus, amen.

THOUGHT TO REMEMBER

Those of each new generation must build a relationship of faith and obedience with God.

Discovery Learning

This page contains an alternative lesson plan emphasizing learning activities. Classes desiring such student involvement will find these suggestions helpful. The next page is a reproducible activity page to further enhance discovery learning.

LEARNING GOALS

After participating in this lesson, each student will be able to:

1. Describe the situation Israel repeatedly faced when the faith held by one generation was not passed on to the next.

2. Compare and contrast Israel's challenge of passing on its faith to the next generation with the twenty-first-century church's challenge to do the same.

3. Identify one way that he or she will help prepare the next generation of church leaders.

INTO THE LESSON

Display the following four scrambled words as your class assembles: AAOPSSTY; CIIRSS; ACEEENNPRT; ACDEEEILNRV. Also display a poster board circle, 12" in diameter, that is centered and attached by a paper fastener to a poster board circle that is 20" in diameter. On the smaller circle have an arrow pointing from center to edge. Work the attached circle until it rotates easily.

As class members decipher the four scrambled words (*apostasy, crisis, repentance, deliverance*), write each respectively at the 12 o'clock, 3 o'clock, 6 o'clock, and 9 o'clock positions on the larger circle. Make a short statement based on the lesson writer's comments on the cycle of destruction from the lesson Introduction.

INTO THE WORD

As today's text pictures the foolish sinfulness of the people of Israel, it also reveals the grand characteristics of God. Display each of the short affirmatives about God below, but don't reveal the verses and thoughts that are in italics. (This can be done with simple paper strips, with an overhead transparency, or as a PowerPoint® presentation.) As each affirmation is revealed, ask your class, "How and in what verses is this attribute of God revealed in today's text?"

Sample verse numbers and explanations are given here, but accept other reasonable and insightful responses. (Though listed in a verse-by-verse sequence, the statements should be displayed randomly.) (1) "God is a moral God" (vv. 11, 12 affirm that God sees evil and it angers him); (2) "God is not bound by time or space" (vv. 11, 12 affirm his relationship with previous generations and his presence in Egypt is a given); (3) "God can

decide not to impose his will over human choice" (v. 13 indicates that he can be ignored, at least temporarily); (4) "God will demonstrate his justice and wrath" (v. 14 pictures his punishment of his wayward nation); (5) "God controls the destinies of all nations" (v. 14 indicates God's use of pagan nations as his agents); (6) "God loves his people" (v. 16 reveals that the judge-deliverers were God's loving idea); (7) "God expects his people to obey his commandments" (v. 17); (8) "God will support individual leaders to fulfill his purposes" (v. 18 states that God was with the judge he called forth to service); (9) "God stays the same; his expectations and his mercy do not vary" (see v. 18); (10) "God deals with people individually, one generation at a time" (v. 19 pictures the failure of succeeding generations and individuals to remain consistent to God's truth); (11) "There is a limit to God's patience with sinfulness" (vv. 20, 21 describe God's decision about his sinful people); (12) "God will test the faith of his people" (v. 22 indicates God's plan to prove his people by allowing sinful nations to continue alongside them); (13) "God can intervene on behalf of his people, or he can choose not to" (v. 23 affirms God's decision not to intervene, not to overwhelm Israel's enemies).

A similar activity is included in the student book. The What Does It Take exercise from the reproducible page can enhance this section of Discovery Learning.

INTO LIFE

As adults, your class members need to take an active role in the Christian education of their own children, grandchildren, and other children of your church and community. "Faithful unto death" should be each generation's goal. But all godly parents will look beyond their own generation to help the next generation to gain a faith that will last a lifetime.

Ask your class to make a list of the various ways that they can participate in the godly nurture of your church's children and teens. When the list is complete, indicate that you will make copies and distribute them next Sunday. Then each class member can choose one way to enlarge his or her presence in the lives of the next generation.

(The Leaders and Enemies activity from the reproducible page can also be used here, time permitting.)

What Does It Take?

What does it take to build and maintain faith? Judges 2:7 affirms that "The people served the Lord throughout the lifetime of Joshua and of the elders who outlived him and who had seen all the great things the Lord had done for Israel." But sadly, verses 10b-12 picture a drastic change: "After that whole generation had been gathered to their fathers, another generation grew up, who knew neither the Lord nor what he had done for Israel. Then the Israelites did evil in the eyes of the Lord and served the Baals. They forsook the Lord, the God of their fathers." What do you suppose happened? Complete each of the following:

1. If they did not know the Lord, it is most certainly true that the blame . . .

2. If they did not know what God had done for Israel, assuredly the _____ had not done what they needed to do.

3. Their choosing false gods above the true God was a sure sign that . . .

4. Does it take seeing "great things" to develop and maintain your own personal faith? If so, what sort of "great things" does it take?

5. What are the "great things" that God has done for his New Testament people? How well are we doing in communicating those things to the next generation?

Leaders and Enemies

No modern Christian has a Perizzite or Caananite lurking as a next door neighbor! But the people of God always have enemies to their faith peering over their backyard fence. Whom (or what) do you consider to be spiritual enemies in your life? Draw or write them on the slats of the fence.

In lieu of "judges," who or what are the spiritual leaders you "invite to your backyard" to help you fend off the attacks of those over-the-fence enemies? Identify these spiritual leaders, and let each one "say" something to you to help you build and maintain your faith.

GOD LEADS THROUGH DEBORAH

LESSON 6

WHY TEACH THIS LESSON?

Intelligence. Physical attractiveness. Eloquence. People skills. Character. The secular world looks at many such elements when evaluating someone's fitness for leadership. Perhaps some personal quality—gender, age, educational background, etc.—may make a person a controversial leadership candidate, either in a secular or a church role.

This uncertainty should lead us to ask which factors God weighs most heavily as he chooses people through whom to work. In today's lesson we see God's heart. He is looking for those who listen to him, who are humble and obedient. He is looking for those whose faith is in him and whose concern is for others.

This lesson depicts two leaders who were successful. Each acknowledged and leaned on the other's strength or expertise, even though one sacrificed personal glory in the process. This is a key element for church leadership today. The best leaders work together in humility and harmony to achieve God's will for us all.

INTRODUCTION

A. WOMEN IN THE OLD TESTAMENT

The Old Testament is treated by some as little more than a book of fantastic children's stories. To do this is to miss the rich treasury of insights into the lives of men and women who struggled in their relationships with God. Sometimes they are heroically successful, and we learn how they are pleasing to God. At other times they are colossal failures, and we can observe the patience and redemptive nature of God in dealing with them.

The Old Testament is dominated by the lives and exploits of men. Because of this, it is common to overlook the crucial and inspirational roles played by women in the history of Israel. Rarely are women presented as recognized community or national leaders. More often we find them in supporting roles as mothers, sisters, and wives of important men.

Consider Moses, the great man, whose life was influenced by women who functioned in all three of these supporting roles. The name of Moses' mother was Jochebed (Numbers 26:59). Exodus 2 relates the story of her daring actions to save baby Moses from a death edict. She stood against Egyptian tyranny, and God providentially rewarded her by allowing her to keep her baby and nurse him before turning him over to the Egyptian princess.

Also involved in this incident was Moses' sister, Miriam. This brave little girl, maybe just five or six years old, hid near her baby brother in the Nile and had the presence of mind to suggest to the princess her mother as a nurse. Later, Miriam played a key leadership role in the exodus. After the destruction of Pharaoh's army in the Red Sea, she led the women of Israel in a celebration of singing and

DEVOTIONAL READING:
PSALM 91
BACKGROUND SCRIPTURE:
JUDGES 4
PRINTED TEXT:
JUDGES 4:4-10, 12-16

Oct
8

LESSON AIMS

After participating in this lesson, each student will be able to:

1. Retell the story of Deborah, noting the qualities that made her a model leader.

2. Point out how leadership qualities like Deborah's can help the church.

3. Create a personal prayer plan for his or her church's leadership.

KEY VERSE

Deborah, a prophetess, the wife of Lappidoth, was leading Israel at that time.   —Judges 4:4

WHAT DO YOU THINK?

What can we learn about the character of godly women through the portions of Scripture that record their words?

[You will need to consider Exodus 15:21; Judges 5; 1 Samuel 2:1-10; and Luke 1:46-55 as you form your answer.]

dancing (Exodus 15:20, 21). In this passage she is referred to as a prophetess, although we have no record of her prophetic activities. Centuries later, the prophet Micah remembered the leaders of the exodus as three: Moses, Aaron, and Miriam (Micah 6:4).

An often-overlooked woman in the life of Moses is his wife, Zipporah. Exodus 4:24-26 tells a sobering story of a time when God sought to kill Moses. Zipporah saved Moses' life. She moved to guard her family in a time of crisis. Had she failed to understand the perplexing threat and act decisively, the history of Israel would have been very different.

Many other women can be identified as examples of faith in action in the Old Testament. Today's lesson is about one of the most famous of them all: the prophetess, judge, and warrior named Deborah.

B. LESSON BACKGROUND

Last week's lesson presented the destructive cycle of Israel that is found repeatedly in Judges: apostasy, crisis, repentance, and then deliverance by a judge raised up by God. After the death of the judge, this cycle began again and grew worse with each repetition (Judges 2:19). This week's lesson examines the story of the judge Deborah.

Many enemies threaten Israel in the book of Judges. The people who pose a threat to the Israel of Deborah's day are called simply the Canaanites. Genesis presents them as descendants of Canaan, the grandson of Noah. This Canaan was cursed because of an unfortunate incident related in Genesis 9:20-27.

The primary city of this particular group of Canaanites was Hazor, a large city located about 10 miles north of the Sea of Galilee. The site of Hazor has been excavated extensively. It is the largest biblical-era site in Israel, covering approximately 200 acres. Archaeologists estimate that ancient Hazor was a city with a population of more than 20,000—very substantial for the time.

The story of Deborah is told twice in Judges. In chapter 4 it is presented in prose form, as if from the hand of a recording historian. In chapter 5 the story is told as a song or in poetic fashion. This is likely the earlier version, for ancient peoples were great storytellers. Their stories were composed in a poetic manner so that they could be more easily learned and remembered.

The triumphal ode of chapter 5 is ascribed to Deborah herself (Judges 5:1). Scholars recognize the Song of Deborah as one of the oldest texts in the Old Testament.

I. DEBORAH THE JUDGE (JUDGES 4:4, 5)

A. PROPHETESS AND WIFE (v. 4)

4. Deborah, a prophetess, the wife of Lappidoth, was leading Israel at that time.

The author introduces Deborah as a *wife, prophetess,* and judge. With all of these jobs, she must have been as "busy as a bee" and indeed her name means "bee" in Hebrew.

The Old Testament gives the title *prophetess,* in a godly sense, only to Miriam (Exodus 15:20), Huldah (2 Kings 22:14), Deborah, and the unnamed wife of Isaiah (Isaiah 8:3). This title is the feminine equivalent of *prophet,* with no real difference aside from gender.

We usually think of a prophet as one who has divine insight into future events, but this is only part of a prophet's function. Old Testament prophets are God's mouthpieces. As such, they are inspired by God to keep Israel on track in religious and moral matters. Deborah, then, is presented as more than a wise judge. She is an inspired judge, used by God to guide the development of the young nation.

Deborah is also presented as a wife. Her husband's name, *Lappidoth,* means "torches" or "wicks." One tradition outside the Bible holds that Lappidoth was responsible for providing the wicks for the sacred lamps of the sanctuary in Shiloh. There is no record that Deborah and Lappidoth had any children.

B. JUDGE OF ISRAEL (v. 5)

5. She held court under the Palm of Deborah between Ramah and Bethel in the hill country of Ephraim, and the Israelites came to her to have their disputes decided.

Deborah and Lappidoth live in a rural area less than a dozen miles north of Jerusalem. This is in the tribal territory of *Ephraim.* It is a semi-mountainous region. Deborah uses an outdoor courtroom under a *palm* tree named after her.

The fact that people come *to her to have their disputes decided* indicates that Deborah's judging is akin to what we would call binding arbitration. It is doubtful that she is dealing with criminal cases. Those would have been quickly resolved in the various communities of Israel, usually at the city gate (see Deuteronomy 17:5; 21:19).

More likely, Deborah is an agreed-upon judge for difficult private disputes (more like our civil litigation). The two disputing parties would agree to abide by her decision before it was given, perhaps having been sent by the elders of a village or city. Deborah likely receives a fee for each judgment.

Such a system would have no strict legal basis, because there is no king or government to appoint and validate Deborah's authority. This makes her judgeship all the more remarkable. Deborah must have a widespread reputation for fairness and wisdom. She would be fulfilling the qualities stated to Moses by his father-in-law, Jethro, for a judge: capable, God-fearing, truthful, and not open to bribery (Exodus 18:21).

She judges the thorniest matters, a role filled by Moses during an earlier period (see Exodus 18:14, 15, 25, 26). The people appreciate this just and impartial judge, because government officials in the ancient world are known for corruption (see Isaiah 1:23).

Visual for Lesson 6. *You may wish to post this chart alongside one of the other charts for the quarter.*

WHAT DO YOU THINK?

What do you think made Deborah such a good judge? Why do you think God used a woman in a role traditionally filled by a man?

HONEST AND DISHONEST JUDGES

A little-known lawyer was sworn in as a U.S. Supreme Court Justice on December 19, 1975. How he got there is an intriguing story.

In 1958 a man by the name of Sherman Skolnick sued a Chicago brokerage firm for allegedly mishandling his life savings. Skolnick lost his case. He also lost his appeal to the Illinois Supreme Court. The experience embittered him against the justice system, and he began a judicial watchdog organization. In 1969 Skolnick accused two state supreme court justices of accepting thousands of dollars' worth of bank stock in return for deciding a case in favor of a powerful Chicago lawyer.

Media pressure forced the state supreme court to appoint a special commission to investigate. John Paul Stevens became the chief counsel. The meticulous care with which he built his case, combined with his courtroom strategy, brought down two previously respected but now-tainted justices. (Ironically, both had ruled against Skolnick in his case years earlier.) Stevens was exactly the kind of person President Gerald Ford was looking for to restore respect for the federal government after the Watergate scandal of 1974.

Deborah was such a judge: careful and honest in her judgments. The common people of every nation are blessed when people of impeccable reputation, practical wisdom, and honest judgment control the judicial system.   —C. R. B.

II. DEBORAH THE ORGANIZER (JUDGES 4:6-10)

A. Recruiting General Barak (v. 6a)

6a. She sent for Barak son of Abinoam from Kedesh in Naphtali

As a leader of the people, Deborah's role extends beyond maintaining an outdoor courtroom. She recognizes a crisis among her people and summons a man who can do what she cannot: lead an army into battle. This man is *Barak,* from the city of *Kedesh* (meaning "sanctuary"). Kedesh is located about 5 miles north of Hazor. Although in the tribal territory of *Naphtali,* Kedesh is one of the six cities of refuge controlled by the Levites (Numbers 35; see Joshua 20:7).

The crisis is a state of Canaanite banditry. That had caused trade caravans to disappear and farming villages to be abandoned (Judges 5:6, 7).

B. Planning a Strategy (vv. 6b, 7)

6b, 7. . . . and said to him, "The Lord, the God of Israel, commands you: 'Go, take with you ten thousand men of Naphtali and Zebulun and lead the way to Mount Tabor. I will lure Sisera, the commander of Jabin's army, with his chariots and his troops to the Kishon River and give him into your hands.'"

Barak is instructed to gather a large army to *Mount Tabor,* which rises about 1,500 feet above the surrounding countryside. It is located in the northeast end of Israel's central Plain of Esdraelon. The army is primarily drawn from the northern tribes of *Naphtali* and *Zebulun;* Judges 5:14, 15 tells us that there are also present men from Benjamin, Issachar, and Makir (a subtribe of Manasseh).

The enemy *army* has gathered under the leadership of *Sisera,* the military expert of King Jabin. Jabin rules from Hazor in the northern Galilean area. Hazor is reckoned as the great city of the Canaanites (compare Joshua 11:10). Although Joshua had defeated and burned the city, it was not conquered. By the time of Deborah, the Canaanites had rebuilt it. Deborah determines the strategy of the coming battle, choosing to engage Sisera on the banks of *the Kishon River,* to the east of Mount Tabor.

C. Traveling with the Troops (vv. 8-10)

8-10. Barak said to her, "If you go with me, I will go; but if you don't go with me, I won't go."

"Very well," Deborah said, "I will go with you. But because of the way you are going about this, the honor will not be yours, for the Lord will hand Sisera over to a woman." So Deborah went with Barak to Kedesh, where he summoned Zebulun and Naphtali. Ten thousand men followed him, and Deborah also went with him.

Barak may be the most able military leader in Israel, but he recognizes the value of having *Deborah* accompany him. Deborah warns him that this will divert the glory of victory from himself to her.

The result will be that the mighty chariot army of *Sisera* suffers defeat at the hand of *a woman.* The biggest disgrace in being defeated by a woman is the fact that women are not participants in the armies of the ancient world. Thus Sisera will lose to a nonmilitary adversary. This will also diminish the recognition of Barak's victory.

III. DEBORAH THE WARRIOR (JUDGES 4:12-16)

A. Powerful Enemy (vv. 12, 13)

12, 13. When they told Sisera that Barak son of Abinoam had gone up to Mount Tabor, Sisera gathered together his nine hundred iron chariots and all the men with him, from Harosheth Haggoyim to the Kishon River.

We now begin to understand the daunting challenge, for Sisera's army is known to have 900 armored *chariots*. These are the most fearsome battle machines of the ancient world (see Judges 4:3). The author paints an imposing picture: the Canaanite forces are spread for several miles across the broad Plain of Esdraelon. Sisera's army is vulnerable, however, because of its dependence upon this chariot force.

B. Confidence in God's Presence (v. 14)

14. Then Deborah said to Barak, "Go! This is the day the Lord has given Sisera into your hands. Has not the Lord gone ahead of you?" So Barak went down Mount Tabor, followed by ten thousand men.

The faith and determination of *Deborah* shine brightly here. She announces that *this is the day*—the day of victory! Deborah understands that God is willing to fight on the side of Israel, and, therefore, "safety is of the Lord" (Proverbs 21:31). With this great blessing of assurance, Barak and his men rush *down Mount Tabor* to meet the Canaanites in battle.

Thoughts into Action

Matthew Nagle is a quadriplegic. He made history in June 2004 when surgeons implanted a silicon wafer into his brain. The wafer, known as BrainGate, is one-sixth of an inch square and has 100 electrodes that extend one-sixteenth of an inch into Nagle's brain. When he thinks about moving his arm, the brain signals are sent to another device on the outside of his head. From there an electronic message is sent to a computer that translates it into code that enables a machine to do things such as change the TV channel or perform simple tasks on Nagle's computer.

The device is far from perfect. Scientists had to figure out the signals Nagle's brain sends before the computer could be programmed. Because brain patterns are always changing, the device has to be "retuned" every time Nagle uses it. Still, the technology enables him to turn his thoughts into action and gives him some control over his life that he has been missing.

Deborah's role in Israel's victory started with her being in touch with the will of God, hearing the message God gave her for Israel's good, and using her wisdom and strength of character to turn God's thoughts into human action. Not all of us have Deborah's gifts, and, like Nagle's machine, we don't respond perfectly to "divine input." But when we are "properly tuned," we each have the ability to use what God has given us to turn his thoughts into action.   —C. R. B.

C. Victory with God's Power (vv. 15, 16)

15, 16. At Barak's advance, the Lord routed Sisera and all his chariots and army by the sword, and Sisera abandoned his chariot and fled on foot. But Barak pursued the chariots and army as far as Harosheth Haggoyim. All the troops of Sisera fell by the sword; not a man was left.

Despite Sisera's superior technology, Barak's army is able to defeat the enemy. There is both an earthly and a heavenly reason. First, the mighty *chariots* become bogged down in the sandy soil in and around the Kishon River, rendering them ineffective (Judges 5:21). Judges 5:20 may indicate that this was made worse by a providential downpour of rain.

Second, the superior forces of *Sisera* were *routed*. This is a panic sent from God himself. The deep fear that follows causes Sisera's troops to flee chaotically. God is fighting on Israel's behalf. This is the opposite of the periods in Judges where God withdrew his blessing and fought against Israel (Judges 2:15).

What Do You Think?

How are Deborah and Barak models for Christian faith? How do their stories mirror ours? (Remember that Barak is among the heroes of the faith in Hebrews 11:32.)

Daily Bible Readings

Monday, Oct. 2—*The God in Whom I Trust (Psalm 91)*

Tuesday, Oct. 3—*No Need to Fear (Psalm 27:1-6)*

Wednesday, Oct. 4—*Othniel Judges Israel (Judges 3:7-11)*

Thursday, Oct. 5—*Courageous Leaders (Hebrews 11:1, 2, 32-34)*

Friday, Oct. 6—*Deborah Leads the People (Judges 4:1-10)*

Saturday, Oct. 7—*Success Assured (Judges 4:12-16)*

Sunday, Oct. 8—*Deborah's Song of Praise (Judges 5:1-12)*

PRAYER

Holy God, we are in your hands. We pray that you will provide our church with leaders who are brave and strong, yet humble and obedient. Give those called to leadership the wisdom to trust you fully. We pray in Jesus' name, amen.

THOUGHT TO REMEMBER

Tough times require strong leaders.

WHAT DO YOU THINK?

What problems are the leaders of our church facing right now? How can we support them in the battles they face and the service they provide to God's people?

The victory is complete, for *not a man* is *left*. Sisera himself is reduced to fleeing on foot. He will die at the hand of another woman: Jael, the wife of Heber. She will drive a tent stake through sleeping Sisera's head (Judges 4:21).

CONCLUSION
A. FAITHFUL WOMEN TODAY

Are there lessons for the church in this Old Testament story? Is Deborah a model for women today? These are good questions, and there are thorny problems of interpretation regarding the role of women in church leadership (see 1 Timothy 2:12). Perhaps, however, this story can give us at least partial insight into how God views these issues.

First, we see that God is not opposed to using women to help his people. Deborah enjoyed God's blessings in her work as a righteous judge, in her voice as a prophetess, and in her planning as a military strategist. The judges of Israel are overwhelmingly male but not exclusively.

Second, we see that capable women can earn the respect of the people of God. It would be fascinating to learn exactly how Deborah developed her reputation as a judge, but we meet her after this had been accomplished. Undoubtedly, this did not happen overnight. It probably took many years of consistent excellence as a judge for Deborah to achieve her position of authority.

Third, we should understand that it is unnecessary for men to deny women credit for effective service. Barak was warned that his need for Deborah's presence would result in her receiving the people's acclaim for the great victory over the Canaanites. Barak didn't seem to have a problem with this. The wisest players are those who sometimes step aside to let someone else carry the ball and hear the roar of the crowd.

B. OVERCOMING LEADERSHIP CONFLICTS

Why are some churches in constant turmoil? Why is growth sporadic or absent altogether? These are complex issues, and there is no single answer that fits every situation. However, many churches fail to grow and thrive because of conflicts among the leaders. Here are three lessons from the story of Deborah that can help us.

First, egos need to be checked at the church door. Judges 4 and 5 paint a beautiful picture of two cooperating leaders, each recognizing the abilities of the other. Churches that are controlled by isolated, inflexible leaders will have problems. Congregations led by win-at-all-costs personalities will suffer. Some qualities that make a person successful in the business world may become destructive in church leadership.

Second, good leadership decisions have the welfare of the people sharply in focus. Neither Deborah nor Barak are presented as bloodthirsty warriors itching for glory. They pursue the terrible option of war because the people must be freed from oppression. When making leadership decisions, we should ask ourselves, "Why am I doing this? Am I choosing this course because it is most comfortable for me? Am I making a choice that is best for the long-term health of the church?"

Third, leadership success ultimately is determined by God. Deborah knew that the battle would be won because God was fighting for Israel. All church leaders should be accountable to God and open to his leading. The church is not a private little empire for any leader. Whatever leadership roles we are given, we should approach our ministries with the desire to serve people and to serve God.

Discovery Learning

This page contains an alternative lesson plan emphasizing learning activities. Classes desiring such student involvement will find these suggestions helpful. The next page is a reproducible activity page to further enhance discovery learning.

LEARNING GOALS

After this lesson, each student will be able to:

1. Retell the story of Deborah, noting the qualities that made her a model leader.

2. Point out how leadership qualities like Deborah's can help the church.

3. Create a personal prayer plan for his or her church's leadership.

INTO THE LESSON

Display an outline of a person (on roll paper or poster board) as your class assembles. Have the following heading over the drawing: "The Ideal Leader." As students arrive, hand them a marker and say, "Go up to the drawing and write in a characteristic you think is important in the ideal leader." (Make sure the marker won't bleed through the paper and damage the wall.)

As class begins, point to the list and ask, "Are there other qualities you want to add, now that you have had more time to think?" Then introduce Deborah as a judge of Old Testament Israel. (Option: distribute A Look at the Text from the reproducible page for students to work on as they arrive.)

INTO THE WORD

Before class recruit a volunteer to be interviewed as the Israelite judge Deborah. Encourage your volunteer to be well studied on the time period of the judges generally and on the life and work of Deborah specifically. Provide your volunteer a copy of the lesson writer's commentary and the questions that you (or a class member) are going to ask. Be sure to allow some spontaneity from your class and from your interviewee.

Interview questions are provided here, but you may choose to write your own questions to match your class's level of biblical maturity. Of course some answers may be speculative; be sure your students understand that. You should discuss the reasonableness of answers that are not directly revealed in Scripture. Verse numbers from today's text in Judges 4 are given after each question.

(1) "Deborah, what did your husband think about your work on behalf of God's people?" (*v. 4*); (2) "What was the nature of your prophesying? How did you receive the Spirit's Word?" (*v. 4*); (3) "Why was your work done under a tree by the side of the road?" (*v. 5*); (4) "What sort of cases did you handle?" (*v. 5*); (5) "How did you know of Barak, who lived so far away?" (*v. 6*); (6) "What would Barak have known of the Canaanite oppressors?" (*v. 6*); (7) "How could Barak raise an army of 10,000 men from only two tribal groups?" (*v. 7*); (8) "Where exactly is this Kishon River, and why would God want the battle to take place there?" (*v. 7*); (9) "Why do you think Barak refused to go to war without you?" (*vv. 8-10*); (10) "Why did you caution Barak that the honor of victory would come to a woman and not to him?" (*vv. 8-10*); (11) What is significant about the fact that your army was to face 900 iron chariots? Didn't your 10,000 men seem to be the stronger army?" (*vv. 12, 13*); (12) When you assumed command of Barak's army and gave the command to charge, how did Barak respond?" (*v. 14*); (13) "From Mount Tabor you had a good view of the battle. Exactly what happened?" (*vv. 15, 16 and Judges 5:18-22*); (14) "Your poem of victory that we have recorded in Judges 5 is a beautiful expression. How do you account for such a response to the defeat of God's enemies?"

As your "Deborah" responds, stop to discuss key elements of the text. Allow students to interact with her assumptions and conclusions.

INTO LIFE

Give each student an index card. Display a list of the primary leaders of your congregation: ministers, elders, deacons, etc. Pair up each student with a leader's name. If your class is not large enough to cover pairing up all the names, ask for volunteers to take two or more names. If there are more class members than leaders, have more than one student responsible for each leader.

Have students make the following commitment: on one side of their cards, write out a plan for how they will offer prayer support for their chosen leader. On the other side of their cards, write a commitment to visiting with their chosen leader. This visitation may be at the leader's home, by going out for coffee, etc. By participating in this activity, students will have an opportunity to express appreciation for their leaders and enjoy being in their presence. This will reflect Barak's appreciation and reliance on Deborah's leadership. (Option: use the The Secret of Success exercise from the reproducible page as an alternative or additional learning activity.)

A Look at the Text

In the following word puzzle, you will find 20 words from today's text in Judges 4:4-10, 12-16. The words appear in every direction. (Some words combine to make two-word phrases.) You score 5 points for each word you find, for a maximum score of 100. *Caution:* there are also several words in the puzzle that are not in the text; you lose 1 point for each of those that you identify as being in the text but are not!

```
S  T  O  I  R  A  H  C  D  J  H  A  M  R
E  D  D  E  F  R  T  M  L  A  P  P  I  O
B  I  E  D  E  B  O  B  E  B  A  R  A  K
O  S  R  C  N  R  A  O  E  I  D  O  R  B
R  R  D  O  A  O  H  T  R  N  H  P  H  E
E  J  N  D  N  P  H  B  A  A  S  H  P  D
D  A  U  E  H  E  T  S  O  B  W  E  E  R
A  H  H  D  L  H  U  A  I  A  O  T  E  H
E  R  E  A  G  O  A  T  I  K  R  E  A  H
L  F  N  H  H  E  A  M  H  N  D  S  R  O
B  O  I  T  A  B  D  E  A  R  E  S  I  S
E  D  N  W  O  M  A  N  A  R  D  E  B  H
D  E  E  R  A  H  W  A  R  R  I  O  R  A
T  B  O  R  D  E  B  O  R  A  H  B  O  R
```

Words in the puzzle that are also in the Scripture text: Barak, Bethel, chariots, Deborah, Ephraim, iron, Jabin, Kishon, nine, hundred, palm, prophetess, Ramah, Sisera, sword, Tabor, ten thousand, wife, woman.

The Secret of Success

As Deborah and Barak began singing their song of victory in Judges 5, they affirm how godly success happens. Find their conclusion in this regard and summarize it in the box below.

Now answer these questions: In our congregation's work against the enemies of God, do I let the leaders lead? If not, what is the problem? Do I willingly offer myself as a follower and servant? If not, what is the problem? Do I hear praises to the Lord for the victories he accomplishes each day in my life and in the life of our church? If not, what is the problem? (Use a separate sheet of paper as needed.)

GOD ANSWERS SAMUEL'S PRAYER

WHY TEACH THIS LESSON?

God loves us as his children. As children's behavior sometimes disgusts their parents, our behavior often grieves God. A teenager who shoplifts is not only guilty of criminal behavior personally but also brings disgrace to others in the family. I know that our Heavenly Father still loves us when we sin, but we undoubtedly disgust him by our unholy behavior. Our lesson today shows Samuel helping the people of Israel get back on track with God, first by instructing them to give up their God-disgusting idols and then by praying to God on their behalf.

Only those who know what God loves and hates can advise others when they are behaving in ways that displease him. Although this role often seems confrontational and difficult, it sometimes brings another person back into God's peace. Your students are likely to function as Samuel at times, pointing others to God and praying for them. At other times they will assume the role of Israel, hearing the sage advice of godly friends and benefiting from intercessory prayer.

INTRODUCTION

A. NATIONAL REPENTANCE

"Return, O Israel, to the Lord your God. Your sins have been your downfall!" (Hosea 14:1). This type of call to national repentance is found repeatedly throughout Scripture. It was a constant message of the Old Testament prophets (example: "Say to the house of Israel, . . . Repent!" Ezekiel 14:6). Jonah was sent to Nineveh, a non-Israelite city, to call that city to repentance; Jesus used that example in his call for a generation to repent (Matthew 12:41).

We often view calls for repentance from an individualistic perspective. That is, we assume that a call for repentance is a call to each person to get right with God. While individual repentance is vital, the Bible also issues calls of repentance to communities and nations. God will not bless a society that encourages sin. History is littered with stories of communities and nations that descended into depravity and eventually were blotted out by God. A striking example is the city of Sodom (Genesis 19:24; Isaiah 3:9).

Today's lesson relates the story of a period of repentance for the nation of Israel. Israel was called by Samuel, God's prophet and judge, to give up its pagan idolatry and return to God. The resulting repentance brought deliverance from a national threat. It brought a period of revival and spiritual blessing.

We should take encouragement from this story, for such calls to national repentance are not just relics of the biblical world. We need godly voices in modern nations to resist evil and to call for repentance, even in the face of ridicule and disbelief. We cannot predict the success or failure of such appeals, but we can be sure of God's blessings if such calls are heeded.

DEVOTIONAL READING:
PSALM 31:14-24
BACKGROUND SCRIPTURE:
1 SAMUEL 7:3-13
PRINTED TEXT:
1 SAMUEL 7:3-13

LESSON AIMS

After participating in this lesson, each student will be able to:

1. Tell how repentance and prayer were important to the deliverance of the Israelites from the Philistines.

2. Describe how repentance and prayer are important today.

3. Write an intercessory prayer for someone who is plagued by some trouble.

Oct
15

KEY VERSE

Samuel . . . cried out to the LORD on Israel's behalf, and the LORD answered him.
—1 Samuel 7:9

B. LESSON BACKGROUND

Samuel is one of the most multitalented characters in the Bible. His amazing story starts even before his birth. His mother, Hannah, prayed fervently for God to remove her inability to bear a child. She vowed that if a son were given to her, he would be dedicated to the service of the Lord (1 Samuel 1:11). When God answered her prayer, she named her son Samuel, meaning, "his name is God" or perhaps "heard of God." This name is an acknowledgement of the one true God.

Samuel grew up in the tabernacle at Shiloh under the tutelage of Eli the priest. There, as a young boy, Samuel received a message directly from God (1 Samuel 3:1-14). The message concerned God's displeasure with the household of Eli, but its reception confirmed the extraordinary ministry that awaited Samuel.

Beyond that of child prodigy, consider some of the other roles played by Samuel in the Bible. He was a prophet, meaning that he was God's spokesman (1 Samuel 3:20). He was a seer, meaning that he received supernatural visions from God (1 Samuel 9:19, 20). He "continued as judge over Israel all the days of his life" and was the last of the judges (1 Samuel 7:15; Acts 13:20); that fact makes him a transitional figure to the era of the prophets (Acts 3:24; 13:20). Finally, he was a kingmaker, the one who anointed both Saul (1 Samuel 10:1; 15:1) and David (1 Samuel 16:13) as kings of Israel.

Today's lesson is the aftermath of a horrifying incident in the history of Israel in which the ark of the covenant was used as a tool for war (1 Samuel 4:3, 4). This ill-conceived plan resulted in the defeat of Israel and the capture of the ark by the Philistines (4:10, 11). The Philistines are often seen as the traditional enemy of the people of God in the Old Testament. They occupied the seacoast area of Gaza in southwest Israel, south of Joppa. They had five strong cities in this area: Gaza, Ashkelon, Ashdod, Gath, and Ekron.

The Bible and other sources tell us that the Philistines were originally foreign invaders from the land of Caphtor (see Amos 9:7), which some scholars identify as the island of Crete. At the time of the exodus, the Philistines were already well established in their territory (see Exodus 13:17). They appear prominently in Judges and 1 Samuel and are finally conquered by David.

After Solomon, however, the Philistines seem to have a small revival of independence and resume their role as the bane of Israel. Although now gone, they left their name on the region, for *Palestine* is derived from *Philistine*. In matters of religion the Philistines are often pictured as polar opposites to the Israelites. There seems to be no more degrading title than to be called an "uncircumcised Philistine" (see 1 Samuel 17:26).

The recovery of the precious ark is the occasion for Samuel's call for national repentance.

I. CALL AND REPENTANCE (1 SAMUEL 7:3, 4)

A. ABANDONING FALSE GODS (v. 3)

3. And Samuel said to the whole house of Israel, "If you are returning to the LORD with all your hearts, then rid yourselves of the foreign gods and the Ashtoreths and commit yourselves to the LORD and serve him only, and he will deliver you out of the hand of the Philistines."

Repentance is described here as a return to God. Sin is when we wander away from God, disregard his will, and become alienated from him. Samuel was saying in effect, "If you're serious about getting right with God, here is what you must do."

Samuel then outlines a four-part process of national repentance for Israel. First, they are to do this wholeheartedly, not holding anything back. Partial re-

WHAT DO YOU THINK?

What experiences in Samuel's life equipped him to pray effectively? What personal experiences have taught you how to pray?

pentance is false repentance. Second, they are to stop all worship of other, pagan *gods*. God does not allow for multiple allegiances in matters of worship. Third, they are to prepare their *hearts*. Repentance requires determination to change. Fourth, they are to pledge themselves to *serve* God exclusively. Repentance is more than the passive elimination of sinful practices. It is turning to active obedience to God and his will.

B. SERVING THE LORD ONLY (v. 4)
4. So the Israelites put away their Baals and Ashtoreths, and served the LORD only.

Since entering the land of Canaan, the Israelites had struggled with rejecting pagan gods. These gods are summarized here as the *Baals*, or male deities, and the *Ashtoreths*, or female deities. The chief Philistine god was called Dagon (see 1 Samuel 5:1-5).

The author is pleased to tell us that the children of Israel heard Samuel's message. They abandoned their false gods in order to serve and worship *the Lord* God exclusively.

WHEN CHANGE IS NEEDED

Maya Angelou is a well-known professor, poet, and actress. She tells a story that helps to explain her success. Her grandmother was a storekeeper in rural Arkansas. When a person with a reputation for complaining would come into the store, the child Maya would be called inside to listen to the litany of complaints about weather, work, etc.

As an adult, Angelou remembers her grandmother's words to her after the complainer had left: "Sister, there are people who went to sleep last night, poor and rich and white and black, but they will never wake again. And those dead folks would give anything at all for just five minutes of this weather or ten minutes of plowing. So you watch yourself about complaining. What you're supposed to do when you don't like a thing is change it. If you can't change it, change the way you think about it."

The wise old woman's words summarize Israel's actions in today's text. Samuel had told the nation what it should do; the people recognized the change that needed to be made, and they made it! Sometimes the call for change comes from a messenger of God such as Samuel; sometimes it comes directly from the Bible; sometimes it comes from the circumstances of life. In any of these cases, wise people change their ways. They repent. That's when they find that God has blessings waiting for them.

—C. R. B.

II. CRISIS AND VICTORY (1 SAMUEL 7:5-11)

A. PRAYER OF NATIONAL REPENTANCE (vv. 5, 6)
5, 6. Then Samuel said, "Assemble all Israel at Mizpah and I will intercede with the LORD for you." When they had assembled at Mizpah, they drew water and poured it out before the LORD. On that day they fasted and there they confessed, "We have sinned against the LORD." And Samuel was leader of Israel at Mizpah.

Mizpah is a location of special significance in ancient Israel. The city is one of three in central Israel that Samuel uses as locations for his circuit-court judging (the others being Gilgal and Bethel; 1 Samuel 7:16). It was also a site for national assembly (Judges 10:17; 20:1; 1 Samuel 10:17).

Samuel leads *Israel* in a powerful symbolic act before their admission of sin: he has them pour *water* on the ground. This probably is to represent emptying their hearts, purging them of sin. The accompanying call for fasting, a traditional sign of repentance, reinforces this interpretation. After these acts of preparation, the

---

WHAT DO YOU THINK?

What should biblical repentance look like today? Does Samuel's four-part process still apply? Why, or why not?

HOW TO SAY IT

Ashdod. ASH-dod.

Ashkelon. ASH-ke-lon or AS-ke-lon.

Ashtoreths. ASH-toe-reths.

Baal. BAY-ul.

Beth Car. BETH Kar or Beth KAR.

Caphtor. KAF-tor.

Crete. Creet.

Dagon. DAY-gon.

Ebenezer. EB-en-EE-zer.

Ekron. EK-run.

Gath. Gath

Gaza. GAY-zuh.

Gilgal. GIL-gal

Jonah. JO-nuh.

Nineveh. NIN-uh-vuh.

Philistines. Fuh-LISS-teens or FILL-us-teens.

WHAT DO YOU THINK?

If God called you to be a Samuel in the twenty-first century, how would you lead your nation to repentance? Without politicizing the debate, what activities would you call people to participate in?

people confess their sin aloud. This is also an important component in the process of repenting.

B. TREACHERY OF THE PHILISTINES (v. 7)

7. When the Philistines heard that Israel had assembled at Mizpah, the rulers of the Philistines came up to attack them. And when the Israelites heard of it, they were afraid because of the Philistines.

How do *the Philistines* hear about this gathering of *Israel*? The Philistine leadership probably maintains a spy network within Israel. At any rate, the Philistines decide to take advantage of a peaceful national prayer meeting as an opportunity to massacre their enemies. Not surprisingly, the people of Israel are *afraid* when they become aware of this Philistine threat.

C. PRAYER FOR DELIVERANCE (vv. 8, 9)

8, 9. They said to Samuel, "Do not stop crying out to the LORD our God for us, that he may rescue us from the hand of the Philistines." Then Samuel took a suckling lamb and offered it up as a whole burnt offering to the LORD. He cried out to the LORD on Israel's behalf, and the LORD answered him.

Having repented, the Israelites turn to *Samuel* for deliverance. This continues the pattern of judges-as-deliverers that we saw in the book of Judges. Samuel now cries out in a great prayer of intercession for the children of Israel.

Doctrinally, we should not understand this as God rewarding Israel's repentance with deliverance. This mistaken notion is what leads people to "make deals with God" when they are in a desperate situation. "God, get me out of this and I'll give up drinking." Or, "Lord, help me survive this terrible mistake and I'll give money to the church." But it doesn't work this way. God always seeks our repentance.

When we are in proper fellowship with God, we have his favor. When we are at odds with him, he may use adverse circumstances to bring us to repentance.

D. DEFEAT OF THE PHILISTINES (vv. 10, 11)

10, 11. While Samuel was sacrificing the burnt offering, the Philistines drew near to engage Israel in battle. But that day the LORD thundered with loud thunder against the Philistines and threw them into such a panic that they were routed before the Israelites. The men of Israel rushed out of Mizpah and pursued the Philistines, slaughtering them along the way to a point below Beth Car.

God's choice for Israel's deliverance is both powerful and dramatic: a supernatural roar of *thunder*. We should also understand that while this terrifies *the Philistines*, the *men of Israel* are not afraid. Because their hearts are right with repentance, they know that God is fighting for them. This allows them to rally quickly and rout the enemy. When we are right with God, we are able to remain calm and confident in the most frightening situations.

III. PROCLAMATION AND EBENEZER (1 SAMUEL 7:12, 13)

A. LORD'S HELP (v. 12)

12. Then Samuel took a stone and set it up between Mizpah and Shen. He named it Ebenezer, saying, "Thus far has the LORD helped us."

When the battle is over, *Samuel* proclaims victory by erecting a memorial. This memorial is in the form of a large *stone*, which Samuel calls *Ebenezer*. In Hebrew this means "stone of help." (What an irony that Ebenezer Scrooge, the miser character in *A Christmas Carol*, has that name!)

Hitherto hath the Lord helped us.
1 Samuel 7:12

Visual for Lesson 7. *This picture illustrates one way that the Lord helps us. Point to it as you ask your students to list some other ways.*

Samuel's actions are significant for three reasons. First, he clearly gives credit for the victory to God, not the men of Israel. Second, he names the stone to emphasize Israel's dependence upon God. Third, he establishes a tradition of remembering, calling Israel to understand all the events that led to its repentance and subsequent deliverance.

REMEMBERING

Many monuments erected around the world memorialize wars and their victims. America has monuments dedicated to the soldiers who fought in her wars. Napoleon intended the Arc de Triomphe in Paris to memorialize his greatness, but it has since become a French memorial to those who died in World War I. Canada has its National War Memorial in Ottawa.

There are other kinds of memorials. The Statue of Liberty was a birthday gift to America to remind the world of the victory of independence that America had achieved. The Lincoln, Washington, and Jefferson Memorials in Washington, DC remind people of the character and contributions of those men. Many people will never visit such memorials, but it is now possible to view "virtual" memorials on the Internet.

When Samuel raised his Ebenezer, he was creating a reminder for Israel that God had acted to save them from their enemy. A far simpler—but much more profound—memorial than any we have mentioned is the one we Christians have: the Lord's Supper. When we partake of its rudimentary elements, we remember the victory of Christ over sin. And we need not go to Ottawa, Paris, or Washington to appreciate it. —C. R. B.

B. LORD'S PROTECTION (v. 13)

13. So the Philistines were subdued and did not invade Israelite territory again. Throughout Samuel's lifetime, the hand of the Lord was against the Philistines.

This summary statement reflects Israel's continued reliance on God and God's continued protection of Israel. With God as Israel's shield, the strong rival, *the Philistines,* no longer trouble them. The text leaves us with a small sense of foreshadowing, however: this situation continued *throughout Samuel's lifetime.* Repentance is not a one-time thing. It must continue and go beyond generational boundaries through the years. When relationship with God falls into neglect and sin, disaster looms.

CONCLUSION

A. RAISING EBENEZERS

Robert Robinson (1735–1790) was an English preacher. In 1758 he wrote the hymn, "Come, Thou Fount" when he was only 23 years old. Stanza 2 of this famous hymn says, "Here I raise mine Ebenezer; Hither by Thy help I'm come." For Robinson this was a reference to the salvation he had found after a youth of horrible sin. His early years of evil had been so destructive that he nearly lost his life. After conversion, however, Robinson drifted away. He fell back into a life of sin and abandoned the Bible.

Many years later, Robinson was riding in a coach. Seated across from him was a woman deeply engrossed in a hymnbook she had just acquired. She was humming one of her favorites, the tune of "Come, Thou Fount." Having no idea whom she was talking to, she innocently asked Robinson if he knew that hymn. Robinson burst into tears and replied, "Madam, I am the poor unhappy man who wrote that hymn many years ago, and I would give a thousand worlds, if I had them, to enjoy the feelings I had then." Robinson had accidentally stumbled

WHAT DO YOU THINK?

What kind of an Ebenezer could we raise today? In other words what kinds of memorials could we establish that would remind us to pray for our nation and repent of our sins?

DAILY BIBLE READINGS

Monday, Oct. 9—Call to Prayer (Colossians 4:2-6)

Tuesday, Oct. 10—The Psalmist Prays (Psalm 31:14-24)

Wednesday, Oct. 11—Hannah Pays Her Vows (1 Samuel 1:21-28)

Thursday, Oct. 12—Hannah Prays (1 Samuel 2:1-10)

Friday, Oct. 13—The Lord Calls Samuel (1 Samuel 3:1-10)

Saturday, Oct. 14—Israel Returns to God (1 Samuel 7:2-6)

Sunday, Oct. 15—The Lord Helps the Hebrew People (1 Samuel 7:7-13)

O Lord, our help and protector, give us a heart to pray for others. Help us repent of the sins that foul our relationship with you. Please be merciful to us as you were to the people of Israel. Continue to deliver your people in their times of need. In Jesus' name, amen.

back upon that Ebenezer of his. Sitting there beside his own hymn, he realized how far he had wandered and how awful was his journey and destination.

In today's lesson Samuel built a monument to help Israel remember God's providential deliverance from the Philistines. Building a monument is an attempt to ensure that a person or event will be remembered by succeeding generations. The Bible teaches that "the memory of the righteous will be a blessing" (Proverbs 10:7). Monuments can be powerful tools for interpreting and remembering our history. Do you have monuments in your spiritual history? Are there people and places that stand out as turning points for you, where you were rescued from self-destruction or where you made commitments that shaped your future? Take some time to remember.

B. THE MINISTRY OF INTERCESSORY PRAYER

An acquaintance of mine named Paul shared an amazing story with me in church one Sunday. Paul was an older gentleman and not in very good health (a leukemia survivor). He had a heart for missions and frequently traveled to an Asian country to encourage churches and to transport Bibles and materials for a mission agency.

On a recent trip Paul's health problems caught up with him. He returned with an infection that led to pneumonia and a high fever. He was taken to a hospital directly from the airport in San Francisco. After a stay of 11 days, he was finally allowed to go home. But he ended up in the hospital again. The fever would not go away. After a few days Paul was released, but the fever persisted and he got even worse. He was unable to go to work.

On Saturday afternoon he lay down to take a nap, the fever raging. He awoke rather suddenly a few hours later and realized that the fever was completely gone. He was very weak but well.

Why is this amazing? Don't people recover from pneumonia all the time, every day, in every city? My friend Paul didn't understand it either until he began to do some time-zone calculations. One of the churches he had visited in the Asian country had a small intercessory prayer group that had met every Sunday for many years. They had learned of his illness that week. When Paul calculated the time differential, he realized his fever had left him at the precise time they were praying for him.

There are many reasons to pray. We pray as an act of worship. We pray as an act of repentance. We pray in times of personal trial to seek God's help and mercy. But one of the greatest ways to use the marvelous gift of prayer is as an act of intercession: praying for other people.

Any church is stronger if believers know the great needs of fellow believers and take time to petition God on their behalf. That's what Samuel did. This type of praying allows us to move beyond self-centered prayers. Too often our prayers are like a Christmas list to Santa Claus, packed with our own wants and needs. When we pray sincerely for the needs and pains of others, we begin to think more like God, who cares for all. My friend Paul's story (along with many Bible examples) is a witness to the effectiveness and power of intercessory prayer (compare Romans 15:30-32; Ephesians 6:19, 20).

If you have never prayed for other people, start today—it is not difficult. Share some real needs among fellow class members; then agree to pray for those people during the week. Begin by committing to doing it once; then do it. Keep sharing and praying; you may be surprised at how rewarding the ministry of intercessory prayer can be.

Intercessory prayer develops the church into a community of repentance and remembrance.

What are the various kinds of prayers and petitions that we could lift up to God? Which kind do you pray most often? Why?

Discovery Learning

This page contains an alternative lesson plan emphasizing learning activities. Classes desiring such student involvement will find these suggestions helpful. The next page is a reproducible activity page to further enhance discovery learning.

LEARNING GOALS

After this lesson, each student will be able to:

1. Tell how repentance and prayer were important to the deliverance of the Israelites from the Philistines.

2. Describe how repentance and prayer are important today.

3. Write an intercessory prayer for someone who is plagued by some trouble.

INTO THE LESSON

Bring to class a rock that is as large as practical. Write EBENEZER conspicuously on it. Cover the rock with a cloth, and then display the rock as class begins. Lead the class (or have someone else lead) in singing the old hymn, "Come, Thou Fount." Make sure to include the stanza that begins, "Here I raise mine Ebenezer." Point out that today's text includes the Bible verse (v. 12) on which hymn writer Robert Robinson based his poem. Also, plan to use the hymn at the end of class. You may want to include the lesson writer's story of Robinson's writing and re-experiencing the truth of his song.

INTO THE WORD

Establish brainstorming pairs. Give each pair one of the letters of the word REPENTANCE. (Repeat the E and the N if you have an adequate number of students; if you have more than 20 students, repeat the letters R, P, and C.)

Direct the pairs to look at today's text and any other biblical texts on repentance, if they choose. (Option: distribute copies of the "Repent!" Who Says So? activity from the reproducible page to help prod students' thinking.) They are to make a list of components or actions involved in repentance that begin with their assigned letter. Give pairs six to eight minutes to work, and then call for responses.

Though you will get some surprises, expect such responses as the following: R—returning, regretting, restoring, realizing; E—ending, eliminating, embarrassment, examining; P—peace, pain, past, pleading; N—need, necessity, nearness (to God), neglect, newness; T—talking, tears, tenderheartedness, tenacity, thinking, truth; A—abandonment, anguish, accountability, action, admitting, atonement; C—commitment, change, character, choice, cleanness, conscience.

After the pairs have deliberated, ask them to connect their ideas to specific verses in today's text. When they report their decisions, you should hear such connections as these: returning is the call of verse 3; eliminating relates to the call to put away idolatry in verse 3; commitment is shown in verse 4 as the Israelites obeyed God and destroyed their enemies as God had long commanded; etc.

Ask each pair to present its list and its connections to the text. Have the word REPENTANCE displayed in large letters. Point letter by letter, asking for students' comments.

As a visual reminder of the components of repentance, recruit pantomime players to stand in a row and do the following: the first player squints his eyes as he puts a finger to the side of his nose, cradling his chin in his other fingers while slowly nodding his head pensively (to represent thinking); a second player rubs her eyes vigorously with her clenched hands and silently sobs (to represent sorrow/remorse); a third player assumes the classic prayer pose with hands palm-to-palm and head bowed (to represent sharing his decision with God in prayer); a fourth player walks across the room and abruptly turns to retrace his steps (to represent the turning aspect of repentance); a fifth player pulls play money from her purse and starts giving it to the other players (to represent a sacrificial offering aspect of repentance.)

Give your players the freedom to represent their ideas in other ways. As class members identify each component of repentance, write it clearly into a list for display. Come back together once again to ask, "Where do you see these components of repentance in today's text?"

INTO LIFE

Distribute to each class member a small round stone with an E written on it. Tell students that this stone is their "Ebenezer." Ask students to use their stones throughout the coming week as a reminder of this study and as a stimulus to pray for someone they know who needs to repent and receive Christ's forgiveness. (Alternative: use the Ebenezer Stones activity from the reproducible page.)

Finally, lead the class in singing again "Come, Thou Fount," or at least the stanza beginning, "Here I raise mine Ebenezer."

"Repent!" Who Says So?

The urgent call to repentance is heard through all of biblical history, for it is always one thing God requires of anyone who would turn to do his will. Decide who made each of the following calls to repentance; match a name (or names) to each. If you need help, check the references in the box below.

1. __ "In repentance and rest is your salvation" (Isaiah 30:15).

2. __ God "commands them to repent of their evil" (Job 36:10).

3. __ "In the past God overlooked such ignorance, but now he commands all people everywhere to repent" (Acts 17:30).

4. __ "Unless you repent, you too will all perish" (Luke 13:3).

5. __ "[The Lord] is patient with you, not wanting anyone to perish, but everyone to come to repentance" (2 Peter 3:9).

6. __ "If they have a change of heart . . . and repent and plead with you . . . hear their prayer and their plea" (1 Kings 8:47-49).

7. __ "Repent! Turn away from all your offenses . . . . Repent and live!" (Ezekiel 18:30, 32).

8. __ and __ "Repent, for the kingdom of heaven is near" (Matthew 3:2; 4:17).

9. __ "Repent, then, and turn to God, so that your sins may be wiped out" (Acts 3:19).

10. __ "Repent and be baptized, every one of you, in the name of Jesus Christ for the forgiveness of your sins" (Acts 2:38).

A. Elihu

B. Ezekiel

C. Isaiah

D. Jesus

E. John the Baptist

F. Simon Peter

G. Solomon

H. Paul

Ebenezer Stones

Every person has those "Ebenezer stones" that serve as markers for critical points of life change. On each of the stone monuments below, write about such occasions in your life. On the monument with the baby on top, recall the time and place you first affirmed the lordship of Christ and submitted to his will. On the monument with the church building on top, identify the congregation that has been the most significant in your walk with Christ and how it has been so. On the third monument, draw a simple sketch of a third occasion and briefly describe its significance.

God's Living Covenant
Unit 2: God's Covenant with Judges and Kings
(Lessons 5-9)

GOD MAKES A COVENANT WITH DAVID

WHY TEACH THIS LESSON?

Success. Everyone wants it. Many who achieve it these days write a book:

How to Build a Profitable Business
How to Grow a Big Church
How to Raise Great Children

It seems once someone has found success, they write a formula as to how they arrived there. They assume that anyone can follow their prescribed program and replicate their life achievements.

In today's lesson God reminds David of the "secret" of his success: God was with him. You may not end up as the leader of a nation, but God's favor is always a key to the successes that count for eternity. Through the line of David, God sent Jesus Christ. Through him we have victory in all of life's struggles. Like David, we may have times of trials and we may fall to temptation. But God promises to keep safe all that we commit to him. Let's commit our all! It's the sure road to success.

INTRODUCTION

A. KEEPING PROMISES

The word *promise* is capable of many shades of meaning. A coach might evaluate a young player by saying, "He shows lots of promise." This implies that the player has potential, in the opinion of the coach. Yet sports fans are well aware that many players who show promise never deliver.

Another form of this word may be seen when a person takes out a loan and signs a promissory note. This indicates an agreement to pay off the loan. If the person defaults on the loan, he or she will still be held accountable and may be forced to pay the money back. This type of promise speaks of obligation.

Many parents have encountered a third variation on this word when they fail to meet the anticipation of a demanding child. The parent may be confronted with the guilt-inducing complaint, "But you promised!" In this case the word *promise* takes on the idea of "expectation." A hazard of parenting is the failure to live up to the expectations of one's children!

Potential, obligation, and expectation are three components in the range of meaning for the word *promise*. But none of these is adequate to describe the biblical concept of promise when applied to God. God always keeps his promises. God's promises are more than potential; they are assurances. God's promises are not simply obligations; they are vows of commitment. God's promises are far beyond expectations; they are declarations of intention. This week's lesson teaches us that God's promise to one man, David, not only blessed David and his descendants but all who find salvation in Jesus Christ. That includes you and me.

DEVOTIONAL READING:
PSALM 5

BACKGROUND SCRIPTURE:
2 SAMUEL 7

PRINTED TEXT:
2 SAMUEL 7:8-17

LESSON AIMS

After participating in this lesson, each student will be able to:

1. List the major features of God's covenant with David.

2. Explain the importance of God's covenant with David for the New Testament era.

3. State a specific area of personal weakness in which he or she will trust God's promises more fully.

Oct
22

KEY VERSE

Your house and your kingdom will endure forever before me; your throne will be established forever.   —2 Samuel 7:16

B. LESSON BACKGROUND

During the time of Samuel, a major shift occurred in the history of Israel. Since the death of Joshua in about 1365 BC, judges had "run the show." These were God-ordained leaders who often acted as military leaders or coordinators in times of national crisis. But there was no central government for the people of Israel. The nation of Israel was actually a confederation of the 12 tribes. Participation in national events was dependent upon the cooperation of tribal leaders.

The people of Israel finally rejected this style of government and asked Samuel to give them a king. This turning point was a sad day, for God saw this as a rebuff of his rule over (1 Samuel 8:7). Tragically, the people of Israel demanded this so that they could have leadership like "all the other nations" (1 Samuel 8:5). The heartbreak was that Israel became like the nations in more than just its choice of rule by a king; Israel also followed its neighbors in sin. Thus the history of Israel was an ongoing battle against idolatry and failure to be the holy people of God.

This was further compounded by the performance of Israel's first king, Saul. Although chosen by God and anointed by Samuel, Saul did not live up to the heavy responsibilities of making Israel into a godly kingdom. God saw Saul's disobedience as a rejection of his Word, which resulted in God's rejection of Saul as king (1 Samuel 15:26; 1 Chronicles 10:13, 14). Even while Saul was still reigning, God directed Samuel to anoint Saul's successor, a new king who was not Saul's son (1 Samuel 16:1). The dynasty of Saul's house lasted only one generation, approximately 40 years (see Acts 13:21).

David had no royal qualifications to be king. Yet he had personal qualities that added up to the extraordinary credentials that God desired. His bravery was a hallmark (1 Samuel 17). David became a victorious military leader in the service of Saul, so successful that Saul became jealous (18:6-9). David was also a talented musician (see 16:23), the author of many psalms.

Most importantly, though, was the fact that God saw in David "a man after his own heart" (1 Samuel 13:14). Paul explained this phrase to mean that God was confident that David would "do everything I want him to do" (Acts 13:22). Although David, like King Saul, failed and committed sin, his response was unlike Saul's response. Saul responded to sin with arrogance, stubbornness, and rationalizing. David, however, came to God in humility and repentance (see Psalm 51:10). David was spiritually submissive to God. In fact, David's career was characterized by the strong presence of God's Holy Spirit in his life (1 Samuel 16:13). This week's lesson will help us understand why God's love for David has implications for us today.

I. DAVID IS CHOSEN (2 SAMUEL 7:8-11a)

A. GOD'S PREPARATION OF DAVID (vv. 8, 9a)

8, 9a. *"Now then, tell my servant David, 'This is what the LORD Almighty says: I took you from the pasture and from following the flock to be ruler over my people Israel. I have been with you wherever you have gone, and I have cut off all your enemies from before you.*

The message of David's covenant with God is being delivered by Nathan the prophet (2 Samuel 7:4). Nathan plays several important roles in the reign of David. He is the one who risks David's wrath by confronting the king and revealing David's sin with Bathsheba and the murder of Uriah (2 Samuel 12). He also anoints Solomon as David's successor (1 Kings 1:34).

Nathan reminds David that God has been looking out for him since his days in *the pasture.* God raised David from the humblest of occupations, shepherd, to

WHAT DO YOU THINK?

What characteristics that made David a good king (humanly speaking) do we still look for in political leaders today? Which of these characteristics are good and which are bad from a spiritual perspective? Defend your answer.

the pinnacle of success, king of God's chosen nation. In all situations the Lord protects David from danger and treachery.

B. GOD'S PLANS FOR DAVID (vv. 9b-11a)

9b. "'Now I will make your name great, like the names of the greatest men of the earth.

God promises that David will have a *great* name. This is a promise of legitimate fame and respect that will be widespread in Israel and in other nations.

This kind of fame is nothing like the modern "cult of celebrity," where men and women become famous for outrageous behavior or their ability to garner publicity. In the ancient world, fame and respect are built on accomplishment. David is a great man because he is powerful, talented, successful, and just. Yet he is also humble, for he always rules in the fear of the Lord (see 2 Samuel 23:3).

10, 11a. "'And I will provide a place for my people Israel and will plant them so that they can have a home of their own and no longer be disturbed. Wicked people will not oppress them anymore, as they did at the beginning and have done ever since the time I appointed leaders over my people Israel. I will also give you rest from all your enemies.'"

God ties the fortunes of David's house to the fate of the nation of *Israel*. The strength provided by the Davidic monarchy will allow Israel to achieve a much higher degree of stability in the promised land. This land will become a permanent home and a place of safety, for the nation will finally gain relief from its pagan *enemies*.

FROM THE BOTTOM TO THE TOP

Andrew Carnegie (1835–1919) is among the most famous of American philanthropists. His father lost his job when steam-powered looms changed Scotland's textile industry. The family moved to America in 1848, where Andrew got his first job, working in a textile mill for $1.20 per week.

From that point his life became the proverbial "rags to riches" story. His diligence and ability to solve problems creatively soon put him on the road to success. He took a job with the Pennsylvania Railroad, where his innovative style led to further advancement. By the time he was 24, he had become the western superintendent of the railroad. His investments and involvement in the oil, steel, and telegraph industries soon made him rich.

In 1889 Carnegie published his essay "Gospel of Wealth," which argued the moral obligation of the wealthy to serve as society's stewards (see www.pbs.org). He lived up to his credo: by the time of his death in 1919, he had given away 90 percent of his fortune after having become the wealthiest man in the world.

David's humble beginning as a shepherd would not have made anyone predict his rise to the height of power. But godly character and willingness to serve others were traits that served him well, both at the bottom and the top of the social hierarchy. Every society needs people who see their gifts as a trust from God to be used for others.   —C. R. B.

II. DAVID'S HOUSE IS CHOSEN (2 SAMUEL 7:11b-17)

A. COVENANT WILL CONTINUE (vv. 11b, 12)

11b. "'The LORD declares to you that the LORD himself will establish a house for you:

God's plan to establish a royal dynasty beginning with David are made clear.

12. "'. . . When your days are over and you rest with your fathers, I will raise up your offspring to succeed you, who will come from your own body, and I will establish his kingdom.

WHAT DO YOU THINK?

How were David's early years as a shepherd a preparation for him to be king? What was a time when hindsight revealed that God was preparing you for a future task?

WHAT DO YOU THINK?

What are some dangers of a man becoming king? What can we learn from the example of David that will help us curb these dangers in leaders today?

The kings of Israel reigning in Jerusalem will have David's royal blood flowing in their veins. Future kings will be David's son, grandson, great grandson, and so on.

After the death of King Solomon, David's son, the nation unfortunately will split in two. The northern kingdom (usually called Israel) ends up being ruled by Jeroboam. The southern kingdom (usually called Judah) comes to be ruled by David's grandson Rehoboam. The history of Judah's kings shows both good and bad rulers, but all were heirs of David. This stands in contrast to the northern kingdom, where dynasties were short-lived, and coups by military strongmen were common.

B. TEMPLE WILL BE BUILT (v. 13)

13. "'He is the one who will build a house for my Name, and I will establish the throne of his kingdom forever.

The Lord lays out a twofold promise: the privilege of building the temple in Jerusalem and the permanence of the Davidic dynasty. These promises are not made to David directly—as if David would never die—but to his son. At this point in David's life, it is unclear which one of his many sons will be his heir. At one point it seemed that David's third son, Absalom, would succeed David by overthrowing his father (2 Samuel 15). When David became old, his fourth son, Adonijah, tried to become king (1 Kings 1:5). Despite his advanced age, David orchestrated the events to make Solomon the next king (1 Kings 1:28-37).

David was prohibited from building the temple because he had blood on his hands (1 Chronicles 28:3). There is no haste in God's plans. He is infinitely patient, willing to wait until the right king is in place to *build* the temple.

TO THE GLORY OF GOD

St. Paul's Cathedral in London is one of the world's great church buildings. Its architect was Sir Christopher Wren (1632–1723). Wren was trained in anatomy and astronomy and was teaching at Oxford when his architectural career began.

At age 31 he was requested to draw the plans for a chapel in Cambridge. So impressive was his work that more soon followed. After the Great London Fire of 1666, Wren proposed a visionary master plan for rebuilding the city. The plan included the dome of St. Paul's cathedral, which ended up being Wren's most famous work. Over the next half-century he designed more than 50 church buildings in London. He has come to be regarded as Great Britain's greatest architect.

God promised David that his son (whom we know to be Solomon) would build a house for God. And what a house it was! It is said to have been the most magnificent building of ancient times. It reflected the glory of God and the greatness of the kingdom over which Solomon reigned. But that now-gone structure of stone and wood does not compare with God's greatest building project: the church. What part are you playing in its construction? —C. R. B.

C. RELATIONSHIP WILL STAY FIRM (vv. 14, 15)

14, 15. "'I will be his father, and he will be my son. When he does wrong, I will punish him with the rod of men, with floggings inflicted by men. But my love will never be taken away from him, as I took it away from Saul, whom I removed from before you.

Here we see that the relationship between the king of Israel and God has a unique element: the king is considered to be a *son*. This type of situation has parallels and differences with other ancient cultures. The kings of Egypt (the pharaohs) are considered to be gods, direct descendants of the Egyptian deities.

Yet there is no hint of that here. For David or Solomon to be God's son does not mean that these men are some type of demigods themselves.

These verses explain the relationship in some detail. God is the king's *father* in that God intends to take a special, personal interest in such men. As their father he will discipline them and show *love* to them, the qualities all fathers should show to their children.

The most sobering expression of this relationship will come with the reign of King Manasseh, one of David's descendants. That king will stray far from God's will into the evils of bloodshed and idolatry—so much so that he comes to be named as the cause for the destruction of Jerusalem in 586 BC and the deportation of the nation for exile in Babylon (2 Kings 24:2-4). God's discipline will be harsh indeed.

Love includes discipline. It is popular today to refer to this as "tough love." Good parents are sometimes hard on their children, not allowing them to fall into sinful patterns and sloth. But this hardness must be tempered with mercy. Discipline should never be a matter of revenge. This is the painful task of a parent who seeks to keep his or her child on the right path.

D. THRONE WILL BE ETERNAL (vv. 16, 17)

16, 17. "'Your house and your kingdom will endure forever before me; your throne will be established forever.'"

Nathan reported to David all the words of this entire revelation.

This final section of the words of Nathan lays out the three primary elements of God's covenant with David. David is to have an eternal *house,* an eternal *kingdom,* and an eternal *throne.* The eternal house means that the line of David will never die out. There will always be a king with David's royal blood. The eternal kingdom indicates that this king will have subjects and a territory. The eternal throne means that the sons of David will inherit extraordinary authority to carry out the will of God.

All three concepts are reinforced in Psalm 89, the parallel text. There David is promised to have a "throne to all generations" (v. 4). There is a pledge to preserve the kingdom by crushing all "his foes" (v. 23). And the exceptional authority of the Davidic king is strengthened by the mighty "hand" and "arm" of God (v. 21).

The records show that none of David's descendants (except Christ) really lived up to the implications of these promises. God always kept his side of the covenant, but even wise Solomon fell into the sin of false worship due to foreign wives (see 1 Kings 11:4). The three-fold promise of an eternal house, kingdom, and throne is completely fulfilled only in David's descendant Jesus. He is the eternal one who conquered death to ascend to Heaven and take his throne at the right hand of God (see Romans 8:34; Ephesians 1:20; Hebrews 1:3).

CONCLUSION

A. JESUS AND DAVID

God's covenant with David is a major theme in the Old Testament. Not only did the Davidic line of kings continue to reign in Jerusalem without interruption for almost 400 years, but the prophets of Israel began to reveal that a future king would come from David's line to be the redeemer of Israel (compare Luke 24:21).

This future redeemer was referred to in several ways including "my servant David" (Ezekiel 34:23, 24), and the "Branch" of David (Isaiah 11:1; Jeremiah 23:5). This branch image represents the idea of a reborn line of David—new growth from the stump of the tree.

Thine house and thy kingdom shall be established for ever . . . thy throne shall be established for ever (2 Samuel 7:15).

Visual for Lesson 8. *Point to this picture and say, "Some things will endure even longer than mountains. Can you name some of those things?"*

WHAT DO YOU THINK?

Which of God's promises to David are we able to claim for the church? Which are we not able to claim? How will we get into trouble if we don't sort this out properly?

The prophets wrote of future blessings on the "house of David" (Zechariah 12:10). But the most significant of these predictions are the ones that see a coming Messiah (Psalm 132:17; Daniel 9:25). This person has been specially chosen or appointed by God.

The New Testament shows many connections between Jesus and David. Jesus is called the "son of David" (Matthew 1:1; Mark 10:47, 48), the "King of Israel" (John 1:49; 12:13; compare Matthew 27:42; Zechariah 9:9). The most common link is the reference to Jesus as the Messiah or Christ. We have heard the two-word designation *Jesus Christ* so often that we forget that this includes a title: "Jesus the Christ." To claim that Jesus is the Christ is to claim that he is the Davidic king, the promised heir to David's throne.

A central conviction of the New Testament authors is that Jesus meets all the qualifications to be the heir of David. Jesus' earthly father, Joseph, is from the house of David (Luke 2:4). Paul is often found arguing with his fellow Jews that Jesus is the Messiah (see Acts 9:22; 28:23). Peter decisively concludes his Pentecost sermon by declaring that Jesus' resurrection confirms that God had made him Christ (Acts 2:36).

The significance of all this is enormous. Our eternal salvation is not an accident of history. Jesus Christ is much more than an ordinary man who accomplished extraordinary things. The church is much more than the work of creative geniuses like Paul and Peter. God's covenant with David teaches us that God planned the church, that he sent his Son, Jesus, and that our salvation was his intentional design. As believers we should find assurance in God's loving provision for us.

B. THE ETERNAL KINGDOM

The old spiritual sang, "Ride on, king Jesus!" The New Testament frequently speaks of Jesus as a king. The first book tells of the Magi, who came looking for the newborn "king of the Jews" (Matthew 2:2). The last book reveals Jesus as the "King of Kings" (Revelation 19:16).

What kind of king was Jesus, though? Jesus told Pilate, "My kingdom is not of this world" (John 18:36). If not of this world, what kind of kingdom does Jesus rule?

God promised David that he would establish "the throne of his kingdom for ever" (2 Samuel 7:13). Yet Jesus had no interest in being the reigning king of Jerusalem. When his followers tried to make him king, he refused (see John 6:15). His disciples continually failed to understand that he was not going to claim a throne in Jerusalem (see Acts 1:6).

The author of Hebrews shows a strong appreciation for the eternal throne of Jesus (Hebrews 1:8). Jesus reigns in righteousness and truth. His kingdom is far more than a time-bound, earthly kingdom. Jesus is king of the universe in a timeless, cosmic way. For us the eternal nature of Jesus' throne means that a man who walked the earth 2,000 years ago is still alive, still in power, still reigning from Heaven.

His reign is not fully realized on earth, where sinful rebels still operate outside his will. But Christians take comfort in the promise that a day will come in which every creature will acknowledge and submit to King Jesus by bowing before him (Philippians 2:9-11). On that day we will see that "The kingdom of the world has become the kingdom of our Lord and of his Christ, and he will reign for ever and ever" (Revelation 11:15). This is the ultimate vision of the covenant with David (see Revelation 22:16).

Discovery Learning

This page contains an alternative lesson plan emphasizing learning activities. Classes desiring such student involvement will find these suggestions helpful. The next page is a reproducible activity page to further enhance discovery learning.

LEARNING GOALS

After this lesson, each student will be able to:

1. List the major features of God's covenant with David.

2. Explain the importance of God's covenant with David for the New Testament era.

3. State a specific area of personal weakness in which he or she will trust God's promises more fully.

INTO THE LESSON

From a craft shop, toy store, or parents in your congregation, obtain children's alphabet blocks for the following letters: *A, D, D, E, F, H, I, O, O, S, U, V.* Have the blocks stacked as a pyramid, with the letters showing toward your class. As class begins, ask for acrostic responses to the question, "What are the components—let us say 'building blocks'—of the house of David, as God promises to build it?"

Have the class look at 2 Samuel 7:8-17 as an initial source, but also suggest they use their general knowledge of the kingdom of David. Accept reasonable answers; a sample of responses may include A=announced; D=disciplined; D=directed (by God); E=everlasting; F=famous; H=heavenly; I=independent; O=otherworldly; O=optimistic; S=spiritual; U=universal; V=victorious. At the end rearrange the blocks to show HOUSE OF DAVID toward the class.

INTO THE WORD

Prepare the following monologue of David, as if he were revealing today's text to us personally, rather than as a prophet revealing it to David. Some of the phrasing from the lesson Scripture text (in bold below) is used.

Monologue: "The prophet's announcement to me—of course, I knew it came from the Lord—was startling but joyful. I was fully aware that it was God who called me from tending sheep to become **ruler over** his **people Israel.** I always sensed his presence and care; **all** my **enemies** were as good as out of my sight.

"God has made me a name among **the greatest men of the earth.** I thank him! And his people have been planted in **a home of their own.** They will move no more. He has caused us to **rest from all** our **enemies.**

"Even more, the Lord has said, 'I will make you into a royal house, a dynasty.' He has promised that once I die and **rest with** my **fathers,** my own son will see God **establish his kingdom.** That son's great pride will be that he **will build a house for** God's **Name,** a blessing I will not do or see.

"God assures me that he will be **father** to my **son,** as he has been for me. Oh, yes, if my son should do **wrong,** God **will punish him with the rod,** just as I would as his earthly father. He will have the stripes of loving discipline. But he will never be forsaken as Saul was, put away out of God's sight. God's mercy will not depart away from him.

"The royal house he grants to me **will be established forever.** Praise his name! The throne that I sit on, likewise, will seat a king for ever. Who shall that king be?"

At the end, give to each learner a copy of the monologue without any text being marked in bold. Say, "Compare the monologue you have just heard with the printed text and mark all the words and phrases that are identical."

This can be a small-group activity. Allow time to discuss discoveries.

INTO LIFE

Give to each student a "blueprint," as it were, for a simple house. Areas that should be identified are family room, bedroom, living room, laundry room, kitchen, dining room, closets, computer room, etc. Tell the class, "If you have your own little room in David's house, which is it? Why do you say so?"

Direct them to take the sketch and decide where they best fit in David's house, the kingdom of God. Give them an example: "I see myself in the computer room, because I want to communicate the good news to people all around the world." Another possibility is "I see myself in the bedroom, because I am so looking forward to that heavenly rest."

Suggest that students keep their "blueprints" handy in the coming week. After having a day or two to think about it, they may be able to think of better ways to see their places in all the rooms of David's house: service, rest, hospitality, evangelism, and others.

Two alternative or additional activities are on the reproducible page. The This Ol' House activity focuses on the church; the David and Me activity focuses on the individual student.

This Ol' House

Today's text uses "house" to refer to a promise of a royal dynasty to begin with David. This house had some of the following features. Look at 2 Samuel 7:8-17 and indicate *yes* or *no* in the small spaces to the left those you see as true of David's house as God built it.

____*Had a full security system:*

____*Had room for the next generation:*

____*Would last a long time:*

____*Designed by a divine architect:*

____*Was filled with warm and loving relationships:*

____*Was to see a demonstration of firm discipline:*

____*Had a great name "over the door":*

____*Came as a gift of grace:*

To the right, briefly explain what makes the statements true or false. Then consider which features of the house of David are realized in the church; briefly describe how and why.

David and Me

As a son or daughter of God, what things do you have in common with David? As you look at the following list (and perhaps look up the Scripture references given), decide how David has the characteristic and then how you share that characteristic with him.

DAVID	CHARACTERISTIC	ME
2 Samuel 7:8	Called from humble circumstances	1 Corinthians 6:9-11
2 Samuel 7:8	Made a member of royalty	1 Peter 2:9
2 Samuel 7:9, 10	Defended by God against enemies	Ephesians 6:10-13
2 Samuel 7:9	Given a great name	Revelation 3:12

GOD GRANTS WISDOM TO SOLOMON

LESSON 9

WHY TEACH THIS LESSON?

A remote control car, three new DVDs, a motorized skateboard—have you ever listened to a child's Christmas list? Even a thoughtful child who understands his parent's limitations in procuring many gifts may succumb to the myth of Santa's endless resources.

In today's lesson we will see God make Solomon an offer that transcended his wildest imaginings: the God of all creation told him to ask for whatever he wanted. *Whatever!* This word is not used in the flippant sense that we hear so often today; rather, God used it in the sense of open permission. Solomon, in response, acknowledged God's past generosity to himself and his father, David. Then he asked for the wisdom to do well at the task God had set before him.

We should take note of the prayer that God rewarded so richly. Too often our prayers sound like letters to Santa. Before we sit down with our list of wishes and blessings, let's pray that God will help us know what we ought to pray. God promises his assistance (through the Holy Spirit) to guide us into God-pleasing requests.

INTRODUCTION

A. THE EXPLOSION OF KNOWLEDGE

Near the end of his life, King Solomon wrote, "of making many books there is no end, and much study wearies the body" (Ecclesiastes 12:12). The modern world has realized both parts of this observation, perhaps far beyond Solomon's wildest expectations. It is estimated that as many as 2,000 new books are published every week worldwide. Add to this the enormous output of newspapers, journals, magazines, Web pages, and other media. The total is far beyond the capacity of any one individual to keep track of, let alone to read and digest.

This ever-increasing rate of publication has been labeled the information explosion. Its close cousin is called the knowledge explosion: the constantly growing store of facts and theories. These twin phenomena have many implications. One of these is the short shelf life of any education or training. For example, someone who earned a college degree in computer science 20 years ago would be woefully lacking in expertise about today's computers unless he or she had been updating constantly. Every field of study requires constant study to stay current. At times this may feel like it "wearies the body"!

Yet it is important to ask whether or not this avalanche of knowledge has made us any wiser. Has society's increased stock of information solved the basic problems of wars, poverty, or disease? Has more knowledge eliminated the age-old vices of greed, pride, anger, or lust? If anything, we seem to be in a world that is greedier, prouder, angrier, and more sexually oriented than ever before.

DEVOTIONAL READING:
PSALM 119:97-104
BACKGROUND SCRIPTURE:
1 KINGS 3
PRINTED TEXT:
1 KINGS 3:3-14

LESSON AIMS

After participating in this lesson, each student will be able to:

1. Retell the account of Solomon's prayer for wisdom and God's response.

2. Cite other examples, biblical and modern, of God's answering prayer.

3. Suggest one specific improvement he or she will implement in his or her personal prayer life.

Oct
29

KEY VERSE

I will do what you have asked. I will give you a wise and discerning heart, so that there will never have been anyone like you, nor will there ever be.—1 Kings 3:12

LESSON 9 NOTES

WHAT DO YOU THINK?

Share a time in your life when you received either really good or really bad advice. What lesson did this teach you about wisdom?

HOW TO SAY IT

Abiathar. Ah-BYE-uh-thar.
Adonijah. Ad-o-NYE-yuh.
Bathsheba. Bath-SHE-buh.
Ecclesiastes. Ik-LEEZ-ee-AS-teez.
Euphrates. You-FRAY-teez.
Gibeon. GIB-e-un
Jedidiah. Jed-ih-DIE-uh.
Joab. JO-ab.
Judean. Joo-DEE-un.
Nebuchadnezzar. NEB-yuh-kud-
   NEZ-er.
Pharaoh. FAIR-o or FAY-roe.
Pilate. PIE-lut.
shalom (Hebrew). shah-LOME.
Solomon. SOL-o-mun.
Zadok. ZAY-dok.

Remember: the most destructive wars of the twentieth century were fought between the most "educated" countries on earth!

There is a lot of overlap in meaning among the concepts of knowledge, understanding, and wisdom. But one key idea that sets wisdom apart is that wisdom is a godly use of knowledge and understanding. This week's lesson is about a man who requested wisdom from God and was rewarded with godly wisdom and much, much more.

B. LESSON BACKGROUND

The third king of Israel was David's son Solomon. Solomon reigned as king in Jerusalem from about 970 to 930 BC. His name is derived from the Hebrew word *shalom* ("peace"), thus Solomon means "peaceful one." Nathan the prophet also gave him the name *Jedidiah,* meaning "beloved of Yahweh" (2 Samuel 12:25). Solomon's mother was Bathsheba, David's partner in adultery. Bathsheba's first child, the product of their sin, died in his first week. David and Bathsheba's second child was Solomon.

Solomon was the first king of Israel to inherit the throne from his father. After David's death, Solomon acted quickly to remove any threats to his throne by executing Adonijah, his scheming half-brother (1 Kings 2:24) and Joab, a traitorous army general (2:33, 34). He also exiled the high priest, Abiathar, and replaced him with the loyal Zadok (2:35).

During the reign of Solomon, the kingdom of Israel expanded its boundaries to its greatest extent, from the Euphrates River to the border of Egypt (1 Kings 4:21). The kings in some of these territories paid annual tribute to Solomon, providing him with vast wealth.

The riches of Solomon have been the subject of theories and speculation, but the Bible itself has a great deal of information on this subject. His yearly tribute income was 666 talents of gold (1 Kings 10:14). The modern equivalent of this amount is difficult to estimate, but this may have been eight to ten tons of gold every year—and this was only part of his income. His hoard was so plentiful that Solomon made hundreds of ceremonial shields out of gold to adorn his palace (1Kings 10:17).

Solomon is also famous for his building projects. His greatest accomplishment in this area was the construction of a house for the Lord, the Jerusalem temple. The primary purpose of the temple was to provide suitable and permanent housing for the holy ark of the covenant (see 1 Chronicles 28:2). The detailed description of this structure is found in 1 Kings 5–7 and 2 Chronicles 2–4. When finished, this edifice was undoubtedly one of the most splendid buildings of the ancient world.

The Bible also tells us that King Solomon "loved many foreign women" (1 Kings 11:1). It is recorded that he had 700 official wives and 300 concubines (secondary wives). Unfortunately, we are also told that these wives led him away from the Lord in his old age (1 Kings 11:3, 4). We do believe, however, that the elderly Solomon sorted through all these things and returned to God before his death. This seems to be the lesson of the book of Ecclesiastes—a book thought to have been written by Solomon near the end of his life. He finishes this book by admonishing his readers that our primary duties are to love God and to keep his commandments (Ecclesiastes 12:13).

Today's lesson presents a young Solomon who finds himself in a powerful position that exceeds his capabilities. When the weight of his responsibilities is combined with his inadequacy, he does not despair. He trusts God.

I. GOD'S APPEARING (1 KINGS 3:3-5)

A. ABUNDANCE OF SACRIFICES (vv. 3, 4)

3, 4. Solomon showed his love for the LORD by walking according to the statutes of his father David, except that he offered sacrifices and burned incense on the high places.

The king went to Gibeon to offer sacrifices, for that was the most important high place, and Solomon offered a thousand burnt offerings on that altar.

To sacrifice in *high places* is not necessarily an act of paganism or idolatry (compare 2 Chronicles 33:17). The high place at *Gibeon* is the semi-permanent site of "the tabernacle of the Lord" (see 1 Chronicles 16:39). Gibeon is located in the Judean hill country, about seven miles northwest of Jerusalem.

The text does not tell us exactly what the *burnt offerings* are, but likely they are animals, probably young bulls. In this type of offering the entire animal is burned to ashes, giving it all to God. For Solomon to do this with *a thousand* bulls is a large, impressive display of his wealth, his devotion, and the seriousness of the occasion.

B. OFFER TO SOLOMON (v. 5)

5. At Gibeon the LORD appeared to Solomon during the night in a dream, and God said, "Ask for whatever you want me to give you."

The offerings likely take more than one day. Because of the length of time involved, Solomon stays in *Gibeon* overnight. During one of these nights, he is visited by God *in a dream*. This type of communication from God is not unknown, but it is rare. There are fewer than 20 people in the Bible who are said to have received dreams from God, and not all of these are believers (examples: Pharaoh, Nebuchadnezzar, Pilate's wife). Nevertheless, dreams have long been recognized as a powerful way by which God has spoken to humans on rare occasions.

God does not confront Solomon with a call for action or obedience. Instead, God presents Solomon with a blank check: *Ask for whatever you want me to give you.* There are no limits or guidelines given by God. Already, the wisdom of Solomon is being tested. Will he choose wisely or selfishly?

THE MEANING OF DREAMS

An old story tells of a woman who awoke in the morning and told her husband of her dream. "Last night I dreamed that you gave me a diamond necklace and earrings for our anniversary," she said. "Do you have any idea what my dream means?" His cryptic answer was, "Tonight you will know."

After work that evening, he presented her with a small package. Eagerly opening it, she found a book titled, *The Meaning of Dreams.* We can imagine what happened next! Seriously, though, you could spend a small fortune on all the books written about how to interpret your dreams.

Solomon's dream was not about diamond jewelry, although we should consider a vision of God in a dream to be of inestimable value! Just as the fictional woman's dream came in the context of her relationship with her husband, it is likewise significant that Solomon's dream came in the context of his relationship with God.

The day before his dream, Solomon had made an exceedingly large number of offerings to God. That night God came to him in the dream. We shouldn't make the mistake of assuming that we can "buy" God's presence with devotion or sacrifice. However, Solomon's sacrifices were a tangible indication of his love for God. At the very least, we can see that God responds positively to those who seek to please him.

—C. R. B.

DAILY BIBLE READINGS

Monday, Oct. 23—The Value of Wisdom (Proverbs 1:1-7)

Tuesday, Oct. 24—Where Is Wisdom Found? (Job 28:12-28)

Wednesday, Oct. 25—Add to Wisdom Understanding (Psalm 119:97-104)

Thursday, Oct. 26—Solomon Chosen to Be King (1 Kings 1:28-40)

Friday, Oct. 27—Solomon Requests Wisdom (1 Kings 3:3-9)

Saturday, Oct. 28—God Answers Solomon's Request (1 Kings 3:10-15)

Sunday, Oct. 29—Solomon Was Wise (1 Kings 4:29-34)

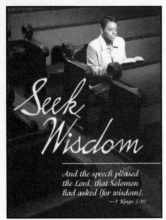

And the speech pleased
the Lord, that Solomon
had asked (for wisdom).
—1 Kings 3:10

Visual for Lesson 9. *Use this
picture to open a discussion
about prayer requests that do
and do not please the Lord.*

II. SOLOMON'S REQUEST (1 KINGS 3:6-9)

A. SOLOMON AS DAVID'S SUCCESSOR (VV. 6-8)

**6. Solomon answered, "You have shown great kindness to your servant, my father
David, because he was faithful to you and righteous and upright in heart. You
have continued this great kindness to him and have given him a son to sit on his
throne this very day.**

Solomon does not blurt out a request, like "Gimme a new Cadillac!" Instead,
he evaluates his needs by talking them through with God. (Isn't this what prayer
should be?) In this process he rehearses the marvelous relationship his *father,
David,* had had with the Lord. Being king gives Solomon occasion to remember
how God had kept his promise to David by allowing his *son* to become king.

**7. "Now, O LORD my God, you have made your servant king in place of my father
David. But I am only a little child and do not know how to carry out my duties.**

Solomon has come to a strong conviction that he is inadequate for the task he
has been given. Who could possibly fill the shoes of the great and famous *David?*

**8. "Your servant is here among the people you have chosen, a great people, too nu-
merous to count or number.**

Solomon is aware that Israel is the chosen nation of God and that it has grown
to be a very populous *people.* These factors combine to make him feel like a little
child, unequal to his responsibilities. We may experience something similar
when we observe the children of capable and powerful leaders. Sometimes a
child is expected to live up to the legacy left by the father but cannot possibly fulfill these expectations. Following a famous father is not an easy path.

B. SOLOMON SEEKS WISDOM (V. 9)

**9. "So give your servant a discerning heart to govern your people and to distin-
guish between right and wrong. For who is able to govern this great people of
yours?"**

David had left Solomon with the instruction that "When one rules over men
in righteousness, when he rules in the fear of God, he is like the light of morning
at sunrise" (2 Samuel 23:3, 4). Solomon understands that a major component of
being a successful king is related to his judgment. Therefore he asks for divine
understanding in dealing with his *people.* He cannot do it by himself. Solomon
asks, rhetorically, *Who is able to govern this great people of yours?* The answer is
that only the Lord himself can do this. Solomon desperately needs God's help.

In this request Solomon submits his heart to God. Any cry to God for help is a
cry of faith. He is following the advice of his father, to rule "in the fear of God."
He understands that even the greatest leaders are answerable to a higher authority and need God's assistance to rule justly. We don't have many kings left in our
world, but any nation with a leader who depends on God will receive blessings
because of this relationship.

III. GOD'S PROMISES (1 KINGS 3:10-14)

A. SOLOMON'S REQUEST PLEASES GOD (V. 10)

10. The Lord was pleased that Solomon had asked for this.

Oh, to please *the Lord*! All too often we find ourselves in need of humility and
repentance because we have displeased God. That Solomon is able to set aside
petty, personal, selfish desires and pinpoint what he will need to serve God effectively is a display of wisdom at a young age. He has already learned the lesson he
later teaches to others: "The fear of the Lord is the beginning of wisdom" (Proverbs 9:10).

B. SOLOMON'S REQUEST GRANTED (vv. 11, 12)

11, 12. So God said to him, "Since you have asked for this and not for long life or wealth for yourself, nor have asked for the death of your enemies but for discernment in administering justice, I will do what you have asked. I will give you a wise and discerning heart, so that there will never have been anyone like you, nor will there ever be.

God well knows that Solomon could have *asked for* personal favors: longevity, *wealth*, or victories. God promises to make Solomon a unique individual in history: the wisest man who ever lived.

There are related yet distinct qualities that are promised here. When we see that Solomon is granted *a wise . . . heart*, we should realize that wisdom goes beyond the ability to discern good from evil. The wise person recognizes the difference and chooses to do the good. The one who understands but chooses evil is a fool (see Proverbs 14:16; Romans 16:19). Solomon's gift is more than just the ability to know righteousness. He is enabled to choose righteousness.

Solomon's heart is also to be one of *discernment*. This has the sense of clear perception of a situation and insight into its implications. This means that Solomon will be able *in administering justice*. The word *administering* is based on the Hebrew word for "to hear." It has the implication of one who listens judiciously, evaluating all factors carefully.

The three Hebrew words that are behind these qualities are repeated in Proverbs 1:5: "Let the wise listen and add to their learning, and let the discerning get guidance" (see also 1 Kings 4:29). Wisdom builds on wisdom. Wise choices lead to more wise choices. Deeper understanding results from listening to wise teachers.

C. SOLOMON'S REQUEST EXCEEDED (vv. 13, 14)

13. "Moreover, I will give you what you have not asked for—both riches and honor—so that in your lifetime you will have no equal among kings.

There are those who attain great wealth but are despised. There are others who gain great honor and dignity yet die penniless. And, of course, there are many who perish being neither rich nor honorable. But few are recognized as persons with *both riches and honor.* Such ones are doubly blessed by God. Here God makes a promise to Solomon: he will be a person of vast wealth and someone respected very highly.

As mentioned above, Solomon's wealth becomes legendary. God's gift of wisdom, however, causes Solomon's reputation to spread far and wide. His wisdom is unlimited (1 Kings 4:29-31). He is the author of 3,000 wise sayings (proverbs) and over 1,000 songs (1 Kings 4:32). Some of these are preserved in our Bible books of Proverbs, Ecclesiastes, and the Song of Songs (see also Psalm 72).

SUDDEN WEALTH SYNDROME

"In a lot of ways, I was happier living a simpler life." Those are the words of a multimillionaire who had made an amazing amount of money in the high-tech stock market boom of the 1990s. His household was one of some 275,000 in America with assets of over $10 million at the end of that decade—a group that was five times larger than it had been just 15 years earlier.

Psychologists say people who become very rich very quickly complain about becoming isolated from their former friends; they even feel alienated from their sense of who they are (www.webmd.com). One man who sold his company for tens of millions of dollars said he felt a "gnawing anxiety that his money could disappear

---

WHAT DO YOU THINK?

Why is wisdom so far superior to anything else, both then and now?

WHAT DO YOU THINK?

God gave Solomon more than he asked for. Do you think that those who seek and practice the wisdom of God are also blessed with earthly rewards? Why, or why not?

[Ephesians 6:2 may get you started on your answer.]

PRAYER

O Lord, we can never be wise without your presence. Give us hearts that seek wisdom, even when the wise choices are the hard choices. Give us peace in knowing that your ways transcend the ways of the world, the paths of foolishness. We pray in the name of your Son, Jesus, amen.

as quickly as it had come." He found it hard to talk to his old friends about things they had easily conversed about before he was struck with sudden wealth. Many poorer people would be willing to change places with the rich, but they obviously aren't aware of the psychological and relationship costs of having lots of money!

God's promised gift to Solomon could have been an unparalleled blessing. But it turned out to be a responsibility that Solomon was not fully prepared to exercise. He did not always "walk in my ways," as God had said he must if he were to enjoy the blessings fully. Solomon's experience proves once again that who you are— your character, etc.—is far more important than how much you have.   —C. R. B.

14. "And if you walk in my ways and obey my statutes and commands as David your father did, I will give you a long life."

While the promises of wisdom and honor are unconditional, God does place conditions on the gift of a *long life*. This promise is contingent upon Solomon's obedience to God's laws, an obedience that God had seen in Solomon's father, *David*. God had not seen in David a perfect record of obedience, of course. But God had indeed seen a general life pattern of obedience, described as to walk in my ways.

Unfortunately, Solomon will not match his father David. Solomon's disobedience causes God to be very angry. God then modifies his earlier promise to David of a continuing king in Jerusalem from David's family: much of Solomon's kingdom will be taken away from his son Rehoboam (1 Kings 11:9-13). This promise is made good after the death of Solomon, and the kingdom is split.

CONCLUSION

Solomon apparently was not content with God's gift of wisdom. Ecclesiastes is a record of his wretched search for the meaning of life in many different areas. He confessed that he denied himself nothing (Ecclesiastes 2:10) and concluded that he hated life (2:17). "Everything is meaningless" he said (1:2). How can wise people sometimes be so stupid?

Fortunately Solomon overcame the cynicism of his foolish quest and regained some of the wisdom he displayed at a younger age. Solomon was able to reaffirm that our purpose is to be found in our fear of God and in our obedience to him (Ecclesiastes 12:13).

In modern society we find people seeking wisdom from curious sources. The media bombards us with the opinions of celebrities, as if being famous automatically brings wisdom. Why do we think the ability to hit home runs or make music videos gives a person understanding and discernment? Conversely, people who live wisely, fearing God and striving to keep his commandments, are rarely seen as those who should be honored and followed. Solomon knew that sinners were fools and fools were sinners.

So how do we seek and find wisdom? An obvious treasure, yet one we often ignore, is to study God's Word. We are promised that Scripture is able to make us "wise for salvation" (2 Timothy 3:15). The people of God should be people of his Word.

We should also seek to be taught by those whose lives display God's wisdom. Solomon's story teaches us that great wisdom will attract disciples. Great understanding and discernment is not often found in the very young, so we should listen to those whose faith has been tested, "refined by fire" (1 Peter 1:7). Not all old people are wise. But we are more likely to strike the rich vein of wisdom among our elders than among the young.

WHAT DO YOU THINK?

Why do you think wisdom is so hard to attain? What are the obstacles to acquiring it in our world today?

THOUGHT TO REMEMBER

Recognition and development of true wisdom is tied directly to our relationship with God.

Discovery Learning

This page contains an alternative lesson plan emphasizing learning activities. Classes desiring such student involvement will find these suggestions helpful. The next page is a reproducible activity page to further enhance discovery learning.

LEARNING GOALS

After this lesson, each student will be able to:

1. Retell the account of Solomon's prayer for wisdom and God's response.

2. Cite other examples, biblical and modern, of God's answering prayer.

3. Suggest one specific improvement he or she will implement in his or her personal prayer life.

INTO THE LESSON

Display an image of a genie rising from a magic lamp. Ask the class, "Given three wishes, what would most people name?" Give time for responses, noting the ego-centric, materialistic nature of most. Then say, "Given a much greater opportunity to satisfy personal needs and wants, Solomon made an altogether different request."

Transition by saying in a manner similar to PBS's Sesame Street, "Today's lesson is brought to you by the number 3 and the letter I." Display large images of both.

INTO THE WORD

Direct the class to read silently today's text in 1 Kings 3:3-14, noting elements that appear in threes. After a time of reading and pondering, ask the following questions, either in the order of the verses (as given here) or in some random order. Suggested answers are in italics.

(1) "What three attributes of Solomon indicate his relationship with God?" (*loved the Lord, walked in the statutes of his father David, and offered sacrifices—vv. 3, 4*); (2) "What three attributes of God are indicated to Solomon at Gibeon?" (*God appeared, God spoke, God offered a gift—v. 5*); (3) "What three characteristics of David are noted in verse 6?" (*faithful, righteous, upright—v. 6*); (4) "What three expressions of humility and inadequacy does Solomon make in response to God?" (*too young, not smart enough, overwhelmed by the number of people—vv. 7, 8*); (5) "What three end results does Solomon want when he asks God for an understanding heart?" (*for governing wisdom, for ability to distinguish good and evil, and for strength to deal with so many people—v. 9*); (6) "What three things does God commend Solomon for not asking?" (*long life, wealth, and victories over enemies—v. 11*); (7) "What three 'extra' things did God grant Solomon?" (*riches, honor, and long life—vv. 13, 14*).

First Kings 4 ends with a summary statement of the nature and extent of the wisdom God granted to Solomon. Arrange with a student before class to do the following: After surveying the lesson text (having used the preceding activity), turn to your prearranged helper and ask, "[Student's name], did God grant Solomon's request for wisdom?" Tell your helper to answer enthusiastically and emphatically with words such as, "Did He? Why . . ." and then have the helper read 1 Kings 4:29-34. Once the helper finishes, affirm, "God does answer prayer—especially when it is not self-centered and when it is for the welfare of his people."

Now ask the class to explain how "this class is brought to you by the letter I." Accept reasonable answers. These will certainly include the ideas that Solomon's request refused to focus on "I" (himself) and that God's "I" statements clearly revealed his personal intentions of what he would do for Solomon.

(Alternative: use, in small groups, the Readiness Attitudes exercise from the reproducible page.)

INTO LIFE

Note to your class again the unselfish nature of Solomon's request and the abundant grace God showered as a result. After a brief discussion of the things people typically pray for, ask, "What are some of the nonmaterial things the Scriptures admonish us to pray for?" When someone suggests wisdom (based on James 1:5), stop and ask, "Yes, but what kind of wisdom?" Have someone read James 3:13-18. List the characteristics of earthly wisdom: envy, selfish ambition, disorder, every evil practice. Ask, "How do these things keep one from praying for the right things?" (Example: envy certainly keeps one from praying for others, for it is others who are being envied.)

Continue with a list of the wisdom that is "from above." Once that list is made (from James 3:17, 18), ask the class, "And how do these attributes give impetus to praying for the right things? (Example: "full of mercy" gives direction to prayers of compassion for the needy and the distressed.) Recommend that your learners keep this passage open during their times of prayer this week, as a guideline for how to pray in wisdom. (As an alternative prayer exercise, use the Solomon's Train activity from the reproducible page.)

Readiness Attitudes

God's simple direction to Solomon, "Ask for whatever you want me to give you" (1 Kings 3:5) brings forth words from Solomon that indicate he is ready to make the right request. How does each of the following statements about Solomon (from verses 6-9) show his readiness?

He remembers God's kindness in the past to his family.

He realizes that God's grace is related to human faithfulness and righteousness.

He expresses personal humility and inadequacy.

He expresses great concern for the people of God.

He wants to see clearly the difference between right and wrong.

He understands that true discernment is more important than riches and even life and health itself.

If you want to please God with your requests, per verse 10, how should each of those "readiness attitudes" alter your prayer life?

Solomon's Train

When God requested that Solomon choose his gifts for life and service, Solomon realized the difficulty of keeping what we might call "the royal train" in motion. He saw himself as being inadequate for the task. If Solomon was to his train from running out of fuel or jumping the tracks, he needed help from God.

On boxcars of the train below, list some of the heavy demands that your life and ministry are making on you. On the engine, list one feeble strength—something that seems inadequate for the task.

What is your prayer to the God who says, "Ask for whatever you want me to give you"? Write it below.

ELIJAH TRIUMPHS WITH GOD

LESSON 10

WHY TEACH THIS LESSON?

Last night I heard a heart-wrenching story. It seems that my dear friend's granddaughter had been harassed at her middle school after being open about her faith in Jesus. A group of girls, one in particular, made a mission of tormenting her. Among ugly words in e-mail messages, the attacker told her that she believed in a God who doesn't exist.

Minutes before hearing this disturbing story, another friend had told me about an experience he had had at work that day. His dealings with a broken man who had lost a wife, a job, and experienced a health crisis led my friend to want to share his faith with this desperate soul. Yet to do so would breach company rules and risk his job.

Sometimes we, like Elijah, feel alone in representing the one true God to a dark world. And while God may not manifest his power with a downpour of fire, we must pray to God for help. We do that because we know that his power and truth will shine through faithful lives.

INTRODUCTION

A. THE POWER OF ONE

During the summer of 2004, Mike Krzyzewski, head coach of the men's basketball team at Duke University, was approached about becoming head coach of the National Basketball Association's Los Angeles Lakers. "Coach K," as he is known, had gained a reputation as one of the premier coaches in college basketball. The high salary and prestige that accompanied coaching a team like the Lakers were tempting.

In the midst of his deliberations, Krzyzewski received an e-mail that proved to be the pivotal influence in his decision. Andrew Humphries, a junior at Duke, sent an impassioned message for Coach K to stay. The e-mail brought tears to the eyes of Krzyzewski; he rejected the Lakers' offer and chose to remain at Duke.

Andrew Humphries was just one person—yet he had the power to persuade! The prophet Elijah also was just one man. His voice seemed like a whisper in Israel when compared with the powerful, government-backed influence of Baal worship. Yet when just one person chooses to stand firm on behalf of the one true God, the results can be one of a kind! Coach K could well have made a different decision even after Humphries' e-mail. Would the people on Mount Carmel dared to have chosen Baal after seeing the power of God before their eyes?

B. WHAT PROFIT WERE THE PROPHETS?

Many associate the word *prophet* with someone who has the ability to predict the future. The role of the Old Testament prophets, however, went much further than this. Every prophet conveyed a significant message and was raised up by the Lord during a particularly critical time in the history of God's people.

DEVOTIONAL READING:
PSALM 86:8-13
BACKGROUND SCRIPTURE:
1 KINGS 18:20-39
PRINTED TEXT:
1 KINGS 18:20-24, 30-35, 38, 39

LESSON AIMS

After participating in this lesson, each student will be able to:

1. Give the significant details of the account of Elijah's contest with the prophets of Baal on Mount Carmel.

2. Tell why this confrontation was such a crucial event in the history of God's people.

3. Write a prayer that commits him or her to take a stand for God's truth in a situation where doing so will go against an ungodly viewpoint.

NOV
5

KEY VERSE

When all the people saw this, they fell prostrate and cried, "The LORD—he is God! The LORD—he is God!" —1 Kings 18:39

LESSON 10 NOTES

Prophets were raised up by the Lord during periods when paganism became an especially serious threat to God's people. This is one of the reasons that the prophet Elijah's ministry was pivotal. Ahab and Jezebel (particularly Jezebel) were intent on promoting the worship of pagan gods throughout Israel. Baal was considered a god of storms and fertility, meaning that he was believed to be in charge of providing life—to crops, animals, and human beings.

God used Elijah to counter this false and repulsive system of worship. Elijah demonstrated that the God who had called Israel to be his people was still in control.

C. LESSON BACKGROUND

By the time Elijah's ministry began, the nation of Israel had been divided for approximately half a century. (*Israel* is often used to designate the ten tribes that constituted the northern kingdom with *Judah* referring to the two tribes of the southern kingdom.) Elijah himself appears in the biblical record quite suddenly. Nothing is said about his parents, his childhood, or even his call to be a prophet.

The first time he is mentioned is in 1 Kings 17:1, where he announces a period of drought in the land of Israel. This challenge was a slap in the face of the god Baal and of those who worshiped him, since Baal was believed to be the provider of storms that would bring rain.

Elijah was then guided through a series of circumstances that served to prepare him further for his ministry and assure him of God's presence. First, he was told to go to the Kerith Ravine, where ravens brought him food twice a day (1 Kings 17:5, 6). When the brook dried up because of the drought, the Lord told Elijah to travel northward to Zarephath of Sidon. There the Lord used a widow to provide Elijah with food in a miraculous manner. Later when the widow's only son became ill and died, Elijah prayed to the Lord and the boy was brought back to life (vv. 7-24).

Notice that the miracles had something to do with providing food in life-areas where Baal was believed to be in control. Sidon was Jezebel's homeland (1 Kings 16:31). Elijah thus saw God's clear superiority to the pagan gods!

In the third year of the drought, the Lord told Elijah to "Go, and present yourself to Ahab, and I will send rain on the land" (1 Kings 18:1). Elijah sent a message to Ahab through Obadiah, an official of Ahab's who was also a devout follower of the Lord.

When prophet and king met, Elijah issued a challenge to Ahab to summon all Israel to assemble at Mount Carmel. Ahab was also to gather the 450 prophets of Baal "and the four hundred prophets of Asherah" (1Kings 18:19). The goddess Asherah was believed to be Baal's consort.

At this point, Elijah did not specify what he planned to do at Mount Carmel. Our printed text begins by describing Ahab's compliance with Elijah's challenge.

I. PEOPLE ADDRESSED (1 KINGS 18:20-24)

A. THE PLACE (v. 20)

20. So Ahab sent word throughout all Israel and assembled the prophets on Mount Carmel.

Ahab does as Elijah says, sending *word throughout all Israel* and gathering *the prophets on Mount Carmel.* Later Elijah observes that the 450 prophets of Baal are present (v. 22), but he says nothing about the 400 prophets of Asherah. For some unknown reason, Jezebel apparently forbids her prophets to come to

Mount Carmel. Probably her failure to comply with Elijah's challenge is simply an act of defiance. Maybe Ahab is willing to do what Elijah says, but Jezebel is not about to!

One may ask why Mount Carmel serves as the place for this assembly. Mount Carmel is actually a mountain ridge some 12 miles in length. Near the summit of the ridge is a plateau where a contest such as this one can take place. A spring of water is close at hand. It flows even during extremely dry seasons. This is why Elijah can have 12 containers of water poured on his sacrifice (vv. 33, 34, below) even though this incident occurs during drought conditions.

B. THE PLEA (v. 21)

21. Elijah went before the people and said, "How long will you waver between two opinions? If the LORD is God, follow him; but if Baal is God, follow him."
But the people said nothing.

Elijah begins his address to the Israelites with a question: *How long will you waver between two opinions?* Elijah is describing the spiritual unsteadiness of the people in the crowd that day. The alternative to such wavering will be a confident, steady walk with the Lord, which they do not possess.

The issue facing the people on this occasion is remarkably simple. Two options confront them: the way of the Lord and the way of *Baal*. In today's pluralistic religious climate, Elijah's statement is still timely. We may choose a narrow road to salvation or a wide road to destruction (Matthew 7:13, 14).

Observe the audience's passive, apathetic response: *the people said nothing.* Perhaps they are cowering in fear, knowing that to answer in favor of Baal will displease Elijah, while answering in favor of the Lord will ignite the rage of Jezebel. Perhaps their silence reflects their lack of passion for or interest in anything having to do with spiritual matters. It is also possible that Elijah's uncompromising words make all too clear their failure to obey the Lord; thus their silence may indicate a sense of shame or embarrassment. In any case, the safe response (from a worldly point of view) is to keep quiet.

C. THE PLAN (vv. 22-24)

22. Then Elijah said to them, "I am the only one of the LORD's prophets left, but Baal has four hundred and fifty prophets.

Elijah observes that he is *the only one of the Lord's prophets left.* Yet we know from an earlier statement in 1 Kings 18:4 that Obadiah, one of Ahab's officials, has hidden 100 prophets of the Lord from Jezebel's murderous fury. In addition there are prophets such as Micaiah (22:8) and various unnamed men who are part of the group known as the "sons of the prophets" (20:35). Elijah probably means that he is the only one of the Lord's prophets who is present for this confrontation.

Elijah's emphasis on the contrast between 1 and 450 highlights a key principle: truth is not determined by the number of people who embrace a certain position. Truth is truth, no matter how many or how few hold to it at any given time.

23, 24. "Get two bulls for us. Let them choose one for themselves, and let them cut it into pieces and put it on the wood but not set fire to it. I will prepare the other bull and put it on the wood but not set fire to it. Then you call on the name of your god, and I will call on the name of the LORD. The god who answers by fire—he is God."
Then all the people said, "What you say is good."

WHAT DO YOU THINK?

In what ways does our culture waver between a multitude of opinions? How do we respond?

WHAT DO YOU THINK?

In what ways is Elijah's confrontation with 450 ungodly opponents an example for Christians today? In what ways is it not an example?

How to Say It

Ahab. AY-hab.
Asherah. Uh-SHE-ruh.
Kerith. KEY-rith.
Elijah. Ee-LYE-juh.
Jezebel. JEZ-uh-bel.
Krzyzewski. Sha-SHEF-ski.
Micaiah. My-KAY-uh.
Obadiah. O-buh-DYE-uh.
Sidon. SIGH-dun.
Zarephath. ZAIR-uh-fath.

The rules of the contest are simple. Each side is to prepare a bull in the same manner: they will *cut it into pieces,* and lay it *on the wood.* Then each side is to *call on the name* of its deity. The God who responds *by fire* will prove himself to be the true God.

The fire that Elijah mentions may refer to lightning. Remember that the issue at hand is which deity is in control of the rains. Lightning would serve as a signal of the coming of the drought-ending rains. That would demonstrate decisively to those gathered on Mount Carmel which God is in control of the forces of nature.

Perhaps the prophets of Baal relish the opportunity to go first. Should Baal respond to their cries, the contest essentially will be over. However, their going first only sets the stage for what Elijah will do, because it will highlight how powerless Baal really is.

Verses 25-29 (not in our printed text) record the futile efforts of the followers of Baal. The threefold emphasis at the conclusion of verse 29 provides a solemn closure to the failure of Baal's prophets: "there was no response, no one answered, no one paid attention." The stage is now set for a dramatic display of divine power.

II. PREPARATION ACCOMPLISHED (1 KINGS 18:30-35)

A. SETTING UP THE ALTAR (vv. 30-32)

30. Then Elijah said to all the people, "Come here to me." They came to him, and he repaired the altar of the LORD, which was in ruins.

While nothing is said specifically about the altar used by the prophets of Baal, it is noted that Elijah repaired *the altar of the Lord,* which was broken down. No doubt this altar had been a victim of the apathy and neglect of the people toward the worship of the true God.

31. Elijah took twelve stones, one for each of the tribes descended from Jacob, to whom the word of the LORD had come, saying, "Your name shall be Israel."

The use of 12 *stones* by Elijah is noteworthy in light of the fact the nation of Israel has been divided for several decades by this time. Yet Elijah recognizes through this action that God's original intention is that the Israelites be 12 tribes—yet one nation—under him.

SYMBOLIC STONES

In the sixteenth century English royal power increasingly asserted itself over Ireland. That pressure set off some four centuries of political and religious struggle. The Anglo-Irish war of 1919–1921 resulted in two separate countries. Mostly Catholic southern Ireland became independent. Northern Ireland was mostly Protestant and aligned with Britain.

Throughout much of the twentieth century, dissidents hoped for political reunification of Ireland. These dissidents used terrorist methods to try to force the British out of Northern Ireland. One could have hoped that since each side of the Protestant-Catholic divide claimed to be Christian, they could all act as if they were and quit killing each other.

The century-long division of the Irish peoples is somewhat similar to that of God's people of old. Israel and Judah were divided politically and religiously. Israel in the north had turned mostly to Baalism; Judah in the south had remained somewhat faithful to Yahweh (although it had dabbled in idolatry also). By building his altar out of 12 stones, Elijah hoped that the symbolic number would speak to all the tribes of divided Israel. Perhaps they would remember their common heritage before the one true God.

Visual for Lesson 10. *Point to this artwork as an illustration of someone standing alone for God. Use it to introduce the second question on page 93.*

Faithfulness to God is without doubt the best way for any nation to find internal peace. That fact should not be lost on the people of any democracy when they go to the polls to elect their leaders.   —C. R. B.

32. With the stones he built an altar in the name of the LORD, and he dug a trench around it large enough to hold two seahs of seed.

The act described earlier in verse 30 as repairing the altar of the Lord is now described in another way: Elijah *built an altar in the name of the Lord.* Elijah is building an altar under the authority of and in reverence for the true God. God's name has lost none of its power, in spite of Ahab and Jezebel's attempts to stamp it out.

This verse also notes that Elijah makes a *trench* about the altar, as great as would contain *two seahs of seed.* This computes to about 13 quarts. If such an act seems odd to the onlookers, it does not compare with what Elijah does next.

B. SOAKING THE SACRIFICE (vv. 33-35)

33, 34. He arranged the wood, cut the bull into pieces and laid it on the wood. Then he said to them, "Fill four large jars with water and pour it on the offering and on the wood."

"Do it again," he said, and they did it again.

"Do it a third time," he ordered, and they did it the third time.

Elijah proceeds to prepare the sacrifice according to the rules established earlier. But then he does something else quite unexpected: he commands that *four* barrels of *water* be poured *on the offering* three times. As noted earlier, water may be available from the streams that flow at higher elevations, such as that of Mount Carmel, despite the severe drought that is now in its fourth year (Luke 4:25; James 5:17).

35. The water ran down around the altar and even filled the trench.

By soaking completely the sacrifice and *the altar,* Elijah sets the stage for an even more impressive demonstration of the power of the true God. At the same time, Elijah is also putting his own reputation as the Lord's prophet on the line. He will look utterly foolish if God fails to answer.

Elijah's actions also indicate to the audience that he is not engaging in any kind of trickery to ignite his sacrifice. If the sacrifice is ignited, the only possible explanation will be that God has done it.

The prayer of Elijah, recorded in verses 36 and 37, is not part of our printed text. His simple, earnest plea to the Lord contrasts markedly with the frenzied madness of the prophets of Baal. And whereas there was no response of any kind to the prophets of Baal, such is not the case now.

III. PRAYER ANSWERED (1 KINGS 18:38, 39)

A. THE LORD'S RESPONSE (v. 38)

38. Then the fire of the LORD fell and burned up the sacrifice, the wood, the stones and the soil, and also licked up the water in the trench.

In a spectacular display of unmistakably divine power, *the fire of the Lord* consumes everything that is part of the preparation for *the sacrifice.* Even the *water in the trench* is *licked up* by the fire.

B. THE PEOPLE'S REACTION (v. 39)

39. When all the people saw this, they fell prostrate and cried, "The LORD—he is God! The LORD—he is God!"

WHAT DO YOU THINK?

Elijah built an altar to God in the presence of all of the people, including the prophets of Baal. When is public expression of Christian faith especially appropriate today? When can such expressions be counterproductive?

WHAT DO YOU THINK?

What was a time in your life when you stood alone (or nearly alone) for something you believed was right? What was the result for the cause you supported? How did taking this stand affect you personally?

Father, may we have the courage to stand for you in our time as Elijah did in his. When we feel intimidated by the strength or loudness of the opposition, help us to be unmoved. Help us to remain faithful and consistent in our testimony. May we thereby give no one cause to question our devotion to your Son, Jesus. In his name, amen.

THOUGHT TO REMEMBER

God will give us the courage we need for any opposition we face.

WHAT DO YOU THINK?

When was a time that you stepped out so far on faith that you could have been successful only if God intervened?

All the people, who were silent earlier when confronted by Elijah (v. 21), do not hesitate to express their reaction after what they witness. What else could they conclude? *The Lord—he is God.*

The aftermath of the contest on Mount Carmel includes the slaughter of the prophets of Baal. That is in accordance with the Law of Moses concerning false prophets: "a prophet who speaks in the name of other gods must be put to death" (Deuteronomy 18:20). Also comes the long-awaited rains. The drought has ended, and—more importantly—the Lord, his prophet, and his Word have been vindicated.

"DON'T TRY THIS AT HOME"

We've all heard of fire-breathing preachers of the gospel. Colin Davis, a Church of England vicar in Devon, England, is a fire-*eating* preacher! While he was in college training for the ministry, he saw a fire performer and thought he would be able to use the trick to attract attention to the message of Christ. Neither his former work as a banker nor his current work as a preacher would seem to predict this particular avocation!

Davis says he uses the trick for its attention-grabbing impact, comparing the feat to Jesus' use of parables. Only occasionally does his performance take place in church; more often he does it in school assemblies. On those occasions he makes students vow before the demonstration that they will not try it.

In one sense, Elijah's use of fire was like Colin Davis's use of fire: it certainly captured the attention of his audience! On the other hand, there is a striking difference: Davis's performance is just that—a trick that has no physical effect. But Elijah's fire was sent by God from Heaven to consume everything in its path. We can respond, "Don't try this at home" to both. Seeing the constant shower of God's blessings in our everyday lives should be all we need to evoke the same reaction as that of Elijah's audience: "The Lord—he is God!" This bears repeating.

—C. R. B.

CONCLUSION

Perhaps after reading an account such as that of Elijah we may wonder, "Why don't we see demonstrations of God's power such as this today? If we could offer the kind of evidence that Elijah did on Mount Carmel, think of the impact it would have on our culture! Does God no longer provide these demonstrations, or do we as his people lack faith?"

We should remember that as Christians we bear witness to the greatest of all demonstrations of God's power: the resurrection of Jesus his Son from the dead. That always has been the essence of the gospel message (1 Corinthians 15:1-4).

Interestingly, when the New Testament instructs Christians on how to live in light of that event, it points to the quiet, often inconspicuous deeds of service done in the name of Christ. The metaphors of salt and light (Matthew 5:13-16) are hardly noisy or flamboyant in how they function. But no one can question their effectiveness or their necessity.

Elijah's surroundings demanded the kind of highly visible, dramatic manifestation of power that God wrought at Mount Carmel. We see similar demonstrations during other critical periods in biblical history (the plagues in Egypt and the miracles of Jesus, for example). But a primary challenge issued to New Testament believers today is that of a consistently holy lifestyle. Peter challenged the Christians of his time to live holy lives among unbelievers that "though they accuse you of doing wrong, they may see your good deeds and glorify God" (1 Peter 2:12).

Discovery Learning

This page contains an alternative lesson plan emphasizing learning activities. Classes desiring such student involvement will find these suggestions helpful. The next page is a reproducible activity page to further enhance discovery learning.

LEARNING GOALS

After this lesson, each student will be able to:

1. Give the significant details of the account of Elijah's contest with the prophets of Baal on Mount Carmel.

2. Tell why this confrontation was such a crucial event in the history of God's people.

3. Write a prayer that commits him or her to take a stand for God's truth in a situation where doing so will go against an ungodly viewpoint.

INTO THE LESSON

Display a sign saying *Impact—The Power of One!* Tell the class that one person can make a difference in the world, a culture, a church, or in a life. Ask the class members to think of one person who made such an impact. While the class members are thinking about this challenge, tell the story of Andrew Humphries found in the Introduction. Then allow class members to share the name and events of one person who made an impact.

Make the transition to Bible study by telling the class that the prophet Elijah is a wonderful example of just one man making a huge impact on culture. Say, "But Elijah's influence was backed by a miracle of God. That ancient miracle still serves as an encouragement to us."

INTO THE WORD

Give a very brief lecture based on the Lesson Background. Emphasize the division of the tribes, the drought, Elijah's history, and the nature of Baal. As you lecture, write the following words on the board while speaking on each topic: Israel, Drought, Elijah, and Baal.

Prepare a handout as follows (also printed in the student book). The students will need Bibles, since some of the information is found in verses not included in the printed text. Students can complete the handout individually, in pairs, or in small groups as you think best.

Heading: A Contest of Gods
Contestants
   The bad guys (v. 22):
   The good guy (v. 22):
The contest location (v. 20):
The challenge for the teams (vv. 23, 24):
The team strategies

The bad guys (vv. 26-29):
   The good guy (vv. 30-37):
The victor (vv. 38, 39):
The fate of the defeated (v. 40):
The fate of the drought (vv. 41-45):

For follow-up discussion, use these questions: (1) Why do you think Elijah selected 12 stones for his altar (vv. 31, 32)? (2) Why do you suppose Elijah chose to pour water on the sacrifice before offering his prayer (vv. 33, 34)? (3) What lessons about prayer do we learn as we contrast the pleas of Baal's prophets and Elijah's prayer? (4) Why do you think this contest was a crucial event in the history of Israel? (Write answers on the board and discuss as appropriate.)

INTO LIFE

Make the transition to application by saying that God still calls people to take a stand in cultures that value pluralistic religious views. Despite the common view of varied "paths to God," Jesus is the only way to the Father. Like Israel, God calls us to take a stand for the one true God. However, does our stand need always to be confrontational? Why, or why not? (Discuss.)

Tell the students that underneath three chairs are taped Scripture references that have clues that may be helpful in determining how to live an influential life. Have the students find and read the following Scriptures, then ask the attendant questions:

Matthew 5:13-16. Do these metaphors of salt and light suggest an alternative to noisy and flamboyant confrontation? Is there a way to make an impact through quiet and less conspicuous means? How?

1 Peter 2:12. What does this Scripture offer or imply about influencing lives or society? What is the wisdom of this verse and its appeal?

1 Peter 3:1-4. What clues do we find in this passage about a way to influence the unsaved?

Conclude by asking each student to write a prayer that commits him or her to take a stand for God's truth in a situation where doing so will go against the majority, ungodly viewpoint.

(Alternative: use the exercises Making an Impact and Prayerful Preparation from the reproducible page. These two exercises are best used together in sequence.)

Making an Impact

The Bible shows us many people who made impacts while serving the Lord. Some, like Elijah, made their impacts through dramatic confrontation. Some, however, affected others through quieter ways, with a sweet spirit of faithful service. Use the following exercise to discover examples of each. List their names and tell how each made an impact. Make special note of names that appear on both lists!

CONFRONTATIONAL	GENTLE
Exodus 8:1, 2	Genesis 50:19-21
2 Samuel 12	Numbers 12:3
Nehemiah 13:23-28	Ruth 2
Matthew 3:7	Acts 28:2
Acts 4:8-11	1 Thessalonians 2:7
Galatians 2:11-14	3 John 1

Prayerful Preparation

You can make an impact in many ways! Perhaps it will be through dramatic confrontation, or perhaps you may be influential as you put into quiet action Peter's encouragement to "live such good lives among the pagans . . . they may see your good deeds and glorify God" (1 Peter 2:12). Think of a situation that requires godly change. Then write a brief appeal for God's help to use you in ways that seem best to him.

JOSIAH BRINGS REFORM

LESSON 11

WHY TEACH THIS LESSON?

I love my church family! One of the things I find attractive about it is the sign we have in front of our building: "A Place for New Beginnings." That's not just a catchy motto but a belief that our leaders and members hold firmly. What comfort we have knowing that God delights in our returning to him. This lesson is as relevant today as it was in Josiah's time. No matter what failure, sin, or neglect are in your students' lives, God will welcome back every repentant soul.

Reform and repentance happen when people take God's Word seriously. Today's lesson shows us just that. It wasn't just luck that the high priest found the Book of the Law when God-fearing Josiah was on the throne of Israel. Forget luck; God intervened to assist Josiah in his reform efforts. God will also go to great lengths to help us with our efforts to please him yet today.

If we're not watching expectantly, acknowledging God's hand in the big and small events of our lives, we may miss the comfort of seeing his continual interaction with us. Coincidence, as some say, is God choosing to act anonymously.

INTRODUCTION

A. "Accidental" Discoveries

One day in 1947 a young Bedouin goatherd left his companions in order to find a stray goat. Eventually, he came upon a cave with a small opening at its top. Suspecting that the goat may have fallen inside, he threw some stones into the opening. Instead of hearing the sound of a startled goat, he heard the sound of broken pottery.

The goatherd lowered himself into the cave and found some ancient clay jars containing various leather scrolls. He had discovered what came to be called the Dead Sea Scrolls—one of the foremost archaeological discoveries of the twentieth century. These scrolls have since shed significant light on life during the time between the testaments and on the history (and reliability) of the Old Testament text. It is an oddity that often the most important archaeological finds in the field of biblical studies have occurred quite unexpectedly.

Today's Scripture text records another "accidental" discovery that was of enormous significance in the history of God's people. The priest Hilkiah was assisting with the renovation of the temple when he came across a book. It was not just any book; it was the Book of the Law, which was then read to King Josiah.

Josiah was so moved by the book's contents and by the nation's failure to comply with the laws written therein that he intensified his efforts to turn Judah back to the Lord. Sometimes in God's providence what appears to be a chance occurrence is actually a divine appointment.

B. Lesson Background

The incident covered in last week's lesson (the contest on Mount Carmel) took place around 850 or 860 B.C. Today's lesson moves us forward roughly 200

Devotional Reading:
Psalm 103:1-18
Background Scripture:
2 Kings 22, 23
Printed Text:
2 Kings 22:8-10; 23:1-3, 21-23

Lesson Aims

After participating in this lesson, each student will be able to:

1. List the causes and outcomes of Josiah's reform movement.

2. Predict the conditions that would have to be present for a similar reform movement to occur in the church today.

3. Choose one area in his or her personal life in which to make a "Josiah reform."

Key Verse

The king stood by the pillar and renewed the covenant in the presence of the Lord—to follow the Lord and keep his commands, regulations and decrees with all his heart and all his soul, thus confirming the words of the covenant written in this book. Then all the people pledged themselves to the covenant.

—2 Kings 23:3

Nov
12

years. By this time the northern kingdom of Israel (over which the wicked duo Ahab and Jezebel had ruled) already had fallen to the Assyrians; that happened in 722 BC. Judah likely would have suffered the same treatment from Assyria in 701 BC. had it not been for the reign of godly King Hezekiah. It was his cries to the Lord that resulted in a miraculous deliverance (2 Kings 19:35, 36).

The first half of the seventh century BC was a spiritual nightmare for Judah. Most of those years were part of the reign of Manasseh, the son of Hezekiah. He ruled from about 698 to 644 BC, and he was as wicked as his father was righteous. Judah and Jerusalem's eventual downfall is traced to the sinfulness of Manasseh (2 Kings 21:10-15; 24:1-4). There was, however, one last glimmer of hope for Judah—one Hezekiah-like king who sought to call the nation back to its spiritual roots. If he were successful, perhaps his country could avoid a tragedy such as that which befell the ten tribes of the northern kingdom. That king was Josiah, who reigned from 640 to 609 BC.

Today's lesson puts us into the eighteenth year of Josiah's reign. The lesson will focus on a period of revival in Judah that was given additional impetus by the discovery of the Book of the Law. We say *additional impetus* because it is clear that some spiritual renewal had occurred in Judah prior to this book's discovery (2 Chronicles 34:3-7).

I. DISCOVERING A BOOK (2 KINGS 22:8-10)

Second Kings 22 begins with the account of King Josiah's reign. Unlike the Chronicles account, the Kings account does not record the efforts of Josiah to promote righteousness in Judah prior to the discovery of the book of the law. It opens by mentioning Josiah's age at becoming king (eight!) and provides a general analysis of his reign: "He did what was right in the eyes of the Lord and walked in all the ways of his father David, not turning aside to the right or to the left" (2 Kings 22:2).

The account in Kings then notes how Josiah, in the eighteenth year of his reign, had initiated a program to renovate the temple in Jerusalem. (Most likely the temple had suffered from neglect during the reigns of Manasseh and his wicked son Amon, who was Josiah's father.) The high priest Hilkiah had been instructed by Josiah, through the king's secretary Shaphan, to make certain that the workers involved in the project were paid correctly. They were to be provided with the funds to purchase any materials necessary for the rebuilding.

· Apparently, after Shaphan had conveyed these instructions to Hilkiah, the high priest informed Shaphan of a surprising discovery.

A. HILKIAH INFORMS SHAPHAN (v. 8)

8. Hilkiah the high priest said to Shaphan the secretary, "I have found the Book of the Law in the temple of the LORD." He gave it to Shaphan, who read it.

As a *scribe*, Shaphan would be quite interested in the discovery we read about here. Just what constitutes *the Book of the Law* has been the subject of much discussion. Some believe it comprises all of Genesis through Deuteronomy (the Pentateuch). Others suggest that it was made up of a smaller portion of those five, specifically the book of Deuteronomy. The phrase *Book of the Law* is used in Deuteronomy 31:24-26 to refer to the contents of that particular book.

A third possibility is suggested by 2 Kings 23:2, which states that Josiah read in the people's hearing "all the words of the Book of the Covenant." The term *Book of the Covenant* is used in Exodus 24:7 to describe (most likely) the material included in Exodus 20–23.

Visual for Lesson 11. *Ask, "How does this picture illustrate how the Bible can be 'lost' today? What can we do to guard against this?"*

The contents of Deuteronomy certainly would be enough to generate the kind of intense response that Josiah later spearheaded. For example the references to the "Lord's anger" (2 Kings 22:13) and to promises to bring correction (vv. 16, 20) would fit with the list of curses pronounced in Deuteronomy 28:15-68 as a punishment for disobeying God's law.

Deuteronomy 31:26 says that a copy of the Book of the Law originally had been placed in the ark of the covenant. Deuteronomy 17:18 stipulates that a king, upon beginning his reign, should "write for himself on a scroll a copy of this law, taken from that of the priests, who are Levites." Perhaps it is a copy of this law produced under these circumstances that was ignored by kings such as Manasseh and Amon. Now, by the providence of God, it has been discovered. Its discovery comes during the reign of a king who will take its message seriously.

"LOSING" THE BIBLE

In 1985 a church building in Braham, Minnesota, burned to the ground. The church's brass bell, weighing 1,400 pounds, was sold to a scrap metal company as a result. Church members thought they had seen the last of the bell, and most of them forgot about it.

About 15 years later an employee at the scrap metal company discovered the bell hanging on the company's property. The employee saw the inscription on the bell and recognized it for what it was. Communications between the church and the scrap company were interrupted when both went through reorganizations.

Thus the bell was forgotten about again. Everyone assumed it had been melted down for scrap. In 2004 the bell was "re-rediscovered" and returned to the church, nearly 20 years after it had first been "lost."

Doesn't it seem strange that something as significant as a church bell could be overlooked for so long? And doesn't it strike us as unbelievable that a much more significant treasure—the Book of the Law—could get lost in ancient Judah? But here is something else that is amazing: churches and individuals who have abundant copies of the Bible, yet still disregard what it says when it comes to some of the moral issues of our time!

In effect, these churches and individuals have "lost" the Bible. How do you think such a thing can happen?
—C. R. B.

B. SHAPHAN INFORMS JOSIAH (vv. 9, 10)

9. Then Shaphan the secretary went to the king and reported to him: "Your officials have paid out the money that was in the temple of the LORD and have entrusted it to the workers and supervisors at the temple."

After reading the contents of the book (v. 8), *Shaphan* then returns to King Josiah and reports on his conversation with Hilkiah. Shaphan first mentions the matter that Josiah had instructed him to address concerning *the money that was in the temple.* This is to make sure that *the workers and supervisors* receive proper compensation for their labors.

10. Then Shaphan the secretary informed the king, "Hilkiah the priest has given me a book." And Shaphan read from it in the presence of the king.

Though not included in our printed text, it is important to observe King Josiah's reaction upon hearing the Lord's Word: "he tore his robes" (2 Kings 22:11). This is worth noting because Josiah's son, Jehoiakim, will exhibit a brazen contempt for the Lord's message that comes through Jeremiah by cutting it up, casting it into the fire, and refusing to tear his robes (Jeremiah 36:22-24).

WHAT DO YOU THINK?

In Western cultures there is no shortage of Bibles. Yet widespread biblical illiteracy means that the Bible often is effectively "lost." What would you suggest to address the problem?

WHAT DO YOU THINK?

What advantages are there to having a godly person in a position of political power? What are the disadvantages or potential pitfalls?

II. DEDICATING A PEOPLE (2 KINGS 23:1-3)

Following his anguished response to the law of the Lord, King Josiah tells some of his officials, including Hilkiah and Shaphan, to inquire of the Lord. Huldah the prophetess confirms the message of judgment found within the book. But she also promises that King Josiah will be spared from seeing all of this because of his desire to obey God and his law (2 Kings 22:14-20).

A. RALLYING THE PEOPLE (vv. 1, 2a)

1. Then the king called together all the elders of Judah and Jerusalem.

How easy it would be for King Josiah simply to allow the nation to continue on its downward path toward judgment, secure in the knowledge that at least he himself is going to escape the wrath of God! But Josiah is not one to rest on his laurels by focusing on himself. He determines, rather, that the entire nation needs to hear the same solemn message that he has heard.

So *the king* calls together *all the elders of Judah and Jerusalem.* Jerusalem is singled out because of its status as the capital city of Judah. The elders are probably local leaders of towns or villages. Josiah knows that the support of these men is crucial. The king by himself cannot generate any renewal of interest in God's law that will have a lasting impact.

2a. He went up to the temple of the LORD with the men of Judah, the people of Jerusalem, the priests and the prophets—all the people from the least to the greatest.

Various groups take part in this ceremony of rededication. The reference to *the men of Judah* may highlight the vital part that godly men must play in any effort to promote national spiritual renewal. The presence of *the priests and the prophets* at such a public ceremony testifies of their desire to obey God's law.

Later, however, the prophet Jeremiah (who lives during the reign of Josiah) will lament over how corrupt the priests and the prophets had become throughout Judah (Jeremiah 5:30, 31; 6:13; 23:11). When the leaders are unstable spiritually, there is little hope that the general populace will be any better.

At this point, however, *all the people from the least to the greatest* are in attendance. Distinctions based on social class or income are meaningless on an occasion such as this. Everyone needs to hear what the law of the Lord says!

B. READING THE BOOK (v. 2b)

2b. He read in their hearing all the words of the Book of the Covenant, which had been found in the temple of the LORD.

The Book that *had been found* earlier by Hilkiah now is being "found" by the general populace through Josiah's public reading of it. Since many people in the ancient world are illiterate, the public reading of documents is quite important for communicating vital information.

C. RENEWING THE COVENANT (v. 3)

3. The king stood by the pillar and renewed the covenant in the presence of the LORD—to follow the LORD and keep his commands, regulations and decrees with all his heart and all his soul, thus confirming the words of the covenant written in this book. Then all the people pledged themselves to the covenant.

The fact that the king stands *by a pillar* indicates a specific place to stand (compare 2 Kings 11:14; 2 Chronicles 23:13). The term *pillar* could refer to one of the two pillars that Solomon erected at the main entrance of the temple (1 Kings 7:15-22). Or, it may be a special pillar built for special occasions associ-

WHAT DO YOU THINK?

How should a leader go about gaining consensus for change in today's church? Or is it better just to proceed with a majority, since building a consensus is often time consuming or even impossible?

WHAT DO YOU THINK?

Josiah met with "all the people from the least to the greatest." What elements of society tend to be overlooked by churches? How can we make sure that we are communicating the gospel to everyone?

ated with royalty. Whatever the specific location is, from that place Josiah leads God's people in a special ceremony of dedication. It is there that Josiah renews *the covenant in the presence of the Lord.* Here is the kind of leadership that God's people so desperately need!

III. DECLARING A PASSOVER (2 KINGS 23:21-23)

The passage between verse 3 and verse 21 (not in today's text) gives an account of the various steps taken by Josiah in obedience to the law of the Lord. Pagan shrines of worship are destroyed. Pagan priests are removed from office. Josiah's efforts include the fulfillment of a prophecy given some 300 years earlier by an anonymous man of God from Judah (2 Kings 23:15-18). That man of God had even mentioned Josiah by name: "O altar, altar! This is what the Lord says: 'A son named Josiah will be born to the house of David. On you he will sacrifice the priests of the high places who now make offerings here, and human bones will be burned on you'" (1 Kings 13:2).

A. COMMAND (v. 21)
21. The king gave this order to all the people: "Celebrate the Passover to the LORD your God, as it is written in this Book of the Covenant."

Another important phase of Josiah's rededication of all the people involves the observance of *the Passover.* Instructions may be found in Exodus 12:1-20, 43-49 and Deuteronomy 16:1-8. The Exodus passage deals with how families are to observe this feast, while the Deuteronomy passage deals more with observing the Passover on a national level. The latter of these two circumstances fits the occasion described in the passage before us. This may support the view that the book discovered in the temple was Deuteronomy.

B. COMPARISON (vv. 22, 23)
22. Not since the days of the judges who led Israel, nor throughout the days of the kings of Israel and the kings of Judah, had any such Passover been observed.

These verses provide an assessment of the significance of this *Passover* observance under Josiah's leadership. Josiah's celebration surpasses any that has taken place since the days of the *judges* or during the time of the divided monarchy.

Why is this so? What is so special about the way Josiah observes the Passover? Second Chronicles 35:1-19 provides additional details about Josiah's celebration and includes an evaluation similar to that found in 2 Kings: "The Passover had not been observed like this in Israel since the days of the prophet Samuel; and none of the kings of Israel had ever celebrated such a Passover as did Josiah with the priests, the Levites and all Judah and Israel who were there with the people of Jerusalem" (v. 18). Josiah's compliance with the law's requirements is especially noted; for example, the Chronicles account records that all the Passover lambs are slaughtered exclusively by the Levites, as the law stipulates (2 Chronicles 35:3, 5, 6).

Josiah's devotion to the Law of Moses is also emphasized in 2 Kings 23:25. That passage provides this evaluation of one of Judah's most godly kings: "Neither before nor after Josiah was there a king like him who turned to the Lord as he did—with all his heart and with all his soul and with all his strength, in accordance with all the Law of Moses."

Such a one-of-a-kind tribute may appear to contradict what is said of Hezekiah, who receives similar praise in 2 Kings 18:3-5. Hezekiah, however, is specifically commended for his trust in the Lord, while Josiah's scrupulous

HOW TO SAY IT

Amon. AY-mun.
Bedouin. BED-uh-wun.
Hezekiah. Hez-ih-KYE-uh.
Hilkiah. Hill-KYE-uh.
Huldah. HUL-duh.
Josiah. Jo-SIGH-uh.
Manasseh. Muh-NASS-uh.
Pentateuch. PEN-ta-teuk.
Shaphan. SHAY-fan.

WHAT DO YOU THINK?

What circumstances would make a command to corporate worship effective? Why do we seldom hear these kinds of commands from political or spiritual leaders today?

PRAYER

Father, thank you for your holy Word and its truth. Like King Josiah, may we be so convicted by what it says that we will do all we can to apply its truth to our lives and share its message with others. This is the best way to treat your Word with the respect that it deserves. In Jesus' name, amen.

THOUGHT TO REMEMBER

Reform happens when God's Word transforms us.

observance of the law of Moses is stressed. Each king is exemplary in a different area of devotion to the Lord. Such kings are a primary reason why Judah lasts approximately 130 years longer than the northern kingdom, Israel.

A ONE-OF-A-KIND CELEBRATION

Lakshmi Mittal, an Indian magnate in the steel industry, is listed by *Forbes* magazine as one of the richest people in the world. As such, he was able to offer his daughter a one-of-a-kind celebration when he spent $60 million on her wedding just a couple of years ago.

The wedding took place in the environs of Paris and lasted for six days. There were 1,500 invited guests. One night a banquet and theatrical performance was held in the rented Tuileries (*twee*-luh-reez) Garden in Paris. Another venue for the celebration was a made-for-the-occasion castle that the proud father had erected in a Paris suburb. One dinner was held at the palace at Versailles (Ver-*sigh*) and another at the Vaux-le-Vicomte (Voh-luh-Vee-*kohnt*), considered by some to be one of the finest chateaus and gardens in all of France.

Mittal probably said to himself, "Now that's the way to celebrate a wedding!" Perhaps it is, if one has unlimited wealth. But most of us would shy away from such an ostentatious display (even if we could afford it!).

Josiah's elaborate celebration of the Passover was also a one-of-a-kind event. The difference was that its purpose was not to display one's wealth, but to help a whole nation recommit itself to God. The world has a twisted sense of what makes a celebration! How should those who belong to the family of God demonstrate that they have a different set of priorities?   —C. R. B.

23. But in the eighteenth year of King Josiah, this Passover was celebrated to the LORD in Jerusalem.

This verse notes the time that *this Passover* celebration occurs: it is *in the eighteenth year of King Josiah*. Mentioning the timeframe at this point serves to call attention to the urgency of Josiah's efforts at spiritual renewal in Judah since that was the same year that the book of the law was found (2 Kings 22:3, 8).

The discovery of the Book of the Law in that same eighteenth year, along with Josiah's wholehearted commitment to its contents, gives Judah a reprieve from the judgment of God. Sadly, it is only a reprieve, for Josiah is the last of Judah's godly kings.

CONCLUSION

Someone has wisely observed that the Bible has been given to us not merely for information but for transformation. The example of Josiah in today's lesson provides a powerful illustration of that principle.

Transformation involves allowing the words of the Bible to come across in the language and conduct of our daily lives. It is one thing to know what the Bible says about its people, places, and events. It is quite another to know what the Bible says to me about the people, places, and events that are a part of my life today.

A little boy heard an announcement concerning the upcoming revival services at his church. Later he told one of his friends in the neighborhood, "We're going to have a 're-Bible' at our church!"

Although it's clear that the young fellow hadn't heard the original statement quite correctly, his unintended revision wasn't bad! Let's take a close look at our lives and ask whether we need to be "re-Bibled." The need is urgent; the time is now.

Discovery Learning

This page contains an alternative lesson plan emphasizing learning activities. Classes desiring such student involvement will find these suggestions helpful. The next page is a reproducible activity page to further enhance discovery learning.

LEARNING GOALS

After this lesson, each student will be able to:

1. List the causes and outcomes of Josiah's reform movement.

2. Predict the conditions that would have to be present for a similar reform movement to occur in the church today.

3. Choose one area in his or her personal life in which to make a "Josiah reform."

INTO THE LESSON

Option #1: Write "New" on the board. Ask, "What are sights, sounds, smells, or symbols that remind you of newness?" (Some ideas include new car smell, butterflies, eggs, fresh paint.)

Option #2: Write "Old Car/New Car" on the board. Ask, "What are some of the steps needed to refurbish or restore an old car back to its original newness?" Interact with responses.

Make the transition to Bible study by saying that God tells us that newness, or restoration, can be brought to people's lives, churches, or even nations. This restoration, of course, happens through God's wonderful grace. The truest restoration of people or of churches is grounded in a renewed commitment to God's Word. We'll discover that principle as we read of an adventure in the life of God's chosen people.

INTO THE WORD

Provide the following resources to three study groups: to Group #1, a photocopy of the lesson background, Bible dictionary, a marker, and poster board; to Group #2, string, letter-sized paper (punch holes in two corners of the paper), and a photocopy of the lesson commentary; to Group #3, a marker, poster board, and a Bible dictionary. Distribute the instructions below to the groups. (If you have a large class, you may create extra groups to divide up activities for #1 and #3, but only one group should do #2.)

Group #1: Deliver a brief background of today's Scripture to the rest of the class. Study the lesson commentary and outline your remarks about the timing of the event, the impact of some of the kings, the spiritual condition of Judah, and a snapshot of Josiah's influence. A Bible dictionary is available, if needed.

Group #2: Prepare a dramatization of 2 Kings 22:8-11; 23:1-3, 21-23. String and paper is provided for name tags to hang around the character's necks. Feel free to insert dialogue that gives clues to why or how things may have happened. But be sure to tell the story clearly enough so the class understands what happened.

Group #3: Deliver a report about how Josiah worked to change Judah's worship focus. You will read a portion of Scripture that is not included in today's printed text, namely 2 Kings 23:4-19. Be sure to include a brief definition of Baal and Asherah. A Bible dictionary is available as a resource.

Allow groups to share discoveries. (Alternative: use the Revival exercise from the reproducible page to provide Into the Lesson and Into Life exercises combined.)

INTO LIFE

Transition to application by writing "Re-Bible" on the board. Tell the story included in the lesson commentary of the little boy saying to his friends they were going to have a "Re-Bible" (revival) at his church. Explain the irony of his statement. The Bible is at the core of spiritual revivals, including Josiah's. It is also the basis of personal spiritual renewal and of a church's renewal.

Ask the groups that worked together earlier to choose one of the following two tasks. (If short on time, you may choose simply to do choice #1 as an entire class.)

Choice #1: Develop a worship program for your church that emphasizes renewed commitment to the Lord and his Word. What special feature would you include? What songs? What would be the sermon theme or text? How would you issue a call to commitment?

Choice #2: Suppose you have a friend who has drifted away from the Lord. This friend still attends church occasionally but has not been growing spiritually. He or she seems to be focusing energies on work and family. Your task is to develop a plan to encourage this person to renew a commitment to the Lord. What are some steps you might take to help bring this about?

Conclude by reminding class members that spiritual renewal is important in each person. Ask each person to identify two or three steps to take to refresh his or her relationship with the Lord. (Option: use the Take Some Giant Steps exercise from the reproducible page for this segment of Into Life).

Revival

After reading today's printed text, list in the *Judah News* some of the elements, activities, and leadership decisions that contributed to Judah's revival. Then in the *Journal News* jot some of the elements, activities, or leadership decisions that would contribute to your own church's revival.

Take Some Giant Steps

To make a "Josiah reform" in my own life, I propose the following steps:

THE PEOPLE GO INTO EXILE

LESSON 12

WHY TEACH THIS LESSON?

"Oh, I can't drink these days. I'm allergic to alcohol and narcotics. If I use them I break out in handcuffs." The harsh reality behind that humor from actor Robert Downey, Jr. spells out the truth in today's lesson: often we fail to correct wrong behavior until circumstances force our hand. If we would only listen to God's message to us at the warning stage, we might avoid calamity.

This lesson will hit people differently. For those experiencing loss it is a reminder that God—then, now, and always—is in control and is working through the hard times as well as the good times to accomplish his will. For those in a period of calm, this account can encourage a time of soul searching.

Are you neglecting any warnings in your life? Is God speaking to you through his Word, through Christian friends, through your circumstances, or through nudges by his Holy Spirit? Give attention to his warning before sin's consequences make an unfriendly visit.

INTRODUCTION

A. ONE UNFORGETTABLE DAY

Some older Americans will remember where they were and what they were doing on December 7, 1941—the day Pearl Harbor was attacked. A more current example of an unforgettable day would certainly be September 11, 2001. Who can forget what he or she was doing or the emptiness that was felt upon hearing and seeing the Twin Towers in New York City being attacked?

Whatever you feel inside when such events occur, it may be similar to how the people of Jerusalem felt as they witnessed the Babylonians ravaging their holy city and setting Solomon's magnificent temple on fire. We should not miss what the religious implications of this action were at the time it took place. The Babylonians' destruction of the temple of the God of Judah implied that their pagan gods were mightier than Judah's God. After all, so the thinking went, if the Lord were stronger, wouldn't he have intervened to protect his sacred dwelling place?

Of course, that was not at all the case. Prophets such as Jeremiah repeatedly emphasized that the Babylonians were not conquering Jerusalem through their own might; the Lord was giving Jerusalem into their hands as punishment for the sins of his people (Jeremiah 27:5-7; 34:2). Even some Babylonians recognized this truth (see Jeremiah 40:2, 3).

The destruction of Jerusalem and the captivity of God's people did not signal the absence of the Lord; on the contrary, these events provided evidence of his control. The events validated his prophets as messengers who conveyed his truth.

B. LESSON BACKGROUND

Conditions in Judah deteriorated rapidly following the death of Josiah in about 609 BC, the last godly king in that country. Here is a summary of the reigns of Judah's last four kings:

DEVOTIONAL READING:
PROVERBS 1:20-33

BACKGROUND SCRIPTURE:
2 CHRONICLES 36:15-21;
PSALM 137

PRINTED TEXT:
2 CHRONICLES 36:15-21;
PSALM 137:1-6

LESSON AIMS

After participating in this lesson, each student will be able to:

1. Retell the events leading up to and following the destruction of Jerusalem.

2. Review how God continues to warn humanity of the consequences of sin.

3. Write a personal "psalm" confessing one specific area of spiritual need.

WHAT DO YOU THINK?

What is your most vivid personal memory of a national tragedy? How did this tragedy affect you spiritually, if at all?

Nov
19

KEY VERSE

By the rivers of Babylon we sat and wept when we remembered Zion. —Psalm 137:1

Jehoahaz, also called Shallum, was a son of Josiah. He reigned over Judah only three months. He was taken captive to Egypt, where he died (2 Kings 23:31-34; Jeremiah 22:11, 12).

Jehoiakim was put on the throne by the Egyptians after they had removed Jehoahaz from power. This was another son of Josiah. He ruled for 11 years (609–598 BC). He was a striking contrast to his father. Jehoiakim lived in personal extravagance (Jeremiah 22:13-15), pursued dishonest gain, and set his eyes and his heart "on shedding innocent blood and on oppression and extortion" (22:17). During Jehoiakim's reign, King Nebuchadnezzar came to power in Babylon as Egypt declined in influence. Jehoiakim switched his loyalty to Babylon in an attempt to keep up with the times, but rebelled after three years (2 Kings 24:1). The Scriptures do not indicate how Jehoiakim died; possibly he was assassinated.

Jehoiachin, Jehoiakim's son, ruled for only three months. He was taken captive to Babylon by Nebuchadnezzar in 597 BC. His later release from prison and elevation to a position of honor in Babylon is mentioned in 2 Kings 25:27-30 and Jeremiah 52:31-34.

Zedekiah, the last king of Judah, was another son of Josiah. Zedekiah reigned for 11 years until Jerusalem fell in 586 BC. Weak and unstable, he refused to heed the counsel of Jeremiah to surrender to the Babylonians (Jeremiah 27:12-15; 38:17, 18). When the Babylonians finally overtook Jerusalem, Zedekiah watched as they slaughtered his own sons. The Babylonians then put out his eyes and took him to Babylon (39:5-7), where he most likely was at the time of his death.

The two printed texts for today examine the fall of Jerusalem from two perspectives. The first, from 2 Chronicles, summarizes why this tragedy occurred. It also provides a somber description of the Babylonians' destruction of the city and the exile of its residents.

The second passage is taken from Psalm 137. Though the author of this psalm is not named, the contents clearly reflect the perspective of someone experiencing the anguish of living as a captive in a foreign land. However, the psalm also conveys the dogged determination not to forget the beloved city of Jerusalem. Jerusalem may have been out of sight, but it was certainly not out of mind.

I. PLEAS OF THE PROPHETS (2 CHRONICLES 36:15, 16)

The verses immediately preceding the section covered in our printed text recount what took place during the reign of Zedekiah, the last king of Judah. In particular, it is noted, "all the leaders of the priests and the people became more and more unfaithful, following all the detestable practices of the nations and defiling the temple of the Lord" (2 Chronicles 36:14).

A. GOD'S MERCY (v. 15)

15. The LORD, the God of their fathers, sent word to them through his messengers again and again, because he had pity on his people and on his dwelling place.

The Lord has responded by giving *his people* fair and frequent warning of the judgment they face if they continue in their sinful practices. God is described as repeatedly sending these faithful *messengers.* As noted earlier, these messengers include prophets such as Jeremiah. Others who serve at this time include Habakkuk and Zephaniah.

Notice that God's *pity* extends not only to his people, but also to *his dwelling place.* God had promised to put his name in Jerusalem after the temple had been completed (1Kings 9:3; 2 Kings 21:4). In addition the identity of the people is so

OLD TESTAMENT WORLD

Visual for Lesson 12. *Keep this map posted throughout the quarter to help set the geographical context.*

closely bound to the temple in Jerusalem that God knows that its destruction will be an especially devastating burden for them to bear. Yet, as 2 Chronicles 36:14 tells us, the people have defiled the temple through their pagan practices. The time has come when God's judgment can no longer be avoided.

B. PEOPLE'S MOCKING (v. 16)

16. But they mocked God's messengers, despised his words and scoffed at his prophets until the wrath of the LORD was aroused against his people and there was no remedy.

Here is how God's efforts to reach out in pity to his people have been received: *they mocked the messengers of God, despised his words, and scoffed at his prophets*. When the Son of God comes to save mankind from sin, a similar response is noted in John 1:11. See also Stephen's description in Acts 7:52.

What patience God has! Yet eventually such callous treatment of the Lord's messengers results in God's wrath. He is aroused against his people and there is *no remedy*. No remedy is available, not because God cannot supply one, but because the people's sinfulness has reached the stage where they are not willing to accept any remedy (compare Romans 1:24, 26, 28).

II. POWER OF BABYLON (2 CHRONICLES 36:17-21)

The Babylonians defeated the Egyptians at the Battle of Carchemish in 605 BC (see 2 Chronicles 35:20; Jeremiah 46:2). This epic battle changed the balance of power in the ancient world. After defeating the Egyptians, the Babylonians turn their attention to Judah.

A. LIVES LOST (v. 17)

17. He brought up against them the king of the Babylonians, who killed their young men with the sword in the sanctuary, and spared neither young man nor young woman, old man or aged. God handed all of them over to Nebuchadnezzar.

Both the beginning and the conclusion of this verse highlight a pivotal truth: it is the Lord who brings up *against* his people *the king of the Babylonians*, and God hands his people *over to Nebuchadnezzar*. A secular historian may explain the Babylonian triumph over Jerusalem as the exercise of sheer political and military supremacy. The Bible reveals the primary cause to be the Lord's deliverance of his people to be judged.

B. TREASURES TAKEN (v. 18)

18. He carried to Babylon all the articles from the temple of God, both large and small, and the treasures of the LORD's temple and the treasures of the king and his officials.

Suppose you pulled into the driveway of your home after work one day only to see someone dousing your home with gasoline and preparing to strike a match and set it on fire. What would you do? The answer is obvious: you would do all you could to stop him! As noted earlier, the mind-set of the time would ask why Israel's God does not come to the rescue of his *house*—his *temple* and its *treasures*. The answer has nothing to do with the weakness of the Lord. He allows these tragedies to occur in fulfilling his promises of judgment.

C. BUILDINGS BURNED (v. 19)

19. They set fire to God's temple and broke down the wall of Jerusalem; they burned all the palaces and destroyed everything of value there.

WHAT DO YOU THINK?

What sins do you think could bring God's judgment upon our country today? How would we be able to tell the difference between the judgment of God and what may be called "natural consequences"?

WHAT DO YOU THINK?

In what ways have you benefited from God's patience?

WHAT DO YOU THINK?

In reaction to a national tragedy, someone says, "I guess this is God's punishment." How do you respond?

[Make sure to consider Luke 13:1-5 in your response.]

The two main structures of many cities of the time are the *temple* (a spiritual landmark) and *the wall* (the primary source of defense). The Babylonians destroy both. *The palaces*—symbolic of status and wealth—suffer the same tragic end.

BURNING TREASURES

It was February 13, 1945, and it seemed as if the sky itself was on fire. By the end of the two-day bombing raid, 650,000 incendiary bombs had fallen on Dresden, Germany. Dresden's cultural treasure had been epitomized in the *Frauenkirche* (frau-in-kur-kuh), the "Church of Our Lady," built in 1743. It had been called one of the most remarkable buildings in the world. Now it was a burning treasure.

The morality of the Dresden attack is still debated. At best, the bombing of Dresden can be said to be an example of the consequences of warfare. The nation of Judah felt similar consequences when Babylon's forces sacked Jerusalem. Those forces burned its greatest treasure, the temple, and either destroyed or pillaged everything of value in the temple and in the city.

There is a similarity of cause in the burning of the treasures of these two cities: the cause, somewhere along the line, was sin. None of us can say whether a calamity such as the burning of Dresden was an act of God. But Scripture is clear why Jerusalem was destroyed. We should heed the warning.   —C. R. B.

D. REMNANT REMOVED (v. 20)

20. He carried into exile to Babylon the remnant, who escaped from the sword, and they became servants to him and his sons until the kingdom of Persia came to power.

"The doctrine of the remnant" is one of the most important in Old Testament prophecy. In spite of God's judgment, he does not completely destroy his people. Just as he speaks warnings through his prophets (see v. 15), so also he speaks hope and promise. In time a remnant will return (Isaiah 10:21; Jeremiah 23:3; Ezekiel 6:8; Micah 2:12). That remnant eventually will be the source from which the Messiah comes to offer deliverance to all peoples from the captivity of sin.

This verse reveals another important truth: the Babylonians' days on the center stage of world history will reach their limit—just as the Assyrians reached theirs before being overthrown by Babylon. Eventually, the Persians will take control of the Babylonian empire. Under the Persian ruler Cyrus the Great (next week's lesson), the remnant will be granted the opportunity to return to their homeland and start anew.

E. REST REMEMBERED (v. 21)

21. The land enjoyed its sabbath rests; all the time of its desolation it rested, until the seventy years were completed in fulfillment of the word of the LORD spoken by Jeremiah.

The law of Moses prescribed a *sabbath* year for the promised land—a time (every seventh year) during which *the land* was to be given a rest. It was not to be cultivated or harvested. The people were instead to eat what grew in the Sabbath year (Leviticus 25:1-7). Such a procedure gave the land the opportunity to be replenished for further use. This law also reminded the people of Israel that they were caretakers who cared for the land according to the giver's stipulations.

However, like many of the laws God gave to his people, this one had been ignored. In a sense the land cried out for God's judgment to be administered, for it had not been treated according to the giver's directives. The punishment for violating this law is found in Leviticus 26:34, 35, the language of which is very similar to the wording found here in 2 Chronicles.

III. PASSION OF GOD'S PEOPLE (PSALM 137:1-6)

This psalm captures the bitter sentiments of one who is enduring captivity in a foreign land.

A. BITTER MEMORIES (v. 1)

1. By the rivers of Babylon we sat and wept
  when we remembered Zion.

Memory can be a wonderful gift, but it can also be a source of unbearable heartache. Tragedy often causes one to look back and long for happier days. Emotions run high whenever the captives in pagan *Babylon* remember the sacred site of *Zion*. Zion gained significance because of David, who brought the ark of the covenant there (2 Samuel 6:12). Eventually the term *Zion* comes to mean the entire city of Jerusalem (2 Kings 19:21).

It should be noted that Jeremiah, known as the weeping prophet, had shed countless tears while warning God's people of the coming judgment (Jeremiah 13:17; 14:17). Now, because they had refused to heed the prophet's tears, they are the ones weeping.

B. BRUTAL MASTERS (vv. 2, 3)

2, 3. There on the poplars
  we hung our harps,
 for there our captors asked us for songs,
  our tormentors demanded songs of joy;
  they said, "Sing us one of the songs of Zion!"

The people's despair in their captivity is multiplied by the way their *captors* are making light of their sorrow. *Sing us one of the songs of Zion!* they say mockingly. But this is hardly a time for songs of joy, whether vocal or instrumental.

C. BETTER MEMORIES (vv. 4-6)

4. How can we sing the songs of the LORD
  while in a foreign land?

Some music is just not appropriate in certain settings. *Songs of the Lord* do not seem right when sung on *foreign* soil or sung simply to comply with the sarcastic requests of one's oppressors.

5, 6. If I forget you, O Jerusalem,
  may my right hand forget its skill.
 May my tongue cling to the roof of my mouth
  if I do not remember you,
 if I do not consider Jerusalem my highest joy.

In verse 1 the memory of Zion had brought tears to the captives. But that memory is also the source of hope to them. Here the writer expresses his fierce loyalty to Jerusalem in an oath, pronouncing a kind of curse on his *right hand* and on his *tongue* if he should forget Jerusalem. Having earlier mentioned the harps (v. 2) and the songs of Zion (v. 3), the writer says, in effect, "May I lose the ability to play the harp and sing if I allow the circumstances of captivity to affect my devotion to the beloved city of God—*Jerusalem!*"

LONGINGS, WORTHWHILE AND OTHERWISE

Between 1830 and 1850, the total mileage of railroad track in the United States went from 23 to 9,000. At the same time steamboats were providing a new form of transportation. In 1844 the first telegraph message was sent. It was about the year

WHAT DO YOU THINK?

When is it appropriate to hold on to and nurture a bitter memory, and when is it better to try to let go and move on with our lives? How could our decision be different if the memory is of a shared community event rather than of a more individual, personal tragedy?

1850 that former New York City mayor Philip Hone, age 69, bemoaned, "The world is going too fast!" He longed for the good ol' days when horse-drawn coaches sped along at the rate of six miles an hour (*Newsweek*, Nov. 29, 2004).

The nineteenth-century Industrial Revolution was just the beginning. The rate of change has been accelerating ever since. Some of us lament the increasing complexity of technology. The classic example is the inability of some of us to program our VCRs. We might as well give up: DVDs are now the state of the art. Yet even they will likely be outmoded soon by another technology.

"Even nostalgia ain't what it used to be!" That comic's quip says a lot about our longing for a more peaceful past, or a healthier past, or an [add your own longing here] past. We catch some of that spirit in Psalm 137. But it contains more than a longing for days past, lost in the "daze" of imperfect memory. There is a recognition that some values of the past are worth keeping. When we think wistfully about the past, is it to long for something important—something that is "of God"—or is it for something trivial?

—C. R. B.

CONCLUSION

A. THE ENEMY IS US!

From the comic strip "Pogo" by Walt Kelly comes an often-quoted line: "We have met the enemy and he is us." That statement could be applied to a variety of situations, including the history of God's people in the Old Testament.

From the beginning of its existence as God's holy nation, Israel was warned repeatedly of the need to remain faithful and obedient to the Lord. The people's worst enemy would not be any of the peoples cited in Deuteronomy 7:1—the various names ending in "ites," whom they were commanded to destroy. The "ites" who became their worst enemy were the Israelites themselves! Today's text from 2 Chronicles highlighted this tragic truth: God's people had no one to blame for their captivity but themselves.

To what extent is this principle applicable to the church? While it is true that our world has grown increasingly hostile to the Christian faith, is it not also true that at times Christians have brought some hostility upon themselves? Think of our arrogance toward others, our infighting, our general lack of love (John 13:35). These have caused many to treat the Christian faith as if it were a disease instead of the hope of the world.

B. LOOK IN THE MIRROR

The story is told of a minister who began serving a church in a small town. After he arrived, he spent a few days visiting the homes of the members and urging them to attend his first service that coming Sunday. But only a few people came.

After several Sundays like this, the minister placed a notice in the newspaper announcing that the congregation appeared to be dead, thus it was his duty to give it a decent burial. The funeral was to be held the following Sunday afternoon.

The next Sunday the building was filled nearly to capacity. (Many had come simply out of curiosity.) In front of the pulpit was an open casket. The minister read an obituary and delivered a eulogy. He then invited those present to step forward and pay their respects to the deceased.

Each mourner who filed by peered into the casket and then turned away with a sheepish look. In the casket, tilted at just the correct angle, was a mirror. Each person saw himself or herself as the reason for the death of the congregation.

Discovery Learning

This page contains an alternative lesson plan emphasizing learning activities. Classes desiring such student involvement will find these suggestions helpful. The next page is a reproducible activity page to further enhance discovery learning.

LEARNING GOALS

After this lesson, each student will be able to:

1. Retell the events leading up to and following the destruction of Jerusalem.

2. Review how God continues to warn humanity of the consequences of sin.

3. Write a personal "psalm" confessing one specific area of spiritual need.

INTO THE LESSON

Begin the lesson by reminding the class that losing someone or something precious to you is a very traumatic moment. Then ask class members to form small groups of four or five and share a time they lost someone or something dear to them. They may also share how God helped them get through this difficult time. Keep this portion of the lesson brief.

After this time of sharing, expand the discussion by saying, "Times of loss are traumatic to individuals and to nations." Ask about traumas that are specific to your country (examples: Pearl Harbor, December 7, 1941; terrorist attacks, September 11, 2001). Make a transition to Bible study by saying, "Our feelings about these events help us understand the emotional impact on God's people when they lost their beloved Jerusalem."

INTO THE WORD

Form five or more groups to do the following tasks and report conclusions to the class as a whole. Give each group written instructions, a marker, poster board, and the materials mentioned. Before the groups begin their work, read the printed text to the class and include a brief explanation of the background for this text. The notes in the Lesson Background will be helpful.

Group #1. Read the printed text and answer the following questions: Why did Jerusalem fall? Who were the major players in this drama, and what were their roles? Who ultimately was responsible for Jerusalem's destruction? You will find it helpful also to read 2 Chronicles 36:1-14 and Jeremiah 27:5-7; 32:28; 34:2.

Group #2. (Provide for this group a photocopy of the lesson commentary for 2 Chronicles 36:17 and a Bible dictionary.) Tell the class about the Babylonians. Use the Bible dictionary and lesson commentary to prepare your summary about this powerful nation.

Group #3. (Give this group a photocopy of the lesson commentary for 2 Chronicles 36:20 and a Bible dictionary that includes an article on "the remnant.") Do research and tell the class about the group known as "the remnant." What was the experience and significance of this group in Israel's history?

Group #4. (Give this group a Bible dictionary and a copy of the lesson commentary for 2 Chronicles 36:21. Mark the article or section of the article that talks about the land having a Sabbath rest.) Focus on the comments about the Sabbath in 2 Chronicles 36:21. Read about Sabbath rests in the Bible dictionary and lesson commentary. Describe this topic for the class and tell why you think this was specifically mentioned in today's text.

Group #5. (Give this group a copy of the lesson commentary on Psalm 137:1-6.) Read Psalm 137:1-6 and explain the significance of this passage that speaks of singing about Zion. If time permits, you can also explain a few of the colorful word pictures used in this psalm.

Allow time for group presentations. With five groups, you will need to keep things moving along briskly. (Alternative: use small groups for the Powerful Pictures in Words activity from the reproducible page.)

INTO LIFE

Activity #1: Keeping in the groups established earlier, have each group discuss and address the following: God's chosen people brought this sorrow and captivity upon themselves. Apply the lessons learned to today's church. What actions or inaction of today's believers have brought negative consequences to the church in general?

Activity #2: Give each person a piece of paper and ask students to write a personal psalm that expresses a need, sorrow, or regret. Encourage students to use the colorful language of Psalm 137:1-6 as a model. The psalm should include a need or regret in his or her personal life, the life of the church, or the nation (v. 1); a place to express the sorrow or need (vv. 1. 2); a creative expression of the need or sorrow (vv. 3, 4); a statement of commitment or determination (vv. 5, 6).

Allow each person to share his or her "psalm" with members of the group. (Alternative: use the Repentant Response activity from the reproducible page.)

Powerful Pictures in Words

Today's printed text contains powerful images painted by words. Read the printed texts. On the left side, list the word pictures that describe the atrocities and damages done to the Israelites and their properties. On the right side, list all of the colorful expressions of grief and sorrow felt by the Israelites.

Atrocities and Damages: 2 Chronicles 36:15-21 | Grief and Sorrow: Psalm 137:1-6

Repentant Response

Dear Lord, today's lesson helps me understand your expectations of faithfulness in my life. I have sometimes turned away from your way to follow my own will. Today, I confess my sin of _____ and promise I will try to be more faithful to you. I pray this in the name of my Savior, amen.   signed, _____

God's Living Covenant

GOD OFFERS RETURN AND RESTORATION

LESSON 13

WHY TEACH THIS LESSON?

Today's lesson spells it out clearly: God is the master planner behind world leaders, policies, and programs. The will of God will be accomplished. Temples will be rebuilt. Nations will rise and fall. His Word will be spread. Who can doubt his sovereignty? He designs the decisions of kings; he places desires and passions on people's hearts.

What if we choose to ignore what God puts on our hearts? No problem for him . . . he can accomplish his perfect goals in many ways. His plan will come about right on schedule. But if we are willing, he'll use us flawed servants in his grand restoration plan.

Many times we come to God with so many agenda items of our own that we forget to be still and hear what he is putting on our hearts. God is sovereign in the universe. If we will let him be sovereign in our lives, we can be a part of his master plan. All it takes to join him is a willing heart. That message from the year 538 BC is still valid today.

INTRODUCTION

A. THE GOD WHO REBUILDS

Most of us have watched a small child play with building blocks. He or she takes great delight in stacking a certain number, and then with one gleeful swipe scatters the blocks everywhere. Then the child gathers the blocks together and does it again—each time squealing with delight until boredom sets in. Then it becomes time to move on to some other form of entertainment.

Rebuilding scattered building blocks is one thing; rebuilding a place of worship is quite another matter. Solomon's temple had been constructed with great care and much effort. First Kings 6:38 records that this magnificent structure took seven years to build. Yet once the Babylonian army had entered Jerusalem (following a siege of about 18 months), it required far less time to demolish what had been so carefully erected and so prayerfully dedicated (1 Kings 8:22-61). Tearing down always takes much less time than building.

But God had other plans for the temple; destruction would not be the final word. The same prophets who spoke so passionately of God's coming judgment on his people and his temple were just as passionate about the promise that a remnant would return and rebuild.

On one occasion, Jesus used the language of destroying and rebuilding to describe what would eventually happen to him: "Destroy this temple, and I will raise it again in three days" (John 2:19). The text later notes, "But the temple he had spoken of was his body" (v. 21). The same language can be applied to what God can do with our broken, sin-ravaged lives. What we have ruined he can

DEVOTIONAL READING:
JEREMIAH 29:10-14

BACKGROUND SCRIPTURE:
2 CHRONICLES 36:22, 23;
EZRA 1:5-7

PRINTED TEXT:
2 CHRONICLES 36:22, 23;
EZRA 1:5-7

LESSON AIMS

After participating in this lesson, each student will be able to:

1. List the divine and human factors in the return of God's people from captivity.

2. Explain why the terms *return* and *restoration* are appropriate to describe people's response to the gospel message today.

3. Prepare a testimony of how God has restored his or her life through Jesus, and share that testimony with an unsaved person.

KEY VERSE

This is what Cyrus king of Persia says: "The LORD, the God of heaven, has given me all the kingdoms of the earth and he has appointed me to build a temple for him at Jerusalem in Judah. Anyone of his people among you—may the LORD his God be with him, and let him go up."
—*2 Chronicles 36:23*

NOV
26

LESSON 13 NOTES

rebuild, restore, and renew. Paul writes of our bodies as a temple in which God's Spirit dwells (1 Corinthians 3:16; 6:19). We are not our own; we are under new management.

Whether the damage has been done to sacred structures or to sin-marred souls, God is in the business of rebuilding and restoring.

B. THE CHRONICLES FACTOR

At first glance the books of 1 and 2 Chronicles may seem to be unnecessary additions to the Old Testament. After all, don't they cover the same period of history covered by much of 1 and 2 Samuel and 1 and 2 Kings? And why the extensive genealogies that take up the first nine chapters of 1 Chronicles? (Those aren't exactly the most thrilling portions of the Bible to read!)

Most students of the Bible believe that the books of Chronicles were written after the Babylonian captivity and after God's people had returned home to rebuild their temple in Jerusalem. (Their return is the topic of today's lesson.) It is worth noting that the final two verses of 2 Chronicles and the first three verses of the book of Ezra are virtually the same. Because of this, some have proposed that Ezra may have been the author of the books of Chronicles as well as the book that bears his name. Certainly Ezra was well qualified for such a task (see Ezra 7:6, 10).

Why would Ezra (assuming him to be the author) compose such a record as that found in the books of Chronicles? Consider the following hypothetical situation: A congregation experiences an especially trying set of circumstances, such as a fire that destroys its sanctuary, a split of some kind, or a crisis within the leadership. The result would likely be a keen sense of loss of purpose and direction within the congregation. Questions would surface, such as, "Where do we go from here?" and "What is God's will for us now?" How would a church in such a situation get the people back on track and restore a sense of direction and purpose?

One answer might be to call attention to the history of the congregation and review God's faithfulness over the years in preserving the people through other difficult times. By considering such examples from the congregation's history, the people may be encouraged to continue to "fight the good fight." They would do what was necessary to see themselves through the current series of events.

A similar scenario confronted God's people following the crisis of the Babylonian captivity and the return to their homeland. They too must have wondered, "Where do we go from here? Does God still have a purpose for us?" For God's covenant people, there were other burning issues as well: "Is God's covenant still intact? Are the promises made to Abraham and David still binding?"

The material found in 1 and 2 Chronicles seems especially intended (through the guidance of the Holy Spirit) to address these and other crucial issues in the minds of those who were part of the rebuilding effort in Judah. The genealogies in 1 Chronicles 1–9 would not have been dull or boring to the original readers; they would have given the postexilic generation a sense of identity with their past. They would have been encouraged by realizing that the link with the individuals and tribes mentioned in these chapters had not been severed by the captivity and exile.

There is a special emphasis in 1 and 2 Chronicles on the reigns of David and Solomon and all their achievements. This let the postexilic community know that this was still a part of their history and their identity. God was not finished with them yet!

DAILY BIBLE READINGS

Monday, Nov. 20—Prayer for Deliverance (Psalm 57)

Tuesday, Nov. 21—God Promises to Lead and Heal (Isaiah 57:14-19)

Wednesday, Nov. 22—God Forgives (Psalm 130)

Thursday, Nov. 23—God's Plan Revealed (Jeremiah 29: 10-14)

Friday, Nov. 24—King Cyrus Plans to Rebuild (2 Chronicles 36:22, 23)

Saturday, Nov. 25—The Exiles Return (Ezra 1)

Sunday, Nov. 26—Rebuilding the Temple (Ezra 5:6-14)

C. Lesson Background

The conclusion of 2 Chronicles, from which our text for today is taken, is a key part of the previously mentioned encouragement to the postexilic community. As we learned from last week's text, God's people had repeatedly spurned the appeals of his prophets to turn from their sins. Eventually, his judgment fell. God used the Babylonians to destroy the temple—believed by some in Jerusalem and Judah to be indestructible. That belief was based on a theory that God would never allow his people to be overtaken by pagans (compare Jeremiah 7:4).

I. DECREE ORDAINED (2 CHRONICLES 36:22, 23)

Did the destruction of the temple mean that God had turned his back completely on his chosen people? The end of 2 Chronicles provides the answer, and it is a resounding *no!* That the temple will be rebuilt indicates that God still has a purpose for his people.

A. God's Working (v. 22)

22. In the first year of Cyrus king of Persia, in order to fulfill the word of the LORD spoken by Jeremiah, the LORD moved the heart of Cyrus king of Persia to make a proclamation throughout his realm and to put it in writing:

Cyrus king of Persia is the human instrument whom God uses to keep his promise to bring his people home. Second Chronicles 36:20 records that Nebuchadnezzar exiled the remnant of God's people to Babylon where "they became servants to him and his sons until the kingdom of Persia came to power." Persia came to power in 539 BC through the series of events described in Daniel 5.

King Cyrus possesses a discernment and fair-mindedness that many rulers in the ancient world lack. He understands that it will enhance his reputation and get his reign started on a positive note if he provides some measure of relief from the cruel tactics of the Babylonians.

Thus Cyrus demonstrates an attitude of diplomacy and tolerance in his dealings with conquered peoples. He gives these peoples a wide latitude in allowing them to practice their religions. Thus it should be noted that what the Scriptures describe Cyrus as doing for the Jews, he does also for other peoples: permitting them to return to their respective homelands. There they may reestablish themselves and be free to practice their religious beliefs.

Secular historians may view Cyrus's actions as simply the exercise of capable and discerning leadership. The Scripture, however, is clear in emphasizing that the Lord uses this policy of Cyrus to accomplish his own purpose. This is all part of his plan as announced by *the word of the Lord spoken by Jeremiah*. That Word, mentioned in the previous verse (v. 21, not in today's text), describes the captivity as lasting 70 years (also Jeremiah 29:10). Cyrus is not acting alone; the Lord, the heavenly king, has moved the heart of the earthly king to implement a program of restoration for the Lord's people.

It is noteworthy that another prophet gave Spirit-inspired insight into the Lord's master plan some 100 years before Jeremiah uttered his prophecy. Isaiah prophesied not only before Persia became a dominant force, but also he prophesied even before Babylon gained such a stature! Yet Isaiah gave a message from the Lord that specifically named Cyrus (Isaiah 44:28; 45:1). Thus, some 160 years before Cyrus conquered Babylon and issued his decree, Isaiah's prophetic perspective named that ruler as the man whom God would use to fulfill his own plan.

What Do You Think?

What are some things that can be rebuilt only by the power of God? How are humans sometimes arrogant in thinking that such power belongs to them?

[Daniel 4:28-33 and Acts 12:21-23 can enrich your answer.]

How to Say It

Babylonians. Bab-ih-LOW-nee-unz.

Bethlehem. BETH-lih-hem.

Caesar Augustus. SEE-zer Aw-GUS-tus.

Cyrus. SIGH-russ.

Ezra. EZ-ruh.

Jerusalem. Juh-ROO-suh-lem.

Judah. JOO-duh.

Levites. LEE-vites.

Marduk. MAR-duke.

Nebuchadnezzar. NEB-yuh-kud-NEZ-er.

Persia. PER-zhuh.

B. CYRUS'S WORDS (v. 23)

23. *"This is what Cyrus king of Persia says:*

"'The Lord, the God of heaven, has given me all the kingdoms of the earth and he has appointed me to build a temple for him at Jerusalem in Judah. Anyone of his people among you—may the Lord his God be with him, and let him go up.'"

As noted previously, Cyrus allows other captive peoples to return to their homelands—not just the Jews. Thus the acknowledgment of *the Lord* as the *God of heaven,* etc., should not be considered as a sign of any kind of conversion to the God of Israel on Cyrus's part. That ruler uses equally grand language of other deities. For example, on the famous Cyrus Cylinder, unearthed by archaeologists, are inscribed these words: "Marduk, king of the gods [the leading deity of the Babylonian gods] . . . designated me to rule over all the lands."

Nevertheless, it is clear that Cyrus is indeed God's instrument to carry out his purpose. This is also true of Caesar Augustus, a later ruler whom God will use to issue a decree that results in Joseph and Mary's journey to Bethlehem. There Jesus will be born in fulfillment of prophecy (Micah 5:2; Matthew 2:6).

Following the claim to be authorized by the Lord, Cyrus's decree grants permission to any of the Lord's people to *go up* to *Jerusalem.* There they can participate in the rebuilding effort. The Hebrew word translated as *go up* occurs elsewhere in the Old Testament in the context of another significant movement of God's people: the exodus from bondage in Egypt (see Exodus 3:8, 17; 33:1).

To *go up* thus has a special meaning for God's people and gives them a sense of kinship with the exodus event that established them as a "holy nation" (Exodus 19:5, 6). In a sense they can consider themselves reborn as a nation, for they are coming out of bondage in Babylon much as they had come out of Egypt under Moses. The promise of God's presence (*the Lord his God be with him*) was also a key source of encouragement during the exodus and subsequent events (Exodus 3:11, 12; 33:14-17; Numbers 14:9).

II. DECREE OBEYED (EZRA 1:5-7)

The remainder of our printed text describes the compliance of God's people with the decree of Cyrus.

A. GOD'S ACTION (v. 5)

5. *Then the family heads of Judah and Benjamin, and the priests and Levites—everyone whose heart God had moved—prepared to go up and build the house of the LORD in Jerusalem.*

This verse lists those who prepare to go up and *build the house of the Lord in Jerusalem* (just as the decree had stated). *The family heads* are probably the leaders of the various tribal clans, or extended families, within the tribes of *Judah and Benjamin.* These two tribes provide the primary makeup of the southern kingdom of Judah, which the Babylonians had conquered and taken captive.

Included in those who return are the *priests* and *Levites.* Their spiritual leadership will be necessary in guiding and mentoring those who choose to return. Sadly, some of these priests and Levites eventually commit sin by marrying women from outside the covenant people. This causes great distress to Ezra and others among those who return (Ezra 9:1-4).

In this verse it is also important to note the guidance of the Lord's hand. Those who choose to return include everyone *whose heart God had moved.* The same God who has "moved the heart" of a pagan king (Ezra 1:1) now moves

WHAT DO YOU THINK?

Cyrus said that God had given him a mission to rebuild the temple, but other decrees from Cyrus gave equal credence to other deities. Is this an early form of "political correctness"? Why, or why not?

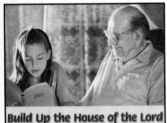

Build Up the House of the Lord

Visual for Lesson 13. *Point to this picture and ask, "How does this illustrate one way we build the Lord's house today? What are some other ways?"*

among his people to stir them to action. This also means that the same God who had brought the king of Babylon *against* his people (2 Chronicles 36:17) is now working *for* his people. He is fulfilling his promise to bring them home.

B. NEIGHBORS' ASSISTANCE (v. 6)

6. All their neighbors assisted them with articles of silver and gold, with goods and livestock, and with valuable gifts, in addition to all the freewill offerings.

Here one sees another parallel to the events surrounding the exodus of some 900 years before. Exodus 11:2 records these instructions given by the Lord to Moses: "Tell the people that men and women alike are to ask their neighbors for *articles* of silver and gold." And now, as a kind of "second exodus" unfolds for God's people, all their neighbors assist them with numerous contributions and offerings. The *livestock* that are provided most likely include animals that can be used for the various sacrifices required by the law of Moses.

SKIPPING CHRISTMAS

Crossroads Christian Church in Lexington, Kentucky, recently took a different approach to Christmas: they encouraged skipping it (the bad parts, that is). What triggered the new thinking was that the church staff was hearing people say such things as "I wish we didn't spend so much on gifts" or "I feel like I have to buy gifts for some people even though I don't want to." So they took a page from John Grisham's recent book, *Skipping Christmas*. (The book was made into the 2004 movie *Christmas with the Kranks*.)

Crossroads's response to the laments was *not* to tell people that they shouldn't give gifts or put up Christmas trees. Instead, the church leadership decided that what it really needed to do was to help people change their focus. The fivefold emphasis was skip excess, find simplicity; skip obligations, find joy; skip rush, find rest; skip loneliness, find belonging; skip Christmas, find Christ. The foundational idea was to bring back the joy that should be in a season that celebrates giving (www.skipchristmas.net).

When the leaders of Judah and Benjamin began the task of rebuilding the temple, all whose hearts were moved by God's gift of freedom caught the spirit of the occasion and freely gave to the cause. They had found the true focus of giving: gratitude for what God had done. We detect no sense of "Aw, do I have to?"

Christmas is right around the corner. How many of us have that same mind-set?

—C. R. B.

C. CYRUS'S ASSISTANCE (v. 7)

7. Moreover, King Cyrus brought out the articles belonging to the temple of the LORD, which Nebuchadnezzar had carried away from Jerusalem and had placed in the temple of his god.

Furthermore, *Cyrus* brings out the *articles* that rightfully belong to the *temple of the Lord*. This shows his personal support for the return home. Second Chronicles 36:18, part of last week's printed text, describes how Nebuchadnezzar carried these items to Babylon. That king's successor had used some of those articles in a most unholy way (Daniel 5:1-4).

Now these actions are reversed, as the temple articles are removed from Babylon and taken to their original, rightful home in *Jerusalem*. This will give the returning captives some sense of continuity with the past when they are in a position to place the items in the new temple.

The removal of articles from a conquered people's place of worship is a significant religious statement in the ancient world. It is interpreted as a sign of the

WHAT DO YOU THINK?

Material support for this "second exodus" came from the gifts of fellow Jews. Support for the original exodus came from non-Jews (Exodus 12:36). When should a church rely on support from the world to accomplish a ministry, if ever?

[Make sure to consider 3 John 7 in your answer.]

WHAT DO YOU THINK?

In what ways can a non-Christian ruler become an agent for God?

superiority of the conqueror's gods. In this case the Lord God of Israel, who had allowed the Babylonians to remove the articles from his temple, now allows the Persians to send them back!

REBOOTING

One of the most famous lines in English literature was uttered in *Macbeth*, which is one of Shakespeare's darker works. Evil piles upon evil throughout the play. At one point Lady Macbeth pushes her husband to kill King Duncan of Scotland so that Macbeth might be king. With Duncan dead Lady Macbeth goes back to the scene of the assassination and smears blood on guards (who had been drugged). This implicates them in the crime.

But then her conscience begins to work. She starts sleepwalking, rubbing her hands as if trying to wash away the blood that remains. In this state she admits her part in the murder and utters the famous words, "Out, [foul] spot! out, I say!" Guilt over the murder is driving her insane as her fevered mind tells her that there is no atoning for the evil she has done. In computer terminology her mind is desperately trying to "reboot," to no avail.

Many atrocities had been committed against the people of Judah by the Babylonians. Now, many decades later, Cyrus performs an act of atonement for what his predecessor had done. Does he feel a sense of shared guilt? We don't know. For whatever reason seems best to him personally, Cyrus is trying to "reboot" the situation as he gives back the sacred vessels that had been looted.

Perhaps we may be tempted to say "Not my fault" or "Not my problem" when confronted with the need to clean up someone else's mess. When that happens, stop to consider if God needs to "reboot" your thinking!   —C. R. B.

CONCLUSION

A few years ago, a certain brand of spaghetti sauce advertised its product by making the claim, "Homemade taste—it's in there!" The same can be said of the idea of *grace* in the Old Testament. Most Christians associate that concept with the New Testament. And while the doctrine of grace is most clearly expressed through the coming of Jesus, grace is not absent from the Old Testament. It is most definitely "in there." A powerful example comes from today's lesson.

As noted earlier, the books of 1 and 2 Chronicles were most likely written to encourage the returning exiles that God still had a purpose for them and that the captivity did not spell "the end." Both the conclusion of 2 Chronicles and the beginning of Ezra highlight the fact that God took the initiative in fulfilling his promise. He did that by moving the heart of Cyrus and then moving his people to take the necessary steps to return to Judah and rebuild. If ever there were doubts in the minds of those who returned from captivity concerning God's intentions, they needed only to look back and remember God's grace in using the right man at the right time to achieve his holy purpose.

Christians have a similar perspective, based on what Jesus Christ has done for us through his death and resurrection. Sometimes circumstances we encounter may cause us to doubt the validity of our faith. In those situations we can remind ourselves, as Paul did the Roman Christians, that nothing "will be able to separate us from the love of God that is in Christ Jesus our Lord." (Romans 8:39).

That love—and that grace—were also revealed during the Old Testament era. It was revealed from the time of Adam and Eve receiving the promise of what the woman's seed would accomplish (Genesis 3:15). Is grace found within the pages of the Old Testament? Make no mistake—it's in there!

Discovery Learning

This page contains an alternative lesson plan emphasizing learning activities. Classes desiring such student involvement will find these suggestions helpful. The next page is a reproducible activity page to further enhance discovery learning.

LEARNING GOALS

After participating in this lesson, each student will be able to:

1. List the divine and human factors in the return of God's people from captivity.

2. Explain why the terms *return* and *restoration* are appropriate to describe people's response to the gospel message today.

3. Prepare a testimony of how God has restored his or her life through Jesus, and share that testimony with an unsaved person.

INTO THE LESSON

Have the following question displayed before students arrive: "Can God use non-Christian or ungodly people to accomplish his purpose? Give examples." Have small groups of three to five discuss the question. Then ask groups to share their conclusions and illustrations with the whole class.

Next, make the transition to Bible study by saying, "Yes, God can use ungodly people to accomplish his purpose. We'll find another example of God's sovereignty in this regard in today's lesson from Israel's history." (Option: place a copy of the Now I Know My ABCs activity from the reproducible page in each chair for students to work on as they arrive.)

INTO THE WORD

Begin with a brief lecture titled "The Chronicles Factor," using the Lesson Background. Have on display a picture of Solomon's temple while you speak.

Next, use three or more groups of four to five people each to do the following tasks.

Group #1: Decree Ordained: God's Working—2 Chronicles 36:22. Read today's printed text and focus on your assigned verse. Prepare and deliver to the class a brief lecture with outline. A possible outline is

    I. Babylon and Persia

    II. Cyrus's Attitude

    III. The Lord's Will

    IV. Isaiah's Prophecy

Group #2: Decree Ordained: Cyrus's Words—2 Chronicles 36:23. Read today's printed text and focus on your assigned verse. Prepare and deliver to the class a brief lecture with outline. A possible outline is

    I. Cyrus: Instrument of God

    II. "Go Up"

Group #3: Decree Obeyed—Ezra 1:5-7. Read today's printed text and focus on your assigned verses. Prepare and deliver to the class a brief lecture with outline. A possible outline is

    I. Those Who Went

    II. Neighbors Who Helped

    III. Cyrus, Who Helped

In addition to the written assignments above, give each group a poster board with the group headings (but not the possible outlines) already written, a marker, and a photocopy of the lesson commentary on the verses assigned. Explain that their combined efforts will provide a comprehensive outline and study of today's text.

Each group will select two people to make the presentation to the class. One will deliver a brief lecture on the assigned passage and another person will write the outline for all to see as the report is being delivered.

INTO LIFE

After group reports, offer the following for discussion: (1) The doctrine of God's grace is often thought of as a New Testament doctrine. However, God's grace is often demonstrated in the Old Testament too. How do you see God's grace powerfully at work in this piece of history? (You may need also to ask for a definition of *grace*.) (2) The terms *return* and *restoration* are key concepts in this Old Testament picture of God's grace. How are those terms appropriate for describing people's response to the gospel message today? (The Grace and Restoration notepad from the reproducible page is useful here.)

After discussion, say, "We can personalize the concepts of return and restoration in our own testimonies." Give each student an index card and ask him or her to write "My Journey" at the top. Ask each student to jot notes about his or her life's spiritual journey, including them in a personal testimony.

Testimonies should include the concepts of return and restoration. Students who have accepted Jesus as Savior should include that in the testimony. Those who haven't can still make notes about their heart's movement toward or away from him. Ask two volunteers to share their testimonies. Then ask the class as a whole, "How will you share your testimony this week?"

Now I Know My ABCs . . .

Use the ABCs to unfold today's wonderful demonstration of God's grace, human faith, and even a surprise in today's printed text.

A   The Lord A _ _ _ _ _ _ _ _ _ Cyrus (v. 23)

B   B _ _ _ _ a temple (v. 23)

C   The king of Persia was C _ _ _ _ (v. 22)

D   The word of the _ _ _ D (v. 22)

E   The _ E _ _ _ of Cyrus (v. 22)

F   The F _ _ _ _ year of Cyrus (v. 22)

G   The G _ _ of Heaven (v. 23)

H   Let H _ _ go up (v. 23)

I   Cyrus, king of _ _ _ _ _ I _ (v. 22)

J   The word of the Lord was spoken by J _ _ _ _ _ _ _ _ (v. 22)

K   The K _ _ _ _ _ _ _ of the earth (v. 23)

L   The L _ _ _ _ _ _ prepared to build the temple (v. 5)

M   God had M _ _ _ _ hearts (v. 5)

N   All their N _ _ _ _ _ _ _ _ _ assisted them (v. 6)

O   _ O up and build (v. 5)

P   The P _ _ _ _ _ _ prepared to build (v. 5)

Q   A Free Space!

R   Everyone _ R _ _ _ _ _ _ to go up and build (v. 5)

S   S _ _ _ _ _ and gold (v. 6)

T   Goods and _ _ _ _ _ T _ _ _ (v. 6)

U   The _ _ U _ _ of the Lord (v. 5)

V   V _ _ _ _ _ _ _ gifts (v. 6)

W   _ _ _ _ W _ _ _ offerings (v. 6)

X   A Free Space!

Y   Articles had been carried _ _ _ Y from Jerusalem (v. 7)

Z   He looted the temple: _ _ _ _ _ _ _ _ _ _ Z _ _ _ (v. 7)

Grace and Restoration

God's grace showed in the return of his people and the restoration of the temple. Why or how are the terms *return* and *restoration* appropriate to describe people who respond to the gospel message today?

_____

_____

_____

_____

Winter Quarter 2006–2007

Jesus Christ:
A Portrait of God

Special Features

Lessons

Unit 1: Christ, the Image of God

Unit 2: Christ Sustains and Supports

Unit 3: Christ Guides and Protects

About These Lessons

When a fashion from the past comes back into style, we call it a *retro look*. We may also use the term *throwback*. Jesus lived 2,000 years ago, but those terms do not apply to Him. The simple fact is that His message never goes out of style. The texts about Jesus this quarter are ever new!

Dec
3

Dec
10

Dec
17

Dec
24

Dec
31

Jan
7

Jan
14

Jan
21

Jan
28

Feb
4

Feb
11

Feb
18

Feb
25

Jesus This Christmas

by Tom Thatcher

One of my favorite things about Christmastime as a child was the holiday TV specials. I can hardly think of Christmas without recalling the Grinch, Rudolph and Yukon Cornelius, and Frosty the Snowman. My favorite holiday program yet today is Charles Schulz's *A Charlie Brown Christmas.*

As is so often the case, Charlie Brown has the blues. This time it's because he "just doesn't know what Christmas is all about." Lucy tells him it's about getting presents; his sister, Sally, says it's about Santa Claus; Snoopy thinks it's about winning the neighborhood lights and display contest. Even the Christmas pageant turns into a dance-a-thon, with all the kids complaining about their parts.

One proposal is that Christmas must have something to do with a Christmas tree, a big artificial tree. But all this celebration only leaves Charlie Brown more miserable. Eventually he cries out in despair, "Isn't there anyone who knows what Christmas is all about?"

When we look around and see what Christmas means in our culture, we're often forced to ask the same question. Even in Japan, a country where there never have been many Christians, Christmas is celebrated with decorations and parties and presents as a commercial holiday. In many ways it's hard to see how things are any different where we live. Did Jesus come so that we could celebrate his birthday with expensive cards and presents and parties? And, honestly, do we really need Jesus to have Christmas, or would it be just as much fun without him?

At the end of the show, Linus steps into the spotlight with an answer. In a bold move that barely got by the censors when the program was first aired in 1965, Schulz insisted that his TV special end with a summary of the true meaning of Christmas. "And there were in the same country shepherds abiding in the field," Linus begins. Then, after quoting the rest of Luke 2:8-14 (*King James Version*), he says, "That's what Christmas is all about, Charlie Brown. 'For unto you is born this day in the city of David a Saviour, which is Christ the Lord'" (v. 11). What better summary could there be of the meaning of Christmas and, indeed, of the meaning of Jesus?

This quarter's lessons explore the identity of this remarkable person whose birth we celebrate every December 25. Who was Jesus? What was his mission? What did he say about himself? What blessings come to those who accept him?

DECEMBER

UNIT 1: CHRIST, THE IMAGE OF GOD

Lesson 1 focuses on Colossians 1 to establish Jesus' complete equality with God the Father. We will see Paul stress that Christ is the perfect image of God, and that he shares all of God's power and authority. Jesus was not just a great rabbi while he walked the earth; he is, in fact, the one who created the universe and who now sustains everything we see by his unmatched power.

Lesson 2, from Hebrews, explores Jesus' role as the ultimate revelation of God on earth. In Old Testament times God revealed himself through the words of prophets. Sometimes he even sent messages through angels, special agents of God who move between Heaven and earth. In Christ, however, God revealed himself to the world in a unique way.

Lesson 3 focuses on a popular text from 1 John that tells us several things about Jesus Christ. Although Jesus is fully God, he was also fully human during his time on earth. People saw him, heard him, and touched him. As a man he died on a cross; as God he rose and returned to Heaven. Knowing that he did all this for us should lead us to confess our sinfulness and attempt to walk as he walked.

Lesson 4, our Christmas Eve lesson, will examine the prologue to the Gospel of John (1:1-18). John's Gospel does not include a Christmas story but instead opens by showing the role that Christ has filled from the beginning of time. Drawing on Old Testament imagery, John reminds us that Jesus was involved in the creation of the world.

Lesson 5, our New Year's Eve lesson, allows us to explore the mind and attitude of Christ through Paul's great letter to the Philippians. What better way to bring the year 2006 to a grand close than to learn to think as Jesus thought!

UNIT 2: CHRIST SUSTAINS AND SUPPORTS

JANUARY

Lesson 6 discusses Jesus' claim, in the Gospel of John, to be the ultimate revelation of God's truth. Often we know in our hearts that we should behave a certain way, yet we constantly fall prey to temptations and the influences of the world around us. Jesus' teaching helps us here. His words are true, and in them we find clarity and freedom from sin.

Lesson 7 touches on a familiar theme from the Gospel of John: Jesus' spiritual authority. While on earth, he didn't just make up new doctrines and force them on people. Instead, as God's Son, he spoke directly on God's behalf. For this reason we can be sure that his words will either save us or condemn us on Judgment Day.

Lesson 8 examines two of the best known images of Christ from the Gospel of John: "Bread of Life" and "Living Water." Just as our bodies require food and water to live, our spirits require nourishment from Christ. Even though none of us has had a chance to meet Jesus face-to-face, we continue to experience his presence and power in our lives through the Holy Spirit.

Lesson 9 closes this unit on Christ's provision by looking at his role as "Light of the World." The Bible often describes the world as a dark place in the sense that it's hard for us to know the right thing to do. Where is God in all the evil and chaos that surround us? How do we know what God has called us to do? In John 8 and 12 Jesus promises to light our path if we look to him. His teaching and example show us the way to the Father.

UNIT 3: CHRIST GUIDES AND PROTECTS

FEBRUARY

Lesson 10 looks at Jesus' role as the good shepherd from the Gospel of John. He is the one who loved his sheep so much that he gave his life for them (us). Some religious leaders seek to "fleece the flock." They claim to speak for God when they really only want to increase their own power and influence. Others have good intentions but act like part-time, hired babysitters. They abandon the job when things get tough.

Jesus, though, is a "good" shepherd. He is forever loyal to his sheep, proving his love by dying for them (us). We can therefore always trust him to give us guidance and protection.

Lesson 11 looks at the Gospel of John to explore Jesus' ability to meet our ultimate need. What happens to us when we die? Is this the end, or can we hope for something beyond the grave?

Before Jesus proved his power over death by calling Lazarus from the tomb, Martha found her faith tested by the death of her brother. The pain and hardship of this world will test our faith as well. Will we remain confident that Christ will make it all worthwhile in the end?

Lesson 12 takes us to the upper room. There Jesus and the disciples gather for their final meeting the night before his death. After washing their feet and urging them to love one another, Jesus assures his followers that he is "the way, the truth, and the life." He is the only route to the Father. No other person in history can make and prove such a claim. For this reason we find salvation in Christ alone. Jesus shows us how to live lives pleasing to God, lives founded on the truth of his message.

Lesson 13 closes our series with a familiar passage from John 15. Here Jesus compares himself to a grapevine and his disciples to the branches that bear clusters of grapes. As the branches draw life from the vine, believers draw strength from Jesus to serve God.

If we fail, it is not because Christ has abandoned us. Rather, it is because we have separated ourselves from him. Also in this passage Jesus shows his care for the disciples by saying that he no longer calls them servants but friends. What an awe-inspiring privilege! This should reflect the way that we work with Christ to bring glory to God.

ONE TRUE WAY

We live in a world where many voices call us to follow their lead. Our jobs, friends, hobbies, habits, and family members all demand our loyalties. In the process it's easy to get confused and off track. Even at Christmastime, when we should be focusing on the coming of Christ, the demands of the season make it hard to remember who Jesus is and what he is all about. The lessons in this series should serve as a reminder that the son of Mary was also the only-begotten Son of God.

Rome

Philippi

ASIA MINOR

Ephesus • Colossae

Mediterranean Sea

Capernaum •

Sea of Galilee

GALILEE

Mediterranean Sea

Jordan River

Jerusalem •

Bethlehem • • Bethany

JUDEA

Dead Sea

The Holy Land in the Time of Christ

I Am...

I Am ... the true vine. —John 15:1

the bread of life. —John 6:35

the good shepherd. —John 10:11, 14

the resurrection, and the life. —John 11:25

Alpha and Omega. —Revelation 1:8; 21:6; 22:13

the way, the truth, and the life. —John 14:6

the living bread. —John 6:51

the light of the world. —John 8:12; 9:5

Unit 1: Christ, the Image of God
(Lessons 1-5)

WHO IS JESUS CHRIST?

LESSON 1

WHY TEACH THIS LESSON?

It is often said that knowledge is power. This is true, and some knowledge is very powerful. There's great power and fruitfulness in having knowledge of Jesus.

In this lesson, we will look closely at the person and character of Jesus Christ. In this process of coming to know more about the Lord, we grow in our understanding of who he is and what he has done for us. Growing in our knowledge of him helps us better to see all that he is to us and what he has come into our lives to do. Having a growing knowledge of Jesus Christ draws us closer to him in deeper fellowship.

As we study this lesson, we will not merely be learning information about an important person. We will gain knowledge of the Son of God, knowledge that will bless and empower us daily.

INTRODUCTION

Jesus. Although secular society continually attempts to exclude him, he still seems to be everywhere. We see him as a plastic dashboard statue in a passing car. We watch him portrayed in Hollywood productions. We observe him in many variations as the manger baby for Christmas. In spite of all of this attention, we sometimes neglect to ask the most crucial question: "Who is Jesus Christ?" The lessons for this quarter will explore this vital question.

A. THE PATH TO HERESY

Perhaps you have heard the word heresy at some time in your life. Merriam-Webster says that heresy is "an opinion, doctrine, or practice contrary to the truth." Heresy is dangerous false teaching that negates or denies the central truths of the Christian faith (see 2 Peter 2:1).

Many heresies that have arisen in the history of the church are centered on Jesus Christ himself. The first major heresy about Jesus came from a collection of false teachings we call *gnosticism*. While there were several false doctrines within gnosticism, the most dangerous was the belief that Jesus was not really human—he just seemed or appeared to be human. Gnostics had no problem with the divinity of Jesus; they denied his humanity. But, as Hebrews 2:14 teaches, if Jesus had not been a man, he could not die. Thus, acceptance of gnostic beliefs would deny the basic doctrine that Jesus died on the cross to pay the price for our sins, the doctrine of the atonement.

A second major heresy that was centered specifically on Jesus was a fourth-century teaching we call *Arianism*. Arians taught that while Jesus was indeed a powerful, supernatural being, he had not always existed. He was a created being. This was recognized as a heresy because it ultimately denied the divinity of Christ. If he were a creature, then he could not be the creator—he could not really be God. If this were true, then Jesus' claims about himself were delusions or lies, and he should be rejected as a false teacher.

DEVOTIONAL READING:
ISAIAH 9:2-7
BACKGROUND SCRIPTURE:
COLOSSIANS 1
PRINTED TEXT:
COLOSSIANS 1:15-23

LESSON AIMS

After participating in this lesson, each student will be able to:

1. Tell how the creation is dependent on the creator.

2. Explain why Paul emphasized the doctrine of Christ in his battle against heresy in the church.

3. Write a prayer that expresses worship for Jesus in his role as creator.

KEY VERSE

He is the image of the invisible God, the firstborn over all creation. For by him all things were created: things in heaven and on earth, visible and invisible, whether thrones or powers or rulers or authorities; all things were created by him and for him.
—Colossians 1:15, 16

Both of these heresies can be found in the church today. There are those who do not like to think of Jesus as a man, thus falling into a modern gnosticism. For example, this viewpoint has trouble thinking about the baby Jesus of Christmastime without also thinking that he never cried or while assuming that he was spouting words of wisdom while in the cradle.

There are others today who see Jesus as the ultimate man but not as God, thus agreeing with the Arians. These modern Arians admire Jesus as an advocate for the downtrodden, a wise teacher, or even as a revolutionary leader. This line of thought stops short of seeing Jesus as God in flesh.

Biblical Christians are called to affirm that Jesus was fully human and fully divine. To do anything less sets one on the path of heresy and departure from the Christian faith.

B. LESSON BACKGROUND

Paul's letter to the Colossian church was sent primarily to combat a growing threat of heresy within that group of believers. Paul never says exactly what the heresy is, but we can see that he refers to it as a type of "philosophy" (Colossians 2:8); it seems to have been an early form of gnosticism, perhaps combined with a type of Judaizing. Judaizing was the belief that Christians were obligated to keep every aspect of the Old Testament law, including circumcision. Paul wrote to correct the problem and call the church to a return to the simple faith in Christ (2:6, 7).

Today's lesson text comes on the heels of Paul's opening prayer for the needs of the Colossian church. Paul has asked God that the Colossian believers would be spiritually wise (1:9), live upright lives (1:10), show endurance in the face of persecution (1:11), and be thankful for their glorious salvation through Jesus Christ (1:12-14). Having ended his prayer on this high note, he then proceeds to discuss the true nature of Christ and what this means to his readers.

I. DIVINE CHRIST FOR CREATION (COLOSSIANS 1:15-20)

The six verses in this subsection (1:15-20) have been labeled the "Christ Hymn" or the "Hymn to Christ."

A. JESUS: IMAGE OF GOD (v. 15)

15. He is the image of the invisible God, the firstborn over all creation.

This extraordinary verse is one of the most profound doctrinal statements of the entire New Testament. Yet it is susceptible to misunderstanding in at least two ways.

First, when Paul says Jesus is the *image of . . . God,* he does not mean that Jesus is some type of "copy" of God. We know from our experience with copy machines that the copying process always causes degradation, and each copy is less perfect than the original. Such experiences do not apply here. Paul means that Jesus is "imaging" or revealing the unseen God, the creator who does not normally allow human eyes to see him (compare John 1:18). Jesus is the visible expression of God. See also John 14:9.

Second, when Paul describes Jesus as the *firstborn over all creation,* he is not saying that Jesus himself is a created being. Rather, this is his way of saying that Jesus is the ruler over all creation. In the ancient world the firstborn son has authority over the father's household that is essentially equal to that of the father himself. The only one who can overrule the firstborn son is the father. Since there is complete unity of purpose between Jesus and his Father, the authority of the

Son over creation is equal to that of the Father. The word translated *firstborn* here is also in Hebrews 1:6. There it is even clearer that Jesus enters the world of humans from the outside as an uncreated being.

Thus Paul begins the Christ Hymn with a robust statement of the divinity of Christ. He does this by affirming two mighty characteristics of Jesus: his role in revealing the true God and his authority over creation.

THE INVISIBLE GOD

Most religions in the ancient world worship gods represented by idols. Yet the God of the Bible refuses to be represented by an idol of any kind; he commanded that his people not make an idol of any kind (see Exodus 20:4). When the Romans first occupied Palestine, some officers entered the Holy of Holies in the temple and were dismayed that there was no image there. They concluded that these Jews did not worship any God at all and thus were atheists.

Today many people doubt God's existence because they cannot see him. Yet in other areas of life we readily accept what we cannot see. We cannot see carbon monoxide, but we know that this gas can be lethal. We cannot see love, but we feel its presence and power. We cannot see radio waves, but that does not stop us from tuning in our favorite stations. Even though all these things are invisible, we still order our lives around them because we know they are real.

God too is real. And Jesus is the image of God. That means that what we see in Jesus is a picture of what God is like. The apostle John tells us that no one has even seen God, except as God's Son has revealed him (John 1:18). What a privilege to see Jesus in the pages of Scripture!   —J. B. N.

The Holy Land in the Time of Christ

Visual for Lesson 1. *Use this map to help your students gain a geographical perspective of this quarter's lessons.*

B. JESUS: CREATOR AND SUSTAINER (vv. 16, 17)

16. For by him all things were created: things in heaven and on earth, visible and invisible, whether thrones or powers or rulers or authorities; all things were created by him and for him.

Paul expands upon Jesus' role as creator by giving an inclusive statement with important implications. First, *by him all things were created*. Paul makes sure that his readers do not exclude anything from this broad statement. There are no exceptions. Paul wants the Colossians to know that this includes both the physical realm (*on earth*) and the spiritual realm (*in heaven*).

Paul also insists that all things were created *for him*. This, of course, further excludes Jesus from the realm of created beings and things. While the full purpose of creation is not laid out here, we know from elsewhere in Scripture that creation was undertaken by God for his glory. Paul includes Jesus in this goal; there is no separation of purpose.

17. He is before all things, and in him all things hold together.

Paul's mighty statements about Christ continue at an intense pace. In this verse he asserts the preexistence of Christ. The affirmation that Jesus *is before all things* tells us that the divinity of Christ is not limited by time or space. This statement is similar to Jesus' own claim that "before Abraham was born, I am!" (John 8:58).

Paul goes on to declare that Jesus is not only the creator but is also the sustainer of all things. The word translated *hold together* has the sense of "continue to exist." The Bible never sees God-the-creator as some kind of divine clockmaker who makes the clock, winds it up, and then abandons it. Christ continues to be involved in the ongoing affairs of the created order. Without this involvement the world would quickly cease to exist.

HOW TO SAY IT

Arianism. AIR-ee-uh-nih-zim.
Bethlehem. BETH-lih-hem.
Colossians. Kuh-LOSH-unz.
Corinthians. Ko-RIN-thee-unz.
Ephesians. Ee-FEE-zhunz.
gnosticism. NAHSS-tih-SIZZ-
   um.
gnostics. NAHSS-ticks.
heresy. HAIR-uh-see.
Nazareth. NAZ-uh-reth.
shalom (Hebrew). shah-LOME.

WHAT DO YOU THINK?

How would you compare and contrast Christ's role within the church with the roles that church leaders are to fill? How well do your church's leaders recognize what their roles should be? How can you support them?

C. JESUS: PREEMINENT ONE (v. 18)

18. And he is the head of the body, the church; he is the beginning and the firstborn from among the dead, so that in everything he might have the supremacy.

Having established that Christ is the creator and ruler of the world, Paul now narrows the focus of the Christ Hymn to Jesus' role in *the church*. As elsewhere, the church is seen as *the body* of Christ (see Romans 12:5, 1 Corinthians 12:27), a beautiful metaphor. Compare Ephesians 1:22, 23; 4:15; 5:23.

In regard to Christ's relationship to the church, Paul lifts up three important concepts. First, Christ is *the beginning* or originator of the church. He founded the church (Matthew 16:18) and purchased it with his own blood (Acts 20:28).

Second, Jesus' resurrection is the crucial doctrine of the church. Without the resurrection of Jesus, the faith of Christian believers is futile and useless (1 Corinthians 15:14), and the church is based on fraud. The doctrine of the resurrection emphasizes the flesh-and-blood side of Jesus. As a man Jesus died, but God raised him *from among the dead*. As *the firstborn* of the resurrection, he will lead all believers to victory over death.

Third, Paul states that all of these things work to establish Christ's *supremacy*. This word means first place or highest rank. There is no authority in the church that exceeds the authority of Christ in any matter. It is his church, not ours. We must remind ourselves that we exist as the church for his service and for his glory.

D. JESUS: DWELLING OF DEITY (v. 19)

19. For God was pleased to have all his fullness dwell in him,

This verse lifts up the doctrine of the incarnation. Although we may not be able to understand this teaching completely, it is a foundational doctrine for the Christian faith. This is the belief that the deity of God was present in the person of a man, Jesus of Nazareth.

Paul adds more detail to this statement in Colossians 2:9: "For in Christ all the fullness of the Deity lives in bodily form." In Christ we find all the fullness of God. Jesus did not merely have a "spark of the divine," or "a more intense relationship with God." Christ was and is God. As the apostle John wrote, "the Word [Christ] was God" (John 1:1), and this Word "became flesh and made his dwelling among us" (John 1:14).

E. JESUS: PEACE OFFERING (v. 20)

20. . . . and through him to reconcile to himself all things, whether things on earth or things in heaven, by making peace through his blood, shed on the cross.

From the doctrine of the incarnation, Paul continues the Christ Hymn with the equally foundational doctrine of the atonement. Briefly stated Paul teaches that Jesus' death on the cross was an act that paid the price for human sins; it thereby returned all creation back to God.

There are many aspects to the doctrine of the atonement, and Paul draws on three of them here. First, the cross of Christ served as a type of peace offering to God. The biblical concept of peace can mean more than lack of hostilities. In the Old Testament peace (Hebrew *shalom*) could be used in the sense of "satisfaction of a debt." For example, a landowner who failed to cover a pit, thus allowing his neighbor's ox to fall to its death, was obligated to give the neighbor a new ox. To do so was to make peace with the neighbor (see Exodus 21:34, where the idea of payment is represented by the Hebrew *shalom*). Elsewhere, Paul teaches that Christ is our peace, having breached the wall of sepa-

WHAT DO YOU THINK?

The cross is the means through which peace entered the world. How do you explain this to an unbeliever? What roadblocks might you expect?

ration between Jews and Gentiles and between God and humanity (Ephesians 2:11-22).

Second, Paul uses the concept of Jesus' death as a *blood* offering for sins. The Bible teaches that without the shedding of blood there is no forgiveness of sins (Hebrews 9:22). This is the essence of Paul's "message of the cross" (1 Corinthians 1:18), that the blood of Jesus serves as an ultimate, once-for-all sin offering (see Hebrews 10:10).

Third, this verse speaks of the atonement in terms of reconciliation. Two parties who were once on good terms but who have been alienated from one another need to be reconciled. They are reconciled when the cause for alienation is removed. We were alienated from God because of sin but reconciled when Jesus' death covered our sin (see Romans 5:10). What is even more remarkable is that Jesus' death does more than *reconcile* humankind with God; it also reconciles all of creation—*all things, whether* they be *things on earth or things in heaven*—with its creator.

II. HUMAN SAVIOR FOR HUMANITY (COLOSSIANS 1:21-23)

Verse 20 marks the end of the Christ Hymn. Paul now turns to its direct implications for his readers.

A. JESUS: JUSTIFIER AND SANCTIFIER (vv. 21, 22)

21, 22. Once you were alienated from God and were enemies in your minds because of your evil behavior. But now he has reconciled you by Christ's physical body through death to present you holy in his sight, without blemish and free from accusation—

Paul reminds his readers of our side of the problem: we are the ones who caused the alienation by our sin (*evil behavior*). Our movement away from God brings to mind the story of the wife who was riding with her husband in their big old car with the old-fashioned bench seats. She asked, "Honey, why don't we sit next to each other like we did on our honeymoon?" Her husband, who was driving, answered, "Dear, I haven't moved." Alienation from God is not due to any failing or moving away on his part. The moving away has been entirely our work.

When we are *reconciled* to God through the blood of Jesus, he is able to present us completely restored before the throne of God. We are *holy* (cleansed of sin), *without blemish, and free from accusation.*

ALIENATED . . . RECONCILED

Our family likes to watch old movies. One fond memory is the 1968 comedy *With Six You Get Egg Roll,* starring Doris Day and Brian Keith. Day is a widow with three boys; Keith is a widower with one daughter. Day and Keith meet and the chemistry begins to flow. At one point Keith breaks a date with her in order to go to a birthday party. But when Day sees him at a restaurant with a much younger woman, she is furious—not knowing that the young woman is his daughter and her birthday party is at the restaurant.

After that is cleared up, Day and Keith get married. When Keith discovers that his daughter has to spend much of her day doing housework while Day's son plays basketball, the fireworks begin anew! He moves out of the house, and their relationship is on the rocks again. Eventually the misunderstandings are straightened out, and they live happily ever after.

Alienated, and then reconciled. Unfortunately, our alienation from God was more than a simple misunderstanding. We sinned, and this created a great gulf

VISUALS FOR THESE LESSONS

The visual pictured in each lesson (example: page 129) is a small reproduction of a large, full-color poster included in the Adult Resources packet for the Winter Quarter. The packet is available from your supplier. Order No. 292.

WHAT DO YOU THINK?

What are some difficulties that the standards holy, without blemish, *and* free from accusation *have caused for you? How did you (or how will you) overcome these problems?*

WHAT DO YOU THINK?

Verse 23 begins with a conditional "if-statement." What things are most likely to cause you to stray from the faith? How do you guard against these?

WHAT DO YOU THINK?

How do you embrace as your own Paul's calling as a minister to preach "to every creature under heaven"? Or do you see this calling to be relegated to a select few rather than being a general call to all Christians? Explain.

between us and God. But God pursued us. It took the sacrifice of his Son to unite us once again with God. It was that great sacrifice that makes it possible for us to live happily—and eternally—ever after.   —J. B. N.

B. JESUS: CORE OF THE GOSPEL (v. 23)

23. . . . if you continue in your faith, established and firm, not moved from the hope held out in the gospel. This is the gospel that you heard and that has been proclaimed to every creature under heaven, and of which I, Paul, have become a servant.

Here Paul speaks of the *faith* as the body of doctrine that is to be believed by Christians (see Jude 3). If we depart from the central doctrines of Jesus Christ as contained in the Christ Hymn, then we abandon the faith (see 1 Timothy 4:1). The danger that is in view here is not that we will quit believing altogether, but that our beliefs will become false as we drift into heresy.

While Paul's books (letters) may have different emphases, they are consistent concerning these central doctrines, as is all of the New Testament. This is why we are able to use verses from one part of Scripture to help us understand a verse in another book. This is known as the "analogy of faith," since Scripture never fights with itself. Scripture speaks with one voice in teaching us about the implications of Jesus' life, death, and resurrection. These teachings are both secure and timeless, serving with equal value every generation of Christian believers.

CONCLUSION

A. THE AGELESS JESUS

"Jesus Christ is the same yesterday, and today, and for ever" (Hebrews 13:8). Some things about the church must change as culture and society changes. For example, no churches in the first century AD had Web sites or parking lots. However, the church has no need for new, updated doctrines about Jesus. Those doctrines as taught in the New Testament were adequate for Paul's churches and they remain sufficient for ours.

Church history tells sad stories of teachers who wanted to redefine what the church taught about Jesus. Gnosticism and Arianism were only two of several threats that the church battled to retain "the faith": the true doctrines concerning Christ. Until Jesus returns there will be false Christs (Mark 13:22). These may be flesh-and-blood impostors. They may be teachers presenting warped views of the nature of Christ and his work of salvation. Church leaders should always be on guard against the infiltration of such false teachings into the congregation (see Titus 1:9).

B. THE CHRIST OF CHRISTMAS

Paul never tells the Christmas story of baby Jesus, either in his letters or in his recorded preaching in the book of Acts. (The closest he comes is in Galatians 4:4: "But when the time had fully come, God sent his Son, born of a woman, born under law.") Yet Paul would agree that the basic story of a baby born in Bethlehem is essential to our understanding of who Jesus is.

Jesus did not appear on the scene as a full-grown man, like gods of Greek mythology. The story of Jesus is an account both of human frailty and of divine, awe-inspiring power. He was born on the road and cradled in a feed trough. Yet he was worshiped by wise kings, and his birth was heralded by an angel choir. Even at his birth he was truly God and truly human.

THOUGHT TO REMEMBER

Jesus was both fully human and fully divine.

Discovery Learning

This page contains an alternative lesson plan emphasizing learning activities. Classes desiring such student involvement will find these suggestions helpful. The next page is a reproducible activity page to further enhance discovery learning.

LEARNING GOALS

After participating in this lesson, each student will be able to:

1. Tell how the creation is dependent on the creator.

2. Explain why Paul emphasized the doctrine of Christ in his battle against heresy in the church.

3. Write a prayer that expresses worship for Jesus in his role as creator.

INTO THE LESSON

Before class begins display a large wall sign titled, "The Path to Heresy." Begin the lesson by asking for a definition of heresy. After the discussion, summarize and write on the sign the definition(s) that your class comes up with. Compare it (or them) with the dictionary definition given in the lesson Introduction. Then ask for examples of heresy within modern Christianity.

Make a transition by reminding the class that there were heresies in the church of the New Testament that still persist today. Deliver a brief lecture to include discussion of gnosticism and Arianism, based on the lesson Introduction.

INTO THE WORD

This activity is an opportunity to develop leadership in your class. Assign the following phrases to eight class members during the week before class. Ask each to be ready to give a brief definition or explanation of his or her assigned phrase. Give each of these students a copy of appropriate part of the lesson commentary. Encourage them to read the lesson Introduction to help them understand the significance of their assigned phrases.

The eight phrases to assign are the image of the invisible God (v. 15); the firstborn (v. 15); by him all things were created (v. 16); he is before all things (v. 17); the supremacy (v. 18); God was pleased to have all his fullness dwell in him (v. 19); reconcile to himself all things (v. 20); peace through his blood (v. 20). (If your class is small, you may wish to double up on verses 16, 17 and/or verses 19, 20.)

Before asking the assigned students to share their findings, distribute to all class members a copy of the printed text with each of the phrases mentioned above underlined. Have a wide margin available for students to write notes. Read Colossians 1:15-20 together and ask the assigned class members to help clarify the phrases mentioned above. (Option: use the Truth About Christ exercise from the Reproducible Page as a substitute activity.)

Next tell the class that in verses 21-23 Paul explains the implications for this wonderful snapshot of Jesus. Read these verses and ask these questions:

1. How would you describe reconciliation in everyday language to an unbeliever?

2. How is this a "before and after" story?

3. What are the differences among, and implications of, the three ideas concerning how Christ presents us to God as "holy," "without blemish," and "free from accusation"?

4. What does the word *if* imply in verse 23?

INTO LIFE

Allow class members to form small groups of no more than five people each. Each group will choose to do either Activity #1 or Activity #2 below. Because you may not know how many groups will choose to do each activity, it will be necessary to have several sheets of each of the following instructions available. You will also need several hymnals and chorus books for Activity #1.

Activity #1. Your task is to select hymns or choruses for a worship service that will focus on the supremacy of Jesus Christ. Today's printed text will be the text for the sermon in this service. Find several hymns and choruses that speak of some of the qualities or characteristics of Jesus that are mentioned in today's study. Be ready to share with the rest of the class the reasons you chose these songs based on the specific lines or words in the songs that reflect today's text.

Activity #2. Your task is to write a prayer of worship based on the concepts of today's printed text. The prayer of worship will be incorporated into the worship service that those doing Activity #1 are working on. It will become the prayer that many class members will pray throughout the week; for this, have someone from your group go to the church office and make a photocopy of the prayer for each member of the class.

Allow time for discussion. Make sure to give each group equal time. Wrap up with a quiet time as students fill out the Immanuel: God with Us exercise from the Reproducible Page.

Truth About Christ

One kind of false teaching denies Jesus' divinity. Another kind of false teaching denies Jesus' humanity. Read Colossians 1:15-29 and jot a note in each banner about how that verse teaches us that the Christ child who cried in a manger was not only human but also fully divine.

Colossians 1:15

Colossians 1:16, 17

Colossians 1:18

Colossians 1:19, 20

Immanuel: God with Us

What are some of the characteristics of Jesus' humanity that provide a wonderful model for life? For which qualities of Jesus' divinity are you especially grateful? Write your thoughts below.

Jesus Christ: A Portrait of God

Unit 1: *Christ, the Image of God*

(Lessons 1-5)

WHAT GOD
SAYS ABOUT JESUS

LESSON 2

Dec
10

WHY TEACH THIS LESSON?

Modern culture seems to have an insatiable appetite to know the details of the lives of celebrities. The tabloids and talk shows feed this voracious desire. Are we as hungry to know about Jesus?

Today's lesson offers a clear portrait of the Son of God. It is a portrait painted by the loving hand of a Father who wants the world to know what his Son "looks like." God says, in effect, "See my Son, learn from him, come and grow closer to him. As you do, you will prepare yourself to live eternally with him."

INTRODUCTION

A. THE SELF-REVEALING GOD

Have you ever been part of a "secret sisters" program (or the men's counterpart)? In this type of program, each participating member is assigned secretly the name of another woman. The secret sister then sends notes and gifts to her counterpart during a set period of time. When time is up a party is held in which the secret sisters are revealed. It can be a fun way to get to know another person and to practice spiritual disciplines such as generosity and encouragement.

Revelation is based on the idea that something hidden has been uncovered and can now be known. In the case of God, we should remember that we know nothing about him except that which he has chosen to reveal to us. God is sovereign even with regard to our knowledge about him. There is much about God that we do not know but might like to know. We can speculate on such things, but we know with certainty only what God has graciously chosen to reveal to us.

Reliable knowledge about God is not discovered by accident or chance. It has come to humanity through the process of revelation. We know about God because he is the God who reveals himself. Our knowledge of God is not due to our brilliance or our worthiness.

In this sense human knowledge about God is *progressive*. This means that God reveals himself in stages. There are some striking examples of this in the Old Testament. In his experience with the near-sacrifice of his son, Abraham learned that God is both demanding of faithful obedience and ultimately merciful (Genesis 22). At the burning bush God revealed to Moses that his name is I Am. This places God outside human existence controlled by time (Exodus 3). In his vision of God on his throne in Heaven, Isaiah learned that God seeks those who will speak for him, delivering even difficult messages (Isaiah 6). In his sufferings Job learned that God is great and that he (Job) had no right to challenge God's actions (Job 38). Through his experience of adultery and the death of a son, David learned that only God can truly cleanse a person's heart and renew the human spirit (Psalm 51).

DEVOTIONAL READING:

LUKE 1:46-55

BACKGROUND SCRIPTURE:

HEBREWS 1

PRINTED TEXT:

HEBREWS 1:1-9

LESSON AIMS

After participating in this lesson, each student will be able to:

1. List ways that Jesus is superior to angels.

2. Predict how the church could be damaged if the natures of Jesus and angels are misunderstood.

3. Write a testimony that articulates how his or her faith in Christ is stronger because of today's lesson.

KEY VERSE

In the past God spoke to our forefathers through the prophets at many times and in various ways, but in these last days he has spoken to us by his Son, whom he appointed heir of all things, and through whom he made the universe.

—Hebrews 1:1, 2

LESSON 2 NOTES

To speak of revelation as *progressive* or *ongoing* has certain dangers, however. Christians who are faithful to the Bible need not look to modern "prophets" to reveal more and more about God. Historically the church has believed that the Old Testament serves to prepare for God's ultimate revelation in Jesus. The New Testament is the testimony of this revelation in Christ.

Today's Scripture text teaches us that God has revealed himself in his Son, Jesus Christ. In other words, God has told us everything about himself that we need to know for our earthly existence. We can assume that we will understand God even more fully when we join him in Heaven. But for now we have no need to know more than that which has been revealed in the Old and New Testaments.

B. LESSON BACKGROUND

While there is some early tradition that concludes that the book of Hebrews was written by the apostle Paul, many scholars today do not accept this conclusion. The book does not begin with Paul's personal name, as all his other letters do. Furthermore, the author of the book seems to place himself in the second generation of Christian believers, not as an apostle (see Hebrews 2:3). It is doubtful that Paul would do this, since elsewhere he defends his apostleship vigorously. For these reasons and others, the great scholar Origen (AD 185–254) concluded, "Who wrote Hebrews, only God knows."

The anonymous nature of this book in no way lessens its importance or authority as a major source for our understanding of Christ. The author appears to have been writing to a community of Jewish Christians who were in danger of abandoning their faith in Jesus in order to return to the community of the Jewish synagogue. The author addresses this potential apostasy by carefully laying out the roles of Jesus in relationship to the Old Testament Scriptures. Hebrews is a uniquely significant New Testament book, for it delves into explanations about Jesus that are not found anywhere else in the Bible.

Hebrews has two primary functions overall. First, it defends the church's teachings about Jesus from outside attacks. Hebrews in particular shows that Jesus is superior to the older system of the Jews.

Second, Hebrews shows that Jesus and the Old Testament system are not in conflict with each other. Rather, the Christian system grows out of and is a fulfillment of the Jewish system. Hebrews does this by using many Old Testament texts and allusions to show that Christians should understand themselves as heirs to a faith that began long before the first century AD.

I. JESUS: GOD'S SELF-EXPRESSION (HEBREWS 1:1-3)

Hebrews begins with no preliminary material. Instead it plunges immediately into its main topic: a doctrinal presentation of the nature and role of Christ in relationship to previous revelations of God.

A. REVELATION BEFORE JESUS (v. 1)

1. In the past God spoke to our forefathers through the prophets at many times and in various ways,

The author begins by describing the partial nature of revelation before Christ. Two rare and unusual Greek adverbs, translated *at many times* and *in various ways*, present themselves. Before Jesus, God's revelation of himself came in bits and pieces, delivered sporadically over a long period of time.

These revelations of God were delivered to the *forefathers* of Israel's history. The messages came via God's spokesmen, *the prophets*. The author of Hebrews does

God, who . . . spake in time past unto the fathers by the prophets, hath in these last days spoken unto us by his Son. —Hebrews 1:1

Visual for Lesson 2. *As a background sketch point to this poster and ask for names of prophets who came before Christ.*

not minimize the importance of this prophetic voice. Rather, the author wants the readers to realize that there is incompleteness if we stop with the Old Testament. The Old Testament tells of many people who were commended for their faithfulness, yet "none of them received what had been promised" (Hebrews 11:39). Thus they were at a certain disadvantage compared with Christians.

B. Revelation in Jesus (v. 2a)

2a. . . . but in these last days he has spoken to us by his Son,

By *last days* the author is not intending a reference to the final few days or weeks just before the second coming of Jesus. Rather, *last days* refers to the final period of human history, the era of Christ. This period is characterized by a new age of revelation. No longer do we receive our knowledge of God in bits and pieces. God now speaks through *his Son.*

There are two major implications to this statement. First, the ministry of Jesus was strategically chosen by God as a way to reveal himself. As John wrote, by experiencing Jesus, "We have seen his glory, the glory of the One and Only, who came from the Father" (John 1:14). Later in this same Gospel, Jesus declared, "Anyone who has seen me has seen the Father" (14:9).

The second implication is that Jesus is the perfect and complete revelation of the Father. The Old Testament prophets, for all their virtues, were able to give only a fragmentary picture of who God is. God has revealed himself fully by sending his Son; we neither need nor should expect further revelation about God while we're still in our earthly existence. Therefore Jesus is the culmination of God's revelation about himself in this, the final period of human history.

C. Revelation Through Jesus (vv. 2b, 3)

2b. . . . whom he appointed heir of all things, and through whom he made the universe.

Understanding the exact relationship between Jesus and God is difficult. One of the best ways to understand it is the frequent biblical description of the Father-Son relationship. This passage matches this description in two ways. First, as *heir of all things,* Jesus is the unique Son of God. He shares this level of sonship with no one else. We are able to become sons and daughters of God through faith (John 1:12; Galatians 3:26), but not in the way that Jesus is God's Son.

This unique relationship is further explained by the second description: Jesus as co-creator with the Father. In the ancient world a son commonly worked with his father in the family business. The Son has worked with the Father, even in creating *the universe.* This serves as a further confirmation of Jesus' sonship and also affirms his preexistence. The Son is not a created being but rather the creator himself.

3. The Son is the radiance of God's glory and the exact representation of his being, sustaining all things by his powerful word. After he had provided purification for sins, he sat down at the right hand of the Majesty in heaven.

To define and explain the true nature of the Christ completely is impossible because of the limitations of human language and understanding. However, the author gives four powerful images to help us.

First, the Son is the *radiance* of the Father's *glory.* This could also be translated as the "reflection of God's glory." In this the author emphasizes that Jesus was a visible revelation of God. The glory of God in Jesus was partially uncovered at the transfiguration for the disciples to see (Mark 9:2, 3). The miracles of Jesus also were partial revelations of God's glory (John 2:11).

What Do You Think?

How does the concept of Jesus as an heir help you understand more about him and draw closer to him? How do we bring this imagery from the first century into the twenty-first?

[Make sure to use Matthew 25:34 and Romans 8:17 to inform your answer.]

WHAT DO YOU THINK?

Which parts of God's revelation of himself through Jesus Christ help you gain a better understanding of who he is?

Second, the Son is *the exact representation* of the Father's *being*. The original, Greek word used is the one from which we get our English word *character*. In the ancient world it was used to describe an exact imprint of a coin, a complete and faithful reproduction stamped from the original, engraved coin die. The author is saying that Jesus is a full and faithful representation of the Father, without flaw.

Third, the description *sustaining all things by his powerful word* expands upon Jesus' role as creator (see Colossians 1:17, last week's lesson). In some religions the creator and the sustainer are different gods. The fully revealed truth is that the Son shares in both functions.

Fourth, the author reminds his readers that after Jesus' death and resurrection, he ascended to Heaven to be seated *at the right hand* of the throne of God. This presents the Son as a ruler and judge equal to the Father. It also shifts the focus to the realm of Heaven, where the position of Jesus is far superior to that of any angel. This is the next topic of discussion.

ON THE RIGHT HAND

In the English language the phrase *right hand* is rich in symbolism. It can mean the hand that is normally stronger (than the left). The *Oxford English Dictionary* cites a source from the year 1000 with this connotation. Another meaning is to symbolize friendship or alliance. This connotation is cited as early as 1591. We normally shake hands with the right hand.

A third meaning is to indicate a person of usefulness or importance, an indispensable or efficient helper. We use the phrase *right-hand man*, a usage that goes back to 1537. In 1863 General Thomas J. "Stonewall" Jackson's left arm was amputated after a wound (which eventually proved fatal); to this General Robert E. Lee exclaimed, "You have lost your left arm, but I have lost my right!"

A similar meaning is that the right hand is the position of honor. This is probably the meaning intended in Hebrews 1:3. After he had fulfilled his task on earth, Jesus ascended and was seated at the right hand of the Father. Jesus represents the right hand of God in all ways—in strength, in alliance, and in honor. Do we hold Jesus in as much honor as the Father does?   —J. B. N.

II. JESUS: SUPERIOR TO CREATED BEINGS (HEBREWS 1:4-9)

Recently we have experienced a renewed fascination with angels. Television programs, movies, and novels are filled with fanciful accounts of divine visitations. Cards, pictures, and artwork have used angels as a decorative motif.

The Bible has comparatively little information about angels. We know that they are a class of beings with supernatural powers. They serve at the pleasure of God. We even know the names of a couple of them: Gabriel (Luke 1:19) and Michael (Revelation 12:7). While our knowledge of angels is limited, some things about them are very clear in the Bible. First, they are not to be worshiped. Worship is for God alone (see Revelation 19:10). Second, Jesus Christ is not some type of glorified angel. He is the divine Son and far superior to any angel. Apparently the author of Hebrews is aware of misunderstandings related to both of these things. He seeks to correct them in the following verses.

A. NAME ABOVE ANGELS' (vv. 4, 5)

4. So he became as much superior to the angels as the name he has inherited is superior to theirs.

What does your *name* mean? I recently learned that the name "Tiffany" does not mean "expensive jewelry." It comes from the Greek word *Theophanos*, meaning "presence of the divine." What a powerful name for a baby girl!

The author's first point in showing that Jesus is *superior to the angels* has to do with his name. We treat names casually in the modern world. We use nicknames, shortened names, informal names, and other variations. In the biblical world, however, names were highly significant. They were chosen carefully and usually had a clear meaning. For example, Pharaoh's daughter named her adopted baby "Moses" (meaning *drawn*) because she "drew" him out of the water (Exodus 2:10). The *superior* name in mind here is not "Jesus" or "Christ" but "Son," as will be explained in the following verses.

5. For to which of the angels did God ever say,
  "*You are my Son;*
    today I have become your Father"?
Or again,
  "*I will be his Father,*
    and he will be my Son"?

The author draws upon two well-known Old Testament passages to make his point: 2 Samuel 7:14 and Psalm 2:7. Jesus is designated *Son* by God himself. This is a name and (more importantly) a title that Jesus shares with no one else, not even angels. Although these verses probably applied to Kings David and Solomon in their original context, Jesus had discussed this question during his ministry (see Matthew 22:42-45). In so doing he had shown himself to be the ultimate Son of God, superior to David (compare Acts 2:25-32).

B. WORTHY OF WORSHIP (v. 6)

6. And again, when God brings his firstborn into the world, he says,
  "*Let all God's angels worship him.*"

The author uses another Old Testament quotation to show the readers what it means to be the Son of the Father in Heaven: he is worthy of worship. See Revelation 5:13, where worship includes both God and the Lamb (Jesus). The source of this quotation is probably the Greek (Septuagint) version of Deuteronomy 32:43. In that version heavenly beings are commanded to *worship* God. No creature, including *angels*, is exempt from the obligation of worshiping God and his Son.

C. RULES IN HEAVEN (vv. 7-9)

7. In speaking of the angels he says,
  "*He makes his angels winds,*
    his servants flames of fire."

The author now quotes Psalm 104:4 to define the glorious function of *angels*. They are powerful spiritual beings who are *servants* of God. To describe them as *flames of fire* reminds us of passages such as Genesis 3:24 and Exodus 3:2.

8, 9. But about the Son he says,
  "*Your throne, O God, will last for ever and ever,*
    and righteousness will be the scepter of your kingdom.
  "*You have loved righteousness and hated wickedness;*
    therefore God, your God, has set you above your companions
    by anointing you with the oil of joy."

The author now uses his most formidable quotation: Psalm 45:6, 7. David and Solomon had been promised an eternal *throne* or dynasty (see Psalm 89:4, 29, 36). But neither of these esteemed kings was ever promised he would be a god. Thus their promise of an eternal throne is fulfilled only in Jesus.

There is another important detail in this quotation that should not be missed. When God the Father anoints God the Son, he literally makes him Christ. The

WHAT DO YOU THINK?

Why do you think that there is such a modern interest in angels? How can we use this infatuation to point people to Jesus instead?

WHAT DO YOU THINK?

One who holds a scepter is a king on a throne. Yet we who live in democratic societies may balk at the idea of having a king. If you live in a democratic society, what challenge does this pose for you?

WHAT DO YOU THINK?

Today's text directs the readers to Jesus as the true object for worship. How well is your church doing at pointing people toward Jesus? How will you help it do better?

term *Christ* (or its Old Testament counterpart, *Messiah*) means "Anointed One." Jesus is not a self-anointed messiah. He is anointed by God for a special ministry, the most important ministry in the history of the world. Jesus himself proclaimed, "The Spirit of the Lord . . . has anointed me to preach" (Luke 4:18).

The sweeping claims about Jesus Christ in this beautiful text still serve today as guideposts in our quest to know him more fully. He is the unique Son of God, the ultimate revelation of God the Father, the co-creator and sustainer of our world.

WHAT DO YOU LOVE?

When I was a youngster, I used to love going to my grandfather's farm. There were fascinating animals, and the wooded area at the rear of the farm was an exciting place to a suburban kid. When I got older, I used to love riding my bike and exploring residential and factory areas several miles away. I loved eating banana splits. I also loved playing baseball; the kids on our block often would play several hours every day, all summer, straight through the heat and humidity of July and August.

In my adult years my tastes have changed. Now I love to sit in a comfortable chair with a tall, cold glass of caffeine-free diet cola and a big bowl of popcorn, and read a book. Other people love to go to NASCAR races. I have a friend who loves to participate in Civil War reenactments. Some people love watching sunsets. Others love taking walks along the beach or in the woods.

What do you love? Jesus loved righteousness. That's a much more lofty value, isn't it? We tend to love things. Jesus loved virtues. He loved doing God's will. He loved doing what was right in God's sight. When he was baptized, he said it was to fulfill all righteousness. He did not live just to fulfill his own selfish desires or seek his own pleasures; he wanted to fulfill God's will in all things. He loved righteousness. Do we?

—J. B. N.

PRAYER

Holy Father, thank you for sending your Son to help us understand you better. Because of his death, we need never doubt your love for us. He has revealed your heart to us, and we rejoice in that revelation. We pray in his name, the name far above any angel's, amen.

CONCLUSION

A recent newspaper story claimed that a majority of people have hidden aspects to their lives that would embarrass them if revealed. The classic example of this is the traveling salesman who has two wives and families residing in different cities. He may operate for years by spending part of each week at the different locations. When such arrangements are made public, the result is tragic, with strong feelings of betrayal.

Many people, however, have "dirty little secrets" on a smaller scale. The ability to remain anonymous in our electronic age has led many into online pornography, affairs, and other secret yet sinful behavior. An overemphasis on the "right to privacy" has proved to be a stumbling block to some Christians, even Christian leaders. The secular press delights in uncovering these transgressions and revealing the hypocritical lifestyles of guilty believers. There is nothing more comical to the critics of the church than the preacher who rails against adultery on Sunday morning and visits his mistress Sunday night.

There are some things about God that remain hidden to us. There are, however, no foul details that are hidden. God is pure and holy and righteous consistently, without any deviation at any time.

We can learn much about God from studying the Old Testament, but even more by looking at Jesus. The life of Jesus shows us that God is loving and compassionate. God loved us enough to send his only Son to redeem the world as an offering for human sin (see John 3:16, 17; Romans 5:8). God's self-revelation in Jesus Christ is the sure foundation of all Christian faith and hope. This stands as a great assurance and comfort to all believers.

THOUGHT TO REMEMBER

Jesus is God's ultimate revelation and is far superior to the angels.

Discovery Learning

This page contains an alternative lesson plan emphasizing learning activities. Classes desiring such student involvement will find these suggestions helpful. The next page is a reproducible activity page to further enhance discovery learning.

LEARNING GOALS

After participating in this lesson, each student will be able to:

1. List ways that Jesus is superior to angels.

2. Predict how the church could be damaged if the natures of Jesus and angels are misunderstood.

3. Write a testimony that articulates how his or her faith in Christ is stronger because of today's lesson.

INTO THE LESSON

Fill the classroom with as many pictures, images, and knickknacks of angels that you can find. Also attach two posters to the wall with the following headings: "What We Know About Angels" and "Angels at Work in the Bible."

As class begins, appoint two "scribes" to be ready to write on these posters as class members brainstorm answers. Ask students to share what they know about the nature of angels and to cite appearances of angels in the Bible. After the exercise ask students what songs they know that include references to angels (examples: "Angels from the Realms of Glory," "Angels We Have Heard on High"). Ask, "What do those songs teach us about angels, if anything?"

Make the transition to Bible study by saying, "While the world has a special fascination with angels, we really don't know a lot about them. But the existence of angels becomes part of a great revelation about the nature of Jesus. That revelation about Jesus, as it speaks of his distinction from angels, is found in today's text."

INTO THE WORD

Give to four study groups copies of their respective instructions below and copies of their assigned passages from the lesson commentary. Also give Groups #2 and #3 poster board and markers. Ask each group to appoint a spokesperson to report the group's conclusions. Larger classes may have more than one group working on each task. Keep group sizes to five people or fewer.

Group #1. Your task is to give a report on how God revealed himself progressively before the arrival of Jesus (Hebrews 1:1). You will find the lesson commentary on verse 1 and the Introduction to the commentary to be helpful. Also discuss the dangers of believing in progressive (ongoing) revelation after Christ.

Group #2. Your task is to focus on verse 2a of our printed text as you describe how God has revealed himself in Jesus. Write on the board the two major implications of this verse for our understanding of Christ; be ready to explain these to the class. Illustrate on the poster board each implication, if possible. The attached lesson commentary will be helpful.

Group #3. Your task is to report how God has revealed himself through Jesus' many roles and attributes (vv. 2b, 3). The lesson commentary on these verses will be helpful. Write the four images of Christ from verse 3 on the poster board and be ready to explain them to the class.

Group #4. Your group will discuss the significance of angels as the writer of Hebrews uses them to illustrate the superiority of Jesus. The attached lesson commentary will be helpful. Be sure to include remarks about the significance of Jesus' name (v. 4), the significance of Jesus' being called God's Son (v. 5), the issue of who is worshiped (v. 6), and the heavenly roles of Jesus and angels (vv. 7-9).

Allow each group to share its conclusions with the class. (Alternative for a small class: divide the class in two; have each group complete one of the "Jesus and Angels" and "Jesus and God" activities from the Reproducible Page.)

INTO LIFE

Use the following discussion questions to help make this lesson personal. Say, "The focus of today's lesson is on Jesus rather than on angels. Nevertheless, we learn some things about angels and their relationship with Jesus. What have you learned about angels in this study? Why do you think it is important that today's church understands the relationship of Jesus and angels? Why would God include this teaching in his everlasting Word? Of all the qualities of Jesus mentioned in verses 2-4, which grabs your attention? Why?"

Give each student an index card. Remind the class that several issues have been discussed that are important to their faith. Ask class members to jot down key words they could use in a testimony about how their faith is stronger because of this study. Allow volunteers to share their thoughts. (Alternative: use the "What a Savior!" activity from the Reproducible Page.)

Jesus and Angels

What does Hebrews 1:1-9 teach you about Jesus in comparison with angels? What key phrases support this teaching? Jot your ideas below.

_____

_____

_____

_____

_____

_____

_____

Jesus and God

What does Hebrews 1:1-9 teach you about the relationship of Jesus and God? What key phrases or words support this teaching? Jot your ideas below.

_____

_____

_____

_____

_____

_____

_____

What a Savior! Worthy of Honor!

Jesus is the best revelation of our heavenly Father ever given. Jesus is the "exact representation of his being" (Hebrews 1:3). It is no wonder the angels and all created beings sing "Worthy is the Lamb, who was slain, to receive . . . honor and glory and praise!" (Revelation 5:12). Use the space to write key "faith strengthening" words you would use in your own song of praise to Jesus.

LIGHT THAT CONQUERS

LESSON 3

Dec
17

WHY TEACH THIS LESSON?

Positive relationships add to our lives. It is easy to see that many people, such as parents, brothers, sister, friends, and teachers, have strengthened our lives and made them better. All these relationships are a blessing. Rare is the person who avoids all relationships!

Without question, our relationship with God is the most empowering and encouraging relationship we have. "God is light." This light overflows with grace, blessing, strength, and glory. This lesson will encourage us to "walk in the light." And as we walk in the light we walk in close relationship with God in obedience to him. May his grace, blessing, and strength rub off on us as we do!

INTRODUCTION

A. UNRESOLVED GUILT

She sat on the tailgate of a pickup in the parking lot, her body shuddering with silent sobs. In the nearby park the rest of the church was enjoying the annual picnic, but she didn't participate. She just sat there, hugging herself tightly, staring into nothing.

The preacher sat down next to her and asked, "What's wrong, dear? Can I help?" She gained control for a minute and blurted, "I take shower after shower, but I still feel dirty." Her problem? She had recently committed adultery with her best friend's husband. Her sin made her feel guilty and unclean, and she felt there was no way to get over it.

Counseling professionals say that unresolved guilt is one of the great problems facing troubled adults. The church knows the cause of unresolved guilt: sin. Some secular counseling theories deal with sin problems by saying, "That's who you are. Just accept yourself and be happy." They believe that clients want a therapist who will say that their sin is OK. Actually, no one needs to spend money to hear this. All you have to do is find a bunch of drinking buddies to party with, and they will tell you this for nothing!

God, who made us, knows that sin cannot be ignored or explained away. It must be confronted and overcome. Ignoring sin is a sin itself and is ultimately destructive. The apostle John has a strategy for dealing with sin that we will see today. This week's lesson uses bold symbolic language to guide us into a fellowship with God. This fellowship moves beyond paralyzing guilt to a joyous walk with the Lord.

B. LESSON BACKGROUND

The apostle John was one of Jesus' closest associates. Jesus trusted him enough to task him with the care of his own mother, Mary, at the cross (see John 19:26, 27). Church tradition says that John later moved to the great city of Ephesus, taking Mary with him. There he ministered for many years, dying sometime between AD 95 and 100. His exile to Patmos is also well known (Revelation 1:9).

DEVOTIONAL READING:
EPHESIANS 5:8-14
BACKGROUND SCRIPTURE:
1 JOHN 1:1–2:6
PRINTED TEXT:
1 JOHN 1:1–2:6

LESSON AIMS

After participating in this lesson, each student will be able to:

1. Quote 1 John 1:8, 9 from memory.

2. Discuss the personal implications of what it means to walk as Jesus did.

3. Describe one way that he or she will walk as Jesus did.

KEY VERSE

This is the message we have heard from him and declare to you: God is light; in him there is no darkness at all. —1 John 1:5

LESSON 3 NOTES

HOW TO SAY IT

Ephesus. EF-uh-sus.
Galatians. Guh-LAY-shunz.
gnosticism. NAHSS-tih-SIZZ-um
koinonia (Greek). koy-no-NEE-uh.
Patmos. PAT-muss.
propitiation. pro-PIH-she-AY-shun
synagogue. SIN-uh-gog.

WHAT DO YOU THINK?

Since Christ is the "Word of life," what life changes have you experienced after coming into a relationship with him? What changes do you yet expect?

There are five books in the Bible written by the apostle John: the Gospel of John; 1, 2, 3 John; and Revelation. We are not sure who the intended audience was for 1 John, but apparently they were confronted with many threats to their faith. Some may have been Jewish believers who had denied Jesus in order to return to the synagogue (see 1 John 2:22). Others may have been former pagans who were being lured back into the worship of idols (see 1 John 5:21).

Still others were being tempted by an early form of the attractive heresy we call *gnosticism* (see discussion of this in the first lesson of this quarter). For this reason John emphasized his personal contact with the human Jesus, including seeing and touching (1 John 1:1).

First John deals with both extremes on the issue of sin: *legalism* and *license*. On the one hand, John confronts a legalism that refuses to recognize the sufficiency of Jesus to deal with sin. On the other hand, John will not stand for those who think that they have a license to sin because they believe that personal righteousness and lifestyle are unimportant (compare Romans 6:1, 2).

John's solution to both extremes is to combine forgiveness with godly living. If we try to live righteously but do not feel forgiven for those times we have failed, we will be miserable. If we glory in our forgiveness but disdain God's standards of personal purity and integrity, then we have given up the possibility of a close relationship with God. We too will ultimately be miserable. These issues of John's day are amazingly current for us today. The message of 1 John still has a place in the church and should be heard.

I. THE WALK OF FELLOWSHIP (1 JOHN 1:1-4)

John begins his letter by outlining a dual purpose. First, he writes to bring about true fellowship among his readers. This is fellowship not only with one another but also with God (1 John 1:3). Second, he wants his readers to have hearts full of joy from hearing his words (1 John 1:4). John has no joy in knowing that some of his readers lack true, intimate fellowship. He wants to break down the barriers that destroy fellowship and cause joy to be stifled.

A. EXPERIENCING THE WORD OF LIFE (vv. 1, 2)

1. That which was from the beginning, which we have heard, which we have seen with our eyes, which we have looked at and our hands have touched—this we proclaim concerning the Word of life.

This verse contains strong echoes of the first verses of the Gospel of John. In both places the apostle opens with an affirmation of the preexistence of Christ: He *was from the beginning*. When the universe was created and time began, he was already there. John identifies the Christ as *the Word of life,* combining his descriptions of *Word* (John 1:1) and *life* (John 1:4). These are strong statements of Jesus' deity.

Also important are John's eyewitness reports of the humanity of Jesus. Jesus was not a divine being who merely seemed to be human. John employs three of the five senses to confirm how humanly real Jesus was: John has *heard* him, *seen* him, and even *touched* him. These things are burned into John's memory, and he shares them freely with his readers.

2. The life appeared; we have seen it and testify to it, and we proclaim to you the eternal life, which was with the Father and has appeared to us.

John now explains further what he means when he calls Jesus the "Word of life" in verse 1. First, he describes him as *eternal life*. In Jesus we both find and receive eternal life. Jesus is life (John 11:25), and Jesus grants life (see John 10:28).

Second, true life cannot be found apart from a relationship with God *the Father.* One of the great promises of the Bible is that, in the end, we will be given renewed access to the tree of life that is in the presence of God (see Revelation 2:7). Believers, though, don't need to wait until Heaven to experience life. John wrote to assure us that Jesus brings us life in the here and now (John 20:31). By walking with Jesus, we will experience LIFE in all capital letters!

B. EXPERIENCING FELLOWSHIP (v. 3)

3. We proclaim to you what we have seen and heard, so that you also may have fellowship with us. And our fellowship is with the Father and with his Son, Jesus Christ.

Fellowship is the Greek word *koinonia.* This word has the sense of "mutual sharing." Fellowship is not a matter of being part of an audience. How much fellowship can you have with strangers while watching a movie in the theater? *Koinonia* fellowship involves closeness and caring. A church with this type of fellowship will have members who care about one another far beyond the casual, "How are you doing?" on Sunday morning.

John teaches us that fellowship in the church must exist on two levels. First, we must have fellowship with God. God has already initiated this. He has revealed himself through his prophets and, finally, through his Son (Hebrews 1:1, 2, last week's lesson). We can know the heart of God if we study the Scriptures.

Second, we will begin to have fellowship that is more authentic with fellow believers when we allow our relationship with God to flourish. We have much stronger mutual ties and learn to care for each other as God does. Christian fellowship, then, is experienced on both the vertical level (with God) and the horizontal level (with other believers).

C. EXPERIENCING JOY (v. 4)

4. We write this to make our joy complete.

John has no ulterior motives, no hidden agendas, in writing to his friends. He is seeking neither personal gain nor personal vindication over his critics. He simply wants his readers to experience the *joy* that comes from having a secure relationship with God. That result should control their relationship with others. This is the walk of fellowship. It is the abundant, joyous life (see John 10:10).

II. THE WALK IN THE LIGHT (1 JOHN 1:5-10)

Another powerful theme that 1 John shares with the Gospel of John is the image of Jesus as the light (see John 1:4; 8:12). Walking in his light implies two things for believers. First, it means that we walk without hiddenness, without private sin. We live with integrity, with no fear of public exposure of even the most intimate details of our lives. Darkness for John is equated with sin and ignorance. Walking in the light means we walk in truth and holiness.

Second, walking in the light means walking with God. God allows no darkness in his presence. The great barrier to walking with God, then, is sin. John outlines a two-part process to deal with sin: cleansing and confessing.

A. FULL CLEANSING (vv. 5-7)

5. This is the message we have heard from him and declare to you: God is light; in him there is no darkness at all.

We begin to understand personal spiritual cleansing by remembering that the cleanser (God) is without any taint of sin. John's image *God is light* means that

WHAT DO YOU THINK?

How has your relationship with God affected your relationship with other Christians thus far? Have you discovered that your relationship with others serves as a barometer of your relationship with God? Or is it more the other way around? Explain.

God is pure and holy in every possible way. We should not understand this as an exclusive, absolute statement that conflicts with John's other basic declarations about God. For example, John can say "God is light" here and "God is love" later (1 John 4:8), and both statements are completely true.

6. If we claim to have fellowship with him yet walk in the darkness, we lie and do not live by the truth.

The church always has had false believers among its members. These are the ones who claim to be God's children but engage in behaviors that God abhors. We, from our human perspective, cannot always tell who is a true believer and who is a false believer. Sometimes the person with many chronic and visible sin problems is struggling sincerely to change his or her life every day.

In other cases a person who presents the appearance of great righteousness and piety may be living a secret life of evil and disdain for God. For John this is the person walking *in the darkness.* His or her relationship with God is a sham as life is lived only for self. Jesus labeled such people hypocrites and reserved his strongest condemnation for them (see Mark 7:6). Elsewhere Jesus indicated that such evil persons may coexist with believers now, but they will be condemned at the time of judgment (Matthew 13:30).

7. But if we walk in the light, as he is in the light, we have fellowship with one another, and the blood of Jesus, his Son, purifies us from all sin.

John follows the discussion of the hypocrite with a message of hope for the one struggling with sin (and this includes every believer). This is not addressed to the nonbeliever.

How does the Christian deal with sin? First, we maintain a strong relationship with God, walking *in the light.* But, furthermore, we never lose sight of the fact that our sins have been paid for by *the blood of Jesus,* shed for us (see Revelation 1:5).

B. FULL CONFESSION (vv. 8-10)

8. If we claim to be without sin, we deceive ourselves and the truth is not in us.

It is unlikely that John is dealing with a hypothetical situation here. There apparently are false teachers trying to convince the church that they are completely *without sin.* We know this is not true, both from our experience and from God's Word. Even the strongest, most mature believers can stumble. Remember that Paul had to confront Peter over a matter of hypocrisy (Galatians 2:11-14).

9. If we confess our sins, he is faithful and just and will forgive us our sins and purify us from all unrighteousness.

John offers another key to how Christians can overcome sin problems. We must *confess our sins.* To confess means to acknowledge our sin before God. It means we are not comfortable with it, nor do we ignore it. We come to God and say, "What a wretched man I am! Who will rescue me from this body of death?" (Romans 7:24).

We acknowledge our sinfulness and our helplessness. God cleanses us, meaning he forgives us. We who are unrighteous are reckoned by God as righteous because of his cleansing power.

10. If we claim we have not sinned, we make him out to be a liar and his word has no place in our lives.

John now presents the most awful consequences of falsehood: if we deny our sinfulness, we are calling God *a liar.* We are saying that we don't need a Savior and that God didn't need to send Jesus to die for our sins. This is the complete, polar opposite of confessing our sins.

WHAT DO YOU THINK?

Think of some ways that light is used today that were not part of the daily life of John's contemporaries. How would you use these to illustrate how Jesus' light guides us today?

WHAT DO YOU THINK?

Although the blood of Christ purifies us from all sin, later verses remind us that we are sinful creatures. How do these two facts affect your relationship with God and with others?

III. THE WALK OF LOVE (1 JOHN 2:1-6)

Our lives as believers are to be controlled and characterized by love (John 13:35). When we truly understand what God has provided for us in Jesus, our lives will radiate his love to others.

A. JESUS OUR ADVOCATE (v. 1)

1. My dear children, I write this to you so that you will not sin. But if anybody does sin, we have one who speaks to the Father in our defense—Jesus Christ, the Righteous One.

We have another advantage when it comes to sin. In the heavenly court of judgment, we have the finest defense attorney available: Jesus our advocate.

AN ADVOCATE

It was a common practice in my neighborhood when I was a youngster. If you wanted to do something with some of the other kids and you believed Mom might not approve, you brought in one of the other kids to ask her, "We're going to ride our bikes over to the park. Can Johnny come with us?" You could ask her yourself, of course, but you knew you had a better chance of getting her approval if one of the other kids asked. We wanted someone to stand alongside us and speak our request to Mom.

The word *advocate* suggests a lawyer who represents someone in court. Such a one stands alongside, speaks to the judge, and argues the case. The picture that emerges out of all this is that Jesus is our defense attorney, so to speak.

Jesus pleads our case. As he does he stresses that we can go free with no penalty, because he has paid sin's price on the cross. He knows our desire to live right, but he also knows how poorly we have been able to do it. Yet in all this he faithfully represents our best interests. What an advocate we have!   —J. B. N.

B. JESUS OUR ATONING SACRIFICE (v. 2)

2. He is the atoning sacrifice for our sins, and not only for ours but also for the sins of the whole world.

John uses doctrinally heavy language to state a basic truth: Jesus is *the atoning sacrifice for our sins.* (The word for "atoning sacrifice" in more literal translations is *propitiation.*) In the doctrine of the atonement, God's penalty for our sins is paid by the sacrificial death of Jesus on the cross. The statement here is remarkably similar to the declaration of John the Baptist about Jesus: "Look, the Lamb of God, who takes away the sin of the world!" (John 1:29). See also 1 John 4:10.

C. JESUS OUR STANDARD (vv. 3-5)

3. We know that we have come to know him if we obey his commands.

A confused brother or sister may wonder, "Am I really a believer? Sometimes I doubt my own faith." John says the time for self-delusion is over. You know whether you are a believer by looking at your own life. Jesus said, "By their fruit you will recognize them" (Matthew 7:16). John says that you can know yourself by your actions as you *obey his commands.*

OBEYING COMMANDS

Some years ago a friend of mine mentioned an incident that had occurred in his family. His children had various chores they were to do around the house. His youngest son, Jimmy, was to take the garbage each evening and put it in the garbage can at the back of their yard. His mother usually wrapped it in a newspaper and placed it on the corner of the kitchen cabinet.

WHAT MESSAGE DO YOU SEND?

Visual for Lesson 3. *Point to the nativity scene that is "buried" behind the secular glitz. Ask your students if their Christmas is like this.*

PRAYER

Gracious and merciful God, thank you for loving us in spite of our sin. Thank you for being willing to allow us into your close fellowship despite our weaknesses. And thank you for cleansing us despite our spiritual filthiness. We pray in the powerful name of Jesus, your Son and our advocate in Heaven, amen.

One night Jimmy went out to play, and my friend asked his daughter, "Did Jimmy pick up the garbage?" She looked into the kitchen and noticed the garbage was still on the kitchen counter. My friend said, "Tell Jimmy to come back and get the garbage." She went to the back door and yelled out, "Jimmy, come back and get the garbage." Jimmy yelled back, "Who says so?" She replied, "Dad says so." Only at that point did Jimmy came back and pick up the garbage!

Jimmy had heard his sister's command, but there was no obedience because he did not respect her authority. When he understood whose authority lay behind the command, he obeyed readily. John says that if we know Jesus, we will obey his commands. Do we?

—J. B. N.

4, 5. The man who says, "I know him," but does not do what he commands is a liar, and the truth is not in him. But if anyone obeys his word, God's love is truly made complete in him. This is how we know we are in him:

Why do we *do what* God *commands*? Out of fear? To earn heavenly merit badges? No, there is only one valid reason: We follow God's will because we love him. Some children obey their parents primarily out of the fear of punishment. Other children obey primarily because they love their parents and do not want to disappoint them or hurt them.

To obey out of love is a godly motivation, for God loves us consistently at all times. When we truly appreciate God's great love, the enjoyment of sin grows less and less enticing. We are moving toward what John sees as perfect *love*. When we achieve this type of relationship with God, we no longer fear him (1 John 4:18).

D. JESUS OUR TRAILBLAZER (v. 6)

6. . . . Whoever claims to live in him must walk as Jesus did.

The section concludes by looking to the example of Jesus. When we don't know what to do, we should look at the pattern of Jesus' life. In this he is "the author and perfecter of our faith" (Hebrews 12:2). He has walked before us and shown us how to live.

CONCLUSION

Over a century ago Charles Sheldon penned the classic Christian novel *In His Steps*. The main character, a minister named Henry Maxwell, is confronted by an angry poor man who asks, "But what would Jesus do? Is that what you mean by following his steps?"

This challenge sets off a series of events that transforms a town because the people begin to ask themselves, "What would Jesus do in this situation?" They allow the answer to determine their decisions.

The "What Would Jesus Do?" fad passed through many churches a few years ago, accompanied by WWJD? wristbands and other paraphernalia. The question WWJD? doesn't always work because Jesus did some miraculous things that we cannot; Jesus even died on a cross to pay sin's price—something we cannot and need not do. But by and large the WWJD? phenomenon was a good thing. Even if it is now out of fashion, the question still is worth asking.

Are you willing to do what Jesus would do, to live as Jesus lived, to walk as Jesus walked? Are you willing to act in a manner that acknowledges Christ's presence in your life and let him be the controlling influence for your actions? This is the message of this lesson. When we do this, we are not automatically perfect. But we have yielded to God's conquering light in our lives, and we are truly walking with him.

WHAT DO YOU THINK?

Sometimes Christians talk about how they hope they are doing what Jesus wants them to do. John suggests our relationship with Christ should be built on knowledge rather than just hope. What are some steps you need to take to increase both your knowledge of Christ and your hope in him?

THOUGHT TO REMEMBER

Walking with Jesus means living with his presence in our lives.

Discovery Learning

This page contains an alternative lesson plan emphasizing learning activities. Classes desiring such student involvement will find these suggestions helpful. The next page is a reproducible activity page to further enhance discovery learning.

LEARNING GOALS

After participating in this lesson, each student will be able to:

1. Quote 1 John 1:8, 9 from memory.

2. Discuss the personal implications of what it means to walk as Jesus did.

3. Describe one way that he or she will walk as Jesus did.

INTO THE LESSON

As class members enter the room, blindfold each of them and tell them not to remove their blindfolds until asked to do so. Say that this experience is a part of today's lesson. Tell class members to find a place to sit (have a helper ready to assist with this) and to feel free to visit with the people around them.

While the students remain blindfolded, tell them that both darkness and blindness bring special challenges and dangers. Ask, "What has your experience of being blindfolded been like? Tell us what has happened to you." Also ask, "What are some of the dangers of not being able to see?"

Have students remove their blindfolds. Make the transition to Bible study saying, "The contrast between darkness and light is not only something that relates to seeing. In the Bible darkness and light are often metaphors for sin and righteousness. The phrase 'walking in the light' has its roots in Scripture and is the core of today's study."

INTO THE WORD

Before class begins hang four signs from the ceiling. Each sign will have one of the following headings: Appreciating Jesus; Rich Fellowship; Light and Darkness; Walking Like Jesus.

Begin the Bible study by reading the printed text. Tell the class that this text will be explored by looking at key phrases (these key phrases are also included in the student book). Ask class members to divide into study groups by standing underneath one of the signs hanging from the ceiling. Give each study group one set of the following printed instructions:

Group #1: Appreciating Jesus. Your task is to look at the following phrases from our text and to explain the significance of each. Be sure to read the entire text to glean information that will be helpful. Be prepared to share your conclusions with the class. The phrases are *That which was from the beginning* (1 John 1:1) and *The Word of life* (1 John 1:1, 2).

Group #2: Rich Fellowship. Your task is to look at the following phrases from our text and to explain the significance of each. Be sure to read the entire text to glean information that will be helpful. Be prepared to share your conclusions with the class. The phrases are *Fellowship with us . . . with the Father . . . with his Son* (1 John 1:3) and *Make our joy complete* (1 John 1:4).

Group #3: Light and Darkness. Your task is to look at the following phrases from our text and to explain the significance of each. Be sure to read the entire text to glean information that will be helpful. Be prepared to share your conclusions with the class. The phrases are *God is light,* and *In him there is no darkness* (1 John 1:5) and *Walk in the light* (1 John 1:7).

Group #4: Walking Like Jesus. Your task is to look at the following phrases from our text and to explain the significance of each. Be sure to read the entire text to glean information that will be helpful. Be prepared to share your conclusions with the class. The phrases are *Atoning sacrifice for our sins* (1 John 2:1, 2) and *Must walk as Jesus did* (1 John 2:3-6).

If time allows, you can have groups also work on one or both of the activities on the Reproducible Page.

Alternative activity. Prepare eight posters, each featuring one of the eight key phrases from the above group assignments. Affix the signs to the wall before you lead a discussion of each phrase in turn.

INTO LIFE

Prepare cloth ribbons to be used as wristbands. Use adhesive-backed hook-and-loop dots for fastening the wristbands. Also have numerous cloth markers available. Tell the class that today's text reminds us of the WWJD? ("What Would Jesus Do?") phenomenon. Have class members assemble their wristbands and write on them: "WWJD? Walk in the light!"

Ask class members to wear their wristbands for the week as reminders to walk faithfully and enjoy the light that God brings to life. (If you think your class members will resist wearing wristbands, make bookmarks instead.)

Walking in the Light

Every believer will agree with John that walking in the light is better than walking in darkness. Look for word clues in our text to show how to accomplish that walk in our lives. Write these key words in the two acrostics below. One example is given to get you started.

W   L

A   I

L   G

K   FellowsHip

                     T

The Atoning Blood

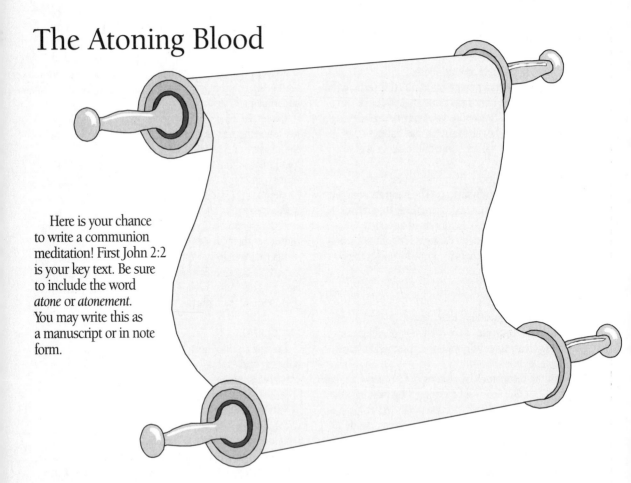

Here is your chance to write a communion meditation! First John 2:2 is your key text. Be sure to include the word *atone* or *atonement*. You may write this as a manuscript or in note form.

THE WORD BECAME FLESH

LESSON 4

WHY TEACH THIS LESSON?

How would you react if you saw an individual walking down the street and knew that it really was God, in human form, coming toward you? How do you think others would react? Would people just stare at him? Would they run to him? Would they run from him? What would people do?

Today's lesson does not ask us to imagine what it would be like if God walked and lived among us. It tells us that God did, in fact, walk and live among us. An even more profound truth lies behind this fact: if we open the door of our hearts, God will come to live inside of us.

INTRODUCTION

A. REJECTION

I once arrived in a distant city very late for a convention. After the usual hassle of departing the airport, I finally arrived at my assigned hotel near midnight. I had been up since before dawn and was dead tired. I gave the hotel clerk my name and waited as she clicked away on her computer. My heart sank, though, when she said, "I'm sorry, sir. I have no record of your reservation." This was not the reception I was hoping for or expecting!

The Bible teaches that God had a plan for redemption when the first human couple sinned and was expelled from the garden. God planned for this by preparing the nation of Israel to be the people who would receive his redeemer, his Son Jesus. Yet in one of the terrible ironies of history, this chosen people did not recognize their own promised Messiah. His reception was instead a rejection.

The apostle John begins his Gospel by putting the person and mission of Jesus into the perspective of a panoramic review of human history. This week's lesson looks at the first 18 verses of this great book. There John introduces his themes about Jesus from the broadest possible historical viewpoint.

B. JOHN'S TITLES FOR JESUS

The Gospel of John is a treasure trove for Christians who want to understand Jesus Christ more fully. Consider the many titles or descriptions that John uses in explaining Jesus. A brief survey of some of these could start with the designation of Jesus as *the Word*. This emphasizes the communication element in the nature of the Christ (John 1:1, 14; compare Revelation 19:13).

Second, John often describes Jesus as *the Son*, emphasizing his relationship with God. This takes several forms. He may be *the one and only Son* (John 3:16; compare 1 John 4:9), *the Son of God* (John 1:34, 49; compare 1 John 4:15), or *the Son of Man* (John 1:51; 12:23; compare Revelation 1:13). Third, John depicts Jesus as the Jewish Messiah. This may be simply as *the Christ* (John 1:41) or as *the King of Israel* (John 1:49; 12:13).

Fourth, we find Jesus as *the Lamb of God* (John 1:29, 36; compare Revelation 5:6), highlighting Jesus' role as the sacrifice for human sins. Fifth, the

DEVOTIONAL READING:
ISAIAH 53:1-6
BACKGROUND SCRIPTURE:
JOHN 1:1-34
PRINTED TEXT:
JOHN 1:1-18

Dec
24

LESSON AIMS

After participating in this lesson, each student will be able to:

1. List three of John's titles for Jesus.

2. Paraphrase John's explanation of Jesus' preexistence and incarnation.

3. Choose one personal behavior to transform from darkness to light.

KEY VERSE

The Word became flesh and made his dwelling among us. We have seen his glory, the glory of the One and Only, who came from the Father, full of grace and truth. —John 1:14

LESSON 4 NOTES

most dramatic title of Jesus is *Lord and . . . God* (John 20:28; compare Revelation 19:16), emphasizing his deity and sovereignty.

This is not an exhaustive list. You may want to study John's titles further by reading through the Gospel of John, looking only for the various ways the author portrays Jesus.

C. LESSON BACKGROUND

We have four Gospels in the New Testament that tell the story of Jesus. The first three Gospels (Matthew, Mark, and Luke) are very similar in their general structure. The fourth Gospel, John, is quite different from the other three. John wrote 30 or so years after those other three, and he was well acquainted with their material. For this reason he seems to avoid repeating most of their content. Instead, he chooses to give new information from his wealth of eyewitness recollections (see John 21:24, 25). About 90 percent of John's material is not found in the other three Gospels.

A significant difference among the four Gospels is the way the writers choose to begin their accounts. Mark begins with the ministry of John the Baptist, without any reference to the birth or childhood of Jesus. Luke begins with the birth of John the Baptist and includes the nativity story of Jesus. Matthew begins with Jesus' genealogy, thus pushing the story of Jesus back into the Old Testament.

John, for his part, pushes the story back to the very beginning of the Old Testament. Thus John's Gospel is an inclusive account of the entire sweep of human history, beginning before creation itself. Most of this is accomplished in John 1:1-18, the prologue of John. Today's lesson explores the issues of the doctrine of the incarnation. We will try to understand how God could assume a human form.

I. THE WORD BEGINNING THE WORLD (JOHN 1:1-3)

A. THE WORD FROM ETERNITY PAST (vv. 1, 2)

1, 2. In the beginning was the Word, and the Word was with God, and the Word was God. He was with God in the beginning.

John's opening statements retell the Genesis account of creation with an important addition: John includes the preexistent Christ. There are hints of the threefold nature of God in Genesis 1:26: "Let us make man in our image." But the relationship between God the Father and God the Son is not explored there.

In order to tell his story of Jesus more fully, this is where John must start. Genesis 1:1 begins, "*In the beginning* God." To this John adds three clarifications: (1) *the Word* was at the beginning, (2) this Word was in fellowship *with God*, and (3) the Word, in some way, *was God*. These three in combination give us enormous truths about Jesus.

WHAT DO YOU THINK?

We get our word logic *from* logos. *Yet there are many who would say that belief in Jesus is anything but logical. Why do they say this? How do you respond?*

We may begin by asking what exactly it means for John to describe the preexisting Christ as *the Word*. The Greek term behind this is *logos*. This was a well-known term in Greek philosophy, where it means something like "the ordering principle of the universe." The Greeks saw *logos* as that which caused the universe to hold together and make sense. It is from *logos* that we get our term *logic*.

While these ideas may touch some of John's Greek readers, this is probably not what he has in mind by using *logos*. For John logos is the creative Word of God. In Genesis God speaks the universe into existence (compare Psalm 33:6). God's Word is powerful and creative.

Also, there is no beginning for the Word. The preexistent Christ *is* the beginning (see Revelation 22:13). Just as Genesis begins creation with God already in place, so John starts his telling of the beginning with the Word already present.

John can say further that *the Word was God* while making a careful distinction between the Word and God. From a logical point of view, this seems curious: How can the Word be *distinct from* God, yet *be* God at the same time? Perhaps the best we can do is to say that there are three centers of consciousness in the Godhead (Father, Son, and Holy Spirit) and that these three share a single essence.

In any case, John expects us to believe that *the Word was God.* For John no other way of describing this will do. We must accept the truth of this relationship, even if it seems to strain our understanding. Remember: John walked side by side with Jesus. John knows what he is talking about!

IN THE BEGINNING

A friend once asked me, "Did you know that baseball is mentioned in the Bible?" I was rather dubious, so I asked him where. He replied, "The Bible says, 'In the big inning.'"

Poor humor aside, the first phrase in both the Gospel of John and Genesis is significant: In the beginning. The beginning—what an appropriate place to start! It's far better than the fairy tale introduction, "Once upon a time." A story that begins "once upon a time" actually means that it has no historical framework. There is no attempt to place it in context with other events.

The ancient world normally dated things by the year of the ruler (compare 1 Kings 6:1; Isaiah 6:1; Luke 3:1; etc.). Yet how would one refer to events before there were any rulers or when there was as yet no means of measuring time? In talking about the absolute beginning of things, the Bible writers do it very simply—in the beginning.

This is an acknowledgment that not only was God active in creation, he also preexisted before there was the concept of time, as did Christ. The Arian controversy in the fourth century AD wanted to make Christ less than God and so argued "there was when he was not." The other side responded with a double negative: "there was not when he was not." John puts it very simply—"In the beginning . . . the Word was with God." This is truth.   —J. B. N.

B. THE WORD AT CREATION (v. 3)

3. Through him all things were made; without him nothing was made that has been made.

John explicitly defines the Word's (that is, Christ's) role in creation. The Word is uncreated and is fully involved in creation. There is no created thing that exists apart from the Word's creative power. Paul wrote that creation is both a testimony to God (Romans 1:20) and waits for God's redemption (Romans 8:22).

II. THE WORD BRINGING LIGHT (JOHN 1:4-13)

A. SHINING LIGHT (vv. 4, 5)

4, 5. In him was life, and that life was the light of men. The light shines in the darkness, but the darkness has not understood it.

The Word does not become inactive when creation is completed. So John moves to the function of the Word as communication and enlightenment for humanity.

God's initial act of creation was to make *light* (Genesis 1:3). In so doing God separated light from *darkness.* Here light is the life-giving presence of God. Light is goodness, righteousness, and truth (see John 3:21). Darkness symbolizes evil, unrighteousness, and ungodliness (John 3:19).

WHAT DO YOU THINK?

John pointed to the creative ability of Jesus as a reason that we should believe in Him. What's the difference between human creativity and that of Jesus? How is this distinction important to your personal faith walk?

WHAT DO YOU THINK?

The apostle John chose to approach the study of Christ in a certain way. How and why should we adjust John's approach for today? Or should we leave well enough alone? Explain.

The word *understood* is a good translation, but other possible translations are "conquered" or "overcame." Jesus' mission among men and women was to rescue them from spiritual darkness (John 12:46).

LIGHT IN DARKNESS

Thomas Kinkade has become known as The Painter of Light. His paintings have become so popular that his name has become virtually a household word. Other than prints of the pictures themselves, his paintings adorn Christmas cards, greeting cards, book covers, and various other items. His web site claims that he is "America's most collected living artist."

Part of his attraction is his unabashedly Christian and family orientation. He credits Christ for the inspiration of many of his subjects as well as his talent to depict them. Nostalgic views of faith, hope, and familial warmth shine forth from his canvases. He pays tribute to his wife, Nanette, by hiding the letter *N* in many of his scenes. The names of his four daughters also show up in his work. He has donated his efforts to numerous charitable and religious organizations and has helped raise millions of dollars for their projects.

Central in all his paintings is some feature of light—be it old-fashioned streetlights, lighted windows, sunlight, or reflected light. One finds few darkened windows, brooding clouds, stormy landscapes, or tempestuous waves of emotion. Instead, the central features are calm, serene, restful, and heartwarming. While Norman Rockwell painted humorous and inspiring personality sketches, Kinkade specializes in idyllic scenes of town and country living—all delivered through an imaginative use of light. His works of art display the point that the apostle John makes: light will overcome the darkness.   —J. B. N.

B. WITNESS TO THE LIGHT (vv. 6-8)

6. *There came a man who was sent from God; his name was John.*

This *John* is John the Baptist, not John the apostle who writes this Gospel. We are told that John the Baptist was commissioned by God; he was not self-appointed. This puts him in the tradition of the great prophets of Israel (see Matthew 11:7-15; Luke 7:28).

7, 8. *He came as a witness to testify concerning that light, so that through him all men might believe. He himself was not the light; he came only as a witness to the light.*

Elsewhere Jesus describes John the Baptist as "a lamp that burned and gave light" (John 5:35). But he *was not the light,* the ultimate manifestation of God that was Jesus. John had a specific function: he was *a witness.* This means that he was to testify about Jesus, to be a reliable witness of his identity. When John the Baptist pointed out Jesus, some of John's own disciples followed him (John 1:35-37).

C. LIGHT IN THE WORLD (vv. 9-11)

9. *The true light that gives light to every man was coming into the world.*

John combines two of his most important concepts in this verse: truth and light. This helps us understand what the light imagery is all about. God is a God of light and truth, and he brings these into the created world to help men and women be "enlightened." This means he has not abandoned us to darkness. Instead he continues to create light to banish our dark world of sin. God's enlightened truth is our way out, our guide to how we should live (see John 8:12).

10, 11. *He was in the world, and though the world was made through him, the world did not recognize him. He came to that which was his own, but his own did not receive him.*

HOW TO SAY IT

Alexandria. Al-iks-AN-dree-uh.

Athens. ATH-unz.

Jerusalem. Juh-ROO-suh-lem.

logos (Greek). LAW-goss.

Messiah. Meh-SIGH-uh.

Nazarenes. NAZ-uh-reens.

Nazareth. NAZ-uh-reth.

Nicodemus. NICK-uh-DEE-mus.

prologue. PROH-lahg.

synagogue. SIN-uh-gog.

In terse words these verses depict the greatest irony of history: when visited by its creator, *the world* did not recognize him. It rejected him instead. The phrase *his own* refers to the nation of Israel, the people chosen by God to be the receiving nation for his Messiah.

Undoubtedly, Jesus did not meet many people's expectation of Messiah. He was not born in a king's palace, but in a stable. His parents were not rich and powerful, but young and poor. His early education was not at the great centers of learning such as Alexandria, Athens, or Jerusalem, but at the local synagogue. The real reason for the rejection, however, was not Jesus' humble human origins but spiritual blindness (Romans 11:25).

D. FAITHFUL RESPONSE TO THE LIGHT (vv. 12, 13)

12, 13. Yet to all who received him, to those who believed in his name, he gave the right to become children of God—children born not of natural descent, nor of human decision or a husband's will, but born of God.

Jesus' rejection was not universal, however. Even though the vast majority of Jews did not receive their Messiah, there were believers. The opposite of "did not receive him" in verse 11 is to believe *in his name*. In the ancient world the name of a person is symbolic of the full identity of that person. To trust a person fully, one might even adopt that person's name. This is seen when the early believers in Antioch take up the name *Christians* (Acts 11:26), meaning "one loyal to Christ."

The result of receiving and believing in Jesus is to be adopted by God. We become his children. We are reunited and reconciled with our creator. We become co-heirs with Jesus (Romans 8:17).

John introduces the concept of new birth at this point. Spiritually we *become* God's *children* by a rebirth. This is not any type of physical birth related to the conception of a child through normal means. This birth comes from God.

The idea of new birth comes up later in Jesus' conversation with Nicodemus. There Jesus says that without this new birth one "no one can see the kingdom of God" (John 3:3).

III. THE WORD BECOMING FLESH (JOHN 1:14-18)

A. INCARNATION OF THE WORD (v. 14)

14. The Word became flesh and made his dwelling among us. We have seen his glory, the glory of the One and Only, who came from the Father, full of grace and truth.

This verse is John's way of expressing what we call "the incarnation." It is the divine putting on *flesh*, God taking human form. This is a very difficult concept to understand, but it is vital for the Christian faith. It is only by becoming human that the Son of God could die for the sins of the world (Hebrews 2:14).

John and companions were witnesses to the *glory* of God in this regard. Jesus, the Son, reveals *the Father* in a way that allows Jesus to say that seeing him means seeing the Father (John 14:9). This is a vision of grace and truth, which is explained in the next verses.

B. REVELATION OF GRACE AND TRUTH (vv. 15-17)

15. John testifies concerning him. He cries out, saying, "This was he of whom I said, 'He who comes after me has surpassed me because he was before me.'"

John the Baptist's testimony is recorded here. What is important for this passage is John the Baptist's knowledge of Jesus' true identity. Jesus *was before* John

WHAT DO YOU THINK?

John 3:19 says that "men loved darkness instead of light because their deeds were evil." What was a time when you resisted Christ's light? What helped you change to prefer his light?

"The Word was made flesh."
—John 1:14

Visual for Lesson 4. *Point to this passage as you ask, "Why is John 1:14 important to the twenty-first century AD?"*

the Baptist, meaning that he existed before his incarnation. Therefore, John the Baptist knew well that Jesus deserved precedence over him in all things.

16. From the fullness of his grace we have all received one blessing after another.

John now expands upon one of the central concepts of the New Testament: *grace* (introduced in 1:14). *One blessing after another* conveys the image of gifts being piled upon one another endlessly. The grace that came through Jesus was not something we earned. It was given freely by the Father.

17. For the law was given through Moses; grace and truth came through Jesus Christ.

The *law* in mind here is the Jewish law, the various commandments *given through Moses*. Laws can result in doing the right thing with no relationship with the lawgiver. Thus, while the law is not bad, it does not do what *Jesus* does. Jesus allows us to become true children of God through faith, far beyond any attempts to earn God's favor by keeping his rules. Jesus is the true light of the world.

C. DECLARATION OF THE FATHER (v. 18)

18. No one has ever seen God, but God the One and Only, who is at the Father's side, has made him known.

This final verse of John's prologue sums up everything he has said so far. God exists far above any possibility of human perception and experience. There are a few Old Testament descriptions of people seeing a kind of manifestation of God (Genesis 32:30: Jacob "saw God face to face"; Exodus 24:11: "leaders of the Israelites . . . saw God"). But in a more profound sense *no one has ever seen God* because "You cannot see my face, for no one may see me and live" (Exodus 33:20).

Even so, God has revealed himself in a way that we can understand and believe. He has done this by Jesus, God in flesh, God's only *Son*. Jesus reveals God in a way that no other human ever could. Through Jesus we have access to God.

CONCLUSION

What is the amazing thing we call grace? While that word is common in Paul's writings, it is used only a few times in the Gospel of John (1:14-17). This word gets tossed around in many ways in the church. Some people seem to equate grace with the Holy Spirit, as supernatural power ("I was overcome by grace"). Others see it as the same as God's presence ("God's grace is in this place"). Still others associate it with a mealtime prayer ("Bow your heads while I say grace").

An old acronym for grace is helpful: God's Riches At Christ's Expense. But this only gives a partial sense of this rich concept. There are two essential components to a biblical concept of grace. First, it always denotes an element of "gift." It is never something we earn or deserve. Second, grace involves both attitude and action. God's grace means that God determined to do something beneficial; then he did it.

I have another acronym for grace (which, unfortunately, doesn't make a real word): BUA. This is Beautiful Undeserved Action. John tells us that everything about God's self-revelation in Jesus is gracious. We didn't deserve him. He is beautiful in ways we cannot even appreciate. The incarnation is a decisive act of enormous significance.

How much did it really cost God to sacrifice his Son? We cannot possibly know. But we can understand that this is not the way things normally work. Fathers don't usually sacrifice their sons for others. If anything, a father will sacrifice *for* his son. Yet God sent his Son to become a man and die on a cross to pay the price for sin. That is BUA grace!

Discovery Learning

This page contains an alternative lesson plan emphasizing learning activities. Classes desiring such student involvement will find these suggestions helpful. The next page is a reproducible activity page to further enhance discovery learning.

LEARNING GOALS

After participating in this lesson, each student will be able to:

1. List three of John's titles for Jesus.

2. Paraphrase John's explanation of Jesus' preexistence and incarnation.

3. Choose one personal behavior to transform from darkness to light.

INTO THE LESSON

Display three posters of multiple-choice questions. A religious Christmas card attached to each poster will help students connect the season with the activity. Give each student three colored, self-adhesive dots when entering the classroom. Ask students to stick a dot on each poster near or on the best answer for each question.

Poster #1. The word *Messiah* is the Hebrew form of (a) Christ, meaning "creator-God"; (b) Christ, meaning "anointed one"; (c) Christ, meaning "redeemer"; (d) a song written by a man named Handel.

Poster #2. The word *incarnation* refers to (a) God becoming a man; (b) the virginity of Mary when giving birth to Jesus; (c) another name for communion; (d) a nation with lots of cars.

Poster #3. Immanuel means (a) "redeemer"; (b) "anointed one"; (c) "God with us"; (d) "God against us."

After the class members have made their choices by placing stickers on the posters, review each question. Give the correct answer and comment on the significance of each.

The answer to question #1 is *b.* Ask, "What does the title *Messiah* tell us about Jesus—his nature and mission?" The answer to question #2 is *a.* Say, "The incarnation is a difficult concept. Today's text, however, enthusiastically explains this key to understanding Jesus' identity and origin." The answer to question #3 is *c.* Say, "The title *Immanuel* was introduced in Isaiah 7:14, teaching us even more about the nature of Jesus."

Transition to Bible study by stating that these and other titles given to Jesus in the Gospel of John help us know our God and Savior better.

INTO THE WORD

Begin this section of study with a brief lecture on some titles given to Jesus in the Gospel of John. Also touch on the purpose of John's Gospel. On the board or overhead write "Titles for Jesus." As you speak, write some titles as found in the lesson Introduction. Give a brief explanation of each.

Next read today's printed text. Then ask the discussion questions that follow. You may wish to announce the focus of each group of questions. (These questions are also in the student book; this can be a small-group activity, one group per Focus.)

Focus: Jesus as the Word (John 1:1-5): (1) Why do you think John chose to call Jesus "the Word"? (2) What truths do verses 1-5 teach us about the nature of Jesus? (3) Why do you think John chose this way to introduce Jesus rather than beginning with Jesus' birth?

Focus: Jesus as the Light (John 1:6-13): (1) Why do you think John chose to insert John the Baptist into these verses? (2) What do verses 10-13 teach us about how people respond to Jesus? What comfort or challenge does this bring to your life? (Option: if using the focus exercises for the class as a whole, you can work in the My Christmas Bumper Sticker! activity from the Reproducible Page at this point.)

Focus: Jesus in the Flesh (John 1:14-18): (1) What are some of the implications of the incarnation—of God becoming a man? (2) What do you think is the main point of this passage of Scripture? (3) Why is the story of the incarnation precious to Christians at this time of year?

INTO LIFE

Point to the three posters used at the beginning of class as you remind students that they have discovered a new and rich appreciation for words such as Immanuel, incarnation, Messiah. Say, "What happened was nothing less than God becoming flesh. This is our time to use that fact to help us walk more closely with him."

Ask the class to work in teams of two or three to write an acrostic. This acrostic will provide some steps that will help change personal behavior from darkness to light, based on the word Messiah.

Give each team a poster board and marker with the letters to the word Messiah written vertically. Examples for the first three letters could be Maintain personal holiness, Expect God's blessings, and Spend time in prayer.

If time allows, distribute the Christmas Blessings activity from the Reproducible Page for students to work on.

My Christmas Bumper Sticker!

After reading today's printed text, create a bumper sticker that will help teach non-Christians a little bit about Jesus. Use either the word *Light* or *Life* in your bumper sticker. You may use up to two lines, but for bumper stickers the briefer the better!

Christmas Blessings

Today's text holds wonderful words that have blessed all of Christendom. After each of the phrases printed below, write two or three of the blessings that have come to us through the fulfillment of those words.

The Word was God (v. 1)

The light shines in the darkness (v. 5)

Children of God (v. 12)

The Word became flesh (v. 14)

We have seen his glory (v. 14)

The fullness of his grace (v. 16)

HUMILIATION AND EXALTATION

WHY TEACH THIS LESSON?

Cast the words *humiliation* and *exaltation* against a backdrop of modern culture, and certain images will leap out. Most so-called "reality" TV shows are about humiliation as people are "voted off," "fired," etc. Exaltation is what happens to the few who make it all the way to the end of such artificial experiences. The fact that audiences revel (or wallow) in such shows points to a need for a biblical understanding of humiliation and exaltation.

The lesson today will teach us just that. As we consider the example of Christ, we will come to understand what humiliation and walking in humility really mean. Followers of Christ are to live lives of humility—lives of humble submission, obedience, and service to and for Christ. Christ will, in his own time, exalt us to the place he desires us to be in.

INTRODUCTION

A. SERVANT LEADERSHIP

I was recently shopping in a "big box" retail store for an electronics item. I briefly overheard three young employees of the establishment discussing an employee meeting that had been held that morning. They were making fun of the concept of "servant leadership," which apparently had been stressed at this meeting. As one put it, "If they think I'm here to serve customers, they're crazy. I'm just here for a paycheck until I can find something better." This got a good laugh of agreement from the other two.

Some retail establishments have found that a way to thrive is by offering fabulous customer service. A large department store chain where I live has been practicing this policy for years and is legendary for its customer service. It does not have the best prices, but loyal customers flock to this store because they are always treated with courtesy and respect. There is no hassle for a return or a special order, and salespeople go out of their way to please customers.

While most people enjoy being served, to be a servant is another matter! Modern society has demeaned the role of servant. Young people rarely aspire to be career servants. They all want to be boss. Even in the church we have allowed a "serve me" culture to dominate in many congregations. The paid church staff is under enormous pressure to provide many types of services for the members. Worship services sometimes degenerate into entertainment, with an audience that must be pleased. If a church is providing inadequate services, members may go elsewhere or cut down on their giving.

Yet the church, as a whole and individually, is tasked with cultivating a "mind of Christ." This is an attitude of service, of valuing others more than self. Today's lesson seeks to understand how Jesus can be Lord of all yet servant of all.

DEVOTIONAL READING:

1 PETER 3:8-12

BACKGROUND SCRIPTURE:

PHILIPPIANS 2:1-11

PRINTED TEXT:

PHILIPPIANS 2:1-11

Dec
31

LESSON AIMS

After participating in this lesson, each student will be able to:

1. Tell of ways that Christ humbled himself.

2. Discuss how Christ's humility gave way to his exaltation.

3. Identify one specific area in which he or she will adopt an attitude of service to others.

KEY VERSE

Do nothing out of selfish ambition or vain conceit, but in humility consider others better than yourselves. —*Philippians 2:3*

B. LESSON BACKGROUND

Philippians is an unusual letter for Paul. Unlike most of his other writings, he was not writing to defend himself from attacks or to combat major doctrinal errors. Instead, it has been called "Paul's joy letter" because of his frequent use of the terms *joy* and *rejoice*. This peaks when Paul commands his readers to "Rejoice in the Lord always. I will say it again: Rejoice!" (Philippians 4:4), one of the best-loved verses of all Scripture.

The historical circumstances behind the letter help us to understand Paul's upbeat spirit. Paul had founded the Philippian church on his second missionary journey (Acts 16:11-40). Philippi was an important Roman city in the province of Macedonia.

Unlike most large Roman cities, Philippi had a very tiny Jewish population. The Bible doesn't say that Paul was able to locate a synagogue in Philippi when he visited that city. This leads us to presume that no synagogue existed there. Instead, he found a group of faithful Jewish women that included a prominent merchant named Lydia. We believe that Lydia became a close ally of Paul, and that the Philippian church met in her home. Acts also tells the dramatic story of Paul and Silas being thrown into the Philippian jail and gaining release through God's miraculous intervention.

The result was the conversion and befriending of the Gentile warden of the Philippian jail. Paul was asked to leave the city by the Philippian authorities, but he left behind a strong group of friends and fellow believers. His relationship with this congregation was in no way strained, so much so that he could begin the letter by saying, "I thank my God every time I remember you" (Philippians 1:3).

Paul wrote Philippians while he was imprisoned. The Philippian congregation became aware of Paul's circumstances and sent one of its trusted young men, Epaphroditus, to assist the apostle personally. This young man fell ill and nearly died (Philippians 2:25-30).

Paul sent Epaphroditus back to the Philippian church with a letter that expressed deep thanks for their long-time support of his ministry (Philippians 4:15, 16). Paul was unable to bless them financially but instead gave them a marvelous letter full of wonderful statements of faith. As a result, the verses from Philippians are among the most popular for Scripture memorization (examples: Philippians 1:6, 21; 2:5; 3:7, 10, 14; 4:4, 7, 13).

One of the gems of this book is known as the Philippian Hymn (Philippians 2:6-11). As with the Christ Hymn in Colossians 1:15-20 (see the first lesson of this quarter), we can imagine Paul teaching this song to the new Christians at Philippi nearly a decade earlier. This hymn is full of beautiful and profound information concerning our Lord Jesus Christ.

I. THE MIND OF CHRIST (PHILIPPIANS 2:1-5)

A. ATTITUDE OF UNITY (vv. 1, 2)

1. *If you have any encouragement from being united with Christ, if any comfort from his love, if any fellowship with the Spirit, if any tenderness and compassion,*

Paul begins this section with four rhetorical *if*-statements. These are rhetorical in the sense that Paul does not question whether these things are true but wants his readers to ponder them for a moment. Can we find *encouragement* in knowing Christ? Yes. Can we find *comfort from his love*? Yes. Can we find sweet *fellowship* through the Holy *Spirit* with God and other believers? Yes. And are we blessed recipients of *any tenderness and compassion* from God? Yes.

Paul uses four rhetorical "if-statements" to depict an attitude of unity. Which of the four do you find most helpful personally? Why? What other phrases would you use to describe your relationship to the Lord?

2. . . . then make my joy complete by being like-minded, having the same love, being one in spirit and purpose.

Paul is hundreds of miles away from his beloved Philippian brothers and sisters. But there is still something they can do to bring him great *joy*: they can be united in their thinking and controlled by a spirit of love. Paul is leading up to the great uniting factor: everyone trying to be like Christ. Unity is not achieved when we try to copy each other. In that case the strongest example will prevail temporarily but may change quickly and create ongoing disunity. True, lasting unity comes when all copies are made from an ultimate, unchanging pattern. For the church this pattern is Christ.

B. ATTITUDE OF SERVANTHOOD (vv. 3, 4)

3. Do nothing out of selfish ambition or vain conceit, but in humility consider others better than yourselves.

Why do we do the things we do? Almost any action has an underlying motivation. Why do we mow our lawns? One man does it because he loves things to be neat and tidy. Another man does it because he is afraid his neighbors will speak negatively of him if his home looks unkempt. A third man does it because that's the way his dad taught him, and he still wants to do things to please his father.

Paul uses the phrases *selfish ambition* and *vain conceit* to describe improper motives. The meanings of these two words overlap to a great degree. The combined idea is to avoid doing things out of motivation of selfish recognition. Self-aggrandizement is just that! The Bible has a lot to say about the dangers of pride (examples: Proverbs 8:13; 11:2; 13:10; 14:3; 16:18; 29:23). Conceit brought down some high and mighty rulers in the Bible (Daniel 4:28-33; Acts 12:21-23). Church leaders must resist those who push personal agendas at the expense of the long-term health of the body of Christ.

Then Paul gives a single motivation for correct actions: we should do things out of our esteem for others, placing their interests above our own. I was once talking to an older Christian man about changes in worship style. I sensed that he was not happy about the direction his church had taken. I asked him, provocatively, "What do you think about having drums in worship?"

For a moment his countenance was angry, and he admitted, "I hate the drums." Then his face softened; he smiled and said, "But if that's what we need to reach young people for Jesus, I'll put up with drums." He was considering *others better than* himself.

ESTEEMING OTHERS

Charles Dickens's classic *A Tale of Two Cities* centers on the figure of Sydney Carton, a drunken, listless attorney who helps acquit Charles Darnay of a mistaken charge of treason. Both wind up in love with Lucie Manette. But Carton steps aside when he realizes that he has nothing to offer her, and that she loves Darnay anyway.

At the height of the French Revolution, they are all in Paris. There Darnay is arrested because of crimes committed by his father and uncle. Convicted by the revolutionary court, he is sentenced to death by guillotine. Carton, who bears an uncanny resemblance to Darnay, trades places with him in prison so that Darnay, Lucie, and their family can escape. Carton then goes to the guillotine and dies in the place of Darnay.

The story is filled with the themes of unjust retribution as well as the redemption of the self-deprecating Carton. In essence he esteemed others better than he esteemed himself. Paul encourages the same attitude in the Philippians. Indeed,

WHAT DO YOU THINK?

Wouldn't it be great if those in the church were always of one mind! What are some things that cause dissonance within the church? What actions can we take to keep dissonance and disunity from gaining a foothold?

WHAT DO YOU THINK?

Well-intentioned counselors often equate good psychological health with certain assertive behaviors. How does verse 3 help you respond to this kind of philosophy?

"Be like-minded, having the same love, being of one accord, of one mind."
—Philippians 2:2

Visual for Lesson 5. *Point to this visual as you ask, "How can acts of service demonstrate that we are like-minded?"*

the fictional Carton's self-sacrifice bears a resemblance to what Jesus did. Dickens had a make-believe character gave up his life to save the earthly life of a friend; God sent his only Son to give up his life to save us for eternity. Do you live each day with that fact in view? —J. B. N.

4. Each of you should look not only to your own interests, but also to the interests of others.

Our motivations must extend beyond the desire to avoid offending others. We must truly look out for *the interests of others,* even though they may be at odds with our own interests. In the church this can be difficult. Should we spend our limited funds to hire a youth minister or a senior citizens minister? Should we be funding our church's own food pantry or the local food bank? Paul gives his answer in the next verse.

C. ATTITUDE OF CHRIST (v. 5)

5. Your attitude should be the same as that of Christ Jesus:

All of our attitudes should be patterned after the attitudes of *Jesus.* This is why it is important to study his life; that is the only way to understand what he did.

This is a consistent message in Paul's writings. Earlier Paul warned the Christians in Rome not to "conform" to the selfish ways of the world. Instead, they were to be "transformed" by having new minds, minds that were in line with the mind of Christ (Romans 12:2). He told the Corinthian church that even though Christ in Heaven was rich beyond all measure, he became poor for our sakes (2 Corinthians 8:9).

II. THE HYMN TO CHRIST (PHILIPPIANS 2:6-11)

A. CHRIST'S PREEXISTENCE (v. 6)

6. Who, being in very nature God,
    did not consider equality with God something to be grasped,

Many newer translations such as the *New International Version* format this section as poetry, attempting to give the sense of how it may have been used in worship. The hymn begins with an affirmation of Jesus' divine status before he came to earth as a man. He was like *God* in both *nature* and *equality.*

The seeming paradox of the nature of the Godhead is present here: Jesus is both distinct from God and at the same time equal to God. This verse is not talking about two equally powerful gods who are united only in purpose, a thought that might be at home in Greek philosophy. There is equality between the Father and the Son.

B. CHRIST'S INCARNATION (vv. 7, 8)

7. . . . but made himself nothing,
    taking the very nature of a servant,
    being made in human likeness.

The hymn now gives us one of the most profound explanations of the incarnation in all of Scripture. *Made himself nothing* is literally "emptied himself." Christ debased himself. Why? The answer has been given already: he esteemed others (us) more important than himself.

Another insight into the significance of the incarnation is that Jesus ministered to others as *a servant*—literally, a slave. A slave is someone with no rights and is considered to be property of the master. Jesus, the King of kings, did not come as a conqueror. Instead he taught that the way to be great in the kingdom of God was to be the servant of all (Mark 10:44).

This was a prophesied role for the Messiah. Isaiah said that Jesus would be "despised and rejected by men" (Isaiah 53:3). This reflects the ancient attitude towards slaves. They were looked down upon as the lowest rung of the ladder of humanity. We see the servant attitude of Jesus in his final meal with his disciples. At this dinner Jesus himself took on the role of a household slave and washed the feet of all present, a demeaning and odious task (John 13:14).

8. And being found in appearance as a man,
    he humbled himself
      and became obedient to death—even death on a cross!

The hymn moves to Jesus' *death on a cross,* the ultimate act of servanthood and self-sacrifice. Jesus died an innocent man, guilty of no crime. His crucifixion was not an act of triumph or strength in a human sense. It was an act of self-humiliation and weakness (see 2 Corinthians 13:4). Even on the cross, Jesus could have rescued himself by summoning legions of angel warriors (see Matthew 26:53). Instead, he chose not to assert his equality with God but died for our sins (1 Corinthians 15:3).

C. CHRIST'S EXALTATION (vv. 9-11)

9. Therefore God exalted him to the highest place
    and gave him the name that is above every name,

The crucifixion was therefore necessary, and it required that Christ become human and submit obediently to this horrible, unjust death. That was not the end of the story, however. God honored Jesus, first by raising him from the dead (Acts 2:32) and then by exalting him to God's right hand, a position of honor and authority (Acts 2:33). He has a position unchallenged and unequaled by any other: King of kings and Lord of lords (1 Timothy 6:15; Revelation 19:16).

HIGHLY EXALTED

Mark Twain's novel *The Prince and the Pauper* tells the story of Tom Canty and Edward Tudor. Tom was born into poverty; Edward was born into the royal family, the son of King Henry VIII, and was the heir to the kingdom. Becoming acquainted in a chance meeting, the boys traded clothes, and circumstances soon traded their experiences. Edward, dressed in Tom's rags, was thrust from the palace; Tom, dressed in Edward's finery, dwelt in luxury.

Edward soon experienced the deprivation of the impoverished. Beaten, starved, and humiliated, he learned what it was like to become part of the urban poor. Through various experiences he discovered how the other side of England lived. When Henry VIII died, Edward was able to make himself known and was placed on the throne as king. From barely existing in the lowest levels of poverty, he was exalted to the highest station in the kingdom.

Although Jesus was in quite different circumstances, the change in his position also was startling. He gave up his position in Heaven to live in economic poverty on earth. He became poor (2 Corinthians 8:9). Living as a man among men, he came to know firsthand our struggles and failures. He was beaten, humiliated, and even crucified. Yet God took Jesus from that lowly position, raised him from the dead, highly exalted him, and restored him to his rightful place in Heaven. This is the one we serve.

—J. B. N.

10, 11. . . . that at the name of Jesus every knee should bow,
    in heaven and on earth and under the earth,
   and every tongue confess that Jesus Christ is Lord,
    to the glory of God the Father.

WHAT DO YOU THINK?

The ultimate test of Jesus' humility came as he submitted to the atrocities leading to the cross. How will you use Jesus' humility as a model in your own life?

WHAT DO YOU THINK?

Before Jesus' exaltation to the right hand of the Father, he led an earthly life of humility. What are one or two specific things you will do this week to model that humility?

HOW TO SAY IT

Corinthians. Ko-RIN-thee-unz.

Epaphroditus. Ee-PAF-ro-DYE-tus.

Gentile. JEN-tile.

Lydia. LID-ee-uh.

Macedonia. Mass-eh-DOE-nee-uh.

Philippi. Fih-LIP-pie or FIL-ih-pie.

Philippians. Fih-LIP-ee-unz.

synagogue. SIN-uh-gog.

PRAYER

Loving God, help us to begin the new year with a deeper desire to serve you by serving others. May your Spirit always be working within us to remake our minds to be like the mind of our Lord Jesus Christ. We pray this in his name, the name above all names, amen.

THOUGHT TO REMEMBER

Submitting to the lordship of Jesus means we are willing to humble ourselves and serve others.

The implications of Jesus' exaltation are now given. First, every created being, whether in the physical realm or the spiritual realm, will *bow* before *Jesus*. We should understand this bowing as more than a mere act of respect or courtesy. It is an act of worship (see Revelation 5:14). The Bible teaches that worship is for God and God alone (see Revelation 22:9). For the hymn to envision universal worship of Jesus is a strong affirmation of his deity.

Second, the worshiping will be accompanied by a confession. This word *confess* is sometimes misunderstood. This is not a confession of our sins or crimes. It is confession in the sense of acknowledgment, a statement of strong and passionate belief. All creatures, including all men and women, thus will acknowledge that Jesus is indeed the *Lord*. The saved will do so gladly, eagerly. The unsaved will have no choice; resistance will be futile. The truth that they rejected in their earthly lives will be all too clear, to their eternal disgrace.

CONCLUSION

Have you ever heard a tune that stuck in your head for days? Every time I visit a certain famous theme park and ride a particular ride, I am haunted by a song about a "small world" for days. But I still do it because I enjoy the ride.

What makes us think the way we do? How do certain thoughts (or tunes) get stuck in our minds? Why do we think some things to be trivial and other things to be important? What causes us to care about some things and ignore other things? To push this even further, why do we sometimes have thoughts we don't want to have (or, at least, that we regret later)?

"The unwanted thought" seems to be part of the human condition. We get angry and think terrible things about an irritating coworker. Later, though, we may be ashamed at what we thought. We see an attractive person and our minds flash inappropriately. Later we are ashamed for thinking that way. We lose patience with our spouse and blame him or her for our inadequacies. Later, when we reflect, we are ashamed of such thoughts and appreciate this person deeply.

Paul speaks elsewhere about taking every thought captive to make it obedient to Christ (2 Corinthians 10:5). What he means is that we must make Jesus the Lord of our thought life. Our minds are not fortresses of solitude where Jesus is not welcome. If he is truly our Lord, then our minds must be open to his presence without shame or fear.

How can we accomplish this on a practical level? The Philippian Hymn outlines a very clear strategy: we begin to think like Jesus. This does not mean we try to imagine what we would do if we were the King of kings as he is. It means we look for ways to serve others. We think of how we can help others, not just help ourselves.

Jesus declared that he came to serve, not to be served (Matthew 20:28). When we adopt this attitude, we have made a giant leap toward adopting the mind of Christ. Paul described this attitude as the difference between being sinfully minded and having a "mind controlled by the Spirit" (Romans 8:6). Those thoughts that cause us to be ashamed will not be welcome in the mind that is set on Christ and acknowledging his presence.

How can you improve your thought life in the new year ahead? Are there things you need to avoid, things that pull you from having your mind open to Jesus? Specifically is there an area in your church or family life where you have been selfish? Take a minute to think of a concrete example; then be resolved to eliminate this unchristlike attitude by fixing your mind on Jesus and adopting the desire to serve others rather than to be served.

Discovery Learning

This page contains an alternative lesson plan emphasizing learning activities. Classes desiring such student involvement will find these suggestions helpful. The next page is a reproducible activity page to further enhance discovery learning.

LEARNING GOALS

After participating in this lesson, each student will be able to:

1. Tell of ways that Christ humbled himself.

2. Discuss how Christ's humility gave way to his exaltation.

3. Identify one specific area in which he or she will adopt an attitude of service to others.

INTO THE LESSON

Before class begins, cluster the classroom chairs into groupings of two to five chairs. Prepare one slip of paper for each group with the phrase, Why We Do the Things We Do. Also write one of the following categories on each slip: mow the lawn; paint the house; get a college degree; clean and wax the car; buy new clothes; take a family trip. (Feel free to shrink or expand the list based on class size.)

Tape one slip of paper underneath a chair in each group. Write *Why We Do the Things We Do* on the board or overhead.

At the beginning of class, ask each group to pick a "scribe" to take notes for their group and to be ready to report. At your signal each group will find the slip of paper taped under one of its chairs. They then will have only two minutes to create a list of the reasons or motivations for accomplishing the task written on their paper. After two minutes only the group with the longest list will be allowed to share its list with the class.

Make the transition to Bible study by saying, "The kind of motivation and the strength of motivation we have for a task often determines what we do and how well we do it. God calls us to a task that is often difficult to accept or understand in a world that encourages us to be self-serving. God calls us to be servants as well as to be leaders. To accomplish that commission of being servant-leaders, we need to understand motivation: why Christians do (or should do) the things we do."

INTO THE WORD

The class will continue to work in their groups. Have one of your good readers read the entire text aloud; then give each team one of the following group assignments.

Team #1: Attitude of Unity (Philippians 2:1, 2). Paul begins this passage on servant-leadership with four "if-statements." While the statements are rhetorical in nature, we know that Paul wants us to think about these truths. Examine verses 1 and 2; summarize your interpretation and application for the rest of the class.

Team #2: Attitude of Servanthood and of Christ (Philippians 2:3-5). Your group will address the theme "why we do the things we do." Paul lists reasons why not to do things in church while also telling us what to do. Discover what Paul teaches about motivation for servant-leadership and give examples of why these actions/attitudes are or are not important.

Team #3: Christ's Preexistence (Philippians 2:6). Your task is to examine one portion of this hymn and interpret its significance for the rest of the class. Keep in mind the hymn's theme of servant-leadership.

Team #4: Christ's Incarnation (Philippians 2:7, 8). Your task is to examine one portion of this hymn and interpret its significance for the rest of the class. Keep in mind the hymn's theme of servant-leadership.

Team #5: Christ's Exaltation (Philippians 2:9-11). Your task is to examine one portion of this hymn and interpret its significance for the rest of the class. Keep in mind the hymn's theme of servant-leadership.

Allow time for each group to report its conclusions. With five groups you will need to keep the reports somewhat brief. If you have a small class, double up some assignments. (Alternative: have each group do the same task by distributing the Heart Medicine—Key Words! activity from the Reproducible Page.)

INTO LIFE

Ask and discuss these questions with the entire class:

1. Why and how is the concept of servant-leadership of value in the business world?

2. What do those "business world values" teach us about why servant-leadership is good for the church and for Christians—or is the teaching the other way around? Explain.

3. What project or class activity could we do together that demonstrate servant-leadership?

Following discussion of the last question, select an activity and assign a planning team; then make that activity happen in the near future. Close the class in a devotional manner by having each student complete the Heart Exercises! activity from the Reproducible Page.

Heart Medicine—Key Words!

The heart is often considered to be the seat of attitudes and values. Paul reminds us that our "attitude should be the same as that of Christ Jesus" (Philippians 2:5). The question, of course, is how do I develop a heart or attitude like Jesus? Search Philippians 2:1-11 for clues. Write the words or phrases you discover in the heart below.

Heart Exercises!

Let Paul's encouragement to become a servant-leader meddle in your daily life. First, identify at least three possible, practical ways you can demonstrate servant-leadership. Second, place a checkmark by one way you wish to demonstrate servant-leadership within the next few days. Then, in the box at the right, outline the steps you must take to accomplish that goal.

Let's see . . . three ways I can demonstrate servant leadership are:

1. _____

2. _____

3. _____

Steps to Take:

"I AM FROM ABOVE"

LESSON 6

WHY TEACH THIS LESSON?

Every parent knows that no matter how much freedom a child is given, he or she will want more! Balancing the enjoyment of freedom with responsible, godly living is a lifelong challenge. Two old clichés are true: freedom isn't free, and with freedom comes responsibility.

In Christ we have freedom. But this freedom isn't free. Our spiritual freedom cost Christ his life. Our responsibility is to be slaves to the freedom and the righteousness that he purchased for us. As you move through this lesson, reflect on the freedom you have in Christ. Rejoice in it! But also remember the price paid for this freedom. As you do so, consider what price you are willing to pay to prove that you remain in him.

INTRODUCTION

A. SLAVES TO SIN

Ron is a longtime Christian who worked for many years as an information technology director for a large company. His boss and coworkers admired his dedication, honesty, and integrity. One day, however, Ron was called to his supervisor's office to be told that he was being fired for violating the company's "fair use" policy: a colleague had discovered a huge number of pornographic images stored in Ron's computer.

Ron confessed that he had become addicted to Internet porn. His technical expertise had enabled him able to hide the files for some time. Ironically Ron had become aware of Internet porn while investigating other employees, several of whom had been fired for similar violations. Ron lost his job but saved his marriage and family by confessing his sin and seeking counseling. He told his counselor that he was glad he had been caught because he had felt for a long time that the porn had taken control of him.

Ron's situation illustrates the irony of addiction to sinful habits: we fear the loss of short-term gratification if we quit, but at the same time we fear the long-term consequences if we don't. This is true not only of "high profile" sins such as pornography and drug abuse, but also of more common sins like anger, gossip, and lying. Once we develop a habit of doing the wrong thing, it becomes very difficult to change on our own. In our lesson today Christ offers us freedom from the power of sin and the fear of death.

B. LESSON BACKGROUND

The events and teachings recorded in John 7 and 8 occurred during one of Jesus' visits to the Feast of Tabernacles in Jerusalem (see John 7:1, 2, 37; 8:20). God instituted this festival for two reasons. First, it was a time of thanksgiving during the season of the olive and fruit harvests (the September–October time frame). Second, it was as a time to remember deliverance from slavery in Egypt (see Leviticus 23:33-44).

DEVOTIONAL READING:
JOHN 14:23-31
BACKGROUND SCRIPTURE:
JOHN 8:31-59
PRINTED TEXT:
JOHN 8:31-38, 48-56, 58, 59

LESSON AIMS

After participating in this lesson, each student will be able to:

1. List some reasons people rejected Jesus.

2. Explain the concepts of spiritual slavery and freedom.

3. Move from slavery to freedom through Jesus in one area of thought or habit.

Jan
7

KEY VERSE

To the Jews who had believed him, Jesus said, "If you hold to my teaching, you are really my disciples. Then you will know the truth, and the truth will set you free."
—John 8:31, 32

LESSON 6 NOTES

As something of an object lesson, many who celebrated this festival would live in tents ("tabernacles") outside the city to reenact the 40 years that the Israelites had lived in tents while wandering in the wilderness. It is against this backdrop of deliverance from physical bondage that Jesus proceeds to demonstrate the way to deliverance from spiritual bondage.

I. ABOUT THE JEWS' STATUS (JOHN 8:31-38)

A. DISCIPLESHIP AND TRUTH (vv. 31, 32)

31. To the Jews who had believed him, Jesus said, "If you hold to my teaching, you are really my disciples.

The word *Jews* seems somewhat out of place here because both Jesus and John (the author of this Gospel) are Jews by race, culture, and religion. Why would a Jewish person refer to other Jewish people as "Jews," as though they were somehow different from himself?

Scholars generally see this unusual terminology as evidence that John had been persecuted by Jewish people by the time he writes, just as Jesus had predicted (John 16:1-4). The story of the blind man in chapter 9 reveals that this sort of persecution already had begun during Jesus' ministry (see especially John 9:22).

Here at John 8:31 we see that some Jewish people have gone against the grain and have taken a positive view of Jesus. These are the ones *who had believed him* (see also v. 30). Jesus proceeds to test their faith by stressing that they must accept his teachings if they wish to be *disciples*. The verses to follow will reveal that they are not quite ready for that level of commitment.

32. "Then you will know the truth, and the truth will set you free."

Truth refers back to Jesus' "teaching" in verse 31, which he now says will give freedom to believers. The context reveals that John is not referring to Jesus' ethical commands about lifestyle issues (the Gospel of John actually includes very little of that sort of teaching). In John 8:12-29 Jesus has been speaking about his identity as the light of the world, the one who reveals God in a special way. Believers *know the truth* in the sense that they accept what Jesus claims about himself; they recognize him as the unique Son of God.

This is the truth that gives us freedom. Our acceptance of Christ through his plan of salvation allows us to become children of God. This liberates us from the power and consequences of sin and death (see John 1:12).

B. SERVANTS AND SONS (vv. 33-36)

33. They answered him, "We are Abraham's descendants and have never been slaves of anyone. How can you say that we shall be set free?"

At first glance, the Jews seem to be very forgetful. Their people, in fact, had been enslaved many times over the years: *slaves* in Egypt; oppressed by foreign powers many times during the judges period; taken in exile to Babylon; dominated by Rome even as they spoke. The reference to Abraham suggests, however, that they are thinking of their spiritual status with God.

Ancient Jews believe that having God's favor comes from being born as *descendants* of Abraham, the person to whom God had made covenant promises (Genesis 12:1-3). Jesus, however, seems to say that their descent from that great man is not enough. So they want to know how he can make such a preposterous claim.

34. Jesus replied, "I tell you the truth, everyone who sins is a slave to sin.

Jesus challenges the Jews' claim to spiritual freedom by stating that *everyone who sins* is enslaved by sin. Everyone does indeed sin (1 John 1:8). The fact that everyone sins should eliminate any prideful belief that a person can somehow get to God through ancestral connections.

Even if the Jews do think of themselves as "born into God's family," every subsequent sin should have underlined how far away from God's will they had gone. Sin alienates us from God and enslaves us to carnal desires. This is a problem that our parents cannot solve for us.

35, 36. *"Now a slave has no permanent place in the family, but a son belongs to it forever. So if the Son sets you free, you will be free indeed.*

Jesus' words refer to legal relationships in ancient households. A *son* and a *slave* may live in the same house, and both serve the same person (the father, who is also the master). But the slave is, ultimately, not a permanent part of the family. He or she has no legal rights. The fact that the Jews are slaves of sin shows that they do not enjoy full status as God's heirs.

A son, however, is heir to everything the father has. A son carries the family name from generation to generation. The son's status in a household is thus permanent (*belongs to it forever*) because he is a true member of the family. The genuine *Son* in view here is Jesus himself.

Jesus as this Son has the power to grant full membership in the family. Abraham, himself a sinner and a servant, cannot grant true spiritual freedom. The phrase *free indeed* brings with it the sense, "I am the one who can set you free from sin and its power forever."

C. ATTITUDE AND TESTIMONY (vv. 37, 38)

37. *"I know you are Abraham's descendants. Yet you are ready to kill me, because you have no room for my word.*

The word *yet* highlights the irony of the situation. As the Jews well know, Abraham was famous for his faith (compare Genesis 12:1-4; 22:1-3). The Jews are not doing a very good job of following their famous forefather's example. When they hear God's message through Jesus, they respond not with belief but by trying to silence him (compare John 5:18; 7:19, 25, 32, 44).

38. *"I am telling you what I have seen in the Father's presence, and you do what you have heard from your father."*

Jesus stresses again and again that he speaks and acts in complete harmony with the Father (see John 4:34; 7:16; 10:38; 12:44; 14:9-11). Jesus' power both to do great works and to offer freedom from sin finds its source in this unity.

Similarly, the Jews' refusal to accept him reveals the true source of their thinking. They claim to be Abraham's descendants. But their lack of faith in the one whom God sent reveals that they actually are children of the devil (John 8:43, 44, not in today's text). The Jews will remain under Satan's power as long as they reject Jesus' words.

II. ABOUT JESUS HIMSELF (JOHN 8:48-56, 58, 59)

A. FIRST ACCUSATION (v. 48)

48. *The Jews answered him, "Aren't we right in saying that you are a Samaritan and demon-possessed?"*

Just before this verse, Jesus had stressed again that his words come from God. Thus he condemns *the Jews* for their disbelief. He can only interpret their stubbornness as evidence that "you do not belong to God" (v. 47).

This claim is extremely offensive to the Jews, but they do not know how to refute it. Jesus invited them to prove him guilty of sin, but instead they resort to name-calling. The Samaritans are a people of mixed Jewish and Gentile descent

WHAT DO YOU THINK?

How can admitting that sin is slavery help us in our battle against temptation?

WHAT DO YOU THINK?

What are some ways that we, like the ancient Jews, might be tempted to allow ancestry and tradition to produce an inaccurate view of our spiritual status before God? How do we guard against this?

who live just north of Judea and worship at Mount Gerizim. The hostility between Jews and Samaritans is well documented both in the Bible (Ezra 4:1-5; Nehemiah 4:1-8; John 4:9) and in other literature.

Jews and Samaritans each claim to be God's elect people. The accusation that Jesus is *a Samaritan* follows from his statement that the Jews are not acting as true children of Abraham. The accusation that Jesus is *demon-possessed* is an attempt to contradict Jesus' statement in verse 38. The Jews think that Jesus' words do not come from God but rather from the devil, because surely neither God nor a true prophet would call them slaves to sin!

YOU ARE A SAMARITAN

The *ad hominem* argument is one of the oldest fallacies in the history of logic. The name of this argument literally means that it is an argument against the person, rather than against the logic of the person's argument. It is an easy and convenient way of scoring points off an opponent.

Sometimes it can be used in a humorous way. As children we could end an argument by stating, "Your grandmother wears combat boots!" Modern politicians can dismiss certain issues by claiming their opponents are "left wing" or "right wing." Valid points can be ridiculed by commenting, "You're only a truck driver; what do you know about international diplomacy?" By giving people labels with negative overtones, we can dismiss their observations unfairly.

Jesus' opponents found it hard to respond to his discussion on the proper behavior of the children of Abraham—with the implication that the Jews were not acting as true children of Abraham should. So they simply dismissed his comments by saying that he was a Samaritan. In their minds that ended the discussion. Ethnic Samaritans could not be expected to contribute intelligently to a discussion on Judaism, so Jesus' comments could be ignored.

Yet *ad hominem* arguments don't prove anything. They are a fallacy and therefore irrelevant to the discussion. The observations that Jesus makes are still valid. His critique cannot be overlooked simply by name-calling. Neither can modern society dismiss him by thinking of him as a mere first-century carpenter.   —J. B. N.

B. FIRST RESPONSE (vv. 49-51)

49, 50. "I am not possessed by a demon," said Jesus, "but I honor my Father and you dishonor me. I am not seeking glory for myself; but there is one who seeks it, and he is the judge.

Jesus, unlike the Jews, does not reject the word of the *Father*. Further, while the Jews are seeking affirmation of their own spirituality, Jesus is seeking only to do God's will. God, however, is seeking to glorify Jesus. God knows that what Jesus says is true. The Jews will therefore be in a dangerous situation unless they repent. *51. "I tell you the truth, if anyone keeps my word, he will never see death."*

Obviously Jesus is using the word *death* in a way other than in a physical sense, since everyone dies. Death here refers to the lost state of those who do not accept Christ (compare 1 John 3:14). That condition will become irreversible once we leave this world. Only those who believe Jesus' claims about himself will escape this fate and enjoy eternal life (John 6:63, 68).

The verse before us follows logically from Jesus' earlier remarks in verse 34 about slavery to sin. As Paul notes in 1 Corinthians 15:56, "the sting of death is sin." Those who accept Jesus need not fear judgment. Their belief in him frees them from sin's power and makes them God's children.

The phrase *I tell you the truth* appears often in the Gospel of John to draw attention to particularly important sayings by Jesus. As is the case here (and in v.

WHAT DO YOU THINK?

What are some practical lessons the example of Jesus can teach us regarding how to present the exclusive claims of the gospel?

WHAT DO YOU THINK?

How should you as a Christian witness to someone who fears death? How would your witness to a Christian and a non-Christian differ, or would it?

[Make sure to consider 1 Corinthians 15:26.]

34), comments followed by this formula often relate to Jesus' divine identity or the need to accept him in order to receive salvation (see John 1:51; 3:3, 5, 11; 5:19, 24, 25; 6:47; 12:24; 13:20).

C. Second Accusation (vv. 52, 53)

52, 53. *At this the Jews exclaimed, "Now we know that you are demon-possessed! Abraham died and so did the prophets, yet you say that if anyone keeps your word, he will never taste death. Are you greater than our father Abraham? He died, and so did the prophets. Who do you think you are?"*

Taking Jesus' discussion of *death* in a physical sense, *the Jews* mock his claim. Even their great heroes of the faith, *Abraham* and *the prophets*, could not grant life; in fact these people died themselves. The Jews' comment suggests that it would be impossible for any human being to do what Jesus claims he can do.

Apparently the Jews' earlier "faith" that we saw in John 8:31 was based on the idea that Jesus was some sort of prophet or holy man (compare John 7:40). Now, however, they suspect that he may be claiming something more.

D. Second Response (vv. 54-56, 58)

54. *Jesus replied, "If I glorify myself, my glory means nothing. My Father, whom you claim as your God, is the one who glorifies me.*

Jesus responds by pointing out that *God*, working through him, is making Jesus' true identity plain to the world. Many people may refer to God as *Father* because they recognize him to be the creator of the universe, yet Jesus is God's Son in a unique way. Thus the Jews (and others) reject God's offer of freedom and life when they refuse to believe Jesus. God *glorifies* Jesus both by empowering his miraculous works and, ultimately, by raising him from the dead and restoring his divine glory in Heaven (John 17:5).

55. *"Though you do not know him, I know him. If I said I did not, I would be a liar like you, but I do know him and keep his word.*

Jesus now exposes the real reason that the Jews cannot accept him: their misunderstanding of Jesus reflects a deeper misunderstanding of God. Everything that Jesus does and says reveals the Father in a dark world, so that one can see God in Jesus (John 14:7-10). Those who reject Jesus, then, actually are rejecting the God who sent him. John raises this point at the very beginning of his gospel by noting that Jesus' "own [the Jews] did not receive him" (John 1:11). They refuse to recognize God's power at work in him.

Knowing God

I know that World War II happened. I have read books about it, seen pictures taken during it, listened to recordings of speeches by Roosevelt and Churchill. Yet if my father were to say, "I know World War II happened," he could speak with more authority than I could. In 1943 he was drafted into the army and saw service in New Guinea and the Philippines. I know about the war, but he knew it firsthand.

The verb *to know* has two meanings, both in English and in Greek. On the one hand it can mean to know something intellectually, or to have what we often call "head knowledge." This applies to facts, information, etc. Another meaning of *to know* is to have experience of something. This goes beyond mere head knowledge. This has to do with life experience and awareness.

The Jews had knowledge of God. They had learned the Old Testament; they had studied the law. They performed the ritual cleansings; they practiced tithing. The Jews knew factual data and information *about God*. But had they really experienced God in their hearts?

What Do You Think?

In what ways can Jesus' example help us in our efforts to share the gospel with Jewish people today? What are some cautions?

How to Say It

Abraham. AY-bruh-ham.
ad hominem. add HAH-muh-nem.
Babylon. BAB-uh-lun.
Egypt. EE-jipt.
Ezra. EZ-ruh.
Gentile. JEN-tile.
Gerizim. GAIR-ih-zeem or Guh-RYE-zim.
Judea. Joo-DEE-uh.
Nehemiah. NEE-huh-MY-uh.
Samaritans. Suh-MARE-uh-tunz.

Visual for Lesson 6. Point to this visual as you ask, "Which of these 'I am' statements do you find most meaningful personally? Why?"

Jesus could claim, "I know him," because he had firsthand experience with God. Jesus invites us to go beyond mere knowledge about him and experience him in our hearts.

—J. B. N.

56, 58. "Your father Abraham rejoiced at the thought of seeing my day; he saw it and was glad." . . . "I tell you the truth," Jesus answered, "before Abraham was born, I am!"

Jesus confirms the Jews' suspicions by noting two ways in which he is superior to *Abraham*. First, *Abraham rejoiced at the thought of seeing* Jesus' *day*. Some ancient rabbis believed that God had revealed the secrets of the messianic age to Abraham in a vision (compare Genesis 15:17-21). A better idea may be that Jesus is referring to the joy that Abraham experienced when told by God that "all peoples on earth will be blessed through you" (Genesis 12:3). The Jews of Christ's day have the opportunity to see that promise fulfilled in the coming of Abraham's descendant Jesus. Abraham, then, was looking forward to what Christ would do.

Second, and much more substantially, Jesus existed before Abraham. Such a statement would be absurd if Jesus were a normal human being (compare John 8:57, not in today's text). But it is obvious that Jesus is claiming something more. *I am* is drawn from Exodus 3:13, 14, where God refers to himself as Yahweh, meaning "the one who exists."

The ancient Jews came to treat that "I am" phrase as God's sacred name. Many times in the Gospel of John, Jesus describes himself with a statement that begins with *I am*—"I am the light of the world," "I am the good shepherd," etc. But when *I am* is used in the absolute sense—alone and with no other words following—Jesus is applying God's sacred name directly to himself. Jesus can offer freedom from sin because he is, in fact, completely one with the God who existed before Abraham. It is therefore pointless for the Jews to appeal to Abraham as their spiritual forefather; Jesus is much greater than he is anyway.

E. ACTIONS (v. 59)

59. At this, they picked up stones to stone him, but Jesus hid himself, slipping away from the temple grounds.

The Jews' actions reveal that they finally have come to understand the implication of Jesus' words. Stoning was prescribed in the law for blasphemy (Leviticus 24:16). Clearly they realize that Jesus is claiming to be God; sadly they reject that claim and the eternal life that he offers.

CONCLUSION

Recently a new museum opened in Cincinnati, Ohio, called *The Freedom Center*. This museum celebrates those who led the Underground Railroad before America's Civil War. Those heroes helped escaping slaves secretly make their way northward to freedom. The Ohio River—a natural boundary marker between North and South—symbolized a new life of liberty. Many pre–Civil War houses and buildings in northern Kentucky and southwestern Ohio still include secret rooms, trap doors, and concealed crawlspaces for hiding. The Underground Railroad provided a means of escape from a world of harsh servitude.

How much more profound is the eternal freedom that Jesus offers! He, and only he, is our "eternal underground railroad." To reject his route to freedom is both sad and amazing. Yet that's just what we see people doing in today's lesson. It is a pattern that continues today.

Discovery Learning

This page contains an alternative lesson plan emphasizing learning activities. Classes desiring such student involvement will find these suggestions helpful. The next page is a reproducible activity page to further enhance discovery learning.

LEARNING GOALS

After participating in this lesson, each student will be able to:

1. List some reasons people rejected Jesus.
2. Explain the concepts of spiritual slavery and freedom.
3. Move from slavery to freedom through Jesus in one area of thought or habit.

INTO THE LESSON

Display the word *FREEDOM* in letters large enough to be read across your assembly area. Use a separate sheet of paper for each letter. Next write the following letters on seven separate sheets of paper: *A, E, L, R, S, V, Y*. As class begins, show these seven letters one at a time in the order given.

As you show each letter, ask, "What is a common sin that begins with this letter?" Accept group answers. (Answers could include the following: swearing and stinginess for *S*; lying and lasciviousness for *L*; adultery and avarice for *A*; violence and vengeance for *V*; envy and exclusion for *E*; ritualism and rebellion for *R*.)

As sins are identified write them on the sheet bearing the letter under discussion. Then stick each sheet over the letters in *FREEDOM* as follows: *A* over the first *E*; *E* over *D*; *L* over *R*; *R* over *O*; *S* over *F*; *V* over the second *E*. When you show *Y*, say, "Do you see 'Y' we're doing this? The simple answer is 'Sin takes away our freedom and makes us slaves to evil.' That's the theme of today's study and Jesus' words in John 8:32-34."

INTO THE WORD

Now display a large copy of the word *IF*, either written to fill a poster board or cut out from two poster boards. As you display it, say, "Now here is a BIG word! Today's text is filled with the word *if*."

Assign a verse from the text to each learner. Then say, "Look at your verse and write an 'If-statement' based on your verse's idea; then personalize it." Give this example, based on verse 31: "If I hold to Jesus' teaching, then I truly am his disciple." Allow a few minutes for consideration. Ask for responses in verse order.

Though responses for most verses are probably obvious, expect such things as the following:

Verse 32: "If I know the truth, then I will be truly free."
Verse 34: "If I commit sin, sin becomes my master."

Verse 36: "If I am made free from sin by the Son of God, then I can't be any freer."
Verse 48: "If I think Jesus to be less than the Son of God, then why would I listen to him or follow him?"
Verse 50: "If I seek my own spiritual glory, then I am substituting self for God."
Verse 52: "If there is no life after death, then I have believed a lie."
Verse 53: "If Jesus can give me life after death, then he obviously is greater than Abraham or any prophet."
Verse 54: "If I honor myself, then I am not acting as Jesus did."
Verse 55: "If I know something and then deny its truth, then I have made myself a liar."
Verse 56: "If I want to be like Abraham, then I will rejoice in God's plan as he reveals it!"
Verse 58: "If Jesus is indeed the great 'I Am,' then I must accept him as God."

(As an alternative exercise, use small groups to complete the Why Would Anyone Reject Jesus? activity from the Reproducible Page.)

INTO LIFE

Call attention back to the Into the Lesson activity, which used the words *freedom* and *slavery*. Give each student a sheet of paper and ask him or her to draw seven squares. On the front of the paper students are to write the letters of the word *SLAVERY*, one letter per square. On the back of the paper, students are to write the word *FREEDOM*. Say, "Place the letters of each word in order back to back: *F* on the back of *S*, *R* on the back of *L*, etc."

Then suggest to your students that they use this paper for repentance and prayer times in the week ahead. They can use one block on each of the seven days of the upcoming week. Give the following instructions: "On Monday tear off the block that has *S* on one side and *F* on the other. Consider a personal sin that begins with *S* (such as stinginess), and then flip the square over and use the letter *F* to ask God for forgiveness. Follow the same pattern each day as a reminder of freedom that we have in God's grace and forgiveness." (An alternative exercise is the Slavery and Freedom activity from the Reproducible Page.) Close with a prayer that includes those two ideas.

Why Would Anyone Reject Jesus?

Examine John 8:32-38 and John 8:48-59. Identify a verse number where the following "reasons" for rejecting Jesus are implied or stated.

_____ They believed they were already saved.

_____ They had believed a lie.

_____ They didn't understand the spiritual meaning of Jesus' words.

_____ Their sins had blinded and bound them.

_____ They were acting just like their father.

_____ They thought that Jesus was a representative of the devil, not God.

_____ They believed that death was final.

_____ They did not truly know God and God's plan.

_____ They could not accept that Jesus was God in the flesh.

_____ They preferred taking matters into their own hands, rather than submitting.

In what ways do these same reasons keep people from accepting Jesus' claims today?

Slavery and Freedom

Jesus makes it clear: sin enslaves. On each link of the chain below, identify a sin that—in times past or presently—tends to enslave and restrict you.

Next, use your concordance—and your Christian friends—to identify verses of Scripture that are part of the Christian's "weaponry" for dealing with a sin that you wrote in the chain. Write the reference inside the chain link.

JESUS IS AUTHORITY AND JUDGE

WHY TEACH THIS LESSON?

"Question authority!" The 1960s introduced a revolution that did just that. And, unfortunately, some in authority gave every reason for their authority to be questioned. From the riots and rebellions of the 1960s to the tolerance and terrorism of the first decade of the twenty-first century, authority has been questioned and, at times, abhorred.

Many of your students just don't like rules! The authority of God's Word has not escaped this questioning. But what God has said authoritatively and what the Son of God has done through the authority given him by his Father always results in good, never in evil. Today's lesson reveals the ultimate authority of Father God and Jesus, his Son. It is by living under this benevolent authority that the followers of Christ find the true meaning and significance of life.

INTRODUCTION

A. LIKE FATHER, LIKE SON

People who know my father often say that I bear a very strong resemblance to him. We look very much alike, and people can match us up as parent and child in a crowd.

I also resemble my father in other very notable ways that have nothing to do with our appearance. For example, I inherited my father's energy and work ethic, and people are often surprised at how much I will take on. I also share some of his tastes and interests: we both like auto racing, and both of us eat way too much candy.

In many respects a person who knows me well will also come to know many things about my father, as his traits are reflected in my life. We often say that someone is a "chip off the old block" when a child is very much like a parent. In such cases we can learn a lot about someone just by looking at his or her children. This fact is evident to teachers and youth workers, who often see kids do and say things that they could have learned only at home.

Jesus frequently appeals to this principle in the Gospel of John to discuss his "sonship"—his unique identity as God's only-begotten Son. While we often think of Jesus' "sonship" in terms of his virginal conception, etc., Jesus usually mentions the sonship issue to highlight his complete unity with, and obedience to, the Father. As such we learn what God is like by looking at Jesus.

B. LESSON BACKGROUND

Our text today follows the story of the healing at Bethesda (John 5:1-9). While in Jerusalem for a feast (v. 1), Jesus visited a pool where many sick people gathered for medical care. There he met a man who had been lame for 38 years. To the

DEVOTIONAL READING:
2 TIMOTHY 4:1-5
BACKGROUND SCRIPTURE:
JOHN 5:19-29
PRINTED TEXT:
JOHN 5:19-29

LESSON AIMS

After participating in this lesson, each student will be able to:

1. Describe the authority that Jesus has.

2. Discuss how Jesus expects us to live in this world in anticipation of eternity.

3. Write a plan to honor Jesus' authority in one specific way.

Jan
14

KEY VERSE

"I tell you the truth, whoever hears my word and believes him who sent me has eternal life and will not be condemned; he has crossed over from death to life."
—John 5:24

great surprise of the crowd—and especially to the surprise of the man himself—Jesus commanded him to rise, take his cot, and walk.

The miracle generated controversy, however, because it took place on the Sabbath. That was the weekly day of rest (v. 9). Some Jewish authorities who believed that carrying cots and healing were works prohibited on the Sabbath confronted the man and learned what Jesus had done.

When those authorities challenged Jesus, he justified his actions by noting God's power at work (v. 17). If God chooses to work on the Sabbath, who can object? The Jews considered this blasphemous. So they conspired to kill Jesus for "making himself equal with God" (v. 18). Jesus' comments in our printed text are a response to this persecution.

I. FATHER AND SON (JOHN 5:19-23)
A. UNITY (vv. 19-21)
19. Jesus gave them this answer: "I tell you the truth, the Son can do nothing by himself; he can do only what he sees his Father doing, because whatever the Father does the Son also does.

Jesus begins his defense by noting that he and *the Father* work together in complete harmony. Verse 19 describes something that Jesus does to reveal this unity, while verse 20 (below) highlights something that God does. While Jesus is equal to the Father in nature, he is completely obedient to him in service. An implication of this fact is that any complaint about Jesus' words or actions is ultimately a complaint against God the Father.

Jesus portrays himself, in a way, as God's apprentice. In Jesus' day sons normally follow the family trade. Such trades include farming, fishing, and carpentry. Often a boy is apprenticed to his father, who teaches him the skills of the job. Jesus, as the faithful *Son*, follows his Father's every step. The result is that Jesus perfectly implements the Father's will. "I do nothing on my own but speak just what the Father has taught me" (John 8:28).

FROM THE SAME TIMBER

"He's cut from the same timber" is a familiar old saying. A variation is "He's cut from the same piece of cloth." These are usually said of blood relatives who have the same characteristics. It could be two brothers or a father and son. The mannerisms, virtues, and qualities of one individual show up equally as well in the other.

My wife and I have two daughters. In many ways the older daughter resembles me (fortunately she's prettier than I am!); the younger daughter resembles my wife. It is sometimes uncanny how my older daughter has many of the same characteristics that I do. Obviously there are some things that she has copied from my own behavior. But some things have gone beyond mere copied behavior. I remember how amazed I was when she was a preschooler, and I saw her do some things that I know she had never seen me do. Some things have simply been genetically programmed into her that she probably has little control over.

If such things are true between an earthly father and his children, we should not be surprised that Jesus says that the same is true between himself and God the Father. The divine Son of God does the same things as his Father. John relays to us that whatever the Father does, these are the same things the Son does. "Like father, like son" is just as true in the spiritual sense as it is in the human world. Thus when we obey the Son, we also obey the Father. —J. B. N.

20. "For the Father loves the Son and shows him all he does. Yes, to your amazement he will show him even greater things than these.

Jesus shows his unity with *the Father* through faithful service, and the Father shows that unity by revealing *all he does* to Jesus. If Jesus is, in a sense, the apprentice, then God is the caring mentor who teaches Jesus everything he knows (compare Luke 2:52).

The word *for* at the beginning of this verse has the sense of "because" as an explanation of what Jesus has just said in verse 19: he is able to do the Father's works because God loves him and shows him everything. In the immediate context this would refer to the healing of the man at Bethesda (John 5:1-9); the *greater things than these* would then refer to the surpassing miracles yet to come. These include the raising of Lazarus (John 11:39-44) and, ultimately, Jesus' own resurrection. The greater works must also include the granting of eternal life, as we see in verse 21, next.

THE APPRENTICE

As I write in early 2005, the television show *The Apprentice* is all the rage. The formula is unique and clever; there has never been a television show quite like it.

A handful of contestants compete with one another for the sole privilege of becoming Donald Trump's apprentice. The competition also involves cooperation since the participants must work in teams. Their tasks include everything from selling lemonade to designing lines of clothing to fixing up old motels—whatever the writers of the show can dream up.

The team that loses each week must then present itself before Trump in the dreaded "boardroom." It is a dark and somber place. It is the place where the losing team must answer for its failure. It is a place where one person each week will hear Trump say the words that no one wants to hear: *You're fired!*

Trump picks his apprentice through a process of elimination. In effect his apprentice is the one who has failed the least. How different it is with Jesus! He never failed at a single task; he proved himself to be God through his own resurrection. Jesus, as the Father's "apprentice" (if it's appropriate to use that term for him), has the Father's complete confidence. That's where our confidence should be as well.

—R. L. N.

21. *"For just as the Father raises the dead and gives them life, even so the Son gives life to whom he is pleased to give it.*

The ability to raise the dead belongs to God alone. It is he who controls the final destiny of every human being (compare 2 Kings 5:7).

Jesus obviously is claiming this divine power for himself. Yet the exact meaning of the phrase the Son *gives life to whom he is pleased to give it* needs to be examined. In a physical sense the phrase could refer to the upcoming resurrection of Lazarus. Some suggest that Jesus is referring to the healing power that he has just demonstrated at Bethesda—although the man who was lame was not physically dead, his life was restored to wholeness in a remarkable way.

In view of the discussion to follow, it seems that Jesus is most likely claiming that he even shares God's power to grant eternal life, not just physical healing. This being the case, it is hardly relevant to accuse him of breaking the Sabbath (John 5:16). If he has ultimate authority over eternal judgment, he certainly can heal someone whenever he wants!

B. TRUST (v. 22)

22. *"Moreover, the Father judges no one, but has entrusted all judgment to the Son,*

The Jewish authorities have taken it upon themselves to judge Jesus a sinner and a blasphemer. They reach this judgment because he does not meet their

HOW TO SAY IT

Bethesda. Buh-THEZ-duh.
Ezekiel. Ee-ZEEK-ee-ul or Ee-
   ZEEK-yul.
Jerusalem. Juh-ROO-suh-lem.
Lazarus. LAZ-uh-rus.
Pharisees. FAIR-ih-seez.

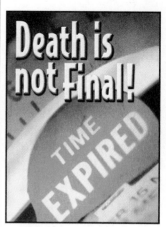

Visual for Lesson 7. *Use this visual to ask students to list things that "expire." Then ask how life in Christ is different.*

expectations. But God has not called them to judge the world; rather, God has given the power of *judgment to the Son.*

Following verse 21 the judgment in question clearly refers to the final judgment at the Last Day. That is when God will assign eternal rewards and punishments. For this reason Christians treat Jesus' teachings as the ultimate authority.

At first glance this verse would seem to conflict with John 3:17. There Jesus says that he did not come to judge the world, but rather to save the world. The tension is resolved easily when we note the difference between Jesus' purpose and his role. In terms of purpose, John 3:16 tells us that Jesus came to earth to proclaim and provide salvation. Two verses later, however, John clarifies that "whoever does not believe stands condemned already" (3:18). This means that those who do not accept Jesus' teaching have no other hope of salvation.

Consistent with this emphasis John 5:22 stresses Jesus' role as judge. Although Jesus wants everyone to be saved—so much so that he died for the world—he eventually will sit in judgment to condemn those who reject him.

C. HONOR (v. 23)

23. "*. . . that all may honor the Son just as they honor the Father. He who does not honor the Son does not honor the Father, who sent him.*"

This verse is a warning to those who deny Jesus' claims or who criticize his actions. Common sense tells us that only a fool would show disrespect to a judge who is about to pass sentence. The opponents of Jesus should therefore carefully consider what they are saying about him.

Any disrespect these opponents show to Jesus automatically dishonors God. This is so because Jesus is God's designated agent who speaks on the Father's behalf. Ironically the Jews have been trying to protect God's honor by persecuting Jesus. In fact that very persecution shows disrespect for God's authority.

II. DEATH AND LIFE (JOHN 5:24-29)

A. IMPORTANCE OF BELIEF (vv. 24, 25)

24. "*I tell you the truth, whoever hears my word and believes him who sent me has eternal life and will not be condemned; he has crossed over from death to life.*"

Eternal life is something that begins in this world. When we accept Jesus according to the biblical plan of salvation, we pass *from death to life.* The word *death* as used here refers to separation from God, while life refers to the relationship with God that comes through Christ. "I tell you the truth, if anyone keeps my word, he will never see death" (John 8:51; compare Colossians 1:13).

Physical death will not change this relationship, although it will finalize our decision. Those who accept Christ have everlasting life that begins now. They begin to enjoy the benefits of salvation and will continue to enjoy God's love eternally in the age to come.

25. "*I tell you the truth, a time is coming and has now come when the dead will hear the voice of the Son of God and those who hear will live.*"

Following the teaching of the Pharisees, most ancient Jews believe that God will one day judge the world. When he does he will resurrect all good Jews for eternal life in a renewed world (compare Acts 23:6-8). Jesus affirms this belief but revises the doctrine at key points. The hour of judgment, when the *dead will hear* God's voice, is now. Those who are spiritually dead but choose to listen to Jesus' words are granted eternal life. Those who are (or were) spiritually dead include people like the Jews and the man at Bethesda. It also includes all other, later readers of John's gospel (us!) who must make a decision about Jesus.

WHAT DO YOU THINK?

Think about the lesson's comparison between John 3:17 and John 5:22. How does this comparison help you approach texts that seem to conflict?

WHAT DO YOU THINK?

How does recognizing that eternal life *begins in this world* make a practical difference in your life right now?

WHAT DO YOU THINK?

How should recognizing that judgment *occurs now* make a practical difference in your life?

The Pharisees naturally attribute the power of resurrection to God alone. Yet Jesus establishes his own role and authority in the judgment. It is *the Son* who proclaims the arrival of the *time* of judgment and salvation. What a crucial point this is!

HEARING AND LIVING

A couple of years ago, there was a series of television commercials featuring cell phones and phone service. In numerous variations a man talking on a cell phone would move to different locations and ask, "Can you hear me now?"

The commercials thus depicted the technician trying to discover locations where the cell-phone transmission wouldn't reach. The point of the commercials was that that particular phone service was superior to that provided by other companies having inadequate technology or equipment. That *Can you hear me now?* phrase became a cultural staple for a brief time.

"To hear," however, means more than merely listening. When a parent is laying down the law to a child, the parent may say, "Do you hear what I'm saying?" This is not a question of just hearing. It means, "Do you recognize the significance of what I am saying, and is it going to change your behavior?"

The old message from the herald, "Hear ye, hear ye," meant more than just mere listening. The herald was providing information that should result in action. The U.S. Army uses the phrase *HUA* (pronounced who-ah). This stands for *Heard, Understood, Acknowledged*. "To hear" properly leads to obedience.

That is the impact of what Jesus is saying: "They that hear shall live." Merely listening is not sufficient. If we properly hear the words of Jesus, we will incorporate them into our thinking and modify our behavior accordingly. Those that hear appropriately shall then live because their actions will be in tune with God's will.

—J. B. N.

B. SON OF MAN (vv. 26, 27)

26, 27. *"For as the Father has life in himself, so he has granted the Son to have life in himself. And he has given him authority to judge because he is the Son of Man.*

Some have suggested that the phrase *Son of Man* is used here in the general sense of "a human being." That is the way that God uses this term to refer to the prophet Ezekiel numerous times (example: Ezekiel 2:1). This approach would suggest that Jesus is given power to judge human beings because he, as a man, can sympathize with our experiences and temptations (see Hebrews 4:15).

While this may be the case as far as it goes, it seems likely that John has a more specific idea in mind. Following Daniel 7:13, 14, many ancient Jews believe that God will send a special agent to judge the world at the end of time. This agent is to be called the Son of Man.

We see this title used in the Gospel of John to highlight Jesus' divinity and *authority* (see John 1:51; 3:13, 14; 6:27, 53; 8:28; 13:31). By calling himself Son of Man in a unique sense, Jesus is claiming to be the one whom God has appointed to judge the world at the end of time.

C. HIS VOICE (v. 28)

28. *"Do not be amazed at this, for a time is coming when all who are in their graves will hear his voice*

As noted earlier, eternal life is a present reality; it is something that those who accept Jesus can begin to experience in the here and now. Jesus clarifies, however, that his authority to grant life goes beyond this world and into eternity. Whereas "the dead" in verse 25 referred to those who are spiritually dead, Jesus

WHAT DO YOU THINK?

How does John's portrait of Jesus as judge provide encouragement to you?

PRAYER

Lord, please help us to live lives that will honor Christ the way that Christ honored you. In times of temptation and stress, help us remember that eternal life is a gift we already have in this world. Keep us mindful at every moment that the things we do now have eternal consequences. In Jesus' name, amen.

WHAT DO YOU THINK?

How can we avoid making mistakes similar to those of Jesus' opponents, who thought they were protecting God's truth yet actually were violating it?

THOUGHT TO REMEMBER

We experience the blessings of resurrection life in every moment that we honor Christ.

now speaks of the situation of those who have physically died—those who are *in their graves.*

Even in the face of death, we can be confident in Christ's power to save. We know that we will one day *hear his voice* and rise to eternal life (see the next verse). Jesus thus has authority over both our present and our future. Hallelujah —what a Savior!

D. OUR STATUS (v. 29)

29. . . . and come out—those who have done good will rise to live, and those who have done evil will rise to be condemned."

Those who respond positively to Jesus and his call in the current life will be glad to hear his call in the next world. "For my Father's will is that everyone who looks to the Son and believes in him shall have eternal life: and I will raise him up at the last day" (John 6:40; compare 6:54).

The same hope does not belong to those who reject him. Their resurrection will be one of condemnation. Indeed they have been *condemned* already. "This is the verdict: Light has come into the world, but men loved darkness instead of light because their deeds were evil" (John 3:19).

We must stress that the phrase *have done good* is not referring to a system of salvation by works. In this context the phrase *have done good* is defined by verse 24: "Whoever hears my word and believes him who sent me has eternal life." See also Jesus' declaration in John 6:29: "The work of God is this: to believe in the one he has sent."

By contrast, those who challenge Jesus' claims and refuse to accept him will suffer eternal judgment. Jesus regrets this situation, but it cannot be otherwise in view of God's justice. The choice is ours.

CONCLUSION

A good friend of ours is a police captain. I once asked him what we should do if a policeman came to our house or we were stopped for a traffic violation. He said, "In one word, 'cooperate.' You're not going to argue with a cop, so don't." My wife very recently profited from this advice when she parked momentarily in a fire lane to pick up a large item in a store. A police officer came in looking for her, and she avoided an expensive fine by listening quietly and following his orders.

Jesus offers similar advice in our passage today. God is the boss, and he has given Jesus all authority to judge us. We're not in a position to argue with him or to question what he says. If we want to stay out of trouble, our only hope is simply to follow his instructions. Make no mistake: there won't be any arguing about the situation on Judgment Day!

But people foolishly try to argue with God, don't they? Such arguments can take several forms. The most serious way we argue with God is through sin itself. God, the judge and lawgiver, has defined what sin is. He has commanded us to avoid it. When we go ahead and commit sin anyway, we are saying, in effect, "I know better than you do, God." Thus our sin becomes our argument against him and his will.

Such sin is obvious when we break one of the "Thou shalt not" commandments. A less obvious way to argue with God is in resisting his will for us after we become Christians. Jonah knew God's direction for his life but chose to do something different (Jonah 1:3). Is God calling you into a particular ministry or service? Don't argue—go!

Discovery Learning

This page contains an alternative lesson plan emphasizing learning activities. Classes desiring such student involvement will find these suggestions helpful. The next page is a reproducible activity page to further enhance discovery learning.

LEARNING GOALS

After this lesson, each student will be able to:

1. Describe the authority that Jesus has.

2. Discuss how Jesus expects us to live in this world in anticipation of eternity.

3. Write a plan to honor Jesus' authority in one specific way.

INTO THE LESSON

Procure a small dart board and pair of darts. Over the board's bulls-eye, place a picture of a beloved member of your congregation (be sure to get the person's permission). Display the board. As class begins, ask a person who you know will refuse to do so to throw darts at the board.

When you sense the hesitancy and reluctance, say, "I thought it would be difficult for anyone to throw darts at our beloved [name]. Imagine those in Jesus' day attacking him and his good deeds." Note that that is what happens in today's text, as the religious leaders attack Jesus for healing on the Sabbath. They also attack him for making himself equal with God, which in fact, he is (see John 5:18).

As an alternate beginning, ask the class to describe the ideal father/son relationship, using only adjectives or abstract nouns. Expect such responses as respectful and submissive. Another alternative beginning is to use the Authority Symbols exercise from the Reproducible Page.

INTO THE WORD

Prepare a copy of the following table for each student. (The table is included in the student book.)

John 5	Father	Son	Jewish Leaders/Us
19	_____	_____	_____
20	_____	_____	_____
21	_____	_____	_____
22	_____	_____	_____
23	_____	_____	_____
24	_____	_____	_____
25	_____	_____	_____
26, 27	_____	_____	_____
28, 29	_____	_____	_____

Ask students to fill in the chart, briefly noting what each at the top will do or not do according to each verse.

Note that most verses will not use all three columns. For example, for verse 22: the Father does not judge; it is the Son who judges.

To continue the examination of the text, read aloud the following expressions in random order, one at a time. Ask the class to identify a related verse from today's text. (Do not read aloud the verse numbers provided in parentheses after each expression.)

"Escape with a pass key" (v. 24). "Like Father, like Son" (v. 19). "Dead men's ears—what shall they hear?" (v. 28). "Love shows" (v. 20). "Life and death; Father and Son" (v. 21). "Who gets to judge? The judge!" (v. 22). "Honor one, honor the other" (v. 23). "Listen up; come alive!" (v. 25). "Full of life; full of life" (v. 26). "See good; do good" (v. 19). "Just because" (v. 27). "Risen up, risen down" (v. 29). "Hear . . . believe . . . live!" (v. 24).

As the class identifies verse numbers, discuss the meaning of each.

Display the phrase *The Second Coming of Christ*. Ask the group to quote from the Bible some facts about that grand event. Make a quick list. Then say, "OK, this is a good list, but do we have everything Jesus reveals in today's text?" Have students look especially at verses 24-29. Add any important ideas to the earlier listing.

Decide in advance which of the above three activities you will allow the most time for, depending on what content you wish to stress. An alternative activity is the Father and Son exercise from the Reproducible Page.

INTO LIFE

Put the following fill-in expression on display: "I Res____t Jesus' Authority!" (A similar activity is found in the student book.) Ask for letter combinations to fill in the blank (such as is, en, pec, and tric). Discuss how people's lives demonstrate how they would fill in the missing letters.

Next, give each student a slip of paper with the same phrase and have each fill in letters appropriate to his or her own attitude toward Jesus' authority. Then have each add an affirmation, "so I (will) _____." Each should complete the idea either with a description of how his or her life is being lived or how he or she will commit to begin living it.

Authority Symbols

Authority is often represented in a symbol. What authority does each of these symbols represent? Write your answers under the symbols.

What symbol do you think best represents the authority of Christ? Which is most unlike the authority of Christ? Defend your answers.

Father and Son

In John 5 Jesus' authority is attacked. As John explains in verse 18, Jesus was breaking the Sabbath from the Jews' perspective. He was even "even calling God his own Father, making himself equal with God." Jesus then teaches them about his relationship with the Father. In which verse(s) does Jesus give each of the following explanations?

____ I only do what I see the Father doing.

____ The Father loves the Son.

____ The Father shows the Son all he is doing.

____ Just as the Father gives life, so does the Son.

____ I have the Father's authority to judge.

____ I deserve the same honor the Father does.

____ To dishonor me is to dishonor the Father.

____ Accepting my Word is the same as believing the Father who sent me.

____ I have the power to call to the dead, even as the Father does.

____ The essence of my existence is the same as that of the Father.

____ The Son's first motive is to please the Father.

JESUS IS THE BREAD OF LIFE AND LIVING WATER

LESSON 8

WHY TEACH THIS LESSON?

Food and water are basic. But people who have plenty of both don't think about them much. Instead, they turn their hunger and thirst toward luxuries—gadgets such as MP3 players or the latest new sports car. When people focus on such things it can be difficult to redirect their attention to their spiritual needs.

Scripture teaches us that we are to seek that which is truly important: spiritual bread and water. This lesson helps the "hungry learner" see the source of these basic spiritual necessities: Jesus. It also helps those who are distracted by other things to recognize a hunger and thirst that they may be only vaguely aware of.

INTRODUCTION

A. THE GOD WHO IS

Exodus 3 records Moses' encounter with God at the burning bush. Before this event Moses had sacrificed his privileged position in the Egyptian government in order to protect one of his Hebrew kinsmen. As a result Moses fled the country (Exodus 2:11-15). He became a shepherd. One day while tending the sheep on Mount Horeb, he suddenly heard God's voice speaking from a flaming bush.

God had good news: he would rescue his people after years of suffering and slavery. Moses would have the special privilege of leading the people out of Egypt to the promised land. This would be the fulfillment of God's ancient covenant with Abraham (Genesis 15:18-20). One can easily understand why Moses was shocked by this information (especially from a bush!). He questioned his own ability to fulfill the task. He pointed out that his name carried no weight with Pharaoh or the Jews. He was certain that he lacked the skills needed for the job. God assured him that he would empower him.

Moses also raised another significant problem. The Hebrews had lived in Egypt for centuries, and the Egyptians worshiped many gods. Over the course of time, the Hebrews had been exposed to this corrupt practice. They would therefore want to know which "god" Moses was talking about.

God replied "This is what you are to say to the Israelites: 'I AM has sent me to you'" (Exodus 3:14). In other words: "Tell them that the one God who actually exists—the one 'who is'—sent you to deliver them."

This one-and-only God delivered the Hebrews from Egypt. He continues to work through his people to reveal himself to the world.

B. LESSON BACKGROUND

In the Gospel of John, we notice Jesus making frequent statements about himself that involve God's sacred name, I Am. For the sake of convenience, we can call these "the 'I am' sayings."

DEVOTIONAL READING:
EPHESIANS 3:14-21
BACKGROUND SCRIPTURE:
JOHN 6:25-59; 7:37-39
PRINTED TEXT:
JOHN 6:34-40; 7:37-39

LESSON AIMS

After participating in this lesson, each student will be able to:

1. Identify the hunger and thirst that Jesus meets.

2. Discuss how the Holy Spirit is a "river of living water" in our lives.

3. Interview a spiritually mature Christian to discover how Christ meets that person's spiritual and emotional needs.

Jan 21

KEY VERSE

Jesus declared, "I am the bread of life. He who comes to me will never go hungry, and he who believes in me will never be thirsty." —John 6:35

These sayings form an important distinctive in John among the four Gospels. For those interested in statistics, Greek "I am" is used 5 times in Matthew, 3 times in Mark, 4 times in Luke, but 30 times in John. If we take off the "am" part and just consider how often Jesus refers to himself as "I" in an authoritative way, then the occurrences are 29 times in Matthew, 17 times in Mark, 23 times in Luke, but 134 times in John!

These sayings take two forms. We will explore both forms in our lessons over the next several weeks. The first form occurs when Jesus simply applies God's divine name, I Am, directly to himself. He does this to stress his complete union with the Father (John 8:24, 28, 58; 13:19). For those interested in technical things, this is known as the *absolute use* of I am.

The second form occurs in instances where Jesus uses this phrase to start a sentence in which he compares himself to something else. Some examples are "I am the vine" and "I am the good shepherd." Technically speaking these *I am* statements are said to have *explicit predicates*.

Jesus' *I am* remarks in our passage today follow John's account of the miraculous feeding of the 5,000 (John 6:1-13). Impressed with his power, the people sought to make Jesus king. Perhaps they hoped that he would lead them in a revolution against the Romans. To avoid this Jesus first withdrew to a mountain (v. 15), then to Capernaum (vv. 16-25). But the crowds found him anyway. When they did Jesus advised them not to focus on the bread that they had eaten but rather on food that is eternal (vv. 26, 27).

I. FEASTING ON THE BREAD (JOHN 6:34-40)

A. WHO JESUS IS (vv. 34, 35a)

34, 35a. "Sir," they said, "from now on give us this bread."

Then Jesus declared, "I am the bread of life.

The manna in Moses' day was food for the body (see John 6:31, 32). Rather than focusing on this kind of nourishment, Jesus' hearers need to receive "the bread of God" that "comes down from heaven and gives [eternal] life" (John 6:33). Of course Jesus' hearers want to eat *this bread*. So they ask Jesus to give it to them.

Clearly, however, Jesus' audience does not understand fully that Jesus himself is the source of eternal life. Jesus uses an *I am* saying to show that he is superior to the old covenant. While Moses fed people bread in the wilderness, and while this was an incredible miracle of God, none of the people who ate that physical bread lived forever as a result of ingesting it. Jesus, by contrast, is *the bread of life*. The phrase *of life* has important implications, as we see next.

WHAT DO YOU THINK?

How can the example of Jesus help Christians deal with the temptations that accompany popularity and power?

BREAD

We often refer to bread as "the staff of life." In our current culture with all the concern about carbohydrates, perhaps that is not as true as it once was.

But in first-century Palestine, bread was a crucial ingredient in the daily diet. The average family had meat only three times a month—it simply was too expensive. People subsisted on milk, cheese, vegetables, and bread. Of these, bread was probably the most important. Wheat flour for making bread was expensive. So most people ate bread made from barley (notice that in John 6:9 Jesus fed the 5,000 from barley loaves).

The Egyptians were the first to discover the effect of yeast spores in raising the dough. The result was a softer, lighter bread that most people considered a major improvement over the previously flat, unleavened loaves. The Egyptians were also the first to build ovens for baking bread; this was an improvement over baking in the open air and covering the dough with hot ashes. The importance of bread throughout history is demonstrated by how much attention has been paid trying to improve it!

Comparison to bread is thus a natural way for Jesus to illustrate truth. Throughout the Scriptures bread stands for food in general. "Breaking bread" stands for the entire meal. "Give us today our daily bread" refers to more than merely loaves. When Jesus says he is the bread of life, he is making a major statement to the people of his time and ours. Our souls hunger for spiritual nourishment, and Jesus promises that he is that food. He is the "required daily allowance" in our spiritual diet.   —J. B. N.

B. WHAT JESUS OFFERS (v. 35b)

35b. "He who comes to me will never go hungry, and he who believes in me will never be thirsty.

The bread to which Jesus refers is "living bread" (John 6:51). It's alive and standing right in front of them. (The two uses of *me* makes this emphatic.) This kind of bread is most unlike the inanimate manna that God provided through Moses! This bread gives life to those who accept it—to those who believe in Jesus.

Because the bread (Jesus) is eternal, the life that he provides is also eternal. Anyone who believes in him will never be *hungry* or *thirsty* again in a spiritual sense because Jesus will satisfy his or her desire for God forever. This too is quite different from the manna that Moses provided, which quickly spoiled (Exodus 16:20).

C. WHAT PEOPLE DECIDE (vv. 36, 37)

36. "But as I told you, you have seen me and still you do not believe.

At first glance it seems odd that Jesus would say this to people who have just tried to make him king because of the miraculous feeding in John 6:14, 15. The crowd clearly is impressed with Jesus, yet Jesus clarifies that their faith thus far is inadequate. It is not enough simply to believe that Jesus is a prophet or a great teacher; rather, one must accept that his miracles are signs that he is God's unique Son.

Those standing before Jesus believe that he can feed them with miraculous bread. But they have not yet come to understand his true identity as the one sent from Heaven. They do not grasp that Jesus is so much greater than Moses (compare Hebrews 3:3).

37. "All that the Father gives me will come to me, and whoever comes to me I will never drive away.

This verse can be perplexing. Jesus seems first to imply that only certain people receive a special, mandatory calling from God to believe in him; then immediately Jesus insists that he will not reject (*will never drive away*) anyone who chooses to believe.

We can reach a reasonable solution by first recognizing that God knows the future. Through his foreknowledge God is aware of who will and who won't accept Jesus by their freewill choice. Those whom the Father knows will accept Jesus are the ones whom *the Father gives me.*

Jesus' words thus provide assurance to those who believe—to those who recognize that the one who does miracles is actually God in the flesh. Jesus will never relinquish his love for them (us!). As Paul says, nothing can separate us from his love (Romans 8:37-39).

DAILY BIBLE READINGS

Monday, Jan. 15—May Christ Dwell Within (Ephesians 3:14-21)

Tuesday, Jan. 16—Do Not Be Afraid (John 6:16-21)

Wednesday, Jan. 17—Jesus, the Heavenly Bread (John 6: 25-34)

Thursday, Jan. 18—I Am the Bread of Life (John 6:35-40)

Friday, Jan. 19—Sustained by Living Bread (John 6:41-51)

Saturday, Jan. 20—Sing for Joy (Isaiah 49:7-13)

Sunday, Jan. 21—Living Water (John 7:37-41)

WHAT DO YOU THINK?

The phrase I will never drive away *provides great comfort! But at times some may ask,* "If that promise is really true, then why did such and such happen to me?" How do you respond?

WHAT DO YOU THINK?

What are some ways that the example and teaching of Christ can help you assess the will of God for your life?

D. WHAT THE FATHER WANTS (vv. 38-40)

38. "For I have come down from heaven not to do my will but to do the will of him who sent me.

Jesus now returns to a theme that we have seen several times in this series: he does not come to do his own *will*, but God's will. In this context doing God's will relates very specifically to his mission of providing eternal life to all who accept him. This mission is explained in more detail in the next two verses.

39. "And this is the will of him who sent me, that I shall lose none of all that he has given me, but raise them up at the last day.

The idea of "losing" refers to the separation of a believer from Christ and, consequently, from the eternal life that Jesus provides. In Jesus' great prayer in chapter 17, he will stress that he has protected his disciples so that none of them was "lost" except Judas, who betrayed him. But even that case wasn't really an exception (in the sense of Jesus failing at his task) since Judas Iscariot was "doomed to destruction" by his own choice (John 17:12; compare 6:70, 71).

Jesus' assurance will be of great comfort as churches are persecuted for their Christian faith (John 16:1-4). Such persecutions can create fear and discouragement. But Jesus reminds us that these experiences do not affect his love for us or our ultimate safety in him.

Raise them up refers back to theme of John 5:25-29 (see last week's lesson). There Jesus assured believers that he would reward their perseverance with eternal life on *the last day.* Jesus is able to provide!

LOSE NOTHING

A friend of mine who went through medical school told me that many of his classes were like getting a drink from a fire hydrant without being able to spill a drop. I realize that's a bit of an exaggeration, but it points out how much he was required to learn—and lose nothing in the process. I have known only one person in my life who claimed to have a photographic memory. I'm not sure he remembered absolutely everything he had ever read but his memory was awesome, particularly for trivia.

I heard once that when Mozart was only about eight years old, he attended a concert and was fascinated by a ten-minute piece he had heard. Having heard it only once, he then went home and proceeded to write it out—every note for every instrument. He went back the next day to hear the piece again just to be sure he had transcribed it accurately. He had—every note for every instrument. How incredible to remember everything after just one hearing, and not lose a single note!

Jesus said that out of everything the Father had given to him, he would lose nothing. If humans can mentally remember vast amounts of information and lose nothing in the process, it should not be surprising that Jesus is able to do much the same thing with all the responsibilities the Father has given to him. We can be sure that our lives and our souls are safe in his hands.   —J. B. N.

40. "For my Father's will is that everyone who looks to the Son and believes in him shall have eternal life, and I will raise him up at the last day."

While many people do not accept Christ, this does not reflect on God's *will* for them. John 3:16, 17 stresses that God loved the world and sent his Son to save the world. This is clear evidence of his desire for all people to have everlasting life.

Regrettably, however, many people reject this gift and refuse to accept Jesus' offer. Jesus thus challenges his audience to see past the miracle of the bread itself and realize what the miracle points to: he is God's only Son.

HOW TO SAY IT

Abraham. AY-bruh-ham.
Capernaum. Kuh-PER-nay-um.
Egypt. EE-jipt.
Horeb. HO-reb.
Jerusalem. Juh-ROO-suh-lem.
Judas Iscariot. JOO-dus Iss-
    CARE-ee-ut.
Leviticus. Leh-VIT-ih-kus.
Moses. MO-zes or MO-zez.
Pharaoh. FAIR-o or FAY-roe.
Siloam. Sigh-LO-um.

II. DRINKING FROM THE RIVER (JOHN 7:37-39)

A. COME AND DRINK (vv. 37, 38)

37, 38. *On the last and greatest day of the Feast, Jesus stood and said in a loud voice, "If anyone is thirsty, let him come to me and drink. Whoever believes in me, as the Scripture has said, streams of living water will flow from within him."*

The Feast in question here is the great Feast of Tabernacles in Jerusalem. Jesus has been impressing the crowds with his teaching during this feast. On each day of this celebration, a group of priests carries buckets of water from the pool of Siloam to the temple. There they pour the water on the altar as an offering while reciting Isaiah 12:3, "With joy you will draw water from the wells of salvation."

Jesus uses this ceremony as a symbol of the new life that is available to those who believe in him. This feast lasts seven days, with a closing assembly on the eighth day (Leviticus 23:33-36). The phrase *On the last and greatest day of the Feast* could refer to either the seventh or the eighth day—we're not certain.

Another uncertainty is the possibility of interpreting these verses in two different ways. Jesus begins with an invitation for those who thirst for God to come to him and be filled. The way our English text is punctuated suggests that the person who drinks from Jesus (that is, the one who believes in him) will then become a source of *living water.* This rendering appeals to verse 39, making Jesus' words a promise of the indwelling Spirit: every believer will have the Holy Spirit as an inner spring of life.

Some say, however, that the period in verse 37 should not come after *and drink* but after *come to me.* Without getting too technical about English and Greek sentence structure, this view promotes Jesus to be the source of the water; it emphasizes his unique authority to give the Spirit to those who accept him. This interpretation makes Jesus the source of the Spirit that gives life to those who believe.

We should not be too concerned with the differences in these two possibilities. In either case Jesus emphasizes the fact that the spiritual water that he provides is *living.* The Spirit that Jesus gives is active in the life of the believer.

The Scripture that Jesus has in mind could be Isaiah 58:11: "The Lord will guide you always; he will satisfy your needs in a sun-scorched land and will strengthen your frame. You will be like a well-watered garden, like a spring whose waters never fail."

THIRST

Most of us live in areas where water is abundant. When I was a youngster, our neighborhood did not have city water; each house had its own shallow well that supplied all its water needs. The water had a high iron content that soon stained drinking glasses orange—but at least we had water.

Not everyone is so fortunate. Areas of California face water shortages. Much of the Central Valley of California was unable to sustain agriculture until canals brought water from the snow packs in the Sierras. When I lived in California a number of years ago, we often had to endure water rationing.

An abundance of water does not guarantee a lack of thirst, however. Those stranded at sea know this all too well. As *The Rime of the Ancient Mariner* has it, "Water, water, everywhere, Nor any drop to drink." Trying to drink seawater is a big mistake. The high salt content of seawater will leach water out of a person's internal organs. Then the thirst gets worse rather than better.

Desert areas are also dangerous. People who live in the Near East are familiar with the acute need for water. Witness the fame of an "oasis." Therefore when

Visual for Lesson 8. Point to this refreshing waterfall imagery as you introduce the question at the conclusion on page 188.

PRAYER

Lord, help us never forget that you already have met all of our spiritual needs through Christ. Give us strength as we feed on the bread and water that you have provided. We ask for your forgiveness for those times when we have not been satisfied with what Christ provides. In Jesus' name, amen.

Jesus said that he could relieve the thirst of anyone who needed a drink, they understood the significance of the imagery.

Yet Jesus was talking about a spiritual thirst rather than a physical one. People might misunderstand what he really was talking about, as did the woman at the well in John 4. Is our comprehension any better than those who originally heard Jesus' words?   —J. B. N.

B. PROMISE OF THE SPIRIT (v. 39)

39. By this he meant the Spirit, whom those who believed in him were later to receive. Up to that time the Spirit had not been given, since Jesus had not yet been glorified.

Jesus' glorification refers to his forthcoming death and resurrection. In John 14:15-19 Jesus promises the disciples that *the Spirit* will come to take his place as their Comforter after his death.

The Spirit will act as the ongoing source of power and authority for the church as a whole and for individual believers. He will bring to mind Jesus' promises so that his followers may enjoy peace in the face of trial (John 14:25-27). In this way Jesus continues to provide for our needs long after he leaves this world. We enjoy this comfort until his return!

CONCLUSION

In times past, and in many countries yet today, bread and water was the food of criminals. Prisoners and captives in wartime were kept barely alive on a sustenance diet of minimal amounts of these two. This fact reflects, however, the essential role that bread and water play in human life: they are things that we must have to survive. Human beings can live a long, long time on only air, bread, and water.

In our passages for today, Jesus uses bread and water figuratively to stress that he provides everything essential for our spiritual lives. When we need to know God's will, we look to the one who "came down from heaven"; when we seek strength and guidance, his Spirit refreshes us with "living water." And unlike physical bread and water, we never grow tired of the heavenly food that Jesus gives us. It tastes new and exciting every day.

But how do we communicate these facts to an unbelieving world? Bread is viewed with disdain by the low-carbohydrate diet plans. Bread is hardly a centerpiece of meals in the industrialized West. Many people let the bread sit untouched in a basket off to the side of the table when they go to a restaurant. We may even caution ourselves "don't fill up on bread" before the main course arrives. The bread that most of us ingest these days seems to come in the form of pizza crusts.

Water imagery also causes problems. On the one hand pure, bottled water is all the rage in some quarters. This value enhances the image of Jesus as living water. On the other hand, we also see television commercials by companies selling sports drinks that attack the adequacy of water. They say we should buy their products instead, so we don't miss out on electrolytes, etc. Soft drinks also attract our attention from every vending machine we see. Water did not have this kind of competition back in the first century AD!

Jesus spoke with images that were vital to the people of his day. It is not our prerogative to change that imagery (as in "I am the pizza crust of life"). Our task, rather, is to explain that imagery carefully. The Scripture will come alive when we do! This honors God

WHAT DO YOU THINK?

In what ways have you found the Holy Spirit's indwelling presence to be an encouragement in living the Christian life?

WHAT DO YOU THINK?

How do you intend to use the images of hunger and thirst to communicate the gospel in the twenty-first century?

THOUGHT TO REMEMBER

Christ is the source of everything that we should long for.

Discovery Learning

This page contains an alternative lesson plan emphasizing learning activities. Classes desiring such student involvement will find these suggestions helpful. The next page is a reproducible activity page to further enhance discovery learning.

LEARNING GOALS

After this lesson each student will be able to:

1. Identify the hunger and thirst that Jesus meets.

2. Discuss how the Holy Spirit is a "river of living water" in our lives.

3. Interview a spiritually mature Christian to discover how Christ meets that person's spiritual and emotional needs.

INTO THE LESSON

Give each student a sheet of lined paper with the heading *Survival List.* Say, "You are stranded on an isolated isle. You know that you will not be rescued for at least seven days. What do you want included in the survival kit you have fortunately brought with you?"

Give the students a few minutes to list the items that they consider to be essential. Then let them share their lists, along with any explanation considered necessary. Expect such items as food, water, and matches.

After all have shared, say, "Certain things are essential for earthly existence, but certain things are also essential for heavenly preparation. In today's study Jesus makes it clear: he himself is the bread and water that we need!"

INTO THE WORD

Read aloud John 6:28-33, the verses preceding today's text. In those verses the context for today's teaching about bread are given.

Then have two of your better oral readers read Exodus 16:11-31 and Exodus 17:5-7. These passages relate to the bread and water God provided for the Israelites during the wilderness wandering. Have one volunteer read the words spoken by God, Moses, and the people; the other volunteer will read the narrative. After looking at today's text, you may wish to return to these texts for a comparison and contrast between the desert bread and water and the bread and water that is Christ himself. (For example, both were sent by God for the welfare of his people; both came while the people were in sin—see Exodus 16:1 and 1 Timothy 1:15.)

Establish "Bread" and "Water" groups of five people per group. Give each group a stack of five cards, bearing either B-R-E-A-D or W-A-T-E-R, one letter per card. Give the cards to one person in each group with the direction to shuffle the cards and distribute one to each member.

Announce, "The goal of your group is to develop an acrostic for your word, bread or water. Each word or phrase of the acrostic must be related to today's text (John 6:34-40; 7:37-39) or to the nature of Jesus. Each group member is responsible to create the word or phrase for the letter on his or her card. OK, those with the B or the W, get started!"

Give the groups five minutes. Then ask the person who holds the last letter of either word (D or R) to report the group's acrostic to the whole class, with any explanation deemed necessary.

Though you will accept the creations of each group, here is a sample for each: B equals "broken," as the body of Christ will be; R equals "requested," as in 6:34; E equals "eternal," also from 6:34; A equals "all," for he is all we need; and D equals "delightful," for tasting Jesus always is; W equals "wonderful," because it differs from the water we drink each day; A equals "anticipated," because 7:39 reveals "living water" as a reference to the Spirit to be given after Jesus' glorification; T equals "thirst-quenching," from 7:37; E equals "enough," for the bread and water that is Christ himself is totally sufficient; R equals "required" for eternal life.

INTO LIFE

Before today's session collect empty personal water bottles so that you have one for each student. Also have on hand some blank peel-and-stick labels (at least 2 inches by 3 inches), two per student. After you distribute bottles and labels, direct students to prepare a name label reflecting the truths of John 6:35b and/or John 7:37, 38. If they need an example or two, suggest "Thirst Quencher" (from 6:35) and "Never Dry" (from 7:38). After students finish and attach their labels to their bottles, have several class members read the names they have chosen.

For the second label ask students to write, "What's in it?" Suggest that for the next several days each student should look at his or her bottle and add to the label one attribute of Jesus that "fills his or her bottle of living water." Examples are "divine vitamins," "pure grace," or "100 percent daily requirements." (For alternative Into Life exercises, you can use either or both of the From Now On or Bread Stamps activities from the Reproducible Page.)

From Now On

Think about the people who stood with Jesus "on the other side of the lake" (John 6:25) from where he had miraculously fed them. Jesus said to them, "the bread of God is he who comes down from heaven and gives life to the world" (6:33). The people pled with Jesus, "from now on give us this bread" (6:34). They had the right request, even if they misunderstood the full import. "The bread of God is he" is a big idea that our minds struggle with. What are some of the big ideas Jesus expressed that your mind struggles to comprehend, even though you want the promise "from now on"?

I struggle with this big idea	I struggle with this big idea	I struggle with this big idea

Bread Stamps

At one time bread stamps were popular. These stamps were made of plastic and were shaped like slices of sandwich bread. The stamps carried raised symbols and words to be pressed into a fresh slice of bread. After toasting, the image would be revealed. Now think about it the other way around. If you were designing stamps to show what our lives would look like once the bread of life (Jesus) had made his imprint on us, what would they look like? Sketch your ideas in the boxes.

"I AM THE LIGHT OF THE WORLD"

LESSON 9

WHY TEACH THIS LESSON?

In John 3:19 Jesus speaks about those who "loved darkness instead of light." This appears to be truer in the spiritual realm than in the physical. Thieves love darkness, but most people can't wait until the power is restored during an outage. In such times people quickly become impatient waiting for light in the midst of the darkness. People grope around seeking candles and flashlights. Light switches are flipped, to no avail. When it comes to spiritual darkness, however, many of these same folks are amazingly unconcerned. They blunder on, seemingly unaware of, or totally indifferent to, the darkness in which they live and move.

But light is available to those walking in darkness! Christians become a source of light in the world by reflecting the eternal light of the Son. This light gives boldness to the Christ-follower to maintain the walk, even through the valley of the shadow of death. It is vital, though, that the Christian stays plugged into the source of this power for light. This lesson describes the means by which this power connection stays in place.

INTRODUCTION

A. THE POWER OF A MATCH

Kentucky's Mammoth Cave is one of the largest complexes of underground passages in the world. Many of the cave's farthest recesses have yet to be explored, but the largest known entrance is home to a national park. On one of the guided tours, rangers lead guests to a cavern deep below the surface and ask them to remain silent while they turn off the lights.

The resulting darkness is overwhelming. It is impossible to see anything at any distance. The ranger then illustrates the power of light by striking a single match. I have been on this tour several times, and on each occasion I find that it is impossible to look away from this tiny spark of light. Human beings were not made to live in utter darkness. We readily grasp for anything to light our way.

Darkness is a powerful figure of speech. At least part of the reason is because we fear the dark and what may be lurking there. The Bible often uses the imagery of darkness to describe the spiritual state of those whose lives are not directed by God. A few such passages are Acts 26:18; Colossians 1:13; 1 Thessalonians 5:4, 5; and 1 John 2:11. In today's lesson Jesus discusses his role as the light of the world.

In that role, he is the one who brings hope by revealing God to us. "In him was life, and that life was the light of men" (John 1:4). "This is the message we have heard from him and declare to you: God is light; in him there is no darkness at all" (1 John 1:5).

DEVOTIONAL READING:
ISAIAH 35:3-10
BACKGROUND SCRIPTURE:
JOHN 8:12-20; 12:44-46
PRINTED TEXT:
JOHN 8:12-20; 12:44-46

LESSON AIMS

After participating in this lesson, each student will be able to:

1. List ways in which Jesus was and is a source of light in our dark world.

2. Explain Jesus' use of the "light" metaphor as proof of his unique authority.

3. Change one habit to better reflect Jesus' light.

Jan
28

KEY VERSE

I am the light of the world. Whoever follows me will never walk in darkness, but will have the light of life. —John 8:12

LESSON 9 NOTES

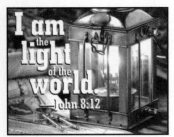

Visual for Lesson 9. *Point to this imagery of a light-producing apparatus as you introduce either the second question on page 193 or the question on page 196.*

B. LESSON BACKGROUND

John 8 seems to follow directly on Jesus' teaching at the Feast of Tabernacles. There he promised the gift of "living water" (the Spirit) to those who believe in him (last week's lesson).

Up to that point the crowds were divided on his message. Some had concluded that Jesus was the "Prophet" (Deuteronomy 18:15-18; John 7:40). Others thought him to be the Messiah or Christ (John 7:41). The chief priests sent the temple guards to arrest him, but they returned empty-handed after being overwhelmed by his authoritative teaching (John 7:45, 46).

Some of the leading Pharisees, including Nicodemus (compare John 3:1-10), debated among themselves about Jesus' identity (7:50-52). Jesus then explicitly identified himself as the one sent to reveal God in the midst of a dark world.

I. LIGHT OF THE WORLD (JOHN 8:12)

A. JESUS' IDENTITY (v. 12a)

12a. When Jesus spoke again to the people, he said, "I am the light of the world.

Jesus' illustration here, one of John's great *I am* sayings, is likely drawn from the celebrations during the Feast of Tabernacles. During this feast four huge lamps are lit in the temple courts. People then dance through the night with burning torches, singing songs of praise, accompanied by the music of the temple orchestra.

The glow from these festivities can be seen all over the city of Jerusalem. It is against this backdrop that Jesus proclaims himself to be the true *light of the world.*

B. OUR RESPONSE (v. 12b)

12b. "Whoever follows me will never walk in darkness, but will have the light of life."

Jesus' claims probably reflect two aspects of his ministry. First, he brings *light* by revealing God and his nature in a fallen world. This revelation is vastly superior to the Old Testament system, for Jesus comes as the unique Son of God rather than as a mere prophet or priest. He thus shows people the way to eternal *life* through faith in him. "The Lord will be your everlasting light, and your God will be your glory" (Isaiah 60:19).

Second, Jesus' teaching and example provide moral guidance, showing believers how to live in a way that pleases God. Ancient Israelites should be very familiar with such imagery. They undoubtedly know Isaiah 42:16: "I will turn the *darkness* into light before them and make the rough places smooth. These are the things I will do; I will not forsake them."

FOLLOW THE LIGHT

When the children of Israel left Egypt, they were led by God in a pillar of cloud by day and a pillar of fire by night to give them light (Exodus 13:21). The cloud and the fire were important, for they were the evidence of God's leading.

Equally important, however, was the fact that the people had to follow. They could have stayed in one place and enjoyed the phenomenon of the cloud and fire. No one had ever seen such a thing before. Perhaps they could have built a viewing stand and sold tickets. They could have advertised far and wide for people to come see this strange event—a pillar that changed from cloud by day into a fire by night! What a marvelous thing it would be!

All that would have been pointless, of course. The pillar was not there to fascinate them or become another one of the seven wonders of the ancient world. The purpose of the pillar was to lead them out of Egypt into the promised land. But by the same token, the pillar was not a magic carpet. It would not instantly transport them from Egypt into Canaan. In order to get from Egypt to Canaan, they would have to travel—on foot, every step of the way.

All that should be obvious. The pillar would lead them; but they must follow. Jesus is the light of the world. But we too must follow where he leads.   —J. B. N.

II. TESTIMONY OF THE FATHER (JOHN 8:13-20)

A. PHARISEES CHALLENGE JESUS (v. 13)

13. The Pharisees challenged him, "Here you are, appearing as your own witness; your testimony is not valid."

Not valid means that Jesus has not, in the opinion of *the Pharisees*, sufficiently substantiated his claims about himself. Rabbinic law assumes that such testimony will be biased. The Law of Moses requires that testimony and truth claims in criminal proceedings can be accepted only on the testimony of multiple witnesses (Deuteronomy 19:15). The Pharisees therefore plead that they, and everyone else, are allowed to dismiss Jesus' claims about himself.

B. JESUS REFUTES PHARISEES (vv. 14-18)

14. Jesus answered, "Even if I testify on my own behalf, my testimony is valid, for I know where I came from and where I am going. But you have no idea where I come from or where I am going.

Jesus begins his defense by arguing that his case is unique, simply because no other human being is in a position to *testify* on his *behalf*. This verse looks ahead to John 13:3. That passage specifies that Jesus had come from God and was in the process of returning to God through death and resurrection.

Obviously, no one has ever seen God (John 1:18). It would therefore be impossible for anyone to verify or challenge Jesus' claims in the sense of being "witness" to his preexistence. For this reason Jesus does not depend even on the testimony of John the Baptist (John 5:31-36). This is so despite the fact that John was a prophet who pointed to Jesus as the Lamb of God (John 1:29-36).

Instead it is Jesus' unique origin and destiny that establish his credibility. His origin (*where I came from*) is from the Father (John 5:36, 37; 16:28); his destiny (*where I am going*) is to go back to the Father (John 13:1; 16:28; 17:5). Those hostile to Jesus know nothing about either. They are spiritually blind.

15, 16. "You judge by human standards; I pass judgment on no one. But if I do judge, my decisions are right, because I am not alone. I stand with the Father, who sent me.

In Jesus' view, the Pharisees' objections simply reveal that they are unable to perceive spiritual matters. Instead they are stuck in judging *by human standards*. When the Pharisees look at Jesus, they see a man from Galilee who has remarkable abilities but unorthodox teaching. He doesn't fit their understanding of a prophet or the Christ. They are therefore unable to recognize the source of his power (John 7:52; 9:29).

As a result Jesus disqualifies the Pharisees from passing *judgment* on him. He appeals instead to God as the ultimate witness to his identity. Jesus judges *no one* in the way that the Pharisees do.

17, 18. "In your own Law it is written that the testimony of two men is valid. I am one who testifies for myself; my other witness is the Father, who sent me."

Jesus reminds his accusers that Moses had taught that *two* witnesses are sufficient to establish guilt or innocence (Deuteronomy 17:6; 19:15). On the topic of

WHAT DO YOU THINK?

In what ways do people still say not valid *when it comes to Jesus? Why do they do this?*

WHAT DO YOU THINK?

What causes people to reject Jesus as their source of spiritual guidance in favor of something or someone else? How do you protect yourself from making this kind of mistake?

HOW TO SAY IT

Colossians. Kuh-LOSH-unz.

Deuteronomy. Due-ter-AHN-uh-me.

Galilee. GAL-uh-lee.

Isaiah. Eye-ZAY-uh.

Jerusalem. Juh-ROO-suh-lem.

Judaism. JOO-duh-izz-um or JOO-day-izz-um.

Lazarus. LAZ-uh-rus.

Messiah. Meh-SIGH-uh.

Nicodemus. NICK-uh-DEE-mus.

Pharisees. FAIR-ih-seez.

rabbinic. ruh-BIN-ik.

Thessalonians. THESS-uh-LO-nee-unz.

---

his identity, Jesus has testified on his own behalf, and he now calls *the Father* to the stand in his defense. The Father's *testimony* here most likely refers to the works that Jesus does by God's power (John 5:36). The Gospels use Jesus' miracles as signs of his identity; the signs establish his credibility (John 2:11; etc.).

In the "purpose statement" of this Gospel (John 20:30, 31), the apostle makes clear the reason for the signs. When people watch Jesus turn water into wine or raise Lazarus from the dead, they should see the evidence for his claims about himself.

BEARING WITNESS

Several times I have been a witness in court cases. Once was for a traffic accident that I saw. I was asked to describe what I had seen, and it was used as evidence in the case. Another time I appeared on behalf of one of the parties to a suit because of my academic studies in a particular area. I was asked to give my assessment of the issue because I was considered an "expert" in the field. (I enjoyed that label, but my wife was not particularly impressed.)

A witness is a person who gives testimony in court proceedings. I appeared either because I had personally seen the incident or because I had special experience with the nuances of the situation. The task of witnesses is to relate to the judge and/or jury the facts that they know. The judge and jurors were not present at the incident, and they need to know exactly what happened. Or there may be some technical depth to the case, with the judge and jury needing an impartial, objective "expert" to interpret the situation and give an opinion on it.

Jesus relates that he can be a witness to himself, and even God the Father can be a witness on his behalf. The Pharisees of verse 13 were not willing to accept his testimony, not knowing that he did indeed have first-person experience of the situation. Jesus knew some technicalities of the situation that they did not. He was an excellent expert witness, even though they failed to recognize that fact. Do we recognize it? —J. B. N.

C. KNOW ME, KNOW MY FATHER (vv. 19, 20)

19. Then they asked him, "Where is your father?"

"You do not know me or my Father," Jesus replied. "If you knew me, you would know my Father also."

The Gospel of John often follows the "theme of misunderstanding": frequently, no one, not even the disciples, can figure out what Jesus is talking about. No matter how obvious his remarks seem to be (to us!), usually people "just don't get it."

If John is following this theme here, then the Pharisees have missed the point of Jesus' remarks entirely. Thus they ask him where they can find his *father,* meaning Joseph, so that they may question him about Jesus (compare John 6:42). They are still thinking "by human standards" (John 8:15, above).

Jesus' answer implies what the reader already knows to be true: the *Father* of whom Jesus speaks is God, not Joseph. The fact that the Pharisees either cannot understand or will not accept Jesus does not discount his role as the light of the world. People may choose to close their eyes, but their decision to do so does not say anything about Jesus. It reveals, rather, that they do not know the God whom Jesus came to reveal more fully.

20. He spoke these words while teaching in the temple area near the place where the offerings were put. Yet no one seized him, because his time had not yet come.

The implication of *no one seized him, because his time had not yet come* is that hostility is building but has not yet reached the boiling point. Jesus' *time* in the

Gospel of John refers to the time of his arrest and crucifixion. That is when he fulfills his task of dying on the cross (John 7:30; 12:23, 27; 17:1).

Jesus has complete control over his destiny (John 10:15-18). Jesus' enemies can do no harm because he still has much more to do.

III. ESCAPE FROM DARKNESS (JOHN 12:44-46)

A. GOD'S SPECIAL AGENT (vv. 44, 45)

44, 45. Then Jesus cried out, "When a man believes in me, he does not believe in me only, but in the one who sent me. When he looks at me, he sees the one who sent me.

John 12:37-50 is sometimes referred to as a "saddle" or "bridge" in the outline of this Gospel. The reason for this designation is because it is here that John summarizes Jesus' public ministry before moving on to the private teachings to the disciples in the upper room (chapters 13–17). In John 12:35, 36, Jesus urges the Jews one last time to believe in the light. This exhortation leads John to express disbelief at the Jews' inability to understand who Jesus really is (John 12:37-43).

As a closing refrain to his public teaching ministry, Jesus warns the Jews once again. His warning is that it is impossible to believe in God (*the one who sent me*) while rejecting the Son. There are many different religious systems that claim to reveal God in a variety of ways, yet John insists that none of these, not even Judaism, can really lead us to a true vision of God's love and power. God's true nature is perfectly revealed in Jesus alone, making it essential that people accept him.

HE WHO SENT ME

Major General George G. Meade was commanding officer, Army of the Potomac, as it faced the Confederate army under Robert E. Lee at Gettysburg. On Meade's staff was Brigadier General Gouverneur K. Warren, Chief of Engineers.

Acting on his authority as chief engineering officer, Warren was scouting the front lines on the afternoon of July 2, 1863. He came to the southern end of the Union line on a rocky hill called Little Round Top, where he saw that it was undefended. He also saw a large segment of the Confederate army moving toward the same hill. He knew that if the Confederates seized the height they could roll up the entire Union line, bringing disaster to the entire army.

Warren sent couriers down the hill, and they soon met the brigade of Colonel Strong Vincent. Warren ordered him to go up, defend the hill, and prepare to repel the Confederates. Vincent instantly obeyed, and the defense of Little Round Top became famous. Yet it was a near thing. The Union forces beat the Confederates to the top by only fifteen minutes.

What if Vincent had argued with Warren? He could have said, "You are not my immediate commanding officer; why should I obey you?" Vincent knew that Warren represented the authority of General Meade, and that was sufficient for him. Jesus said that if we believe him, we are really acknowledging the authority of God. To refuse to accept the words of Jesus is to refuse that authority.   —J. B. N.

B. LEAVING THE DARKNESS (v. 46)

46. "I have come into the world as a light, so that no one who believes in me should stay in darkness."

The world is spiritually dark in two senses. First, most people do not adequately understand the nature of God himself. As a consequence they do not really understand who they are as people created in God's image. Of course, the

Jews of Jesus' day claim that they are God's elect people, blessed with a special revelation of his true nature. Even they, however, are walking *in darkness* because only through faith in Christ can they truly know God's nature (compare John 12:35, 36).

Second, the world is dark in the sense that people do not live lives that please God. Instead they stumble blindly in pursuit of worldly pleasures that ultimately leave them longing for fulfillment (compare Romans 1:18-32). Like a thirsty man who is given saltwater instead of refreshing water, this pursuit only increases the thirst. Jesus came to rescue us from this ignorance and despair—for eternity.

CONCLUSION

A. PIERCING THE DEEPEST DARKNESS

The image of Jesus as light is a powerful theme in the Gospel of John. Physical light has some marvelous characteristics that allow this image to function beautifully as a description of Christ. Consider this example: you can go into an utterly dark room and light a tiny birthday candle, and all the darkness of that room cannot stop the little light from shining. The smallest candle can dispel the deepest, blackest darkness.

On the other hand, you cannot go into a brightly lighted room with a box of darkness, open the box, and expect the darkness to dim the brightness. Darkness cannot overcome light (John 1:5). This is the case because darkness is, by definition, the absence of something—the absence of light.

When we speak figuratively of the dark world in which we live, we are highlighting the fact that the world is missing or ignoring God. Just as light always overcomes darkness, God's purposes will always overcome evil in this world. Of course, some people choose to close their eyes. But those who open their eyes will find a way through the darkness to eternal life and peace.

B. AVOIDING COUNTERFEIT LIGHT

The issue of "light vs. darkness" is well defined. Spiritually mature Christians clearly recognize the choice. But another issue we face is what we may call "true light vs. counterfeit light." We face this problem since "Satan himself masquerades as an angel of light" (2 Corinthians 11:14).

Many sincere Christians are determined to avoid the darkness of sin, and Satan knows this well. So instead of offering those Christians something that is obviously in the category of *dark*, he offers something that seems, at first glance, to fit within God's light.

This deception can take many forms, and Satan is very crafty. For example a harmless hobby that provides needed rest and relaxation can become an obsession and an addiction, wrecking the family budget. Eating that extra piece of pie at the restaurant buffet can be rationalized as "good stewardship" since "I'm getting my money's worth." Remember, when Satan offered certain temptations to Jesus, he even backed up his ideas with Scripture! (See Matthew 4:1-11.)

So how do we recognize and avoid counterfeit light? The first line of defense is to know the Scriptures thoroughly. Jesus is our example here, since that was how he refuted Satan during the temptation in the wilderness. "Your word is a lamp to my feet and a light for my path" (Psalm 119:105).

The second line of defense is prayer. Jesus saw this as an important part of avoiding temptation (Mark 14:38). A third line of defense is mutual accountability. Invite a fellow Christian to point out your spiritual blind spots. Then consider his or her counsel very carefully!

WHAT DO YOU THINK?

How can we get people to accept the idea that there is such a thing as "spiritual darkness"? How important is this in getting them to see their need for Jesus?

PRAYER

Lord, we live in a dark and confused world. Sometimes it is hard even to know what we should do, much less to do it. Please light our way as we seek to serve you, and please also help us shine the light of Christ on others. In Jesus' name, amen.

THOUGHT TO REMEMBER

The light of Jesus can—and does—pierce the deepest spiritual darkness.

Discovery Learning

This page contains an alternative lesson plan emphasizing learning activities. Classes desiring such student involvement will find these suggestions helpful. The next page is a reproducible activity page to further enhance discovery learning.

LEARNING GOALS

After participating in this lesson, each student will be able to:

1. List ways in which Jesus was and is a source of light in our dark world.

2. Explain Jesus' use of the "light" metaphor as proof of his unique authority.

3. Change one habit to better reflect Jesus' light.

INTO THE LESSON

Have two sides of your assembly area clearly marked, "This Side" and "That Side." As class begins, ask everyone to stand. Give these directions: "I want all the ____ on "This Side" and all the _____ on "That Side." Fill in an appropriate dichotomy, such as men/women, right-handed/left-handed, local sports team fans/fans of teams from other cities. If you like, you may perform this division two or three times rapidly, using different criteria each time. Then have students sit.

Say, "Many things divide us. But one matter must never divide us: who we consider Jesus to be." Have a student read John 6:40-43. Note, "Today's texts in John chapters 8 and 12 continue Jesus' answer regarding questions of who he is." Remind the class of this quarter's theme, "Jesus Christ: A Portrait of God" and remind them of Lesson 1, "Who Is Jesus Christ?"

Continue with an emphasis on the "I Am" theme of the Gospel of John. Say, "'I Am' is an affirmation of power and position." Ask students to affirm a position or role that each holds. Give them one personal example, such as, "I am the head of the class." Encourage metaphors, to be decoded by other members of the class.

INTO THE WORD

Prepare in advance half sheets of paper with eight blocks drawn vertically down the left side. Each block should feature one of the letters of the word *darkness*. On the right side of the paper make eight numbered lines with a "T/F" by each line. Give each student eight yellow peel-and-stick dots (to resemble small suns), each large enough to cover a letter on the paper. (Such dots are available inexpensively at office supply stores.)

Say, "Read the text silently and then close your Bibles and books. We are going to have a true-false quiz on ele-ments of today's lesson. Your goal is to 'dispel darkness' with the Word of light. For each answer you get correct, you may cover one letter with a 'sunlight' dot."

Read aloud each of the following statements. Allow time for students to mark their answers, and then give the answer and any explanation necessary. (1) Jesus calls himself the light of the world *[True; 8:12]*. (2) This is the first time in the Gospel of John that Jesus has been called "the light" *[False; 1:5, 7-9]*. (3) In the Pharisees' legal system, a person could not testify on his own behalf *[True; 8:13]*. (4) Jesus affirms that the Pharisees had no idea where he came from *[True; 8:14]*. (5) Jewish law required four witnesses to testify to confirm a truth *[False; 8:17]*. (6) The Jewish leaders asked Jesus to bring in his mother as witness *[False; 8:19]*. (7) No one was able to lay a hand on Jesus *[True; 8:20]*. (8) Seeing Jesus is the same as seeing God *[True; 12:45]*. (9) Jesus' discussion with the Jewish leaders in John 8 took place in the temple *[True; 8:20]*. (10) Believing in God requires believing in Jesus, and vice versa *[True; 12:44]*.

INTO LIFE

Introduce the assignment below using this book summary. Say, "In Ursula LeGuin's fantasy *The Tombs of Atuan*, the hero, named Ged, rescues the princess, Arha, who has learned to love the darkness of the catacombs. There she has been made priestess of the dark powers. As Ged delivers her from the tombs, he assures her that she was not made for darkness but for light."

Explain that Arha was taken as a young child to replace a dying princess, but as most children are, she was afraid of the dark. As she grew comfortable entering the dark world of tombs she became fascinated. She gained a sense of power over the darkness, even as it gained power over her. Arha's name means "the eaten one."

Comment on how darkness first scares, then fascinates, then "eats alive." Liken this same sequence to most people in our world who get swallowed up in darkness and need a light bearer to rescue them.

Close with a time of sharing. Ask students how they plan to change one habit in the week ahead to better reflect Jesus' light. (Option: let students fill in the Imperatives! exercise from the Reproducible Page. Then use the third of those imperatives [Follow me!] to lead into the Reflectors exercise.)

Imperatives!

From today's text find three verbs that will fit the following critical imperatives.

Jesus says,

1. "___ ___ ___ ___ me!" (John 8:19)
2. "___ ___ ___ ___ ___ ___ me!" (John 12:44)
3. "___ ___ ___ ___ ___ me!" (John 8:12)

DO IT!

How is this order the logical, necessary one?
Where do you stand in the sequence?

Reflectors

Light can be reflected from certain surfaces. How could and should you reflect his light in the following circumstances? Write your ideas in the boxes.

A coworker is cheating your company by arriving late and leaving early.

Nearly every driver around you is exceeding the speed limit.

You have income sources the government will not discover unless you report them.

The neighbors have noticed your failure to maintain your yard as they think you should.

A customer in front of you at the grocery store is chewing out the cashier for high prices.

In the locker room there are individuals who repeat crude and vulgar stories.

"I AM THE GOOD SHEPHERD"

WHY TEACH THIS LESSON?

We all like to feel that we're "in control," don't we? We can become terrified when we get swept along by events that are beyond our control. Think of the widow who hears someone sneaking around outside her house at night. Think of citizens of a nation that is victimized by terrorist attacks. Think of residents of a coastal area as they watch weather reports of a hurricane advancing relentlessly against them. All these situations involve people desiring protection against "enemies" over which they seem to have no control.

Satan, the great enemy, the awful adversary, is sneaking around. At times he strikes as a terrorist. Spiritual forces beyond our control threaten to overwhelm us. We are weak and vulnerable; we need shelter. In such times the Christian has a sure protector. Jesus is the good shepherd of his flock. From the Scripture lesson today we learn to listen for the voice of the gentle shepherd. Listen as he speaks to you words of encouragement, hope, and comfort. He is in control.

INTRODUCTION

A. KNOWING YOUR OWN

For many years we had a large dog named Sassy. I could always identify Sassy's bark from several blocks away, even though there were dozens of dogs in our neighborhood; Sassy, in turn, could identify my call and would come to me in a crowd of people.

In a similar way my wife and I can identify our young daughter's cry in a room full of toddlers. My son's first-grade class at church, where I volunteer as a youth sponsor, includes a pair of twins who define the word *identical*. Their teachers are constantly in a quandary trying to tell them apart. The teachers insist that the two must never wear matching clothes. Yet the parents of these boys can immediately tell one from the other.

Knowledge of this kind—the ability to pick out a voice or a face in a crowd—is a sign of intimacy: we know those we love and they know us, through constant interaction. In our lesson today Jesus will apply this principle to his loving relationship with his disciples.

B. LESSON BACKGROUND

Most scholars view John 9, just preceding today's lesson text, as critical for understanding the background of John 10. In John 9 Jesus met a man who had been blind from birth and healed him. The healing came about when Jesus covered the man's eyes with mud and sent him to wash at the Pool of Siloam. The cure was effective, but it was impossible for the man to recognize Jesus or know much about him. (Jesus was gone before the man had a chance to see him.)

DEVOTIONAL READING:
ISAIAH 40:10-14

BACKGROUND SCRIPTURE:
JOHN 10:1-18

PRINTED TEXT:
JOHN 10:1-18

LESSON AIMS

After participating in this lesson, each student will be able to:

1. Recite reasons Jesus is the good shepherd.

2. Contrast Jesus as a spiritual shepherd with other religious leaders of his day.

3. Suggest one specific way to participate in the shepherding ministry of his or her church.

Feb
4

KEY VERSE

I am the good shepherd. The good shepherd lays down his life for the sheep. —John 10:11

The Pharisees later interrogated the man who had been healed because Jesus, in their view, had violated the Law of Moses by healing on the Sabbath. The man refused to condemn Jesus and ultimately criticized the Pharisees for ignoring the obvious evidence of his divine power. As a result they excommunicated him (John 9:1-34).

Jesus later found the man and led him to faith, while the Pharisees continued to question Jesus' authority (John 9:35-41). Jesus' teaching in chapter 10 about his role as the good shepherd is a commentary on this situation. It includes several promises that Jesus will protect and save those who believe in him.

This teaching undoubtedly was extremely meaningful to the apostle John. He, along with the other apostles, also experienced persecution and excommunication for faith in Christ (see John 16:1-4).

I. SHEPHERD AND THIEF (JOHN 10:1-6)

A. REACTION TO THE SHEPHERD (vv. 1-4)

1, 2. *"I tell you the truth, the man who does not enter the sheep pen by the gate, but climbs in by some other way, is a thief and a robber. The man who enters by the gate is the shepherd of his sheep.*

The opening phrase *I tell you the truth* leads us to ask a question: to whom is Jesus speaking? The context of John 9:40, 41 seems to indicate that Jesus is still talking to the Pharisees. On the other hand, the phrase "they did not understand" in John 10:6 (below) may indicate that a different audience is in view.

In either case Jesus' parable about *the sheep pen* here in verses 1-6 is a sharp condemnation of the Jewish religious leaders. Jesus compares God's people to *sheep* in a pen; in the immediate context, the specific "sheep" in question is most likely the man whom Jesus has just healed of blindness in chapter 9.

The *shepherd* in this analogy is Jesus himself, while the thieves are the Pharisees and other Jewish leaders who are attempting to prevent people from believing in him (compare John 9:40). Jesus' legitimate spiritual authority is evidenced by the fact that he *enters by the gate.* He displays God's care and love, and people recognize him as the one whom God has sent (compare John 9:30-34).

God's true sheep, however, refuse to accept the false teachings of the Pharisees. These sheep recognize that those teachings do not reflect a correct understanding of Christ in light of Jesus' miracles. Many Pharisees are thieves and robbers, bent on self-preservation at the sheep's expense (compare Ezekiel 34; Jude 12).

3. *"The watchman opens the gate for him, and the sheep listen to his voice. He calls his own sheep by name and leads them out.*

Middle Eastern shepherds lead flocks by voice commands. Consequently *the sheep* know the *voice* of their shepherd. Even when many different flocks graze together, a shepherd can gather his own simply by calling to them. In a similar way those who seek God's will recognize Jesus' voice and willingly follow him.

The *watchman* is the person who guards the gate of the sheep pen. In the context of Jesus' illustration, this character probably does not refer to any specific person. Rather, the reference is to the general fact that Jesus has a legitimate claim to call God's people.

KNOWN BY OUR NAMES

For several years we had a professor on our college faculty who had an amazing gift. He would look at the pictures of all incoming freshmen that the admissions department provided. He would also notice the hometown of each. At freshmen orientation he would then have all new students stand up—usually over two hundred people whom he had never met.

Starting at one end of the group, he would begin to call out names and hometowns. Each student named would then sit down. By the time he got to the other end of the room, only one or two students would be standing—and often they were recent applicants for whom the admissions office did not have a picture!

In addition that man often taught at a particular "high school week" at a nearby Christian service camp. He would have all students who were there the previous year stand up. He had not seen these students in a year, but he called off their names without any mistakes.

In the 1996 movie *Fly Away Home,* Amy Alden raises a flock of orphaned Canada geese. She gives them all names and leads them into winter quarters in the southern United States. To most of us one goose looks just like another.

If a human can have an ability to know names, hometowns, and individual geese, how much more is Jesus able to know us! He is the good shepherd, and he knows the names of his sheep. That comfort will follow us into eternity. —J. B. N.

4. "When he has brought out all his own, he goes on ahead of them, and his sheep follow him because they know his voice.

To heed the call of Christ is vital! Ancient shepherds walk ahead of their flocks to lead them from the pen to safe pasture, and Jesus uses this analogy to describe his leadership of God's people. The twofold emphasis is on knowing *his voice* and on following *him.* The first of these two speaks to the ability to recognize Jesus as the one who has come to reveal God to the world. The second speaks to being obedient to his teaching in all circumstances.

B. REACTION TO STRANGERS (v. 5)
5. "But they will never follow a stranger; in fact, they will run away from him because they do not recognize a stranger's voice."

In John 9 the man healed of blindness stubbornly refused to yield to the Pharisees. He would not condemn Jesus despite pressure. His reaction contrasted sharply with that of his parents, who tried to straddle the fence when called to testify (John 9:18-23).

The attitude of the man healed of blindness parallels the way that sheep will scatter when strangers attempt to lure them away. God's people will listen to Jesus' voice and no other.

C. REACTION OF THE LISTENERS (v. 6)
6. Jesus used this figure of speech, but they did not understand what he was telling them.

Although the meaning of Jesus' analogy seems obvious to us now, it is misunderstood by the original hearers. This confusion may suggest that Jesus is now speaking to a different audience: not to the Pharisees of John 9:40, 41 but to a larger group of Jews of John 10:19.

This view could be supported by the reaction of the chief priests and scribes in Luke 20:19. There we see that those religious leaders are able to understand all too well that Jesus uses a figure of speech against them. Here, however, the audience *did not understand what he was telling them.*

So perhaps this is a larger audience (again, John 10:19) that is not aware of Jesus' earlier discussion with the man whom he had cured of blindness. In either case Jesus proceeds to expand the illustration in order to explain its relevance to all people who are considering whether or not to follow him (next verse).

HOW TO SAY IT
Cornelius. Cor-NEEL-yus.
Ezekiel. Ee-ZEEK-ee-ul or Ee-ZEEK-yul.
Messiah. Meh-SIGH-uh.
Pharisees. FAIR-ih-seez.
Siloam. Sigh-LO-um.

WHAT DO YOU THINK?
The people listening to Jesus were confused by his figures of speech. What subjects in the Bible still cause you confusion? How do you go about getting help to clarify those issues?

WHAT DO YOU THINK?

Christians often fill their lives to the brim with activities and duties. Churches may be partially responsible for this hyperactivity. How is this different from what Jesus meant by having an abundant life? What corrections do you need to make?

II. INDIVIDUALS AND MOTIVES (JOHN 10:7-10)

A. NOW VS. THEN (vv. 7, 8)

7. Therefore Jesus said again, "I tell you the truth, I am the gate for the sheep.

In ancient times *sheep* often are kept in caves or in pens made of rock walls in open fields. The shepherd brings his flock back to the pen at the end of the day. There he counts and inspects them.

These pens may have no physical doors or gates. For that reason the shepherd himself would stand or lie across the opening to prevent sheep from wandering out and wolves from entering. Thus the shepherd himself becomes the door or *gate* of the sheep pen. This is the imagery Jesus uses to describe how he watches over his sheep and guards them from harm.

8. "All who ever came before me were thieves and robbers, but the sheep did not listen to them.

The *thieves* here may refer again to the Jewish religious leaders as depicted in Jeremiah 23:1, 2; Ezekiel 34:2, 3. The term may also refer to the various false messiahs who led anti-Roman revolutionary movements after the death of Herod the Great in 4 BC (compare Acts 5:36, 37). In either case God's people are waiting for the true shepherd, Jesus. Thus the sheep do not heed the imposters who came before Jesus.

B. SALVATION VS. DESTRUCTION (vv. 9, 10)

9. "I am the gate; whoever enters through me will be saved. He will come in and go out, and find pasture.

This verse pictures the sheepfold as the dwelling place of God's redeemed people. *Come in and go out* does not suggest that one falls in and out of salvation. Rather, the reference is to the way that Jesus continually provides for his people by leading them to safe *pasture*—by providing for their spiritual needs. The sheep depend on the shepherd to lead them out of the pen for food and water. In the same way we depend on Christ to provide for us.

The imagery thus emphasizes the shepherd's ongoing, daily care for the flock. Jesus' concern for his people is constant.

10. "The thief comes only to steal and kill and destroy; I have come that they may have life, and have it to the full.

The false messiahs attempt to "call" God's sheep, but they do so for selfish reasons. They want to increase their own power and prestige in service of their own agendas. Jesus, here as elsewhere, stresses that his motives are entirely pure. He does not wish to promote himself at the expense of others. He seeks only to protect the lives and well being of his flock. In fact he is willing to sacrifice his own life to save them (v. 11, next).

III. SHEPHERD AND HIRED HAND (JOHN 10:11-18)

A. SHEPHERD'S ACTIONS, PART 1 (v. 11)

11. "I am the good shepherd. The good shepherd lays down his life for the sheep.

Shepherds give their lives for their *sheep* in at least two ways. First, sheep need constant care and attention, with many long days and nights in the field. The job is all-consuming. Second, and more specifically here, shepherds are called upon to protect the flock from dangerous predators. In these cases the *shepherd* risks *his life* by placing himself between the sheep and the wolves. Ancient Jews can well relate to this sort of imagery because so many of them work with livestock.

The Old Testament frequently refers to God as the shepherd of his people. Often the emphasis is on protection and provision. Perhaps the most famous of these passages is Psalm 23. Jesus calls himself *the good shepherd* against this backdrop to emphasize his loving care for his people. This is in contrast to the religious leaders of his day. It is Jesus alone who literally will give *his life* on the cross *for the sheep* (compare Hebrews 13:20).

LAYING DOWN ONE'S LIFE

On January 23, 1943, more than 900 men sailed from New York on the USAT *Dorchester,* a former luxury liner, now a troop ship bound for Greenland. Most of the travelers were young Army enlistees, plus some officers and Merchant Marine sailors. There were also four chaplains: George L. Fox, a Methodist minister; Clark V. Poling, a Dutch Reformed minister; John P. Washington, a Roman Catholic priest; and Alexander D. Goode, a Jewish rabbi.

About 150 miles from Greenland, at about 1:00 AM on February 3, German submarine U-223 torpedoed the aging transport. The attack killed about 100 men immediately. The rest groped for the openings in the darkness that would lead to the deck. The four chaplains helped where they could, lending some sense of calm to the fear-crazed young men. Lifeboats were readied, and the chaplains went to the lockers to hand out life jackets.

Unfortunately, there were not enough jackets for everyone. The four chaplains had theirs on, but all four removed their jackets and handed them to young men and directed them to the boats. The *Dorchester* sank in less than 30 minutes. As it went down the survivors noticed the four chaplains standing at the railing, arms linked together, singing and praying, giving strength to others.

About 75 percent of the men aboard perished in the sinking, including the four chaplains. Those four had laid down their lives for the men of their "flock." We marvel at their sacrifice, even after more than 60 years. Do we marvel as much about Jesus? He also laid down his life, but in a much more profound way. His sacrifice made it possible for us to live eternally. That's something that even the selfless sacrifice of the four chaplains could not accomplish. —J. B. N.

Visual for Lesson 10. *Point to this visual as you ask, "In what ways do you allow Jesus to be your shepherd? In what ways do you resist?"*

B. HIRED HAND'S ACTIONS (vv. 12, 13)

12, 13. "*The hired hand is not the shepherd who owns the sheep. So when he sees the wolf coming, he abandons the sheep and runs away. Then the wolf attacks the flock and scatters it. The man runs away because he is a hired hand and cares nothing for the sheep.*"

While the thieves and robbers of verse 8 likely allude to the Pharisees who had persecuted the healed man in John 9, we're not really sure who the *hired hand* represents. Whoever this is, such a person works among *the flock* (God's people) but without genuine concern. Jesus, by contrast, knows his people and loves them as his own. The next several verses describe how he expresses this love.

C. SHEPHERD'S ACTIONS, PART 2 (vv. 14-18)

14, 15. "*I am the good shepherd; I know my sheep and my sheep know me—just as the Father knows me and I know the Father—and I lay down my life for the sheep.*"

The verb *know* here refers to more than merely "know about." Of course Jesus knows his sheep in the sense that he knows who we are. But the hireling of verse 13 can also claim that he knows the sheep in this way—how many sheep there are, what they look like, which ones walk slower, etc.

Jesus therefore proceeds to outline two ways in which his ministry is unique. First, he emphasizes the special relationship that he has with his people through comparison with his own relationship to God. Jesus and *the Father* are completely united, and Jesus and his people are united as well (see Matthew 11:27).

WHAT DO YOU THINK?

Jesus distinguished between shepherds and hired hands. How do we use this distinction to help us discern between those who have good and bad motivations for being in leadership roles in the church?

[Make sure to consider Matthew 7:1, 15-20.]

PRAYER

Lord, we know that you call to us in every situation; help us to hear your voice. We live in a world with many false ideas and self-serving teachers. Sometimes it's hard to know what's right. Keep us focused on the one who gave his life for us. In Jesus' name, amen.

Second, Jesus restates his willingness to *lay down* his *life,* sacrificing everything for the well-being of his flock.

16. "I have other sheep that are not of this sheep pen. I must bring them also. They too will listen to my voice, and there shall be one flock and one shepherd.

Who are the *other sheep* of whom Jesus speaks? Most commentators conclude that these are Gentiles (that is, non-Jewish people) who have not yet heard about Jesus and his message. Consider the prediction in Isaiah 42:6: "I, the Lord, have called you in righteousness; I will take hold of your hand. I will keep you and will make you to be a covenant for the people and a light for the Gentiles."

Jesus is thus making a prediction about the mission to the Gentiles that will follow the conversion of Cornelius in Acts 10. That mission ultimately will find its fullest expression in Paul's ministry.

Notice also the emphasis on the unity of the flock. The phrase *one flock* speaks to the unity of Jew and Gentile in Christ, *one shepherd.* Jesus' words are especially meaningful to John's churches in the late first century AD. These churches likely include believers from both Jewish and Gentile backgrounds. Christ cares for all of his people equally.

17. "The reason my Father loves me is that I lay down my life—only to take it up again.

Take it up again refers to Jesus' resurrection. Jesus enjoys the Father's love because he, unlike the Pharisees and false Messiahs, proves his love for God's people. The ultimate proof comes when he lays *down* his *life* to pay the price for sin. After the resurrection Jesus is exalted once again to his heavenly position beside the *Father.*

18. "No one takes it from me, but I lay it down of my own accord. I have authority to lay it down and authority to take it up again. This command I received from my Father."

John stresses throughout his Gospel that Jesus' death was not an accident of circumstance. Despite the fact that he died in a gruesome and humiliating way, Jesus was at every moment completely in control of everything that happened to him. This makes his death so much more meaningful as an expression of his care for the flock.

Many shepherds may have to risk their lives to protect the sheep at a moment's notice; Jesus consciously chooses when and how he will die, confident that he has the power to live again. No one else could make such a claim.

CONCLUSION

Very often we are told (especially in advertisements) that it's bad to be "just one of the crowd." We are supposed to let our individuality stand out. We like to think of ourselves as independent individuals who don't need to rely on anyone else. At the same time, however, it is very comforting to be a member of a group in which we can feel safe and at home. The hit television show *Cheers* (which ran from 1982 to 1993) portrayed a group of close friends at a small bar in Boston. That bar was a place "where everybody knows your name." That was an important part of the show's appeal: it illustrated the type of place that many of us long to find. A place to be "one of the gang." A place to be accepted for who one is.

The sad thing about that television program is that so many people seek these types of relationships in bars rather than in churches. While we are all individuals, together we make up Jesus' flock as we follow his voice. He knows each of our names, and we each have a special place in his family. In him we find an eternal peace and comfort that the world cannot provide.

THOUGHT TO REMEMBER

Jesus still shepherds us today.

Discovery Learning

This page contains an alternative lesson plan emphasizing learning activities. Classes desiring such student involvement will find these suggestions helpful. The next page is a reproducible activity page to further enhance discovery learning.

LEARNING GOALS

After participating in this lesson, each student will be able to:

1. Recite reasons Jesus is the good shepherd.

2. Contrast Jesus as a spiritual shepherd with other religious leaders of his day.

3. Suggest one specific way to participate in the shepherding ministry of his or her church.

INTO THE LESSON

As students arrive give each a piece of blank paper (or have students turn to "What Do You Think?" in the student books if you're using those). Write the following open-ended statements on the board:

To be a good shepherd, a person must . . .

Jesus was the good shepherd because . . .

Ask your students to write down as many responses to each statement as they can generate in a minute or two. Then call on volunteers to share their answers.

As an alternative, have students work on the Wanted: The Ideal Shepherd! exercise from the Reproducible Page. After completion of either, say, "Today's lesson will stress Jesus' role as the good shepherd. We will also learn something about our responsibility to shepherd members of our congregation."

INTO THE WORD

This Yes or No exercise will help students note contrasts among the shepherd, the thief, and the hireling. Hand out copies of this exercise (or direct students to their student books, where this exercise is also found). Each student should study John 10:1-18 and then answer yes or no to each question. Correct answers are in parentheses; do not hand the answers out.

1. Does he access the sheep by the door? Shepherd (Y); Thief (N); Hireling (Y). 2. Do the sheep recognize his voice? Shepherd (Y); Thief (N); Hireling (Y). 3. Do the sheep follow him? Shepherd (Y); Thief (N); Hireling (Y). 4. Does he take care of the sheep? Shepherd (Y); Thief (N); Hireling (Y, to a degree). 5. Does he care about other sheep besides those in his immediate fold? Shepherd (Y); Thief (N); Hireling (N). 6. Will he give his life for the sheep? Shepherd (Y); Thief (N); Hireling (N).

Review the correct answers, and then say, "Jesus made it clear that this figure of speech was about him.

What do we know about Jesus, from this text and from other passages of Scripture, that proves him to be the good shepherd?" Discuss any passages the students mention. Then discuss the following questions:

1. How does Jesus enter "by the gate"? (See John 9:35-41.)

2. How do the sheep recognize his voice? (See Mark 1:21-27.)

3. In what way is Jesus the "gate" of the sheep? (See Acts 4:12; 2 Timothy 2:8-13.)

4. Who were the thieves and robbers?

5. Who were the hired hands?

6. Who were the "other sheep"?

7. How did Jesus have the power to lay his life down for the sheep? (See Matthew 26:53, 54; Hebrews 5:7-9.)

You can follow up on each question by asking, "Why is this important to know?" The above could be a small-group activity.

INTO LIFE

Students will be completing two exercises. Both parts are found in the student book.

Exercise A: What Do Shepherds Do? Ask students to consider what is involved in shepherding a church today. Each student should list as many essential functions as he or she can think of. For example, they might list teaching, counseling, and praying for the sick. Direct students to Acts 20:28-31; 1 Timothy 5:17; James 5:14; and 1 Peter 5:1-3 for more ideas.

When your students are finished, have them share their answers. Write their ideas on the board. Then ask your students to complete the next exercise.

Exercise B: How Can We Shepherd Our Flock? For each of the shepherding functions listed in Exercise A, instruct each student to jot down at least one possible ministry that your congregation can do to fulfill it. For example, a hospital calling program would carry out the function of praying for the sick. (Option: substitute the How's Your Flock? exercise from the Reproducible Page.)

When your students are finished, list their answers as you did before. Ask students which programs your congregation currently performs. Brainstorm ways to begin new ministries that are not currently part of your church's program. Challenge your students to participate actively in a least one such ministry.

Wanted: The Ideal Shepherd!

Imagine you own a flock of sheep and need to hire a shepherd to care for them. In the space provided, write a want ad for your ideal shepherd. Be sure to include the qualities, experience, and training the applicant needs to meet your expectations.

How's Your Flock?

The sheep below represent typical shepherding ministries in a local church. Underline those ministries that your congregation provides. Circle those that you would like to see your congregation add. Put a checkmark beside any ministry in which you participate or would like to participate. Use the unlabeled sheep to add ministries not listed.

small-group teaching

hospital calling

counseling

evangelism

nursing home and shut-in visitation

prison ministry

food pantry

"I AM THE RESURRECTION AND THE LIFE"

WHY TEACH THIS LESSON?

Facing death is not easy. Watching a parent die is hard. Watching your child die is gut-wrenching. Sudden and tragic deaths because of accidents or violence are hard to understand. A suicide opens up a multitude of questions with no answers for those who are left behind.

But through them all, Jesus is continually the same. Your learners need to know this! We will find consolation in him as we share together in this lesson. Jesus is the one who truly is the resurrection and the life.

INTRODUCTION

A. "THE ONE YOU LOVE IS SICK"

My family originally came from western Kentucky. Not so long ago it was common for women there to marry at a young age. My grandmother was married at 14 and had three children by age 17. I was born when my mother was 19, and as a result I enjoyed the blessing of young grandparents.

My grandmother was a second mother to me. She figures large in almost every one of my childhood memories. She loved all of us dearly, and I cannot count the number of wonderful hours I spent in her home. Even now her house symbolizes peace and comfort and love to me.

I recently had the privilege of holding her hand while she died, someone who loved me unconditionally. As we stood by the hospital bed in her final days, I often wondered what Jesus would have done about her situation. I wondered why God had not healed her.

Since then I have come to see that such feelings reflected my own grief and selfish desires more than a real concern for my grandmother. In death she has now found a true life in God that I cannot yet comprehend. Do we maintain our trust in Jesus when death hits so close to home?

B. LESSON BACKGROUND

John 1:19–12:50 has been called The Book of Signs within that great Gospel. The raising of Lazarus is one of the signs in the Gospel of John through which Jesus revealed himself to be the Son of God (compare John 2:11; 4:54). What we may call the "purpose statement" of John's Gospel stresses the importance of the signs: "Jesus did many other miraculous signs in the presence of his disciples, which are not recorded in this book. But these are written that you may believe that Jesus is the Christ, the Son of God, and that by believing you may have life in his name" (John 20:30, 31).

While the earlier signs demonstrated Jesus' divine power, the resurrection of Lazarus revealed Jesus' authority over the grave. One can scarcely ignore a deed

DEVOTIONAL READING:

JUDE 17-23

BACKGROUND SCRIPTURE:

JOHN 11:1-44

PRINTED TEXT:

JOHN 11:1-7, 17-27

LESSON AIMS

After participating in this lesson, each student will be able to:

1. Describe the mind-sets of Jesus, the disciples, Mary, and Martha just before the resurrection of Lazarus.

2. Explain how Martha is a model of faith in Jesus, as well as how her faith fell short.

3. Show how he or she can use Jesus' teaching to comfort someone in grief.

Feb
11

KEY VERSE

I am the resurrection and the life. He who believes in me will live, even though he dies.

—John 11:25

of this magnitude. The account is significant to the larger flow of John's Gospel in that it leads the chief priests and Pharisees to plot Jesus' death (11:45-53). Today's lesson is not about Lazarus's resurrection itself, but rather it is about the facts and attitudes that preceded it.

I. SOBERING NEWS (JOHN 11:1-7)

A. SICKNESS (vv. 1-4)

1, 2. Now a man named Lazarus was sick. He was from Bethany, the village of Mary and her sister Martha. This Mary, whose brother Lazarus now lay sick, was the same one who poured perfume on the Lord and wiped his feet with her hair.

Back in John 1:28 the apostle identified "Bethany on the other side of the Jordan" as the place where John the Baptist had preached and baptized. At the end of John 10, Jesus left Jerusalem for a preaching tour in that same area after the Jews attempted to arrest him for blasphemy (10:39-42). *Mary* and *Martha*, however, live in a different *village* named *Bethany*. This town is less than two miles from Jerusalem, east of the Mount of Olives.

Mary, Martha, and *Lazarus* (sisters and brother) seem to be close friends of Jesus. Perhaps he stays in their home whenever he attends a feast in Jerusalem. On one of these visits, Martha had criticized Jesus for not making Mary help her prepare a meal. In reply he reminded her that food is less important than devotion to his teaching (Luke 10:38-42). The mention here of the anointing by Mary looks forward to John 12:1-3.

HOUSE OF AFFLICTION

I am often fascinated by biblical place names. The name *Bethlehem* means "house of bread." Isn't that an interesting name for the place where Jesus was born—the one who proclaimed himself as the bread of life? *Jerusalem* means "city of peace"—the capital city of the land where the prince of peace walked. *Bethsaida*, on the shore of the Sea of Galilee, means "house of fishing." That is certainly an apt name for a fishing port.

The meaning of *Bethany*, for its part, is a bit uncertain. It could mean "house of dates or figs." Other possible meanings are "house of poverty," "house of the poor," or even "house of the afflicted ones."

There is no indication that Mary, Martha, and Lazarus were poor, but we can assume safely that the town of Bethany at least had its normal share of death, disease, disappointment, marital discord, family squabbles, and other perennial setbacks to human prosperity. Leprosy was a devastating disease, and in Bethany lived Simon the leper (Matthew 26:6). And then there was Lazarus. With his death there were two grief-stricken sisters plus a whole crowd of others weeping with them. Bethany was definitely a house of affliction at that time.

If you stop to think about it, each of us lives in a "house of affliction" of some kind—discord, strife, pain, delusion, fatigue, abandonment, despair. But it is Jesus, and only Jesus, who can move us into a permanent "house of joy." The change that Jesus brought about at Bethany with Lazarus's resurrection was temporary, since Lazarus obviously died again later. The change that Jesus is able bring to us because of his own resurrection can be permanent and eternal, if we will allow it.   —J. B. N.

3. So the sisters sent word to Jesus, "Lord, the one you love is sick."

The exact nature of Lazarus's illness is not specified and is probably not relevant to the story. Clearly, however, *the sisters* believe that his condition is critical —they would not bother Jesus over a minor case of the flu.

Mary and Martha naturally assume that Jesus will be concerned about his friend's condition. They probably expect him to rush back to town for a healing (see comments on John 11:22, below).

In addition to John's overall emphasis on Christ's divine power, we will see this story provide insight into Jesus' humanity. John depicts Jesus as experiencing the ups and downs of human feelings and relationships. Lazarus is his friend, and the sisters know that it will be natural for Jesus to be concerned about him. **4. When he heard this, Jesus said, "This sickness will not end in death. No, it is for God's glory so that God's Son may be glorified through it."**

When the message reaches *Jesus*, he immediately replies with what would seem to be very good news: *This sickness will not end in death.* When that statement is added to the remainder of the verse—*so that God's Son may be glorified through it*—those who are listening probably infer that Jesus will honor the request to go and heal Lazarus. As on so many other occasions, Jesus' power will indeed be revealed. Lazarus's circumstance ultimately will bring greater glory to God—but not in a way that anyone is expecting!

We should pause to stress that this verse should not be taken to mean that God causes all sickness. Of course God is *glorified* by the confidence that believers can display in the face of illness or death. But here Jesus is simply saying that he plans to bring good from a bad situation.

B. DELAY (vv. 5-7)

5. Jesus loved Martha and her sister and Lazarus.

John confirms the sisters' claim in verse 3 ("the one you love") by noting that Jesus really does care deeply for *Lazarus* and family. This verse leads the reader to expect that Jesus will leave for Bethany immediately, just as the sisters suppose. **6, 7. Yet when he heard that Lazarus was sick, he stayed where he was two more days.**

Then he said to his disciples, "Let us go back to Judea."

These verses are stunning in light of what has preceded. Jesus loves Lazarus and seems to have just indicated in verse 4 that he would go to heal him. But after telling everyone, in effect, "Don't worry," Jesus chooses to wait *two more days* before doing anything. The disciples may interpret this delay as a sign of caution, for the Jewish authorities in Jerusalem apparently have put out a warrant for Jesus' arrest (John 10:39; 11:8). But in John 11:14, 15 (not in today's text) Jesus makes it clear that he is "glad" for the delay.

While Jesus' actions (and inactions!) may seem harsh or confusing, they are calculated to glorify God to the fullest possible extent. In the first place this incident illustrates Jesus' claims throughout the Gospel of John that he does not act according to his human desires and interests. Instead he does everything to please God. "My food," said Jesus, "is to do the will of him who sent me and to finish his work" (John 4:34; compare 5:30; 7:17, 18). Everything must proceed on God's plan and God's timing, even if this is painful for Jesus and his friends.

Second, the event as it unfolds will show clearly that Jesus wants this to be more than a healing. He will demonstrate, rather, that his power reaches even beyond the grave.

II. COURAGEOUS BELIEF (JOHN 11:17-27)

A. ALREADY DEAD (vv. 17-20)

17. On his arrival, Jesus found that Lazarus had already been in the tomb for four days.

WHAT DO YOU THINK?

When Lazarus became seriously ill, his sisters Mary and Martha felt free to call upon Jesus to ask for his help. How will you form that kind of relationship with Christ? What things or attitudes in your life will be a help or a hindrance to this?

WHAT DO YOU THINK?

Our timetable isn't always the same as God's timetable. What are some reasons that God may have for not responding immediately to your prayer requests?

WHAT DO YOU THINK?

Jesus expects our faith and obedience even when (or especially when!) he doesn't reveal his plans to us. What was a time or circumstance that you can look back on and say, "Ah, now I see what God's plan was"? How did your faith grow stronger as a result of how God worked?

Jesus' intentional delay ensures that Lazarus has *already been in the tomb for four days*. Jesus has the ability to heal from a distance, if he so desires (Luke 7:1-10). But that is not the plan here. By the time Jesus arrives, the tone has changed from hopeful expectation to that of grief and mourning. The reference to *four days* is significant. Some ancient Jews believe that the soul of a departed person hovers around the body for three days. On the fourth day, when signs of decomposition are clearly evident (such as the stench that Martha will mention in verse 39), the person's spirit supposedly departs for good. To be dead for four days would thus mean something like "really, really dead."

Whether or not this four-day theory is true, no one can doubt that Lazarus is actually dead. There is no reasonable way to suggest that Jesus simply resuscitates Lazarus or brings him out of a coma. The situation calls for a resurrection rather than a healing.

18, 19. Bethany was less than two miles from Jerusalem, and many Jews had come to Martha and Mary to comfort them in the loss of their brother.

The *Jews* place high value on the ethical need *to comfort* the bereaved. Funerals may last for a week. Lazarus's funeral seems to be especially remarkable in this regard. The fact that *many Jews* had come from Jerusalem to the little town of *Bethany* to mourn for him suggests that the family is well known and perhaps wealthy. Clearly Jesus is not the only person who loved Lazarus.

John may also wish to emphasize the size of the crowd in order to stress that a large number of people will witness Lazarus's resurrection (11:45). Bethany is about one and three-quarter miles *from Jerusalem*.

20. When Martha heard that Jesus was coming, she went out to meet him, but Mary stayed at home.

The fact that *Mary stayed at home* does not necessarily mean that she feels angry toward *Jesus*. She is not indifferent about his arrival, as verses 31-33 will reveal. Perhaps the reason that Mary stays home can be explained this way. The house seems to be packed with mourners; a messenger arrives, finds *Martha*, and tells her that Jesus is on his way. In her excitement Martha perhaps goes straight to Jesus without pausing even to tell her sister. Note that Mary does not seem to be aware of Jesus' arrival until verse 28, after Martha goes back to the house.

WHAT DO YOU THINK?

What are some things we can do as a church or as a class to minister to those who have suffered the loss of a loved one?

We may also speculate that Martha does not want to draw too much attention to Jesus right away: when she finally does tell Mary that he has come, she pulls her aside so that the crowd can't hear (again, v. 28). Martha seems to see the need for Mary to have a private moment to share her grief with Jesus.

B. STEADY FAITH (vv. 21-27)

21. "Lord," Martha said to Jesus, "if you had been here, my brother would not have died.

At first glance Martha's comment *Lord, . . . if you had been here, my brother would not have died* may sound like criticism. But in view of the statements to follow, it appears that Martha wishes to reassure *Jesus* that she does not hold Lazarus's death against him. Martha's mind is clouded with grief at the moment. We may guess that she assumes that Jesus had very legitimate reasons for his delay. One reason could include the obvious danger of visiting a town so close to Jerusalem.

HOW TO SAY IT

Bethany. BETH-uh-nee.
Jerusalem. Juh-ROO-suh-lem.
Jordan. JOR-dun.
Judea. Joo-DEE-uh.
Lazarus. LAZ-uh-rus.
Messiah. Meh-SIGH-uh.

WHAT IF . . . ?

History is filled with "what if" situations. What if General Robert E. Lee had remained in the Union Army as the American Civil War broke out? What if the apple had not fallen on Isaac Newton's head? What if Martin Luther had not been frightened by a lightning bolt in a thunderstorm? What if Christopher Columbus had believed that the earth was flat? What if U.S. President John F. Kennedy had not gone to Dallas in November 1963? What if U.S. President Franklin Delano Roosevelt had died of polio in the 1920s before his election? We can speculate endlessly about such situations, but it doesn't change anything now.

Martha told Jesus that if he had been there, then her brother would not have died. But Jesus had intentionally stayed away. In Jesus' wisdom he saw there was more ultimate benefit to Lazarus and his family (and, indeed, for the entire world) for him not to be there.

Since God controls the present as well as the future, he can see things and place them in a perspective that we don't have. As Christians we believe that God is still ultimately in charge of the universe, and everything happens according to his plan. If we had our way, we would want things to work out for our immediate benefit, and we probably would miss out on some of the ultimately better benefits that God has in store for us.

We do well to remember that God is holding out for the grander good that we can't perceive. It's a good thing we can't control all the "what ifs" of history. Instead we can trust that God is in control and managing the world quite nicely in his own way. —J. B. N.

22. *"But I know that even now God will give you whatever you ask."*

This verse is clearly a statement of Martha's continuing faith in Jesus. Even so, commentators are divided on the exact meaning of her words. Lazarus needs more than a healing now, so perhaps by saying *even now God will give you whatever you ask*, Martha thinks that God will empower Jesus to raise Lazarus from the dead. On an earlier occasion Jesus had interrupted a funeral in Nain to bring a corpse back to life (Luke 7:11-15). Is Martha expecting Jesus to do the same thing now for his good friend?

Against this possibility, however, are Martha's comments in verses 24 (below) and 39 (not in today's text). Those verses strongly imply that she does not really expect Jesus to help Lazarus at this point. Thus her words here are intended to show Jesus that she holds no grudge and has not lost faith in him. He did not heal Lazarus, but of course that does not mean that Jesus is not a unique messenger of God.

Martha's remarkable faith in the face of grief is certainly commendable. She seems, however, to underestimate Jesus' power.

23, 24. *Jesus said to her, "Your brother will rise again."*

Martha answered, "I know he will rise again in the resurrection at the last day."

Many ancient Jews expect a final day of judgment, when the Messiah will appear in order to bring an end to this wicked world. At that time the righteous dead will be resurrected to enjoy eternal life. "Multitudes who sleep in the dust of the earth will awake: some to everlasting life, others to shame and everlasting contempt" (Daniel 12:2).

Martha probably assumes that Jesus must be referring to the glorious occasion that the prophet Daniel mentions. So she interprets Jesus' remarks as words of pastoral comfort. It does not yet occur to her that Jesus will raise her brother much sooner than this. She is about to receive more than she expects.

25, 26. *Jesus said to her, "I am the resurrection and the life. He who believes in me will live, even though he dies; and whoever lives and believes in me will never die. Do you believe this?"*

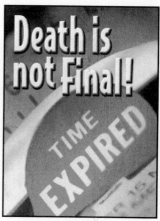

Visual for Lesson 11. *Use this visual to probe your students' views on death. Do they really believe that death isn't final?*

Resurrection and eternal *life* are not blessings that we have to wait until the end of time to enjoy. Rather, we experience their hope right now through faith in Christ, who has all power over death.

The statements about death and life are powerful, aren't they? Believers who die physically (like Lazarus) *will live* eternally through Christ's power to save. If we choose in this life to believe in Jesus, we *will never die* spiritually in the sense that Christ grants us eternal life with him in Heaven—even though our current bodies obviously will fail and decay. For more insight on our physical resurrection, see 1 Corinthians 15:12-55.

27. *"Yes, Lord," she told him, "I believe that you are the Christ, the Son of God, who was to come into the world."*

Martha undoubtedly does not understand why Lazarus had fallen ill or why Jesus had waited before coming to him. She undoubtedly does not understand (yet) what he means by saying that the dead will live.

Even so, Martha is firm in her understanding of one thing: she knows that Jesus is God's Son. This verse is John's equivalent of Peter's confession at Matthew 16:16: "You are the Christ, the Son of the living God." This kind of confession is a vital part of receiving eternal life.

Martha's confession touches on two key elements of John's portrayal of Christ. First, she seems to understand that Jesus is not just a political messiah. Rather, she realizes that he is the one who came from Heaven to reveal the Father to *the world* (John 1:14, 18; 3:13; 6:51; etc.).

Second, Martha's comment parallels John 20:31. That verse is often cited as the "purpose statement" of the Gospel of John that we noted in the lesson Introduction. Nowhere else in the Gospel of John do we see such a strong expression of faith, a fact that testifies to Martha's firm commitment in the face of grief.

CONCLUSION

Perhaps you think it strange that today's lesson text does not include the account of the actual resurrection of Lazarus (John 11:38-44). We all like to read "a happy ending," don't we? That resurrection itself is indeed marvelous. But by leaving out that event, today's lesson has forced us to examine the faith and emotions of Martha. It is a faith that knows something of Jesus but not everything. It is kind of an "in between" faith. It is the kind of faith that says, "Lord, I do believe; help me overcome my unbelief" (Mark 9:24). It's the kind of faith that many of us still have!

Jesus' question *Do you believe?* in verse 26 is applicable not only to Martha but to all of us. It's easy to sit in a Bible study class and say, "Of course, I believe that Jesus can grant us eternal life"; it's harder to feel that way as we stand beside the grave of a loved one.

As we close the lid of the casket, or as we face serious health problems ourselves, how will we answer the question, *Do you believe?* Do we really believe that Jesus has conquered death and that he has the power to grant eternal life? Real faith is tested at the final breath, whether ours or that of someone we love.

Several years ago the wife of a retired Bible college professor died. The funeral exhibited what a Christian funeral should: sadness and grief over the of loss of a loved one, but also a confident realization of an eternity with Jesus into which she had crossed. The husband she left behind said it best: "Of course I'm going to miss her. But let's face it—I haven't been preaching fairy tales all these years!" He had no doubt where she was. He had real faith that passed the test.

Discovery Learning

This page contains an alternative lesson plan emphasizing learning activities. Classes desiring such student involvement will find these suggestions helpful. The next page is a reproducible activity page to further enhance discovery learning.

LEARNING GOALS

After this lesson, each student will be able to:

1. Describe the mind-sets of Jesus, the disciples, Mary, and Martha just before Lazarus's resurrection.

2. Explain how Martha is a model of faith in Jesus, as well as how her faith fell short.

3. Show how he or she can use Jesus' teaching to comfort someone in grief.

INTO THE LESSON

Place copies of the Faith and New Life crossword puzzle from the Reproducible Page in students' seats in advance. Early arrivers can work on this activity before class starts. Begin class by reading the following accounts aloud. Then discuss them with the aid of the questions that follow.

In the early seventeenth century, a certain Marjorie Elphinstone died and was buried. When grave robbers attempted to steal her jewelry, she shocked them by groaning. The robbers fled, and she revived. She walked home under her own power and outlived her husband by six years!

Marjorie Halcrow Erskine died in 1674 and was buried. The church officer (called a sexton) who buried her returned to the grave later to steal her jewelry. While the thieving sexton was trying to cut off her finger to get her ring, Erskine awoke. She lived many more years.

1. What was the mind-set of the robbers just before their intended victims awoke?

2. If you were a family member of one of these women, what would have been on your mind just before she walked through the door?

Tell your class that today's lesson deals with the reactions of loved ones to Lazarus's death and to Jesus' presence after that death.

INTO THE WORD

Read aloud John 11:1-7, 17-27. Divide your class into groups of four. Each group will choose one of three activities described below. Provide pens and paper, or direct them to the student books for the exercises.

Group Activity A. Your group is the staff of a newspaper, the *Jerusalem Post,* covering the events surrounding the death of Lazarus. Write an article based on imaginary interviews with at least two of the following: Jesus, one of his disciples, or Mary. Using information from today's text, describe the state of mind each would have had before the resurrection.

Group Activity B. Your group is the reporting staff for Jerusalem television station WWJD. Write and present to the class an on-the-scene interview with at least two of the following: Jesus, one of his disciples, or Mary. Using information from today's text, describe the reaction each would have had before the resurrection.

Group Activity C. Your group is the editorial staff for a monthly religious magazine, *Judaism Today.* You've decided to do a story on Martha, a true believer in Jesus and the sister of Lazarus. Using information from John 11:20-27, describe Martha's strong faith as well as her spiritual doubts during the time of her brother's sickness and death.

Allow groups sufficient time to complete their activities. Then ask a volunteer "reporter" from each group to share that group's project with the entire class.

INTO LIFE

Read the hypothetical situations described below. Ask your class to suggest scriptural answers, based on the principles Jesus expressed in his teaching before the raising of Lazarus. (This activity can also be found in the student book, if you are using that optional resource.)

1. A member of your congregation has just learned that he has inoperable cancer in an advanced stage. His doctors give him no hope of recovery. How do you help him and his family deal with this crisis?

2. A coworker has lost her teenage son in an auto accident. She and her husband are not Christians, and they are torn between seeking God and blaming him for their son's death. What would be an appropriate way to minister to them in their time of grief?

3. Your friend's mother, a Christian, is reaching the end of her long life due to deteriorating health. She longs to go home to be with the Lord and end her suffering. How can you comfort both your friend and her mother?

4. Your neighbor, a longtime Christian, has been stricken by a mysterious disease that has left his doctors baffled and his faith shaken. He lies in a hospital bed, uncertain of his recovery and doubtful of his eternal destination. How do you reassure his faith?

Faith and New Life

See if you can solve today's puzzle from John 11:1-7, 17-27 without looking at your Bible.

Down

1. Town where Lazarus lived
2. Part of Martha's confession
3. What Lazarus needed
4. What Martha needed to do
5. Number of days in the grave
7. Martha's sister

Across

6. City close to Bethany
8. Location of Bethany
9. Name of the man who died
10. Mary's sister
11. This problem was for the glory of God

1. Bethany; 2. Christ; 3. Resurrection; 4. Believe; 5. Four; 6. Jerusalem; 7. Mary; 8. Judea; 9. Lazarus; 10. Martha; 11. Sickness.

"I AM THE WAY AND THE TRUTH AND THE LIFE"

LESSON 12

WHY TEACH THIS LESSON?

Have you ever heard the phrase "You can't get there from here"? What this usually means is that the destination is a difficult place to reach or that describing how to get there is nearly impossible. When Jesus talked about Heaven, though, he made it clear that you *can* get there from here. You do so by taking THE way, which is Jesus himself.

Along this one, true path are many opportunities for detour. There are many signs alongside the way to Heaven that try to point people in all kinds of directions. But only one sign is the right sign. That sign is Jesus, who points toward the Father. Jesus, as the light of truth, illuminates our journey. The comforting and convicting words of Jesus in today's text are for those seeking direction for life in the here and now and for life everlasting in the presence of God.

INTRODUCTION

A. FAMOUS LAST WORDS

For some reason we attach special significance to the "last words" of a famous person. Good or bad, a person's final words often seem to summarize his or her life. The last words of U.S. President Dwight Eisenhower (1890–1969) were, "I've always loved my wife. I've always loved my children. I've always loved my grandchildren. I've always loved my country. I want to go. God, take me."

Nathan Hale (1755–1776), an American revolutionary spy, said, "I only regret that I have but one life to lose for my country," just before he was hanged by the British. Karl Marx (1818– 1883), reflecting his prideful spirit, came to the end of his life by saying, "Go on. Get out. Last words are for fools who haven't said enough."

As his crucifixion approached, Jesus had "much more to say" to his disciples (John 16:12). But he was no fool, as Marx's statement would suppose! Many of the final words of Jesus, recorded in John 13–17, are notable for their emphasis on the future.

B. LESSON BACKGROUND

Our lessons in this series so far have focused on passages from the first 12 chapters of the Gospel of John. As we noted last week, this section is often called the Book of Signs because it highlights Jesus' public ministry of miracles and teachings; it portrays Jesus' actions as signs of his divine nature.

Yet despite all these great works, most people either did not believe Jesus or refused to confess their faith for fear of persecution (see John 7:13; 9:22). Following this rejection, Jesus met privately with his disciples on the last night of his life in an upper room. There they celebrated the Passover (John 13:1-3).

DEVOTIONAL READING:
EPHESIANS 4:17-24

BACKGROUND SCRIPTURE:
JOHN 14:1-14

PRINTED TEXT:
JOHN 14:1-14

LESSON AIMS

After participating in this lesson, each student will be able to:

1. Describe Jesus' relationship to the Father.

2. Define what Jesus meant by the way and the truth and the life.

3. Develop a plan for meditating on one of Jesus' miracles each day to increase belief.

Feb 18

KEY VERSE

I am the way and the truth and the life. No one comes to the Father except through me.
—*John 14:6*

LESSON 12 NOTES

It is interesting to compare the Gospel accounts here. Matthew, Mark, and Luke focus mainly on the events surrounding the institution of the Lord's Supper (see Matthew 26:17-30; Mark 14:12-26; Luke 22:7-38). John, however, includes lengthy excerpts from Jesus' "farewell address"—his last words for the disciples before his arrest.

The farewell address occupies all of John 13–17. It focuses on the need for unity after Jesus' departure. This includes not only the disciples' unity with Christ but also unity with one another. In today's passage Jesus reminds the disciples that they can come to God only by believing in him and following his example.

I. ULTIMATE COMFORT (JOHN 14:1-4)

A. WHAT TO DO (v. 1)

1. "Do not let your hearts be troubled. Trust in God; trust also in me.

The original, Greek text of this verse can be translated in two different ways. One possibility is that Jesus could be urging the disciples to believe in both God and himself. Following this approach the *New International Version* reads *Trust in God; trust also in me.*

On the other hand, Jesus may be building on their already existing belief in God to encourage them to place complete faith in him as well. *The King James Version* follows this approach: ye [already] believe in God, [now] believe also in me. *The King James Version* seems to be the better translation. As Jews the disciples naturally believe in God and his power; now, however, Jesus asks them to trust in him as well.

Jesus asks this knowing full well that the faith of the disciples will soon be tested by the shocking events of his arrest and crucifixion. The disciples should not lose faith even though most others do not believe. The disciples should maintain belief even when it looks like the forces of evil have won the day.

B. WHAT AWAITS (vv. 2-4)

2. "In my Father's house are many rooms; if it were not so, I would have told you. I am going there to prepare a place for you.

The totality of Jesus' remarks undoubtedly give the disciples both comfort and alarm. The alarm comes with his announcement that he is going to leave them for a time. The alarm leads to confusion in the minds of the disciples when Jesus says that he is going to a place where they cannot come (John 13:33).

Peter, and apparently the others, take this to mean that he is going to go into hiding for a while. Peter then insists that he will follow Jesus even to death (13:37). Now Jesus assures the disciples that he is not leaving forever. He wants them to be with him, so he must *prepare a place* for them in his *Father's house.*

Believers have no permanent place in this world, which hates and persecutes the disciples (John 15:18; 16:1-3). We can take comfort, however, in the fact that Jesus has prepared *rooms* for us in God's house. Then we can be with him forever in Heaven.

3. "And if I go and prepare a place for you, I will come back and take you to be with me that you also may be where I am.

This is the good news: Jesus will not abandon his people. The word *go* clearly refers to his upcoming death, resurrection, and ascension. Jesus' death pays sin's penalty while his resurrection shows his mastery over death (Revelation 1:18). That is how Jesus is able to *prepare a place for* those who love him.

WHAT DO YOU THINK?

In what ways do you think our future, eternal dwelling places will contrast with our current, earthly homes?

Commentators are divided on the meaning of *come back*. Some argue that Jesus is referring to his appearances to the disciples after the resurrection, when he will give them further teaching. Others, however, suggest that the phrase *take you to be with me* refers to our eternal home in Heaven (v. 2), so that *come back* must refer to Jesus' second coming. In either case Jesus stresses that a temporary departure will ultimately make it possible for believers to dwell with him forever.

4. *"You know the way to the place where I am going."*

Based on Jesus' ministry and teaching to this point, the disciples should understand who Jesus is and what is about to happen to him. They should realize that his origin and destination is Heaven (*the place where I am going*) and that he must die (*the way*) in order to prepare their heavenly home. Jesus presumably intends to continue discussing that issue, but Thomas interrupts with a question that reveals a lack of understanding about Jesus and his mission.

II. PROFOUND TRUTH (JOHN 14:5-11)

A. KNOW THE WAY (vv. 5-7)

5. *Thomas said to him, "Lord, we don't know where you are going, so how can we know the way?"*

Jesus' popularity seems to ebb and flow. Jesus was at a height of popularity following the feeding of the 5,000 in John 6:1-14. But then Jesus' popularity in Galilee collapsed following his hard teachings (John 6:60-66).

The resurrection of Lazarus served to refocus attention on Jesus' indisputable power (John 11:45). A huge crowd has just welcomed him to the Passover celebration in Jerusalem (John 12:12-18). Even the Pharisees are forced to admit that "the whole world has gone after him" (John 12:19).

It is against this backdrop that the disciples probably expect that Jesus will now take charge. Will he lead a revolt against Rome? Will he reform the temple? *Thomas* reveals some of this "earthly thinking" with his question. Exactly *where* is Jesus *going* and *how* are the disciples supposed to get there? Is Jesus going home to Galilee for a visit? Is he going into hiding so that he cannot be arrested (see John 10:39; 11:54; 12:9-11)?

Thomas's question shows a lack of spiritual discernment. It has not yet occurred to him that Jesus may be talking about his death and return to Heaven.

6. *Jesus answered, "I am the way and the truth and the life. No one comes to the Father except through me.*

The first part of Jesus' answer to Thomas's question features three nouns: *the way and the truth and the life*. Jesus' statement that he is *the way* to God most directly answers Thomas's question in verse 5, "How can we know the way?" Jesus is *the truth* in that he defines correct beliefs about God. When we look at Jesus, we learn the truth about who God is, how he operates, and what he expects. For this reason, all people must accept Christ in order to come to a proper understanding of the Father.

Finally, Jesus is *the life* because he has life in himself (John 5:26). He is "the resurrection and the life" (John 11:25). Jesus is "the true God and eternal life" (1 John 5:20).

These facts mean that *no one comes to the Father except through me*. Truly John 14:6 is one of the most important verses in the Bible!

7. *"If you really knew me, you would know my Father as well. From now on, you do know him and have seen him."*

Because Jesus is God's Son, and because he follows God's will perfectly, knowing Jesus gives us knowledge of God as well. The verb *know* goes beyond

WHAT DO YOU THINK?

What was a time in your life that you showed a lack of spiritual discernment? How did you grow from this experience?

WHAT DO YOU THINK?

Suppose that you share John 14:6 with a skeptic. In response he or she says, "You're just being narrow-minded. Surely a loving God would make a way for those who have never heard of Jesus!" How do you prepare yourself in advance for this kind of reaction?

[Make sure to consider Matthew 7:14 and Acts 4:12.]

Visual for Lesson 12. *Point to this visual as you ask, "Why is this one of the most confrontational statements that Jesus could possibly make?"*

simple awareness that God exists; rather, it refers to a certain understanding of who God is, how he operates, and how we are to live as his people.

The disciples have learned (or should have learned) all that they need to know about these things through their experience with Jesus. The word *if* opens a criticism of the disciples' failure to understand adequately that Jesus is the true way to the *Father.* Now that Jesus has explained the matter more fully, he expects them to have a better comprehension *from now on.*

B. KNOW THE FATHER (vv. 8-11)

8. Philip said, "Lord, show us the Father and that will be enough for us."

Philip's innocent request reveals that he, like Thomas, is still having a hard time understanding Jesus' plan for the future. His request seems more unusual, however, in light of what Jesus has just said to Thomas.

As a result, students of the Bible are divided on Philip's intent. On the one hand, some believe that *Philip* harbors doubts about Jesus' claims to be the only way to God, and therefore Philip wants to see evidence to confirm his faith. Under this theory, the phrase *show us the Father* would thus be a request for some sort of visionary experience that would allow them to be certain of the truth of what Jesus is saying.

On the other hand it simply could be that Philip does not yet realize that Jesus' "Father" is not Joseph of Nazareth, but rather the eternal God in Heaven (compare John 6:42). If this is the case, then Philip perhaps thinks that Jesus is going back to Galilee to visit his parents. So Philip wants Jesus to explain exactly why he is going to do that. In either case Philip clearly does not yet comprehend fully that God the Father has made himself known in Jesus.

SHOW ME!

There are numerous phrases that mean, "Prove it!" One that was popular a few years ago was "Show me the money!" (from a movie). Enthusiastic talk is one thing. But when the impatient seller wants to close the deal, he or she may say, "Show me the money!" A similar phrase is, "Put your money where your mouth is!" Big talk is not enough.

This "prove it" attitude cuts across many areas of life. For several years I have been active in accrediting associations that review institutions of higher education. At one of our annual meetings a couple of years ago, the staff of the association sported buttons that proclaimed, "Show me the learning." It is not enough for a college to say they educate their students; they have to demonstrate that learning does in fact take place.

Our modern world is filled with demands of "Show me!" The same was true in ancient times, as we see in Philip's request. Jesus had identified himself with the Father and said that the disciples had seen the Father in Jesus' activities. Yet even after three years, Philip still did not understand. "Show me," he demanded.

We are not much different. Our actions constantly request, "show me Your grace," "show me Your forgiveness," "show me Your love," "show me that You understand what I am going through." Before we make too many such requests of God, we should remember that Jesus *did* show us—on the cross.   —J. B. N.

9. Jesus answered: "Don't you know me, Philip, even after I have been among you such a long time? Anyone who has seen me has seen the Father. How can you say, 'Show us the Father'?

At this point in the Gospel of John, Jesus has spent some three years (*such a long time*) with the disciples, teaching and working miracles. Over the course of his ministry, Jesus has explicitly discussed his unity with *the Father* and has said that he came to reveal God to the world.

Jesus is therefore dismayed at the lack of understanding in even his closest followers. They still do not really understand who he is. This is spiritual blindness.

10. "Don't you believe that I am in the Father, and that the Father is in me? The words I say to you are not just my own. Rather, it is the Father, living in me, who is doing his work.

Jesus' question reflects his frustration. His words emphasize his complete unity with God—*the Father* is in Jesus, but Jesus is also *in the Father,* suggesting that the two think and act as one. This has been called a "mutual indwelling."

Jesus points to two areas of his ministry where this relationship should be obvious: the things he says and the things he does. Both Jesus' teachings and miracles reveal God to the world in an unprecedented way.

11. "Believe me when I say that I am in the Father and the Father is in me; or at least believe on the evidence of the miracles themselves.

Jesus did a tremendous miracle in John 6 when he fed the 5,000. But the result was that people sought him out not because of the *miracles* but because they had had their fill (John 6:26). Jesus' miracles should prove that he is more than just a prophet, magician, or a bread king. These mighty deeds should lead people to understand that he reveals God in a new and unique way.

Jesus assumes that his works will eliminate any doubt about his own identity and the identity of his *Father.* If Philip can't understand Jesus' teachings about himself, which seem to be obvious enough, perhaps he should ask himself what it means that Jesus could raise Lazarus from the dead!

III. EXTREME PROMISE (JOHN 14:12-14)

A. WHAT WE CAN DO (v. 12)

12. "I tell you the truth, anyone who has faith in me will do what I have been doing. He will do even greater things than these, because I am going to the Father.

This verse presents us with some interesting challenges of interpretation. First, who is it that will do *greater things* than Jesus? Is it only the original apostles or is it all believers? The phrase *anyone who has faith in me* points to all Christians.

With that identity established we next need to ask, "In what sense will Christians be able to do greater things than Jesus?" The clue to answering this question is found in the last phrase *because I am going to my Father.* That exaltation will happen only after Jesus' death and resurrection. It is Jesus' sacrifice that launches a new era of power. None of Jesus' own miracles or teaching up to the point of the cross and empty tomb could bring about salvation.

Compare the power of the gospel before and after the cross. Even after more than three years of Jesus' teaching, preaching, and miracles, his most dedicated followers were relatively few in number. But after Jesus' resurrection comes Pentecost. Preceding that glorious day, there were only about 120 believers gathered in Jerusalem (Acts 1:15). Peter's sermon and the arrival of the Holy Spirit then add about 3,000 (Acts 2:41)! Whereas Jesus' displayed his power in a limited geographical region, his followers eventually proclaim the gospel across the Roman Empire. Their efforts will reach a much larger number of people, including Gentiles. Christ empowers us to show everyone that he alone is the way to the Father.

B. WHAT JESUS WILL DO (vv. 13, 14)

13, 14. "And I will do whatever you ask in my name, so that the Son may bring glory to the Father. You may ask me for anything in my name, and I will do it."

WHAT DO YOU THINK?

Make a list of some out-of-the-ordinary things that Jesus did in front of his disciples. Despite the miraculous things on this list, what made his disciples linger in their uncertainty about Jesus' identity and authority? How are your own doubts similar?

WHAT DO YOU THINK?

Jesus talked about others doing things even greater than he had done. How do you apply Jesus' expectations in your own life?

HOW TO SAY IT

Galilee. GAL-uh-lee.
Gentiles. JEN-tiles.
Jerusalem. Juh-ROO-suh-lem.
Lazarus. LAZ-uh-rus.
Nazareth. NAZ-uh-reth.
Pentecost. PENT-ih-kost.
Pharisees. FAIR-ih-seez.

These verses must be interpreted both within their immediate context and within the larger context of the John's writings. Jesus has just told the disciples that believers will be empowered to do "greater things." In verses 15-17 (not in today's text), Jesus proceeds to tell his disciples that he will ask God to send "the Spirit of truth" to abide with them. The Spirit will give comfort in the face of persecution (John 14:26, 27) and will work with the disciples to convict the world of sin (16:8-14). Jesus clearly is speaking, then, of the power to proclaim the gospel. This is what brings glory to the Father (7:18; 8:50, 54; 12:28).

Consistent with this theme, 1 John 5:14, 15 states that God will answer prayers that we offer "according to his will"; in that context this apparently refers to prayers for those who have fallen away (1 John 5:16). Jesus is not saying, then, that we can expect God to grant our whims like some sort of heavenly Santa Claus. The emphasis, rather, lies in the phrase in my name: Through Jesus alone we come to God, and through him God grants us power to proclaim the truth in a lost world.

ASK IN MY NAME

My father was a carpenter who spent most of his working years building houses for a contractor. While working on one project, he and his crew experienced significant harassment from the residents of a neighboring house. They threatened to sue because some of the workmen had walked through a corner of their yard, damaging some grass. They refused to allow the workmen to get drinking water from an outside tap. They wanted a ridiculous amount of compensation because they said that the workmen had damaged some vegetables in the garden.

This hostile situation changed dramatically when the neighbors discovered that the workmen were under the contractor rather than under the developer. The neighbors had been cheated by the developer, but they had no grudge against the contractor. The name of the contractor was respected; the name of the developer was despised.

It is important to establish in whose name we operate, isn't it? If we come to God and request things in our own name, or on our own merits, we will not get much response. But when we ask in the name of Jesus according to his will, that's a different story! The name of Jesus opens us up to the marvelous power of God.

—J. B. N.

PRAYER

Father, we live in a world of falsehood. Sometimes we have a hard time saying what the word truth means anymore. Please help us live lives that are pleasing to you. Give us confidence so that we can stand up for you and do the greater works that Jesus calls us to do. In Jesus' name, amen.

CONCLUSION

Many have tried to describe, in song, poem, and prose, what eternity in Heaven will be like. To try to describe the indescribable is quite a job! The hymn "Mansion Over the Hilltop" by Ira Stanphill (1914–1993) is one such attempt. Its well-known lyrics compare the "cottage" the singer has on earth with the "mansion" that awaits in Heaven.

The word mansions occurs in John 14:2 of the King James Version. When that translation came into being in 1611, the word mansion simply meant an "abode" or "dwelling place" or a separate apartment that was not part of a larger building. In this sense an abode in Heaven is the special place that God has prepared for those who are faithful to him. Jesus does not emphasize the material comforts of this heavenly dwelling. Instead he focuses on the essential benefit that we will enjoy: God and Christ will be with us forever.

In the meantime Jesus calls us to live lives that show we are in fellowship with him. As we do we have the confidence that he will give us the power we need to do all that he asks. This may be difficult, but a heavenly home awaits for those who remain faithful.

THOUGHT TO REMEMBER

Believe in Jesus and find God.

Discovery Learning

This page contains an alternative lesson plan emphasizing learning activities. Classes desiring such student involvement will find these suggestions helpful. The next page is a reproducible activity page to further enhance discovery learning.

LEARNING GOALS

After this lesson, each student will be able to:

1. Describe Jesus' relationship to the Father.

2. Define what Jesus meant by *the way, the truth,* and *the life.*

3. Develop a plan for meditating on one of Jesus' miracles each day to increase belief.

INTO THE LESSON

Place copies of the What Is the Truth? exercise from the Reproducible Page in students' chairs in advance so students can begin to think about the text as they arrive. As class begins, distribute the following list of famous last words. Ask students to match each quote with its author. (If you use student books, you will find the exercise printed there.)

1. "How were the [circus] receipts today at Madison Square Garden?" 2. "I have offended God and mankind because my work did not reach the quality it should have." 3. "That was a great game of golf, fellers." 4. "All my possessions for a moment of time." 5. "Lord, help my poor soul." 6. "I . . . am now quite certain that the crimes of this guilty land will never be purged away but with blood!" 7. "Don't turn down the light. I'm afraid to go home in the dark." 8. "Last words are for fools who haven't said enough."

A. Bing Crosby; B. P. T. Barnum; C. O. Henry; D. Queen Elizabeth I, of England; E. John Brown (American abolitionist executed in 1859 for leading a raid); F. Leonardo da Vinci; G. Edgar Allan Poe; H. Karl Marx.

Answers: 1B; 2F; 3A; 4D; 5G; 6E; 7C; 8H

After going over the answers, ask students how these final quotes might reflect the character of their authors. For example Edgar Allan Poe was an alcoholic who also suffered from severe depression for much of his adult life. John Brown was convinced that the only way to end slavery in the United States was to start a revolt. When you have finished your discussion, say, "Today's lesson will focus on some of Jesus' last words to his disciples. Those words will reveal important things about him."

INTO THE WORD

Each student will pair up with another to complete both activities below. Allow pairs several minutes to complete the first activity. Then discuss their conclu-sions as a class, using the lesson commentary to guide the discussion. Follow the same procedure for the second activity. Provide pens and paper, or direct attention to the student books where the activities are printed.

Activity A. Read John 14:1-14 and discuss with your partner the nature of Jesus' relationship with the Father by answering these questions: (1) What do Jesus' statements about preparing a place for us (vv. 2-6) tell us about his relationship to the Father? (2) What did Jesus mean when he said, "Anyone who has seen me has seen the Father" (v. 9)? (3) What reason does Jesus give for the works that he will enable his disciples to do (v. 12)?

Activity B. Read John 14:6 and discuss with your partner what Jesus meant when he said, "I am the way and the truth and the life." (1) How does Jesus constitute the only way to reach God? (Compare to John 10:9; Acts 4:12.) (2) What did Jesus mean when he called himself "truth"? (Compare to Ephesians 1:13; 1 John 2:4.) (3) In what ways does Jesus embody life for the believer? (Compare Matthew 16:25; 19:29; John 3:36; 6:35; Romans 5:10-18.)

INTO LIFE

Using the commentary on John 14:12-14, explain the relationship among Jesus' miraculous works, the works of his disciples, and the Holy Spirit's use of those works to convict the world of sin. You may find that John's "purpose statement" in John 20:30, 31 will enrich your class discussion.

Next, ask each pair of students to write a brief meditation (100 words or less) on one of Jesus' miracles as recorded in John's Gospel. Assign each pair one of these passages: John 2:1-11; 4:43-54; 5:1-15; 6:1-15; 6:16-21; 9; 11:1-44. The meditations should answer these questions: (1) What did Jesus do? (2) What effect did the miracle have on the faith of those who witnessed or experienced it? (3) What effect should it have on our faith today?

Collect the meditations and compile them into a booklet. Distribute copies of the collection to your students at the next class period. Ask them to use them as part of their daily devotions for the week ahead. Suggest that they read one meditation each day. As an alternative, distribute the Daily Meditation exercise from the Reproducible Page for students to use over several weeks.

What Is the Truth?

Jesus said, "I am the way and the truth and the life." Read John 14:1-14 and decide whether each statement is true or false. Circle the T or F to indicate your answer. Don't peek at the answers!

T F 1. Jesus encouraged the disciples to not let their hearts be troubled.

T F 2. Jesus said that in God's house there are exactly 144,000 rooms.

T F 3. Jesus' plan was to go to Heaven to prepare a place for his disciples.

T F 4. Jesus promised to return.

T F 5. Thomas understood what Jesus was talking about.

T F 6. Peter asked Jesus to show the disciples the Father.

T F 7. Jesus said that anyone who had seen him had seen the Father.

T F 8. Jesus told his disciples to believe him because of the miracles he performed.

T F 9. Jesus mentioned doing even greater things than what he had done.

T F 10. Jesus never promised to do what his disciples asked in his name.

Answers: 1. T. 2. F. 3. T. 4. T. 5. F. 6. F. 7. T. 8. E. 9. T. 10. F

Daily Meditation

The calendar below lists 31 miracle accounts from the New Testament that will increase your faith. Commit to reading one of these accounts each day starting tomorrow! Check them off as you go.

Matthew 9:27-31	Matthew 17:1-8	Matthew 17:24-27	Mark 7:24-30	Mark 7:31-37	Mark 8:1-13	Mark 8:22-26
Luke 4:38, 39	Luke 4:40, 41	Luke 5:4-11	Luke 5:12-15	Luke 5:17-26	Luke 6:6-11	Luke 7:1-10
Luke 7:11-17	Luke 8:22-25	Luke 8:26-39	Luke 8:41-56	Luke 9:37-43	Luke 13:11-17	Luke 14:1-6
Luke 17:11-19	Luke 18:35-43	John 2:1-11	John 4:46-54	John 5:1-9	John 6:1-14	John 9:1-7
John 11:38-44	John 20	John 21:1-14				

"I AM THE TRUE VINE"

LESSON 13

WHY TEACH THIS LESSON?

The process of pruning is sometimes not a pleasant sight. What once were beautiful and full trees or plants are suddenly chopped down to almost nothing. At the college where I work, Crepe Myrtle trees go through this kind of pruning from time to time. And each time this happens a notice has to be issued to those unfamiliar with the process to explain that this is not a bad thing but a good thing. It is vital that the bad be cut out. It is also necessary that the whole tree or plant be thinned so that the beauty can continue to be displayed from year to year.

We accumulate lots of spiritual (and material!) "junk," don't we? Yet God, the master gardener, knows how to get the best fruit and the greatest growth from his spiritual garden. As plants in that garden of God, it should be our desire to be cleaned out, pruned, and cultivated by God so that we can be as productive and appealing as possible. This lesson will help you understand the work of the master gardener and the fruit he desires to produce in you.

INTRODUCTION

A. YOU CAN'T DO IT ALONE

Whether we like it or not, there are many things a person can't do alone. You can't sing a duet alone; you can't run a relay race alone; you can't hold a conference alone; you can't do a group presentation alone; you can't play catch alone. As much as it may hurt our pride, there are some things that we can only do with the help and support of other people.

In our passage today Jesus adds something else to the list of things that we can't do ourselves: Jesus insists that we can't please God alone. This is the case because we draw our strength for service from our connection to Christ. God also commands us to love other people. We can't love others as long as we are focused on "going it alone."

B. LESSON BACKGROUND

The three letters that John wrote (namely, 1, 2, and 3 John) reveal sobering news: the churches and people whom John addressed had experienced, or were just about to experience, serious internal crisis. John wrote his Gospel around AD 85–90 and the letters perhaps shortly thereafter. The 55 years or so since the death and resurrection of Christ allowed ample time for false doctrines and false Christs to spring up (compare 1 John 2:18, 22; 4:3; 2 John 7). Church splits were occurring (3 John 9, 10).

John's letters reveal that he wanted to correct these situations. A large part of the solution is found in John's Gospel. There John made sure to include Jesus' teaching about the vine and branches. This reminded believers that they must remain connected to the true Christ and to one another if they wished to please God.

DEVOTIONAL READING:
PSALM 1
BACKGROUND SCRIPTURE:
JOHN 15:1-17
PRINTED TEXT:
JOHN 15:1-17

LESSON AIMS

After participating in this lesson, each student will be able to:

1. Identify what Jesus meant by vine, branches, *and* fruit.

2. Explain why we must remain connected to Christ in order to bear fruit.

3. Correct one situation where he or she has failed to stay connected to the vine.

KEY VERSE

I am the vine; you are the branches. If a man remains in me and I in him, he will bear much fruit; apart from me you can do nothing.
—John 15:5

Feb
25

LESSON 13 NOTES

I. CONNECTED TO JESUS (JOHN 15:1-11)

A. PRUNING THE VINEYARD (vv. 1-3)

1. "I am the true vine, and my Father is the gardener.

Jewish readers would likely detect an allusion here to Isaiah's Song of the Vineyard. In Isaiah 5:1-7 the prophet compares Israel to a choice vineyard that God planted in the promised land. He tended it with special care. Of course God expected a good harvest for his work, as any farmer would. Instead the Israelites produced unrighteousness and injustice.

The vine imagery appears in other Old Testament passages as well (see Psalm 80:8-16; Isaiah 27:2, 3; Jeremiah 2:21; 12:10, 11; and Ezekiel 15). Here in John 15 Jesus now applies Old Testament imagery in a new way: *the true vine,* which will yield a faithful harvest, is Christ himself. Jesus replaces Judaism as the means by which people are connected to God, the keeper (*gardener*) of the vineyard.

2. "He cuts off every branch in me that bears no fruit, while every branch that does bear fruit he prunes so that it will be even more fruitful.

The imagery in this verse outlines God's work as the keeper of the vineyard. Jesus is the vine, and he now pictures the disciples as branches. When a *branch* withers or fails to produce *fruit,* it must be cut off from the vine to protect the overall health of the plant. In a similar way the disciples are forewarned that God expects them to be faithful; if they are not, they may lose their privileged position. Compare John the Baptist's dire warning in Matthew 3:10: "The ax is already at the root of the trees, and every tree that does not produce good fruit will be cut down and thrown into the fire."

On the other hand, the vine keeper also tends to the healthy branches by pruning them back in order to insure the maximum yield. This imagery possibly alludes to the persecution that Jesus will predict for the disciples in John 16:1-4. See also the discussion of God's discipline in Hebrews 12:3-11. Some will respond to suffering by losing their faith; others will become stronger and even more effective through these experiences.

The exact nature of the fruit that Jesus has in mind is not defined here. He may be alluding back to John 14:15. There he said that those who love him will keep his commandments; if this is the case, then the fruit here is similar to Paul's "fruit of the Spirit"—a Christian lifestyle characterized by "love, joy, peace, patience, kindness, goodness, faithfulness, gentleness and self-control" (Galatians 5:22, 23).

Or it may be that Jesus is thinking more of John 14:30, 31, where he speaks of what the world must learn. If this is the case, the fruit would refer to the disciples' evangelizing efforts. Both meanings may be in view, and each is certainly an essential measure of spiritual health.

WHAT DO YOU THINK?

In what ways have you noticed God "pruning" your life? What have you learned from this experience?

WHAT DO YOU THINK?

Bearing fruit (not just foliage) is vital. What kinds, qualities, and quantities of fruit do you think Jesus expects you to bear? How do you avoid the trap of perfectionism in this regard?

[Matthew 7:15-20 and Galatians 5:22-26 can jump-start your thinking.]

WHEN LESS YIELDS MORE

I grew up in suburbia in a family that had no interest in landscaping or beautification. I can't remember either of my parents ever planting any flowers or even maintaining houseplants. We had a happy home, but developing a green thumb was just not part of our family activities.

When my wife and I bought our first house, it was on a small lot in a major city, and the previous owner had planted a rosebush just in front of the house. I didn't know much about gardening. But even I could tell that the rosebush, which carried very few blossoms, was overgrown. The next spring I decided to cut back the plant. There were a lot of branches clustered in the center of the bush, and they were bending across each other.

So I cut out some of the excess branches in the center while thinning some of the outer branches. To my delight that summer the rosebush was covered with blossoms! There were far more blossoms than I would have assumed, even though I knew that was supposed to be the result.

That's the principle Jesus is talking about here. Even healthy plants need to be pruned for maximum productivity. Sometimes Jesus needs to cut some of the "stuff" out of our lives so that we can produce more and better results for his kingdom. We should expect him to do so.   —J. B. N.

3. "You are already clean because of the word I have spoken to you.

The word *clean* refers back to the pruning process in verse 2. The disciples have been cleansed—prepared to serve and to witness—through their constant exposure to Jesus' teaching. Earlier, Jesus had referred to them as clean in order to distinguish them from Judas, whose motives obviously were impure and ungodly (John 13:10, 11).

B. BEARING FRUIT (vv. 4-8)

4, 5. "Remain in me, and I will remain in you. No branch can bear fruit by itself; it must remain in the vine. Neither can you bear fruit unless you remain in me. I am the vine; you are the branches. If a man remains in me and I in him, he will bear much fruit; apart from me you can do nothing.

The ideas of "that which should *remain* in us" and "whom we should *remain in*" are very important to the apostle John (see John 5:38; 14:17; 15:7; 1 John 2:14, 24, 27). The emphasis is on persistent faithfulness. This can come about only through closeness and unity with God.

The first statement in verse 4 is a promise to believers. A good paraphrase might be, "If you continue to be faithful to me, then I will continue to be faithful to you"—Christ will not abandon us. This charge is especially important in light of verse 2. Just as a branch cannot bear grapes without the nourishment provided by *the vine,* so believers cannot live lives that please God without the strength available through Christ.

If we lose that connection, then we lose our power to serve. And once we lose the power to serve and bear *fruit,* we are in great danger. The danger is not just in being pruned back a little but in being pruned away permanently (Luke 13:6-9). Jesus emphasizes this point here in verse 5 so that there can be no misunderstanding: *apart from me you can do nothing.*

6. "If anyone does not remain in me, he is like a branch that is thrown away and withers; such branches are picked up, thrown into the fire and burned.

After the keeper of the vineyard prunes away the dead *branches,* he throws them into a pit and burns them. The wood from vines is useless for anything but burning (compare Ezekiel 15:1-5). Jesus alludes here to ultimate judgment of those who fall away: they are separated from the faithful and cast into eternal fire (compare Matthew 13:37-42).

7. "If you remain in me and my words remain in you, ask whatever you wish, and it will be given you.

Jesus informs his hearers of one way that he will continue to empower them: through his *words* or teachings. By learning what Jesus commanded while on earth, believers will know what they must do to please God. Is there anything more important than learning what Jesus desires of us?

It is important to stress both the context and the condition of the promise in this verse. First, in context Jesus is speaking about our ability to bear fruit through obedience to him. Thus we are invited to *ask* for the power to serve, and

Remain in me, and I will remain in you.
—John 15:4, NIV

Visual for Lesson 13. *Point to this image as you ask, "What have you found that helps keep you close to Jesus?"*

WHAT DO YOU THINK?

What are some specific challenges that your church and her individual members face that cannot be overcome without complete faithfulness?

Jesus will give it. We are not necessarily being promised that physical health or material blessings await just for the asking. In fact the reference to "pruning" in verse 2 may suggest that God will ask us to do without such things at times in order to increase our faith.

Second, the condition of our successful asking is stated in the first part of the verse: we must *remain in* Christ and allow his Word to remain in us. If we remain closely connected to Jesus and meditate on his teaching, then we can have a proper perspective on God's will for our lives. This perspective should focus our prayers on things that please him rather than ourselves (compare James 4:3).

8. "This is to my Father's glory, that you bear much fruit, showing yourselves to be my disciples.

God receives glory when we *bear much fruit* in the sense that our actions reveal his power at work in the world. When we do the right thing, our witness to others shows that we recognize God to be worthy of our service and worship. Jesus' entire earthly ministry has been focused on the glory of God (John 17:4). We show that we are his true followers when we attempt to do the same thing in our own lives.

CHANNELS OF PRODUCTIVITY

We all enjoy the result of fruit trees' productivity. Fruit, however, is not always automatic. I remember we had an old apple tree in our yard when I was a youngster. We did nothing to enhance the fruit, and the result was not very good. There were a lot of apples, but they were wormy, misshapen, blemished, and not worth eating.

Much later I learned that fruit trees require a good deal of care. Spraying controls the worms and blemishes. Pruning the trees helps production. Fertilizer and special applications aid the whole process. Fruit growers spend a lot of time and go to considerable expense to increase the yield of their trees.

But there is one thing that never happens in the process of producing fruit: the tree branches themselves don't have to go to extra effort to produce. Imagine tree branches hunkering down, grunting and groaning like a weight lifter doing a dead lift. Imagine tree branches working up a sweat while trying to increase the size of their fruit. Ridiculous, isn't it?

Yet we often attempt the same thing in trying to produce spiritual fruit. We strain as if the fruit comes from us. It doesn't. It only comes when we (the branches) are tapped into Jesus (the vine). Perhaps that's why Jesus says that the Father is glorified when we produce fruit. We aren't the producers—God is. We are channels of his productivity, if we allow ourselves to be. —J. B. N.

C. ABIDING IN LOVE (vv. 9-11)

9. "As the Father has loved me, so have I loved you. Now remain in my love.

Love is the bond that unites *the Father* and the Son. It is also the bond that unites the branches with the vine. Jesus' entire ministry has been an expression of God's love for him and for the world, and Jesus has shown the same love to the disciples. *Remain* indicates that Jesus' love is our home, the place where we live. Verses 10 and 11 (next) will spell out two effects of this enduring love in our lives.

10. "If you obey my commands, you will remain in my love, just as I have obeyed my Father's commands and remain in his love.

Jesus now explains exactly how it is possible to continue living in his *love*. When we see what Christ has done for us, we should respond by obeying his teachings. This could include all of his ethical commands, such as we see in the

HOW TO SAY IT

Galilee. GAL-uh-lee.

Gentiles. JEN-tiles.

Jerusalem. Juh-ROO-suh-lem.

Lazarus. LAZ-uh-rus.

Nazareth. NAZ-uh-reth.

Pentecost. PENT-ih-kost.

Pharisees. FAIR-ih-seez.

Sermon on the Mount. But the focus here is probably on the "new commandment" that Jesus has just spelled out at John 13:34. He will repeat it in 15:12, below—"love one another." By showing love for one another, we imitate Christ's love for us. (See also 1 John 5:2.)

11. "I have told you this so that my joy may be in you and that your joy may be complete."

The thought of Christian service, love for others, and obedience to Christ's commands often seems overwhelming and impossible. Yet Jesus highlights the benefit of obedience: *joy*. The phrase *my joy* refers to the satisfaction that Jesus receives from knowing that he perfectly fulfills God's will, despite the difficulties he faces.

Such joy remains with us when we know that we also are following Christ's commands and bearing fruit despite circumstances. Of course this is not to say that we always will be happy in this life; we can, however, always be confident in the knowledge that God is pleased with our work.

II. CONNECTED TO ONE ANOTHER (JOHN 15:12-17)

A. NEW COMMANDMENT (vv. 12, 13)

12, 13. "My command is this: Love each other as I have loved you. Greater love has no one than this, that he lay down his life for his friends.

Love each other is Jesus' "new command" of John 13:34, as noted above. Jesus' love is the model for the relationships we are to have with other believers.

Jesus illustrates this love by referring the disciples to what he has done for them already (*as I have loved you*). Up to this point in time, he has allowed them to enjoy a special, privileged relationship with him. He has provided for their needs. He has protected them both physically and spiritually, as they have allowed him to.

Jesus also illustrates the kind of love he is talking about by referring the disciples to what he is about to do in the very near future. He will provide the ultimate sacrifice by laying down *his life* for them on the cross.

Such sacrificial love is the purest expression of the fruit that Christ empowers us to bear. This does not mean that Jesus calls us to die upon a cross as he did. That was a one-time event, not to be repeated. Yet if the type of love that is evident in the cross is not evident in our lives as well, then we clearly are not drawing our power from the Christ, who died for sinners.

B. FRIENDS OF CHRIST (vv. 14-16)

14. "You are my friends if you do what I command.

The term *friends* is used to refer to people sharing the same social status in the ancient world. Viewed in this light the disciples must see this comment as something of a paradox. Technically, a servant (one who follows commands) is not a friend (an equal) to his or her master. We are friends of Christ in the sense that we are privileged to know his thinking, as was Abraham (2 Chronicles 20:7; Isaiah 41:8; James 2:23) and Moses (Exodus 33:11). See the next verse.

15. "I no longer call you servants, because a servant does not know his master's business. Instead, I have called you friends, for everything that I learned from my Father I have made known to you.

The slave or *servant* does not need to understand the *master's* orders; he or she simply needs to obey them without asking questions. Jesus is our Lord, and he does not invite us to question his commands. At the same time, however, he has not simply left us with a code of laws and rules. Rather, Jesus has openly

WHAT DO YOU THINK?

How has obedience to Jesus brought joy to your life?

WHAT DO YOU THINK?

Here Jesus refers to his disciples as friends. But in John 13:13-16, he affirms his role as Lord. How do you harmonize these? How do you fulfill your roles as both a servant and a friend of Jesus on a daily basis?

revealed the Father's will and purposes to the disciples. He has taught them the importance of revealing God's love to the world.

We should therefore be able to understand why it is so important for us to bear fruit and love one another. If we do not understand this, then we really cannot say that we understand anything that Jesus did or taught.

16. *"You did not choose me, but I chose you and appointed you to go and bear fruit—fruit that will last. Then the Father will give you whatever you ask in my name.*

While we can enjoy the privilege of friendship with Jesus, we must never forget that he is the boss. Christ is the one who initiates a relationship with us, and we should not take his offer lightly.

At the same time, however, we should feel secure in the knowledge that Jesus has not set us up to fail: he has not *appointed* that we should be pruned away and cast off (v. 2). He has cleansed us instead (v. 3). He tells us everything that we need to know to *bear fruit.* Because of our relationship with him, we can expect not only God's favor but also his power for service.

C. NEW COMMANDMENT REPRISED (v. 17)

17. *"This is my command: Love each other."*

Jesus closes by repeating the essential element in bearing fruit: that new *command* to *love each other.* By the time the apostle John writes his letters, this new command becomes an old command (2 John 5). Yet it bears repeating!

The disciples will have to depend on one another for support once Jesus is gone. The church will not be able to grow if it is divided. Strangely, Christians often take the command to love one's neighbor (Mark 12:31) more seriously than the command to love one another. That makes us prey to easy criticism from nonbelievers. Who wants to join a divided church?

CONCLUSION

Everyone knows that there are a lot of things we can't have access to unless we know people in "high places." I am devoted fan of NASCAR, and recently I was able to secure a garage pass to a race in Indianapolis. This allowed me full access to all the behind-the-scenes areas at the race. These included the garages where the cars are serviced and the areas where the drivers and crews meet to discuss strategy. I saw many of my favorite drivers up close there, as well as some other celebrities who had come to the race. All this was possible solely because my cousin's husband works as a member of the crew on one of the NASCAR teams. Without his help I would have been watching from the stands or on television.

Our passage today applies that principle to our spiritual lives. If we follow Jesus' teaching, he treats us as "friends," and with Jesus, you really do have "a friend in high places"! With him on our side, there is no limit to what we can do—provided that we stay connected.

How sad it is to see an unconnected Christian! Ironically, it seems sometimes that it is preachers who are in the most danger of losing their connection to the true vine. Preachers are under tremendous pressure to be involved in all the major and minor activities of the church. They scurry from one meeting to another, trying to keep all the programs going. Under all this time pressure, it's tempting for them to start cutting back on their prayer and devotional life.

The cure for the Christian who is relying on his or her own strength to get things done is Zechariah 4:6: "Not by might nor by power, but by my Spirit, says the Lord Almighty."

Discovery Learning

This page contains an alternative lesson plan emphasizing learning activities. Classes desiring such student involvement will find these suggestions helpful. The next page is a reproducible activity page to further enhance discovery learning.

LEARNING GOALS

After this lesson, each student will be able to:

1. Identify what Jesus meant by *vine, branches,* and *fruit.*

2. Explain why we must remain connected to Christ in order to bear fruit.

3. Correct one situation where he or she has failed to stay connected to the vine.

INTO THE LESSON

Before class begins, place copies of the Working in God's Vineyard activity from the Reproducible Page in the classroom chairs for your students to begin working on as they arrive.

To begin class, distribute the following quiz about common biblical metaphors (also printed in the student books). Correct answers are indicated in brackets, but distribute blanks for those. Challenge students to fill in the blanks without looking up the Scripture reference. Remind your class that a metaphor is a figure of speech containing a comparison in which a word or phrase normally used of one thing is identified with another. For example, "The sun is a bright, orange ball."

What's That Metaphor?

1. "I am the [bread] of life" (John 6:35).

2. "I am the [light] of the world" (John 8:12).

3. "I am the good [shepherd]" (John 10:11).

4. "Don't you know that you yourselves are God's [temple]?" (1 Corinthians 3:16).

5. "The Lord is my [rock], my fortress" (Psalm 18:2).

6. "'God is a consuming [fire]'" (Hebrews 12:29).

7. "You are the [salt] of the earth" (Matthew 5:13).

8. "You are the [light] of the world" (Matthew 5:14).

Discuss the quiz. Then tell your students that this lesson will analyze three metaphors that Jesus used to describe a Christian's proper relationship to him and to other Christians.

INTO THE WORD

Before dividing your class for the following two exercises, use the lesson commentary to explain the background of John 15:1-17. Focus on the meaning and significance of the terms *vine, branch,* and *fruit.* Discuss the need to stay "connected" to Christ in order to serve effectively and keep heresy out of the church.

Divide the class into several small groups. Half of the groups will do the activities in Exercise #1. The other half will do the activities in Exercise #2. Provide blank paper and copies of each exercise for the groups. (If you use the student books, you will still need to provide blank paper.) Allow 10 minutes for these exercises. Then ask each group to report its findings to the entire class.

Exercise #1

Activity A: Have someone in your group read aloud John 15:1-8. Identify what you think is the theme of this section.

Activity B: Write a paraphrase of John 15:1-8. "Translate," as much as possible, the key metaphors (vine, etc.) into plain speech.

Activity C: Discuss the following questions about the text: (1) In the church what are the respective roles of Jesus and the Father as vine and husbandman? (2) What will happen to those who do not produce fruit? (3) What constitutes fruit in Christ's kingdom?

Exercise #2

Activity A: Have someone in your group read aloud John 15:9-17. Identify what you think is the theme of this section.

Activity B: Write a paraphrase of John 15:9-17.

Activity C: Discuss the following questions about the text: (1) What are some aspects of the Father's love for his Son? (2) How does Jesus love us the same way? (3) How are we to love one another with this same love? (4) What must we do to remain in Christ's love? (5) What kind of joy comes from having this relationship with Christ?

INTO LIFE

For each hypothetical situation described below, suggest scriptural ways to help these people reconnect with the Lord and his church.

1. Jennifer was a faithful Christian through her high-school years. When she went off to college, however, she drifted away from God. How can you help her reactivate her faith?

2. Bob is a member of your church, but he is inactive. His business is demanding, so he likes to use his Sundays to relax at home, do yard work, or play golf. He talks about returning to church but never seems to get around to it. What can you do to help him?

Working in God's Vineyard

To serve in God's vineyard, a person must have a special relationship with Jesus, our Savior. To explore that relationship, read John 15:1-17 and fill in the blanks from selected verses in that passage.

```
                              V  __ __ __
                     __ __ __  I  __
              __ __ __ __  N  __
                     __ __ __  E  __
                     __ __ __  Y  __
                              A  __ __ __ __ __ __ __ __
                        __ __  R  __ __ __ __
                              D  __ __ __ __ __ __ __ __
```

1. "I am the true _____, and my Father is the gardener" (John 15:1).

2. "No branch can bear _____ by itself; it must remain in the vine" (John 15:4).

3. "If a man _____ in me and I in him, he will bear much fruit" (John 15:5).

4. "As the Father has _____ me, so have I _____ you" (John 15:9).

5. "If you _____ my commands, you will remain in my love, just as I have obeyed my Father's commands and remain in his love" (John 15:10).

6. "You did not choose me, but I chose you and _____ you to go and bear fruit" (John 15:16).

7. "He cuts off every branch in me that bears no fruit, while every branch that does bear fruit he _____ " (John 15:2).

8. "This is to my Father's glory, that you bear much fruit, showing yourselves to be my _____ " (John 15:8).

Spring Quarter 2007

Our Community Now and in God's Future

Special Features

Lessons

Unit 1: Known by Our Love

Unit 2: A New Community in Christ

Unit 3: Living in God's New World

About These Lessons

An old saying goes, "Well begun is half done." Lessons 1–4 show us the key to beginning (and continuing) well: love. We love one another because God first loved us. It was God's love that sent Jesus to the cross (Lessons 5 and 6). That same love creates a new heaven and earth for our benefit (Lessons 7–13). What a great future! What an opportunity to show love *now*!

Mar 4
Mar 11
Mar 18
Mar 25
Apr 1
Apr 8
Apr 15
Apr 22
Apr 29
May 6
May 13
May 20
May 27

Practice for Heaven

by Jonathan Underwood

Our local Christian radio station airs some short pithy statements in between the music and other programs at various times throughout the day. One of them is, "Practice for Heaven: love each other now!" The apostle John, the disciple whom Jesus loved, would have liked that statement. He had much to say about loving one another, and it is he who gives us the grand glimpse of Heaven that we know as the book of Revelation.

For the next three months, our attention will be on some of John's writings (with one text from Luke on Palm Sunday). In March our lessons come from 1 John. The longest of his three short letters near the end of our New Testament, its theme is love and how we practice it day by day. In April we'll make the transition to a study of Revelation with two lessons from the Gospels.

Our recall of the final week of Jesus' life and of his death and resurrection will draw us fittingly to a look at what the book of Revelation has to say about Heaven. And that's what we'll be doing for the remaining seven weeks of the quarter. We'll conclude with a prayer, "Come, Lord Jesus."

MARCH

KNOWN BY OUR LOVE

Lesson 1 reveals "The Light of Love." Anyone who has risen in the night and stumbled over a chair or a stray shoe knows it's better to turn on a light before walking through a dark room. John tells us we likewise don't want to stumble in the darkness of a loveless relationship. To walk and live in the light, we need to walk in love.

In **Lesson 2** we are met with "The Test of Love." We can see that the Father himself passes this test, having lavished his love on us. Now it's up to us to pass the test in our relationships with each other. Our text includes the reminder that we cannot pass the test with words alone. True love is expressed in action.

Lesson 3, "The Source of Love," reminds us that love comes from God. If we are confronted with people who are hard to love, we may think we cannot love them. We can't—on our own. But we're not on our own! We are "born of God."

The unit concludes with **Lesson 4**, "The Way to Love." The title may lead some to expect a few easy steps to achieve a life of love. John says it's more basic than that. If you want to love, simply obey the commands of Christ. Obedience to a leader is usually identified more with faith than with love, but that's the point. When we practice our faith, we practice love.

APRIL

A NEW COMMUNITY IN CHRIST

Lesson 5 launches a new unit and a new book for study: Revelation. But we'll use this lesson on Palm Sunday, so most of our text comes from Luke's account of Jesus' triumphal entry. The lesson is fittingly titled "Christ Is King"; it recalls how the people gave Jesus a king's welcome as he entered Jerusalem at the beginning of a momentous week that would end in Jesus' death and burial. It also recalls that the one who was heralded as a king in Jerusalem is in fact King of much more. He is "the Alpha and the Omega, . . . the Almighty."

Lesson 6 will be used on Resurrection Sunday. It testifies that "Christ Is Risen" by laying John's account of Jesus' resurrection next to a few verses from Revelation. Both accounts give grand testimony to the fundamental truth that

Jesus "was dead, and behold [is] . . . alive for ever and ever!" This is the foundation of our faith; nothing is more basic. If Jesus did not rise from the dead, then we might as well close the doors of our church buildings and put our Sunday-school quarterlies in the trash. But, in fact, he did rise!

From **Lesson 7** on we devote ourselves wholly to texts from Revelation. The first is from Revelation 4 and declares that "Christ Is Worthy of Praise." All of Heaven adores him and declares that he is worthy as creator. This attention paid to him makes obvious another reason Christ is worthy of praise: He is worthy as Lord of Heaven. Actions in Heaven match the words; those who *say* Christ is worthy *act* as though he is worthy. That is an example worth noting.

Being Lord of creation and Lord of Heaven are reasons enough for Jesus to receive our praise, but **Lesson 8** adds another: "Christ Is Able to Redeem." He is, in fact, not merely able—he has done it! People of every tribe and tongue and nation have been redeemed by his precious blood. Praise God that that includes us, because while Jesus is worthy of praise, we are not, of ourselves, worthy to praise him! We would be separated from him forever without his sacrificial grace. In the lesson text, every creature in Heaven bowed to worship the Lamb. In view of our redemption, can we do any less?

Lesson 9 promises "Christ Is Our Protection." This assurance should not be taken to mean Christians will have no trouble in life. Jesus himself warned that, in the world, we will have tribulation. But our text for Lesson 9 promises that this world will have to give an account for that tribulation. Judgment is sure, and it will be severe. But when God measures out his wrath on the wicked, we need not fear. Christ is our protection from God's wrath and punishment. Indeed, for us, "God will wipe away every tear from [our] eyes."

LIVING IN GOD'S NEW WORLD

MAY

In previous lessons we saw grand worship scenes in Heaven (especially from Revelation 4 and 5). In **Lesson 10**, "Taking Our Place at the Table," we see another—and yet there is something different here. Amid the *hallelujahs* for the Lord Jesus, we find that there is a place for us as well! We are not worthy to receive worship alongside him, but we do have a place. He is the bridegroom and the host of the marriage feast. And we, the church, are the bride. We belong at his side. We are his beloved. "Blessed are those who are invited to the wedding supper of the Lamb!"

Lesson 11 promises that we'll be "Finding a Home in Heaven." Our place at the table, then, is not merely as guests. Our dwelling place is there. The lesson text includes the dire warning that not everyone will share this place. There will be some whose place is in the fiery lake. They are the ones who reject the Lord in life. But we need not fear that place, that "second death." When we join the Lord in Heaven, we're there to stay!

Images and symbols are important in the book of Revelation, and many of them are taken from the Old Testament. The image of the temple is one of them. But John tells us he saw no temple in Heaven. In the Old Testament the temple, like the tabernacle that preceded it, symbolized God's presence with his people. Our text for **Lesson 12** tells us that in Heaven we need no symbol for that: we will literally be "Living in God's Presence."

Lesson 13 provides a fitting close to the unit and to the quarter with a focus on "Anticipating Christ's Return." With the grand visions of Heaven and its celestial worship, with the promises and reminders of redemption and protection and belonging, these lessons will already have made us look forward to the time when the promises are all fulfilled. So when we hear again the promise of Jesus, "Yes, I am coming soon," we reply with John, "Amen. Come, Lord Jesus."

WHO WILL BE THERE?

In our lessons about Heaven we have focused primarily on our being in the presence of the Lord. Each one of us wants to see him, to be with him. As the song says, "Face to face with Christ my Savior, Face to face—what will it be? When with rapture I behold Him, Jesus Christ who died for me."

But it's not going to be just Jesus and me—it's Jesus and us, many of us, from every tribe and tongue and nation and people. It's people who speak a different language from mine and whose skin is a different color from mine. But it's also people very much like me, like the person I refused to speak to in church last week, or the person I argued with in Sunday school the week before that.

That's the reason we begin our studies this quarter with the unit on love. The early church was known for its love. Even the enemies of the cross had to admit that the Christians had a special love one for another. Surely John's writings were in part responsible for that behavior. So we look this quarter at some of those writings. Yes, we thrill at the scenes of glory and majesty in Revelation. But we are urged and prodded by his old command, which we have had since the beginning. That command is simply, "Love one another."

As they say on the radio, "Practice for Heaven: love each other now!"

The last week of Jesus' life

Bethany
- Jesus is anointed

Mount of Olives and Jerusalem
- The Triumphal Entry

On the road between Bethany and Jerusalem
- Jesus curses the fig tree

Jerusalem
- Jesus cleanses the Temple

On the road between Bethany and Jerusalem
- Jesus and the disciples discuss the withered fig tree

Jerusalem
- Jesus' authority is questioned by the chief priest's and the elders
- Jesus teaches in the temple using parables and answers questions

Jerusalem
- Chief priest, scribes, and elders plot against Jesus
- Judas agrees to betray Jesus

Jerusalem, the Upper Room
- Preparation for the Passover meal
- The last supper with the disciples
- Jesus washes His disciples' feet
- Judas identified as the traitor
- The Lord's Supper instituted
- Jesus comforts and prays for the disciples and later believers

Jerusalem
- Trials before Annas, Caiaphas, and the Sanhedrin
- Trials before Pilate and Herod; torture by Roman soldiers

Golgotha, outside Jerusalem
- Jesus' crucifixion and death

Joseph's Tomb
- Jesus' burial

Gethsemane, on the Mount of Olives
- Jesus prays in the garden
- Jesus' betrayal and arrest

SAT
SUN
MON
TUES
WED
THURS
FRI

Our Community

(1 John, Revelation)

Known by Our Love

The meaning of God's love

A New Community in Christ

Community

Living in God's New World

Promises

THE LIGHT OF LOVE

| LESSON 1 |

WHY TEACH THIS LESSON?

I owned a classic Ford Mustang for many years. My son and daughter enjoyed driving it to high school. We cared for its appearance and mechanical condition. In a sense, we loved that car. But as it neared 200,000 miles and 25 years of age, we found that we didn't put much money and energy into keeping it in good condition. We thought it foolish to pour our hearts and resources into preserving what would soon die. How true for many things of this world.

Christians are told to not love this world. Since this world will pass away, it is foolish to love it. But what should we love and how? Today's study of God's love will help us focus and practice the art of love.

INTRODUCTION

A. DARKNESS AND LIGHT

Cockroaches love the darkness. So do termites, slugs, and most kinds of mold and fungus. Some really disgusting stuff thrives in places where there is no light. Similarly, people who do evil deeds love the darkness (compare 1 Thessalonians 5:7). Physical darkness may hide misdeeds. Spiritual darkness is both the cause and increasing result of sin.

But God's people are to live in the light. When we live lives of love, we walk in the light. We have nothing to hide. We do not stumble in spiritual darkness. We are not corrupted by the love of the world and the lusts of the world. We gladly choose the ways of God. He is the one who said, "Let there be light." He is the provider of both physical and spiritual light.

B. LESSON BACKGROUND

Light and love are important themes in the writings of the apostle John. He writes near the end of his earthly days, after a long life as a leader of the church. In this first of three letters, he appears to address the church at large, warning people to avoid the darkness of false teaching and to embrace the light of love.

The time of John's writing is perhaps somewhere between AD 85 and 90. At this time, the church began to be troubled by a false doctrine known as *gnosticism*. What we may call "full-blown gnosticism" doesn't really appear until the second century AD. So John was confronting an early version of that heresy. Gnostics thought that they knew more than other believers and that they alone would be saved. They taught that following Jesus was not enough to save. The gnostics claimed that believers had to learn secret knowledge. (See also our discussion of this heresy in Lesson 1 of the winter quarter.)

To set matters straight, John assured his readers that what they had received from the beginning was true. John's epistle, however, is far more than a warning against gnostic heresy. Its truths about light, love, and righteousness are needed in every age. Whenever a new false teaching or a new temptation confronts the church, this letter helps to keep us on course.

DEVOTIONAL READING:
1 PETER 4:1-11
BACKGROUND SCRIPTURE:
1 JOHN 2:7-17
PRINTED TEXT:
1 JOHN 2:7-17

LESSON AIMS

After participating in this lesson, each student will be able to:

1. List ways that people can benefit from the light of love.

2. Explain how the principle of love should act as a beacon to guide his or her life.

3. Articulate one way that the principle of love will guide his or her life in the week ahead.

KEY VERSE

Whoever loves his brother lives in the light, and there is nothing in him to make him stumble. —1 John 2:10

I. LIGHT'S ARRIVAL (1 JOHN 2:7-11)

John wants his readers to know the truth and obey it. He begins his epistle with truth, asserting that he and the other apostles had heard and seen and touched Jesus personally. The second chapter continues to focus on truth—the true light that guides the church.

A. WHAT JOHN STRESSES (vv. 7, 8)

7. Dear friends, I am not writing you a new command but an old one, which you have had since the beginning. This old command is the message you have heard.

John calls his readers *friends* since they share membership in God's community (the church). As such, they must submit to all the commands of God. John reminds them that an important rule of behavior is a *command* that is as *old* as Leviticus 19:18: "Love your neighbor as yourself." (We will see John unpack the content and meaning of this commandment as our lesson continues.)

Unlike the false teachers who trouble the early churches, John has added nothing to this truth, which is part of the gospel of Christ (Matthew 19:19). John is merely reemphasizing the same command that Jesus gave, as we shall see (compare John 13:34; 1 John 3:23; 2 John 5, 6).

8. Yet I am writing you a new command; its truth is seen in him and you, because the darkness is passing and the true light is already shining.

The command to love is as old as the Law of Moses. It is as old as Jesus' earthly ministry, now some 55 or 60 years in the past as John writes. Yet it is as *new* as tomorrow's dawn.

The command is true in Jesus, who demonstrated God's great love at the cross. The command is also true in the church, where believers live out divine love in their own lives. When love points the way, people no longer walk in *darkness*. The gloomy night of sin is over; the *light* of love accompanies the dawn of new life (compare Matthew 4:16). What was true in the life of Jesus is now being put into practice in the lives of believers (compare 1 John 2:5, 6).

The *true light* that is *already shining* is Jesus and truth about him. The apostles have faithfully proclaimed this truth. Now false teachers are trying to extinguish that light. Their darkness must be rejected.

B. WHAT JOHN KNOWS (vv. 9-11)

9. Anyone who claims to be in the light but hates his brother is still in the darkness.

The sharp contrast between light and darkness serves to reveal who a person "really is." Someone may claim to *be in the light*, but the *darkness* of attitude and actions will expose him or her. The one who *hates his brother* is not at all like Jesus; such a person is more like Cain (compare 1 John 3:12). Actions speak louder than words. To God, the heart-attitudes that produce actions speak loudest of all. When a person's deeds show that he or she harbors hatred, that person loves the darkness (compare John 3:19-21).

We should also remember that there is more than one way to hate. For many, hatred is shown by the absence of loving action. When they see their fellow Christians in need, they just do not care. When people who claim to be Christians fail to give anything in Jesus' name, they show clearly that they do not have God's love in their hearts (see Matthew 25:42, 43; 1 John 3:17).

10. Whoever loves his brother lives in the light, and there is nothing in him to make him stumble.

The person who follows Jesus *lives in the light* of life. Such a person tries to imitate the greater love of Jesus, remembering how Jesus laid down his life for his

WHAT DO YOU THINK?

The same imperative of Leviticus 19:18 is before us with the coming of Christ. How can its "newness" be practiced today? What excuses do believers offer in failing to practice this?

WHAT DO YOU THINK?

What happens when Christians "walk the walk" as well as "talk the talk"? How will you repair the damage for past inconsistencies in this regard?

WHAT DO YOU THINK?

What was a time in your life when, because of your faith in Christ, you changed your attitude toward someone from hatred or anger to love? How did things turn out?

friends (see John 15:13). The true believer does not step into the light only on special occasions; rather, such a person abides in the light permanently.

Because the light of love has opened that person's eyes to God's reality, *there is nothing in him to make him stumble.* The word that is translated *stumble* originally referred to a trap of some kind. For deeper study you can explore how John uses this word in John 6:61; 16:1 (verb forms) and Revelation 2:14 (noun form). When we walk in the light with Jesus, we neither stumble nor serve as a trap for others to do so.

11. But whoever hates his brother is in the darkness and walks around in the darkness; he does not know where he is going, because the darkness has blinded him.

The one who *hates* a fellow Christian is someone who perhaps still thinks of himself or herself as part of the fellowship of believers. But such a person actually *walks around in the darkness.* A person who makes this choice gives up the opportunity to walk safely with Jesus in the light. This person little knows (or cares) of the dangers that await in the darkness.

The false teachers whom John opposes make the darkness only worse. They have contempt, rather than love, for people who put their faith in Christ. They are quick to condemn anyone who does not have their "secret knowledge." These false teachers *walk around in the darkness* and do not know it because the darkness has *blinded* them to God's truth.

Visual for Lesson 1. *Post this chart to provide your students with a broad view of this quarter's lessons.*

STUMBLING IN DARKNESS; WALKING IN LIGHT

Paris—the city of light! The city is famed for its brilliantly floodlit monuments and buildings that glow throughout the night. The cost for the lighting is considerable, but it pays for itself in quality of life for the residents and visitors. However, there is another side to Paris. A darker side.

In the city's fourteenth district, down 130 steps of a spiral staircase, one may enter "the empire of the dead." It is a dimly lit catacomb of several city blocks. There stacked in neat piles rest the skeletal pieces of 6 million people—the remains of those who died by plagues, the guillotine, and other causes of times past. For a fee one may walk a dimly lit path through the bones.

Two hundred years ago, the catacombs were totally dark and could be explored only by torchlight. The torch of one unfortunate explorer went out, and he stumbled along, lost in the darkness. Eleven years later his remains were found just a few feet from an exit. John reminds us that the times of darkness should be past because the gospel has come. It is a torch that never goes out.

Yet one can still stumble along in darkness voluntarily, bringing grief to self and others. A clue John offers as to whether we walk in light or darkness is whether we choose to make hatred or love the defining character of our lives.   —C. R. B.

II. LIGHT'S RESULTS (1 JOHN 2:12-14)

The light of God and the love of God are not intended for a chosen few. God's light is for all people. By this light they can see the error of their ways and come to repentance (see 2 Peter 3:9). As the following verses show, everyone can walk in this light and enjoy its results.

A. VARIOUS GROUPS, PART 1 (vv. 12-13b)

12. I write to you, dear children,
   because your sins have been forgiven on account of his name.

Turning to a happier theme, John writes brief notes of celebration to various groups in the church. By using the address *children,* it is possible that John is referring either to those who are young in age or are young in the time they have

VISUALS FOR THESE LESSONS

The visual pictured in each lesson (like the one above) is a small reproduction of a large, full-color poster included in the Adult Resources *packet for the Spring Quarter. The packet is available from your supplier. Order No. 392.*

HOW TO SAY IT

Demas. DEE-mus.

gnostics. NAHSS-ticks.

gnosticism. NAHSS-tih-SIZZ-um.

Thessalonians. THESS-uh-LO-nee-unz.

been Christians. The address *dear children* is a favorite of John's (see 1 John 2:1, 12, 18, 28; 3:7, 18; 4:4; 5:21). This may mean that John thinks of all who receive his letter as his own children in the faith.

In any case, John celebrates the fact that their *sins have been forgiven*. The gnostics falsely tell them that they cannot have salvation until they know "secret truths." But John assures them that they are forgiven already. Moreover, this forgiveness is not a personal accomplishment. Rather, it is by Christ—all *on account of* God's great *name*.

13a. I write to you, fathers,

    because you have known him who is from the beginning.

Next John turns specifically to *the fathers*. These are members of the church who are mature both in years and in faith. They have known Christ *from the beginning*—from the time the church was planted in their area. They know that their beliefs are the original truths. They can refute the assertions of the false teachers. God's community must always adhere to the apostolic truth preserved in the Bible, regardless of what false teachers present as a newer "truth."

We should pause to remember that Jesus cautioned against calling anyone on earth "father" (Matthew 23:9). The apostle John is not violating that restriction since he is not using the term *father* in the sense that Jesus forbids—a sense of a rival to the heavenly Father. For deeper study, you can explore how the New Testament uses this word in Luke 1:55; Acts 7:2; 22:1; Ephesians 6:4; Colossians 3:21; and 2 Peter 3:4.

13b. I write to you, young men,

    because you have overcome the evil one.

Now John addresses the *young men*. As with "children" of verse 12, *young* may refer to chronological or spiritual age (or both). The chief characteristic of young men is their vigor and strength. These young warriors for the faith have *overcome the evil one*, the devil. Through Christ they have resisted temptation. Youth are particularly vulnerable to certain kinds of sin (2 Timothy 2:22). Blessed are the overcomers!

B. VARIOUS GROUPS, PART 2 (vv. 13c-14b)

13c. I write to you, dear children,

    because you have known the Father.

As if writing a second verse to a song, John addresses each group anew. He rejoices with the *dear children* because they have come to know God. As the Gospel of John records, "This is eternal life: that they may know you. the only true God, and Jesus Christ, whom you have sent" (John 17:3). The first benefit of walking in the truth is knowing God.

14a. I write to you, fathers,

    because you have known him who is from the beginning.

Again John addresses the *fathers,* repeating the same important truth. They are the ones who *have known him who is from the beginning*. Walking in the light has given them the privilege of knowing Christ and serving him for many years. Their ability to confirm and preserve the ancient truths makes them vital to the church.

14b. I write to you, young men,

    because you are strong,

    and the word of God lives in you,

    and you have overcome the evil one.

When John addresses the *young men* again, he adds two statements about them. Not only have they *overcome the evil one* (repeated from v. 13b), they are

WHAT DO YOU THINK?

The gospel is for all! Yet the devil tries to sow division in the church. What can we do to recognize, prevent, and heal such divisions?

strong and they have the *word of God* living in them. They are not just casually acquainted with God's Word! Such are the benefits of belonging to the fellowship of believers.

GUIDANCE STILL NEEDED?

A generation ago, the baby boomers (those born between 1946 and 1964) entered adulthood. They wanted to "cut the apron strings." But in college they found they still needed guidance from adults—just not from their parents! So the Dean of Students office came to prominence to help guide students in college.

Now that the boomers' children are in college, the parents still want a level of involvement that colleges must learn to deal with. Thus, many universities have created a Coordinator of Parent Programs position to help parents learn to let go of their children who are becoming adults. The title of a *Wall Street Journal* article was "Tucking Them In—in the Dorm: Colleges Ward Off Overinvolved Parents" (July 28, 2005).

People of every generation have needs that they want addressed. When John writes to children, young men, and fathers, he is telling us the Word of God speaks to the needs of all. That Word helps us sort out the difference between *felt needs* and *real needs*. How will God's Word guide you today?   —C. R. B.

III. WORLD'S DESIRES (1 JOHN 2:15-17)

Tragically, some people reject the light. Some reject it right from the start. Others reject the light after having first accepted it (see Hebrews 6:4-6).

A. STARK CHOICE (vv. 15, 16)
15. Do not love the world or anything in the world. If anyone loves the world, the love of the Father is not in him.

Love should be our finest motive. It is to be a selfless devotion modeled after the nature of God. Yet some people direct their love to the things that are *in the world* rather than to the *Father.* Then love becomes an ugly thing—a distortion and a corruption. This was the problem of Demas (2 Timothy 4:10).

When John charges his readers *do not love the world,* he does not have in mind the world of humanity that God loved and sent his Son to save (see John 3:16). He means the fallen world as it continues defiantly to reject God (John 16:11; 1 John 4:3-5; 5:19).

To love the fallen world and its things is to prefer the company of sinners to the community of saints. It is to prefer living in fallen brokenness rather than being born anew. It is to be "of" the world rather than merely "in" it (John 17:11, 16). If a person loves the fallen world, he or she does not love God. We cannot have two masters (Luke 16:13).

16. For everything in the world—the cravings of sinful man, the lust of his eyes and the boasting of what he has and does—comes not from the Father but from the world.

John has warned his readers not to love the world, and now he specifies what this means. *The cravings of sinful man* are cravings that arise out of our selfish appetites. This includes the more obvious sins of gluttony, drunkenness, and sexual immorality. It also includes sins such as racism (selfishness for one's "own people") and contempt for the poor (selfishness for one's own social level). These cravings are the unholy desire to do any of the works listed in Galatians 5:19-21.

John's second warning is against *the lust of the eyes.* This refers to enticements that come through our sense of sight. The tree of the knowledge of good and evil in the Garden of Eden was "pleasing to the eyes" (Genesis 3:6). There was

DAILY BIBLE READINGS

Monday, Feb. 26—Partakers of the Divine Nature (2 Peter 1:5-11)

Tuesday, Feb. 27—Living in Love (Romans 12:9-21)

Wednesday, Feb. 28—Fulfilling the Law in Love (Romans 13:8-14)

Thursday, Mar. 1—Serve with Love (Galatians 5:13-26)

Friday, Mar. 2—Love Deeply (1 Peter 4:1-11)

Saturday, Mar. 3—Called to Live in Love (1 John 2:7-11)

Sunday, Mar. 4—Live for God (1 John 2:12-17)

WHAT DO YOU THINK?

Give examples of loving the world. *How does* love of the Father *provide an antidote?*

nothing wrong with the tree in and of itself. But Adam and Eve used it for an unholy purpose.

While there is often a sexual element in lust (compare 2 Samuel 11:2), the primary focus here is materialism. Television, movies, and the Internet offer materialistic enticements to our eyes that did not exist in John's day. Believers must remember that their treasures are laid up in Heaven.

The third warning is against the *boasting of what he has and does*. This is not pride in a positive sense, such as taking godly pride in doing the best we can. John refers, rather, to boastful arrogance. This describes those who think they are too good to honor God (see Romans 1:30). Such people become lovers of themselves (see 2 Timothy 3:2). They proudly list their virtues for God (see Luke 18:9-14). This is a fatal flaw of modern society, where status seekers care only about their public image, thinking, "It's all about me."

B. END RESULT (v. 17)

17. The world and its desires pass away, but the man who does the will of God lives forever.

The fallen world is dying. Everything in the world will *pass away*. Even the lust or desire for such things will finally die. Why should God's people care about carnal pleasures that do not bring lasting satisfaction? Why should we care about amassing goods, as did the rich fool (see Luke 12:16-21), only to die and lose it all? Why should we care about our standing in the eyes of humanity, rather than our standing before God (see John 5:44)?

When life is done, only the one *who does the will of God* will endure. People who invested everything in the lust of the world will have nothing; God's people will have everything. The arrogant will perish in their carnal boasting; the meek will inherit the earth. So John warns his readers that love for the world brings failure. The wise choice is to walk in the light of love, to do the will of the Father, and to abide forever.

CONCLUSION

A. IGNORING THE LIGHT OF LOVE

Over the centuries there have been many false teachers who have tried to lead God's people astray. Against this John issues a call to the church to walk in the true light. This light is right for all ages and brings its benefits to all ages. On the other hand, John warns that the one who chooses the darkness and the ways of the world will be exposed. The light of love is God's beacon to guide our lives.

B. FOLLOWING THE LIGHT OF LOVE

What does it mean to us today to follow the light of love? First, it means that to love God is to honor his truth. We must never let the "wisdom" of the world replace divine revelation. The light of love necessarily includes the love of truth. John clearly shows that love is not just a "feel good" emotion; it is inseparably intertwined with acting in accordance with truth. Truth matters!

A second application is found in the way we express love in the church. We can learn to love both from God's nature and from God's command. We get a foretaste of Heaven in a community of godly love. God's people are to be different from those controlled by worldliness. Our happiness does not lie in fulfilling the lust of the flesh; our eternal security does not lie in the size of our earthly estate. The only real satisfaction comes from walking with Jesus in the light—in the light of love.

Discovery Learning

This page contains an alternative lesson plan emphasizing learning activities. Classes desiring such student involvement will find these suggestions helpful. The next page is a reproducible activity page to further enhance discovery learning.

LEARNING GOALS

After participating in this lesson, each student will be able to:

1. List ways that people can benefit from the light of love.

2. Explain how the principle of love should act as a beacon to guide his or her life.

3. Articulate one way that the principle of love will guide his or her life in the week ahead.

INTO THE LESSON

Option #1. Display the following word-find puzzle as class begins (it also appears in the student book).

```
J  E  T  A  H  O
H  V  H  R  N  J
O  O  G  H  U  K
N  L  I  D  R  E
E  S  L  A  F  N
W  O  D  H  O  J
```

Say, "Four sets of John's contrasts can be found in this word puzzle. Check today's text and then find and mark the eight words." Allow time to find these words: DARK, FALSE, HATE, LIGHT, LOVE, NEW, OLD, TRUE. Say, "John uses simple terms to reveal profound truths." You may want to relate this truth to the lesson writer's discussion of the gnostic heresy of the first century.

Option #2. Distribute copies of the Where Do You Stand? Where Are You Going? exercise from the reproducible page for students to work on as they arrive.

Option #3. Introduce the entirety of the first unit (Lessons 1-4) by displaying the following as class begins:

1 John 2:7-17	The ___ of Love	GHILT
1 John 3:1, 2, 11-24	The ___ of Love	ESTT
1 John 4:7-21	The ___ of Love	CEORSU
1 John 5:1-12	The ___ of Love	AWY

Ask the class to unscramble the letters at the end of each line to fill in the blank with the correct word: LIGHT, TEST, SOURCE, WAY.

INTO THE WORD

Note to students that John is emphatically repetitious in his writing—he uses the same key words over and over. Then give them this list of words in a column: Be-cause, Beginning, Brothers, Children, Command(ment), Dark(ness), Fathers, Hate, Light, Love, True/Truth, World, Write. Direct them to go through the text, 1 John 2:7-17, and make a tally of how many times each word (or form of a word) is used. Allow about five minutes, then ask for tallies. Don't get bogged down in disagreements; the point is to see the prevalence of certain ideas.

Establish groups that you call "The Light Group" and "The Love Group." Duplicate the groups as many times as you need to keep each to no more than six people. Give each group a list from a concordance of 10 to 12 biblical references to *light* or *love*. (A concordance will have hundreds of references, so be selective.) If you desire, you can choose from the following two lists.

Light: Genesis 1:3, 4; Exodus 10:21-23; Job 12:24, 25; 29:2, 3; Psalm 27:1; Isaiah 2:5; 5:20; 60:1-3; Daniel 2:22; Matthew 5:16; Luke 11:34-36; John 1:9; 3:19-21; 12:35, 36; Acts 26:17, 18; Ephesians 5:8; 1 Peter 2:9.

Love: Exodus 20:6; Leviticus 19:18; Judges 5:31; Psalms 69:36; 97:10; Proverbs 10:12; 17:17; Jeremiah 31:3; Zephaniah 3:17; Luke 6:32; John 3:16, 19-21; Romans 12:10; 13:10; 1 Corinthians 8:3; Ephesians 4:1, 2; 1 Peter 1:22.

Say, "Cooperate on finding and reading the verses assigned. Note particularly how the key words are used, and then look at today's text in 1 John 2:7-17. Your task is to relate the verses you find to truths John expresses in today's text." If necessary, give this example: "Job 12:24 speaks of a contrast: that of spiritual darkness with light." Allow the groups time to deliberate. Then ask volunteers explain the connections they have made. Discuss.

INTO LIFE

Either buy a package of lighthouse stickers or have a class member sketch a simple lighthouse image onto peel-and-stick labels. Distribute one to each student.

Suggest that each student stick the image in a place where it will serve as a reminder to live and act in the light of God's love in the week ahead. Possible places are the bathroom mirror and the refrigerator door. Say, "When you are tempted by various sinful cravings or to boast of what you have or do, let the light of love show you a different way." Distribute The Urge to Write exercise from the reproducible page as take-home work.

Where Do You Stand? Where Are You Going?

John says that the one who walks in darkness doesn't even know where he is going (see 1 John 2:11). Psalm 119:105 is the psalmist's affirmation of his confidence in the light shed by God's Word: "Your word is a lamp to my feet and a light for my path." The light of God's Word helps one know where one stands ("a lamp to my feet") and the direction to take ("a light for my path"). Use your Bible study aids and your Christian friends to put an appropriate Scripture reference underneath each of the signs below.

_____ _____ _____ _____ _____

The Urge to Write

John felt compelled by circumstances and by the Spirit to write words of encouragement and correction to those he loved in the Lord. Whom do you know who may need your encouraging or corrective word for any of the following circumstances? Write the names in and then consider how and when you will "feel the urge to write."

_____ Someone who has slipped away from the truth of the gospel, who needs to hear the old command that is ever new.

_____ A fellow Christian who is struggling with loving another as he or she should.

_____ A new Christian whose sins have been forgiven in Christ.

_____ An older Christian whose life demonstrates a knowledge of the one who is from the beginning.

_____ A young person who is demonstrating that the Word of God lives in him or her.

_____ A Christian brother or sister who seems to be lured away by the things of the world that appeal to the eye.

_____ A fellow Christian who shows signs of arrogance about what he or she has or has accomplished.

_____ Someone who simply needs to hear that "the world and its desires pass away, but the [one] who does the will of God lives forever."

THE TEST OF LOVE

LESSON 2

WHY TEACH THIS LESSON?

A certain congregation has a volunteer ministry group called *HomeWorks*. This ministry helps church families and neighbors in need of minor home repairs. The group has shingled roofs, built wheelchair ramps, restored a porch, and done many minor plumbing and electrical repairs. Some projects take a few hours while other projects have taken up to two months to complete. All the money for repairs comes from the pockets of the volunteers or from donations to the ministry. What a wonderful demonstration of selfless love for other people! This ministry is a dynamic demonstration of compassion and a fulfillment of Christ's call to love one another.

Christianity is, in a sense, a lifelong test of love. But your students may wonder, "What is the nature of this test, and how do we pass it?" The "final exam" will be on how we have loved the Lord and how we have loved our neighbor as ourselves. We are not saved by works of love, of course. Yet the way we express Christian love demonstrates our faith. Love is the test that reveals whether or not a believer is really walking in the light. This lesson stresses that the practice of Christian love is a priority item with our God.

INTRODUCTION

A. WILL WE BE TESTED ON THIS?

A high-school teacher has spent hours preparing a special lesson. As she launches into her enthusiastic presentation, a hand goes up in the back row. The laziest student in the class raises the predictable question: "Will we be tested on this?" The implication is clear. If the material is not going to be on a test, then the student is not going to bother to learn it.

The apostle John wants his readers to know something for certain: they are going to be tested on the subject of love. God has already shown them his love; now he expects them to show this same kind of undeserved, unearned love to one another.

"The royal law found in Scripture" is "Love your neighbor as yourself" (James 2:8). Love is the defining mark of Jesus' followers. It is the first fruit of the Spirit (see Galatians 5:22); it is the crowning virtue to be added to a Christian's life (see 2 Peter 1:7). Love holds all the other virtues together in "perfect unity" (see Colossians 3:14). Even when measured against faith and hope, the greatest of the three is love (see 1 Corinthians 13:13).

B. LESSON BACKGROUND

John wrote this epistle against a background of false teachers who came to be known as *gnostics*. Among other things, gnostics taught that it did not really matter if a person had morality or love—as long as he or she had "secret knowledge." To combat this false teaching, John emphasized the interconnection of right belief, right actions, and right love. To put it another way, it is the

DEVOTIONAL READING:

1 CORINTHIANS 13

BACKGROUND SCRIPTURE:

1 JOHN 3

PRINTED TEXT:

1 JOHN 3:1, 2, 11-24

LESSON AIMS

After participating in this lesson, each student will be able to:

1. Recite 1 John 3:16 from memory.

2. Compare and contrast John 3:16 with 1 John 3:16.

3. Commit to imitating Christ's love by sharing one possession with a Christian brother or sister in need.

KEY VERSE

Dear friends, now we are children of God, and what we will be has not yet been made known. But we know that when he appears, we shall be like him, for we shall see him as he is.

—1 John 3:2

right involvement of head, hands, and heart. The child of God must believe the truth, obey the commands, and love the brethren.

Of these three areas, John's clear favorite is the emphasis on love (although they cannot really be separated). In last week's lesson John equated the life of love with walking in the light. Today he will examine God's love, the world's lack of love, and the saints' love that meets every test.

I. MAJESTY OF LOVE (1 JOHN 3:1, 2)

Pure, unselfish love is a beautiful thing. The ultimate example of love is the love of God himself, which he showed when he invited unworthy people back into fellowship. John calls his readers to contemplate what kind of love this is and to imagine what the outcome of this love will be.

A. OUR PRESENT (v. 1)
1. How great is the love the Father has lavished on us, that we should be called children of God! And that is what we are! The reason the world does not know us is that it did not know him.

Look! What a wonder! Consider *how great is the love* that God has offered! With these thoughts John calls his readers to ponder the degree of love it took for God to adopt us as his children. How can God love us when we have been sinful and unworthy?

It is through Christ that God has forgiven us and welcomed us into his family. If we will only think about it, we will realize that it is not the having of merit or knowing secrets that will take us to Heaven. Rather, it is the love and grace of God.

The family of God must take note, however, that *the world* does not understand or approve of us. The fallen, unregenerate world refuses to know God, so it is only to be expected that the world will not look favorably on God's people. In spite of this, it is an eternal privilege for believers to be called *children of God*. "Yet to all who received him, to those who believed in his name, he gave the right to become children of God" (John 1:12).

B. OUR FUTURE (v. 2)
2. Dear friends, now we are children of God, and what we will be has not yet been made known. But we know that when he appears, we shall be like him, for we shall see him as he is.

As *children of God*, Christians have a glorious future. We are heirs of a Father who owns the whole universe. We as God's children will be changed (see 1 Corinthians 15:51-54), with bodies transformed into something far more glorious (see Philippians 3:21).

What we eventually *will be* has not yet been disclosed fully. Even so, we do know this: when Jesus *appears* at his second coming, *we shall see him as he is*. At that time *we shall be like him*, with glorious bodies made eternal and incorruptible. Just as God made our bodies in the beginning and pronounced everything "very good," by his same power our bodies will be made even better.

God's immense love was poured out on people who deserved just the opposite. He invites us to come out of our rebellion to live in a heavenly home. The cost to God to issue this invitation was the life of his Son. When we consider the degree of love it took to do that, is God's command that we love one another so burdensome? The other person has not earned our love. But neither have we earned God's love.

WHAT DO YOU THINK?

What are some of the reasons the world regards the church with suspicion? How should we respond?

What Love Can Do

George and Janet had been married for several years but were unable to start the family they so badly wanted. At last they were able to adopt a baby. But this baby had suffered from parental neglect. The little girl was a tragic sight to behold. Her skin was covered with lesions; her frail body bore the signs of abuse.

George and Janet came to visit their minister and his wife to show them the baby. The new parents proudly unwrapped the blankets and thrust the baby into the arms of the minister's wife with the words, "Isn't she beautiful?" The truth was that she *wasn't* beautiful physically; she showed the evidence of the former abuse. It was all the minister and his wife could do to feign an appreciation for a beauty they did not see. They could only state their joy that the three were now a family.

A few months later the family returned for another visit. This time there was no doubt: the baby was indeed beautiful! Tender care had transformed the infant from an object of neglect and abuse into a symbol of what happens when love does its wonderful work. God has brought us into his family, even though the spiritual abuse we suffer is self-inflicted. We cannot imagine how great the difference can be when we let his transforming love work its power on us!   —C. R. B.

II. MESSAGE OF LOVE (1 JOHN 3:11-15)

God shows us the triumph of love at its best, but the fallen world shows us the failure to love at its worst. From a negative example we can learn what it is to reject the message of love.

A. Don't Be Like Cain (vv. 11, 12)

11. *This is the message you heard from the beginning: We should love one another.*

It was God's intention *from the beginning* that we should *love one another.* But what beginning is John talking about? Even before the church was established, Jesus proclaimed that "By this all men will know that you are my disciples, if you love one another" (John 13:35). But John may intend the phrase *from the beginning* to go back even further, as the next verse shows.

12. *Do not be like Cain, who belonged to the evil one and murdered his brother. And why did he murder him? Because his own actions were evil and his brother's were righteous.*

Satan, *the evil one,* tempted Eve and Adam to eat the forbidden fruit. More sin followed, bringing hatred and murder into the lives of their sons. When Cain's offering was rejected and Abel's was accepted, sin was at the door (Genesis 4:7). Refusing to listen to God's counsel, Cain allowed jealousy to overrule love. So he *murdered his brother* out in the fields.

Cain was furious because his own offering from his garden did not win the approval of God while Abel's offerings from his flock did. Abel had made his offering "by faith" (see Hebrews 11:4). The same is not said of Cain's offering. Cain's own actions were evil, but the actions of his brother were righteous (compare Matthew 23:35). "The way of Cain" (Jude 11) is detestable.

The Opposite of Love

Graham Greene wrote the novel *The Quiet American* in 1956. The novel is set in about 1952, when France was fighting a war to hold on to its colonial power in Southeast Asia. In the novel, Thomas Fowler is a British journalist living with his mistress in Saigon. Alden Pyle, "the quiet American," disrupts Fowler's degenerate, opium-smoking, life at ease when he develops a romantic interest in Fowler's mistress. Using political ideology as his rationalization, Fowler conspires to have Pyle murdered.

Visual for Lesson 2. *Point to this visual as you ask, "How do we recognize needs that God expects us to meet?"*

What Do You Think?

Many of us would disavow any connection with Cain and dismiss him as "an extreme case." Why is this a mistake? What can you learn from the story of Cain that can help you in your daily life?

The book and the movies that followed in 1958 and 2002 were subject to speculation about the author's political motivations. Regardless of the political spin, the story echoes the problem of allowing passion and self-interest to cause a person to hate and even murder.

It's a story as old as the one John reminds us of: Cain's attitude toward his brother and the murder that resulted. It is a topic that has timeless relevance. The ugliness of a lack of love in our hearts can cause us to gossip, condemn, backbite, or even do things much worse! —C. R. B.

B. DON'T BE SURPRISED (v. 13)

13. Do not be surprised, my brothers, if the world hates you.

Hatred is nothing new; it has existed in every generation. Therefore, John's readers should not marvel that this hatred is now directed against them. This is particularly true in light of what Jesus said to his disciples in the upper room: "If the world hates you, keep in mind that it hated me first" (John 15:18).

C. DON'T FAIL THIS TEST (vv. 14, 15)

14. We know that we have passed from death to life, because we love our brothers. Anyone who does not love remains in death.

The hatred of Cain is an old story, and the hatred of the world is probably not surprising. But what about hatred within the family of God? It is inconceivable! If a believer doesn't love his brother it signifies that such a person either has never come all the way into life or has gone back and now abides in *death*.

15. Anyone who hates his brother is a murderer, and you know that no murderer has eternal life in him.

To put it more bluntly, anyone who claims to be within the community of God yet hates a fellow believer *is a murderer.* Jesus said something similar in the Sermon on the Mount. The Law of Moses said, "Do not murder," but Jesus added that "anyone who is angry with his brother" is in danger of the same judgment (see Matthew 5:21, 22). John shows the chilling twofold reality of this. First, the person who hates his brother is a murderer. Second, no murderer has eternal life in him. Hatred and murder are in the same moral category.

III. MEASURES OF LOVE (1 JOHN 3:16-24)

Cain and the fallen world failed the test of love. But God's children can pass this test. In the following verses John outlines measures or tests of love. John presents this in a positive way, as if he expects his readers to live up to them. The theme is one of obedience.

A. PRACTICAL TEST (vv. 16-18)

16. This is how we know what love is: Jesus Christ laid down his life for us. And we ought to lay down our lives for our brothers.

The first measure of *love* is a practical test. The love of God is a love that we can perceive in action. When God loved the world, he sent Heaven's greatest gift. Jesus came and *laid down his life for us*—unrepentant enemies of God (see John 3:16; Romans 5:8, 10; Colossians 1:21, 22). Love like God's love could give nothing less. God's children should resemble their Father in this kind of love. We should be willing to do just about anything *for our brothers* (see John 15:12, 13).

17. If anyone has material possessions and sees his brother in need but has no pity on him, how can the love of God be in him?

Sometimes a person claims to be a loving member of the church, but that person's actions (or lack of actions) show otherwise. He or she may have plenty

HOW TO SAY IT

Colossians. Kuh-LOSH-unz.

Corinthians. Ko-RIN-thee-unz.

Galatians. Guh-LAY-shunz.

Hebrews. HEE-brews.

Philippians. Fih-LIP-ee-unz.

of *material possessions* with which to help. But when a fellow Christian is *in need,* the person who is well off does not care. *How can the love of God be in* such a person?

18. Dear children, let us not love with words or tongue but with actions and in truth.

Therefore, love must be put into action. Addressing his readers endearingly as *dear children,* the aged apostle speaks as a loving father (compare 2 John 1). He urges his readers not to love merely *with words or tongue,* paying mere lip service to the Lord's command (compare Matthew 7:21; James 1:22-25; 2:14-17). God wants his children to put their love to work *with actions and in truth.*

The earliest church in Jerusalem was a good example of this. In that community of love, "No one claimed that any of his possessions was his own, but they shared everything they had" (Acts 4:32).

B. INWARD CONVICTION (vv. 19, 20)

19. This then is how we know that we belong to the truth, and how we set our hearts at rest in his presence

The words *this then* link this verse to what has just been said. It is by our actions that *we know that we belong to the truth.* If the Christian's loving actions are genuine and substantive, that is positive evidence of a right relationship to God. Knowing truly that we love produces confidence within our hearts, even to the extent that it will *set our hearts at rest,* so we can stand before God at judgment. This is blessed assurance at its best!

20. . . . whenever our hearts condemn us. For God is greater than our hearts, and he knows everything.

But what if *our hearts* should happen to *condemn us?* What if a tender conscience, manipulated by the devil, fills us with misgivings and doubts? The good news is that God himself is the final court of appeal; the devil cannot go over his head! We can rest assured that God, who knows everything, is well aware that we love him and we are sincerely trying to love his children the best we can.

C. END RESULT (vv. 21-24)

21. Dear friends, if our hearts do not condemn us, we have confidence before God

Now John leads his beloved readers beyond the possible self-doubt of verse 20. *If our hearts do not condemn us*—and there is no reason that they should do so—then we can enjoy *confidence before God.* Having this kind of confidence in the presence of our creator is not unreachable, especially when we remember that it is Jesus himself who makes it possible (Hebrews 4:14-16).

22. . . . and receive from him anything we ask, because we obey his commands and do what pleases him.

John's focus on hands, head, and heart—in whatever sequence—is repeated frequently throughout his epistle. Moving from verses 20, 21 to verse 22 takes us from heart back to hands. When we keep God's *commands,* that is, do what pleases him, we are promised that we will receive *anything we ask.*

Our loving Father will not withhold his blessings from his children. This presupposes, of course, that we ask in a spirit of love and that we ask for things that are according to his will. "This is the confidence that we have in approaching God: that, if we ask anything according to his will, he hears us" (1 John 5:14). Asking for blessings also presupposes that we ask with right motives. "When you ask, you do not receive, because you ask with wrong motives, that you may spend what you get on your pleasures" (James 4:3).

WHAT DO YOU THINK?

You see a shabbily dressed man on a street corner asking for money. His cardboard sign says, "Homeless veteran. Hungry. What would Jesus do?" How do you respond in a way that demonstrates Christ's love and is not counterproductive?

WHAT DO YOU THINK?

How do you counsel a fellow Christian who feels condemned by his or her own heart? How will your counsel be flexible from person to person?

WHAT DO YOU THINK?

Love is probably written and sung about more than any other emotion or action! In what ways will your actions this week demonstrate how the Christian concept of love differs from what the world calls love?

PRAYER

Our Father, we cannot thank you enough for the love that has allowed us to be called your children! Your people have rejected you time and time again over the course of many centuries. Yet you were working through it all to bring your plan to fruition: the redemption of humans from the quagmire of self-inflicted sin.

Forgive us for sometimes treating your great love so casually. Help us to honor your love by reflecting it toward one another. In the name of Jesus, amen.

23. And this is his command: to believe in the name of his Son, Jesus Christ, and to love one another as he commanded us.

Now John moves us from hands to head in declaring what we must *believe*. Jesus was asked on one occasion, "What must we do to do the works God requires?" He answered in these words: "The work of God is this: to believe in the one he has sent" (John 6:28, 29). Similarly, John says that God's command is simply this: *to believe on the name of his Son, Jesus Christ.*

Added to this is the further commandment *to love one another* (compare Matthew 22:36-40). The right belief plus the right love fulfills God's demands.

24. Those who obey his commands live in him, and he in them. And this is how we know that he lives in us: We know it by the Spirit he gave us.

When God's child is obeying, believing, and loving as John has directed, then he or she is keeping God's commands and dwelling in God. More than this, God is also dwelling in him or her. This closely parallels a promise of Jesus: "If anyone loves me, he will obey my teaching. My Father will love him, and we will come to him and make our home with him" (John 14:23).

This divine presence in the life of the believer is identified in this verse as *the Spirit he gave us.* The abiding Spirit confirms to us that God is with us and in us (see Acts 2:33, 38; Romans 5:5; 8:14-16).

CONCLUSION

A. LOVE: THE FINAL EXAM

Love is a verb, not just a noun. It is an action, not just an emotion. We know that faith without actions is dead (James 2:17). We could also say that love without actions is dead. When John writes about love, he writes about *doing* more than *feeling.* The command to love one another is a call to action.

God's "final exam" for his people on Judgment Day will not count how many church services were attended or how many verses were memorized. What he is interested in most of all is how our belief expresses itself in love. If we fail the test of love, we can never make up for it with any "extra credit" we may think we can gain from a flurry of religious activities.

B. LOVE: THE COMMENCEMENT

The context of 1 John suggests many ways that love can be put to work. We can show our love for God by committing ourselves to his Son and clinging to the truth of his Word. If we truly love God, we will not dishonor his Son by lazy discipleship (Hebrews 6:12). If we truly love God, we will not allow false teachings against his Word to stand (1 Timothy 6:3-5). Love and light must walk hand in hand.

We also show our love for God by loving his children. God wants us to combine our love for him with our love for one another. This kind of shared love is what characterizes living in God's community—the church. Our love for one another is to be genuine and practical. Mere lip service cannot feed the hungry or clothe the naked. Real love is always ready to reach out.

Finally, we can show our love for God and his church by "talking up" our eagerness to go to Heaven. It is not a cop-out on this world to be eager to go to the next. When Jesus returns and we are suddenly, gloriously changed, we will live forever in fellowship with God, Jesus, and all our fellow saints. If we really treasure the reward of Heaven, we will want to bring the lost into the community of the saved. Inviting someone to join us on the road to Heaven is the ultimate expression of loving one another.

THOUGHT TO REMEMBER

Love must act.

Discovery Learning

This page contains an alternative lesson plan emphasizing learning activities. Classes desiring such student involvement will find these suggestions helpful. The next page is a reproducible activity page to further enhance discovery learning.

LEARNING GOALS

After this lesson, each student will be able to:

1. Recite 1 John 3:16 from memory.

2. Compare and contrast John 3:16 with 1 John 3:16.

3. Commit to imitating Christ's love by sharing one possession with a Christian brother or sister in need.

INTO THE LESSON

If you have access to a college bookstore, buy copies of the small "blue books" that schools typically use for written exams (they cost about ten cents apiece). Otherwise, prepare copies of a sheet with 20 numbered entries, an *A, B, C, D, E* by each number, and the word *TEST* prominently displayed at the top. Hand a copy to each student as he or she arrives. Also provide pens and pencils. Say nothing about your intentions.

As class begins say, "Please write your name at the top of the test sheet I have given you. While you are at it, also indicate at the top whether you will get a *pass* or a *fail.*" Give time for the grumbles and remarks and then say, "There is only one question on this test, and it is not multiple choice. It is a simple *yes* or *no.* Ready for the question? Here it is: 'Do you love as Jesus loves?'"

Discuss how this concept and this question relate to this lesson on "The Test of Love." (Alternative: distribute copies of John's Theme and Thesis from the reproducible page for students to work on as they arrive.)

INTO THE WORD

Make arrangement in advance for a musically talented member of your congregation to lead the class in singing "Behold, What Manner of Love" by Patricia Van Tine (© 1978 by Maranatha! Music). This song is based on 1 John 3:1. This song will set the tone for today's study: the true test of love in us is how closely we resemble the love God has shown to us in Christ.

Display the lesson writer's outline: I. Majesty of Love (1 John 3:1, 2), II. Message of Love (1 John 3:11-15), III. Measures of Love (1 John 3:16-24). Include in your display two columns conspicuously headed *FAIL* and *PASS.*

Lead a brief discussion of verses 1, 2. Then divide your class into two groups. Say, "Group #1, I want you to suggest a list of attitudes and deeds guaranteed to get the test taker a failing grade, based on verses 11-15 in today's text. Group #2, I want you to suggest a list of at-titudes and deeds guaranteed to get the test taker a passing grade, based on verses 16-24 of today's text."

Allow time to examine the verses, then call for answers. Expect answers such as, "A person who hates fails" (v. 15); "Self-sacrifice for the good of others gets a passing grade" (v. 16); "One who cannot tolerate the success of others fails" (v. 12); and "Compassionate generosity passes" (v. 17). Write the two lists as answers are suggested.

Next, say "1 John 3:16 is an important verse, closely related to John 3:16. Let's dig into what 1 John 3:16 means." Then distribute four index cards that you have prepared in advance with the following phrases: *Card #1*—"How do we perceive the love of God?" *Card #2*—"Because he laid down his life for us"; *Card #3*—"So?" *Card #4*—"We ought to lay down our lives for our brothers and sisters!"

Give the four cards to individuals randomly chosen and not seated next to one another. Direct them to stand, say their phrases as quickly as possible, in order, and then to hand their cards to another. Repeat the procedure five or six times. This will help class members fix this verse in their minds. Finish by reading 1 John 3:16 to the class.

INTO LIFE

Say, "First John 3:17 describes what God did for us: saw us in need (sinners headed to Hell), felt compassion, and acted to meet our needs (sending Jesus as the pure and holy sacrifice to atone for and cover our sins). To be a true child of God, we must see, feel, and act in the same manner."

Give each student a small piece of paper. Indicate that you want each person to write on that paper the name and circumstances of someone in need. Suggest that it could be a young person needing help for a missions trip, a neighbor who has been victimized by fire or other disaster, or a senior saint struggling just to make ends meet.

Collect the papers and put them in a container. Place the container by the classroom exit. Suggest that your students take slips (without looking) as they leave and do their best to meet anonymously the needs identified. Beside the container have copies of Take This Test from the reproducible page available to take home as well.

John's Theme and Thesis

Both in his Gospel and in his first epistle, John makes marvelous statements of the theme of the gospel. The following mixes John 3:16 and 1 John 3:16. Separate the words into a 26-word statement (Gospel) and a 27-word statement (epistle). [Hint: the correct words always flow forward; this means you will never have to go backward from one word to find the next correct word.]

FOR THIS IS GOD SO LOVED HOW WE KNOW THE WHAT WORLD THAT LOVE IS HE JESUS GAVE CHRIST HIS LAID ONE DOWN AND HIS ONLY LIFE SON FOR THAT US WHOEVER AND WE BELIEVES IN OUGHT HIM TO SHALL LAY NOT DOWN PERISH OUR BUT LIVES HAVE FOR ETERNAL LIFE OUR BROTHERS.

_____ _____ _____ _____ _____

_____ _____ _____ _____ _____

_____ _____ _____ _____ _____

_____ _____ _____ _____ _____

_____ _____ (John 3:16).

_____ _____ _____ _____ _____

_____ _____ _____ _____ _____

_____ _____ _____ _____ _____

_____ _____ (1 John 3:16).

Take the Test

How are you doing in the following elements of John's test as he reveals it in today's text? Give yourself an A, B, C, D, or F on the following:

_____ Reveling in your status as a child of God.

_____ Waiting excitedly for Jesus' return to see him as he is.

_____ Loving the brothers and sisters, all of them!

_____ Sharing material possessions with those in need.

_____ Setting your heart at rest because you know your status with Jesus.

_____ Obeying God's commands and pleasing him.

_____ Sensing the presence of his Spirit in your life.

_____ Being willing to lay down your life for fellow believers, if necessary

THE SOURCE OF LOVE

LESSON 3

WHY TEACH THIS LESSON?

How do you know if you actually are a child of those people claiming to be your biological parents? A certain television program was dedicated to discovering whether a man was or was not the father of a woman's child. The producers of the show did not compare facial features or body traits of the adult and the child. They did not look at the color of eyes and hair to discover similarities or differences. The producers of the show used a more reliable form of testing: DNA. This was the final test of paternity of a child.

How does one know if he is a child of God? How do you know if you are actually born of God? Many contradictory answers have been proposed, and your students may be confused. While there may be a number of Christlike traits we would discover in a child of God, one test stands out above all others. We discover that one test in today's fascinating study and application of God's Word.

INTRODUCTION

A. SEARCHING FOR THE SOURCE

Hernando de Soto was the first European to explore the Mississippi River. Despite all his courageous efforts, however, he only got as far up the river as modern-day Memphis, Tennessee. Little did he know that he was less than a third of the way up that mighty river! He died in 1542 of a fever, and his body was buried in the river that was too big for him to trace. David Livingstone was a Christian missionary and explorer of the Nile River in Africa. His final, most famous, journey was a search for that long river's source. When he died in 1873, he still had not found the elusive headwaters for which he was searching.

Sometimes searching for the source of a mighty river has been just too difficult. But what of the great river of love that flows in the community of God throughout the world and throughout history? What is its ultimate source? What inspired this love? The apostle John makes it clear in this lesson that the source of love is God. Love is part of his central nature; love flows from his heart. Whenever we act in love, we are reproducing what we learned first from him.

B. LESSON BACKGROUND

The apostle John is in some ways an unlikely person to be writing about love. He did not show much love when he and his brother wanted to call down fire from Heaven on a village in Samaria (Luke 9:54). He did not show much love when he and his brother tried to secure preferred seats of honor alongside Jesus (Mark 10:35-37). But while John did not show love very well in the beginning, he certainly received it—as "the disciple whom Jesus loved" (see John 21:20). John learned firsthand that we love because he first loved us. In the end John came to be known as *the apostle of love*.

Previously, we saw John demonstrate that love for fellow Christians is a test that reveals whether a person is really walking in the light. Now John goes further: love

DEVOTIONAL READING:
JOHN 21:15-19
BACKGROUND SCRIPTURE:
1 JOHN 4:7-21
PRINTED TEXT:
1 JOHN 4:7-21

LESSON AIMS

After participating in this lesson, each student will be able to:

1. List the actions that God's love took on our behalf.

2. Explain the concept of propitiation, including how this doctrine alleviates fear in the life of the believer.

3. Write a prayer that asks God to help him or her replace fear with trust in his love.

KEY VERSE

We love him, because he first loved us. —1 John 4:19

is also the test that reveals if a person actually is born of God. Since God is the ultimate source and embodiment of love, anyone who is genuinely born of God will reflect his characteristics. A person without love is a person who is not God's child. We will see John establish that such a person does not even know God.

I. EXAMPLE OF LOVE (1 JOHN 4:7-12)

A. OUR PATTERN (vv. 7, 8)

7. Dear friends, let us love one another, for love comes from God. Everyone who loves has been born of God and knows God.

John addresses his readers as people who are dear to him (see also 1 John 3:2, 21; 4:1, 11). John's urging that they *love one another* is a repeat of 1 John 3:11, 23. He is quick to supply a threefold reason. First, *love comes from God;* that is, God is the source of this selfless emotion. Second, those who love show that they are *born of God;* they as genuine children resemble their Father in a vital way. Third, those who love show that they know God; they follow God's love as their pattern.

8. Whoever does not love does not know God, because God is love.

John said previously that the one who lacks love walks in the darkness and abides in death (see 1 John 2:11; 3:14). If someone does not have love, John now asserts, he or she does not even know God. Since the very nature of God *is love,* the person unacquainted with love is unacquainted with God.

This is the same truth that Paul wrote to the Corinthians. Even if a person speaks in tongues, delivers prophecies, and exercises mountain-moving faith, it all means nothing without love (see 1 Corinthians 13:1-3). Love is the most excellent way because it is God's way.

B. OUR SALVATION (vv. 9, 10)

9. This is how God showed his love among us: He sent his one and only Son into the world that we might live through him.

God's love is not just an empty emotion. It is a mighty passion that impelled him to bring salvation to those created in his image. God showed this love in the way *he sent his one and only Son* to take on human flesh and to die on the cross. This will forever be the world's greatest example of love (see John 15:13). God sent—and Jesus came—so *we might live through him.* Exactly how Jesus' death can save us is the subject of the next verse.

10. This is love: not that we loved God, but that he loved us and sent his Son as an atoning sacrifice for our sins.

God is the source, the fountainhead, of love. It is *not that we loved God,* as if we had taken the first steps to make salvation possible. Rather, it is *that he loved us,* even when we were sinful and unworthy (see Romans 5:8). Love begins with God.

When God sent his only begotten Son into the world, he sent him to be the *atoning sacrifice for our sins.* Older and more literal versions of the Bible use the word *propitiation* instead of *atoning sacrifice.* That idea is vital for understanding how God's forgiveness works. God provided Jesus to be the sacrifice for sin. When Jesus gave his life, God accepted Jesus' suffering as payment for sin's penalty. This payment turned God's wrath away from us. We could never have turned away God's wrath on our own (see also Romans 3:25; 1 John 2:2).

God does not just ignore our sins and pretend that they do not exist. His own holiness and justice do not allow this. Holiness and justice require than sin be punished. Yet in his great love for us, God took the necessary steps to deal with

WHAT DO YOU THINK?

Describe someone you know who excels at loving people. How will you follow his or her example?

WHAT DO YOU THINK?

Some may view church attendance and Bible study as good measures of a person's walk with God. What problems can that type of thinking create? Why is love a better test to discern authentic Christianity?

our sins. He sent Jesus, who was both infinite God and sinless man, to give his one great life in our place.

C. OUR CHALLENGE (vv. 11, 12)

11. Dear friends, since God so loved us, we also ought to love one another.

The theme of love is repeated often in this epistle. God, the source of love, has *so loved us* that he gave Jesus for our salvation (John 3:16). Since we have been saved by this love, we ought to be ready to *love one another.* In view of what God has done for us in love, nothing less is acceptable (see also Matthew 18:33).

STEALING JESUS

A few years ago a church in midtown Manhattan (New York City) was burglarized. It was a fairly predictable theft: an offering box and its contents were stolen. Three weeks later a more unusual theft took place: a four-foot plaster figure of Jesus, weighing 200 pounds, was stolen. Stranger yet was the fact that the statue was part of a crucifix, and the cross itself was left behind!

The church custodian commented, "They just decided, 'We're going to leave the cross and take Jesus.'" Think about the implications of that for a moment. Lots of people today like the idea of Jesus as an example of love. They even like the idea (theoretically, at least) of being a person who loves like Jesus. But, as John tells us, God showed his love for us by sending Jesus to be a propitiation or atoning sacrifice for our sins.

If we're going to "take Jesus" as the model for our lives, then we're going to have to "take the cross" as a model as well. "If anyone would come after me, he must deny himself and take up his cross daily and follow me" (Luke 9:23). Is this the model of love and service that directs your life?   —C. R. B.

12. No one has ever seen God; but if we love one another, God lives in us and his love is made complete in us.

Adam heard the sound of God, Abraham heard the voice of God, and Moses stood on holy ground at the burning bush, but *no one has ever seen God.* Moses was even told that no man could see God's face and live. So on the mountain Moses was covered in the cleft of a rock when the presence of God passed by (see Exodus 33:20-23). Some were allowed to see various kinds of manifestations of God (Exodus 24:11). Yet the New Testament reaffirms that no one has ever seen God, both here and in John 1:18.

Even though we cannot see God, we can still have God's presence dwelling *in us.* God's very nature is love, so it is natural for him to live in us if we have *love* for *one another.* This does not mean that we somehow "become" God—creator and creature are still distinct. Even so, we are able to reflect his love for each other. In this way his love is made complete. It reaches completion and fulfills its intended purpose.

II. PROOF OF LOVE (1 JOHN 4:13-16a)

A. SPIRIT WAS GIVEN (v. 13)

13. We know that we live in him and he in us, because he has given us of his Spirit.

Our knowledge *that we live* in God is not based on some mystic, mysterious experience. It is based on the fact that God *has given us of his Spirit* (Romans 8:9; 1 John 3:24). We know that we have the Spirit because God—who cannot lie (Hebrews 6:18)—has given us his firm promise (see Acts 2:38). Thus God's promise of the Spirit and our practice of love join together as proof that we are in

WHAT DO YOU THINK?

In what ways might you face (or have you faced) ridicule or social rebuff while expressing love as Jesus expects? How do you (or did you) react to such attacks?

DAILY BIBLE READINGS

Monday, Mar. 12—*Be Reconciled to God (Romans 5:1-11)*

Tuesday, Mar. 13—*Be Reconciled to One Another (Matthew 5:21-26)*

Wednesday, Mar. 14—*Care for One Another (John 21:15-19)*

Thursday, Mar. 15—*Investing in Eternity (1 Timothy 6: 11-19)*

Friday, Mar. 16—*Knowing God Through Love (1 John 4: 7-12)*

Saturday, Mar. 17—*God Is Love (1 John 4:13-17)*

Sunday, Mar. 18—*Love Brothers and Sisters (1 John 4:18-21)*

HOW TO SAY IT

Boanerges. BO-uh-NUR-geez.

Corinthians. Ko-RIN-thee-unz.

Galatians. Guh-LAY-shunz.

Hernando de Soto. Er-NAN-do da SO-tow.

propitiation. pro-PIH-she-AY-shun.

Samaria. Suh-MARE-ee-uh.

Zacchaeus. Zack-KEY-us.

him and he is in us. Love is the first and greatest fruit that his Spirit produces in us (see Galatians 5:22).

B. SON WAS SENT (v. 14)

14. And we have seen and testify that the Father has sent his Son to be the Savior of the world.

When John says *we have seen and testify,* he reemphasizes the truth of the opening verses of his epistle (see 1 John 1:1-3). He and the other apostles could testify because they knew firsthand that *the Father has sent his Son* into the world. They had seen with their own eyes, heard with their own ears, and touched with their own hands the one sent *to be the Savior of the world.* Jesus did not come just to teach, lead, and befriend—he came to rescue (John 3:17).

C. CONFESSION IS MADE (vv. 15, 16a)

15. If anyone acknowledges that Jesus is the Son of God, God lives in him and he in God.

God sent his Son to save humanity, and God has the right to set certain conditions for salvation. Specifically in this verse, God expects us to acknowledge *that Jesus is the Son of God.* Jesus promised that if a person confesses him before others, he will confess that person before the Father in Heaven (see Matthew 10:32).

Mere acknowledgement is not the entirety of the plan of salvation, of course. As John makes clear, loving action serves as proof that we belong to the truth (1 John 3:17-19). But confessing Jesus is a necessary condition.

16a. And so we know and rely on the love God has for us.

John knows for certain that Jesus really came (v. 14), and because of this he also knows of the great love that God has for us. He and his readers know this love and rely on it; they have put their trust and confidence in it.

III. RESULTS OF LOVE (1 JOHN 4:16b-18)

A. LIVING IN GOD (v. 16b)

16b. God is love. Whoever lives in love lives in God, and God in him.

God does not just "have" love, God *is* love. He embodies everything that is good about love and encompasses the entire range of love's expressions. God and love are so much identified with each other that to live *in love* is to live *in God.* Furthermore, when we live in this love, God himself also lives in us.

B. BOLD AT JUDGMENT (v. 17)

17. In this way, love is made complete among us so that we will have confidence on the day of judgment, because in this world we are like him.

When our *love is made complete,* the final result is that we will have confidence on Judgment Day. We will have nothing to fear when that day comes.

We will have this *confidence* before God because *we are like him* (Jesus). Just as Jesus is pure (1 John 3:3) and righteous (1 John 3:7), by his blood we can also stand before the Father pure and righteous. Jesus abides in the Father (see John 17:21-26), and so can we. Although we live *in this world,* we can have confidence when our love has been made perfect through Christ. Even now, we can approach God's throne of grace in bold confidence (Hebrews 4:16).

C. FREEDOM FROM FEAR (v. 18)

18. There is no fear in love. But perfect love drives out fear, because fear has to do with punishment. The one who fears is not made perfect in love.

Visual for Lesson 3. *Point to this visual as you ask, "In what ways does our love for the heavenly Father drive out fear?"*

Christians can have boldness in judgment, as the previous verse says, because *there is no fear in love.* This fear is not the kind of healthy awe that a person should have for God. Rather, the kind of fear in view is a paralyzing dread and terror. Love and that kind of fear simply have nothing to do with one another; they cannot coexist.

Therefore, love that is perfect or full grown will cast out fear. While fear paralyzes and *has to do with punishment,* genuine love confirms our salvation. The person who still lives in unhealthy fear of God is not yet mature. He or she is not yet made perfect in love.

IV. GRAND SUMMARY OF LOVE (1 JOHN 4:19-21)

A. GOD WAS FIRST (v. 19)

19. *We love because he first loved us.*

Now John sums up his grand teaching about love. God is the source of love. When *we love* him, it is only *because he first loved us.* Without God's initiative we would not have known genuine love; neither would we have known how to love. When we abide in God and his Spirit abides in us, divine love becomes a natural part of our lives.

We return to God the love he has shown us. At the same time, we pass on this kind of love on to our brothers and sisters in Christ.

B. GOD COMMANDS US (vv. 20, 21)

20. *If anyone says, "I love God," yet hates his brother, he is a liar. For anyone who does not love his brother, whom he has seen, cannot love God, whom he has not seen.*

The practical test of love, as seen before, is that God's child must love the *brother* or sister in Christ. A person who says *I love God* but then hates a fellow Christian *is a liar.* There is a logical reason for this fact: we have been made in the image of God. Therefore, this brother or sister whom we should love bears a certain resemblance to God. We have seen this brother or sister, even though we have *not seen* God. If we cannot find anything attractive or lovable in our fellow Christian, then we will not find anything lovable in God. If we fail this practical test of love, our claims to love God are simply lies.

WHAT DO YOU THINK?

Verse 20 implies that "seeing" a person makes it easier to love him or her. Why is this true? What are some things that we can "see" in others that can help us love them?

CLEAN HANDS AND LOVING HEARTS

Millions of people suffer from food poisoning every year. A primary cause is the failure of food-service workers to wash their hands properly. Now "big brother" is here, this time for good! Ultraviolet light scanners developed to detect germs on meat in processing plants are being adapted to show whether we have washed our hands thoroughly. Imagine a parent saying to a child, "Johnny, put your hands under the scanner and let me see if you got them clean"!

Do we need to be reminded that what we can't see *can* hurt us? Yet there are ways to see the unseen, and ultraviolet scanning for germs is only one of them.

A much more important means of "scanning" for both the good and bad of life is found in today's text. John acknowledges that we can't see God. Even so, if we love God then our lives will be a confession of his existence. The Spirit living in us will help us to make this confession. The confession is more than just spoken words. It is also the testimony of our deeds each day of our lives as we exhibit godly character. We reflect God's love in the way we treat others.   —C. R. B.

21. *And he has given us this command: Whoever loves God must also love his brother.*

John concludes as he began: we must love one another. To love God and to love one's neighbor are inseparable. "All the Law and the Prophets hang on these two commandments" (Matthew 22:40).

Moreover, this is our Lord's *command.* It is not optional or negotiable. By observing this love in us, all people will be able to tell that we are Christ's disciples (see John 13:34, 35).

CONCLUSION

A. SOURCE OF LOVE

Love does not just happen. It is a virtue of the highest order, created and demonstrated by God himself. If the world were merely an evolutionary accident and the law of the jungle demanded the survival only of the fittest, then there would be no room for self-sacrificing love. There would be no pattern for such love to exist. But just as God is the creator of the universe and the source of all life, so is he the source of true love.

Without our knowledge of God, searching for the source of love would be an impossible task. We would be like the early explorers who were hopelessly ill-equipped when they searched for the sources of great rivers. If we had only scientific observation to guide us, we would ultimately give up on love and agree with the law of the jungle: the strong devour the weak. If we had only the history of human empires as our guide, we might conclude that there is no real love to be found. It is only in the spiritual realm that we are able to trace love back to its divine source.

But unlike the source of a river, which becomes smaller and smaller as it is traced, the divine source of love becomes greater and greater as we draw nearer. Also unlike the source of a river, the source of love does not need to be increased by tributaries. God's love can never be diminished or depleted; it flows from God's infinite heart.

B. CHANNELS OF LOVE

When we recognize that God is the source of love, we next realize that he intends for us to be the channels of that love. We become the passageways through which the mighty river of God's love flows. This love will bless countless lives, but only as we allow it to flow through us.

God continues to be the dynamic source of the love that flows through us, but he has given us the responsibility to direct that love in ways that would please him. For instance, we know that we should direct generous love toward the widows and the orphans (James 1:27). We should be channels of divine love toward those who are helpless, homeless, and hungry (Matthew 25:34-36).

To be like Jesus means being ready to extend God's love to children (Matthew 19:14), to social outcasts such as Zacchaeus (Luke 19:1-10), and to people of other races such as the woman of Samaria (John 4:9). To be like Jesus means surprising people with the range of our love. To be like Jesus means also surprising people with the intensity of our love. Jesus' love for John marked that apostle for life. He never forgot that he was "the disciple whom Jesus loved."

Finally, we must remember that love begins at home. If we cannot love those who are nearby, we deceive ourselves to think that we can love those who are far away. It is in our own family and in our own church that love builds its foundation (Galatians 6:10; 1 Timothy 5:8). It bears repeating: How can we love the God whom we have not seen, if we do not love our brothers and sisters whom we have seen?

Discovery Learning

This page contains an alternative lesson plan emphasizing learning activities. Classes desiring such student involvement will find these suggestions helpful. The next page is a reproducible activity page to further enhance discovery learning.

LEARNING GOALS

After this lesson, each student will be able to:

1. List the actions that God's love took on our behalf.

2. Explain the concept of *propitiation*, including how this doctrine alleviates fear in the life of the believer.

3. Write a prayer that asks God to help him or her replace fear with trust in his love.

INTO THE LESSON

Prepare 15 sheets of copier paper, each displaying one of the following letters or blanks. Put a number at the bottom of each sheet, as indicated.

S O N   O F   T H U N D E R !
1 10 8 15 11 6 3 14 7 13 9 2 4 12 5

On the back of these sheets of paper, print the following letters and blanks, inverted:

A P O S T L E   O F   L O V E

Affix the 15 sheets to the wall in a single line, with *Son of Thunder!* and numerals showing. Put masking tape along the top of the sheets so each can be lifted to reveal the letter on the back.

Refer to Luke 9:54, in which John and his brother suggested fire from Heaven to punish a village that refused hospitality to Jesus and his apostles. Refer to Mark 3:17, where Jesus gave these two brothers the nickname *Boanerges,* or "sons of thunder."

Lift the flaps in numerical sequence, taping the revealed letters upward. As letters are revealed, encourage students to identify at any time what the phrase on the reverse is. Once the puzzle is solved, ask, "How is it that one called a *son of thunder* became a messenger of love?" Be sure to mention that John, after being in Jesus' company for several years, felt so loved he would call himself the one "whom Jesus loved" (John 21:20).

Option. Distribute the Why Love? exercise from the reproducible page for students to work on as they arrive.

INTO THE WORD

Write all the following statements, drawn from the commentary, on slips of paper. Do not include either the sequence numbers or the verse numbers on the slips.

1. Genuine children resemble their Father in an important way (v. 7); 2. One who does not have love does not know God (v. 8); 3. God's love is a mighty passion (v. 9); 4. Jesus was the *propitiation* or *atoning sacrifice* that restored God's favor (v. 10); 5. God took steps to deal with our sins (v. 10); 6. Nothing less than love for others is acceptable (v. 11); 7. We can have God's presence dwelling in us (v. 12); 8. We have the Spirit because God gave him to us (v. 13); 9. The apostles knew firsthand that the Father sent the Son into the world (v. 14).

10. Jesus did not come just to teach—he came to rescue (v. 14); 11. If a person confesses Jesus, then God dwells in him or her (v. 15); 12. God embodies what is good about love (v. 16); 13. When we dwell in his love, God dwells in us (v. 16); 14. We have confidence to speak boldly in the presence of God (v. 17); 15. If our love is mature, then we can stand pure and righteous before the Father (v. 17); 16. Fear and love cannot coexist (v. 18); 17. The person who lives in unhealthy fear of God is not spiritually mature (v. 18); 18. Without God's initiative we would have not known genuine love (v. 19); 19. The practical test of love is that God's child must love others (v. 20).

20. If we cannot find anything lovable in another, then we will not find anything lovable in God (v. 20); 21. The two great commands of Jesus (love God; love one's neighbor) are inseparable (v. 21); 22. God is the source of love (v. 10).

Put the slips in a box and pass it around for each to take one. (If your class is small, suggest each take two or three.) Then say, "Now turn to 1 John 4:7-21 and find the verse that best relates to the truth on your slip(s)."

As you read through the text, ask students to identify verses they have matched. Because of the emphatic repetition in John's style, students may associate statements with verses other than the ones identified above.

INTO LIFE

Write the letters LFOEVAER on the board. Ask, "What's wrong here?" Once someone notices that the word *fear* is embedded in the word *love,* the answer will be obvious: 1 John 4:18! Ask the class to share in a prayer for God to make our love so perfect or whole that fear will disappear. Suggest that such a prayer is a worthy idea for the beginning of each new day. (Alternative: use the Mutually Exclusive! exercise from the reproducible page.)

Why Love?

First John 4:7-21 reveals a number of reasons why love is the practical and appropriate characteristic for any who would live successfully and joyfully. Look at that text and write the verse number(s) where each of the following reasons is given.

_____ to show our appreciation for God's love

_____ love comes from God

_____ love demonstrates the Spirit in us

_____ to prove that we know God

_____ to verify that we love God

_____ to develop confidence for judgment

_____ to eliminate fear in one's life

_____ because God loved us first

_____ because God is love

_____ it completes God's love

_____ to sense our abiding relationship in him

Mutually Exclusive!

John says simply, "There is no fear in love" (1 John 4:18). Where do you see yourself in relationship to love squeezing out the fear in your life? Mark yourself on this line, from lots of fear and a little love, to a little fear and lots of love.

FEARFEARFEARFEARLOVEFEARFEARFEARLOVELOVEFEARFEARLOVELOVELOVEFEARLOVELOVELOVELOVE

John reveals that as fear is eliminated in love we can have greater confidence as we approach the Day of Judgment at our death or when Jesus comes again. Mark yourself on this confidence line in relationship to that event ("very limited confidence" to the left, "fully confident" to the right).

———C——O——N——F——I——D——E——N——C——E———

Now examine your two scorings in relation to one another. How do you think your score on one scale influences (or is influenced by) your score on the other?

What is your prayer of thanksgiving and petition that you need to make God's love more fully active in your life? Write it here.

_____

_____

_____

_____

THE WAY TO LOVE

LESSON 4

WHY TEACH THIS LESSON?

Your students are bombarded with secular images of (supposed) love. Which of these are pleasing to God, and which are distortions of his will?

A youth minister tells of being last in the cafeteria line on the first day of camp. The only seat left in the cafeteria was directly across from a skinny teenage girl. She had buck teeth, stringy hair, and hunched shoulders. The young minister made small talk during the meal, but the girl seemed quite withdrawn and self-conscious. The young minister was disappointed to hear that the same cafeteria seats would be assigned for all meals during the coming week. But through the mealtime conversations, he discovered a wonderfully spiritual and perceptive Christian beneath that unattractive appearance. They became friends.

When the week-long camp came to an end, the girl hugged the minister and thanked him for his care and friendship. And that minister learned a lesson about how God views his children. The Lord reminded Samuel that, "Man looks at the outward appearance, but the Lord looks at the heart" (1 Samuel 16:7). Learning to love as God loves is a part of our Christian journey. Today's study will sort through the confusion on how to live and love God's way.

INTRODUCTION

A. THE WAY TO DO IT

"No, here's the way it's done." The father, a skilled craftsman, is teaching his son the right way to do a job. If the youngster is too stubborn to listen, he will be slow to make progress. But if he has confidence in his father's ability and pays careful attention, he will learn his lesson well.

God has tried to teach his children the way of love. At the beginning he provided generously for Adam and Eve. He even allowed them to exercise their freewill choice. Time and again in the history of Israel, he lovingly rescued his people from oppression. When they sinned, he corrected them. When they repented, he forgave them. When they prayed, he opened the windows of Heaven to pour out blessings on them. Most of all, he sent Jesus to die on the cross for them. No greater example of love has ever been known.

We have been shown the way to love. Will we be stubborn, or will we learn?

B. LESSON BACKGROUND

This is the final chapter in John's first epistle, written near the end of the first century AD. The special problem of those who originally received the letter was a heresy called *gnosticism*, or at least an early version of it. This teaching placed little value on faith, love, or obedience. Instead, the gnostics said that secret knowledge was the way to Heaven. (The word *gnosis* means "knowledge" and is found within the English words *diagnosis* and *prognosis*.) As John brings his teaching to a conclusion, he puts all his emphasis on being in the right relationship with Jesus Christ. This includes having love for all God's children.

DEVOTIONAL READING:
JOHN 17:1-5
BACKGROUND SCRIPTURE:
1 JOHN 5:1-12
PRINTED TEXT:
1 JOHN 5:1-12

Mar
25

LESSON AIMS

After participating in this lesson, each student will be able to:

1. Describe how love for God and love for others are related.

2. Give an example of how to show love for God and an example of how to show love for others.

3. Apply the two examples from lesson aim #2 in the week ahead.

KEY VERSE

This is the testimony: God has given us eternal life, and this life is in his Son.   —1 John 5:11

LESSON 4 NOTES

I. FOUNDATION OF GOD'S WAY (1 JOHN 5:1-3)

Living God's way involves every part of our lives. As John has indicated previously in this epistle, this includes head, heart, and hands. With our minds we believe the truth; with our hearts we love God and his children; with our hands we do all that righteousness requires. The three areas are inseparably linked as God's design for us to live.

A. FAITH AND LOVE (v. 1)

1. Everyone who believes that Jesus is the Christ is born of God, and everyone who loves the father loves his child as well.

John begins this section with a focus on faith. Anyone who is truly *born of God* will have faith that *Jesus is the Christ*. This faith is not merely an idle opinion about Jesus' identity. It involves sincere confession and commitment to Christ (see 1 John 4:2, 15). It is a trusting, ongoing faith (as shown by John's use of the present tense in the word *believes*). True faith is vital for a lifelong relationship with Jesus.

Everyone who has the proper faith relationship with Jesus, within the biblical plan of salvation, is a child of God. John's immediate point here is that every such child should be an object of our love. After all, if we love *the father,* then we should also love *his child.*

B. LOVE AND OBEDIENCE (vv. 2, 3)

2. This is how we know that we love the children of God: by loving God and carrying out his commands.

John has said that if we love God we will love his children. And how do we know that we *love the children of God*? It is *by loving God and carrying out his commands*. These ideas are reciprocal and complementary as they show both sides of an important truth: we honor God by loving his children; we love his children by loving God as we honor his commands.

The previous verse showed the inseparable connection between faith and love; this verse shows the connection between love and obedience. All three elements must be present to produce the Christian life.

3. This is love for God: to obey his commands. And his commands are not burdensome,

John sees nothing surprising in linking our *love for God* with our obedience to him. It may truly be said that the love of God necessarily, even automatically, requires that we obey his commands. This is the inherent truth of a right relationship with God. How could anyone think he or she loves God while ignoring or disobeying what God says? "If you love me, you will obey what I command" (John 14:15).

John is quick to add that God's commands are *not burdensome*. Jesus himself said, "my yoke is easy and my burden is light" (Matthew 11:30). God's commandments have never been burdensome. This is borne out by Deuteronomy 30:11, 14: "Now what I am commanding you today is not too difficult for you or beyond your reach. . . . No, the word is very near you; it is in your mouth and in your heart so you may obey it." It was the teachers of the law and the Pharisees who made obedience to God a burden. "They tie up heavy loads put them on men's shoulders, but they themselves are not willing to lift a finger to move them" (Matthew 23:4).

None of this should be construed that John is talking about salvation by works or salvation by law keeping. It comes down to motive. We obey God as a

WHAT DO YOU THINK?

Some claim to believe in God, yet do not exhibit a lifestyle that acknowledges God's commands. How do you share with someone of this mind-set what a relationship with God really involves? How do you prepare yourself for a "do not judge" response?

WHAT DO YOU THINK?

Without giving trite, prepackaged answers, what would you say to a believer who is struggling with obedience in some area?

loving response to the salvation that is already ours. We do not obey in order to earn a salvation that God dangles in front of us.

A LOST SCORE

A Japanese music professor announced recently that part of a Bach wedding cantata had been found in the estate of a Japanese classical pianist. J. S. Bach (1685–1750) was a pioneer in classical music, and this cantata had been lost for 80 years. Musicologists believe "Wedding Cantata BWV 216" was copied by students Bach was teaching at the time he composed the piece.

The score contains only the alto and soprano portions of the cantata, and experts believe they were used in the original (and only) performance of the piece played at a wedding in 1728. Historians who specialize in Bach's music hope the lost score can help them reconstruct the full composition so it can be performed as it may have sounded originally.

We can draw a parallel in that the apostle John and the other New Testament writers have given us the "score" for a piece of divinely inspired "music." Believing in Jesus as God's Son, loving God, loving God's children, and keeping God's commandments are the recurrent themes in this composition. If we "lose" the score by neglecting to read it and meditate upon it, then we should not be surprised to find the themes missing from our lives. Those who truly love God will honor him as a composer who deserves to have his "music" played the way he wrote it. —C. R. B.

II. VICTORY OF GOD'S WAY (1 JOHN 5:4, 5)

God's way—the way of love—is the right way. It is the way that brings victory. All the children of God will share in this victory because they have put their faith in Jesus, God's Son. Their faith is an overcoming faith, the kind of faith that trusts in an overcoming Savior.

A. AN OVERCOMING FAITH (v. 4)

4. . . . *for everyone born of God overcomes the world. This is the victory that has overcome the world, even our faith.*

In context the phrase *the world* refers to the powers of evil that take their stand against God. This is what Jesus had in mind when he said, "I have overcome the world" (John 16:33).

By being *born of God*, we share in his *victory* over the world. As members of God's family, we have an overcoming faith. It is a faith that separates us from the fallen world and gives us victory over the temptations of the world. We live in this world in a physical sense, but we are not of the world in an ethical sense (see John 15:19; 17:6, 14-19). Even though we struggle on a daily basis to live godly lives, we can take heart in the fact that the victory has already been won. The outcome is already decided. We are on the winning side.

B. AN OVERCOMING SAVIOR (v. 5)

5. *Who is it that overcomes the world? Only he who believes that Jesus is the Son of God.*

When we overcome *the world*, it is not because we ourselves are so powerful. The true source of our victory is the object of our faith: *Jesus, the Son of God.* Through our faith in him, we are assured that we overcome this world. "But thanks be to God! He gives us the victory through our Lord Jesus Christ" (1 Corinthians 15:57).

Because we have put our trust and confidence in Jesus, "we are more than conquerors through him who loved us" (Romans 8:37). Even though we wrestle

DAILY BIBLE READINGS

Monday, Mar. 19—Jesus Calls Disciples (Mark 1:16-20)

Tuesday, Mar. 20—God's Love Saves Creation (John 3: 16-21)

Wednesday, Mar. 21—Jesus Seeks the Father (John 17:1-5)

Thursday, Mar. 22—We Belong to God (Romans 8:9-17)

Friday, Mar. 23—We Are God's Heirs (Galatians 4:1-7)

Saturday, Mar. 24—Love God's Children (1 John 5:1-6)

Sunday, Mar. 25—God Gives Eternal Life (1 John 5: 7-13)

WHAT DO YOU THINK?

The next time you face temptation, how will it help you to know that everyone who is born of God overcomes the world?

against the forces of spiritual darkness and wickedness (Ephesians 6:12), our final victory is secured. By faith we have chosen to join the victors.

III. BASIS OF GOD'S WAY (1 JOHN 5:6-10)

Christianity stands or falls with Jesus. Either he is who he claimed to be, or he is an imposter. If he is not God's Son, his moral teachings are groundless. If he has not risen from the dead, all Christian faith is in vain. Everything hinges on Jesus. For this reason John emphasizes the testimony to Jesus' identity as God's Son as well as the response to Jesus that we must make.

A. GOD'S WITNESS TO HIS SON (vv. 6-8)

6. *This is the one who came by water and blood—Jesus Christ. He did not come by water only, but by water and blood. And it is the Spirit who testifies, because the Spirit is the truth.*

Our Lesson Background notes the gnostic heresy that was beginning to emerge in the late first century AD. One element of gnosticism was another false teaching called *Docetism*. This word means "to seem" or "to appear to be." This false teaching denies that Jesus came in the flesh, only that Jesus seemed to appear in the flesh. John is very concerned about this kind of error: "Many deceivers, who do not acknowledge Jesus Christ as coming in the flesh, have gone out into the world. Any such person is the deceiver and the antichrist" (2 John 7).

To counter such falsehood, John presents his own, firsthand evidence. From the beginning of Jesus' ministry to its very end, Jesus displayed his deity in bodily form (compare Colossians 2:9). Jesus *came by water* into his public ministry when he was baptized by John the Baptist in the Jordan River. Jesus came by *blood* to the conclusion of his ministry when he was nailed to the cross. The real humanity of Jesus is clearly shown by water and blood.

In addition to the testimony of water and blood, the *Spirit* of God also *testifies* to Jesus. When Jesus was baptized, the Holy Spirit descended from Heaven in the form of a dove and rested upon Jesus. It should not be overlooked that the Father testified about Jesus at that baptism (see Matthew 3:16, 17). The Father bore witness again by raising Jesus from the dead (Galatians 1:1), and the Spirit bore witness through the four Gospels. The veracity of the Gospels is assured by the Spirit who inspired them, for *the Spirit is the truth.*

7, 8. *For there are three that testify: the Spirit, the water and the blood; and the three are in agreement.*

The record borne by *the Spirit, the water and the blood* is powerful! These three witnesses fulfill the requirements for legal testimony as stated in Deuteronomy 17:6; 19:15. Jesus had important things to say about the role of the Spirit, who followed after and confirmed Jesus' earthly ministry (see John 14:26; 15:26). Blood has the same meaning here as in verse 6. The blood signified both payment for sin and the reality of Jesus' flesh. *The three* give unanimous testimony; they *are in agreement.* Jesus is the Son of God who came down to earth in human form.

B. OUR RESPONSE TO HIS SON (vv. 9, 10)

9. *We accept man's testimony, but God's testimony is greater because it is the testimony of God, which he has given about his Son.*

The idea of testimony is important to John's thought (see John 5:31-34, 37; 8:18). Most people routinely *accept man's testimony,* especially in court cases. How much more necessary is it to accept *the testimony of God*!

WHAT DO YOU THINK?

John writes these verses to refute a heresy that claimed Jesus had not come to earth "in the flesh." What other false ideas do we deal with today? What makes some false ideas more serious than others?

The Father testified to the identity of *his Son* on several occasions. We have already mentioned the Father's testimony at Jesus' baptism. At the transfiguration, God said, "This is my Son, whom I love. Listen to him!" (Mark 9:7). Most important of all, "God has raised this Jesus to life. . . . Exalted to the right hand of God, he has received from the Father the promised Holy Spirit" (Acts 2:32, 33).

10. Anyone who believes in the Son of God has this testimony in his heart. Anyone who does not believe God has made him out to be a liar, because he has not believed the testimony God has given about his Son.

The response that God requires is that we must believe in *the Son of God.* We are to trust him, rely on him, and put all confidence in him. The person who does this has accepted the Father's *testimony* and put it in his or her *heart.* On the other hand, if a person does not believe what God has said about Jesus, then he or she pronounces God to be a *liar.* Such a person hears *the testimony God has given about his Son* but rejects it as false. Ultimately, these are the only two responses we can make to the message of God: believe it as true or reject it as false.

IV. OUTCOME OF GOD'S WAY (1 JOHN 5:11, 12)

God's way promises the right outcome. Those who walk the path of faith and love have the promise of eternal life. Those who do not walk this way, however, receive a stern warning: because they have not chosen God's way, they will not have life.

A. IRONCLAD PROMISE (v. 11)

11. And this is the testimony: God has given us eternal life, and this life is in his Son.

God's *testimony* about *his Son* reaches a wonderful conclusion: God *has given* the gift of *eternal life.* We do not earn or deserve this reward; it is a gift. Eternal life is not just an unending quantity of life. It is something far better. It is a whole new quality of life. It is life that *is in his Son.*

This life begins as a person comes to know God. It begins when he or she experiences God firsthand and enters a saving relationship with him (see Acts 2:38; John 17:3). *This is the testimony*—the promise—of God.

B. IRONCLAD CERTAINTY (v. 12)

12. He who has the Son has life; he who does not have the Son of God does not have life.

John does not want his readers to be confused in any way by the false teaching they are hearing. Thus this verse is almost a repeat of John 3:36. John's readers can know this fact for a certainty: *he who has the Son has life.*

The believer can count on receiving life as the gift from God. But whoever *does not have the Son of God* in heart and life should be warned of this fact: he or she *does not have life.* The certainty of reward or punishment on Judgment Day is determined by whether or not a person follows Jesus.

INSURANCE OR ASSURANCE?

Each area of the world has its distinct threats of natural disaster. In the American West, one of those threats is wildfires. Some years are worse than others for these disasters. October 2003 witnessed an especially terrifying fire season in San Diego County, California. The wildfires raged on several fronts for many days, consuming 2,400 houses in the process. The largest of the fires burned over 273,000 acres— that's more than 425 square miles!

Visual for Lesson 4. *Point to this visual as you ask, "How will the truth of this passage influence the way you live?"*

WHAT DO YOU THINK?

How does today's text help you witness to someone who believes in God but feels that insisting on Jesus as the only way is too exclusive? How do cultural trends lure people into this trap?

HOW TO SAY IT

Colossians. *Kuh-LOSH-unz.*
Deuteronomy. *Due-ter-AHN-uh-me.*
Docetism. *Doe-SET-iz-um.*
Ephesians. *Ee-FEE-zhunz.*
Galatians. *Guh-LAY-shunz.*
gnosticism. *NAHSS-tih-SIZZ-um.*
gnostics. *NAHSS-ticks.*
Pharisees. *FAIR-ih-seez.*

PRAYER

Father, we thank you for sending Jesus to live on earth as a man and to purchase our salvation. We praise you for the gift of eternal life we have in his name. Help us to have the faith to love as Jesus loved and to overcome this world. In Jesus' name, amen.

THOUGHT TO REMEMBER

The way of love is the way to life.

The most expensive home to burn was a 20,000 square-foot structure valued at $4,366,000. The house contained the owner's vast art and music collections plus a movie theater. It was all fully insured, but the owner—a self-made millionaire—didn't bother to insure the house he owned next door because, as he later said, it contained only 4,000 square feet and was worth only $1,500,000!

Most of us don't have the kind of resources that enable us to be that blasé about our earthly possessions. But whether rich or poor in this life, our ultimate hope must be for riches in the life to come. Here is where John's message carries its real significance. God has offered us eternal life through Christ, his Son. If we have the Son, we have life. If we don't have the Son, we don't have life eternal. In that case, we don't really have much worth talking about, no matter how much we possess.

—C. R. B.

CONCLUSION

Jesus is the way. He is God's way, the right way. In fact, he is the way, the truth, and the life. No one comes to the Father except through him (see John 14:6). If Christianity is criticized for claiming to be the only true religion, it is only repeating the claims of its founder. It may not be politically correct these days to say there is only one way to Heaven, but that is what the church must say to be faithful to her Lord.

Victorious faith enables us to love as Jesus loved. A review of today's text shows us what this includes. Verses 1 and 2 say that we should love all God's family. When Jesus walked this earth, he extended his love to all who would respond to God's call. We follow Jesus in this way of love.

Verse 3 says that we should keep all God's commandments. Jesus "humbled himself and became obedient to death—even death on a cross!" (Philippians 2:8). "Although he was a son, he learned obedience from what he suffered and, once made perfect, he became the source of eternal salvation for all who obey him" (see Hebrews 5:8, 9). We remember that following the way of love includes obeying God's commands.

Verses 4 and 5 say that we are to have faith to overcome all this world's opposition. When Jesus faced opposition, he put his trust in the Father. He faced the temptations in the desert, for instance, by relying on God's Word. He faced the prospect of death on the cross by turning to God in prayer in the garden. We can be more than conquerors through this kind of overcoming faith.

Verses 6 through 10 say that we are to believe all God's testimony. When Jesus quoted Scripture, he showed that he believed it to be true. He used Adam and Eve to establish what is right in marriage (see Matthew 19:4-6). He used Noah and the flood to teach about the second coming (see Matthew 24:37). He used Jonah to teach about his own resurrection (see Matthew 12:40). Jesus accepted these accounts as true. We should have the same view of God's Word as Jesus did: "Scripture cannot be broken" (John 10:35).

Verses 11 and 12 say that the person of faith will receive God's reward. When Jesus put his trust in God and did as his Father told him, God raised him from the dead. "Therefore God exalted him to the highest place and gave him the name that is above every name, that at the name of Jesus every knee should bow, in heaven and on earth and under the earth, and every tongue confess that Jesus Christ is Lord, to the glory of God the Father" (see Philippians 2:9-11).

Today, "Christ Jesus, who died—more than that, who was raised to life—is at the right hand of God and is also interceding for us" (Romans 8:34). We should take God at his Word and never doubt his promises. Then we will have eternal life in his Son.

Discovery Learning

This page contains an alternative lesson plan emphasizing learning activities. Classes desiring such student involvement will find these suggestions helpful. The next page is a reproducible activity page to further enhance discovery learning.

LEARNING GOALS

After this lesson, each student will be able to:

1. Describe how love for God and love for others are related.

2. Give an example of how to show love for God and an example of how to show love for others.

3. Apply the two examples from learning goal #2 in the week ahead.

INTO THE LESSON

Display several facsimile traffic signs as class begins: STOP, YIELD, NO U-TURN, ONE WAY, or others. Simple hand-drawn and colored ones will be adequate. Ask the class to note their reactions when they see such signs.

Next, direct students to make a quick read of 1 John 5:1-12 and select the sign that best makes a visual for today's study. Allow students to justify their choices with brief explanations. Example: someone may choose *One Way*, because of the exclusive nature of Jesus being the only way to Heaven (v. 12).

INTO THE WORD

Make copies of today's text, with a space after each verse. Distribute one copy to each student. Say, "By now we all have noticed John's style: emphatic repetition of ideas and phrases. I want you to look at today's text and find phrases of three or more words that appear more than once. Circle them and draw a connecting line between the matches."

If students need a start, point out that "born of God" occurs in verses 1 and 4. Others they may find include "believes that Jesus is the" (vv. 1, 5); "his commands" (vv. 2, 3); "overcomes the world" (vv. 4, 5); "by water and blood" (v. 6 [twice]); "anyone who" (v. 10 [twice]) "about his Son" (vv. 9, 10); "Son of God" (vv. 5, 10, 12).

Have students call out their findings; make a list on the board. When the list is complete, go back through and ask how each phrase is completed in the text and what the implications are.

Label this next activity "Ask John" (write those two words on the board). Tell the class that you want them to be John. You will ask "John" questions and you want "John" to answer with one of the verses from today's text. For example, if you ask, "John, many say they are

'born again.' What is a first step to being born of God?" "John" should answer, from verse 1, "Everyone who believes that Jesus is the Christ."

Here are some questions, in random order. "John, sometimes witnesses give conflicting testimony. Isn't that true regarding Jesus' humanity and deity?" (v. 8). "John, what is the most obvious result of loving God the Father?" (v. 1b). "John, how will I know that I truly love God's children?" (v. 2). "John, isn't belief simply a matter for the head? Isn't it only intellectual?" (v. 10a). "John, this world we are in sometimes just overwhelms me . . . with temptation, sickness, death. Can I get out alive?" (v. 4). "John, what is the secret to being an overcomer?" (v. 5). "John, aren't you being a bit exclusive when you say 'life is in his Son'?" (v. 12). "John, I've heard some claim that Jesus could not be both God and man. How do you respond to that?" (v. 6a). "John, I know that more than one witness is required in most legal systems. Do we have that regarding Jesus?" (vv. 7, 8). "John, the Old Testament is full of rules and regulations. How would you characterize God's commandments?" (v. 3b). "John, I know I should tell people that Jesus is the Christ, God's Son, but some won't believe me. What do I do?" (v. 9). "John, do I have to obey the Scriptures in order to love God?" (v. 3a). "John, some reject God's testimony regarding Jesus. What's the bottom line in that circumstance?" (v. 10b).

(Alternative: Use the Grand Doctrinal Truths exercise from the reproducible page in small groups.)

INTO LIFE

Divide your class in two by saying, "I want those whose age is an odd number to help with the first list I am going to request. I want those whose age is an even number to help with the second. OK, here are the questions for our lists: (1) What can a person do this week to show love for God? (2) What can a person do this week to show love for others?"

As ideas are given, write the two lists on the board. Alternate between the two. When lists are completed, recommend that each student pick one entry from each list that is not in his or her typical lifestyle and try to implement both into the coming week of life and service. Distribute copies of the I Love You, God exercise from the reproducible page as a take-home exercise.

Grand Doctrinal Truths

John's words in 1 John 5:1-12 include many of the grand doctrinal truths upon which Christianity is based. For each of the following, identify a verse or verses that speak of the truth given.

_____ Only in Christ can one find eternal life.
_____ Eternal life cannot be earned; it must be received as a gift from God.
_____ It is possible to overcome the world and its ultimate threat—death.
_____ Loving others is an essential component of loving God.
_____ Believing that Jesus is the Son of God is central to Christianity.
_____ Jesus was both divine and human.
_____ The Spirit's testimony is true.
_____ The expectation of God for his children is not a heavy yoke.
_____ Belief in Jesus involves both intellect and emotion.

Optional: look at 1 John 5:13-21 and add two or three other grand doctrinal truths. Again, note the verse numbers.

_____ _____
_____ _____
_____ _____

I Love You, God

John knew that the actions and emotions of love are reciprocal. Complete each of these statements, based on a verse from today's study text.

"I love you, God, so this week I will love your child _____ and will show it by _____." [which verse? _____]

"I love you, God, so this week I will obey this command of yours that I often ignore: _____ _____." [which verse? _____]

"I love you, God, and I will demonstrate my world-overcoming intention this week by _____ _____." [which verse? _____]

"I love you, God, and because I have the testimony in my heart that Jesus is the Christ I will tell _____ that only the one who has the Son has life." [which verse? _____]

"I love you, God, and I will not make you out to be a liar this week, for I will _____ _____." [which verse? _____]

"I love you, God, because you have given me eternal life, and I will express my joy and thanksgiving by _____." [which verse? _____]

CHRIST IS KING

LESSON 5

WHY TEACH THIS LESSON?

What are your students passionate about? Listening to their conversations can be revealing. Sports teams, new possessions, and children's accomplishments will top many lists. The older meaning of the word *passion*, as used in connection with Passion Week, refers to the suffering of Christ. But that is not how we normally use that word today. The word now means an enthusiasm or intense fervor about something.

In the small town where I live, two popular actors recently visited while doing research for a movie project. People were passionate about seeing these celebrities. When the two walked into a local restaurant and made their way to a private dining room for dinner, patrons already seated made cell phone calls to friends and family. The sidewalk in front of the restaurant was soon lined with people hoping to get a glimpse of these men.

As Jesus made his triumphal entry into the city of Jerusalem at the start of Passion Week, both elements of the term *passion* were present. Jesus was entering a week in which there would be intense suffering. But among the people who lined the way there was fervor and enthusiasm. Your students need passion *for* Christ while comprehending the passion *of* Christ.

INTRODUCTION

This week's lesson is the first in a set that begins to focus on Jesus as he is found in the book of Revelation. This lesson and the next come during two important days in the church calendar: Palm Sunday and Resurrection Sunday (Easter). These two Sundays bracket a period in Jesus' life called *Passion Week*—his final week leading up to the crucifixion.

The events of Passion Week are always worth studying and pondering anew. Taken together, the rest of the lessons for this quarter will allow students to see Jesus as more than the main character in the events of Passion Week; he is also the reigning Lord of all creation. This is the glorious picture found in the book of Revelation.

A. PALM SUNDAY AS TRIUMPHAL ENTRY

The title and words of the old spiritual "Ride on, King Jesus" recall the day when Jesus was received into Jerusalem as king. The welcome of Jesus into the holy city on the Sunday before his crucifixion has long been called *the triumphal entry*. This event is found in all four of the Gospels, each having some unique details. Although the Gospels do not make any reference to this event as a "triumph," it does bear some relationship to the ancient custom of welcoming a victorious king or general back to his home city.

The city of Rome had a tradition of staging triumphal processions. This parade would include the Roman legions, enemy prisoners, wagons loaded with booty, and the victorious general in a special chariot. Sometimes a new triumphal arch

DEVOTIONAL READING:
PSALM 118:21-28

BACKGROUND SCRIPTURE:
REVELATION 1:1-8; LUKE 19:28-40

PRINTED TEXT:
REVELATION 1:8; LUKE 19:28-38

Apr
1

LESSON AIMS

After participating in this lesson, each student will be able to:

1. Explain the significance of the Palm Sunday events.

2. Understand how Jesus is king past, present, and future.

3. Determine a specific way to recognize the kingship of Jesus in his or her life.

KEY VERSE

"Blessed is the king who comes in the name of the Lord!"

"Peace in heaven and glory in the highest!" —Luke 19:38

LESSON 5 NOTES

would be created. This custom was revived by the French emperor Napoleon Bonaparte, whose *Arc de Triomphe* in Paris was commissioned in 1806 for the glory of the French army.

The triumphal entry of Jesus was a way of recognizing him as king. What did it mean for those present to acclaim Jesus as king, and what does that mean for us today? This week's lesson will examine some of the implications involved in recognizing Jesus as king in our lives.

B. LESSON BACKGROUND

Jewish law specified three important pilgrimage festivals for which all able-bodied Israelite men were expected to appear at the temple (see Deuteronomy 16:16). They were Passover (very closely associated with the Feast of Unleavened Bread), Pentecost (or Feast of Weeks), and Tabernacles. Passover came at the middle of the Jewish month of Nisan. This was in the spring, in March or April.

Passover was more than just a religious holiday. Since it marked the liberation of the Jews from Egyptian bondage, it was seen as a remembrance of the birth of their nation. Thus, it had strong patriotic and nationalistic overtones. It was ironic, then, to celebrate a national day of freedom when all Jews knew that their nation had again been subjugated, this time by the Romans. This surely made it a bittersweet holiday! As observant and loyal Jews, Jesus and his disciples were expected to celebrate Passover, and they did so willingly.

In Luke 9:51 we see that Jesus "resolutely set out for Jerusalem." For the next 10 chapters of that Gospel, Jesus and the disciples were on the pilgrim's journey to the temple city for the spring celebration of Passover. This was not a quick trip, and they were in no hurry. Traveling south from Galilee they passed through Jericho, a small city just north of the Dead Sea. This was a common route for travelers to Jerusalem from the north, and Jesus' band was doubtlessly a small part of thousands making the journey.

While in Jericho, Jesus was confronted by a blind man who understood Jesus' true identity. The man called out to Jesus as the "Son of David" (essentially the same as saying *Messiah*) and begged to be healed. This healing took place in the presence of the crowd, and they praised God (Luke 18:35-43). In Jericho Jesus also had a dramatic encounter with a height-challenged tax collector named Zacchaeus. Jesus used this occasion to clearly state what he was about: "For the Son of Man came to seek and to save what was lost" (Luke 19:10).

When his business in Jericho was finished, Jesus and his followers began the ascent to Jerusalem. Although Jericho is only about 15 miles from Jerusalem, there is a change in altitude of some 3,300 feet. It was a hot, dusty climb, but we can imagine the growing excitement of the pilgrim throng as it approached the beloved Jerusalem. This is the setting for the primary passage of today's lesson, Luke 19:28-38.

I. CHRIST AS SOURCE AND GOAL (REVELATION 1:8)

A fitting opening to today's study comes from the first chapter of Revelation. Here the apostle John is being introduced to the key figures in his heavenly visions. This includes God the Father and seven spirits (Revelation 1:4). Jesus is introduced and described extensively in 1:5-7. Dramatically, he speaks for the first time to identify himself in the verse before us.

8. *"I am the Alpha and the Omega," says the Lord God, "who is, and who was, and who is to come, the Almighty."*

HOW TO SAY IT

Alpha. AL-fa.

Arc de Triomphe. Ark du treh-ONF.

Bethany. BETH-uh-nee.

Bethphage. BETH-fuh-gee.

Goliath. Go-LYE-uth.

Jericho. JAIR-ih-co.

Maccabees. MACK-uh-bees.

Mardi Gras. MAR-dee Grah.

Napoleon Bonaparte. Nuh-POLE-yun Bo-nuh-PART.

Nazareth. NAZ-uh-reth.

Nisan. NYE-san.

Omega. O-MAY-guh.

Pentecost. PENT-ih-kost.

Philistine. Fuh-LISS-teen or FILL-us-teen.

Zacchaeus. Zack-KEY-us.

Zechariah. ZEK-uh-RYE-uh.

It is striking to see that Jesus does not use the descriptive terms John has employed for him in Revelation 1:5-7. Instead, Jesus uses the terms reserved for God in 1:4: *who is, and who was, and who is to come.* Revelation is never afraid to describe the risen Jesus in terms that remind us of Old Testament descriptions of God.

There are three parts to Jesus' self-description in the verse before us. First, he is *the Alpha and the Omega.* These are the first and last letters of the Greek alphabet, akin to our *A* and *Z.* Jesus is thus *the beginning and the ending.* He is the source and the goal for all of creation. Second, Jesus' claim that he is the one *who is, and who was, and who is to come* is an affirmation of his eternality; he is not bound by the constraints of time (compare Exodus 3:14; John 8:58).

Third, the verse before us refers to Jesus as *Lord* and as the *Almighty.* Often the Old Testament writers referred to God as "God Almighty" or "the Lord Almighty" (see Genesis 17:1). It means that he is the commander of all the armies of angels and that no power in Heaven or earth can stand against him. In the Old Testament, nothing is more powerful than the Lord Almighty. In the book of Revelation, nothing is more powerful than the risen Lord Jesus.

II. CHRIST AS LORD TO BE SERVED (LUKE 19:28-34)

Peter preached that Jesus "went around doing good and healing all who were under the power of the devil" (Acts 10:38). As we move into Luke 19, that period is nearly over. Jesus has come to Jerusalem for the most sobering and important part of the plan for human redemption. Jesus alone is aware of what is about to happen, but his disciples play their parts by making preparations for his entry into the holy city.

A. DISCIPLES GIVEN A MISSION (vv. 28-31)

28. After Jesus had said this, he went on ahead, going up to Jerusalem.

Jesus and his disciples leave Jericho to make the long climb to *Jerusalem.* This is a couple of days before what we call Palm Sunday, for they do not travel on the Sabbath (Saturday), and the trip is difficult to finish in a single day.

We can imagine a large throng of pilgrims making this climb, singing some of the joyous Psalms of Ascent (Psalms 120–134). One they may sing is Psalm 122:1, 2: "I rejoiced with those who said to me, 'Let us go to the house of the Lord.' Our feet are standing in your gates, O Jerusalem."

29. As he approached Bethphage and Bethany at the hill called the Mount of Olives, he sent two of his disciples, saying to them,

Approaching from the east, the band first comes to two small villages near Jerusalem. We do not know the precise location of *Bethphage* (meaning "house of figs"). But *Bethany* ("house of misery" or "house of dates") is at the foot of the *Mount of Olives,* less than two miles from Jerusalem. Bethany is the home of Mary, Martha, and Lazarus (John 11:1). This seems to be Jesus' "headquarters" for the coming week (see Matthew 21:17). Jesus probably arrives in Bethany just before the Sabbath begins (John 12:1).

30, 31. "Go to the village ahead of you, and as you enter it, you will find a colt tied there, which no one has ever ridden. Untie it and bring it here. "If anyone asks you, 'Why are you untying it?' tell him, 'The Lord needs it.'"

The *village* to which the two disciples are sent is Bethphage (see Matthew 21:1, 2). The two men are asked to do something very puzzling: fetch *a colt* belonging to someone else. If accused of being thieves, they are to answer that Jesus, *the Lord,* needs to use the animal.

WHAT DO YOU THINK?

How does realizing that Jesus is almighty and eternal (the one who was, is, and is to come) have a positive effect on your faith? How should this realization affect your daily life as a Christian?

DAILY BIBLE READINGS

Monday, Mar. 26— Jesus Is the Cornerstone *(1 Peter 2:4-10)*

Tuesday, Mar. 27—Jesus, God's Son (Hebrews 3:1-6)

Wednesday, Mar. 28—Children Praise Jesus (Matthew 21:14-17)

Thursday, Mar. 29—Give Thanks (Psalm 118:21-28)

Friday, Mar. 30—The Lord Needs It (Luke 19:28-34)

Saturday, Mar. 31—Blessed Is the King (Luke 19:35-40)

Sunday, Apr. 1—Christ Will Return (Revelation 1:1-8)

This request shows us two parts of Jesus' plan. First, Jesus' simple instructions indicate his authority. To steal a colt is a serious, punishable offense. But that is not what Jesus is doing, and the men obey with confidence. Second, Jesus acts in order to fulfill prophecy. Matthew 21:4 makes it clear that what is about to happen is a fulfillment of Old Testament predictions about Jesus' entry into Jerusalem (see Isaiah 62:11; Zechariah 9:9).

The fact that this animal has never been ridden has a dual significance. First, it offers a sense of holiness for the occasion. This is an ordinary animal but special in that it has never been mounted by any other person. Unknowingly, the owners have been preparing for Jesus' royal ride for many months. Second, Jesus' ability to ride an unbroken donkey is a way of demonstrating his lordship over all of creation. He is the prince of peace, whom even the untamed animals obey.

B. DISCIPLES SERVE THEIR LORD (vv. 32-34)

32. Those who were sent ahead went and found it just as he had told them.

We can imagine the surprise and wonder of the obedient disciples when they find everything exactly as Jesus had predicted. There is no way to explain this except to believe in the supernatural knowledge and authority of Jesus.

33, 34. As they were untying the colt, its owners asked them, "Why are you untying the colt?" They replied, "The Lord needs it."

The details of Jesus' prediction even extend to a confrontation with the *owners* of the colt. Jesus' foreknowledge has already covered this, so the disciples answer as he had advised them. They give no long rationale such as, "Jesus of Nazareth is in town for Passover and needs to borrow a donkey because he wants to ride it into Jerusalem." They merely assert, *"The Lord needs it."* In so answering, they demonstrate both their confident obedience and their submission to the lordship of Jesus the Messiah.

III. CHRIST AS KING TO BE PRAISED (LUKE 19:35-38)

Artists have attempted to illustrate what Jesus' triumphal entry may have looked like. Composers too have worked to bring the event alive musically. All of these efforts fall short of the joyous, even riotous celebration that accompanies Jesus as he enters the holy city. This is shown by the reaction of Jesus' jealous opponents: "Teacher, rebuke your disciples!" (Luke 19:39). Jesus responds that if he did this, "the stones will cry out" (Luke 19:40). This indicates that the joy of this occasion is inspired by God himself. If God is behind such rejoicing, who are humans to stifle it?

A. PREPARING THE WAY OF THE KING (vv. 35, 36)

35, 36. They brought it to Jesus, threw their cloaks on the colt and put Jesus on it. As he went along, people spread their cloaks on the road.

The crowd quickly joins the excitement of the celebration, improvising the best parade possible. There is no royal saddle for the donkey, so the disciples throw their *cloaks* up on the beast. These are their best clothes, their big-city, high holy day celebration clothes. There is no red carpet or newly paved street, so those in the crowd toss their cloaks to cover the dirt and give an air of elegance to the procession. This shows the size of the crowd, which may be sufficient to have garments that cover the mile or so of this march. Matthew 21:8 says the crowd is "very large."

We are reminded that King Jesus does not receive the trappings of human royalty in the Gospel of Luke. At Jesus' birth, he is not laid in a royal bed in a palace

WHAT DO YOU THINK?

How will the faithfulness of those who followed the instruction of Jesus to retrieve the colt inspire you to be faithful in following his instructions?

WHAT DO YOU THINK?

How can you worship Jesus with significant gifts and by speaking up during hostile circumstances?

but in a manger in a stable (2:7). He does not send out his emissaries with troops and lavish transportation but on foot with no money (10:4). Even so, they preach the kingdom of God (10:9). Jesus taught that his ideal kingdom members are not the rich and powerful of the world but those as little children (18:16).

BLEEX

BLEEX—no, that's not the sound of something getting bleeped out of a TV program. It's an acronym for Berkeley Lower Extremities EXoskeleton. The University of California developed the device to help people carry heavy loads. For example, firefighters can use a BLEEX as they struggle up the stairs of a building while carrying heavy rescue equipment.

BLEEX is not a hypothetical science-fiction gadget we have seen in Star Wars–type movies. BLEEX is real. It is a set of strap-on metal legs and power unit. Sensors and a hydraulic system assist the normal motions of the human body. As a result, the 100-pound exoskeleton and a 70-pound load can feel as light as 5 pounds. Imagine the superman impression one could make while transported by a BLEEX!

Had Jesus used something like a BLEEX to enter Jerusalem, the media undoubtedly would have focused on the contraption rather than on Jesus. By riding a humble beast such as a donkey, the attention was appropriately focused on Jesus himself. Jesus' significance came from who he was, not from the technology he used. That's important to remember. People today are enthusiastic about technology, and we use technological innovations at times to further the cause of Christ. But to allow technology to overshadow the message and identity of the king would be a grave mistake.   —C. R. B.

Visual for Lesson 5. *This chart will help your students see how the events of Jesus' final week all fit together.*

B. PRAISING GOD (v. 37)

37. When he came near the place where the road goes down the Mount of Olives, the whole crowd of disciples began joyfully to praise God in loud voices for all the miracles they had seen:

Our age is obsessed by the cult of celebrity worship. Many long to know every detail of the lives of their favorite stars. We often witness the folly of assuming that famous people are wise and/or good examples. This verse shows us that the triumphal entry celebration is much more than celebrity glorification.

The crowd is not praising Jesus because he is famous. They *praise God* because in the ministry of Jesus they have seen the power of God displayed. This is the crowd that traveled with Jesus from Jericho, where he had dramatically healed a blind man just shortly before.

C. BLESSING THE KING (v. 38)

38. "Blessed is the king who comes in the name of the Lord!"

"Peace in heaven and glory in the highest!"

Like the city of Rome, Jerusalem also knew of triumphal processions. The non-biblical passage 1 Maccabees 13:49-53 recounts a triumphal entry into the city with praise, palm branches, and music in 141 BC. Many centuries earlier, David returned to the city in triumph after slaying Goliath (1 Samuel 17:54; 18:6).

This type of victory procession is also reflected in Psalm 118. The psalm begins with a conversation between the king and his army as they approach Jerusalem, giving praise to God for the victory (vv. 1-18). In verse 19 they arrive at the gates of the temple and ask to be admitted. Once inside, they are filled with praise (v. 24). The celebration calls forth a blessing from the priest (v. 26). Then the king's sacrifice is accepted for the holy altar.

PRAYER

God in Heaven, we repeat the refrain: Blessed is he who comes in the name of the Lord! We thank you for sending your Son, Jesus, to bring us salvation. May he reign supreme in our lives, now and forever. In his blessed name we pray, amen.

WHAT DO YOU THINK?

Many who hailed Jesus as king undoubtedly were expecting him to reestablish the realm of an earthly Jewish kingdom. What are some ways that you can safeguard yourself from being lulled into speculating about the events surrounding his second coming?

WHAT DO YOU THINK?

It can be very difficult to reason with skeptics who prefer to focus on the imperfections of Christians. How can we turn the conversation away from criticisms of individual Christians to a focus on Jesus' right to be king of everything?

WHAT DO YOU THINK?

If you decided to live life with the kingship of Jesus always in view, how would your life change?

THOUGHT TO REMEMBER

Celebrate the king!

This mighty refrain is taken up by the crowds of Jewish pilgrims as Jesus enters the city: *"Blessed is the king who comes in the name of the Lord!"* Although Jesus had won no military battles, they recognize and celebrate his kingship.

Jesus' triumphal entry is characterized by more than a Mardi Gras–like party spirit, however. The crowd's spirit is one of worship. The acclamation is not at all inconsistent with that of the angels at Jesus' birth: "Glory to God in the highest, and on earth peace to men on whom his favor rests" (Luke 2:14).

NO P. T. BARNUM, NO APRIL FOOL

Bridgeport, Connecticut's annual Barnum Festival is an upbeat civic event celebrating the life of P. T. Barnum (1810–1891). Barnum was the nineteenth-century circus king and was once the city's mayor. Barnum was called "The Prince of Humbug." He enjoyed playing hoaxes on people, all in the spirit of creative capitalism.

Barnum saw his sideshows as harmless ways of fooling people while giving them their money's worth in good, clean fun. His "Cardiff Giant," his "161-year-old nanny to George Washington," and his "Fejee Mermaid" are legendary. He even wrote a book entitled *Humbugs of the World* (see www.ptbarnum.org).

Jesus of Nazareth was no P. T. Barnum. There was no humbug, no hoax, no April fool in what Jesus offered the crowd that joined his entry into Jerusalem. He was not motivated by the idea of accumulating earthly possessions. Many had seen his miracles, heard his authoritative teaching, and witnessed his humility. Many people joined his procession that day; many probably deserted a few days later; some stuck with him for the rest of their lives and into eternity. Will you follow Jesus today?

—C. R. B.

CONCLUSION

Several years ago, I was in a crowd that was addressed by Queen Elizabeth II, the reigning monarch of Great Britain. I was within a few dozen yards of the queen, and I saw and heard her clearly. She seemed to be a fine woman. The reality, though, is that her authority as queen is very limited. Our world no longer embraces the concept of hereditary monarchs who reign absolutely.

A central theme in the Bible is the kingship of Jesus. Jesus does not inherit a kingdom from an earthly father or win it through his accomplishments. His kingship is not bestowed upon him by adoring citizens of the realm. He *is* king, has *always been* king, and will *always be* king. There will be challengers to his throne, but he will reign supreme (1 Corinthians 15:24, 25). Many rejected him as king (see John 19:15), but in the end he will receive their acknowledgment (see Philippians 2:10, 11).

What are the personal implications of Jesus' kingship? Does he reign in your life? Consider the question this way: When you willingly disobey King Jesus, do you fear his wrath (see Revelation 6:16)? The New Testament teaches that those who reject the reign of the Lord will be crushed in "the winepress of the fury of the wrath of God Almighty" (Revelation 19:15). Those who love him, those who serve him, will be those who obey him. When Christ reigns in our lives, we can be free from the fear of God's mighty wrath (see 1 Thessalonians 1:10).

If you claim citizenship in the kingdom of God and of his Christ, is your allegiance absolute and consistent? Is your loyalty unwavering, even in the face of opposition? Are you able to let go of your own selfish desires to serve the King of kings without reservation? May God bless us as we each strive toward perfect and unreserved service, so that one day we will hear the words, "Well done, good and faithful servant! . . . Come and share your master's happiness!" (Matthew 25:21).

Discovery Learning

This page contains an alternative lesson plan emphasizing learning activities. Classes desiring such student involvement will find these suggestions helpful. The next page is a reproducible activity page to further enhance discovery learning.

LEARNING GOALS

After participating in this lesson, each student will be able to:

1. Explain the significance of the Palm Sunday events.

2. Understand how Jesus is king past, present, and future.

3. Determine a specific way to recognize the kingship of Jesus in his or her life.

INTO THE LESSON

To introduce today's lesson, provide hymnals for the class and lead your students in singing, "All Glory, Laud and Honor." If a certain class member is a good song leader, you may prefer to let him or her lead.

Next, ask your class to identify the New Testament event that is the basis of that hymn. If no one immediately guesses the triumphal entry or Palm Sunday, provide several clues: *Jerusalem, palm branches, a colt, "Hosanna!"* Once someone has guessed the event or you have revealed the answer, inform your class that today's lesson deals with the triumphal entry as it relates to Jesus' divine kingship.

INTO THE WORD

Use the Lesson Background material to explain the setting of the lesson text. Then ask two class members to read Revelation 1:8 and Luke 19:28-38 aloud. One student will read the narration (Luke 19:28-30a, 32, 33a, 34a, 35-38a), the other the dialogue (Revelation 1:8; Luke 19:30b, 31, 33b, 34b, 38b) in the passages. (You may wish to recruit your readers ahead of time, so they have a chance to practice.)

After the reading, tell your students that these two texts highlight some qualities of King Jesus that point to him as being unique among kings. To discover those qualities, have your students work independently to complete the matching exercise below. This activity also is printed in the student book. If you do not use the student book, you will need to make copies of the exercise to distribute to your class.

Each student should match the qualities with the corresponding verses. Mention that a passage may refer to more than one quality. Allow about 10 minutes to complete the quiz.

Why We Call Him King Jesus

___ 1. Omniscient		___ 5. Pre-existed	
___ 2. Fulfilled prophecy		___ 6. Inspired praise	
___ 3. Accepted praise		___ 7. Eternal	
___ 4. Commanded		___ 8. All-powerful	

a. Revelation 1:8; b. Luke 19:29-34; c. Luke 19:37, 38; d. Luke 19:30, 31, 38 (Zechariah 9:9; Psalm 118:26); e. Luke 19:29-31. (*Correct answers: 1. b; 2. d; 3. c; 4. e; 5. a; 6. c; 7. a; 8. a.*)

After your students share their findings, use the lesson commentary and the discussion questions below to explore the text in more detail.

1. How do the terms *Alpha* and *Omega* indicate Jesus' eternal nature and his role in creation? 2. What is implied by the term *Almighty*? 3. How did Jesus' commands in verses 28-31 indicate his omniscience (total knowledge, even of the future) and his lordship? What was significant about the prophecies of Isaiah 62:11 and Zechariah 9:9 in this regard? 4. Why did people praise God at Jesus' arrival (v. 37)? Why did they quote Psalm 118?

INTO LIFE

Divide the class into groups of three or four. Each group will work on the same hypothetical situation below, using information from the Gospel of Luke (not limited to chapter 19) to brainstorm a response designed to convince "Bob" that he should accept Christ as Savior.

Bob is willing to admit that Christianity is probably true. Nevertheless, he is unwilling to surrender his life to Christ. "I would have to give up too much," he says. "Why can't I be a Christian without changing my lifestyle?"

Ask groups to incorporate answers to the following questions: 1. Who is Jesus (his identity) that Bob should *worship* him? 2. What power does he have (his attributes) that Bob should *submit* to his authority? 3. What has he done (his miraculous works) that Bob should *believe* in him? 4. Why should Bob *trust* in him?

Ask volunteers to share their conclusions with the class. Close with prayer, challenging your students to share Jesus with those like Bob. As students leave, distribute the He Is Lord of My Life exercise from the reproducible page as take-home work.

He Is Lord of My Life

In the space provided, indicate how Jesus is Lord of some key areas of your life. Also indicate at least one area you have yet to surrender to his control.

1. Jesus is Lord of my *finances* because . . .

2. I know that Jesus is Lord of my *television and movie viewing* because . . .

3. I made Jesus Lord of my *family relationships* by . . .

4. I believe that Jesus is Lord of my *business or job* because . . .

5. I believe that Jesus should be Lord of my *Web surfing* habits because . . .

6. I invite Jesus to look over my shoulder at what I *read* because . . .

7. I think Jesus should be the one who controls my *tongue* because . . .

8. An area I need to *surrender* to his control is . . .

CHRIST IS RISEN

WHY TEACH THIS LESSON?

A popular method of church growth in recent years is called *the seeker approach*. Non-Christians are referred to as *seekers of God*. The church becomes the instrument to present Christ to them. These churches are geared toward reaching these seekers.

Though many people are indeed seeking Christ, they often seek in the wrong places or in the wrong ways. The wise men sought Jesus in the royal palace; yet Jesus was in a humble stable. In this lesson Mary sought Jesus as a corpse in a tomb; yet Jesus was alive outside. Actually, the non-Christian is not the primary seeker. Jesus is. He says that he came "to seek and to save what was lost" (Luke 19:10). Your students may indeed be seeking Jesus today, but they need to realize that he is seeking them more than they are seeking him!

Your students also need to know whom it really is who seeks them. He is none other than the Jesus who was risen on Easter—the Son of God. This lesson addresses this very issue.

INTRODUCTION

A. THE CROSS AND EASTER

The cross is the most recognizable religious symbol on earth. It appears as jewelry, in logos, on buildings, in cemeteries, and in countless other places. Some churches often use a cross with Jesus included, called a *crucifix*. Other churches prefer an empty cross, symbolizing that Jesus' work on the cross is finished. Still other churches favor another symbol: an image of the risen Christ over the cross. This reflects an understanding that while Jesus' atoning sacrifice on the cross is essential to our salvation, it is his resurrection that validates that work and completes his mission on earth.

This week's lesson is for Resurrection Sunday (Easter). This has been celebrated by the church since her earliest days as the central event in all of human history. We will explore what it means to be a witness to the risen Christ and how such witnesses have continuing significance for us today.

B. LESSON BACKGROUND

After his resurrection, Jesus appeared to some people but not to others. Why was that? We may not understand this completely, but the New Testament does give us some clues. First, we can see that Jesus appeared only to believers. There was no appearance to Pontius Pilate, to Caiaphas, or to the Roman emperor, as dramatic and powerful as such appearances might have been. He did appear to large groups, one group estimated by Paul to have been over 500 in number. But Paul calls these people *brothers,* meaning "fellow believers" (1 Corinthians 15:6). Therefore, the required condition to receive a visit from the risen Christ was faith.

The one possible exception to this first item (the condition of faith) was Jesus' startling appearance to Saul (later called Paul) on the road to Damascus

DEVOTIONAL READING:
ROMANS 14:7-12
BACKGROUND SCRIPTURE:
REVELATION 1:9-20; JOHN 20:1-18, 30, 31
PRINTED TEXT:
REVELATION 1:12a, 17, 18; JOHN 20:11-16, 30, 31

Apr
8

LESSON AIMS

After participating in this lesson, each student will be able to:

1. Describe Mary Magdalene's role as a witness to the resurrection of Jesus.

2. Explain the importance of eyewitness testimony for the resurrection of Jesus.

3. Develop a personal faith-statement in Jesus, which is grounded in the biblical evidence for his resurrection.

KEY VERSES

When I saw him, I fell at his feet as though dead. Then he placed his right hand on me and said: "Do not be afraid. I am the First and the Last. I am the Living One; I was dead, and behold I am alive for ever and ever! And I hold the keys of death and Hades." —Revelation 1:17, 18

(Acts 9). Yet the occasion was clear: Jesus had decided that this was the proper time to call this man of zeal to his service. Paul was a "chosen instrument" for the Lord (Acts 9:15).

Second, we see that Christ alone determined the occasions for his appearances. There was never a sense of Christ appearing at someone's command, like conjuring up a demon or a genie.

Third, the general purpose for Christ's appearances is also clear: He made himself known to those whom he wanted to be witnesses for him. His parting words to the gathered disciples before his ascension served to commission them as "my witnesses" (Acts 1:8), meaning able to testify that Jesus was truly risen from the dead. A necessary qualification for replacing Judas as one of the 12 apostles was that the candidate "become a witness with us of his resurrection" (Acts 1:22). A central person in today's lesson is Mary Magdalene. After her early morning encounter with the risen Lord, she "went to the disciples with the news: 'I have seen the Lord!'" (John 20:18). The many such witnesses to the resurrection are what give us confidence that Jesus really did rise from the grave and that he has the power to save us from death.

John's account of the events of the Sunday morning of the resurrection of Jesus is full of unique details. One of these distinctive aspects is John's interest in the role of Mary Magdalene on that glorious morning. Luke records that Mary was an early follower of Jesus, having been delivered by him from demon possession (Luke 8:2). In John, she is first introduced as one of several women who maintained a vigil at the cross (John 19:25). We can appreciate her great love for the one who freed her from spiritual bondage. We sympathize with her extreme anguish in seeing his suffering and death on a Roman cross.

The commitment of Mary to her Lord can be seen in that she was not just one of the last at the cross but also the first at the tomb. When most of the male disciples abandoned Jesus, Mary and the other women kept the deathwatch without regard to personal danger. While others slept on Sunday morning, Mary arose before daybreak to go to the tomb and finish the proper preparations of Jesus' corpse.

Upon arrival, Mary found the tomb open and empty, and she ran to Peter to report this. John makes it clear that she believed someone had removed Jesus' body (John 20:1, 2, 13, 14). As we study today's lesson, we experience Mary's crushing agony upon her discovery of the empty tomb and her mighty joy when she encounters her risen Lord. We share her emotions on this great day.

I. DEATH IS UNLOCKED (REVELATION 1:12a, 17, 18)

The book of Revelation is made up of a series of visions experienced by the apostle John while exiled on the prison island of Patmos. John signals to the reader the beginning of a new vision by writing that he is "in the Spirit" (Revelation 1:10; also 4:2; 17:3; 21:10). His first vision is of the risen Christ, whom he hears before he sees (1:10-12). This vision includes a description of the Lord that is both awe-inspiring and full of allusions to the Old Testament.

A. PARALYZING FEAR OF DEATH (vv. 12a, 17)

12a, 17. I turned around to see the voice that was speaking to me. . . . When I saw him, I fell at his feet as though dead. Then he placed his right hand on me and said: "Do not be afraid. I am the First and the Last.

We can easily understand the reaction of John. He is experiencing Jesus in all his heavenly glory. This includes a trumpet-like voice (Revelation 1:10). He sees eyes that burn like fire (1:14) and Jesus' countenance glowing like the sun (1:16). John is understandably filled with fear. Jesus taught that this fear is completely justified, for God is the one with ultimate power over a person's eternal destiny (Matthew 10:28). Fear of God is expected of everyone (Revelation 15:4).

John undoubtedly remembers a similar experience of over 60 years earlier, when he was one of three disciples allowed to witness the transfiguration of Jesus. The disciples had fallen down in fear (Matthew 17:6). At that time of deadly terror, Jesus' words had been, "Don't be afraid" (Matthew 17:7). Here again, Jesus lays a comforting *hand* on the cowering John and tells him, "Do not be afraid." His life is not in danger.

B. ENCOURAGING FREEDOM FROM DEATH (v. 18)

18. "I am the Living One; I was dead, and behold I am alive for ever and ever! And I hold the keys of death and Hades."

Jesus gives John three powerful reasons not to fear. First, Jesus reminds John of the event that changed history: Jesus' resurrection. John was likely one of those who helped take down Jesus' body from the cross. John was standing right there when the soldier pierced Jesus' side (John 19:34, 35). John knew, beyond any shadow of doubt, that Jesus' body had been devoid of all life. Yet he had also witnessed Jesus alive again. Jesus *was dead,* but God did not abandon him in the grave (Acts 2:31, 32).

Second, Jesus was raised to eternal life. The Bible tells of several people who were brought back to life after dying (example: Lazarus in John 11). We assume, however, that all of these people eventually died a natural death again. Jesus' resurrection is quite different! He was truly dead, his body lying inert in the grave for days. When he came back to life, it was to be *alive for ever and ever!*

Third, Jesus tells John that he has the keys to unlock the strongholds of death. The word *Hades* as used in this verse does not necessarily refer to the place of ultimate punishment, the lake of fire (Revelation 20:10, 14). It is probably a general reference to the place of the dead, called *sheol* by Jews. To have *the keys of death* means that Jesus is able to lead us from death to life eternal. In this Jesus is the "author" or pioneer of our salvation (Hebrews 2:10; 12:2), the one who has blazed the trail from death to life that we may follow.

When we as believers read these words, we should rejoice. Death has no power over us. We have been rescued from death and from the fear of death by Jesus, our Savior (Hebrews 2:15). Truly, we can sing with the apostle Paul, "Death has been swallowed up in victory!" (1 Corinthians 15:54).

NOT A NEAR-DEATH EXPERIENCE, BUT A . . .

Near-death experiences have been reported by many people. One devout Christian woman relates two such experiences. In both cases she had suffered a deep vein thrombosis that required emergency medical treatment to save her life. She tells of entering into a brilliant room where everything was intensely peaceful and where she was immersed in heavenly music.

These kinds of stories share similar themes. The book *90 Minutes in Heaven* is the story of a Christian minister who was the victim of a horrendous, head-on crash with a semitrailer truck. Rescue personnel found no pulse and declared him dead. Another minister arrived on the scene and prayed for him. Ninety minutes after the crash, the "dead" man showed signs of life and eventually recovered. During those 90 minutes, he saw himself at the gates of Heaven, surrounded by friends and relatives welcoming him home, but he was turned away before he could enter!

WHAT DO YOU THINK?

In what ways has your healthy fear of God helped you to grow in Christ?

WHAT DO YOU THINK?

What are some typical reactions to death or the topic of death? In what ways does knowing of the resurrection of Jesus make facing death easier for you?

WHAT DO YOU THINK?

Many believers who live in dire circumstances long to be with the Lord, while those who are well off sometimes put a lot of time and money into living on earth as long as possible. How can the church help both types stay focused on hope in Christ through his resurrection while remaining grounded in the present?

Do these stories reveal what actually happened, or do they merely describe the vivid imaginings of oxygen-starved brain cells? Regardless of what we make of these stories, they testify to the faith of Christians. Their faith is in the Lord who had not a *near*-death experience but a *through*-death experience. Our Lord is now alive forever. Death could not hold him, and he has the keys to our death as well!—C. R. B.

II. CHRIST IS RISEN (JOHN 20:11-16)

The second Scripture for this week's lesson also comes from the apostle John. But this one is from his Gospel account of the life, death, and resurrection of Jesus. These verses focus on that momentous morning that inaugurated a new era for God's people.

A. WEEPING WITHOUT CHRIST (vv. 11-13)

11. But Mary stood outside the tomb crying. As she wept, she bent over to look into the tomb

The previous verses of this chapter tell of how Mary had visited *the tomb* before dawn, found the tomb empty, returned to tell Peter, and then came back to the tomb herself. This is a moving, emotional time for Mary. Her grief brings tears and sobs. She is *crying* because the shock of Jesus' missing body has rekindled all of the sorrow she felt at his death. It appears that she even has been denied the opportunity to do a final service to her Lord: full preparation of his body for its final rest.

12. . . . and saw two angels in white, seated where Jesus' body had been, one at the head and the other at the foot.

This type of tomb is not like the graves that we find in our cemeteries today. This one is a small room carved into the limestone hillside. In this cave-like room, there probably are several shelves or niches to lay newly deceased bodies. After a body is deposited, such a tomb is sealed with a large stone that has been shaped to fit the entrance snugly. The Gospels tell us that this particular tomb belongs to Joseph of Arimathea (Matthew 27:57-60) and that it has never been used for burial.

Looking inside, Mary sees something she does not expect: *two angels.* These visitors have just appeared because Peter and John found nothing in the tomb but empty grave linens, and then they went home (John 20:3-10). The appearance of these two angels thus is specially designed for Mary's benefit.

13. They asked her, "Woman, why are you crying?"

"They have taken my Lord away," she said, "and I don't know where they have put him."

The angels know what Mary doesn't: that this is a time for rejoicing, not weeping. Mary weeps because the great crush of events has overwhelmed her. Her master has been disgraced and executed as a common criminal. And now the final insult has come: his body has been *taken* away.

Mary's sorrow is so deep that she cannot even marvel at an angel manifestation. She can think only of one thing: find the missing body of her dead *Lord,* Jesus, and rescue it from those who would desecrate it.

B. MEETING THE RISEN CHRIST (vv. 14, 15)

14. At this, she turned around and saw Jesus standing there, but she did not realize that it was Jesus.

Getting no answer from the angels (or perhaps not caring even to wait for an answer), Mary turns away from the entrance of the tomb. She is determined to

---

WHAT DO YOU THINK?

How have the reactions of Mary and John in today's text been a help to you as you review your faith walk?

HOW TO SAY IT

Arimathea. AIR-uh-muh-THEE-uh.

Caiaphas. KAY-uh-fus or KYE-uh-fus.

Hades. HAY-deez.

Magdalene. MAG-duh-leen or Mag-duh-LEE-nee.

Patmos. PAT-muss.

Pontius Pilate. PON-shus or PON-ti-us PIE-lut.

Rabboni. Rab-O-nye.

sheol. SHE-ol.

find Jesus' body. Yet in the dim light of the dawn, she encounters another person. She finds Jesus' body but not in the way she expects.

15. "Woman," he said, "why are you crying? Who is it you are looking for?" Thinking he was the gardener, she said, "Sir, if you have carried him away, tell me where you have put him, and I will get him."

The combination of Mary's extreme grief, tears that cloud her eyesight, and the scant light of early morning combine to prevent her from recognizing Jesus. He repeats the question of the angels, *why are you crying?*

Mary, *thinking* him to be *the gardener,* asks the only question that seems reasonable at the time. Perhaps Jesus' body has been stolen. Or perhaps this gardener has moved it for some good reason. But neither idea is correct.

C. RECOGNIZING THE RISEN CHRIST (v. 16)

16. Jesus said to her, "Mary."

She turned toward him and cried out in Aramaic, "Rabboni!" (which means Teacher).

Knowing that *Mary* has not recognized him, *Jesus* speaks her name in a personal, revealing way. It all comes to her in a rush: Jesus is not dead! This is her Lord, her *Teacher* speaking to her. The realization of a split second changes her life forever.

Notice that Mary does not find the living Christ because of her seeking (remember: she is looking for a dead Christ). Rather, *the living Christ finds her!* This has huge significance for us today. The risen Jesus is alive still and is still seeking disciples. Jesus said he came to "seek and to save what was lost" (Luke 19:10). If we make ourselves available, call on his name, and follow the biblical plan of salvation, Jesus finds us and changes us.

We will never be the same when this happens. We can be transformed from death to life (John 5:24). Our great fear of death no longer paralyzes us, for "Christ has indeed been raised from the dead" (1 Corinthians 15:20) and "in Christ all will be made alive" (1 Corinthians 15:22). Even if we die, we will be raised to eternal life and "so we will be with the Lord forever" (1 Thessalonians 4:17).

III. FAITH BRINGS LIFE (JOHN 20:30, 31)

Have you ever wondered why the Gospels were written? The apostle John now gives his readers a clear statement of his purpose in writing: his purpose is evangelistic.

A. SIGNS OF JESUS (v. 30)

30. Jesus did many other miraculous signs in the presence of his disciples, which are not recorded in this book.

In John *signs* are the miracles of Jesus (see John 2:23; 4:48). The miracle accounts in John tend to be more extensive and detailed than in the other Gospels. John admits that he has been necessarily selective in choosing which miracles to recount (see John 21:25). How wonderful it would be to learn of some of those unrecorded miracles! Jesus' earthly life was not one of carefully chosen good deeds for a public-relations campaign. Rather, it was a pattern of healing and helping wherever he went.

B. FAITH IN JESUS (v. 31)

31. But these are written that you may believe that Jesus is the Christ, the Son of God, and that by believing you may have life in his name.

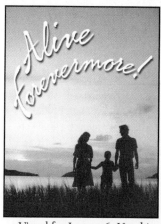

Visual for Lesson 6. *Use this visual to ask, "How is our new life in Christ like a sunrise?"*

WHAT DO YOU THINK?

Some say that Jesus did not come back to life. How can the church equip the average Christian to respond?

In fact, John does indeed tell us why he selects certain miracles and why he writes in general: he does this so *that by believing you may have life in his name.* John thinks his account of *Jesus* is adequate to make his case. The careful reader will see in Jesus the one who is God's *Son,* sent to redeem humanity (John 3:16). Such a reader will see the Lamb of God who takes away the world's sin (1:29). Such a reader will see God's chosen Messiah, who brings living water (4:14). Such a reader will see life and resurrection from the dead (11:25).

The one who believes in Jesus need not fear death, for he has conquered death. Those who believe are called to be faithful, even to the point of death, for they will receive a crown of life (Revelation 2:10).

BELIEVING THE EVIDENCE

Juan Catalan was charged with the murder of a teenage girl in May 2003. He claimed that he had been with his daughter at Dodger Stadium in Los Angeles at the time of the murder, about 20 miles from the scene of the crime. Police did not believe him. Catalan had ticket stubs to the game, and family members testified to his innocence. But police had a witness placing Catalan at the murder site. Catalan's attorney obtained an official Dodger videotape of the game, but Catalan couldn't be identified.

Then the attorney discovered that HBO had also filmed a program at the stadium that evening. In footage that had been cut from the program, one scene clearly showed Catalan and his daughter eating hot dogs. The time codes on the tape were evidence that he had been at the stadium at the time of the murder. Cell phone records placed him near the stadium as well. Nearly six months after Catalan was jailed, the court threw his case out. Catalan was a free man.

Evidence is important! John wrote his Gospel to offer us evidence about Jesus. John says the evidence establishes the fact, without ambiguity, that Jesus is the Son of God and our Savior. Do you believe this evidence?   —C. R. B.

CONCLUSION

Some years ago there was a series of documentary programs produced for TV entitled *The Long Search.* The shows examined the origins and beliefs of the world's religions, including several varieties of Christianity. The premise was that religion consists of the human search for God. This search turns out differently for different searchers, thus producing diverging faiths. In this way of thinking, religion is largely the product of human imagination and experience.

Biblical faith, at its core, is decidedly different. The Bible is not the record of humanity's search for God. It is much more the story of God's search to redeem his lost children. Yet some, like Mary, still search for a dead Christ. Some seek him as only a historical figure from 2,000 years ago. They find an enigmatic figure, a person very difficult to explain using the standard criteria of history.

Others seek Christ only in the pages of tradition. They see him as the originator of a great system of ethical teaching: selflessness and service. Still others seek a Christ that fits their predetermined needs. They want a Savior according to their expectations, not according to his terms and demands. Therefore they seem to serve a dead Christ. He makes no impact on what they do, how they behave, or their future plans.

The great news of Resurrection Sunday is that we serve a risen Savior. He was alive on that morning when Mary visited the tomb. He is alive today and still seeking those who would serve him, love him, and be his disciples. As believers we can walk daily with the confidence of Jesus' presence in our lives. He is not dead! Hallelujah, he is risen indeed!

Discovery Learning

This page contains an alternative lesson plan emphasizing learning activities. Classes desiring such student involvement will find these suggestions helpful. The next page is a reproducible activity page to further enhance discovery learning.

LEARNING GOALS

After this lesson, each student will be able to:

1. Describe Mary Magdalene's role as a witness to the resurrection of Jesus.

2. Explain the importance of eyewitness testimony for the resurrection of Jesus.

3. Develop a personal faith-statement in Jesus, which is grounded in the biblical evidence for his resurrection.

INTO THE LESSON

To open today's lesson, share the following riddle with your class (also printed in the student books). Ask students to guess the answer.

I am both first and last. In the course of time I was, and was not, and am again forever. Who am I?

List your students' suggested answers on the board, then ask them to read Revelation 1:12-18. They should recognize that the answer is *Jesus,* who is the first and the last, who lived, died, and rose again to eternal life.

Next, use the commentary on verse 18 to sketch the three reasons why the Christian should not fear death. Then tell your class that today's lesson deals with the biblical evidence for believing that Jesus did indeed conquer death.

INTO THE WORD

Share the following information: George Rawlinson (1812–1902) was an English historian. He formulated guidelines for historians to follow to determine the value of historical writings. He proposed that (1) the writings of eyewitnesses generally have the highest degree of credibility, (2) the writings of those who get their information from eyewitnesses have the next highest degree of credibility, and (3) writers of a later age, who depend on word-of-mouth (oral tradition) for their information, have the lowest degree of credibility.

Using these guidelines and the questions below, your students should evaluate the historical credibility of the following biblical reports of the risen Jesus. (This exercise is also in the student books.) You can either divide your class into small groups and assign each group one or two passages, or investigate each passage with the entire class.

The passages are (A) John 20:11-20; (B) John 20:26-28; (C) John 21:1-14; (D) 1 Corinthians 15:3-8.

Questions for Each Passage

1. Was the author an eyewitness of the appearance of the resurrected Christ?

2. Did the author get the information from an eyewitness or eyewitnesses?

3. Did the author rely on word-of-mouth from an earlier age?

4. Taking the first three questions together, what degree of historical credibility should we assign to the passage in question?

Answers

Passages A, B, and C: The author, John, was an eyewitness of the resurrected Lord; see John 21:20-24 *(highest degree of credibility).*

Passage D. Paul and others were eyewitness of the risen Lord, though not all were witnesses to the same appearances; see Acts 9 *(highest degree of credibility).*

After you have analyzed each passage, discuss the implications this evidence has for a Christian's faith. Use the lesson commentary on John 20:30, 31 and the questions below to guide the discussion.

1. Why did John record so many miracles, especially the miracle of Jesus' resurrection?

2. Why is it important to have historical evidence of the highest credibility upon which to base one's faith in Jesus?

3. What assurance do we have that death has been defeated, based on the historical evidence we have for the resurrection of Jesus?

Option. Distribute the Christ is Risen! exercise from the reproducible page either for students to work on as they arrive or as a take-home activity at class end.

INTO LIFE

Introduce the last exercise by saying, "It is important for each Christian to be able to explain why he or she believes in Christ. As Peter said, 'But in your hearts set apart Christ as Lord. Always be prepared to give an answer to everyone who asks you to give the reason for the hope that you have' (1 Peter 3:15)."

Then ask students to use the paper you provided (or the space in their student books) to complete the following open-ended statement: "I believe that Jesus is the Christ, the Son of God, because . . ." Ask several volunteers to share their faith statements.

Christ Is Risen!

Mary was bewildered when she stood at the empty tomb trying to figure out what had happened to her Lord's body. Shortly, however, she learned the truth about Jesus' disappearance. Read John 20:11-31 and fill in the blanks below with the missing words. Next, copy the highlighted letters to the line at the bottom to discover what she learned.

1. Mary stood outside the tomb _ ☐ _ _ _ _ (v. 11).

2. Mary saw two _ _ _ ☐ _ _ in white (v. 12).

3. They were ☐ _ _ _ _ _ where Jesus' body had been (v. 12).

4. Mary turned around and saw _ _ _ ☐ _ standing there (v. 14).

5. Mary called Jesus ☐ _ _ _ _ _ _ (v. 16).

6. Jesus said, "Do not hold on to me, for I have not yet _ _ _ _ ☐ _ _ _ to the Father (v. 17).

7. Mary Magdalene returned to the _ _ _ _ _ _ _ ☐ _ with the news (v. 18).

8. Jesus said to them, "_ _ _ ☐ _ be with you" (v. 19).

9. ☐ _ _ _ _ _ was not with the disciples when Jesus came the first time (v. 24).

10. Thomas said, "Unless I see the _ _ ☐ _ marks in his hands . . . I will not believe it" (v. 25).

11. Thomas said, "My _ ☐ _ _ and my God" (v. 28).

12. "But these are written that you may believe that Jesus is the Christ, the _ _ ☐ of God" (v. 31).

Mary learned the truth about the _____.

CHRIST IS WORTHY OF PRAISE

LESSON 7

WHY TEACH THIS LESSON?

Challenge your students with this question: What is the one thing you do in your life that is more important than anything else you do? The answer, for everyone, should be *worship*.

As the door of Heaven was opened to John, the first thing he saw was the worship of God by the people of God. God's majesty and glory leads to worship. As you study this lesson today, reflect upon the worship of your church and the role you personally play in that worship. Is it worship inspired by and offered to the Lamb of God, who alone is worthy? This lesson will show why it should be.

INTRODUCTION

A. WORSHIP IN THE CHURCH TODAY

Is it *worship* or is it *entertainment*? That's the question I have asked myself occasionally as I have participated in Sunday services at several hundred different churches in many different states, provinces, and countries. My judgment? Sometimes it's hard to tell the difference.

In many churches the worship time has evolved from hymns led by a song leader, accompanied by an organ and/or piano, to be a "worship set" led by a well-rehearsed team of singers and musicians. It is not uncommon to see 20 or more people on the stage of the church, leading in 30 minutes of singing, accompanied by lavish video projections of words to the songs. New songs are introduced on a weekly basis and repeated many times in order to allow the congregation to learn them. Auditoriums are now "worship centers," with adjustable mood lighting and fabulous sound systems. One church I visited even had fountains down the center aisle; these fountains exploded with water jets at the pinnacle of the worship set. The worship set is energetic. It's loud; it's emotional; it's invigorating.

This shift in styles has certainly added vitality to the worship experience long missing in some congregations. Churches with great worship attract visitors and may grow rapidly. Thus, some church strategists see investment in professionals to lead worship-with-excellence as a wise investment in a church's future.

Some have noticed, however, that the youngest generation of Christians has a different taste in worship. Their preference seems to lean toward acoustic rather than electronic instruments, subtle hand drums rather than booming drum sets, and simple vocals rather than elaborate vocal teams. Their music is quieter, more reflective. They see an emphasis upon professionalism in worship as phony. They long to restore a sense of mystery and reverence to the worship time. One aspect of this has been the new generation's rediscovery of some old hymns such as "Be Thou My Vision." Where this will lead the church of the future is yet to be seen.

DEVOTIONAL READING:
PSALM 111
BACKGROUND SCRIPTURE:
REVELATION 4
PRINTED TEXT:
REVELATION 4

LESSON AIMS

After participating in this lesson, each student will be able to:

1. Describe the praise offered to the Lord in the throne room scene.

2. Tell the significance of some of the elements of worship in Heaven as presented in Revelation 4.

3. Suggest one specific way to improve his or her personal approach to worship.

Apr
15

KEY VERSE

"You are worthy, our Lord and God, to receive glory and honor and power, for you created all things, and by your will they were created and have their being."   —Revelation 4:11

The central question, however, remains: Is it worship or is it entertainment? As we examine Revelation 4, we will find biblical principles of the nature of worship that will help us guide our worship into being just that—worship.

B. LESSON BACKGROUND

The book of Revelation has long been a source of controversy. It has been combed thoroughly as a source of prophecies concerning the future. Many different systems of interpretation for Revelation have been developed and defended. Because of this controversy, some Christians avoid study of this book.

These controversies are unfortunate, for Revelation is much more than a book of prophecy. It is also the New Testament's great book of worship. In this regard, Revelation has much in common with the Psalms. Throughout the history of the church, writers of songs and hymns for worship have drawn from Revelation. Such varied pieces as Handel's "Hallelujah Chorus" (Revelation 19:1-6), Bridges and Thring's "Crown Him with Many Crowns" (19:12), and Tomlin's "We Fall Down" (4:10) are drawn from Revelation.

Nearly half of the occurrences of the New Testament's Greek verb for *worship* appear in the book of Revelation (24 out of 60). We see in this book that Heaven is a place of worship. Scholars have identified seven hymns of praise and worship in Revelation. The songs of praise are spoken (4:8), sung (5:9), and cried out (7:10).

In the New Testament, the word *worship* implies "giving obeisance, bowing down." Thus worshiping can involve a physical position (see Matthew 4:9). Our English word *worship* has the connotation of "giving worth to someone," or "counting someone to be ultimately worthy." Worship is not an emotion; it is an acknowledgment and commitment. We worship that which is superior and worthy of our honor.

I. PRELIMINARIES OF WORSHIP (REVELATION 4:1)

The first three chapters of Revelation concern John's vision of the risen Christ and letters to the seven churches of Asia. It is helpful, though, to understand these letters as separate greetings to each of the churches. The rest of the book is the letter itself, and all of the churches are intended to receive its messages.

A. DOOR TO HEAVEN (v. 1a)

1a. After this I looked, and there before me was a door standing open in heaven.

John understands his world like everyone else in antiquity. He sees the earth as being covered by a firmament, a large canopy that stretches over the earth (see Genesis 1:6-8; Isaiah 40:22). This firmament barrier prevents humans from seeing what is happening in the heavenly, spiritual realm. In his vision John sees a break in the firmament, *a door* into *heaven*. He sees what mortal eye is not normally allowed to see.

The fact that we now have traveled far beyond the sky into outer space diminishes neither the reality of Heaven nor the validity of John's vision. We still believe that Heaven exists as a definite place but not as a physical location that can be visited in a rocket ship. Heaven remains a place where mortals are normally denied access or viewing, but it is a real place just the same.

B. INVITATION TO KNOWLEDGE (v. 1b)

1b. And the voice I had first heard speaking to me like a trumpet said, "Come up here, and I will show you what must take place after this."

WHAT DO YOU THINK?

In what ways do you think your walk with Christ would be affected if you, like John, could get a personal glimpse through the door of Heaven? Why is it probably a good idea for God not to give you that glimpse?

John is invited by an unnamed voice to view heavenly events. He knows this voice, however. It sounds like a *trumpet*, loud and brilliantly piercing. He has heard it before. It is the voice of the risen Christ (Revelation 1:10).

Christ warns John that what he is about to see in Heaven foreshadows future events. This is not to be an impromptu visit to God's throne to observe daily happenings. It is a vision designed to impart special knowledge of the future so John may share this with his fellow believers. Events in Heaven have an effect on us. People in the ancient world believe this, whether Jew, Roman, or Christian. Modern humanity tends to neglect the spiritual realm. It is good for us to remember what is really the case: God is on his throne as the ruler of Heaven *and* earth.

II. CENTER OF WORSHIP (REVELATION 4:2-5)

John's challenge is to describe the indescribable. So he paints wonderful word pictures, but we can be sure that the reality is far more glorious than what we are able to imagine. He begins his vision with a visit to the very throne room of God.

A. DESCRIPTION OF THE THRONE (vv. 2, 3)

2, 3. At once I was in the Spirit, and there before me was a throne in heaven with someone sitting on it. And the one who sat there had the appearance of jasper and carnelian. A rainbow, resembling an emerald, encircled the throne.

Being *in the Spirit* means that a new vision has begun. This is very real to John. His spiritual eyes immediately focus on the *throne* of God itself. He describes the throne occupant as having the appearance of *jasper* (a gemstone that comes in a variety of colors) and *carnelian* (a bright red gemstone). He does not attempt any physical description of God because that would be sacrilegious. His choice of these two gemstones seems to indicate that God has a fiery, glowing appearance.

The throne itself looks like an *emerald* to John, a brilliant green color. It emanates color as well—a multihued *rainbow* radiance. Such marvelous colors surely overwhelm John's mind as they speak to him of the wonders of this place. Nothing on earth can compare with these marvels.

WHAT WORDS CANNOT DESCRIBE

What is your favorite gemstone? For some, diamond is the first choice (possibly because of the jewelry industry's superb "diamonds are forever" marketing job). Others may name rubies or (as John does) emeralds. John describes the emerald he saw as being like a rainbow—a description that reminds some people of opal.

A scientific description of opal is that "it is made up of layers of precipitated silica spheres . . . [that] sometimes produce a diffraction grating, that creates play of rainbow sparkling light from within the stone" (www.theimage.com). Such a description is pretty dull stuff until we get to the phrase "rainbow sparkling light." That grabs our attention! A cut-and-dried scientific description simply cannot do justice to the beauty of the opal (or most other gemstones, for that matter). You have to see it to believe it.

That's probably what John felt as he was trying to find words to describe for us what it was like to stand in front of the throne of God. Paper and ink descriptions of all of those wondrous phenomena give us only a faint hint of the glory we shall behold when we meet our Lord in Heaven. What a future we have!   —C. R. B.

B. ELDERS AROUND THE THRONE (v. 4)

4. Surrounding the throne were twenty-four other thrones, and seated on them were twenty-four elders. They were dressed in white and had crowns of gold on their heads.

DAILY BIBLE READINGS

Monday, Apr. 9—Praise to a Gracious God (Psalm 145:8-12)

Tuesday, Apr. 10—Great Is Our God (Psalm 111)

Wednesday, Apr. 11—God's Eternal Purpose (Ephesians 3:7-13)

Thursday, Apr. 12—None Is Like God (Jeremiah 10:6-10)

Friday, Apr. 13—Live a Life of Love (Ephesians 4:25–5:2)

Saturday, Apr. 14—Endure Hardships (Revelation 2:1–7)

Sunday, Apr. 15—God Is Worthy of Praise (Revelation 4)

WHAT DO YOU THINK?

What cautions should be given to readers in terms of how the different images of this text are interpreted?

Visual for Lesson 7. *Post this visual to start a discussion about the heart of worship. Ask, "Why is God, and only God, worthy of worship?"*

Surrounding God's throne are 24 *other thrones*, occupied by Heaven's *elders*. Who these elders are is not explained, but we have a few clues. They are not angels (see Revelation 7:11). Instead, they seem to be humans who have been installed into a position of honor. This is shown by their garb and their right to wear *crowns* in God's presence.

Numbers have special significance in Revelation. Twelve is the number for the people of God. Twelve was the number of the tribes of Israel (Exodus 24:4; 28:21). Twelve was also the number of disciples chosen by Jesus to be his apostles (Mark 3:14). Jesus himself had promised these 12 that they would be seated on thrones of judgment (Matthew 19:28). The number 24 is double 12. As a bit of speculation, this group of elders may therefore represent the combined peoples of God from the Old Testament and the New Testament: the faithful of Israel and the church.

C. SPIRIT OF THE THRONE (v. 5)

5. From the throne came flashes of lightning, rumblings and peals of thunder. Before the throne, seven lamps were blazing. These are the seven spirits of God.

In the book of Revelation, *lightning* and *thunder* are signs that a significant event is about to take place (compare Exodus 19:16). Such activity marks the last of the seven seals (Revelation 8:5), the seventh trumpet (11:19), and the seventh bowl of God's wrath (16:18). These supernatural fireworks are tied to the spiritual activity originating from *the throne*.

Seven is the number of perfection in Revelation (compare Zechariah 4:2). *The seven spirits* represent the perfect Spirit, thus the Holy Spirit. John sees the Holy Spirit as attendant before the throne of God, ready to do God's bidding.

III. WORSHIP IN HEAVEN (REVELATION 4:6-11)

The description of the scene of worship and its participants continues.

A. DESCRIPTION OF THE FOUR BEASTS (vv. 6-8a)

6. Also before the throne there was what looked like a sea of glass, clear as crystal.

The *sea* is seen in the ancient world as the most violent, uncontrollable force of nature. God's mastery of his created world is often symbolized by his ability to control the sea (see Psalm 89:9). So also Jesus' ability to calm the raging sea (Mark 4:39), and to even walk on its surface (Mark 6:48), are signs of his divinity and power. This sea in Heaven is in utter submission to God, with a surface as smooth as *glass*. This is a vivid symbol of God's power and authority.

6b. In the center, around the throne, were four living creatures, and they were covered with eyes, in front and in back.

The number *four* in Revelation is symbolic of the entire created world. These *living creatures* have *eyes* that observe everything. They are symbols of God's omnipresence (his presence everywhere) and omniscience (his knowledge of all things). They are able to give coverage to the four corners of the earth, to all of the created world (compare Revelation 7:1).

7, 8a. The first living creature was like a lion, the second was like an ox, the third had a face like a man, the fourth was like a flying eagle. Each of the four living creatures had six wings and was covered with eyes all around, even under his wings.

John notices individual differences in *the four living creatures*. As with many of the things seen by John, the beasts are reminiscent of images from the Old Testament. In this case we are reminded of the four "living creatures" seen by the prophet in Ezekiel 1:5-15. The creatures in that vision each had four faces. The list of faces there is quite similar to the list here.

What do these beasts symbolize? A very old explanation ties them to the four Gospels. In this interpretation Matthew is the *lion*, the king of the beasts, because he presents Jesus as the king of the Jews. Mark is the *ox*, the dependable servant animal, because he presents Jesus as the servant of all humanity. Luke is the *man*, because he presents Jesus as the Son of Man. John is the *eagle*, the imperial symbol of the Romans, because he presents Jesus as the exalted Son of God. This explanation has been used to give a picture symbol for each of the Gospels.

A less complicated explanation is that the faces represent various qualities of God. Under this theory, the lion symbolizes God's power; the ox symbolizes God's faithfulness; the man symbolizes God's intelligence; and the eagle symbolizes God's sovereignty.

A more likely explanation is that these four creatures represent the general categories of creatures on the earth: wild animals (lion), domesticated animals (ox), human beings (man), and creatures of the sky (eagle). Thus, the picture is related to the number four, the symbol for the created world.

The detail of the *six wings* ties this vision to Isaiah's vision of Heaven (Isaiah 6). There the creatures above the throne are described as six-winged seraphim. A seraph is a heavenly creature.

B. Worship by the Four Beasts (vv. *8b, 9*)

8b. Day and night they never stop saying:

> *"Holy, holy, holy*
> *is the Lord God Almighty,*
> *who was, and is, and is to come."*

The four beasts have the function of ceaseless litany concerning the one seated on the throne. The threefold *Holy, holy, holy* is also found in Isaiah 6:3. This is an emphatic way of stressing God's unique holiness. (Interestingly, although the Bible says that "God is love," the Bible never describes him as "love, love, love.")

John must be impressed that he is being allowed to view the center of all holiness. The words of the beasts tie this to John's initial description of God as the ageless one (Revelation 1:4).

9. Whenever the living creatures give glory, honor and thanks to him who sits on the throne and who lives for ever and ever,

We now begin to understand the function of the four *living creatures* more clearly. They serve as leaders of worship for the heavenly throng (especially when we see v. 9 and v. 10 together). There are four aspects to these words of worship. First, they give *glory* to God. The Bible teaches that we are to do this (see 1 Corinthians 10:31). To ascribe glory is to recognize God's greatness and power. Second, they *honor* God. To honor means to recognize sovereignty, to place oneself as a loyal vassal. Those in the ancient world are expected to honor the king (see 1 Peter 2:17). When we honor God, we are acknowledging his kingship in our lives.

Third, they give *thanks* to God. To give thanks is recognition of God's provisions for us and our dependence upon him. Our need to give thanks to God will never end (see Psalm 30:12). Fourth, the four beasts recognize a central attribute of God: his eternality. God, the eternal one, *lives for ever and ever.*

A Heavenly Menagerie

We humans have always found animals fascinating; this probably started when Adam first gave them names in the Garden of Eden. Just look at all the money we

What Do You Think?

Today's lesson might tempt one to assume that the complete spiritual emphasis in Heaven means that secular issues on earth are totally unimportant! How do you resist the temptation to think this way?

THOUGHT TO REMEMBER

Worship of God is primary.

spend on our dogs and cats! From what we can learn of Solomon's knowledge and dealings with animals, we can speculate that he may well have had a royal zoo in Jerusalem (1 Kings 4:33; 10:22).

Modern zoo-keeping has been dated to 1752 with the establishment of the Imperial Menagerie in Vienna. It is still open to the public. Today every large city and many smaller ones have zoos or wild animal parks. What a delight it is to see the "zoo babies" every spring!

Do we find it surprising, then, that the God who created such a huge assortment of beasts in the first place would also take delight in having some of them serving him around his heavenly throne? Whatever symbolism we see in this, one thing seems certain: in Heaven all of God's creatures will join in praising him. Should the only creatures who are created in God's own image not praise him daily?   —C. R. B.

C. ELDERS CAST THEIR CROWNS (vv. 10, 11)

10. . . . the twenty-four elders fall down before him who sits on the throne, and worship him who lives for ever and ever. They lay their crowns before the throne and say:

The 24 *elders* follow the lead of the *living creatures* and now offer their own worship. They do this with a remarkable, unforgettable act: they bow and offer their *crowns*. In so doing they release any claim to their own separate authority and autonomy. They are completely devoted to the service of God.

11. "You are worthy, our Lord and God,
    to receive glory and honor and power,
  for you created all things,
    and by your will they were created
    and have their being."

The words of the elders are similar to those of the beasts, with a couple of additions. For one thing, they emphasize the elders' own *created* nature. They are nothing without God. They would not even exist without a creator.

Another addition is the utterance *you are worthy.* This is the very heart of worship: acknowledging the one who is worthy. In an absolute sense, God is the only one worthy to be praised (Psalm 18:3). When we understand worship as spiritual submission to God, we count him as worthy of any possible praise. He is then our king and master, and we are his blessed servants.

CONCLUSION

Is the worship service at your church real worship or is it entertainment? Evaluate it by asking this question: is the congregation the *consumer* of worship or is it the *producer* of worship? In other words, are those gathered for worship thought of as the audience or as participants?

Worship, whether individual or corporate, should have the same purposes as given in the heavenly scene of Revelation 4. We can use this text to ask these evaluative questions: Is what we are doing in any way ascribing worthiness to God? Specifically, are we either giving God honor by our submission, giving God glory by our praise, or giving God thanks by the gratefulness of our hearts?

There is indeed an audience in the worship service, but it should be an audience of one: the Lord God. We may do other things at the weekly meeting time of a congregation, but let us not mistake them for worship. Let us renew our commitment to worship God "in spirit and in truth" (John 4:24).

WHAT DO YOU THINK?

How can we arrange the content and style of our worship to honor God adequately for all his great deeds?

[Caution: Be careful not to let this question turn into a gripe session about the current way your church conducts worship.]

WHAT DO YOU THINK?

If your church organized its worship to match the worship pattern in Heaven, what would change? How do you think the changes would be accepted? Before we think about changing a current pattern or routine, should we think first about changing our awareness that in worship we are talking and singing to God as our audience? Why, or why not?

Discovery Learning

*This page contains an alternative lesson plan emphasizing learning activities. Classes
desiring such student involvement will find these suggestions helpful. The next page
is a reproducible activity page to further enhance discovery learning.*

LEARNING GOALS

After this lesson, each student will be able to:

1. Describe the praise offered to the Lord in the throne room scene.

2. Tell the significance of some of the elements of worship in Heaven as presented in Revelation 4.

3. Suggest one specific way to improve his or her personal approach to worship.

INTO THE LESSON

Distribute paper and pencils (or direct attention to the student book, if using those). Ask students to draw two pictures or write two descriptions. The first will be a picture or description of worship in Heaven as it is portrayed in popular culture. The second will be a picture or description of worship in Heaven as the student imagines it will be. Each picture or description should relate what the scene will look like, who will be there, and what they will be doing. (Caution your students not to attempt to draw a picture of God himself.)

When they finish, ask volunteers to display their artwork or read their descriptions to the class. Discuss the most common images (perhaps floating on clouds, playing harps, singing hymns) and ask your class why those images are so widely held. Then tell your students that today's lesson will deal with a vision of worship in Heaven described by John in Revelation 4.

INTO THE WORD

Select 10 students to read Revelation 4 aloud. One will read the statements made by John (the "I" passages). Another will be the voice "like a trumpet." Four more will read, together, the words spoken by the 4 living creatures. The remaining 4 students will represent the elders. If you have fewer than 10 students, use the same 4 students to represent the living creatures and the elders.

After the reading, discuss the meaning of the text. Use your lesson commentary and the questions that follow to guide the discussion.

1. Whose voice was like a trumpet (v. 1)? See Revelation 1:10-18.

2. Knowing that God is invisible (Colossians 1:14; 1 Timothy 1:17), what is the significance of John's description of his appearance and of the appearance of his throne in verse 3?

3. Who are the 24 elders? What is represented by their number and dress?

4. What is the significance of the thunder and lightning (v. 5)? Who are (or is) the seven spirits of God?

5. What is the meaning of the sea of glass in verse 6?

6. How similar are the four living creatures to the creatures in Ezekiel 1:5-15? What do these beasts represent? What are the four aspects of their worship listed in verse 9?

7. Why did the elders cast their crowns before God's throne? How do their words of worship compare with those of the four living creatures?

8. From this passage, what key elements or aspects of heavenly worship can we deduce? Why is each essential to proper worship?

As you discuss question eight, list this heading on the board: *Key Elements of Worship*. Under the heading, list the four aspects of worship mentioned in verses 9-11: *GLORY* (giving glory to God for his greatness and power); *HONOR* (honoring God for his sovereignty); *THANKS* (thanking God for his provision); *RECOGNITION* (recognizing God's eternality). Discuss.

INTO LIFE

Say, "One of the initiatives of the sixteenth-century Reformation was the renewed emphasis on congregational involvement in worship, including congregational singing. Many believed the New Testament pattern for worship included the participation of every member of the congregation. With that in mind and in light of today's text, how do you respond to the following situations?"

1. Tim doesn't like to sing or participate in worship. He prefers to sit back and enjoy the music from the praise team, choir, and soloists. He just wants to be part of the audience and "soak it all in." How do you get him involved?

2. Jennifer loves to sing, and she considers that to be the "real" worship in the worship service. She doesn't see a reason to read Scripture in church ("We do enough of that in Bible school"), and she thinks the sermons are boring. Prayer is for private devotions, not public worship. How would you correct her misconceptions?

What to Do in Heaven?

What will we do in Heaven? Read Revelation 4:1-11. Then unscramble each of the words on the left and write the word in the spaces provided to the right. After unscrambling all the words, copy the emphasized letters to the designated spaces below to find out what we will do in Heaven.

METTRUP (v. 1) 1. _ _ _ _ ☐ _ _

HOTNER (v. 2) 2. _ ☐ _ ☐ _ _

BRANWOI (v. 3) 3. ☐ _ _ _ _ _ _

RIPSSIT (v. 5) 4. ☐ _ _ _ _ _

MYTHALGI (v. 8) 5. _ _ _ ☐ _ _ _

WRONCS (v. 10) 6. _ _ _ ☐ _ _

___ ___ ___ ___ ___ ___ ___
6   2   3   4   2   5   1

Worship Covenant

After studying the key elements of worship for today's lesson, plan to emphasize one in your personal worship each day this week. You might sing an appropriate hymn, read a relevant passage of Scripture, and/or pray a particular prayer to focus on that element. If you agree to do this, sign the worship covenant below and put it where it will remind you.

I, _____, agree to spend a portion of my devotional time each day this week focusing on a key element of worship. That key element for me will be _____.

Signed: _____

Date: _____

CHRIST IS ABLE TO REDEEM

LESSON 8

WHY TEACH THIS LESSON?

When I was completing my Master of Divinity degree, I had to travel about 500 miles for my oral exams. Some students from the Bible college where I teach went with me, because we were going to attend a conference as well. On the trip they knew of my anxiety concerning facing one of the professors, a well-known and well-respected man. The students kept saying that when they saw this man they would talk to him on my behalf, and everything would be fine.

When we arrived in the city, the first thing we did was go to a restaurant near the seminary for lunch. We were seated, and at the next table was this professor. I introduced these "big talking" students to him, but they said not a word beyond "It's nice to meet you." When they were in the presence of this professor, they were in awe and did not follow through on any of their promises.

How much more awe is due to Christ, our redeemer! An attitude of humble worship is always called for when we are in the presence of Christ. Today's lesson will show us why.

INTRODUCTION

A. JESUS AS THE LAMB

"Look, the Lamb of God," proclaimed John the Baptist (John 1:29, 36). This introduces a major theme in John's Gospel: Jesus as our Passover lamb. The apostle John (who is not the same as John the Baptist) ties the death of Jesus closely to the celebration of the Passover in Jerusalem (see John 13:1; 19:14, 15).

The lamb of Passover was a tradition the Jews had observed for over a thousand years by the time Jesus arrived on the scene. It was at the center of the feast of Passover, a commemoration of God's deliverance of Israel from Egyptian slavery. In Egypt the children of Israel had been commanded to kill lambs and smear their blood outside their doors. This act of faith caused God's agent of death to "pass over" marked dwellings and not inflict God's final plague: the death of the household's firstborn son.

Paul wrote that, "Christ, our passover lamb, has been sacrificed" (1 Corinthians 5:7). When we look at the regulations for the Passover lamb, some striking parallels to Christ are found. The lamb was to be without defect (Exodus 12:5); the apostle Peter described Jesus as "a lamb without blemish or defect" (1 Peter 1:19). The Passover lamb was to have no bone broken (Exodus 12:46); John included this detail into his account of Jesus' death, telling us that his legs were not broken by the Roman executioners (John 19:36).

The most remarkable parallel is that, according to Jewish tradition, the Passover lambs were killed by priests within the Jerusalem temple precincts, and then taken to homes for the feast. At 3 PM on Passover day, the high priest would slaughter the final lamb, saying, "It is finished." If we combine Mark 15:34 and John 19:30, we can see that it was at 3 PM on (what we call) Good Friday when Jesus uttered the words "It is finished" as he died for the sin of the world.

DEVOTIONAL READING:
PSALM 107:1-9
BACKGROUND SCRIPTURE:
REVELATION 5
PRINTED TEXT:
REVELATION 5:1-5, 8-14

LESSON AIMS

After participating in this lesson, each student will be able to:

1. List the three titles of Jesus as found in Revelation 5.

2. Identify how the titles of Jesus explain his power and authority to redeem.

3. Design a worship service that incorporates the titles of Christ.

Apr
22

KEY VERSE

"You are worthy to take the scroll and to open its seals, because you were slain, and with your blood you purchased men for God from every tribe and language and people and nation."
—Revelation 5:9

The designation of *Lamb* is the most common way of referring to the risen Jesus in the book of Revelation, used some two dozen times there. A marvelous picture emerges if we examine these verses: the Lamb shares the judgmental wrath of God (Revelation 6:16); the Lamb's blood cleanses his people from sin (7:14); the Lamb is the author of the book of life (13:8); the Lamb has a song akin to the song of Moses (15:3); the Lamb leads the victorious armies of Heaven (17:14); and the Lamb will be the light of new Jerusalem (21:23). A central, climactic event in Revelation is the marriage supper of the Lamb (19:7-9).

The Passover lambs of the Jews symbolized purity, sacrifice, and escape from God's wrath. The book of Revelation uses all of these attributes in drawing its picture of the Lamb. The book adds truths that the Christ-Lamb is victorious over death and over the enemies of God. This mighty image deserves our study!

B. LESSON BACKGROUND

Last week's lesson looked at the opening scene of John's vision of Heaven. We found a breathtaking tableau of worship before the throne of God, led by the 4 creatures that attend the throne. The worship was joined by 24 honored elders. Study of this scene allowed us to understand the heart of true worship. This week's lesson continues in that vein, but worship has ceased temporarily. The reasons for its pause and for its resumption are key elements of Revelation 5.

A central item in this chapter is a certain scroll (compare Isaiah 29:11). This scroll represents the mystery of God's gracious salvation and of his judgmental wrath. The scroll is closed by seven seals.

The breaking of each seal in the following chapters brings about symbolic events tied to the grim judgments of God. While the images are terrifying, we who are in Christ can rest assured that God's punishing anger will not be visited upon us. Our names are written in the Lamb's book of life. We have overcome by the blood of the Lamb (Revelation 12:11).

I. LAMB REVEALED IN HEAVEN (REVELATION 5:1-5)

The first part of Revelation 5 focuses on a mysterious scroll. We are not told where it originated. We (like John) desire to know its hidden meanings. But we cannot know the scroll's content unless it is revealed and "decoded" for us.

A. SCROLL (v. 1)

1. Then I saw in the right hand of him who sat on the throne a scroll with writing on both sides and sealed with seven seals.

The scroll in view has leaves sewn end to end and rolled around a wooden rod. This makes it possible to seal the outer edge. This is similar to what we find on a new roll of paper towels, where the beginning of the roll is stuck to the main body and must be peeled away for use. Another theory is that the *seven seals* are found one after the other, in a sequence, as the scroll is unrolled a little at a time.

The *seven seals* give a high sense of the importance to the scroll's contents. The book of Revelation uses the number *seven* 55 times. Seven is this book's number for perfection. The number *seven* here tells us that the scroll contains the perfect message of God. It awaits its revelation to John and the heavenly audience.

A further intriguing detail is that the scroll has *writing on both sides*. We can imagine the practical difficulties in using a scroll that has text on both sides, so this is not the common practice of ancient scribes. Usually a scroll has writing only on the inner side for ease of use. Writing on both sides gives the sense that the scroll is crammed with very important information, more data than a normal scroll can contain (compare Ezekiel 2:9, 10). This heightens our desire to know the contents.

B. CRISIS (vv. 2-4)

2. And I saw a mighty angel proclaiming in a loud voice, "Who is worthy to break the seals and open the scroll?"

The *scroll* cannot be opened without breaking *the seals*. The seal on government correspondence in the ancient world is more than a way of keeping the document closed. The nature of the seal determines who has the authority to break it and read the document. For example, a document sealed with the emperor's imprint can be viewed only by an official of the highest level (compare Esther 3:12; 8:10).

This scroll is rated top secret, and not just anyone can break its seals. The one who opens it must have the proper authority—that is, must be found *worthy*. This question of worthiness is tied to worship in these chapters. The one with ultimate authority is worthy, and therefore properly deserving of worship.

3. But no one in heaven or on earth or under the earth could open the scroll or even look inside it.

Presumably, the one seated on the throne (God) can *open the scroll*. But he is the one who has prepared and sealed it in the first place. God waits for someone with adequate authority to come for it, someone having authority approved by him. John is aware that none of his fellow creatures, whether human or angelic, has the requisite authority to break the seals and open the scroll. This is because none of them is worthy.

4. I wept and wept because no one was found who was worthy to open the scroll or look inside.

The facts of verse 3 cause what we may deem to be a strange reaction in John: weeping. He feels the crisis deeply. We can infer that he is sad for two reasons. First, he has a strong desire to know the contents of the scroll, both for himself and so that he may be able to share the contents with his fellow believers (see Revelation 1:1). When that happens, humans may know better how to proceed with God's plans. Second, John realizes that no human is *worthy* of this task, not even him. Much like Isaiah, John is overwhelmed by his own unworthiness (Isaiah 6:5). God has established the standard of worthiness, and apparently no one measures up to it.

C. LION AND ROOT (v. 5)

5. Then one of the elders said to me, "Do not weep! See, the Lion of the tribe of Judah, the Root of David, has triumphed. He is able to open the scroll and its seven seals."

John's weeping is short-lived. There is indeed one worthy to break the seals and unroll the scroll. He is called the *Lion of the tribe of Judah* (compare Genesis 49:9) and the *Root of David*. Both of these are obvious titles for the Messiah, the risen Christ. However, the exact phrase *Root of David* is not found in the Old Testament (see Isaiah 11:10, "Root of Jesse," realizing that Jesse was King David's father). Sometimes the Old Testament prophets refer to the Messiah as the *Branch* of David who originates from David's dynasty (see Jeremiah 23:5; 33:15). This was true of the earthly Jesus, a rightful descendant of David (Matthew 1:1).

But in his eternal fullness, the Messiah is not derivative of the house of David. Rather, just the reverse is true: that house is dependent upon him. The preexistent Christ is the source of the promise to David. This was taught by Jesus when

WHAT DO YOU THINK?

In what ways could an observer tell by your actions that your heart has ached because God's plans were seemingly thwarted and that he was not being glorified as he deserves?

HOW TO SAY IT

Antipas. AN-tih-pus.

Corinthians. Ko-RIN-thee-unz.

Domitian. Duh-MISH-un.

Ezekiel. Ee-ZEEK-ee-ul *or* Ee-ZEEK-yul.

Isaiah. Eye-ZAY-uh.

Navajo. NA-vuh-ho.

he pointed out that David prophetically referred to the Messiah as "my Lord" (Luke 20:41-44).

NAVAJO CODE TALKERS

Navajo code talkers took part in every U.S. Marine battle in the Pacific between 1942 and 1945. Fewer than 30 non-Navajos could speak the language at the time. One of them was Philip Johnston, son of a missionary who grew up on a Navajo reservation. He persuaded the U.S. government that Navajo was the perfect code language (www.history.navy.mil). An unwritten language, Navajo uses a very complex syntax and tonal system.

To make the code work, a series of unrelated Navajo words were first translated into English equivalents. Then the first letters of the equivalents were used to spell English words. To make the code even harder to crack, most English letters could be signified by more than one Navajo word. The skilled Japanese code breakers couldn't break this one!

Some have seen the Bible as a book of codes—codes that we should try to "break." Indeed, the idea of *mystery* or *secret* is found in many places in the Bible (examples: Daniel 2:18, 19, 27, 30; Romans 11:25; 16:25; Colossians 1:26, 27). The secrets of the book that John saw revealed were more inscrutable than those protected by any human code. We should not be surprised that only God can reveal those secrets. This might also be good advice to heed when someone offers the supposedly "one-and-only true" interpretation of the book of Revelation!

—C. R. B.

II. LAMB WORSHIPED IN HEAVEN (REVELATION 5:8-14)

The Messiah now appears. But he is not as a muscle-bound superhero. He is a lamb. He is not a cute, docile lamb, however, but a powerful, bold being. He has the appearance of having been slaughtered (Revelation 5:6, not in today's text), probably meaning his white wool is smeared with blood. He has seven horns, symbolizing perfect, absolute authority. He also has the seven spirits, the Holy Spirit of God, at his disposal (again, 5:6). His authority and worthiness are unquestioned. The enthroned God gladly allows him to take the scroll in preparation for its opening (5:7).

A. BEASTS AND ELDERS (v. 8)

8. And when he had taken it, the four living creatures and the twenty-four elders fell down before the Lamb. Each one had a harp and they were holding golden bowls full of incense, which are the prayers of the saints.

With the appearance of *the Lamb* on the scene, the worship resumes. Now, however, the Lamb himself is the object of worship as signified by the *elders* bowing before him. There are two added elements: *harps* and *bowls*. Now we can imagine the beautiful strains of a heavenly harp orchestra. Present in the bowls are *the prayers* of believers, which add the aroma of sweet incense to the worship (compare Psalm 141:2).

B. NEW SONG (vv. 9, 10)

9. And they sang a new song:
    "You are worthy to take the scroll
        and to open its seals,
    because you were slain,
        and with your blood you purchased men for God
        from every tribe and language and people and nation.

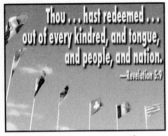

Thou . . . hast redeemed . . . out of every kindred, and tongue, and people, and nation.
—Revelation 5:9

Visual for Lesson 8. *This visual can remind your students that there are more than six billion people on the earth. Ask, "How will we reach them?"*

Further evidence of the level of worship given the Lamb is found in the singing of a *new song*. In the Old Testament, the new song was always sung to God as an act of worship (Psalm 33:3; 40:3; 96:1; 98:1; 144:9; Isaiah 42:10).

Two things motivate this great worship celebration for the Lamb. Most basic, He appears in Heaven as the redeemer for the people of God. He has been slain as an atoning sacrificial victim. The price of his blood has brought redemption to many, both Jew and Gentile. Jesus' death is not seen as a defeat but as a victory (Revelation 5:5, he has "prevailed"). Second, he is acclaimed because his triumphant sacrifice has made him worthy to solve the current crisis: break the *seals* and *open* the scroll.

10. "You have made them to be a kingdom and priests to serve our God, and they will reign on the earth."

The idea of a priestly kingdom has already been introduced (Revelation 1:6; compare 1 Peter 2:5, 9). This was the ideal for Israel as God's holy nation (see Exodus 19:6). The promises we see here are encouraging to John's first readers, who are under persecution from the Roman Empire.

C. Host of Angels (vv. 11, 12)

11. Then I looked and heard the voice of many angels, numbering thousands upon thousands, and ten thousand times ten thousand. They encircled the throne and the living creatures and the elders.

The song of the elders is now joined by a seemingly infinite host of heavenly *angels*. Saying *ten thousand times ten thousand* is not a precise mathematical formula but is more like our exuberant expression "gazillions." They are innumerable (compare Daniel 7:10; Hebrews 12:22). This glorious scene is beyond our imagination.

12. In a loud voice they sang: "Worthy is the Lamb, who was slain, to receive power and wealth and wisdom and strength and honor and glory and praise!"

The worship from the angels is sevenfold, the perfect combination. It encompasses vitally important qualifications for worthiness: *power* (ability), *wealth* (riches), *wisdom* (intellect), *strength* (might), *honor* (esteem), *glory* (majesty), and *praise* (approval). See 1 Chronicles 29:11, 12.

D. Universal Chorus (vv. 13, 14)

13, 14. Then I heard every creature in heaven and on earth and under the earth and on the sea, and all that is in them, singing:
"To him who sits on the throne and to the Lamb
be praise and honor and glory and power, for ever and ever!"
The four living creatures said, "Amen," and the elders fell down and worshiped.

The worship chorus is now joined by *every creature*. The celebration is so great that even *heaven* cannot contain it! The acclamation of the creatures is fourfold, symbolic of the entire world, repeating four of the items from the angelic song.

This song is also reminiscent of the original song of God's worthiness in Revelation 4:11, with one key difference: the worship now includes *the Lamb*—Jesus Christ, the risen one. The redeemer of humanity is worthy of worship, and no human king is similarly deserving. The scene ends on a high note with the worship by the 4 *living creatures* and the 24 *elders*. They worship unreservedly, counting the Lamb as worthy as the one who sits on the *throne*.

This powerful, moving description of heavenly worship is as inspiring today as it was when John first wrote it. We see in it the great esteem and worthiness that all Heaven accords to the risen Jesus, our redeemer and Lord.

WHAT DO YOU THINK?

Do you think we should limit the types of our praise to the model found in the book of Revelation? Why, or why not? (In addition to Revelation 5, see also chapters 4 and 7.)

WHAT DO YOU THINK?

How can your church use the imagery of Jesus' sacrifice to persuade young people to enter missionary service? How hard would it be for you personally to see your child go overseas for missionary work?

WHAT DO YOU THINK?

There is no doubt: Christians have specific preferences about how worship should be conducted! How can we help one another become more open to different ways of worship?

PRAYER

To God, the one who sits on the throne, we offer our praise, our honor, and our blessings. To the Lamb, our redeemer, we offer our deepest thanks and devotion. In Jesus' name, amen.

HEAVENLY MUSIC

Is there any piece of music composed by a human being that would be worthy of being sung before the very throne of God? Some believe that the "Hallelujah Chorus" could be it!

Handel composed this chorus in 1741 as part of his famous *Messiah* oratorio. That was a difficult year for Handel. He was trying to get by on a very small income and it was bringing him to despair. Creditors were hounding him. But one day he received a thick envelope from Charles Jennens, a wealthy admirer of Handel's music. Inside the envelope was page after page of carefully chosen Scripture passages that Jennens thought should be set to music.

Handel was inspired! Over the next few weeks he worked day and night on the piece of music that was burning in his soul. When he had finished, he exclaimed, "I do believe I have seen all of Heaven before me and the great God himself!" Audiences since Handel's day have seemed to agree, especially given the tradition of rising to one's feet during the "Hallelujah Chorus." We may be sure that the great chorus of praise in Heaven will be even more glorious!   —C. R. B.

CONCLUSION

One of the burning issues of John's day was the danger of worshiping false gods. Under the reign of Emperor Domitian, citizens were required to do a yearly act of worship to the "genius" of the emperor—something Christians refused to do. For this they were persecuted, some even to death. John knew that one of the seven churches of Asia had suffered the martyrdom of a faithful member named Antipas (Revelation 2:13). Revelation tells the horrible story of people who worshiped a false god. This may be code language for emperor worship (see Revelation 19:20; 20:4).

There are two sides to the coin of worship. On one side is the principle that *worship is for God and only for God.* If there is another recipient of worship, worship has become idolatry, the most grievous sin in the Bible. When John falls down to worship an angel, he is admonished, "Do not do it . . . worship God!" (Revelation 19:10). This is an absolute in the Bible. There is only one God, and he alone is worthy of worship.

The other side of the coin is that acts *of worship clearly reveal who a person's god is.* We may claim to worship God, but the way we live our lives will show what we really count as worthy. It may be ourselves. It may be a political philosophy. It may be wealth and pleasure. We see Paul's awareness of this when he writes of those whose "god is their stomach" (Philippians 3:19).

With these principles in mind, we are confronted with a difficult dilemma. If there is only one God, and he alone is worthy of worship, where does Jesus, the redeeming Lamb, fit in? If we worship God and his Son, are we guilty of worshiping two Gods?

We may not have an exhaustive answer to this question because it hinges on the mystery of God's Trinitarian nature. The doctrine of the Trinity defies human logic, because it claims in a certain sense that $1+1+1=1$. Some have therefore had an aversion to doing anything that seems like direct worship of Jesus.

This is not what we find in the picture of worship supplied by John. Once the Lamb enters the scene, worship is directed, unreservedly, to the one sitting on the throne (God) *and* to the Lamb (Revelation 5:13). This combination appears several times in the book (example: Revelation 22:1). It is proper and fitting to worship Jesus the Lamb, who redeemed us by taking away our sin. This is the Jesus we have a relationship with today. He is seated at the right hand of God in Heaven. Jesus should be counted as worthy in our hearts and in our worship.

WHAT DO YOU THINK?

How does today's text provide you hope to face ongoing struggles? In what ways does it help you resist the temptation to follow another religion and the temptation to trust materialism instead of Christ?

THOUGHT TO REMEMBER

Honor Jesus in your worship.

Discovery Learning

This page contains an alternative lesson plan emphasizing learning activities. Classes desiring such student involvement will find these suggestions helpful. The next page is a reproducible activity page to further enhance discovery learning.

LEARNING GOALS

After this lesson, each student will be able to:

1. List the three titles of Jesus as found in Revelation 5.

2. Identify how the titles of Jesus explain his power and authority to redeem.

3. Design a worship service that incorporates the titles of Christ.

INTO THE LESSON

To begin today's lesson, ask your students to match each U.S. president listed below with his nickname or description. Also ask your students if they can explain the origin of each nickname. This exercise also is found in the student book.

___ 1. John Adams	a. Old Hickory
___ 2. Andrew Jackson	b. Peanut Farmer
___ 3. W. H. Harrison	c. Ol' Tippecanoe
___ 4. Abraham Lincoln	d. Comeback Kid
___ 5. James A. Garfield	e. His Rotundity
___ 6. Theodore Roosevelt	f. Emancipator
___ 7. Harry Truman	g. The Gipper
___ 8. Jimmy Carter	h. Preacher
___ 9. Ronald Reagan	i. Rough Rider
___ 10. Bill Clinton	j. Haberdasher

Answers: 1e. Adams was chubby! 2a. Jackson was a strict military disciplinarian, "as hard as hickory"; 3c. Harrison won the battle of Tippecanoe in 1811; 4f. Lincoln, The Great Emancipator, authored the Emancipation Proclamation to free slaves; 5h. Before his entrance into politics, this Preacher President was a Disciples of Christ minister; 6i. Roosevelt led the Rough Riders during the Spanish-American War; 7j. "Haberdasher Harry" Truman was co-owner of a hat store following World War I; 8b. Carter owned a peanut farm; 9g. Reagan played George Gipp in the film *Knute Rockne, All American;* 10d. Clinton was defeated following his first term as governor of Arkansas but then came back to win re-election to several more terms. (*Alternative:* distribute the His Name Is . . . activity from the reproducible page for students to work on as they arrive.)

After you review answers, say, "Today's lesson includes three titles or descriptions of Jesus found in Revelation 5. Presidents' nicknames are related to their accomplishments, background, etc. So too Jesus' titles are related to his accomplishments and background."

INTO THE WORD

Introduce this section with a brief lecture on Revelation 5:1-5, using both the Lesson Background and the commentary. Focus on the significance of "Lion of . . . Judah" and "Root of David."

Next, divide your class into small groups. Each group will research the title "Lamb of God." Distribute the following questions and Scripture passages to each group (or direct their attention to the student book). Suggested answers follow each question, but don't distribute those.

1. For what sacrifices and rituals did the Old Testament specify the use of a lamb? See Exodus 12:21; 13:1-16; Leviticus 4:32-35. (*For Passover; to redeem the firstborn; for sin offerings.*)

2. What were important characteristics of such a lamb? See Exodus 12:5, 46. (*Had to be without blemish and could not have its bones broken.*)

3. What characteristics did Jesus have in common with the sacrificial lambs of the Old Testament? See John 19:36; Acts 8:32-35; 1 Peter 1:19. (*Bones were not broken on the cross; had no blemish [sin]; was led to slaughter [cross].*)

4. What did Jesus accomplish by his death that relates to the title *Lamb of God*? See John 1:29; Colossians 1:14; Hebrews 9:11-15, 28; 1 Peter 1:18, 19; 1 John 1:7; Revelation 5:9, 10. (*Redeemed us from sinful lives by securing forgiveness for our sins.*)

Ask for volunteers to share answers. Next, direct your students' attention to Revelation 5:8-14. Have a student read the passage aloud and then ask the class how the beasts, elders, and angels around the throne react to the appearance of the Lamb. Why do they worship him? How significant is this, considering that John was commanded to worship only God (Revelation 19:10)?

INTO LIFE

Ask your small groups to design a worship service to honor Christ as the Lamb of God. Provide hymnals or chorus books; have each group choose Scriptures to be read and songs to be sung that reflect that theme. Challenge your students to design creative ways to praise the Lamb with skits, poems, responsive readings, etc.

Have groups share their results. Choose one, or a combination of two or more, to offer to your church's leadership for use.

His Name Is . . .

Match the title, name, or description used for Jesus with the Scripture where it is found. What is the significance of each title or name? Write your ideas at the far right.

Significance

___ 1. Hebrews 5:9	A. Head over everything for the Church	
___ 2. John 6:35	B. Our Passover lamb	
___ 3. 1 Peter 5:4	C. Rock	
___ 4. John 10:7	D. Resurrection and Life	
___ 5. Ephesians 1:22	E. Word of God	
___ 6. Mark 1:24	F. Source of Eternal Salvation	
___ 7. John 8:58	G. Prince of Peace	
___ 8. 2 Corinthians 4:4	H. Messiah	
___ 9. 1 Timothy 6:15	I. King of Kings	
___ 10. John 8:12	J. Bread of Life	
___ 11. 1 Corinthians 5:7	K. Gate	
___ 12. Isaiah 9:6	L. Chief Shepherd	
___ 13. John 11:25	M. Light of the World	
___ 14. 1 Corinthians 10:4	N. Savior	
___ 15. Luke 2:11	O. I Am	
___ 16. Matthew 1:1	P. The Righteous One	
___ 17. Revelation 19:13	Q. Deliverer	
___ 18. John 1:41	R. Image of God	
___ 19. Romans 11:26	S. Holy One of God	
___ 20. 1 John 2:1	T. Son of David	

Answers: 1. F; 2. J; 3. L; 4. K; 5. A; 6. S; 7. O; 8. R; 9. I; 10. M; 11. B; 12. G; 13. D; 14. C; 15. N; 16. T; 17. E; 18. H; 19. Q; 20. P

CHRIST IS OUR PROTECTION

LESSON 9

WHY TEACH THIS LESSON?

Symbols of protection are all around us. Police uniforms, fire trucks, insurance policies—the list is endless. But why does protection seem to disappear just when we need it? When we broke that arm? When we were laid off? When that drunk driver came into our lane?

Through all these troubles, Christ is still our protection! The uniform of protection we wear is a spiritual robe provided by Christ himself. Today's lesson will challenge your students to consider how well their uniform "fits."

INTRODUCTION

A. THE HISTORY OF BLOOD

Blood is a "hot commodity" today—the Red Cross always seems to need blood donors. Yet blood is a dangerous fluid because of medical risks. As a diabetic who travels frequently, I have experienced the discomfort many people feel at the thought of my blood touching them if they have to deal with my blood-soaked testing strips. The HIV/AIDS crisis has made us wary of contact with anything tainted by blood. Yet there is no substitute for whole blood and blood derivatives for many medical procedures. We are scared by blood, but we need it.

In the religions of the ancient world, blood was viewed as sacred. Some ancients saw blood as containing the life principle, even the soul. They did not understand the function of blood. The fact that blood circulated in the body was not well understood until William Harvey's conclusions in about AD 1615.

Blood was widely consumed as a food in the first century AD. This practice was abhorrent to the Jews (Leviticus 7:26; 17:12, 14; 19:26) and was forbidden by the early church (Acts 15:20). Like many of their contemporaries, ancient Jews believed a person's blood contained his or her life. If the blood drained from a person, they knew that that person would die.

Thus life and blood were tightly linked (Deuteronomy 12:23). This helps us understand the frequent phrase *innocent blood*. From our modern, scientific point of view, we cannot imagine blood itself being guilty or innocent any more than hair can be. Yet *innocent blood* conveys the idea of the violent death of an innocent person. To slay an innocent person would bring guilt of bloodshed upon the perpetrator (see Deuteronomy 19:10; compare Psalm 106:38).

The Old Testament taught that human blood was not to be shed in violence (see Genesis 9:6, part of the covenant with Noah). Murder was more than a criminal act; it was an offense against God. There was a sense, then, that all the human blood belonged to God and that humans had no right to abuse it (see Genesis 4:10).

Yet animal blood was an integral part of the Jewish religious system. A dramatic example of this is found in Exodus 24:3-8. In this ceremony of commitment, Moses took fresh animal blood and sprinkled it on the crowds of people (warning: don't try this at your church!). Thus their vow was sealed. The Old Testament

DEVOTIONAL READING:
PSALM 121
BACKGROUND SCRIPTURE:
REVELATION 7
PRINTED TEXT:
REVELATION 7:1-3, 9-17

LESSON AIMS

After participating in this lesson, each student will be able to:

1. Describe the image of Christ as our protector as given in Revelation 7.

2. Explain how Christ serves as his or her protector now.

3. Write a prayer of thankfulness for Christ's protection.

Apr
29

KEY VERSE

"These [in white robes] are they who have come out of the great tribulation; they have washed their robes and made them white in the blood of the Lamb." —Revelation 7:14

WHAT DO YOU THINK?

For the church to talk about the blood of Christ may seem "uncivilized" to some. How would you defuse this problem before it arises? Or have you found this even to be a problem?

taught that blood purifies, as summarized in the New Testament passage Hebrews 9:22: "without the shedding of blood there is no forgiveness [of sins]."

Blood—on the one hand, so abhorrent; on the other hand, so important. Today's lesson looks at Revelation 7, which gives a spectacular picture of the importance of the blood of Jesus for John's readers and for us today.

B. LESSON BACKGROUND

Last week's lesson (Revelation 5) saw a crisis in Heaven resolved by the appearance of the redeeming Lamb of God, the risen Christ. He was deemed worthy to break the seven seals of the mysterious scroll held by God. The Lamb could unroll the scroll to reveal its contents.

Revelation 6 is the account of the breaking of the first six seals. When a seal is broken, various symbolic things happen. The first seal, the white horse, represents the lust for conquest; a good example of this is the Roman Empire (Revelation 6:1, 2). The second seal, the red horse, symbolizes war; this is both the ancient and modern plague of humanity (6:3, 4). The third seal, the black horse, stands for famine; this is a usual consequence of war (6:5, 6). The fourth seal, the pale horse, denotes death; this is the ultimate result of war (6:7, 8). These four seals are a distinct set, sometimes called the Four Horsemen of the Apocalypse.

The fifth seal (Revelation 6:9-11) presents a question from the people of God, "How long, Sovereign Lord?" (6:10). The answer is that they must wait "a little longer" (6:11). While they wait, their confidence is found in the way they address God: "Sovereign Lord, holy and true" (6:10).

The sixth seal (Revelation 6:12-17) is summed up in the statement, "wrath has come" (6:17). It presents a frightening picture of cosmic upheaval when the wrath of God and of the Lamb is unleashed on sinful humanity. Those caught in this cataclysm ask, "Who can stand" against it? (6:17). The answer is not given but is obvious: no one can withstand the unleashed fury of God. This is the day of God's final vindication of his righteousness (see Amos 5:18-20).

The seventh seal does not come until Revelation 8:1. It does not have a distinct event attached to it. Rather, it is the beginning of the next series, the seven trumpets. Chapter 7, our focus in this lesson, is an interlude between the terrifying images of the first six seals and that next sequence. It comes back to answer for the people of God the question, "Who can stand?"

The people of God are the saints pictured in the fifth seal. While no one can withstand God's wrath, there is a protection for the people of God so that they will not have to face it. This protection comes through the blood of the Lamb, our blessed Savior, Jesus Christ.

I. SEAL OF PROTECTION (REVELATION 7:1-3)

While some styles of dress may identify persons as nonbelievers, most Christians look and dress like their non-Christian neighbors. This text teaches that there is a spiritual seal on God's people that somehow marks them.

A. ANGELS CONTROLLING NATURE (v. 1)

1. After this I saw four angels standing at the four corners of the earth, holding back the four winds of the earth to prevent any wind from blowing on the land or on the sea or on any tree.

The number *four* symbolizes the whole *earth* in Revelation. This may be represented by the *four angels* charged with the earth, *the four corners* or quarters of the land (see Revelation 20:8), or *the four winds* that blow upon the earth (compare

Jeremiah 49:36; Ezekiel 37:9; Daniel 7:2; Mark 13:27). The four angels seem to be stewards of the earth. Their actions demonstrate a pause in the furious activities of the previous chapter.

B. ANGEL WITH GOD'S SEAL (vv. 2, 3)

2. Then I saw another angel coming up from the east, having the seal of the living God. He called out in a loud voice to the four angels who had been given power to harm the land and the sea:

Another angel enters the scene like the rising sun (*coming up from the east*), symbolizing the dawning of a new stage in the drama. This angel possesses God's *seal*, giving him the ability to place a spiritual mark on people. This angel also has authority over the four earth-steward *angels*.

3. "Do not harm the land or the sea or the trees until we put a seal on the foreheads of the servants of our God."

The spiritual seal of God is pictured as a mark on the *foreheads* of God's *servants*. Any destruction to be done by the four earth-steward angels is "on hold" until the project of marking all servants of God is accomplished.

This seal on the forehead is a repeated image in this book (see Revelation 9:4; 14:1; 22:4; compare Ezekiel 9:4). It stands in contrast to the "mark of the beast," a type of sealing done on those who are not covered by the blood of the Lamb, whose names are not written in the Lamb's book of life (see Revelation 14:9; 16:2). This mark is equivalent to having worshiped the false god of the beast. The lake of fire awaits those who do (19:20; 20:10, 15).

What is this seal? We should not understand it as a physical mark, like a tattoo or brand. It is spiritual in nature. Many Bible students have equated the sealing with the act of baptism. Paul taught that when we are baptized, we have "clothed [ourselves] with Christ" (Galatians 3:27). Baptism into Christ is connected with receiving the gift of God's Holy Spirit (Acts 2:38); having the Holy Spirit is a type of seal for believers (see Ephesians 1:13).

Those who maintain their trust in Christ are not in danger of having the mark of the beast stamped on their souls. As the next verses show, Christians are protected by the blood of the Lamb.

EXTREME MAKEOVERS

Just a few years ago, *Extreme Makeover* was a popular television program. The concept was to take a person who was "aesthetically challenged," so to speak, and provide cosmetic surgery to help change that person's looks and outlook on life.

One of the people featured on the show was Ray Krone. He had been wrongfully convicted of a murder not once but twice! His first conviction, in 1992, carried the death penalty. But it was overturned because of procedural errors. At his second trial, in 1996, he was again convicted but given a life sentence. DNA testing in 2002 exonerated Krone.

A key piece of the evidence against Krone in both of his convictions was his crooked smile, which supposedly matched bite marks on the victim. That was the feature that led to his being called "the snaggle-tooth killer." So Krone was a perfect candidate for an "extreme makeover"—dental work, hair transplant, nose job—so no one would misidentify him again.

The seal on the foreheads of the righteous is probably not a physical feature. Yet it symbolizes the "extreme makeover" that God does to our spirits when we accept Christ and become his disciples. From that time on, we are different people with a new outlook on life. No one should be able to call us by any of those old epithets we carried when we were rebellious sinners. —C. R. B.

HOW TO SAY IT

Apocalypse. Ah-POCK-uh-lips.
Deuteronomy. Due-ter-AHN-uh-me.
Ephesians. Ee-FEE-zhunz.
Ezekiel. Ee-ZEEK-ee-ul or Ee-ZEEK-yul.
Galatians. Guh-LAY-shunz.
Leviticus. Leh-VIT-ih-kus.

II. PANOPLY OF THE PROTECTED (REVELATION 7:9-12)

Revelation 7:4-8 (not in today's text) introduces the concept of God's people numbering 144,000. This is not to be taken literally, as if Heaven were run by census takers. The number 12, which occurs 35 times in Revelation, is an important number relating to God's people. (See the discussion of the 24 elders of Revelation 4:4 in Lesson 7.) The number 144,000, or 12 times 12,000, refers to the ultimate, multiplied people of God. These are pictured as coming from the nation of Israel, but they are not alone.

A. WHITE-ROBED MULTITUDE (vv. 9, 10)

9. After this I looked and there before me was a great multitude that no one could count, from every nation, tribe, people and language, standing before the throne and in front of the Lamb. They were wearing white robes and were holding palm branches in their hands.

Added to the 144,000 is a countless crowd. The crowd defies any attempt to *count* it. This *multitude* comes from all the families and peoples of the earth, not just Israel. They are uniformly *wearing white robes* (which will be explained later).

They are also carrying palm fronds. This reminds us of Palm Sunday and Jesus' triumphal entry into Jerusalem (John 12:13). It is customary in the ancient world to carry palm branches at celebrations (see Leviticus 23:40 and the non-biblical 1 Maccabees 13:51).

SYMBOLS

A white robe is the customary baptismal garb in many churches. The color white has long symbolized purity.

One of the grim ironies of life is how symbols of goodness and holiness have been misappropriated by the forces of evil. An example is how white robes became a symbol of virulent racism. After America's Civil War, men dressed in white robes and wearing white hoods brought a reign of terror on African-American citizens.

Such ideology continues to have influence even in the early twenty-first century. How ghastly it is that some members of such organizations even thought of themselves as "good Christians." Some even were ministers!

In today's text John sees a multitude of God's people dressed in white standing before his throne. Their robes are a symbol of the righteousness they had found in Christ; their robes are not cloaks for evil deeds and attitudes. Can you think of other ways in which holy symbols are misappropriated to disguise sin?   —C. R. B.

10. And they cried out in a loud voice:
   "Salvation belongs to our God,
   who sits on the throne,
   and to the Lamb."

The Palm Sunday cry of "Hosanna" meant "God, save us!" Understandably, the Jews of Jesus' day were hoping for God's miraculous saving of their nation. The cry, *"Salvation belongs to our God"* is a fulfillment of that Palm Sunday appeal. In Heaven the people of God shout "Salvation!" to celebrate an accomplished fact. They are the multitude of the saved, and the salvation is attributed both to God and to *the Lamb*.

B. HEAVENLY THRONG (vv. 11, 12)

11. All the angels were standing around the throne and around the elders and the four living creatures. They fell down on their faces before the throne and worshiped God,

The multitude of the saved is now joined by the heavenly cast of characters who worship. We saw *angels, the elders, and the four living creatures* back in chapters 4 and 5. As before, they assume a prostrate posture of worship.

12. . . . saying:

"Amen!
Praise and glory
and wisdom and thanks and honor
and power and strength
be to our God for ever and ever.
Amen!"

The throng sings a sevenfold worship chant. It is like their earlier praise song (Revelation 5:12) with the change of *riches* to *thanks. Amen* means "it is true." The long-anticipated salvation of God is now finalized.

III. BLOOD OF PROTECTION (REVELATION 7:13-17)

Most men are not experts at doing laundry. If they are like me, they end up with white sheets tinged pink because they washed them with a new red T-shirt. However, even the worst launderer knows that you need clean water to get clean clothes. You cannot wash white linens in muddy water and make them bright white. Yet Scripture offers an amazing image: robes washed in blood that become purest white.

A. WASHED IN BLOOD (vv. 13, 14)

13. Then one of the elders asked me, "These in white robes—who are they, and where did they come from?"

John again draws the attention of one of the *elders* (see Revelation 5:5). Perhaps John looks confused at this vast array of *white robes*, so the elder poses a question that is already in John's mind: What's going on with all these white-robed people?

14. I answered, "Sir, you know." And he said, "These are they who have come out of the great tribulation; they have washed their robes and made them white in the blood of the Lamb.

John wisely lets the elder answer his own questions. The robed persons have survived *great tribulation*. Some interpreters see this as referring to a specific tribulation period related to Christ's second coming, but that is probably not what is meant. These are the saints who have endured to the end. They have been faithful to the point of death (Revelation 2:10); they have received their crown-of-life reward. This reward is pictured here as the privilege of wearing a *white* robe. It is white, the symbol of purity, because of the cleansing power of the *blood* of Jesus.

We therefore have a startling picture: washing a robe in red, staining blood and having it come out the purest white. The blood of Jesus was the price for our sins. The Bible teaches that blood must be shed for sins to be forgiven (Hebrews 9:22). The blood of Jesus is thus a divine means for our forgiveness. The shedding of Jesus' blood paid the price that God decreed for sin's punishment. We can have our guilt taken away (Hebrews 10:19; 12:24; 1 John 1:7).

B. FULFILLED IN GOD'S SERVICE (v. 15)

15. Therefore,
  "they are before the throne of God
    and serve him day and night in his temple;
  and he who sits on the throne will spread his tent over them.

WHAT DO YOU THINK?

There will be unity in Heaven among all people, creatures, and angels! How does that fact inspire you to build up the kingdom of Christ and work for the unity on earth for which Jesus prayed (John 17:20, 21)?

WHAT DO YOU THINK?

How can we pray for fellow Christians who are being persecuted? Do you think God listens to generalized prayers such as "O Lord, please help all the suffering Christians"? Why, or why not?

WHAT DO YOU THINK?

The church can teach Christians how to remain faithful during times of persecution and ridicule. But will the same techniques work during times of great prosperity, when the temptations of "the good life" on earth distract us? Explain.

God shall wipe away all tears.
—Revelation 7:17

Visual for Lesson 9. *You can use this visual as a lead-in to the question below. Ask, "How will God lead you through your tears today?"*

WHAT DO YOU THINK?

In what ways have you found that the promise of God taking care of your needs in Heaven has helped you deal with the tough spots in life on earth?

PRAYER

O Jesus, your blood, your blood, your cleansing blood! It is a mystery and a marvel to us; what power it has! Father we thank you for providing our salvation through the blood of your only Son, Jesus, in whose name we pray, amen.

THOUGHT TO REMEMBER

Our eternal protection is the blood of the Lamb.

This is not simply a picture of future bliss in Heaven. This can also be seen as a possibility for us today. Worship is our acknowledgment of the Holy God and submission to him. We don't need to wait for the afterlife in order to *serve him day and night.* Do it now!

C. PROTECTED BY THE MIGHTY LAMB (vv. 16, 17)

16, 17. *"Never again will they hunger;*
never again will they thirst.
The sun will not beat upon them,
nor any scorching heat.
"For the Lamb at the center of the throne will be their shepherd;
he will lead them to springs of living water.
And God will wipe away every tear from their eyes."

This too is not simply a picture of future bliss. Much of this is a spiritual image of our lives today. We are sheltered by our Savior. We suffer no eternal damage from the natural world. We live with the comfort of *God* in our lives. We do indeed suffer the daily sorrows of life, but God overcomes these.

We now live lives of protection and purpose. The center of the throne is *the Lamb,* and the Lamb is the center of our lives (compare Isaiah 49:10). Our purpose is to trust, obey, and follow him (John 21:22). Jesus bids us follow him today and every day (Matthew 16:24). We thus die to self and rejoice in our service to him (1 Corinthians 15:31).

CONCLUSION

From a medical perspective, blood has several functions for our bodies. It protects us in that it contains white cells that fight against invasive infections. Blood carries away wastes created by the various cells and allows the kidneys and other organs to eliminate them. Sometimes a person administering first aid will allow a small wound to bleed a little in order to "clean" it, that is, flush out impurities.

Paul taught that since we are justified by Christ's blood, we are saved from God's wrath (Romans 5:9). Peter wrote that we have been redeemed from futile lives by the blood of Jesus (1 Peter 1:18, 19). The author of Hebrews advised his audience that the blood of Christ purifies us so that we can worship God (Hebrews 9:14). In John's opening statements of Revelation, he affirmed that the blood of Jesus makes us free from the enslavement of sin (Revelation 1:5).

These are just a few of the rich ways that the New Testament authors use the image of the blood of Christ to help us understand how our salvation has been made secure. And this is not just "any blood" of Jesus. If Jesus had had a bad hangnail that bled and we possessed the bloody rag that he wrapped it in, this would have no more spiritual value than any other historical curiosity. The blood of Jesus had no magical properties. It did not glow in the dark or have sparkly glitter in it. It is what that blood represents that is important: Jesus' atoning death on the cross for our sins.

Paul put it very plainly when he said, "Christ died for our sins according to the Scriptures" (1 Corinthians 15:3). Without the blood of Jesus, we would be overwhelmingly dirty because of our sin. As we consider God's marvelous provision, may we offer thanks to the one who still sits on the throne and to the Lamb who gave his blood for us.

"Dear dying Lamb, Thy precious blood shall never lose its pow'r. Till all the ransomed Church of God be saved, to sin no more."

—William Cowper (1731–1800)

Discovery Learning

This page contains an alternative lesson plan emphasizing learning activities. Classes desiring such student involvement will find these suggestions helpful. The next page is a reproducible activity page to further enhance discovery learning.

LEARNING GOALS

After this lesson, each student should be able to:

1. Describe the image of Christ as our protector as given in Revelation 7.

2. Explain how Christ serves as his or her protector.

3. Write a prayer of thankfulness for Christ's protection.

INTO THE LESSON

Put the following quiz in students' chairs. They can begin to work on them as they arrive. If you use student books, you will find the quiz printed there.

1. Which cells defend against infection? a. Red blood cells; b. White blood cells; c. Platelets. 2. Which cells carry oxygen? a. Red blood cells; b. White blood cells; c. Platelets. 3. Which plays the most vital role in the blood-clotting process? a. Red blood cells; b. White blood cells; c. Platelets. 4. What is the life span of red blood cells? a. 3 to 4 weeks; b. 3 to 4 months; c. 3 to 4 years. 5. Red blood cells get their color from what? a. Hemoglobin; b. Oxygen; c. Plasma. 6. The adult body contains about how many quarts of blood? a. 5; b. 10; c. 15. 7. What are the four basic blood types? a. A, B, C, D; b. A, B, A+, B–; c. A, B, AB, O. 8. Blood cells are produced by which of these? a. Heart; b. Kidneys; c. Bone marrow.

Answers: 1b; 2a; 3c; 4b; 5a; 6a; 7c; 8c.

After your students complete the quiz and you have graded it together, say, "Today's lesson will focus on the importance of Jesus' blood to those who trust in him for salvation." (*Alternative:* use the We Need Protection! exercise from the reproducible page instead.)

INTO THE WORD

To begin exploring today's text, prepare a brief lecture on the history of blood using the Lesson Background. Your lecture should cover:

1. Why eating blood was forbidden by the early church (Acts 15:20).

2. The meaning of the terms *innocent blood* and *guilty of bloodshed* (Deuteronomy 19:10).

3. The reasons for the prohibition against murder (Genesis 4:10; 9:6).

4. The role of animal blood in the Jewish religious system, especially in covenant-making and purification (Exodus 24:3-8; Hebrews 9:22).

5. The identification or purpose of the six seals in Revelation 6.

After you finish the lecture portion of this lesson, lead a discussion of Revelation 7:1-3, 9-17. Use your lesson commentary and these questions: *1.* What do the four angels symbolize in this passage? *2.* What is the purpose of the seal on the foreheads of God's servants? What protection does it offer? *3.* Who are the 144,000 and the great multitude? What is the significance of their white robes? Why are they carrying palm fronds? *4.* What is the significance of their cry, "Salvation"? *5.* Why do those around the throne say, "Amen"? *6.* How were the robes made white? *7.* To what service does Jesus call those who have washed their robes in his blood? What protection does he offer?

Distribute slips of paper with the following references (or direct the class to the student books where they are listed): Romans 3:25; 5:9; Ephesians 1:7; Hebrews 9:12-14; 13:11, 12; 1 Peter 1:18, 19; 1 John 1:7; Revelation 1:5, 6. Ask that these Scriptures be read aloud. Comment on each in turn, as appropriate, using your lesson commentary and the remarks below.

Romans 3:25; 5:9—Jesus turned away God's wrath by taking the punishment we deserved; *Ephesians 1:7; 1 Peter 1:18, 19*—Jesus bought us back from slavery to sin by offering his blood as the purchase price; *Hebrews 9:12-14; 13:11, 12*—Jesus' blood accomplished what no animal blood could: purification; *1 John 1:7; Revelation 1:5, 6*—Only the blood of Jesus has the power to cleanse us from all sin.

INTO LIFE

Ask your students to write either a prayer, hymn, or chorus (their personal choice) of less than 10 lines; it is to praise Christ for the forgiveness and protection we have through the power of his blood. For inspiration, direct them to hymns and choruses such as "There Is a Fountain," "Nothing but the Blood," "But for the Blood," "The Blood Will Never Lose Its Power," "There Is Power in the Blood," and "Are You Washed in the Blood?" If you don't use student books, provide pens and paper along with the hymnals or chorus books. Ask volunteers to share their work.

Option: conclude class with the Amen, and Amen! antiphonal prayer from the reproducible page.

We Need Protection!

Many dangers threaten us every day. Match the product or prevention on the left with the threat it is supposed to protect us from on the right.

___ 1. N, N-diethyl-m-toluamide (DEET)

___ 2. Nomex® coveralls

___ 3. Deadbolt locks

___ 4. Lead

___ 5. Kevlar® vest

___ 6. Ground Fault Circuit Interrupter (GFCI)

___ 7. Salk vaccine

___ 8. Aspirin

___ 9. Chromated-copper-arsenate (CCA)

___ 10. Zinc oxide

A. Bullets

B. Polio

C. Electricity

D. Heart attack

E. Burglars

F. Ultraviolet radiation

G. Termites

H. Mosquitoes

I. Radiation

J. Fire

Amen, and Amen!

Use Revelation 7:9-12, below, as the basis for an antiphonal prayer from today's text. One individual or group should read the lines marked A and another should reply with the lines marked B.

A: After this I looked and there before me was a great multitude that no one could count,
B: from every nation, tribe, people and language, standing before the throne and in front of the Lamb.

A: They were wearing white robes and were holding palm branches in their hands.
B: And they cried out in a loud voice: "Salvation belongs to our God, who sits on the throne, and to the Lamb."

A: All the angels were standing around the throne and around the elders and the four living creatures.
B: They fell down on their faces before the throne and worshiped God, saying,

A & B: "Amen! Praise and glory and wisdom and thanks and honor and power and strength be to our God for ever and ever. Amen!"

Answers: 1. H; 2. J; 3. E; 4. I; 5. A; 6. C; 7. B; 8. D; 9. G; 10. F

TAKING OUR PLACE AT THE TABLE

LESSON 10

WHY TEACH THIS LESSON?

"Where do I fit in?" is a lifelong question. This question seems to be particularly painful in the Junior High years, but it never really goes away. Adulthood is filled with job transfers, layoffs, continuing education, marriages, etc. Each major life change is a shock that causes that question to come up all over again.

The Bible tells us where we fit in! We are the church. As the church we anticipate that great wedding feast with our groom, Jesus Christ. This lesson provides a foretaste of the glory and gladness of that day.

INTRODUCTION

A. "SENIORITIS"

A few years ago, I had a very capable senior-level student in my class—let's call him Jason—who simply could not bring himself to complete one last, easy, two-page assignment. Jason had a case of *senioritis*. If you know a student, then you've no doubt heard that term. Right when it counts the most, college and high-school seniors find that the repetition and hard work begin to take their toll.

As a professor, I see this all the time at this time of year. Even our very best students can succumb to the effects of senioritis. Their hard work begins to wear on them, they lose the plot, they take their eyes off the prize of graduating. Before long we have bad grades and a halfhearted effort that characterizes their work.

Jason's senioritis caused him to think that such a small assignment wouldn't really matter. But while it was only a small assignment, it was still very much a part of the course and thus the degree. And you can't graduate without completing all of your courses. Jason and his parents were horrified to find out the day before graduation that he was going to fail the course and thus not graduate. He had family coming in from around the country to celebrate, and his friends assumed everything was fine. Sadly, Jason failed to achieve what he had worked hard for. It was all because he lost his focus and thus his motivation.

The daily rigors of life take a toll on our ability to stay the course. It may be finances, relationships, or "everything in general"; all of us sometimes find that we just want to give up. And, of course, this is only too true of our spiritual journeys. The terrain becomes difficult to traverse and we begin to falter and fall. We often don't want to get up again.

But there is a solution. The same solution that enables students to complete their requirements is what can help us continue our spiritual journeys. That solution is a confident expectation of the future. Students keep working because they *know* that if they stay the course, they'll earn a degree. And we can keep going in our spiritual lives because we *know* that there is an eternal reward waiting for those who are able to stay the course.

DEVOTIONAL READING:

PSALM 148:1-14

BACKGROUND SCRIPTURE:

REVELATION 19

PRINTED TEXT:

REVELATION 19:1-10

LESSON AIMS

After participating in this lesson, each student will be able to:

1. Describe the hope that is available for God's faithful as John reveals it.

2. Explain the imagery that John uses to describe how the faithful can have confidence in their future.

3. Be able to correct false popular ideas of what worship should be.

May
6

KEY VERSE

I heard what sounded like a great multitude, like the roar of rushing waters and like loud peals of thunder, shouting: "Hallelujah! For our Lord God Almighty reigns."

—Revelation 19:6

LESSON 10 NOTES

B. LESSON BACKGROUND

As we come to the next stage in our discussion of the book of Revelation, let's consider where we've been so far. John's Revelation has been a story of hope. John repeatedly makes the same point throughout Revelation: if you are faithful to God, then you will be a part of God's eternal victory.

In the chapters previous to Revelation 19, we encounter Babylon, the great prostitute. Historically speaking, the early church used *Babylon* as a way to refer to Rome (1 Peter 5:13). The reason for this was that Babylon, in the history of Israel, was a place that brought about the destruction of many of God's people. Babylon thus stood as an icon of human arrogance, a place that put itself before God in its pursuit of worldly pleasure and success (even though God used it as his instrument). The early Christians referred to Rome as Babylon because they believed it represented the same sort of worldly values.

Worldly pleasures—fame, possessions, etc.—appeal to virtually all of us on some level, don't they? And this appeal is characterized as the lure of a prostitute; thus we have Babylon as the great prostitute who lures people away from God. As we look into the next part of the story, we find John using this image of the great prostitute to contrast the virtuous character of the bride of Christ.

I. GOD DESTROYS (REVELATION 19:1-5)

A. PRAISE FOR JUSTICE (vv. 1, 2)

1, 2. After this I heard what sounded like the roar of a great multitude in heaven shouting:
> **"Hallelujah!**
> **Salvation and glory and power belong to our God,**
>   **for true and just are his judgments.**
> **He has condemned the great prostitute**
>   **who corrupted the earth by her adulteries.**
> **He has avenged on her the blood of his servants."**

These two verses comprise the first of a series of praises. Note that the praise has two components. Verse 1 shows us the worshipful attitude of those who belong to God. This praise is a personal statement of acceptance of God's authority and an appreciation for his provision. Worship at its core is the recognition of the nature of our reigning God.

Verse 2 provides us with the reason that God's creation should praise and give honor to him: *for true and just are his judgments.* Thus we worship God because of who he is (v. 1) as we recognize that a central feature of God's nature is his justice (v. 2).

As John pens these words, it is easy for Christians of his day to think of Babylon from chapters 17–18 as a reference to Rome. The *great prostitute* of the pagan Roman culture tempts and ravages the people of God. However, the fact that John uses another, very broad figure of speech (*corrupted the earth*) to describe unholy effects indicates a concern for any influence that leads people away from their heavenly Father. In the final analysis, Babylon and the great prostitute thus can refer to anyone or anything that opposes God's purposes. So this first praise is recognition for the way God destroys any who work against his mission of salvation for his people.

Anyone who does not submit to God's authority is an opponent of God. There is no neutral ground in the spiritual world (see John 1:5; 12:46; Ephesians 5:8; 1 Thessalonians 5:5; 1 John 1:5-7). Verse 2 emphasizes the fact that God's destruction of the great prostitute is a just act.

It is important, however, not to take this as a morbid celebration of death. Instead, John is emphasizing the way God is proven to be who he claims to be: a just and righteous God. John does this to show his original readers, who are under persecution, that God is all-powerful and able to keep his promises.

If we remain faithful to him, then God will save us for all eternity. The multitudes of Heaven see the destruction of the great prostitute for what it really is: a magnification of the power of the God who is faithful to keep his promises to those who are faithful to him.

B. PRAISE FOR COMPLETE PUNISHMENT (v. 3)

3. And again they shouted:
    "Hallelujah!
    The smoke from her goes up for ever and ever."

The praise for God's victory over his opponents continues. John uses repetition to bring home the point: God is truly victorious and thus truly worthy of our praise! The phrase *for ever and ever* emphasizes the idea of completeness and permanence (compare Isaiah 34:10). The destruction of those who reject God's authority will be just that.

C. PRAISE FOR VICTORY (vv. 4, 5)

4. The twenty-four elders and the four living creatures fell down and worshiped God, who was seated on the throne. And they cried:
    "Amen, Hallelujah!"

Following the "great multitude" of verse 1, the *twenty-four elders and the four living creatures* are two more groups who praise God for his victory. We were introduced to the elders and the creatures in Revelation 4 (Lesson 7). They are always found giving special recognition to God.

Again, this worship of God emphasizes that God really is victorious. Those who appreciate that fact will have eternal blessing.

5. Then a voice came from the throne, saying:
    "Praise our God,
        all you his servants,
    you who fear him,
        both small and great!"

The *throne* always refers to the presence and authority of *God* (examples: Psalm 9:7; 11:4; 45:6; 47:8; Hebrews 1:8). The voice we hear from the midst of God's presence issues a direct call to all the faithful to yield *praise*. If we understand the true nature of God, then we can still praise him even in the midst of our deepest sorrow and toughest trial. We can do this because we understand that he is worthy.

We also offer praise because we know that his purposes are eternal, that his salvation is sure, and that his victory is guaranteed and complete. We have a hope that transcends our temporary, earthly existence and daily difficulties. How marvelous is his eternal salvation and deliverance! How can we not worship? Worship in spirit and in truth reflects the fact that we understand the true nature and purposes of God. Fear of the Lord is related to our praise of him in Psalm 22:23.

DESERVED PRAISE

A cartoon showed two teenage slackers reading a newspaper. The headline read, "Asian Students Superior to Americans in Science and Math." The caption to the cartoon has one teenager saying, "That may be, but I'll hold our self-esteem up

WHAT DO YOU THINK?

What are some of the victories for which we should fall down and worship God, both as individuals and corporately as the church? Why do we fail to do this as often as we should?

WHAT DO YOU THINK?

How do you praise God when you are going through tough times?

HOW TO SAY IT

Babylon. BAB-*uh-lun.*
Ephesians. Ee-FEE-*zhunz.*
Isaiah. Eye-ZAY-*uh.*
omnipotent. ahm-NIH-*poh-tent.*
senioritis. seen-your-EYE-*tuss.*
Thessalonians. THESS-*uh-*LO-
nee-unz.

against theirs any day!" This points up an ongoing debate within American culture concerning how to motivate children, how to bring out the best in them. The relationship among praise, self-esteem, and accomplishment is frequently debated.

Culture makes an idol out of self-esteem. We praise children disproportionately for minor accomplishments, assuming this will create high self-esteem and make the children successful. We outlaw comparisons between children in order to save the self-esteem of underachievers. A few years ago, schools in Nashville, Tennessee, decided to do away with honor rolls. Low academic achievers might be embarrassed to see their names missing!

We can debate the role that praise plays in the lives of youngsters. But there is no debate about God's worthiness to receive praise! Such praise is not an attempt to manipulate an underachiever into thinking well of himself. God is not an underachiever, and he suffers no self-esteem problems. Praise will be offered by a multitude who have experienced the greatness of God because he has saved them from their sins. He deserves our praise.   —C. R. B.

II. GOD PROVIDES (REVELATION 19:6-10)

A. EVERYBODY LOVES A WEDDING (vv. 6-8)

6. *Then I heard what sounded like a great multitude, like the roar of rushing waters and like loud peals of thunder, shouting:*

     "*Hallelujah!*

         For our Lord God Almighty reigns.

The praise that results from the command in verse 5 is indeed loud! The sounds of *a great multitude, like the roar of rushing waters and like loud peals of thunder,* overlap to create a sense that this is an intense moment of praise. And why not? This is the moment all the faithful have been waiting for, as verse 7 will show. It is the moment when the faithful servants of God enter into eternal, heavenly fellowship with their Savior, Jesus Christ. Such joy! This will be the time when all of God's work throughout history moves toward its magnificent conclusion.

And all this can come about because the God we serve is *omnipotent* (all-powerful). His power is demonstrated by the overwhelming and complete victory over his opponents; now his all-powerful nature brings his promises to their completion. Thus John shows us why we can have courage to be faithful, even in the midst of great trouble: our God reigns over all and will always be able to deliver us. No wonder the praise from the multitude is thunderously loud! How can it be anything less?

WHAT DO YOU THINK?

In what ways have you experienced God's awe-inspiring power at work? How do you know when the power at work is from God and not your own ability?

7a. "*Let us rejoice and be glad*

         and give him glory!

     For the wedding of the Lamb has come,

John now shifts to a picture of a wedding. Using our "sanctified imaginations," we can see that our spiritual lives parallel the practice of getting married. We may say that the cultural practice of becoming engaged parallels the occasion when we first give our lives to Christ. Then the period between the engagement and the wedding parallels the period in which we faithfully await and prepare for the Lord's return. The wedding itself parallels the time when the faithful are finally with Christ for all eternity.

The groom here is identified as *the Lamb.* A pure and spotless lamb has always been the ideal sacrifice offered to God. The Passover, in particular, celebrated God's deliverance with the slaughter of a lamb (Exodus 12:21; 2 Chronicles 30:15; 35:1; Luke 22:7).

John the Baptist referred to Jesus as "the Lamb of God" (John 1:29). The apostle Peter said that Jesus was "a lamb without blemish or defect" (1 Peter

1:19). And in Revelation, the apostle John frequently uses the term *Lamb* to refer to Jesus (Revelation 5:6; etc.). The idea of Christ as the sacrificial lamb lies at the very heart of our redemption and our salvation.

7b. "... and his bride has made herself ready.

John also draws our attention to the fact that the *bride* of the Lamb has been busy getting *herself ready.* She is the community of the redeemed. She consists of the faithful who have submitted themselves to Christ's authority. Their faithfulness is their preparation. Thus the marriage that John now describes unites Christ, who sacrificed his life for humanity, with all those who accepted this sacrifice.

But let us pay attention to the implicit warning in this verse: there will be no person at the wedding who is not ready to be there. Jesus used the image of a wedding to warn about the need to be ready. Matthew 25:1-13 offers the Parable of the Ten Virgins, five of whom were unprepared for the groom's arrival and so failed to enter into the wedding celebration. When they begged to be let in, the groom's response was "I tell you the truth, I don't know you" (Matthew 25:12). Jesus also told the Parable of the Marriage Feast. One man who had not made himself ready through proper attire was thrown out (Matthew 22:1-14).

8. "Fine linen, bright and clean,
        was given her to wear."
(Fine linen stands for the righteous acts of the saints.)

This verse develops the previous verse's idea of the bride's readiness for the Lamb. The nature of the clothing projects an image of purity: *fine linen, bright and clean* (compare Isaiah 1:18; Revelation 3:4, 5; 6:11; 7:9-14). This wedding attire is not something the bride herself could have acquired. Instead, as John says, it is *given her* to dress in this manner.

The final phrase of verse 8 reveals that the description of the fine wedding outfit reflects the *righteous acts of the saints.* We don't have a righteousness of our own. Rather, it is the sacrifice of the Lamb of God that enables the bride to present herself in the white and clean wedding dress (compare Philippians 3:9). The imagery of Isaiah 61:10 is powerful: "He has clothed me with garments of salvation and arrayed me in a robe of righteousness." (See also Romans 1:17; 3:21, 22; 5:17-21; 1 Peter 2:24.)

DRESSED FOR THE WEDDING

Brides usually spend a great amount of time and money getting ready for the ceremony. Choosing the attendants, musicians, and menu for the reception demands attention. Not to be overlooked are personal elements—getting rid of those extra pounds, choosing a good hair style, etc., will make everything "just perfect."

But the centerpiece of all the preparations is the bridal gown. White seems to be an enduring color of choice. Years ago, a wedding advice columnist observed that while white wedding gowns were traditional, gowns in off-white and other colors had gained in popularity. Even so, the color white has shown its staying power.

The purity of the bride of Christ is an important, vivid image in this Bible text. Her "fine linen, bright and clean" signifies this purity. But the bride of Christ doesn't have to try to construct her own gown. We can't make ourselves pure enough; our faith in the Lamb is the means by which his purity becomes ours. Thus we are counted worthy of the pure white linen robes he shall provide.   —C. R. B.

B. EVERYBODY LOVES A MEAL (v. 9)

9. Then the angel said to me, "Write: 'Blessed are those who are invited to the wedding supper of the Lamb!'" And he added, "These are the true words of God."

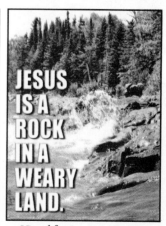

Visual for Lesson 10. *Jesus the lamb is also Jesus the rock! Point to this visual as you ask, "How has Jesus been your rock?"*

WHAT DO YOU THINK?

We readily say that Jesus alone is Lord and that only he is to be worshiped and praised. But like John, we too can be guilty of falling down and worshiping the wrong one. In what ways have you done this? How have you guarded yourself against this error?

The "bride" of verse 7 is an image of the faithful who join Christ forever. Now John refers to the same group as *those who are invited*. There is a slight change in the dynamics of the story here because now John tells us that he has been asked to write *the true words of God*. While all Scripture has its origins in God, John now draws even more attention to the vital nature of the message. His readers must know of the utter reliability of the point that anyone who is faithful to God, and thus participates in this *wedding supper of the Lamb*, is truly *blessed*.

We recall that John's original readers are in the midst of suffering and are in desperate need of maintaining hope. John helps them, and us, with a reminder of the reliability of God's promises. This is a major theme of the book of Revelation: God is faithful and true to those who are faithful and true to him. The book of Revelation is thus a source of hope for all Christians of all centuries who suffer and experience attacks against their relationship with God.

C. ONLY GOD IS TO BE WORSHIPED (v. 10)

10. At this I fell at his feet to worship him. But he said to me, "Do not do it! I am a fellow servant with you and with your brothers who hold to the testimony of Jesus. Worship God! For the testimony of Jesus is the spirit of prophecy."

We may think that the apostles were not prone to make mistakes, but here John reveals his own error. John is so overcome by the magnificence of God's blessing of his people that he attempts *to worship* the angel who is delivering the message. The angel rebukes John for the mistake but also helps John to understand the problem (see also Acts 10:25, 26; 14:11-18; Revelation 22:9).

The final statement, *for the testimony of Jesus is the spirit of prophecy*, is difficult. There are numerous explanations that attempt to take in the various ways of dealing with the original language. For example, does the phrase *testimony of Jesus* (used twice) mean "testimony that comes from the lips of Jesus" or "testimony that is about Jesus" or both?

Perhaps the best way to approach this is to note first that the angel recognizes that he is a *fellow servant* of the *brothers who hold to the testimony of Jesus*. We take the word *brothers* to refer to all faithful believers, understanding that they represent Christ to the world. These faithful people have a *testimony* or witness about Jesus that results in their persecution (Revelation 6:9; 12:11; 20:4).

The word *prophecy* also can cause confusion. It is important to understand that the word translated *prophecy* does not always signify "telling the future." The idea, rather, is one of "speaking on behalf of God" (it's just that sometimes God speaks about the future). So, speaking on behalf of God in testimony is prophecy. The angel thus is talking about the faith of the saints as they live out their relationship to Christ. The Holy Spirit enables them (us) to do so.

CONCLUSION

The Christian life is filled with challenges that wear us down and threaten our ability to remain faithful. Satan knows all our weaknesses, and he doesn't hesitate to exploit them. The book *The Screwtape Letters* by C. S. Lewis offers us a hypothetical account of demons trying to figure out the best ways to tempt humans. We may see ourselves as willing victims on every page!

If we understand the true nature of God—that he really is victorious, destroying his enemies and blessing his faithful—then we have what it takes to remain steadfast, even in the face of suffering. If we are steadfast in our faith, then we will be ready for the groom's arrival. Our eternal future is under his protection. What a reason for praise this is!

THOUGHT TO REMEMBER

Be ready for the wedding feast.

Discovery Learning

This page contains an alternative lesson plan emphasizing learning activities. Classes desiring such student involvement will find these suggestions helpful. The next page is a reproducible activity page to further enhance discovery learning.

LEARNING GOALS

After this lesson, each student will be able to:

1. Describe the hope that is available for God's faithful as John reveals it.

2. Explain the imagery that John uses to describe how the faithful can have confidence in their future.

3. Be able to correct false popular ideas of what worship should be.

INTO THE LESSON

Ask each student to take a piece of paper (or use the student book) and draw or describe something he or she really wished for as a child, as an adolescent, and as an adult. (This could be one, two, or even three different things.) Ask volunteers to share their answers. Were any of these dreams fulfilled? Why, or why not? How did your students feel when their dreams were fulfilled or not fulfilled? How are we affected by such gratifications and disappointments? (*Option:* distribute copies of the Praise Acrostic exercise from the reproducible page for students to work on as they arrive.)

Transition by saying, "Today's lesson deals with the fulfillment of every Christian's greatest hope and the effect it should have on our faith."

INTO THE WORD

Pair off your students to answer the following questions (also listed in the student books). Assign the first five questions to half of your pairs and the last four to the other half. (Suggested answers are italicized; don't distribute those.)

1. Why is the multitude praising God (vv. 1, 2)? (*His judgments are true and righteous.*)

2. Who is the great prostitute who corrupted the earth (vv. 1, 2; see also Revelation 17:1, 18; 18:1, 2)? (*Babylon, or any influence that leads people away from their heavenly Father.*)

3. What will happen to those condemned by God (v. 3)? (*Their destruction will be certain.*)

4. The 24 elders and the 4 creatures represent what 2 groups (v. 4; also Revelation 4:1-11 in Lesson 7)? (*The elders signify all believers and the living creatures point to all the creatures of the world.*)

5. Why did the multitude praise God (vv. 6, 7)? (*Because God reigns and has all power to accomplish his will.*)

6. What is the wedding of the Lamb? To whom is he to be married (v. 7; see also Revelation 18:23; 21:2, 9; 22:17)? (*The Lamb's bride is the church, those who have submitted themselves to Christ's authority.*)

7. What does fine linen represent? How do people receive it (v. 8; see also Isaiah 61:10)? (*It represents the righteousness of the saints, which comes from Christ on the basis of his sacrifice; Christ gives the clothing to his bride.*)

8. Why are those called to the marriage supper considered "blessed"? On what basis are they invited to the supper (v. 9; Matthew 22:1-14)? (*They are blessed because they have God's promise of eternal life if they remain faithful to Christ. They are those who accepted Christ as Lord.*)

9. Whom did John attempt to worship (v. 10)? Why was he rebuked? (*John tried to worship an angel but was rebuked because all worship should be directed only to God.*)

After pairs have finished their research, reassemble the class to discuss their findings. Focus especially on verses 7-11 and what is involved in being invited to the marriage supper of the Lamb. Be sure that students grasp the importance of this question: Why should knowing that our righteousness is not self-achieved increase our confidence in God's promise of eternal life?

INTO LIFE

Ask each pair from the previous exercise to write a brief response to one of the viewpoints below. Make sure to assign all viewpoints.

1. Dave thinks that the weekly worship service is a form of entertainment. If the music is great and the sermon keeps his attention, he considers it real worship. Otherwise, it's a waste of his time. What would you say to him?

2. Jennifer believes that every worship service should be geared to meet the needs of "seekers." She was converted at such a service and feels that any other focus fails to fulfill the Great Commission (Matthew 28:19, 20). How would you respond to her?

3. Ted doesn't understand why the church bothers to include an invitation in every service. "After all, nearly everyone's going to be saved anyway, so why should we worry? Let's just focus on praising God," he says. How do you respond to Ted?

Allow time to discuss suggestions.

Praise Acrostic

Fill in the blanks in the acrostic with words from Revelation 19:1-10. Then circle today's key praise-word that is spelled out in the vertical column with the boxes.

1. The multitude shouts here (v. 1a).

2., 3. _____ and _____ and power belong to our God (v. 1b).

4. Twenty-four of these worshiped (v. 4).

5. God avenged their blood (v. 2).

6. Four of the _____ creatures fell down and worshiped (v. 4)

7. John heard a great _____ (v. 6).

8. Let us _____ and be glad and give God glory (v. 7).

9. Whose wedding supper has come (v. 9)?

10. The testimony of Jesus is the spirit of _____ (v. 10).

FINDING A HOME IN HEAVEN

WHY TEACH THIS LESSON?

Many hymns and choruses have been written about Heaven. It is spoken of as the true home for the Christian, as a place of rejoicing and gladness, and as a place for which there is great anticipation. But though Heaven is considered a wonderful place, many people really don't want to go there just yet. Sometimes when Christians go to conduct worship services at nursing homes, they are told not to sing songs about death and Heaven because it would depress these folks, who are so close to that time in their life. But in actuality, some of the most energetic singing takes place when hymns such as "When We All Get to Heaven" or "When the Roll is Called Up Yonder" are sung.

Most of your students realize that Heaven is a desirable place to be. But some would prefer that Christ not come back just yet and take them there anytime soon! This lesson will help them examine why they feel that way.

INTRODUCTION

A. THANK THE LORD FOR SOLID GROUND

I grew up in Australia, and thus it was practically required that I have a passion for surfing. But any person who has ever had the pleasure of enjoying the sea is a person who also knows the wonderful security of *terra firma*: solid ground!

On a stormy day in 1989, I learned to appreciate solid ground in a way I never had before. The reports of cyclones (hurricanes) and helicopter rescues made others sense danger. But all my best mate and I could think about was big, fun waves. After only a few minutes in the surf, we realized that we had misjudged the situation!

Having drifted three-quarters of a mile up the coast, we were no longer staring back at the golden sands of the beach but at an unforgiving rocky wall. I suddenly lost all interest in surfing and developed a very healthy interest in just staying alive.

We struggled against the current and the waves for about two hours; the sun had set, the waves becoming only silhouettes. We were about a quarter of a mile offshore and could see only a few lights here and there. A huge set of waves loomed in the distance, blackening what was left of the horizon.

My friend made it over the waves, but I did not. The lip of one wave picked me up and slammed me down through the water and onto the rocky ocean floor. Somehow I made it back up to the surface only to have two more waves crash down and do the same thing all over again.

I genuinely thought I was going to die right there in the dark water. I decided all I could do was to make a desperate swim straight for the lights on the shore. Whether it was all rocks or sand, I didn't care. I just wanted something solid and secure. My friend and pieces of my surfboard were waiting for me there as I crawled onto the beach. I laughed nervously at escaping death but then fell down

DEVOTIONAL READING:
2 PETER 3:10-18
BACKGROUND SCRIPTURE:
REVELATION 21:1-8
PRINTED TEXT:
REVELATION 21:1-8

LESSON AIMS

After participating in this lesson, each student will be able to:

1. Identify the Alpha and Omega.

2. Contrast the first heaven and earth with the second.

3. Teach one unbeliever about the differences between the first heaven and earth and the second heaven and earth.

May 13

KEY VERSE

I heard a loud voice from the throne saying, "Now the dwelling of God is with men, and he will live with them. They will be his people, and God himself will be with them and be their God."

—Revelation 21:3

and hugged and kissed the shore. It was so good! At that moment in my life there was simply nothing better than wonderfully solid ground.

Today's lesson offers a similar message. The world is fraught with danger and suffering. But we know the shore is there, even though it is hard to see. If we persevere, by the grace of God we will emerge from the struggle victorious. The things causing our suffering will be put behind us in the end. We will stand firmly for all eternity on wonderfully solid ground.

B. LESSON BACKGROUND

In Revelation 20 we read of Satan's final downfall. Anyone who has ever suffered has felt the power of Satan, because all suffering finds its origin in Satan's influences. That began with the fall of humanity in the Garden of Eden. Satan has set himself up in this world as the enemy of God. Satan actively seeks to destroy us all (1 Peter 5:8). Jesus came to put an end to Satan's project (1 John 3:8). For all who experience Satan's influences through our suffering, pain, and trials, the book of Revelation is a great comfort.

God understands what it means for us to suffer. Jesus, as "the Lamb, looking as if it had been slain" (Revelation 5:6), knows what it means to suffer and experience trial (also Mark 1:13; Luke 22:41, 42). He knows our pain (Hebrews 4:15). The book of Revelation is his Word, and this book shows us that we are given what is necessary to overcome. In the book of Revelation, God tells us that he knows that we suffer. But he promises to destroy the source of our suffering: Satan. Those who embrace Jesus and this promise are able to remain faithful; they surely will be delivered to an eternal life—a life free from the trials and sufferings that Satan brings.

I. NEW HEAVEN AND NEW EARTH! (REVELATION 21:1-5)

A. CHANGED REALITY (vv. 1, 2)

1. Then I saw a new heaven and a new earth, for the first heaven and the first earth had passed away, and there was no longer any sea.

Our passage begins with an important contrast between what is *new* and what is *first*. As we consider what this image conveys, we should note that the word *heaven* as used here is a reference to what we call "the skies." This is very much along the lines of the word *expanse* in Genesis 1:8. The image thus presents a contrast between what we see when we look out the window right now (what John calls the *first*) and what will be *new*.

The word translated *new* in our text can be interpreted in two ways. One way is as a reference to *time*, like when a recently purchased secondhand car is called "new." (I may say that such a car is "new to me.") Another way is to take new as a reference to *quality*, like when someone buys a brand new car that no one has ever owned before. Such a car has the quality of never having been used—it is "factory fresh."

This particular word for *new*, based on the way John uses it, refers to quality. So when John uses the image of a *new earth*, we're not to take that as a reference to an updated version of our own current earth. Rather, it refers to a new kind of earth altogether. The word *new* signals this change from corruptible to eternal (see also Isaiah 65:17; 66:22; 2 Peter 3:13).

The *sea* figures prominently as a symbol in Revelation. About 40 percent of all the references to the sea in the New Testament are in this book (if we don't count "Sea of Galilee," which is actually a lake). The sea in the ancient world is a place of mystery, danger, and vulnerability. Those of John's day use the sea for industry and travel, but it is a strange place that is thought by some to span the gap between the worlds of "gods" and humans. Revelation uses the ancient ideas of the sea as both the thing between God and humans (Revelation 4:6), and as a place of great evil and fear (13:1). Revelation also uses the image of sea to show God's absolute power over all evil (10:1-6). Jesus used the image of the disturbance of the sea as a sign of great turmoil (Luke 21:25).

So the comment *there was no longer any sea* makes a lot of sense in the context of the ancient culture. With the final passing away of this first, temporary world, the new world will be a place without fear and danger that the sea represents.

SOMETHING REALLY NEW

The newspaper ad of a house for sale read, "3br, 2ba, newer kitch, ocn vu." Anyone familiar with real-estate jargon can translate *3br* into "three bedrooms" and *2ba* into "two bathrooms." *Ocn vu* is plain enough: it means that if you climb on a chair in one of the bathrooms and look out of the upper corner of the window, you can view the ocean in the distance—easily adding $10,000 to the price!

But what is a "newer kitch"? *Kitch* stands for kitchen, of course. But what about that slippery word *newer*? Newer than what? That bit of real-estate jargon means that the kitchen is not as old as the rest of the house. Thus it signifies that the house has had its kitchen redone sometime in the indefinite past.

John tells us that the dwelling place he saw in his vision will not be merely *newer*—as a piece of real estate that had been updated a while back. Rather, it will be *qualitatively* new—different in every important way from what we have known before. Everything that could remind us of the pain and sadness of this old, fallen world will be completely gone. Our new, heavenly dwelling place will be *really* new!

—C. R. B.

2. I saw the Holy City, the new Jerusalem, coming down out of heaven from God, prepared as a bride beautifully dressed for her husband.

John's use of geographic locations to depict the coming new world becomes more focused in this verse. As with the new heaven and new earth, the reference here is not to the renewal of the Jerusalem that exists in John's day or even now. It is a reference to a brand *new Jerusalem*. There are two important points made about this new kind of Jerusalem: it comes *from God* and it is *prepared*.

The earthly Jerusalem has a special place in the history of God's people. But as Christianity developed, early believers increasingly used the name *Jerusalem* to refer to the coming promise. For example, Paul can use the word *Jerusalem* to refer both to the city of his day and to the Jerusalem "that is above" (Galatians 4:25, 26). The author of Hebrews uses the term *Jerusalem* in this latter sense (see Hebrews 12:22).

The reason Jerusalem is thought of in this way by first-century Christians is that this city was known in the Old Testament as the place of God's temple, where God put his name (2 Chronicles 6:4-6). This was a place where God was present with his people in a special way. The early Christians drew upon this idea; thus *Jerusalem* could refer to the promise of eternal life with God. John uses the term in this way Revelation 3:12 (compare Isaiah 52:1; Hebrews 11:10, 16).

John further defines the idea of the new Jerusalem by saying that it is *prepared as a bride*. We came across this concept in the previous lesson. Revelation 19 uses wife or bride imagery to refer to the faithful. Here *bride* means the same thing. That is, the new Jerusalem that comes from God is in fact the gathering of the faithful who dwell with God in eternal peace. It is we who are the holy city of God.

WHAT DO YOU THINK?

What are some of the figurative "seas" of life that you face now? How does anticipation of the great, last day help you overcome these?

HOW TO SAY IT

Abraham. AY-bruh-ham.
Alpha. AL-fa.
Ezekiel. Ee-ZEEK-ee-ul or Ee-ZEEK-yul.
Galilee. GAL-uh-lee.
Isaiah. Eye-ZAY-uh.
Jeremiah. Jair-uh-MY-uh.
Jerusalem. Juh-ROO-suh-lem.
Leviticus. Leh-VIT-ih-kus.
Omega. O-MAY-guh.
Patmos. PAT-muss.
Zechariah. ZEK-uh-RYE-uh.

Visual for Lesson 11. *Probe your students' understanding by asking, "How does the work of Christ assure us of life?"*

WHAT DO YOU THINK?

How do you as a Christian deal with death and sorrow? What help do you need in this regard? How have you helped others?

B. DWELLING WITH GOD (vv. 3-5)

3. And I heard a loud voice from the throne saying, "Now the dwelling of God is with men, and he will live with them. They will be his people, and God himself will be with them and be their God.

Essentially, *dwelling* is a repetition of the ideas "holy city" and "new Jerusalem" mentioned in the previous verse. Older versions of the Bible use the word *tabernacle* instead of *dwelling*. God had given very specific instructions to Moses to set up a tabernacle and its furnishings (Exodus 26–27, 35–38). It was to be a focal point of God's presence (Exodus 29:44-46). After Moses had carried out all that the Lord asked of him, "the glory of the Lord filled the tabernacle" (Exodus 40:34). God was with his people in a special way.

It has been God's desire all along to live with his people (compare Leviticus 26:11, 12; Ezekiel 37:27; Zechariah 2:10; 2 Corinthians 6:16). Putting these ideas together reveals that John is making a point that is similar to his point in the previous verse: we are the dwelling place of God!

4, 5. "He will wipe every tear from their eyes. There will be no more death or mourning or crying or pain, for the old order of things has passed away." He who was seated on the throne said, "I am making everything new!" Then he said, "Write this down, for these words are trustworthy and true."

With the passing of the first heaven and earth will also come the passing of Satan's power and influence. And this is the hope to which we all cling: this world and its suffering are only temporary. Suffering tempts us to lose our focus on the eternal. Thus it is a great tool used by Satan to distract God's people and tempt them to question their relationship to him.

People often find cause to blame God for their suffering. But in reality, suffering comes to all of us because we live in a world that has fallen to Satan's temptation and is therefore subject to decay (Genesis 3:1-19; Romans 8:18-22). When a loved one is dying from a terrible disease, who does not long for that person's healing? When we suffer physically, our perspective swiftly turns toward the physical and temporary. The tragedy of suffering drives our minds to obsess about the physical. Thus we become prime targets for the temptation to allow the temporary to dominate our thinking and values.

John's solution is to help us understand that our future with the Lord is utterly free from suffering (compare Isaiah 25:8; 35:10; 65:19). And because John understands the deep and eternal significance of this for us, he reminds us that these are not his words but the Lord's. The words are of the one who is *seated on the throne*!

We can have absolute confidence in our future, new life because *these words are trustworthy and true*. It is worth noting that John emphasizes the reliability of the message three times toward the end of this book (here and in Revelation 19:9; 22:6).

II. NEW LIFE OR SECOND DEATH? (REVELATION 21:6-8)

A. LIFE FOR THE GODLY (vv. 6, 7)

6. He said to me: "It is done. I am the Alpha and the Omega, the Beginning and the End. To him who is thirsty I will give to drink without cost from the spring of the water of life.

In this verse John again emphasizes the reliability of the message, only from a different angle. This time he embeds into the story the point of God's activity in history. God is the one speaking, and he refers to himself as *the Alpha and the Omega*. Those are the first and the last letters of the Greek alphabet. So when

God calls himself *the beginning and the end* we understand it to be a repetition of Alpha and Omega. God is not, however, admitting that he himself has a beginning and an end. Rather, he announces that all beginnings and ends are in his control (Isaiah 44:6; 46:9, 10; 48:12).

The second part of this verse offers two important ideas: a certain problem (spiritual thirst) and its solution (*water of life*). These two concepts are not unique to Revelation. They are found throughout the Bible (examples: Psalm 65:9; Isaiah 41:17, 18; 55:1; Jeremiah 2:13; Zechariah 13:1). For clarity we can look to John's Gospel. In John 7:37, 38, Jesus speaks to the problem of spiritual thirst and then offers the solution in terms of believing on him. Here, those who are thirsty are those who understand their need for Jesus. See also John 4:13, 14.

7. "He who overcomes will inherit all this, and I will be his God and he will be my son.

He who overcomes is mentioned both here and in each of the seven "letters" of Revelation 2 and 3. The phrase comes from the Greek word for "the one who is victorious." In Revelation 2 and 3 the overcomer is the person who has been able to remain faithful in spite of opposition to his or her faith. And the concept of overcoming is a key to the entire book of Revelation. We could even say that a purpose of Revelation is to enable its readers to overcome.

To overcome is the essence of faithfulness. The primary biblical example of this (other than Jesus) is Abraham. Abraham's trust in God was repeatedly challenged. But Abraham's unwavering belief that God would deliver on his promises proved Abraham to be faithful and the father of all who are faithful (Genesis 12:1–25:8; Romans 4:16-22). Faithfulness means overcoming any challenge to one's relationship with the Lord. Thus the overcomer is the person who does not melt away when faith is under fire (1 Peter 4:12-19). Such a person stands firm, knowing that the Lord will always win.

But we must not assume that challenges to faith always come in the obvious form of persecution. Faith is tested by anything that threatens our relationship with God. Money problems, family issues, health problems, etc. can all erode the foundation of that relationship. In short, *all of us* are constantly being challenged in our faith. The good news is that every time we withstand a challenge, we become stronger in our faith. In this way we become true overcomers who remain faithful to God. Thus we will inherit all things and be forever God's children.

BETTER OR BITTER?

Louise Ashby, age 21, had a dream of becoming an actress and model. So she moved to Hollywood, California. That is the place where such dreams are supposed to come true. But it is also a place where physical beauty often is required for success.

Suddenly her dream crashed—literally—in a head-on auto accident. Following the brain surgery that saved her life, Ashby was in a coma. A week later came a lengthy surgery that started the reconstruction of her face. Her first look in a mirror revealed an unrecognizable person with a watermelon-sized head. Fourteen reconstructive surgeries and 238 small titanium plates later, she ended up with a million-dollar face. She was once more a physical beauty. You would never guess what she has had to overcome.

But today the beauty goes deeper. Ashby still models and acts, but she also became involved with an organization that offered counsel and financial help to children who need surgery to correct facial birth defects. She began to make frequent

WHAT DO YOU THINK?

What are some inadequate ways you sought to have your spiritual thirst quenched in the past? What turned you around?

WHAT DO YOU THINK?

What are some ways that our heavenly inheritance differs from an earthly inheritance? How do these differences comfort you?

visits to UCLA's Craniofacial Clinic, encouraging the patients there by telling them what she had overcome.

Ashby affirms that her ordeal made her stronger. That's what happens when we overcome obstacles, whether in a physical or spiritual sense. Whatever spiritual challenges we must overcome in this life, we become stronger with the help of God. Rather than becoming bitter, we can become better—fit for eternity. Blessed are the overcomers!   —C. R. B.

B. DEATH FOR THE UNGODLY (v. 8)

8. "But the cowardly, the unbelieving, the vile, the murderers, the sexually immoral, those who practice magic arts, the idolaters and all liars—their place will be in the fiery lake of burning sulfur. This is the second death."

This list of those who are doomed to an eternal *death* is another encouragement to readers. Removal of evil people removes their persecutions of Christians as well (compare Matthew 25:41). To the degree that the unbelieving will be doomed forever, those who are faithful will be blessed forever.

This list of ungodly people works like many lists in the New Testament: we are better off taking it as a whole rather than scrutinizing it on a point-by-point basis. As we read the list, we're supposed to get an impression of the *kind* of person who is doomed to eternal death. These are people who live in rebellion against God.

Further, we must not forget that the book of Revelation was originally written to people suffering physical persecution. John himself is a prisoner in exile on the island of Patmos as he writes. In such a circumstance we can easily appreciate how the announcement of doom for those who bring pain and suffering to Christians will help strengthen the faith of the readers. That is, if you are being persecuted but you know that in the end you will be delivered and your persecutor will be punished, then it becomes a way for you to endure.

The *second death* idea is the counterpart of "the first heaven and the first earth" in verse 1. But note that John does not call this death a *new death*—he says *second death*. John will often use synonyms to refer to similar things in order to create a sense of distinct value. For example, John describes in Revelation 11 two witnesses of God. John uses "42 months" (11:2) to describe a time of persecution and "1260 days" (11:3) to refer to the time of their prophecy.

John describes this same time period in two different ways to show how the Christian experience is double-sided. On the one hand, we serve Christ and experience his peace; on the other hand, we live in a temporary world filled with pain and suffering. Thus the second death is an eternal death to which the unfaithful must go in the same way that the new Heaven and earth is an eternal destiny for the faithful.

CONCLUSION

When we look at our earthly homes, we often think in terms of what they don't have—we dwell upon what they lack. "It doesn't have central air." "It doesn't have a basement." "It doesn't have an attached garage." "It doesn't have a sun room." Too much thinking like this can lead to envy and unhappiness.

But what our heavenly homes will lack will be glorious indeed: these homes will lack all the evil people, attitudes, and practices that we see in Revelation 21:8. There won't be any bad neighbors in Heaven! What a glorious encouragement this is.

Discovery Learning

This page contains an alternative lesson plan emphasizing learning activities. Classes desiring such student involvement will find these suggestions helpful. The next page is a reproducible activity page to further enhance discovery learning.

LEARNING GOALS

After participating in this lesson, each student will be able to:

1. Identify the Alpha and Omega.

2. Contrast the first heaven and earth with the second.

3. Teach one unbeliever about the differences between the first heaven and earth and the second heaven and earth.

INTO THE LESSON

As your students arrive, give each one a copy of the following agree/disagree exercise (or direct their attention to the student book, where it is printed).

1. Old hymns are much better than new praise choruses. Agree or disagree?

2. Younger preachers are better speakers than older preachers. Agree or disagree?

3. Older church buildings have a more worshipful atmosphere than newer buildings. Agree or disagree?

4. Life 50 years ago was better than it is today. Agree or disagree?

After you discuss their answers, tell your students that today's lesson deals with the contrast between the old heaven and earth and the new. (Feel free to change any questions you think will be too controversial!)

Alternative: begin class with the When We All Get to Heaven skit from the reproducible page.

INTO THE WORD

Distribute "The New Resident's Guide to Heaven" set forth below (also printed in the student book); do not include the parenthetical answers. Then read Revelation 21:1-8 aloud. Ask students to indicate who/what is either present or absent from Heaven, as indicated.

The New Resident's Guide to Heaven

What/Whom You Will Find There: v. 1 (newness); v. 2 (new Jerusalem); v. 3 (dwelling of God; God himself); v. 6 (fountain of water of life); v. 7 (overcomers).

What/Whom You Won't Find There: v. 1 (sea); v. 4 (tears; death; sorrow; crying; pain; former things); v. 8 (the fearful; the unbelieving; the abominable; murderers; whoremongers; sorcerers; idolaters; liars; lake of fire/ second death).

When your students have completed the guides, use the following questions to discuss their answers.

1. What is "new" about the new heaven and earth, compared to the old?

2. Why is there no sea in Heaven?

3. What is the new Jerusalem, and why is it compared to a bride?

4. What does verse 3 mean by "the dwelling" [or tabernacle] of God is with men"?

5. How will God do away with all suffering?

6. What does the reference *the Alpha and the Omega* signify?

7. What is the water of life? How does someone who is spiritually thirsty drink from it?

8. What does it mean to be an overcomer?

9. What is the second death? Who will suffer it? Why? Compare Revelation 21:8 with 1 Corinthians 6:9-11. What does Paul say about those who will or who won't inherit the kingdom of God?

INTO LIFE

Divide your class into pairs or groups of three, depending on how many students you have. Assign one of the following scenarios to each pair or trio. Say, "Write a brief letter to the character in the scenario, using today's text to challenge him or her to follow Christ." Have several volunteers share their suggestions.

1. Jim no longer believes in God. He has been suffering from inoperable brain cancer and endures such pain that he can rarely leave his bed. Jim sees life as nothing more than torture, with death as the only release from that agonizing existence. What hope can you offer him?

2. Sharon is into the occult. She relies on her daily horoscope for guidance, she worships nature with a group of pagans, and she spends much of her free time digesting occult literature and films. How can you reach her with the truth?

3. Dave belongs to a cult that teaches that the only way to reach God is through special meditation. They consider all religions to be equally valid. No matter what faith one chooses to follow, that religion will lead to salvation with proper meditation. How do you respond?

4. Rachel claims to be a Christian but is notoriously dishonest. She cheated to get through school, she lies to friends and family, and she steals from her employer. She admits to these offenses, but considers them justifiable means to an end. How can you convince her to change?

When We All Get to Heaven

For this skit you will need three chairs, arranged in a row at the front of the class, facing the back of the classroom. Dave and Carrie are arguing in Sunday school, just before class begins. They are joined by Phil.

CARRIE: Well, Dave, that's just how I feel about it. What do you think, Phil?

PHIL: Hi, guys! Think about what?

DAVE: Oh, Carrie and I have a little debate going on about who's going to Heaven.

PHIL: Well, is anyone I know, like yours truly, on the list?

CARRIE: I think anyone who believes in Jesus is going to Heaven, regardless of how he or she has lived, because the Bible says we are justified by God's grace.[1]

DAVE: And I think it matters very much how you have lived, because the Bible says that murderers, liars, and immoral people will not go to Heaven.[2]

CARRIE: But clearly, Jesus can forgive any sin. After all, he pardoned the cross-eyed thief.

PHIL: Don't you mean the thief on the cross?[3]

DAVE: Yet Jesus also said, "My reward is with me, and I will give to everyone according to what he has *done*."[4] Therefore, only *good* people can go to Heaven.

CARRIE: Wait a minute! Didn't Paul say that "the wages of sin is death, but the gift of God is eternal life in Christ Jesus our Lord"?[5]

DAVE: OK, Phil. Settle this. Which of us is right?

PHIL: Well, Carrie is right when she says we are justified, or forgiven, by grace. The Bible also says we are justified by Christ's blood.[6] It works like this: God's grace provided Jesus as the sacrifice to pay the penalty for our sins.[7] That's a gift we cannot earn or deserve. When we accept Christ as our Savior and follow the biblical plan of salvation, our sins are covered by his blood. We continue to be forgiven as long as we maintain our faith in Christ.[8]

DAVE: So how do works fit into this?

PHIL: The Christian is not saved by doing good works—none of us could ever do enough to be saved anyway. Rather, a person does good works *because* he or she is saved.[9] James says the works that Christians do demonstrate that they truly do believe in Jesus.[10] The unbeliever, however, has no faith in Christ. He or she will be judged and punished for sin because of refusal to accept God's gift of salvation through Christ.[11]

References: [1]Romans 3:24-28; [2]Revelation 21:8; [3]Luke 23:43; [4]Revelation 22:12; [5]Romans 6:23; [6]Romans 5:9; [7]Romans 3:24, 25; [8]Colossians 2:12; Galatians 3:26, 27; 1 John 1:7; [9]Ephesians 2:8-10; [10]James 2:14-26; [11]John 3:18, 36

Our Community Now and in God's Future
Unit 3: Living in God's New World
(Lessons 10-13)

LIVING IN GOD'S PRESENCE

WHY TEACH THIS LESSON?

We live in God's presence now, but we will live in God's presence in a much more profound way later. How does God expect us to do the former while we anticipate the latter?

For the Christian, life here on earth is to be spent preparing for the ultimate trip, the journey to the celestial city, the new Jerusalem. Preparations are made daily as we live in the presence of God. Two extremes are to be avoided. One is to get so focused on Heaven that we fail to live the life God has for us while we are still here on earth. This is called "being so heavenly minded that we are of no earthly good." The other extreme is to live in the here and now as if this were the only reality.

Today's lesson will give us a taste of God's eternal perspective. When we allow that perspective to sink in, we'll know how to live!

INTRODUCTION

A. A RUN IN THE COUNTRY

I have no trouble admitting that I'm a city person. I love the country, but the fact is it does scare me. I grew up where the streetlights came on as soon as the natural light faded. I grew up close to convenience stores, hospitals, fire houses, and police stations. It was an ordered, safe, and predictable environment.

Recently my wife and I decided to get out into the country. So we drove up to "Amish country" in central Ohio. There we stayed in an old log cottage located at the back of a working farm. Fortunately the cottage had satellite TV, a weather radio alarm, fire extinguishers, a telephone, smoke and carbon-monoxide detectors, security lights, and all the conveniences of the city—right there in the country!

While enjoying the country life late on the first afternoon, I thought I would go out for a run through the woods at the back of the farm. I was a long way out when I realized that the sun had almost set. I found myself running along an old isolated road in the dark and not really sure of where I was. My idea was to keep running and hope I didn't miss the gap in the trees that I had come out of an hour earlier.

I did, of course, miss that gap. So I ran and walked for a few hours. Every time I saw a house light, I'd run up and find that I was not in the right place. There were no shops to stop at, no water fountains to drink from, no food that was not still alive. Dogs ran after me, strange noises freaked me out, and I thought I saw a bear (in central Ohio?!). In short I was terrified. Suddenly I had a new appreciation for the city.

Although the city comes with its own dangers, my run in the country taught me something about John's world. In today's lesson John contrasts being inside with being outside the city to show us the security and abundance that will come when we enjoy the eternal presence of God in the new Jerusalem.

DEVOTIONAL READING:
EPHESIANS 1:15-23
BACKGROUND SCRIPTURE:
REVELATION 21:9–22:5
PRINTED TEXT:
REVELATION 21:9-11; 21:22–22:5

LESSON AIMS

After participating in this lesson, each student will be able to:

1. Recite ways that life in God's eternal presence will provide peace.

2. Contrast the security of Heaven with the insecurity of earthly life.

3. Describe one way to bring the peace of Heaven into daily life.

KEY VERSE

There will be no more night. They will not need the light of a lamp or the light of the sun, for the Lord God will give them light. And they will reign for ever and ever.   —Revelation 22:5

May
20

DAILY BIBLE READINGS

Monday, May 14—The Hope of Our Calling (Ephesians 1:15-23)

Tuesday, May 15—The Glory of the Lord (Isaiah 60: 18-22)

Wednesday, May 16—An Unshakable Kingdom (Hebrews 12:22-28)

Thursday, May 17—The Hope of Glory (2 Corinthians 3:7-18)

Friday, May 18—John Sees the Heavenly City (Revelation 21:9-14)

Saturday, May 19—God Will Be the Light (Revelation 21:22-27)

Sunday, May 20—Blessings to Come (Revelation 22:1-5)

B. LESSON BACKGROUND

We must always remember that Revelation was written to encourage first-century Christians who were being persecuted for their faith. Like all biblical prophecy, its primary value is in its original context. So our interpretation of Revelation must begin with the original readers.

The figures of speech that John uses come from the world of the first century AD. They are strange to us, and so we often miss the real value of the imagery. In Revelation 21–22, we have John's description of Heaven as he experiences his revelation. Yet for John to describe the vision, he has to use images and terms from the then-current, physical world. He wrote Revelation so that his readers could appreciate the next world in such a way that it would make a difference in how they were living out their lives at the time.

John's description of Heaven helps us appreciate its wonders. We should be cautious about taking the descriptions of our eternal home too literally, however. To make this mistake would be to limit Heaven to only the earthly things that we can imagine are valuable.

For example, consider how John describes the foundations of the wall of the city (Revelation 21:19, 20). City walls were valuable things in the ancient world, because they were physical barriers against enemies—it is an impression of security. Today, however, very few cities depend on walls for safety. Instead, we may think of safety in terms of early-warning radar (both military and weather). John uses ideas from his first-century world to create the most meaningful impression he can. When we allow John's intended impression to shape our hearts, we will fall at the feet of Jesus in praise.

I. PEOPLE OF GOD (REVELATION 21:9-11)

A. THEIR STATUS (v. 9)

9. One of the seven angels who had the seven bowls full of the seven last plagues came and said to me, "Come, I will show you the bride, the wife of the Lamb."

We have already considered the image of *the bride, the wife of the Lamb* in earlier lessons; in Revelation 19:7 and 21:2, we saw this terminology used as a reference to all who belong to God. The focus was on the bride's preparation, the way the faithfulness of those who belong to God prepared them for eternal life. When John refers to the Lamb, he draws attention to the fact of whose we are.

The counterpart of the bride is the great prostitute of Revelation 17:1. The purity of the bride is in sharp contrast to the filthiness of the great prostitute (compare Revelation 19:7, 8 with Revelation 17:2). Mention of *the seven angels who had the seven bowls full of the seven last plagues* harks back to the judgment of God in chapters 15 and 16.

B. THEIR FUTURE (vv. 10, 11)

10. And he carried me away in the Spirit to a mountain great and high, and showed me the Holy City, Jerusalem, coming down out of heaven from God.

In order for John to see divine things, he must see them from a spiritual perspective. John started off his experiences "in the Spirit" (Revelation 1:10). Then when he was called into the presence of God, he also was "in the Spirit" (4:1, 2). When John was shown the demise of the unfaithful, it too was "in the Spirit" (17:1-3). Now for him to see the future of the faithful, it likewise must be in the *Spirit* (compare Ezekiel 40:2).

The significant point of this passage is what John sees while he is in the Spirit: *the Holy City, Jerusalem, coming down out of heaven from God*. In the previous verse the angel said that he was going to show John the bride, the Lamb's wife. What John subsequently sees means that the bride of verse 9 is the same thing as the holy Jerusalem of verse 10.

11. It shone with the glory of God, and its brilliance was like that of a very precious jewel, like a jasper, clear as crystal.

John uses breathtaking language to describe what he sees. What makes this city so beautiful is God's presence among his people. John sees the future of all who have remained faithful and how they manifest God's glory.

The *glory of God* is more than mere *brilliance*. The glory of God is also what he achieves, what he does, and what represents him (compare Isaiah 60:1, 2, 19). The opening phrase *it shone* indicates that the community of the faithful (the new Jerusalem) shows God's glory by being in this place with him forever.

The image of precious stones creates a sense of a value beyond measure. And if you read this and feel like jumping up and down with excitement, you should! This is a place beyond compare, and we the faithful really will all be there one day.

II. CITY OF GOD (REVELATION 21:22-27)

A. LIVING IN THE LIGHT (vv. 22-26)

22. I did not see a temple in the city, because the Lord God Almighty and the Lamb are its temple.

John uses images that reflect important ideas for our understanding of eternity. The first is that there is no *temple*. The original audience of Revelation lived in a world where temples were the norm. Temples were thought to be the way to communicate with your god. Even those who served the true God in Solomon's time and thereafter understood that if you wanted to be closest to God you should go to the temple in Jerusalem.

As John writes, the Jerusalem temple has lain destroyed for at least 20 years. But John emphasizes that there is no need for a temple because the faithful will live in the presence of God. The truth of this is seen in the descriptions of city, bride, and dwelling [tabernacle] up to this point.

John's reference to *the Lamb* should remind us that we are forever dependent upon Christ's sacrificial work. Our future abundance already has been secured through the cross; what is necessary for us to have eternal life Jesus already has provided! We can live a victorious life *now.*

23. The city does not need the sun or the moon to shine on it, for the glory of God gives it light, and the Lamb is its lamp.

A pre-electricity world is a dark world. And darkness naturally hides all sorts of dangers. Since the ancient world relied more on natural light than we do today, the difference between *light* and dark has greater significance to the ancients. The New Testament writers use this significance in their writings. Their light vs. dark imagery contrasts people who belong to God (those in the light) and people who do not (those in the dark); see examples in John 8:12; Ephesians 5:8-13; Colossians 1:12, 13; 1 Thessalonians 5:4-8; and 1 John 1:5-7.

This is also a contrast in the Old Testament; see examples in Job 29:3; 30:26; and Isaiah 5:20. The light that Jesus is said to bring in Matthew 4:15, 16 is a quotation of Isaiah 9:1, 2.

GOD'S BRIGHT IDEA

A composite photo taken from space shows the world at night glowing with light from thousands of cities. Yet well-ordered artificial illumination has been de-

WHAT DO YOU THINK?

The church, the people of God, will reflect God's glory in the new Jerusalem, the heavenly city. But how can we reflect his glory while here on earth?

WHAT DO YOU THINK?

In what ways has the church in general—or your church in particular—lost her "shine" for God? How can she get it back?

[Hint: some solutions can be found in 1 John 3:18; 2 John 4-11; 3 John 11; Revelation 2:5, 16, 25; 3:3, 11, 18.]

veloped only within the last two centuries. In 1807 London could boast of the first gas street lamps. By the 1880s electric lighting was replacing gas lighting.

But with progress comes problems, and eventually the first blackout occurred. That happened in New York City on October 14, 1889. Headlines read, "A Night of Darkness—More than One Thousand Electric Lights Extinguished." However, it wasn't a power failure that caused the darkness; it was the outraged mayor who ordered all the lights shut off!

Streets of the time were illuminated by high voltage, carbon arc lights fed through a tangle of overhead wires. Several people had been accidentally (and publicly) electrocuted by the poorly maintained system. Something better was needed, and eventually the shift was made to safer technology. As a result, we can live in the relative security of lighted homes, streets, and public buildings.

We take light for granted, but the new Jerusalem will be illuminated by a light more brilliant than anything we have experienced. This light will be so bright that sunlight will no longer be needed. This light will never be dimmed by power failure, will never cause pain or death, and will signify absolute safety and security. There will be no danger of blackouts. What a bright idea that is!   —C. R. B.

24-26. The nations will walk by its light, and the kings of the earth will bring their splendor into it. On no day will its gates ever be shut, for there will be no night there. The glory and honor of the nations will be brought into it.

WHAT DO YOU THINK?

The nations will be gathered together as one in the new Jerusalem! What impact should that fact have on your church today?

The reference to the open *gates* and the absence of *night* reinforces the idea of security. Further, John now specifies that it is the *nations* that *will walk by its light.* The important concept of *nations* is woven throughout biblical history. A key part of God's plan of salvation came into being when he called Abraham to be the father many nations (Genesis 17:5).

In particular, Abraham became the father of the nation of Israel. That nation bore the responsibility of preparing itself to usher in the Messiah, who would bring God's light to the rest of the world (Acts 13:47, quoting Isaiah 49:6). Today, the church functions as a kind of new Israel as she communicates the light of the gospel to those in darkness (compare Acts 26:17, 18).

The allusion to this final gathering of the saved from among the nations is clear in Isaiah 60:1-5. While Isaiah 60:5 refers to humans bringing their "riches" John magnifies the idea by saying that *kings* bring their *glory and honor.* This glory they bring or offer has always belonged to God in the same way that all power has always belonged to God. This is the ultimate point of the Isaiah passage: any power or wealth that seems to belong to us truly belongs to God. The faithful will surrender it all to him.

B. PROMISE AND WARNING (v. 27)

27. Nothing impure will ever enter it, nor will anyone who does what is shameful or deceitful, but only those whose names are written in the Lamb's book of life.

John's Revelation is for those believers struggling to live in this world, to give us the hope we need to endure trials. But as we saw in Revelation 16–18, this book is not good news for everyone. John issues a warning for anyone who would dare to reject what God has provided.

WHAT DO YOU THINK?

How has the warning given in verse 27 affected the church in both negative and positive ways?

On the one hand, we see a promise to the faithful that their future in the presence of God will not be compromised by his enemies. On the other hand, we see a warning that is especially pertinent to modern culture. Many seem to believe that they can avoid the consequences of their actions. But John's message is clear: God will not overlook those who have rejected him. We see similar warnings in Isaiah 52:1 and 1 Corinthians 6:9, 10.

The *book of life* belongs to the Lamb because it is Christ's work that saves us. Those covered by Christ's blood are those whose names are written in that book (compare Psalm 69:28; Exodus 32:32, 33; Daniel 12:1; Philippians 4:3).

III. PEACE OF GOD (REVELATION 22:1-5)

A. ETERNAL ABUNDANCE (vv. 1, 2)

1. Then the angel showed me the river of the water of life, as clear as crystal, flowing from the throne of God and of the Lamb

As John moves the book toward its close, he brings together many of his previous points to help us understand the message. Thus he reintroduces the *water of life* image discussed previously (Revelation 21:6). The point of the image is that those who worship God will never have any want. John sees this abundant supply of our needs to originate from the presence *of God*. John's frequent reference to *the Lamb* is a constant reminder that our eternity will always be founded upon Christ's sacrifice.

2. . . . down the middle of the great street of the city. On each side of the river stood the tree of life, bearing twelve crops of fruit, yielding its fruit every month. And the leaves of the tree are for the healing of the nations.

A river sustains life, and John describes "the river of the water of life" (v. 1) as the sustainer of *the tree of life* (compare Genesis 2:9). The images are overlapped in order to reinforce the message: our eternal home will be abundantly supplied with all that we need.

John's world is not technologically advanced. As a result, the food supply in his day is much less predictable than in ours. A bad harvest to John's contemporaries means everyone will be dieting. Famine, common to the ancient world, is almost unheard of in Western democracies today. This fact can make it difficult for us to appreciate John's point. This tree has not one but *twelve* kinds of *fruit*, and these twelve kinds of fruit aren't produced just annually but *every month*! It's always harvest time in Heaven, and the crop is always bountiful.

STENCH OF DEATH, PROVISION OF LIFE

God has created some very unusual plants! Do you suppose he did this for his own amusement or for our amazement? One of the strangest examples is known as *titan arum*—the "corpse flower." It gets that name because its fragrance (if that is the right term!) is reminiscent of rotting flesh. The reason for the smell is that it attracts carrion beetles to pollinate the plant. Such beetles normally feed on—you guessed it—rotting flesh.

The plant was discovered in the jungles of Sumatra in 1878. Horticulturists subsequently brought the plant to botanical gardens in the western world. The tuber from which the blossom grows may weigh 170 pounds; the blossom can be from 6 to 10 feet tall and lasts only 2 days.

The blossom is rare in cultivated examples of the plant, but huge crowds will visit exhibits in spite of (or maybe because of) the smell. In 2003, some 16,000 visitors came to see the two-day bloom at the United States Botanic Garden in Washington, D.C.

How different this flower is from the trees that John saw! There will be no smell of death in Heaven. Instead, the tree of life will delight us with its unending provision.

—C. R. B.

B. ETERNAL SECURITY (vv. 3-5)

3a. No longer will there be any curse. The throne of God and of the Lamb will be in the city, . . .

HOW TO SAY IT

Colossians. Kuh-LOSH-unz.
Corinthians. Ko-RIN-thee-unz
Ephesians. Ee-FEE-zhunz.
Ezekiel. Ee-ZEEK-ee-ul or Ee-ZEEK-yul.
Isaiah. Eye-ZAY-uh.
Jerusalem. Juh-ROO-suh-lem.
Philippians. Fih-LIP-ee-unz.
Solomon. SOL-o-mun.
Thessalonians. THESS-uh-LO-nee-unz.

WHAT DO YOU THINK?

God wants us to produce fruit constantly and he empowers us to do so. How effective are you at producing the fruit of new souls? How can you do better?

The Lord God giveth them light: and they shall reign for ever and ever.

—Revelation 22:5

Visual for Lesson 12. *Point to this visual as you ask, "In what ways does God give you a light right now that is better than sunlight?"*

In this one remark John spans the entirety of history, from the fall in the Garden of Eden to the final redemption. The fall of humanity occurred when Adam and Eve decided to privilege their own interests over God's (Genesis 3:6). The resulting *curse* was not so much the hard work and pain (Genesis 3:16-19) as it was being banished from God's presence (Genesis 3:22-24).

What happened after that is the long story of the Lord preparing for our return to his presence. That could come about only via the redemption from the effects of our sin. And now John makes this point: a time comes when the curse is finally gone. We will at last be back with our creator, where we should have been all along.

In the end, there will be no separation from God's presence as there is in this fallen, temporary world. We cannot fail to note that John refers once more to *the Lamb.* It is the work of Christ that has rescued us from the effects of the curse.

3b. . . . and his servants will serve him.

Being in the presence of God is an experience we cannot fully comprehend. But John tells us that our natural joyful response will be to *serve* God.

4. They will see his face, and his name will be on their foreheads.

John's world does not have the experience of televised images or photographs. So for him and his original readers, the only practical way to see people's faces is to be in their presence. Thus seeing God's *face* repeats the previous point that we shall be in the presence of God (compare Psalm 17:15; Matthew 5:8).

By saying that God's *name* will be *on their foreheads,* John reinforces that the future of the faithful will be abundant and secure. That is because we will be in the presence of God. A name or identity written on the forehead is a powerful image (compare Exodus 28:36-38; Ezekiel 9:4-6; Revelation 13:16; 14:9; 17:5). A mark on a forehead designates a certain identity; in this case, it identifies someone as belonging to God. God knows who we are, and we know we belong to him. We will forever be designated as God's and thus forever enjoy his presence, his abundance, his protection. What a comfort!

5. There will be no more night. They will not need the light of a lamp or the light of the sun, for the Lord God will give them light. And they will reign for ever and ever.

John reemphasizes the point that he has been making all along: the faithful shall experience the presence of God and enjoy the eternal security and protection that his presence affords. While it's impossible for us to fathom exactly what John sees, we can still get the message from our limited perspective. Even though we may suffer now, even though our relationship with God may be tested, even though we may have fear now, our faithfulness will ultimately lead us to eternal security and abundance. "The saints of the Most High will receive the kingdom and possess it forever—yes, for ever and ever" (Daniel 7:18).

CONCLUSION

If you ever take a class in ethics at a secular university, you may discover that the teaching is absorbed with the so-called *gray areas.* These are areas where right and wrong are determined by the individuals in the situation under consideration—and almost all situations are thought to be gray areas in some way!

Make no mistake: there will be no gray areas when it comes to determining who will live in God's presence and who won't. God knows those who are his and those who aren't. The choice to stay within the love of Christ or reject him confronts us daily. What does your choice today say about where you intend to spend eternity?

Discovery Learning

This page contains an alternative lesson plan emphasizing learning activities. Classes desiring such student involvement will find these suggestions helpful. The next page is a reproducible activity page to further enhance discovery learning.

LEARNING GOALS

After participating in this lesson, each student should be able to:

1. Recite ways that life in God's eternal presence will provide peace.

2. Contrast the security of Heaven with the insecurity of earthly life.

3. Describe one way to bring the peace of Heaven into daily life.

INTO THE LESSON

Distribute pencils and paper and ask students to design the safest home they can imagine. It should protect their families from intruders, accidents, and disasters. Give your students the choice of drawing a blueprint of the home or simply listing the safety features. (This activity is also found in the student books.)

When your students finish their drawings or lists, ask for volunteers to share their ideas. List these on the board. Some safety features they may mention include burglar alarms, smoke and carbon-monoxide detectors, childproof locks, fire-retardant building materials, deadbolt locks, and ground-fault interrupters on electrical outlets. Ask your class which safety features provide them with the most peace of mind.

Make a transition by saying that today's lesson will draw a sharp contrast between the insecurity of this life versus the security of Heaven.

(*Option:* place a copy of the Word Search activity from the reproducible page in each seat for students to work on as they arrive.)

INTO THE WORD

Divide your class into small groups. Half of your groups will complete Exercise #1; the other half will complete Exercise #2. If you do not use the student books, instruct your students to use paper and pencils from the previous activity.

Exercise #1: Life's Trials. Read the following passages and briefly describe the trials faced by Christians in the late first century AD: 3 John 9, 10; Revelation 2:9, 10, 13; 6:9, 10; 12:13-17; 13:5-7. Next, discuss within your group the questions that follow.

A. What do these trials have in common with those faced by Christians today?

B. What trials did early Christians face that we may not have to endure today, if any?

C. What trials do we face today that early Christians may not have endured, if any?

Exercise #2: Heaven's Security. Read Revelation 21:9-11, 22-27; 22:1-5. What are the images of security that the faithful Christians will enjoy in Heaven?

When the groups finish their research, ask each to share its findings. Potential responses for Exercise #1 include (A) martyrdom (in some parts of the world) and enemies within the church; (B) widespread and overt persecution (absent at least in Western democracies); (C) subtle discrimination and harassment—being passed over for job promotions, being excluded from social groups, being denied government grants, etc.

Potential responses for Exercise #2 include the safety of the walled city; the city's illumination against the evils of darkness; the presence of God and the Lamb; exclusion of all the unholy; no hunger or thirst for the saved; permanent absence of the curse of sin. Ask those who did the second exercise to choose which "security measures" they consider most important—that is, which features of Heaven will make them feel most secure about being there.

INTO LIFE

To close today's lesson, ask each student to complete the following statements. (Space is provided in the student books.)

1. I feel secure in my faith because _____.

2. Because I, as a Christian, enjoy the promise of Heaven, I no longer fear _____.

3. Because I no longer fear _____, I can do _____ for God. (Note: ask for specifics in the last two questions. Do not allow answers such as "anything" or "all things"!)

Allow a minute or two for your students to complete their work. Then ask for volunteers to share their answers to each statement. Make a list of these answers on the board, then discuss the implications of their answers. In particular, focus on their answers to the third statement, discussing what they can do for God because they have the promise of Heaven. Encourage your class to be bold in their daily service of Christ because they have his promise of heavenly security.

Word Search

Read Revelation 21:9-11, 22-27; 22:1-5. All the words in this list are found in the Scripture passages from today's lesson. Look across, up, down, and diagonally. Draw lines around the words as you find them.

```
S E R V A N T S U O I C E R P L
P H E A V E N A T I O N S A I E
L I P O U K O O B O W L S F W Y
E A S S E M A N R E I O E E R T
N U A S W Y A L I G H T V E G E
D I J E R U S A L E M O E U N M
O J W T Y E A C L E A R N S I P
R E E A U F R U I T T I A G L L
O W U G L O R Y A W H Y N N A E
A E A I O U H O N O R N G I E R
W L L A T S Y R C Y O A E K H A
P M A L B R I D E E N M L A M B
A L M I G H T Y I O E E S U W Y
```

seven angels; bowls; plagues; bride; lamb; Jerusalem; heaven; glory; brilliance; precious; jewel; jasper; crystal; temple; almighty; light; nations; kings; splendor; gates; honor; names; book; life; clear; throne; tree; fruit; healing; servants; name; lamp; reign

Our Community Now and in God's Future

Unit 3: Living in God's New World
(Lessons 10-13)

ANTICIPATING CHRIST'S RETURN

LESSON 13

WHY TEACH THIS LESSON?

Most all Christians are aware that the Bible teaches of Christ's return. Somehow we're supposed to live with that fact in mind. But most of the things we do on a daily basis seem so mundane, don't they? Studying for exams, changing the oil in the car, shopping for new socks—we don't usually meditate on Christ's return while doing any of these!

Yet the certainty of Christ's return is to influence the entirety of our lives. As a result, we don't cheat on exams, we don't throw out our used motor oil in a way that pollutes God's creation, and we demonstrate Christian patience (and maybe even evangelism) while in a long checkout line to pay for our new socks. Living life in view of Christ's return is a lifelong discipline. It starts with being convinced of the certainty of that great event. That's where today's lesson comes in. May we each allow the Holy Spirit to use today's text to convict us in this regard.

INTRODUCTION

A. THE BIGGER PICTURE

Everything seemed normal early on September 11, 2001, when a certain passenger jet took off. But soon a group of terrorists seized control of the plane and directed it toward Washington, D.C. The plan apparently was to ram the jet into the White House, the symbol of U.S. freedom and power. This was to be the last of four planes scheduled to wreak destruction on U.S. values that day.

When passengers began receiving cell phone calls from concerned family members, those aboard the plane soon realized that this hijacking was not motivated by the desire to extort money. This was an attack against the U.S. itself. A group of ordinary citizens began to see their present situation in light of the bigger picture. They decided to ignore their self-preservation instincts and attack the attackers. The result was a jet that crashed into a field in Pennsylvania rather than into a building in Washington, D.C.

We often get so busy with our lives that we let our busyness drown out the bigger picture of life. Yet every now and then something makes us look up and see that picture. Once the passengers aboard that jet became aware of the bigger picture, they made right decisions because they understood what was at stake.

Today's lesson focuses on the end of the book of Revelation. It calls Christians everywhere to "look up." It is a call to get out of the smallness of our individual circumstances and start acting with reference to the magnitude of eternity.

B. LESSON BACKGROUND

The point at the end of the book of Revelation is the same point that John has made all the way through: the Lord's victory is certain. His future return is the

DEVOTIONAL READING:
JOHN 16:17-24
BACKGROUND SCRIPTURE:
REVELATION 22
PRINTED TEXT:
REVELATION 22:6-21

LESSON AIMS

After participating in this lesson, each student will be able to:

1. Identify the main purpose of the book of Revelation.

2. Summarize how Revelation 22 describes Christ's return.

3. Suggest one specific area of life in which he or she will focus to keep "the sayings of the prophecy" of Revelation.

KEY VERSE

He who testifies to these things says, "Yes, I am coming soon."

Amen. Come, Lord Jesus. —Revelation 22:20

May 27

LESSON 13 NOTES

hope that enables us to remain faithful in the face of trial. It is important, though, that we understand the meaning of *hope*. In modern English this word often means something like "wishful thinking," as in "I hope I win a new car." But *hope* in biblical contexts means something more like "expectation." Christian hope is not wishful thinking but rather is confident expectation. As the writer of Hebrews notes, "Now faith is being sure of what we hope for and certain of what we do not see" (Hebrews 11:1).

Thus, Christian hope is our certainty that the Lord will indeed return. If we know friends are coming for dinner, we are expecting them and that means action is required. An important aspect of expectation is the way that our awareness of what is to happen affects how we prepare for that event. Christian hope reveals its true colors in how we live our lives in the here and now.

The book of Revelation helps the reader develop this true Christian hope. As John comes to the end of the book, all his points will support this major thrust.

I. TRUST THIS MESSAGE (REVELATION 22:6-10)

A. NATURE OF THE MESSAGE (vv. 6-9)

6. The angel said to me, "These words are trustworthy and true. The Lord, the God of the spirits of the prophets, sent his angel to show his servants the things that must soon take place."

The point John now makes is one he has made before: the Word of the Lord is reliable. It is *trustworthy and true* (compare Revelation 3:14; 19:11; 21:5). Christians of all eras can stake their lives on the truth of this prophecy!

While all of Revelation is faithful and true, the context requires us to observe what the angel has in mind specifically at this point. The angel is about to show John *the things that must soon take place*. The idea of *soon* (mentioned four times in Revelation 22) normally can refer either to a brief interval of time (as in "shortly" or "without much delay") or to speed (as in "quickly" or "swiftly"). Here, however, it is likely that John is simply suggesting that these things will certainly occur. Thus he communicates to his readers a sense of urgency. It's another way of saying that something must indeed take place.

We recall that "With the Lord a day is like a thousand years, and a thousand years are like a day" (2 Peter 3:8). This cautions us against imposing our view of time on God. Rather than computing time lines, we will do well to focus on how faithful and true the Lord's words are.

7. "Behold, I am coming soon! Blessed is he who keeps the words of the prophecy in this book."

Again, the overall point is that Jesus will certainly return. We should note carefully the implicit warning in this verse. The person for whom Jesus' return will be a *blessed* occasion is the person who is prepared. Such a person pays attentions to and keeps the message of the *book* of Revelation. For anyone not prepared, Jesus' return undoubtedly will be "too soon" (compare Matthew 25:1-13).

8, 9. I, John, am the one who heard and saw these things. And when I had heard and seen them, I fell down to worship at the feet of the angel who had been showing them to me. But he said to me, "Do not do it! I am a fellow servant with you and with your brothers the prophets and of all who keep the words of this book. Worship God!"

John is overcome by the experience and makes the mistake of attempting to *worship . . . the angel*. Even given all that the apostle John has seen and experienced, he still makes big mistakes! Even when we try our best, we too will make mistakes.

WHAT DO YOU THINK?

How will you live your life with the fact of the Lord's soon return in mind? What mistakes will you be careful to avoid?

[You may find Matthew 24: 36-51; Mark 13:35-37; and Acts 1:11 useful in your answer.]

John undoubtedly knows of the occasions when Cornelius bowed down to Peter (Acts 10:25, 26) and when villagers tried to offer sacrifices to Paul and Barnabas (Acts 14:11-18). Thus it is interesting that John makes his mistake not once but twice (see Revelation 19:10). John's mistakes come from the overwhelming nature of his experience. Even when we have the best of intentions, even when our heart is just right, we can still make significant mistakes that contradict the nature of our faith. A person may be *sincere* while being *sincerely wrong*. Just because we mean well does not mean that our actions are correct.

B. URGENCY OF THE MESSAGE (v. 10)

10. Then he told me, "Do not seal up the words of the prophecy of this book, because the time is near.

Interestingly, this is the exact opposite of the instructions given to the prophet Daniel (see Daniel 12:4). The directions that John receives speak to the very heart of the book of Revelation: it is a *revelation* from God for us. We bear a responsibility to study this message and gain from it what the Lord wants to give to us.

That John refers to the *time* being *near* should not mislead us into thinking in terms of "right away." As previously, the word *time* has a qualitative value. Hebrews 1:2 refers to "these last days." The apostle John speaks of his day as "the last hour" (1 John 2:18). If we don't sort through this issue carefully, we may end up asking arrogantly, "Where is this 'coming' he promised?" (2 Peter 3:4).

A mistake of some readers of the Bible is to think that they can predict when the Lord will return. Every one of them has failed (see Matthew 24:36; Acts 1:7; 1 Thessalonians 5:1, 2). The point is that it *will* happen. Thus our appropriate response is not to guess when but to be ready for it. We are to expect it!

COMING SOONER, OR LATER?

In one sense, time is *static*: it moves forward second by second for everyone. But in another sense, time seems to be *relative*: the pace of life has not always moved as rapidly as it seems to do for most of us today.

Think about automobile speeds. In the early twentieth century when the automobile was a new invention, people were amazed at how fast they could go. The fact that this was not very fast was demonstrated in 2003 by a cross-country parade of Model T Fords in celebration of the Ford Motor Company's one-hundredth anniversary. Fifty of the antique cars traveled from southern California to Dearborn, Michigan, taking 19 days to do so. Their top speed was 45 miles per hour.

Today we routinely travel much faster when we are able to break free from the gridlock of large cities. Yet in the early 1900s, some speculated that people would die, perhaps from a heart attack or asphyxiation, if they were to exceed 60 miles per hour. We chuckle at such quaint ideas.

The insistence of some that Christ will return soon—meaning "by such-and-such a date"—is an example of how rapidly we expect things to move. The fact that 2,000 years have elapsed since Christ's first coming makes some folks impatient. That seems like a long time, relatively speaking. Yet church history has proven the folly of trying to solve our impatience with date-setting. Christ may not be coming tomorrow, but he *is* coming *certainly!*   —C. R. B.

II. CHOOSE YOUR DESTINATION (REVELATION 22:11, 12)

A. BEYOND THE POINT OF NO RETURN (v. 11)

11. "Let him who does wrong continue to do wrong; let him who is vile continue to be vile; let him who does right continue to do right; and let him who is holy continue to be holy."

If we're not paying attention, we can easily misread this verse to mean that God has no interest in allowing people to be transferred out of "the dominion of darkness" and "into the kingdom of the Son he loves" (Colossians 1:13). John is seeing the final outcome of all things; there will be at a certain, particular point in the history of salvation no opportunity for second thoughts. It will all be finished.

The end result of those who are not faithful, who prefer to *do wrong*, is that they will *continue to do wrong*. The end result of the faithful, who are made righteous, is that they also remain in that state. This verse thus views eternal destinies from a perspective that is past the point of no return.

If in this life we obstinately chose to be spiritually *vile*, then we will forever be condemned as vile. If, however, we deny ourselves and prefer to serve Christ and his purposes in this world, then we will forever be justified.

B. BEFORE THE POINT OF NO RETURN (v. 12)

12. "Behold, I am coming soon! My reward is with me, and I will give to everyone according to what he has done.

John starts by repeating the *"I am coming soon!"* (or "certainly") theme, and then he moves to the subject of Jesus' *reward*. The point is that the certainty of Jesus' return will be accompanied by the certainty that he will repay each *according to what he has done*. This is not "works salvation" but is a recognition that our works demonstrate our faith—or lack thereof (James 2:14-26).

The idea of reward or recompense occurs frequently in the Bible (Psalm 28:4; 62:12; Isaiah 40:10; 59:18; 62:11; Ephesians 6:8; etc.). And before we assume that all is well for us in this area personally, let's give close attention to Matthew 25:31-46. There Jesus offers a clear warning to those who think that they are serving God when in reality they are not.

III. EXPECT CHRIST (REVELATION 22:13-15)

A. IDENTITY OF HE WHO COMES (v. 13)

13. "I am the Alpha and the Omega, the First and the Last, the Beginning and the End.

For the last few verses, John has described the final outcome of the decisions we make in this life. Now John puts the spotlight on the God of history; this is the God who makes known "the end from the beginning" (Isaiah 46:10; compare 44:6; 48:12). He knows our past, present, and future. This imagery reaffirms the power of God to do exactly what he says he will do: repay all people according to the choices made in this life. (We discussed *the Alpha and the Omega* in Lesson 11.)

B. IDENTITY OF THE BLESSED (v. 14)

14. "Blessed are those who wash their robes, that they may have the right to the tree of life and may go through the gates into the city.

While John's vision is in the Spirit and of the future, everything he writes is for the benefit of his readers in this world. We've now read that the Lord will certainly come. By the time the end comes there will be no chance of changing our minds. He will certainly repay us according to our choices in this life.

Thus we understand the significance of the verse before us: we will be *blessed* if we choose the Lord now while we have a choice. For those who remain faithful, their reward from Jesus will be the blessing of the *tree of life* and entrance into the holy *city*. This means eternity with our creator, never to be separated again.

WHAT DO YOU THINK?

What are some ways that keeping the commandments of Christ has enriched your life?

C. IDENTITY OF THE CURSED (v. 15)

15. *"Outside are the dogs, those who practice magic arts, the sexually immoral, the murderers, the idolaters and everyone who loves and practices falsehood."*

Here we have the flip side of the situation. Those who persist in making unholy choices in this life will not enter the eternal city. They will not experience abundance and security. They will not experience the eternal presence of God. If you choose God in this life, then your identity will be blessed. But if you choose yourself and your own desires in this life, then you will be identified for all eternity as having made that choice.

IV. LISTEN TO THE FINAL WORDS (REVELATION 22:16-21)

A. TESTIMONY (v. 16)

16. *"I, Jesus, have sent my angel to give you this testimony for the churches. I am the Root and the Offspring of David, and the bright Morning Star."*

Most of the announcements in Revelation come from divine messengers sent from God. But this is one of the occasions in which the Lord himself speaks. It is further confirmation for the reader that this is a reliable message. This brings Revelation full circle, since it is a repetition of how the book began (Revelation 1:1, 2).

During Christ's earthly ministry, people generally expected that if he were the Messiah, then he would mount some kind of political or military campaign (compare Acts 1:6). That he did not do so probably was a disappointment to many. However, when Jesus now announces that he is *the Root and the Offspring of David*, his kingship is beyond doubt. We have to appreciate that the culture of the ancient Jews understands this phrase to be a reference to a warrior Messiah.

The reference begins in Isaiah 11:1-10, where the prophet refers to a new growth springing up from Jesse, the father of King David. The image there is of a felled tree, most likely referring to the apparent end of David's line of kings. But there is still life in these roots and they allow for the growth of a successor: the Messiah. "The root of David has triumphed" (Revelation 5:5). Jesus is indeed a victorious warrior, but not in the way many in the first century expect.

The title *bright Morning Star* has been rather difficult for many commentators to explain. It seems best to understand this title as being based on Numbers 24:17. That verse was understood by Jews to be a reference to a coming Messiah who would destroy God's enemies. Thus, both of these titles refer to Jesus as a victorious, conquering Messiah. This divine warrior-king blesses those who accept him, but he also punishes those who don't.

B. PLEA (v. 17)

17. *The Spirit and the bride say, "Come!" And let him who hears say, "Come!" Whoever is thirsty, let him come; and whoever wishes, let him take the free gift of the water of life.*

Much has already been said to the reader of Revelation, and much has been repeated for emphasis. Throughout the book we've heard the warnings of eternal death that come with rejecting the truth of Christ. We've heard of eternal blessings that are available for all who embrace that truth. What is our obvious response? Here in the final verses of the book we are told that we respond correctly when we *come*.

The book of Revelation is a message of hope. Hope enables us to remain faithful, and our faithfulness ensures our hope. Our hope is in Christ's ability to secure us for eternity. Our hope is in Christ and his victory over sin and death. This

Visual for Lesson 13. *Use this visual to introduce the second discussion question on page 338. Ask, "Do we really want Jesus to 'come quickly'?"*

is what impels us to come and to *say, Come* to others who are *thirsty.* Who can turn away from such a plea?

C. WARNING (vv. 18, 19)

18, 19. I warn everyone who hears the words of the prophecy of this book: If anyone adds anything to them, God will add to him the plagues described in this book. And if anyone takes words away from this book of prophecy, God will take away from him his share in the tree of life and in the holy city, which are described in this book.

To ignore *the words* of the *book* of Revelation is bad enough. How much worse will it be for the one who hears the words of Revelation then obscures or abuses that message! Such a person will be cursed.

D. AFFIRMATIONS (vv. 20, 21)

20, 21. He who testifies to these things says, "Yes, I am coming soon."
   Amen. Come, Lord Jesus.
The grace of the Lord Jesus be with God's people. Amen.

We come to the last words of the Bible. The final point is that the one who is behind the revelation of this message will certainly *come* again. (Note our earlier discussion concerning the word *soon.*) The importance of this fact is embedded deeply within the fabric of this book. The Lord really will return, and all that we have read really will come about. We do well to expect his return and prepare for it through our faithfulness.

NO ASTERISK

On September 24, 1919, Babe Ruth hit home run number 28 of the season. That feat broke a record that had stood for 35 years. In 1920 and 1921 he raised that single-season record to 54 and 59, respectively. Ruth's final record came in 1927, when he hit 60 homers. His record held until 1961, when Roger Maris hit 61. However, Maris's feat was brought into question by the fact that 8 games were added to the schedule.

Mark McGwire broke Maris's record in 1998, hitting 70 homers. Barry Bonds passed McGwire in 2001 with 73. But these records are tainted by scandals relating to the alleged use of drugs to enhance performance. So the argument among baseball fans has been, "Does scheduling additional games or ignoring rules against drug use disqualify later records? Shouldn't we add an asterisk to those later records, with a note of explanation at the bottom, to say 'maybe, maybe not'?"

In the eternal scheme of things, arguments about baseball records mean little. However, John writes a warning that is of eternal significance: the revelation he received is God's message and its provisions do not change. We are either with Christ or against him. As a result of this choice, a person's name is either written in the book of life or it is not. There is no asterisk, either there or after the last *Amen* in the Bible, to say "maybe, maybe not."   —C. R. B.

CONCLUSION

The last word in the Bible is *Amen.* With that word the aged apostle John finished his earthly writing ministry before the Lord called him home. Yet the challenges offered by what John wrote are ever new. We worship and serve the Lamb because the Lamb is worthy. We tell others about the Lamb for the same reason.

There comes a time when the eternal destiny of a person is "locked in," never to change. That day comes either when a person dies or, for those still living, when Jesus returns. Eternity beckons. What is your choice?

Sidebar:

WHAT DO YOU THINK?

How do you make sure that you are not adding to or subtracting from the Bible? Was there ever a time when you slipped up in this regard? How did you get back on track?

WHAT DO YOU THINK?

Can you honestly say, "Come, Lord Jesus" as if you wanted him to return today? Why, or why not?

PRAYER

Lord, help us to prepare the world for the hope that you have for us. In our own lives help us to use the message of Revelation to overcome all that stands between us and serving you and your people. In Jesus' name, amen.

THOUGHT TO REMEMBER

Christ's return is certain.

Discovery Learning

This page contains an alternative lesson plan emphasizing learning activities. Classes desiring such student involvement will find these suggestions helpful. The next page is a reproducible activity page to further enhance discovery learning.

LEARNING GOALS

After this lesson, each student will be able to:

1. Identify the main purpose of the book of Revelation.

2. Summarize how Revelation 22 describes Christ's return.

3. Suggest one specific area of life in which he or she will focus to keep "the sayings of the prophecy" of Revelation.

INTO THE LESSON

Open today's lesson by sharing the following notorious predictions of the end of the world: In 793, Beatus, abbot of Liébana, Spain, prophesied on Easter day of the end of the world. His prediction started a riot. In 1719, Jacques Bernoulli, a famous Swiss mathematician, predicted the return of a comet that passed the Earth in 1680. This time the comet was supposed to strike and destroy the planet.

The July 20, 1993, issue of a supermarket tabloid predicted that asteroid "M-167" would strike the Earth on November 11, 1993, and possibly end life on the planet. There is no asteroid M-167. In 1999, a self-proclaimed prophet warned that solar flares would strike the Earth in April of that year and kill most of the population.

Ask your students to complete the following open-ended sentence (also printed in the student books): *If I knew for certain that the world would end next week, I would . . .*

Ask several volunteers to share their answers. Then say, "As you may have guessed by now, today's lesson deals with the return of Christ and the end of the world."

(*Option:* place a copy of the Puzzled by Christ's Return exercise from the reproducible page in seats for students to work on as they arrive.)

INTO THE WORD

Divide your class into groups of three or four. Direct the groups to the activity "The Return of Christ" in the student book. If you don't use the student books, provide paper and pencils; then assign each team one of the following passages: Revelation 22:6-10; Revelation 22:11-15; Revelation 22:16-21.

Instruct each group to write a brief, two- or three-sentence paraphrase of its assigned passage. Then each group is to answer the following questions about its assigned text.

Revelation 22:6-10. 1. How could John have been told that Jesus is coming "soon" (v. 7) if it has been nearly 2,000 years since that revelation? 2. Why was John told not to worship the angel (vv. 8, 9)? 3. What do you think verse 10 means when it says, "the time is near"?

Revelation 22:11-15. 1. What do you think verse 11 means when it talks about a person who does wrong/is vile or a person who does right/is holy? 2. What is the most important work that we are called to do? (See also John 6:29.) 3. Who identifies himself as "the Alpha and the Omega" in verse 13? (See also v. 16.) Why is this significant in light of Revelation 21:5, 6? 4. What is signified by the tree of life (v. 14)?

Revelation 22:16-21. 1. How does Jesus identify himself in verse 16? Recall the lesson on Revelation 5. What is significant about Jesus' descent from David? (See Isaiah 11:1-10; Matthew 22:42-45.) 2. Who are the Spirit and the bride (v. 17)? What invitation do they offer? 3. What will happen to those who attempt to modify the book of Revelation? Why?

When your teams finish their studies, use your lesson commentary and the questions above to discuss findings. Especially emphasize the lesson writer's key to understanding the entire book of Revelation: The Lord's victory is certain. His future return is the hope that enables us to remain faithful in the face of trial.

INTO LIFE

Remind your students of their answers to the first exercise in today's lesson. Then direct the class to the two open-ended statements below. (Write them on the board.)

1. *If I knew for certain that Jesus would return one week from today, I would . . .*

2. *Because I believe the New Testament's promise that Jesus will return someday, and I know that it could be today, I will . . .*

Ask for volunteers to share their thoughts. Stress why answers to the second statement are much more important than answers to the first. Pray with your class for the faith to expect the return of Christ, the wisdom to prepare for that return, and the resolve to live with that expectation in mind.

Puzzled by Christ's Return

Read Revelation 22:6-21 to find the answers to this crossword puzzle.

Across:

1. Means "beginning"; 5. Jesus intended this for the churches; 6. The first of creation; 8. Not practiced in Heaven; 11. Close or shut; 13. Last word of Revelation; 15. John's guide in Heaven; 16. Another name for the church; 18. A source of life in Heaven; 20. Jesus is the bright ____ ; 22. Those who crave the water of life; 24. Some love and practice this; 26. Reserved for God; 28. Jesus is bringing this; 29. Bids us to "come"; 30. The angel said this is near; 31. Separated from sin.

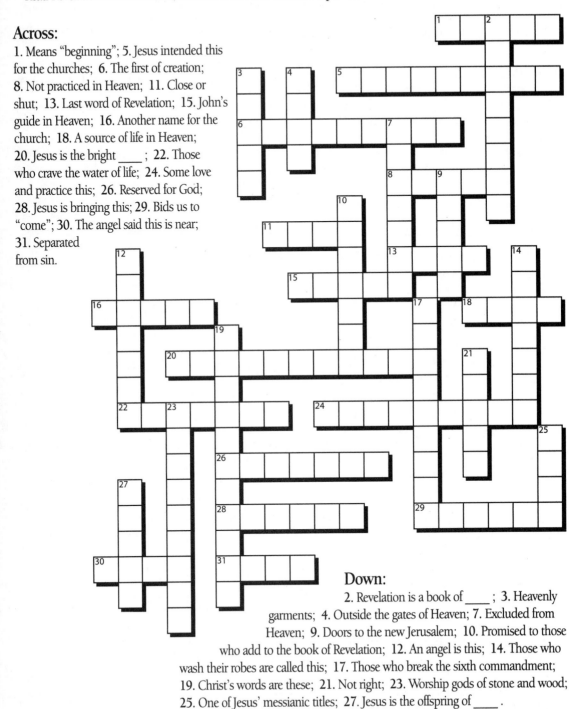

Down:

2. Revelation is a book of ____ ; 3. Heavenly garments; 4. Outside the gates of Heaven; 7. Excluded from Heaven; 9. Doors to the new Jerusalem; 10. Promised to those who add to the book of Revelation; 12. An angel is this; 14. Those who wash their robes are called this; 17. Those who break the sixth commandment; 19. Christ's words are these; 21. Not right; 23. Worship gods of stone and wood; 25. One of Jesus' messianic titles; 27. Jesus is the offspring of ____ .

Summer Quarter 2007

Committed to Doing Right

(Prophets, Lamentations, and 2 Kings)

Special Features

Lessons

Unit 1: Life as God's People

Unit 2: What Does God Require?

Unit 3: How Shall We Respond?

About These Lessons

To *commit* means "to obligate or pledge oneself." Many people have no problem doing that when it comes to signing a contract for a car loan. But to commit one's life to God—that can be a different story! Yet nothing is more important. This quarter's lessons show us why.

Jun 3

Jun 10

Jun 17

Jun 24

Jul 1

Jul 8

Jul 15

Jul 22

Jul 29

Aug 5

Aug 12

Aug 19

Aug 26

Back to Basics

by Doug Redford

A series of studies on doing right may seem a bit pointless. Isn't it kind of like reinventing the wheel? Shouldn't we be studying something deeper? The sobering truth is that God's people have always had to guard against compromising their commitment to doing what is right. As someone once observed, too many Christians are like thermometers, merely reflecting the moral and spiritual temperature around them. Often the problem is not that we become engaged in blatant, outright sin; instead, we simply lose our first love (see Revelation 2:4). We compromise our standards and are no longer committed to doing right.

Instead of being thermometers, we are to resemble thermostats, setting (with God's help) the moral and spiritual standards. We do this by word and example, encouraging others to pursue a God-honoring lifestyle.

Perhaps no group of people can shake us out of spiritual apathy better than the Old Testament prophets. Most of the Scripture texts this quarter are drawn from the books that record the timeless messages of these courageous men of God (with additional passages from the books of 2 Kings and 2 Chronicles). This series of lessons encourages us to rekindle the commitment to doing right—even when wrong appears to be the more popular choice.

Lesson 1 stresses that we cannot pursue what is just and right unless we let God determine what those terms mean.

Lesson 2 uses the language of the courtroom to describe how the Lord had a charge against his people (Hosea 4:1).

Lesson 3 allows us to consider that God's primary concern with worship is the gap between what his people say in worship and how they live daily.

Lesson 4 encourages seeking God. To become a Christian is not the end of a search; it is a never-ending adventure to be carried out on God's terms, not ours.

In **Lesson 5** we hear the prophet Micah pose the question, "What does the Lord require of you?" (Micah 6:8). God has always wanted obedience.

God's judgment is an important theme in **Lesson 6**. A day of reckoning is unavoidable, and each will be held accountable.

A key theme of **Lesson 7** is the righteous will live by faith. This was expected of the ancient Judeans and is expected of us as well.

Lesson 8 focuses on accountability. Yes, God will hold accountable those who reject him; but he will also richly bless all who repent.

Lesson 9 is entitled "Committed to Trusting God." In God's own time he brought his people back from captivity. Will we trust him to bring us through?

Lesson 10 reminds us that even in tragedy, "It is good to wait quietly for the salvation of the Lord" (Lamentations 3:26).

Lesson 11 teaches us that the road to reconciliation with God begins with the acknowledgment that we are sinners.

In **Lesson 12**, God's loving invitation was "Return to me . . . and I will return to you" (Zechariah 1:3). This invitation is echoed in James 4:8.

Lesson 13 highlights another phase of God's plan: a messenger of a new covenant will come. We know him to be Jesus Christ. Today we Christians are God's messengers on behalf of that messenger—commissioned to be his witnesses to a world that desperately needs to follow the right way. May we be faithful to the task before us!

The Assyrian Empire

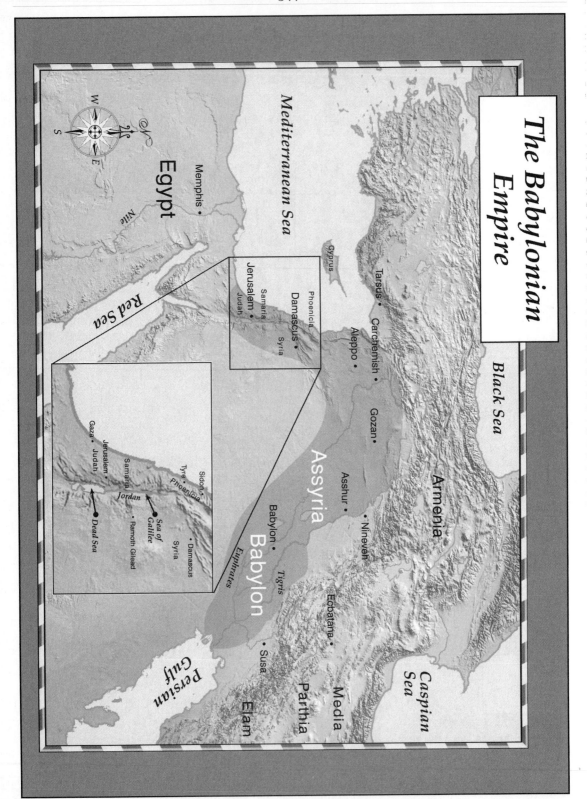

The Babylonian Empire

Committed to Doing Right

Unit 1: Life as God's People
(Lessons 1-4)

COMMITTED TO JUSTICE

WHY TEACH THIS LESSON?

Drivers have to deal with blind spots on the road. A blind spot is the area between the view of the mirrors of a vehicle, where the driver cannot see. Safety demands that a driver be aware of these blind spots.

Similarly, believers sometimes have spiritual blind spots. A believer may think that he or she correctly perceives a situation, while actually being out of step with God's truth. Yet blind spots are very real! Amos' ministry was, in part, to point out spiritual blind spots to the Israelites. They didn't seem to realize that they had missed his Word and his will. Today's lesson points to a very crucial truth for believers: once our eyes have been opened to spiritual blind spots, we need to change and follow God's Word.

INTRODUCTION

A. THE PRICE OF TELLING THE TRUTH

Have you ever had to tell someone an unpleasant truth? Have you ever paid a price for telling the truth? Amos the prophet was a truth-teller. He paid the price of ridicule, even direct repudiation (Amos 7:12, 13).

Telling the truth was dangerous in Amos's world. Even today, a person with a message like Amos's might be dismissed or killed. Yet what the world needs today are more people like Amos, willing to stand up for the truth when it is inconvenient or even dangerous.

Amos is often ignored in the contemporary church. This might be understandable if we had solved all the problems Amos talked about, but we haven't. Maybe we ignore Amos today for the same reason people ignored him in his own time—he hit too close to home.

B. LESSON BACKGROUND

Amos is one of what are often called the *Minor Prophets*. These prophets are not called minor because their books are insignificant. They are called minor because the books are relatively short. The Minor Prophets are collected in a group of 12 books that could be contained on a normal-sized scroll.

Amos prophesied around 760 BC. He prophesied to the northern kingdom of Israel, about 38 years before it fell to Assyrian invaders. It appears that Amos prophesied around the same time as Hosea and Zechariah, perhaps a little before Isaiah and Micah. Those desiring to know more about those times should study 2 Kings 14:23–15:7 and 2 Chronicles 26.

Amos is, in certain respects, a rather unusual choice to deliver prophecy. First, Amos himself confessed that he was not a trained prophet, nor was he related to any prophet (Amos 7:14). In some places in the ancient world, there were schools for prophets, where groups of men studied under a prophet. Other places had a notion of succession—that children of those who prophesied might well be prophets themselves. Amos had neither of these credentials. He was a

DEVOTIONAL READING:
PSALM 82

BACKGROUND SCRIPTURE:
AMOS 5:10-24; 8:4-12; 2 KINGS 13:23-25

PRINTED TEXT:
AMOS 5:10-24

LESSON AIMS

After participating in this lesson, each student will be able to:

1. Describe the evils that Amos condemned.

2. Compare and contrast the evils cited in today's text with those seen in modern society.

3. Make a plan for his or her church to help correct one societal injustice.

KEY VERSE

Let justice roll on like a river, righteousness like a never-failing stream!
—Amos 5:24

simple farmer and shepherd. Yet God had written on Amos's heart a message he could not suppress (Amos 7:15).

Second, Amos was from Tekoa, a small town about 20 miles south of Jerusalem (Amos 1:1; compare 2 Chronicles 11:6). That makes him a Judean, yet he was called to go northward from Judah to Israel. There was friction between the two nations, and the northern kingdom was quite resistant to a prophet from the south calling them to account (Amos 7:10-13). Yet God gave Amos a burden. Thus Amos had to speak up.

To the casual observer, it seemed that things in Israel were going quite well at the time. It was a time of general prosperity, and many had become quite wealthy. But Amos looked beneath the veneer and saw great social and religious corruption. The real picture was one of decadence (Amos 2:8; 4:1; 6:1-6), immorality (2:7), and—worst of all—idolatry (8:14).

In chapters 1 and 2, Amos indicts eight regions for their sins. At the end of the book, chapters 7–9 relate certain visions that Amos received. They contain images of grasshoppers, fire, a plumb line, fruit, and God and the altar. All of these visions relate to Israel's judgment.

In the middle of the book, chapters 3–6 appear to contain three sermons. Scholars have different methods by which to distinguish the three. One common method separates the sermons by the phrase "hear this word" in Amos 3:1; 4:1; and 5:1. So the first sermon is chapter 3; it deals with the sinful affairs in Israel. The second sermon is chapter 4; it speaks of Israel's past sinful conduct. The third sermon is chapter 5; it warns of Israel's punishment if they do not change.

Today's lesson comes from this third sermon. This entire section of Amos 5:1-17 is also called a *lament* (see v. 1). The tone of the sermon in chapter 5 is set in verse 5. There Amos warned the people not to go to Bethel. Bethel was historic; it was the place where Jacob saw the vision of angels (Genesis 28:10-22). Nevertheless, Amos did not want the Israelites to go there because of corrupted worship in that place. People had turned Bethel into a substitute for Jerusalem. The worship in Bethel was blatantly idolatrous.

This fact leads Amos to condemn Bethel, Gilgal, and Beersheba as a group. Amos looks for evidence of genuine worship in these places and finds none (compare Hosea 4:15; Amos 8:14). This condemnation continues through Amos 5:6. In verse 7 the concern switches from one of false religion to one of false justice. With the tone of the sermon now set, we break in at Amos 5:10.

Assyrian. Uh-SEAR-e-un.
Beersheba. Beer-SHE-buh.
Bethel. BETH-ul.
Ephraim. EE-fray-im.
Hosea. Ho-ZAY-uh.
Malachi. MAL-uh-kye.
Manasseh. Muh-NASS-uh.
Obadiah. O-buh-DYE-uh.
Tekoa. Tih-KO-uh.
Zechariah. ZEK-uh-RYE-uh.
Zephaniah. Zef-uh-NYE-uh.

I. BEWARE OF SOCIAL SINS (AMOS 5:10-15)

A. INDICTMENT (vv. 10, 11)

10. You hate the one who reproves in court
    and despise him who tells the truth.

We catch Amos in the middle of a strong indictment against the behavior of God's people. Translations that are more literal use the word *gate* instead of *court* because legal proceedings are held at the city gate. That is where many business and legal transactions take place. It is where the city elders meet (examples: Deuteronomy 21:18-21; Ruth 4:1-11).

One who reproves is someone in authority who renders verdicts. Amos thus charges his listeners with being completely uninterested in justice and truth. In modern terminology we could say that people don't want honest judges or witnesses (compare Proverbs 24:23-25; Isaiah 29:21).

11. You trample on the poor
    and force him to give you grain.

Therefore, though you have built stone mansions,
    you will not live in them;
though you have planted lush vineyards,
    you will not drink their wine.

The rich have robbed *the poor* of their livelihood. Tying in with verse 10, the picture is of the rich abusing the court system to steal *grain* from the poor. There will be punishment! Though the rich may build fine houses, one day they will stand empty. Though the rich may plant *vineyards,* one day they will stand unpicked. The ancient curse of Deuteronomy 28:30 is about to be fulfilled!

B. Warning (vv. 12, 13)

12. For I know how many are your offenses
    and how great your sins.
You oppress the righteous and take bribes
    and you deprive the poor of justice in the courts.

God's anger is justified because the people have committed such injustice. One of the *great . . . sins* is the rich giving *bribes* to those who pass judgment. Thus the rich use the court system to *deprive the poor* of their livelihood. If the legal system is corrupted so that those who can afford a bribe can get the outcome they want, then there is no hope for the poor. Denial of justice is specifically forbidden in the covenant (Exodus 23:1-8; Deuteronomy 16:18-20). The penalty for such denial is severe (see Isaiah 10:1-4; 29:20, 21).

Taking a Bribe

In the 1980s a major American city was hit by *Operation Greylord,* an effort to expose corruption among public officials. The facts disclosed were frightening. Corrupt lawyers conspired to request bribe money from their clients to pay off cooperative judges. In the corridors of the court building, courtroom personnel often bickered over the split of the bribes that were flowing into the judge's chambers.

A young state's attorney took $50 from misdemeanor defendants on the "understanding" that they would not be prosecuted vigorously. A secret FBI recording caught one judge requesting help from city politicians to get a different assignment, promising to help support the proposed political slate of new judges. One judge accepted $10,000 to acquit a man accused of assassinating a labor union official. Another judge was accused of "fixing" at least three murder trials.

By the time the investigation ended, 92 individuals were indicted. They consisted of 17 judges, 48 lawyers, 8 policemen, 10 deputy sheriffs, 8 court officials, and 1 member of the state legislature (www.fbi.gov).

Amos would not have been surprised by such revelations. Even in his time, officials afflicted the just, accepted bribes, and denied the poor their rights. Amos calls these "offenses" and "great . . . sins." What do we call them? —J. B. N.

13. Therefore the prudent man keeps quiet in such times,
    for the times are evil.

This seems to be a strange verse at first glance. Aren't we supposed to speak up when we see injustice and not *keep quiet?*

Amos is merely describing the situation as it exists at the time as he observes it. He is not recommending that people stay quiet—he himself certainly hasn't! He is illustrating that things have become so corrupt that even sensible people are afraid to speak the truth. Things have become so bad that *prudent* people just keep quiet. They don't want to make trouble for themselves. They live in a society that does not reward tellers of truth—it punishes them.

What Do You Think?

Jesus said, "The poor you will always have with you" (Matthew 26:11). What are some proper and improper ways to react to this verse?

[Be sure to consider James 1:27 and 2 Thessalonians 3:10 in your answer.]

Daily Bible Readings

Monday, May 28—A Plea for Justice (Psalm 82)

Tuesday, May 29—Where Is Justice and Truth? (Isaiah 59: 9-15)

Wednesday, May 30—Do What Is Just (Jeremiah 22:1-5)

Thursday, May 31—God Admonishes Israel (Amos 3:1-10)

Friday, June 1—Protect the Poor (Amos 8:4-8)

Saturday, June 2—Seek Good, Not Evil (Amos 5:10-15)

Sunday, June 3—Let Justice Roll Down (Amos 5:20-25

C. PLEA (vv. 14, 15)

14. *Seek good, not evil,*
    that you may live.
Then the LORD God Almighty will be with you,
    just as you say he is.

The people think that *God* is with them. But Amos points out that God is with them only if they decide to pursue *good*. Those who pervert justice have a powerful enemy!

15. *Hate evil, love good;*
    maintain justice in the courts.
Perhaps the LORD God Almighty will have mercy
    on the remnant of Joseph.

Not only are the people to pursue *the good*, they also are to *hate the evil* (compare Romans 12:9). This suggests that the commitment to righteousness, while involving the behavior of the people, finds its source ultimately in the heart.

The phrase *remnant of Joseph* hearkens back to Amos 5:6, which has "house of Joseph." Joseph was father to Ephraim and Manasseh, after whom 2 of the 12 tribes are named (Joshua 14:4). The dire predictions against the house of Joseph in verse 6 are balanced against a promise of hope. It's not too late to repent!

II. BEWARE THE DAY OF THE LORD (AMOS 5:16-20)

A. THERE WILL BE WEEPING (vv. 16, 17)

16. *Therefore this is what the Lord, the LORD God Almighty, says:*
    "There will be wailing in all the streets
        and cries of anguish in every public square.
    The farmers will be summoned to weep
        and the mourners to wail.

Amos paints a picture of a nation that will be in total despair. Everyone will cry out, from the city dwellers to the simple *farmers* to the professional *mourners*.

17. *There will be wailing in all the vineyards,*
    for I will pass through your midst,"
                        says the LORD.

What makes the judgment all the more poignant is that the *wailing* will take place as God walks through their *midst*. Leviticus 26:6 speaks of what happens when people obey the Lord—it is a time when "the sword will not pass through your country." The case before us is just the opposite. The defeat that will come shortly in 722 BC will indeed be severe (2 Kings 17).

B. THERE WILL BE DARKNESS (vv. 18-20)

18. *Woe to you who long*
    for the day of the LORD!
Why do you long for the day of the LORD?
    That day will be darkness, not light.

The phrase *day of the Lord* appears about two dozen times in the Bible. It is a popular concept at various times in the history of prophecy. In addition to Amos, the prophets Isaiah, Jeremiah, Ezekiel, Joel, Obadiah, Zephaniah, Zechariah, and Malachi use this phrase.

The Day of the Lord is that time when God balances the scales and defeats the enemies of his people. Usually the ancient Israelites anticipate this to be a great day. But Amos warns that that day will be bad news for all who oppose God, even if they are of Jewish descent. What Amos's audience fails to see is that the

WHAT DO YOU THINK?

Why do you find it difficult at times to hate the evil and love the good? How do you overcome this difficulty?

WHAT DO YOU THINK?

If God were to come walking through the garden of your life or the life of your church, in what areas would he find you lamenting your state of affairs? What would you confess to him? How do you think he would respond?

Day of the Lord is a time for God to judge sins. (In the New Testament, see Acts 2:20; 1 Corinthians 5:5; 2 Corinthians 1:14; 1 Thessalonians 5:2; 2 Peter 3:10.)

19. *It will be as though a man fled from a lion*
    only to meet a bear,
  as though he entered his house
    and rested his hand on the wall
    only to have a snake bite him.

Amos uses two figures of speech to illustrate what happens on the Day of the Lord. The images could be almost humorous were it not for the real tragedy that awaits. Think about it: first *a man* flees from a *lion* only to run into a vicious *bear*. The one who escapes from the lion must feel a sense of relief. "Whew, that was close!" he says. But this is a false sense of security.

The second figure is of a man who makes it to what he thinks is the safety of his home. The pain of a snakebite then jolts him out of his false sense of security!

Out of the Frying Pan

The old adage *out of the frying pan, into the fire* is familiar. This adage applies when people try to get out of a very negative situation only to discover themselves in an even worse one. The 1964 movie *Father Goose* demonstrates this. Cary Grant plays Walter Eckland, an unshaven runaway from Western civilization who is forced into the role of a coast watcher for the Royal Navy in the South Pacific during World War II. (Fire #1: he escapes civilization and winds up in the middle of a war.)

Then Grant is asked to remove a fellow coast watcher from another island. But instead he rescues a diplomat's daughter (played by Leslie Caron) and seven school children, all girls. (Fire #2: he avoids capture by the Japanese but winds up responsible for eight females.) The list of fires goes on!

Father Goose is a charming comedy, but the situation Amos describes is neither charming nor funny. Fleeing a lion, you meet a bear; safe at home, you're bitten by a snake. You survive the travails of life only to experience the Day of the Lord— finding yourself in a time of darkness, rather than light. God's judgment will not be what many delude themselves into believing! Are you ready for it? —J. B. N.

20. *Will not the day of the Lord be darkness, not light—*
    pitch-dark, without a ray of brightness?

The ancient Israelites may assume that only the non-Jews have anything to fear on the Day of Judgment. But Amos says, "Not so fast." When God passes judgment, he will have to do so on the people of God themselves. To Amos this is more than just a maybe—it is a certainty. *Darkness* stands for distress and trouble in many Old Testament passages (examples: 1 Samuel 2:9; Job 5:14; Psalm 35:6).

III. BEWARE OF SPIRITUAL SINS (AMOS 5:21-24)
A. False Feasts (vv. 21, 22)
21. *"I hate, I despise your religious feasts;*
    I cannot stand your assemblies.

God established three yearly pilgrimage celebrations (see Exodus 23:14-17; 34:22-25; Deuteronomy 16:10-16). God also established Sabbath days, new moon festivals, etc. (see Nehemiah 10:33; Hosea 2:11). God now hates what the people have done to those days. God hates the very things the people think are pleasing to God. The people have made a mockery of God's holy days.

22. *"Even though you bring me burnt offerings and grain offerings,*
    I will not accept them.

Visual for Lesson 1. *Keep this map of the Assyrian Empire posted for several lessons to help your students gain a geographical perspective.*

Visuals for These Lessons

The visual pictured in each lesson (see example above) is a small reproduction of a large, full-color poster included in the Adult Resources packet for the Summer Quarter. The packet is available from your supplier. Order No. 492.

Though you bring choice fellowship offerings,
   I will have no regard for them.

The opening chapters of Leviticus established various kinds of *offerings*. God himself is the author of what those offerings are to be and what they are to represent.

Yet Amos says that these offerings have become completely unacceptable to God. God has not "canceled" the offerings in and of themselves in Amos's day. Rather, it is improper motives and unholy lives of the people who offer false acts of worship that disgust God.

B. INSINCERE SONGS (v. 23)

23. *"Away with the noise of your songs!*
   I will not listen to the music of your harps.

Music is a vital part of Old Testament worship (Ezra 2:65; Psalm 150; etc.). Usually God delights in our music of praise but not if offered insincerely. *Songs* of praise that don't match holiness in one's life are so displeasing to the Lord that he demands they be removed from his presence.

Many churches are struggling these days over styles of worship and music. While that concern is understandable, a greater concern should be the kind of person the music comes from rather than the kind of music that comes from the person.

C. BLESSED BEHAVIOR (v. 24)

24. *"But let justice roll on like a river,*
   righteousness like a never-failing stream!"

This may well be the most familiar verse in the book of Amos. The great civil rights leader Martin Luther King, Jr. quoted it. The verse describes what God wants: *justice* and *righteousness* to permeate the land *like a never-failing stream* bringing life-giving water to the people. Justice must flow continually—day and night. Justice cannot be an intermittent, three times out of four, proposition.

CONCLUSION

Amos was not a professional prophet. He was not even a citizen of the northern kingdom of Israel. He might well have contented himself with pruning the fruit trees and watching sheep. But he could not keep silent. He chose to tell the people the truth, an unpopular truth at that.

The people's complacency was exactly why they needed a prophet like Amos. Gary Smith says that Amos's challenge was much like a doctor telling a patient he has a terminal disease. Sometimes people get angry with the messenger. Instead of being angry with the messenger, they need to take the cure. Amos did not just diagnose, he also prescribed. The problem is that the people did not want the prescription.

Amos drew a lot of attention when he came north. His activities were reported to the king himself (Amos 7:10-12). By coming north and condemning the worship in Bethel, he was coming to the center of idolatrous religion in the northern kingdom. Amos caught the ire of the lead priest at Bethel. That man told Amos to go home and prophecy to his own people if he was determined to preach (Amos 7:12, 13).

We know that Amos's prophecy was true, for history reveals Amos was right. We don't know if Amos remained a prophet for the rest of his life or if he went back to farming. One thing is sure: his message has not been forgotten. Or has it?

WHAT DO YOU THINK?

In what ways do our twenty-first-century offerings and assemblies please and displease God? How can we do better?

WHAT DO YOU THINK?

How will your songs offer worship that is acceptable to God?

PRAYER

Dear Father, help me to be concerned about the things that concern you. Help me to live in a way that reflects my commitment to you. In my worship let not my rituals be isolated from my behavior and my devotion of the heart. In the name of Jesus, amen.

THOUGHT TO REMEMBER

Repentance, not ritual. Commitment, not complacency.

Discovery Learning

This page contains an alternative lesson plan emphasizing learning activities. Classes desiring such student involvement will find these suggestions helpful. The next page is a reproducible activity page to further enhance discovery learning.

LEARNING GOALS

After participating in this lesson, each student will be able to:

1. Describe the evils that Amos condemned.

2. Compare and contrast the evils cited in today's text with those seen in modern society.

3. Make a plan for his or her church to help correct one societal injustice.

INTO THE LESSON

Prepare and post three bold and garish signs that say *BEWARE!* One of the signs should be at the entrance to your learning space. When students voice some interest or concern, explain that the lesson writer outlines today's study with three *bewares*. Encourage the adults to figure out the three dangers for which they are to be on the alert. (You will be returning to these words of warning in the Into Life section of today's study.)

Have also a *NO MINORS ALLOWED!* sign near your room's entrance. After the *beware* introduction, point the class's attention to the other sign to introduce the *Minor Prophets*, books from which most of this quarter's texts are drawn. Be certain the learners know in what way these Old Testament books are "minor" and what ways they are not. The lesson writer has an explanatory note in the Lesson Background.

INTO THE WORD

List the following phrases and ideas on separate sheets of paper, perhaps as cartoon dialogue balloons:

Hate the message? Kill the messenger!
You cannot have your cake and eat it too
Under the table and out the door
A time to speak
What are you looking for?
It's a love-hate relationship
Crocodile Tears
Passing Through
Some wanted things are not desirable
It couldn't get any worse, could it?
Dark? How dark was it?
A holding-the-nose stench
Is a gift truly given if it is not accepted?
Some music is nothing more than noise
No muddy water here

These phrases are designed to summarize a truth of each verse of today's text, from verse 10 ("Hate the message . . . ") to verse 24 ("No muddy . . . "), respectively.

You may choose to display all the above statements at once (in random order), or you may shuffle them and display them one at a time. Say, "Look at Amos 5:10-24 and decide to which verse each of these ideas best relates." If students see a relationship to a verse other than the one intended, ask for an explanation.

To help your students see the sins that brought God's words of wrath and condemnation, identify these items as drawn from the lesson writer's outline: the social sins of Israel (vv. 10-15), bad doctrine regarding the Day of the Lord (vv. 16-20), and spiritual sins (vv. 21-24). Ask the class, "What are these sins?"

For social sins, expect such responses as rejection of truth, oppression of the poor, self-centeredness, sensuality, prejudice, and cowardly silence. For bad doctrine regarding the Day of the Lord, expect responses such as expecting God to overlook sins because the Israelites were "his people" plus believing that everything was going to be all right when the Lord comes, even though their sins were blatant and persistent. For spiritual sins, expect such responses as ritualism substituting for true worship, hypocritical songs, and unrighteousness.

INTO LIFE

From an office supply store, buy sheets of stick-on lettering for the letter *B*. Give each student one or more of the letters; say that it is their *B-wear!* as you stick one to your own lapel. Suggest they "wear their Bs" to heighten their sensitivity to *Beware!* of the three elements highlighted today: social sins, doctrine about the Day of the Lord, and spiritual sins. A short discussion of how these dangers are seen in personal lives and society will enhance the value of wearing these letters.

Read the Key Verse in unison with the class. After the recitation, ask, "How well are we doing in letting that happen in our community?" Following the responses, ask, "What can we do as a class and individually to enhance the free flow of justice?" Make the list and then ask, "What steps can we take to make these happen?" Create an action plan from this list. (Option: the two activities on the Reproducible Page will enhance the Into Life section of the lesson. Use as time allows.)

How Bad Can It Get?

In the words of Amos, the Day of the Lord—His day of reckoning and justice— will be for some as if "a man fled from a lion only to meet a bear, as though he entered his house and rested his hand on the wall only to have a snake bite him" (Amos 5:19). Paraphrase Amos's figures of speech for modern culture:

"As if a person fled from a _____

only to meet a _____ *, as though*

that person entered his or her house and

_____ !"

Obstructions in the River

Consider the following "river of justice." Draw in and label some various obstructions that impede the flow of justice in our society.

Now ask yourself, "What actions can I take that will facilitate the flow? With which one will I begin?" Write your ideas below.

RECOMMITTED TO GOD'S WAYS

LESSON 2

WHY TEACH THIS LESSON?

Your students need to know that sin is bad for them. Spiritually, physically, emotionally—sin is harmful in all areas. Sin damages relationships, life perspectives, and finances. Any way you look at it, sin works against us in the long run. On the other hand, God's way is the best way to do anything.

If those facts seem obvious, we should pause and ask ourselves why people keep on sinning. Often it's because sin *seems* to be profitable, at least in the short run. Your students need "the long view" of life in order to commit or recommit themselves to God's ways. That is what Hosea will teach us today.

INTRODUCTION

A. ORDER IN THE COURT

Have you ever noticed how many courtroom dramas are on TV? From *Perry Mason* in the 1950s and 1960s to today's *Law & Order,* this is an enduring staple of secular entertainment. An entertainment-oriented culture even looks upon such shows as *Court TV* as a source of reality-based amusement.

Hosea wasn't a scriptwriter for a courtroom drama. His book wasn't designed to be entertaining. Hosea wasn't a lawyer, but he could have been. Much of his teaching is like an indictment that would be presented in court. It is a bill of particulars confronting Israel for sinfulness.

Hosea's focus in both the positive and negative sections of his book is on the relationship between God and his people. The prophet Amos talked about God, Israel, and the surrounding nations, but Hosea largely focused on the theme of God and Israel. (In this context, *Israel* refers to the northern kingdom of God's divided people as distinct from the southern kingdom of *Judah*.)

B. LESSON BACKGROUND

To put Hosea's words in context, it will be helpful to understand what the people of Israel had done to their religion. In some cases they had rejected God and their traditions outright. In other cases they had merged the religion of the one true God with a regional religion that worshiped a god named *Baal* (Hosea 2:8). This greatly disturbed Hosea and the other prophets.

Hosea probably began his prophetic ministry just as Amos's ministry (last week's lesson) was drawing to a close. Hosea thus prophesied between about 760 BC and the fall of the northern kingdom in 722 BC.

This period of time seemed like a golden age to the people living in it (compare Isaiah 2:7; 3:16). Yet Hosea saw it, as did Amos and Isaiah, as anything but a golden age. Yes, there was prosperity, but the rich took advantage of the poor. Yes, there were religious observances, but they were corrupted.

DEVOTIONAL READING:
HOSEA 14
BACKGROUND SCRIPTURE:
HOSEA 4:1-4; 7:1, 2; 12:1-9; 14:1-3; 2 KINGS 15:8-10
PRINTED TEXT:
HOSEA 4:1-4; 7:1, 2; 12:6-9; 14:1

LESSON AIMS

After participating in this lesson, each student will be able to:

1. Describe the conditions that Hosea saw in his society.

2. Compare and contrast the conditions of Hosea's society with conditions today.

3. Identify one area in his or her own life to conform to God's ways.

KEY VERSE

Hear the word of the LORD, you Israelites, because the LORD has a charge to bring against you who live in the land: "There is no faithfulness, no love, no acknowledgment of God in the land."
—Hosea 4:1

Hosea's name means "salvation," and he certainly preached that the people were in need of that! Yet the people did not see themselves as vulnerable. "Salvation from what?" they probably asked themselves. The relatively stable reigns of Uzziah in the south and Jeroboam II in the north bred complacency.

But the prophets of God were not fooled. Just as Amos had seen the truth, so did Hosea. As a patriotic dweller of the north, he warned the people of the problem. And his warning would later prove to be valid.

In some ways Hosea is the most intriguing prophet in the Old Testament. Hosea's tumultuous family life, as noted in Hosea 1:2-11; 3:1-3, became almost a metaphor of what was happening between God and his people. God had commanded Hosea to marry a woman who would prove to be unfaithful. This was so that Hosea's family could be an example of God's willingness to love and take back his faithless people. Thus Hosea's own family became a kind of object lesson of human faithlessness and God's forgiveness.

The book of Hosea itself can be studied in three divisions. The first division, chapters 1–3, describes the personal information about Hosea and his family life.

The second division is chapters 4–13; this contains the oracles, or sermons, of Hosea. These messages are very tough condemnations of what was going on in Israel. The lesson for today is taken primarily from this section.

The final section is chapter 14. It deserves its own designation because a bit of hope is introduced. Even so, no more than 10 percent of this book deals with God's blessings. The book is overwhelmingly a message of condemnation.

I. SERIOUS CHARGES (HOSEA 4:1-4)

A. ABSENCE OF GOODNESS (v. 1)

1. Hear the word of the Lord, you Israelites,
    because the Lord has a charge to bring
    against you who live in the land:
"There is no faithfulness, no love,
    no acknowledgment of God in the land.

The opening phrase *hear the word of the Lord* begins the indictment. What follows is a bill of particulars about things the people are lacking. We may call these "sins of omission."

First, the Lord says *there is no faithfulness*. The word used for *faithfulness* carries the idea of fidelity, honesty, or reliability (compare Genesis 24:49; 47:29; Exodus 18:21; Joshua 2:12, 14).

Neither is there any *love* in the land. The word used here is one of the most beautiful and interesting words in the Old Testament. It is sometimes translated *mercy, kindness, goodness,* etc. (example: Jeremiah 9:24). The Hebrew words translated *faithfulness* and *love* in this passage occur together (translated in various ways) in dozens of other Old Testament passages. One interesting example is Exodus 34:6: "The Lord, the Lord . . . abounding in love and faithfulness." What the Lord himself abounds in is precisely what his people disdain!

Third, Hosea says there is no *acknowledgment of God*. This describes lack of an intimate mindfulness of God and his requirements. In place of this acknowledgment the people have substituted meaningless ritual. "For I desire mercy, not sacrifice, and acknowledgment of God rather than burnt offerings" (Hosea 6:6).

Do we see any of these omissions in our own age? Faithfulness is scoffed at. There is too little merciful love. While there are few genuine atheists in the world, there is still a dearth of the acknowledgment of God. God has made knowledge of himself available, but many suppress it (Romans 1:18-23).

What Do You Think?

Though Christians claim to be faithful, what are some ways in which it may appear that we are unfaithful? How can we do better?

B. PRESENCE OF WICKEDNESS (v. 2)

2. *"There is only cursing, lying and murder,*
    stealing and adultery;
  they break all bounds,
    and bloodshed follows bloodshed.

Here Hosea describes the presence of serious sins. We would call these "sins of commission." He describes a decay that is illustrated by the people's ignoring basic morality and decency, such as what is prescribed in the Ten Commandments (Exodus 20:1-17; Deuteronomy 5:6-21).

At least four of those commandments are mentioned here by use of the words *lying and murder, stealing and adultery.* The word *cursing* probably does not refer to using obscenities but to pronouncing a curse on someone. *Break all bounds* is the idea of violating boundaries (compare 1 Samuel 25:10).

This corrupt society can trace its problems to a single cause: the rejection of God. The kinds of qualities that are missing (v. 1) are foundational to a healthy society. The sins that are present inevitably serve to weaken a society. Since Hosea is a resident of the land, this must fill him with both anger and sorrow.

Visual for Lesson 2. *Use this visual as a discussion starter by asking, "What do tree rings and the dating of the prophets have in common?"*

ROGUE'S HARBOR

Peter Cartwright (1785–1872) spent several decades as a frontier Methodist circuit-riding preacher, first in Kentucky and then in Illinois. In 1856 he wrote his autobiography, which has become a classic on the history of frontier religion.

Cartwright was still a child when his parents moved from Virginia to Kentucky, much of which was untamed wilderness at the time. Logan County, where his parents settled, was known as *Rogue's Harbor.* It was the home of many individuals who came to escape justice or punishment. Law could not be enforced. Murderers, horse thieves, highway robbers, and counterfeiters formed a majority of the population. Honest citizens tried to prosecute them, but the outlaws just provided alibis for each other and always escaped justice.

Finally the law-abiding citizens formed a group known as the Regulators to establish their own code of bylaws. One day the two groups met in town and a battle ensued, fought with knives, pistols, and clubs. Many were wounded, some were killed. The rogues were victorious and drove the Regulators out of town.

Sound like a nice place to live? It is similar to the situation Hosea described: a community of killing, lying, adultery, and murder. That is the result of a community that does not know God. When there is no knowledge of God, morals and social stability disappear just as quickly as the outward formalities of religion. This may lead you to reflect on how much knowledge of God remains in your city.   —J. B. N.

C. PRESENCE OF MOURNING (v. 3)

3. *"Because of this the land mourns,*
    and all who live in it waste away;
  the beasts of the field and the birds of the air
    and the fish of the sea are dying.

The faithlessness of God's people is to be punished by a drought—that is a secondary meaning of the word *mourns* in this context. This same Hebrew verb is used in Jeremiah 4:28; 12:4; Joel 1:10; and Amos 1:2. Also notice Hosea's description of an environment in the process of ruination. All creatures that live in the land will waste away or, literally, wither. Even *the fish* are threatened.

Isn't it interesting that God associates judgment for sin as being the occasion for general decline even in the realm of nature? Paul speaks of creation groaning as a result of sin (Romans 8:20-22).

HOW TO SAY IT

Amos. AY-mus.
Baal. BAY-ul.
Beth Aven. Beth AY-ven.
Bethel. BETH-ul.
Ephraim. EE-fray-im.
Hosea. Ho-ZAY-uh.
Isaiah. Eye-ZAY-uh.
Jeroboam. Jair-uh-BOE-um.
Jerusalem. Juh-ROO-suh-lem.
Uzziah. Uh-ZYE-uh.
Zephaniah. Zef-uh-NYE-uh.

D. ABSENCE OF INTEGRITY (v. 4)

4. *"But let no man bring a charge,*
    let no man accuse another,
  for your people are like those
    who bring charges against a priest."

At first glance, the first two lines of this verse may make us think that God is forbidding the readers to reprove one another with regard to the moral decay. The idea, rather, is that finger-pointing and blaming others will not solve the problems. Great revivals begin not when we put the spotlight of the sins of others but when we dare to indict ourselves.

The last two lines are also a bit difficult. Is Hosea condemning his readers for being the kind of people who would dare to bring charges even *against a priest*? Considering how angry Hosea is toward the priests, that is not likely (Hosea 4:6-9; 5:1; 6:9; 10:5). Many commentators say the verse should be seen as an encouragement to confront the priests. Under this theory, it might be read as, "Your people should be as they who bring charges against a priest." A different theory is that this is another reference to finger-pointing, as in, "Any problems are the fault of the priesthood, not me!"

II. SPURNED OFFER (HOSEA 7:1, 2)

A. HEALING WAS REJECTED (v. 1)

1. *"Whenever I would heal Israel,*
  the sins of Ephraim are exposed
    and the crimes of Samaria revealed.
  They practice deceit,
    thieves break into houses,
    bandits rob in the streets;

The name *Ephraim* is another way to refer to the northern kingdom of *Israel*. Ephraim is a prominent tribe in the northern kingdom. Adding the word *Samaria* to the mix serves to emphasize the entirety of the 10 tribes that are situated north of Judah. God is saying to them that he is willing to heal all Israel. But as God makes this attempt, the sins of the people become even more apparent.

The primary way God attempts to heal Israel is by sending them prophets. Rather than causing the people to repent, the work of the prophets just reveals more and more sin and guilt. The prophets are persecuted (Amos 7:10-13) not welcomed (compare Acts 7:52).

The last part of the verse speaks of people being robbed inside their own *houses* as well as while out on the city *streets*. While practicing *deceit* may be a sneaky, somewhat hidden crime, other kinds of banditry are all too clear. There is no social justice anywhere.

B. REPENTANCE WAS REJECTED (v. 2)

2. *". . . but they do not realize*
    that I remember all their evil deeds.
  Their sins engulf them;
    they are always before me."

The people of Israel erroneously assume that God does not know or care about the evil they are doing. How often human beings have deceived themselves into thinking they can hide their sins from God! Yet God does not suffer from Attention Deficit Disorder. Nor does he have a faulty memory (Leviticus 26:42; Psalm 105:8).

WHAT DO YOU THINK?

What are some ways that you rejected the healing that God desired to provide? How did you turn this around?

WHAT DO YOU THINK?

What factors can cause us to think we can hide our sins from God? How do you avoid this trap?

III. STERN COMMAND (HOSEA 12:6-9; 14:1)

A. TURN FOR A BLESSING (v. 6)

6. But you must return to your God;
    maintain love and justice,
    and wait for your God always.

This verse follows a discussion of Jacob's encounter with God at Bethel (Hosea 12:2-4; compare Genesis 28:10-22; 35:1-15). Hosea is highly critical of what has been going on at Bethel. See Hosea 10:5, which refers to *Beth Aven*, a sarcastic name for Bethel. While *Bethel* means "house of God," *Beth Aven* means "house of wickedness."

In Hosea 12:4, the prophet reminds his audience that Bethel was once a holy place. The people need to return to the kind of religion first celebrated there.

To *return to your God* involves repentance. The people are also to *wait on God*. Why the delay? They need for God to bless them again. They need the blessing that God once gave to Jacob.

WHAT DO YOU THINK?

In what areas do you need to repent? How did you receive God's blessings at a time you repented?

WHAT DO YOU THINK?

What are some ways that God has provided for you? for your church?

AXELS OR U-TURNS?

Normally the words *return* and *turn* brings to mind a change in direction. But not all turns are alike. In figure skating there is a maneuver known as an *axel*, named after Norwegian figure skater Axel Paulsen (1856–1938). The axel features a jump with a turn in the air that results in the skater still going in the same direction upon landing. It is just for show. Though the axel takes a good deal of skill, it does not result in a change of direction.

Curves on an interstate highway sometimes do not take any effort on the part of the driver. The road may be banked sufficiently for the car to change direction almost by itself. The turn is done by the road conditions, not by the driver.

Then there is a U-turn. This is a 180-degree change of direction. It occurs only when the driver takes a very deliberate action. There is nothing happenstance or accidental about it. It is a conscious effort by the driver to follow a new course.

When Hosea urged the people to turn back to God, he was not talking about a showy axel that would impress others. Nor was he talking about a situation where the people were turned merely by force of external circumstances, without any conscious effort on their part. Hosea confronts his audience (and us) with the need to make a deliberate change of direction—a U-turn.   —J. B. N.

B. TURN FOR PERSPECTIVE (vv. 7, 8)

7. The merchant uses dishonest scales;
    he loves to defraud.

The Hebrew word translated *merchant* is literally *Canaanite*. Canaanites are known as shrewd traders, thus the translation *merchant* captures the sense very well. Canaanites inhabited the promised land before the Israelites arrived (Exodus 3:8). Greedy merchants are known for their *dishonest* balance *scales*. This is very offensive to God (Deuteronomy 25:13-16; Proverbs 11:1; 20:23). The children of Israel think they are quite superior to the previous inhabitants of the area, but the message is that they have become the same as them. They love *to defraud*.

8. Ephraim boasts,
    "I am very rich; I have become wealthy.
    With all my wealth they will not find in me
      any iniquity or sin."

In a state of arrogant pride, *Ephraim* believes itself to be *rich* and righteous. The people are indeed rich in a material way in the manner of unjust merchants. Not only do they see themselves as rich, they do not see that they had committed any *sin*. "What harm did we do in accumulating these riches?" the Israelites ask themselves. They have so manipulated the laws that they can maintain that technically they are not guilty (compare Mark 7:9-13). *They will not find in me any iniquity* is an arrogant, self-righteous confidence. Yet God knows better (Amos 6:1-7). Several decades after Hosea writes, the message to Jerusalem to the south will be about the same (Zephaniah 1:11-13).

C. TURN OR FACE JUDGMENT (v. 9; 14:1)

9. "I am the LORD your God,
    [who brought you] out of Egypt;
  I will make you live in tents again,
    as in the days of your appointed feasts."

The word *tents* refers to the tents that the Israelites lived in while in the wilderness wanderings after they had left *Egypt*. Thus the Lord promises a severe reduction in Israel's standard of living: they will give up their cozy houses for tents.

The *appointed feasts* here probably includes the Feast of Tabernacles. During this festival, people set up booths or tents as a reminder of wilderness wanderings (Leviticus 23:33-44). How sad: the Israelites will return to tents not as a memorial but as a punishment.

1. Return, O Israel, to the LORD your God.
    Your sins have been your downfall!

Be glad that the book of Hosea has a fourteenth chapter! It is in this chapter that hope is restored. That hope is more evident in the verses that follow (not in today's text). There are only seven "blessings sections" in Hosea, and this is one of them. If the people *return* to God, he can help them walk in the right paths.

This is a note of hope in an otherwise very dark book. Yet it is not the only note of hope. Remember that in Hosea's own experience he bestows forgiving love to an errant wife (Hosea 3). Thus Hosea uses his own life as an example that God also can forgive the people who have been unfaithful to him.

CONCLUSION

Hosea taught that evil can become pervasive. Evil affects the fabric of society. We see in Hosea God's sense of hurt, betrayal, and disappointment. God suffers when his people sin. Hosea also discovered and taught that God is both holy and merciful. God thundered against sin, but he could be warm and forgiving to the repentant sinner.

Here is where we need to remind ourselves of Hosea's marital situation. Hosea sought out his wife, bought her out of prostitution, and took her back into his household (Hosea 3). Hosea could not understand how Israel could so callously choose not to love the God who had loved them so much.

Combining his own personal insight and hurts with God's revelation, Hosea realized the depth of the meaning of *unfaithfulness*. Unfaithfulness toward another human and toward God can be forgiven, but it takes sincere repentance and profound love. Hosea's love for his wife was a picture of God's love for his people. No Christian looking at this can fail to see that Jesus did something similar for us. He paid a price to bring us back home. He did this even though we did not deserve it. "While we were yet sinners, Christ died for us" (Romans 5:8).

This is why some commentators say that Hosea begins to put into our minds what will come into sharper focus in the New Testament: the doctrine of grace. "For the law was given by Moses, but grace and truth came by Jesus Christ" (John 1:17).

Discovery Learning

This page contains an alternative lesson plan emphasizing learning activities. Classes desiring such student involvement will find these suggestions helpful. The next page is a reproducible activity page to further enhance discovery learning.

LEARNING GOALS

After this lesson, each student will be able to:

1. Describe the conditions that Hosea saw.

2. Compare and contrast the conditions of Hosea's society with conditions today.

3. Identify one area in his or her own life to conform to God's ways.

INTO THE LESSON

Invite a man of your congregation who enjoys drama to present the following as an opening monologue. Ideally, costume your actor as an Old Testament figure.

I am Hosea, a heartbroken man and God's prophet to Israel.

My nation is a lawless place where kings are assassinated and the assassin is also murdered. The Israelites seem bent on destroying themselves, all the while considering themselves to be the privileged and protected people of Almighty God. Assyria licks her lips. Egypt slyly says, "Let us help."

God named my children after the tragedy of Israel. My daughter Lo-Ruhamah—you would know her as *Not Pitied*. There is also Lo-Ammi, God's declaration that Israel was no longer his people. You could have called Israel *Not Mine!*—an illegitimate child.

I am Hosea, God's heartbroken prophet. "Ephraim has sold herself to lovers." But God continues to love, and so must I. So must I!

Conclude with any other background information you see as essential. (Option: distribute copies of either [or both] of the Love and Lovers or Loving the Unlovable activities from the Reproducible Page for students to work on as they arrive.)

INTO THE WORD

Questions are important in God's confrontation with Israel (see Hosea 6:4; 9:5; 11:8; 13:10). As noted by the lesson writer, much of Hosea's teaching is like a courtroom indictment, a lawyer and judge asking the accusatory questions of wrongdoers.

Prepare the following pairs of questions (Q) and follow-up questions (FQ) on 12 separate slips of paper, one pair for each verse of the text. Distribute them to class members.

Q: What are the first three indictments God makes against Israel in Hosea 4:1? FQ: How many violations of the Ten Commandments are represented?

Q: In Hosea 4:2, what is meant by the statement, "They break all bounds"? FQ: How does the expression relate to the fact that "Sin is lawlessness" (1 John 3:4)?

Q: How is drought in Hosea 4:3 an excellent figure for spiritual ruin? FQ: In what sense is deterioration of natural environmental systems related to sin?

Q: In Hosea 4:4, what common practice is alluded to that occurs often when things go wrong? FQ: What recent examples of finger-pointing can you name?

Q: What crime does Hosea 7:1 reveal, a crime common in sinful cities? FQ: How is the frequency of robbery a good indication of general sinfulness?

Q: What does Hosea 7:2 say will happen even when people refuse to believe that God sees their sin? FQ: How common is the belief that God sees all that we think and do?

Q: What significant Old Testament event is described by Hosea before he calls for repentance in Hosea 12:6? FQ: What is it that every believer is waiting for when he or she "waits for God"?

Q: Why would Hosea highlight the sin of a dishonest merchant as he does in 12:7? FQ: In what ways do you see "dishonest scales" in modern business practices?

Q: How common is the self-deceit we see in Hosea 12:8? FQ: What is the root of self-deceit when it comes to sin and its consequences?

Q: As 12:9 affirms, how can living in tents be a good thing? FQ: How can thinking about an earlier, even harder time help one's spiritual life?

Q: How is Hosea 14:1 the fundamental message of the prophets? FQ: How is 14:1 the message every evangelist must use with every sinner?

Ask students holding questions to ask them aloud, pausing for answers between Qs and FQs.

INTO LIFE

Say, "People fall away from the church and from Christ for various sinful reasons. How do we intervene when that happens? How do we make sure that we are not being hypocritical in this regard?" Discuss a preventive plan for both questions. Be cautious about mentioning names!

Love and Lovers

Hosea's message to Israel is all about love and lovers (holy and otherwise). God loved Israel, in spite of the nation going after illicit lovers. In a parallel circumstance, Hosea continued to show love for his wife. The two words *love* and *lovers* occur repeatedly in Hosea's writing. Look at each of the following verses and write which of the two words (or both) appears and why.

2:4 _____   6:4 _____

2:5 _____   8:9 _____

2:7 _____   9:1 _____

2:10 _____   9:15 _____

2:19 _____   10:12 _____

2:23 _____   11:1 _____

3:1 _____   11:4 _____

4:1 _____   12:6 _____

4:18 _____   14:4 _____

Loving the Unlovable

God's pattern for us is that "When we were still powerless, Christ died for the ungodly" (Romans 5:6). To Hosea God said, "Love her [his adulterous wife, Gomer] as the Lord loves the Israelites, though they turn to other gods" (Hosea 3:1). Describe situations when you saw the following examples of love demonstrated.

Someone who forgave and was reconciled to a wayward spouse.

A parent who continued loving for a child who had chosen a lifestyle that offended the parent.

A teacher who continued to want the best for a student who had greatly disappointed him and others.

A child who persisted in loving a parent who had a drug or alcohol addiction.

Someone who accepted the return of a spouse who had abandoned home and children.

In what ways is each of these examples either a good or not-so-good picture of God's love for the wayward sinner?

COMMITTED TO TRUE WORSHIP

LESSON 3

WHY TEACH THIS LESSON?

Say the word *worship* and your students likely will think of what they do for an hour or two on Sunday morning. But could it be that worship is broader than this? Could our worship of God include the way we treat other people? Is it possible that our worship of God is validated by how we work to bring about justice in the lives of people who are being oppressed or even killed?

Your students need to embrace worship as a lifestyle to be lived. Today's lesson should help your students come to understand better the true scope of their worship of God.

INTRODUCTION

A. SURPRISED BY TROUBLE

As a child, I once came cheerily into the house, only to be confronted by my parents. They clearly were upset with me. My mother said, "Well, it looks to me like he is ready for a spanking!" I do not remember what wrong I had done. I do not even remember what happened thereafter. However, I do remember vividly that my heart began pounding and my toothy grin dissolved. I came in thinking everything was great; but suddenly I was surprised by trouble.

In today's text, Judah is also surprised by trouble. Isaiah had a message from the Lord that was designed to wipe the grins off their smug faces, as though saying, "It looks to me like they are ready for punishment." Isaiah 1 is a vision designed to move people to repentance.

B. LESSON BACKGROUND

Isaiah 1:1 allows us to date Isaiah's lengthy prophetic ministry between 740 and 680 BC. Last week we saw Hosea, an older contemporary of Isaiah, tell the northern kingdom of Israel to repent and recommit their ways to the Lord. Sadly, they refused. Within a few years after Hosea's ministry, the northern kingdom was defeated and dispersed. That happened in 722 BC.

Isaiah's ministry to the southern kingdom of Judah had only slightly better prospects. The Lord told Isaiah that his preaching to Judah would also fall on deaf ears. But though they would also be taken into exile, the Lord would preserve a small remnant (Isaiah 6:9-13).

Isaiah's book contains glorious passages of this restoration of Judah, one of which is the text for next week. Apparently the original readers latched on to the good news and ignored the warnings and calls for repentance. They mistook the miraculous deliverance from the Assyrian army in 701 BC as a sign that God would never allow Judah to fall. By seeing the temple as something of a good-luck charm, they deviated from true worship (compare Jeremiah 7:4).

DEVOTIONAL READING:
ISAIAH 58:6-12
BACKGROUND SCRIPTURE:
ISAIAH 1:10-20; 2 KINGS 15:32-35
PRINTED TEXT:
ISAIAH 1:10-20

LESSON AIMS

After participating in this lesson, each student will be able to:

1. Identify worship attitudes and practices that Isaiah said pleased the Lord and those he said did not.

2. Explain the relationship between attitude and practice in worship.

3. Identify one area in his or her life that hinders true worship and make a plan to change it.

KEY VERSE

Learn to do right! Seek justice, encourage the oppressed. Defend the cause of the fatherless, plead the case of the widow. —Isaiah 1:17

Isaiah 1:2-31 introduces the entire book of Isaiah. Therefore it was probably written after 701 BC, when the people clearly had failed to understand the Lord's message. So the Lord presents to Isaiah a vision in a form of a lawsuit.

Ancient law courts were different from modern ones, but many roles are similar. It is important to identify the role that each character may represent (judge, plaintiff, defendant, witness, etc.) and the purpose for the scene (to level charges, to prove guilt, to announce a verdict, to impose a sentence). Within the drama of the trial, both the Lord and the prophet may take more than one role. When the prophet steps out of the drama, he speaks to the reader.

Isaiah 1:10-20 forms the central part of the trial scene. The author seems to interrupt the trial drama with interludes, something like a reporter may do. Here is one possible way to identify the back-and-forth of Isaiah 1:

Trial Scenes	Prophetic Interludes
2, 3	4
5-8	9
10-20	21-23
24-26	27, 28
29-31	

In verse 10, where we begin today, the defendants are called to trial. Charges are leveled in verses 11-15. Then the trial motif takes an unusual turn: the offer of a chance for a stay of sentence in verses 16-20.

I. DEFENDANTS SUBPOENAED (ISAIAH 1:10)

10. Hear the word of the LORD,
        you rulers of Sodom;
    listen to the law of our God,
        you people of Gomorrah!

Sodom and *Gomorrah* are used figuratively for Judah. These cities were destroyed because of extreme wickedness (Genesis 19). The references to both the *rulers* and the *people* show the same to be true of Judah. The Lord threatens punishment because his chosen people are sinful at all levels of society. *The word of the Lord* is parallel to *the law of our God*, both referring to the specific charges in the next section.

HEAR!

As I get older (don't we all!), more and more infirmities come my way. I won't bore you with the whole organ recital, but a recent concern has been my hearing. I still believe my hearing is good. No one has suggested I need a hearing aid. Certain loud noises, however, give me a headache and I avoid them.

Another problem is background noise. This can take the form of road noise in a car, conversations at adjacent tables in a restaurant, or even other conversations during a social gathering. All this can prevent me from really hearing what a person is saying. I sometimes have to say, "I'm sorry; I can't hear you." But technically, that's a matter of definition. In the sense that the sounds being made are registering on my eardrum, I actually can hear the other person. But I can't decipher these sounds sufficiently to understand the words being used. It helps to remove the distracting noise and concentrate on the speaker.

The same applies in the spiritual realm. When the Lord speaks to us, there sometimes are so many other background noises that we do not hear with enough clarity for the message to register in our consciousness. We may then need to eliminate the distracting noises and concentrate on the speaker. "Hear the word of the Lord!"
                                                                            —J. B. N.

WHAT DO YOU THINK?

How can you better prepare yourself to hear the Word of the Lord? What progress have you made in this regard?

[Make sure to consider Proverbs 8:34; Ecclesiastes 5:1; and Matthew 6:7, 8 in your answer.]

II. PLAINTIFF READS CHARGES (ISAIAH 1:11-15)

A. DISGUSTING SACRIFICES (vv. 11-13a)

11. *"The multitude of your sacrifices—*
what are they to me?" says the LORD.
"I have more than enough of burnt offerings,
of rams and the fat of fattened animals;
I have no pleasure
in the blood of bulls and lambs and goats.

The Lord begins his testimony with a rhetorical question—a question that actually makes a statement. The expression *what are they to me* occurs only two other times in the Old Testament in the Hebrew original: Genesis 27:46 and Job 30:2. In all three cases the phrase has to do with importance or value.

The problem is not the number of *sacrifices* (a *multitude* of them) nor the type of sacrifices (*burnt offerings* prescribed in the law). Neither is the quality of the animals at issue. The phrase *fattened animals* is merely descriptive of the good quality of the animals (compare 2 Samuel 6:13; 1 Kings 1:9). It must shock the readers to learn that even though they offer sacrifices that are plentiful, correct, and good in and of themselves, God is not pleased (compare Proverbs 28:19).

12. *"When you come to appear before me,*
who has asked this of you,
this trampling of my courts?

To *appear before* refers to the offering of the sacrifices mentioned in verse 11. The *trampling* may be that of the animals, but more likely it is the unfitness of the worshipers themselves.

13a. *"Stop bringing meaningless offerings!*
Your incense is detestable to me.

Offerings is a general term for sacrifices, both grain and animal. The Hebrew behind the adjective *meaningless* is translated "misuse" in the Third Commandment (Deuteronomy 5:11) in connection with the use of God's name. *Incense* can refer generally to spices (Exodus 30:1, 7-9) or to specific sacrifices. But here it probably refers to sacrifices generally (as in Psalm 66:15) that are supposed to be as pleasant to the Lord as incense.

The nation's offerings are useless; worse, they are all *detestable* to the Lord. He is disgusted with them all.

B. INSUFFERABLE GATHERINGS (vv. 13b, 14)

13b. *New Moons, Sabbaths and convocations—*
I cannot bear your evil assemblies.

Observances of *New Moons* and *Sabbaths*, along with various other *assemblies*, were established by God himself (Exodus 20:8; Leviticus 23; Numbers 10:10; 28:11, 14). These are various religious gatherings under the Law of Moses.

Even though God had established these observances, he now says *I cannot bear* the way his people conduct these events. The Lord cannot tolerate any sacred assembly that is characterized by wrong motives and evil intent.

14. *"Your New Moon festivals and your appointed feasts*
my soul hates.
They have become a burden to me;
I am weary of bearing them.

The blistering indictment continues with strong statements of the Lord's contempt. On page after page of Scripture, we can see the Lord's patience. But his patience has limits.

WHAT DO YOU THINK?

What offerings have you brought to God in the past that you think he was dissatisfied with? What spiritual blind spots did you become aware of in getting back on the right track?

[Isaiah 29:13 and Matthew 5:23, 24 can help you frame your answer.]

WHAT DO YOU THINK?

How might our assemblies become iniquities in the eyes of God? What safeguards can we implement?

C. Disregarded Prayers (v. 15)

15. "When you spread out your hands in prayer,
    I will hide my eyes from you;
even if you offer many prayers,
    I will not listen.
Your hands are full of blood;

To *spread out your hands in prayer* is to extend the arms with palms up, as in a plea to receive from God. But no matter the physical posture, the Lord intends to *hide his eyes*. Does it surprise you that the Lord doesn't always heed prayer? The Lord explains that the people themselves are the problem: *your hands are full of blood*. This can mean the guilt for various kinds of killings (Deuteronomy 19:10; 22:8). Here it probably refers more broadly to all kinds of injustice that harm others (compare Isaiah 33:15; Ezekiel 9:9; Nahum 3:1).

All their acts of worship (sacrifices, gatherings, prayers) are detestable because the people are guilty of sin against others; they refuse to connect ritual with obedience. They expect God somehow to have "selective vision"—seeing their pious sacrifices while ignoring the daily injustice they practice. Such arrogance!

III. JUDGE OFFERS A CHANCE (ISAIAH 1:16-20)

A. Stop the Bad (v. 16)

16. "Wash and make yourselves clean.
    Take your evil deeds
        out of my sight!
    Stop doing wrong,

The verse offers specific commands to the people. To *wash* can be used of simple bathing or of ceremonial washing. The context requires this to refer to the ceremonial. We see ceremonial washing in the New Testament in Matthew 27:24; John 13:1-17; etc.

Make . . . clean has a moral sense in the Old Testament. Thus *wash* refers to more than mere ritual washing; moral cleansing must be involved (compare Luke 11:39). God's faithful people will actively pursue both a genuine inward and outward righteousness because they love their God and want to be like him.

B. Start the Good (v. 17)

17. "Learn to do right!
    Seek justice,
        encourage the oppressed.
    Defend the cause of the fatherless,
        plead the case of the widow.

The Lord now gives five positive commands concerning the character of the true worshiper. These move from general to specific, the last three being applications. *To do right* may mean "to be pleasing," "to be skillful," or "to do what is moral or ethical." The context of unethical behavior makes clear that the Lord means the latter. *Learn* implies growth. The readers are surprised by trouble because they are very shallow in their understanding of what it means to relate to God. Changing one's moral fiber is going to involve will and effort.

The people of Judah are to promote *justice* in dealings with one another. Deuteronomy 16:20 insists that the people are to "follow justice and righteousness alone" as a condition for inheriting the land.

The application *encourage the oppressed* seems clear enough, but another translation is possible. The Hebrew word translated *oppressed* occurs only here in the

---

What Do You Think?

What can you do to assure that God hears your prayers? Conversely, how do you make sure that nothing hinders your prayers?

How to Say It

Assyrian. Uh-SEAR-e-un.
Babylon. BAB-uh-lun.
Deuteronomy. Due-ter-AHN-uh-me.
Ezekiel. Ee-ZEEK-ee-ul or Ee-ZEEK-yul.
Gomorrah. Guh-MORE-uh.
Hosea. Ho-ZAY-uh.
Isaiah. Eye-ZAY-uh.
Judeans. Joo-DEE-unz.
Leviticus. Leh-VIT-ih-kus.
Nahum. NAY-hum.
Sodom. SOD-um.

Old Testament, though the same root occurs in one other place, namely Psalm 71:4: "Deliver me, O my God, from the hand of the wicked, from the grasp of evil cruel men." There this root occurs behind the word *cruel*. This fact leads some to believe that *encourage the oppressed* here in Isaiah 1:17 may be translated something like "rebuke the oppressor." Surely the Lord expects both!

The next two applications involve the protection of the powerless of society: *defend the cause of the fatherless* and *plead the case of the widow*. God's faithful people will seek to deal ethically with all people and pursue justice. Christians may not be able to rectify all wrongs. Yet we are to seek justice for all and protection for the defenseless at every level of society. This is a continuing battle.

INNER MISSION

Johann Wichern (1808–1881) was a German minister who was moved by the suffering of children in the impoverished sections of the city of Hamburg. Convinced that something ought to be done for them, he helped organize the Rough House as a home for boys in 1833. This was similar to an orphanage but based on the principles of family education to provide for both spiritual and physical needs.

Under Wichern's expert organizational skills, the Evangelical Church in Germany formed the Inner Mission in 1848. It supervised 1,500 various charitable activities of the German Protestants. Ultimately this Inner Mission included nursing centers, prison reform activities, orphanages, and homes for those who had mental retardation. Before the Nazis closed down the system in 1938, there were 3,800 institutions under the umbrella of the Inner Mission.

Similar to Wichern is the story of George Mueller (1805–1898), a German who came to London in 1829. In 1832 he established an orphanage in Bristol that ultimately cared for more than 2,000 children. These are just two examples of the kind of thing God pleads for through Isaiah: "encourage the oppressed. Defend the cause of the fatherless, plead the case of the widow." They are examples that speak to us—and convict us—yet today.   —J. B. N.

C. THE ONLY CHANCE (vv. 18-20)

18. *"Come now, let us reason together,"*
     says the LORD.

Properly understanding this well-known verse requires that the reader remember that the Lord is still speaking in his role as judge. When he says to Judah, *Come now, let us reason together*, he does not mean to invite these people to sit down over coffee and doughnuts to discuss things. This is not a give-and-take negotiation. Rather, the Lord is challenging them in court to consider the truth of what he has been saying, to realize the peril in which they find themselves!

18b. *"Though your sins are like scarlet,*
     they shall be as white as snow;
   though they are red as crimson,
     they shall be like wool.

After confronting his people with the reality of their sin, the Lord now holds out the hope of the good they may experience. He then lays out the condition for that good (v. 19) and warns them of the punishment for failure to repent (v. 20).

The colors *scarlet* and *crimson* are synonyms. *Scarlet* may be used positively, as in parts of the tabernacle (Exodus 25:4; 26:1; etc.), of good quality clothing (Proverbs 31:21), or even the color of beautiful lips (Song of Songs 4:3). It may be used neutrally simply of thread (Genesis 38:28, 30). However, *scarlet* thread also is used in a purification ritual (Leviticus 14:4, 6, 49, 51, 52; Numbers 19:6) and may also have the suggestion of sin, as it clearly does here.

WHAT DO YOU THINK?

What are some ways your church can help the oppressed, the fatherless, the widow, and the widowers? What should your own part be in this ministry?

DAILY BIBLE READINGS

Monday, June 11—Praise for God's Goodness (Psalm 65:1-8)

Tuesday, June 12—Doing Right in God's Sight (2 Kings 15:32-36)

Wednesday, June 13—Here Am I; Send Me (Isaiah 6:1-8)

Thursday, June 14—The Fast That Pleases God (Isaiah 58:6-12)

Friday, June 15—Comfort for God's People (Isaiah 40:1-5)

Saturday, June 16—Not Desiring Sacrifices (Isaiah 1:10-14)

Sunday, June 17—Learn to Do Good (Isaiah 1:15-20)

True Worship
• Learn to do right
• Seek justice
• Encourage the oppressed
• Defend the fatherless
• Plead for the widow

Visual for Lesson 3. *Use these five elements of true worship as discussion starters. For each ask, "What is a specific way to implement this one?"*

Yet there is good news: the scarlet color of sin can change to *be as white as snow!* Snow is a descriptor of a degree of whiteness; it is a symbol of moral purity that also is found in Psalm 51:7. Likewise *wool* is used as a descriptor of whiteness parallel to that of snow in Daniel 7:9 and Revelation 1:14.

Though not named, it is clear that only the Lord can transform the impure into pure (compare Romans 3:21-26; 12:1, 2). The Lord offers hope for true renewal. However, the Lord leaves a vital part for us to play: choice.

19. "If you are willing and obedient,
     you will eat the best from the land;

The conditions for blessing are that the people be *willing and obedient*. The willingness involves consent to obey the Lord.

The phrase *eat the best from the land* is similar to "eat the good things of the land" in Ezra 9:12. The idea in both places is "to live well from the land, to prosper." This blessing from the Lord is that the Judeans remain in the land of promise. Their role, as God's chosen people, is to bring the Messiah into the world. All the punishments that Isaiah has been preaching can be avoided if they repent. Sadly, we know from history that this repentance didn't happen. The people had to go into exile in Babylon. Yet even after that exile is finished, Ezra 9:12 reaffirms this promise. God is a God of second chances!

20. "But if you resist and rebel,
     you will be devoured by the sword."
     For the mouth of the LORD has spoken.

To *resist and rebel* is the opposite of being willing and obedient. To refuse the Lord's will has serious consequences! Notice what happened to Pharaoh (Exodus 12:29). The idea of refusal is found numerous times in Jeremiah. Most refer to the refusal of the people to admit their sin or repent (Jeremiah 8:5; 9:6; etc.).

The word *rebel* should remind the readers of how both Moses and Aaron were not allowed to enter Canaan because of their respective rebellions (Numbers 20:10-12, 24; 27:14). Very commonly, the idea of rebellion is applied by the prophets to God's people (examples: Isaiah 3:8; 63:10).

The opposite of "eat the best from the land" in verse 19 is to *be devoured by the sword.* Judah was delivered miraculously from Assyria in 701 BC. It had seemed like certain disaster. Now the Lord is warning them that unless their ritual is accompanied by a heart that proves its love for him, they will suffer even greater devastation in war. They can prove their love by obedience in their personal lives and in their behavior toward others. The threat is real because *the mouth of the Lord has spoken* it.

CONCLUSION

The rage on television these days is the "reality show." The idea is to show people in states of raw emotion by placing them in very stressful circumstances. Other than that, though, this type of show has very little to do with what we may call *everyday reality*. But even *everyday reality* is not the same as *ultimate reality*. The sacrifices, gatherings, and prayers that the people of Judah were participating in were "real" in the sense that they happened. But these things were not genuine or sincere.

God's people today must be genuine. Giving money to good causes (even to the church), going to church, and praying do not prove that a person has a genuine relationship with the Lord. Real relationship means that these actions will be accompanied by a heart and lifestyle consistent with the character of God himself. God is not mocked; no person can manipulate the Lord to get into Heaven.

Discovery Learning

This page contains an alternative lesson plan emphasizing learning activities. Classes desiring such student involvement will find these suggestions helpful. The next page is a reproducible activity page to further enhance discovery learning.

LEARNING GOALS

After this lesson, each student will be able to:

1. Identify worship attitudes and practices that Isaiah said pleased the Lord and those he said did not.

2. Explain the relationship between attitude and practice in worship.

3. Identify one area in his or her life that hinders true worship and make a plan to change it.

INTO THE LESSON

Display the word *WORSHIP* vertically on the board. As class begins, ask, "What are the components of true worship? Use the letters of the word to develop your list." Allow learners to express their own ideas, but you can expect such responses as *willingness, orderliness, reverence, relationship, songs, submission, heart, head, honesty, integrity, prayer, praise.* (A similar activity is included in the student book.)

Transition to a study of the text by saying, "In Isaiah 1:1-10, Isaiah and God are describing the defective practice of worship seen in the land. As we study, contrast our list with what is found there. How many 'opposites' do we see?"

INTO THE WORD

Prepare the following 12 "quotes" of bad attitudes on separate slips and distribute them to various people. *1.* "Well, I don't live in Amsterdam or San Francisco; I'm one of God's children" (v. 10). *2.* "I give more than 10 percent to the church plus all the good jobs I do there. What more do you want?" (v. 11). *3.* "Every time the church door is open, you'll see me there" (v. 12). *4.* "No one has more prayer candles lit than I do" (v. 13a). *5.* "I'm here at church for all the special events, in addition to all the regular services" (vv. 13b, 14). *6.* "My hands are up, my head is down, my tears flow, my prayers are constant. What more could you ask?" (v. 15). *7.* "Well, we're all sinners. So we all carry a few sins into every worship assembly. No big deal" (v. 16). *8.* "My time is limited. As for projects like painting at the children's home and visiting shut-ins, I'll leave those to others. But I always have time for the Lord" (v. 17). *9.* "I listen to what God says in his Word; it's just that sometimes I kind of disagree with his decisions" (v. 18a). *10.* "Hey! My sins are all small and hardly noticeable. They're in the barely-stained range" (v. 18b). *11.* "I want it all, especially God's blessings, but he's going to have to overlook some things; I am just human" (v. 19). *12.* "You don't really believe God is going to punish anyone, do you? What kind of God is that?" (v. 20).

Introduce the exercise by saying, "Deeds are important! Yet God's rejection of Israel's worship as pictured in Isaiah 1:10-20 focused on attitudes and motives. Their defective character and lack of submission were primary." Assign to other students the verses and verse portions indicated on the slips. Ask those holding the "quotes" to stand one at a time at random and say their quotes with the implied emphasis. Then ask for the one who has the Scriptural "match" to stand and read his or her verse or verse segment.

Verse numbers are given after each "quote" for confirmation, but, of course, those should not be read with the quote. Your goal is to draw students' attention to the text and its implications.

Next, return to the Into the Lesson acrostic activity. Ask students for contrasts between the positive attributes of their definition and the negative characteristics rampant among the Judean worshipers.

When students suggest opposites, expect such items as the sincerity of true worship in contrast with the hypocrisy of false worship; the willing nature of true worship in contrast with the mechanical nature of the false; the preoccupation with forms and quantity of prayer in Israel's worshipers contrasting with the heartfelt passion and quality of prayer in proper worship.

(Alternative: use the Bad Practices and Attitudes Then activity from the Reproducible Page as the contrast to the Into the Lesson exercise; follow with the Bad Practices and Attitudes Now activity as an Into Life exercise.)

INTO LIFE

Return to the attitude "quotes" from above. Have students read these again. Suggest to the group that as the quotes are read, each should prayerfully ponder how often the sentiment or a similar one runs through their minds and even over their lips.

The "Been There, Heard That" activity in the student book also has a list of expressed (bad!) attitudes that could be used, or you as teacher may prepare another list reflecting attitudes you have heard and seen.

Bad Practices and Attitudes Then

Look at Isaiah 1:10-20 and see if you can think of seven concepts that detract from true worship, beginning each concept with one of the eleven letters of *anti-worship*. One idea is included to get you started.

A_____

N_____

T_____

I_____

-

W_____

O_____

Ritualized

S_____

H_____

I_____

P_____

Bad Practices and Attitudes Now

When you look at the practices and attitudes of worship in Isaiah's day, what elements to you see that, sadly, continue in today's personal and congregational practice of worship? What are your solutions?

Bad Practice or Attitude #1:

Bad Practice or Attitude #2:

Bad Practice or Attitude #3:

My positive solutions are:

COMMITTED TO SEEKING GOD

WHY TEACH THIS LESSON?

Your students probably already know many words and phrases that describe the heavenly father's character. He abounds in goodness, loving-kindness, and mercy. He is just, righteous, and holy. Despite this magnificent list, most of us don't trust him as much as we could. Why don't we seek him more? Why don't we follow him more faithfully? Today's lesson sketches for us more fully the character of our heavenly father. It will encourage your students to seek him in ever deeper ways.

INTRODUCTION

A. THE DREAM TEAM

The film *The Dream Team* is a 1989 comedy about mental patients who meet for group therapy. When their psychiatrist takes them on an outing, he witnesses a slaying and is nearly killed by the perpetrators. The group, not knowing what happened to their doctor, is left in New York City alone. They soon learn they are wanted both for the slaying and for the attempted murder of their doctor, who has ended up in a hospital.

The humor results from the need of this "dream team" to grapple with reality. How will they find their way out of the trouble they are in? In our days of psychiatrists, support groups, and self-help books, it sometimes makes us wonder where previous generations got mental and emotional help. What did Christians do in all those centuries before professional Christian counselors came along?

Once I came across an ancient work entitled *Conferences*. It was written by John Cassian, a monk who lived about AD 365–433. In this book, monastery leaders are portrayed as meeting with Cassian in groups to discuss issues of how to live the Christian life. In other words, they would counsel together for the spiritual benefit of themselves and for those to whom they ministered. Those with greater spiritual maturity could help guide others.

Today's lesson also offers us a picture of members of a group coming together for counseling. Chief among the group members are the future Jewish exiles. The prophet Isaiah writes 100 years before the Babylonian exile, but Isaiah knows that the Judeans will find themselves in deep trouble. They will not know where to turn.

The counselor, however, is the Lord himself. His wisdom and knowledge are infallible. We often wonder, as though in a dream, where to turn in times of trouble. God often uses our Christian friends who are wise enough to help us deal with reality. At other times he provides those with professional training to help. But behind any of these counselors must be the wisdom of the Lord, who alone can bring hope from despair.

DEVOTIONAL READING:
2 CORINTHIANS 9:10-15
BACKGROUND SCRIPTURE:
ISAIAH 55:1-11
PRINTED TEXT:
ISAIAH 55:1-11

Jun
24

LESSON AIMS

After participating in this lesson, each student will be able to:

1. Tell what Isaiah says God expects of a holy people.

2. Compare the moral climate called forth in Isaiah 55 with the moral climate of his or her own society.

3. Create a prayer list of people who need to heed the invitation to accept Christ.

KEY VERSE

Seek the LORD while he may be found; call on him while he is near. —Isaiah 55:6

DAILY BIBLE READINGS

Monday, June 18—Parable of the Great Banquet (Luke 14:15-24)

Tuesday, June 19—God's Banquet (Isaiah 25:6-10)

Wednesday, June 20—The Year of the Lord (Isaiah 61:1-6)

Thursday, June 21—Delight in the Lord (Isaiah 61:7-11)

Friday, June 22—Blessed to Bless (2 Corinthians 9:10-15)

Saturday, June 23—God Invites Us (Isaiah 55:1-5)

Sunday, June 24—Seek the Lord (Isaiah 55:6-11)

B. LESSON BACKGROUND

In last week's text, the Lord sought to shock Judah into repentance. Their acts of worship were in vain unless their lives demonstrated inward purity and outward righteousness. Isaiah's ministry was a call to repentance. Failure to repent meant destruction. Isaiah was told two things about Judah. First, since his preaching would fall on deaf ears, destruction would occur. (In fact, it did in 586 BC.) Second, in order to keep his covenant, the Lord would preserve a remnant of faithful people in spite of this destruction (Isaiah 6:8-13). This remnant was the exiles surviving the Babylonian captivity, which ended in 539 BC. This week's lesson stresses that message again.

The first section of Isaiah, chapters 1–39, is mostly judgment. The second section, chapters 40–66, is mostly blessing; almost all of it is poetry (except for 66:17-24), which means there is much use of figures of speech. Commentators have proposed many different outlines of these last 27 chapters, but most see 3 units of 9 chapters each. Isaiah 55 falls within the second unit, namely Isaiah 49–57. One way to look at these chapters is as a group discussion involving five parties: the Lord, the Messiah, Isaiah, Zion, and the Gentile nations.

The fourth party requires a little discussion. *Zion* can refer specifically to the city of Jerusalem, but also may be used to refer to the nation as a whole. In this part of Isaiah, *Zion* probably refers to the faithful remnant in the (to them, future) Babylonian exile. This remnant is idealized in those who accept the Messiah.

During the discussion, the Lord reveals the fact, method, and scope of his salvation. In Isaiah 55, the reader must identify speakers and those being addressed by carefully noting the pronouns and then identifying the main point.

I. BLESSING OFFERED (ISAIAH 55:1-5)

A. INVITATION (vv. 1, 2)

1. *"Come, all you who are thirsty,*
    come to the waters;
and you who have no money,
    come, buy and eat!
Come, buy wine and milk
    without money and without cost.

The phrase "come to me" in verse 3 (below) leaves no doubt that it is the Lord speaking. He is the one offering the covenant. The people of Judah are the ones being addressed as the plural *all you* shows.

The first address, to those *who are thirsty,* describes those who are invited to *come to the waters;* those who have need will be satisfied (compare Revelation 21:6; 22:17). The second address, to those *who have no money,* refers to those who are in abject poverty; they will need no money to buy what they need. What a future the Lord promises!

The word *wine* is used in both positive and negative ways in the Old Testament. Isaiah 56:12 offers us a negative sense, but in the verse before us the image is plainly positive. *Milk* also symbolizes great blessing (compare Exodus 3:8). Wine and milk are found together in Song of Songs 5:1 as a great delicacy. The Lord is calling his people to buy these desirable things at no cost to them, a symbol of plenty provided by the Lord.

Guaranteed *water* is comfort for the poor and needy (Isaiah 41:17-20); wine is a part of the feast that celebrates for all people the end of death forever (Isaiah 25:6-8); milk is a symbol of blessing in the promised kingdom of the one born of a virgin (Isaiah 7:14, 22). Isaiah 55:2, 3 (below) make clear that these are symbols here as well. To recognize these as figures of speech is not to make them unreal. On the contrary, what they symbolize is very real and very important.

Though water, wine, and milk will have literal significance for the future returnees from the Babylonian exile, Isaiah can use these images to symbolize spiritual blessing. The return from the Babylonian exile many years after Isaiah writes will indeed be a blessing for God's people.

The church age, inaugurated at Christ's first coming, is the beginning of a much more profound period of blessing. Being saved from the guilt and sickness of sin is something no one has money enough to buy. Thanks be to God for his gracious free gift that saves us from our spiritual poverty!

BUY WITHOUT MONEY

There was a time in my younger days when I had a powerful financial fantasy. We were struggling with money problems, as happens often to young couples raising a family on one income. My fantasy was that I had become a personal friend to the owner of a major department store, and I had been given a special card that permitted me to enter the store at any time. I could take whatever I wanted and never be charged for it. All my money problems would magically disappear, since I could now acquire whatever I needed (or wanted!) and never have to pay for it.

Then I realized that some people believe they have a card like this. It's called *a credit card*. They can go into any store, acquire whatever they need (or want!) and not have to pay for it. The major difference, however, is that ultimately they do have to pay for it. That's the reality of credit cards.

But Isaiah describes a situation much more like my original fantasy. God gives us a situation where we can buy without money. In fact, the items do not even have prices and there will never be a monthly statement. God supplies all the spiritual items we could ever need or want, and his credit covers them all. Do you live with that truth in mind?

—J. B. N.

2. "*Why spend money on what is not bread,*
    and your labor on what does not satisfy?
Listen, listen to me, and eat what is good,
    and your soul will delight in the richest of fare.

To *spend money* or exert one's own *labor* summarizes the human pursuit for happiness. The Lord uses a rhetorical question to stress that these yield what is not really *bread*. Whatever the Judeans are striving for is not food that truly nourishes. It *does not satisfy* the deepest human need.

The urgently repeated command to *listen* means to understand and heed. The structure of the Hebrew indicates that both of the next two statements will be the results of obeying him. First, the readers will *eat what is good*. Second, they will experience *delight in the richest of fare*.

These images may be taken in a physical sense, since the future exiles will return physically to "the land of milk and honey" that the Lord provides. But as figures of speech the implications are much more profound: godly living will bring great spiritual blessings. To take the promise merely in a physical sense would be to miss the main message.

B. BENEFITS (v. 3)

3. "*Give ear and come to me;*
    hear me, that your soul may live.
I will make an everlasting covenant with you,
    my faithful love promised to David.

WHAT DO YOU THINK?

How has God quenched your own spiritual hunger and thirst? Did you find this surprising? Explain.

WHAT DO YOU THINK?

What are some ways that people today spend money for that which does not satisfy? How can we guard ourselves against stumbling into such foolishness?

Visual for Lessons 4 & 5.
Keep this map of the Babylonian Empire posted for several lessons to help your students gain a geographical perspective.

Every parent knows the frustration of giving instructions and warnings to a child, only to have the child blithely skip off to do whatever he or she wants to do anyway. That must be how God feels on occasion. The people will behave sinfully right in the midst of the exile itself! Yet the result of their coming back to the Lord will be that he *will make an everlasting covenant.*

That which is *promised to David* is mentioned also in Acts 13:34. There the idea is applied to the resurrection of the Messiah. The name *David* usually refers to the human king in historical writings. *David* may also stand for his royal descendant. However, *David* is sometimes used by the prophets in an ultimate sense as a title for the Messiah (see Jeremiah 30:9; Ezekiel 34:23, 24; 37:24, 25; Hosea 3:5). The next two verses offer clues as to which the Lord intends here.

C. Agent (vv. 4, 5)

4. *"See, I have made him a witness to the peoples,*
    a leader and commander of the peoples.

The tense of *have made* does not rule out a later event; the context is future. Therefore the historical King David cannot be in view. A strictly human king of the line of David could be possible, except that no such ruler is ever the cause of the actions in verse 5, below. Therefore, the name *David* as used in verse 3 (*him* here in v. 4) seems to refer to the ideal, ultimate one: the Messiah. As *witness* to the love of God, the Messiah will make plain God's love to his people. As *leader and commander,* the Messiah is qualified to rule *the peoples.*

5. *"Surely you will summon nations you know not,*
    and nations that do not know you will hasten to you,
  because of the Lord your God,
    the Holy One of Israel,
    for he has endowed you with splendor."

As we work through our lesson text, remember that we are trying to figure out who is speaking and who is being spoken to at every point. Here the word *you* may refer to Zion being spoken to. If so, then the Lord's future kingdom, redeemed Zion, will call a nation it previously did not know. This seems to look forward to the time when redeemed Zion is the church.

If *you* refers ultimately to the church, then *will summon* refers to the preaching of the gospel by the church, and *will hasten* refers to the Gentiles' inclusion into the church. From Isaiah's perspective, this will happen *because of the Lord your God.* From our perspective, this has indeed happened and continues to happen.

The phrase *for he has endowed you with splendor* probably also refers to redeemed Zion and to the church. Isaiah 46:13 predicts the glorification of redeemed Zion (Israel; see also Isaiah 61:3). Romans 11:11-24 describes the glorification of the church in terms of a restored relationship between God and all believers, both Jewish and Gentile.

We should realize, however, that it is also attractive to understand *you* as indicating that the Lord now turns to speak to "David," meaning the Messiah, while in the presence of Zion. If this is the case, then it is the Messiah who will call nations to the Lord; the nations will run to the Lord because he will have glorified his Son (see Acts 3:13; Hebrews 1:1-3). Hebrews 5:5 implies that the Son was glorified by the Father. Under this idea, the divine Messiah calls a nation that *you know not* and nations *that do not know you* in the sense of establishing relationships. The Messiah will indeed have that relationship with the Gentiles under the new covenant. That relationship was not really a part of the old covenant (Hosea 1:10; 2:23; both quoted in Romans 9:25, 26; see also 1 Peter 2:10).

II. ACCEPTANCE URGED (ISAIAH 55:6, 7)

A. SEEKING REQUIRED (v. 6)

6. Seek the LORD while he may be found;
    call on him while he is near.

The speaker is now the prophet Isaiah. This is indicated in verse 7 (below), where he refers to "our God." The idea in the verse before us is not that the reader should *seek* God before God moves away and becomes distant. Rather, the idea is for the readers to seek God while their hearts are soft and willing to believe. They need to seek him and grow in their faith. In Hebrew poetry, the center of a poem often is the main point. Isaiah's urge to Zion is the center of the chapter. Therefore, this appeal to *seek the Lord* is the main point.

B. FORSAKING REQUIRED (v. 7)

7. Let the wicked forsake his way
    and the evil man his thoughts.
  Let him turn to the LORD, and he will have mercy on him,
    and to our God, for he will freely pardon.

Isaiah tells Zion that two things are involved in seeking the Lord. First, *the wicked* must *forsake his way;* that means that unrighteous lifestyles are to be left behind. Second, *the evil man* must forsake *his thoughts;* this is a challenge to abandon the internal sins of the heart. These are summarized with the challenge to *turn to the Lord . . . and to our God.* The results of returning to the Lord are twofold: first, the Lord *will have mercy on* the one who does so. Second, the Lord *will freely pardon.*

What comfort this must bring the exiles while they are suffering! They will be in exile some 70 years. When that time comes (in about 100 years from Isaiah's perspective), many will see no hope of restoration. The years will drag on and on. Well may they wonder, "Has the Lord rejected us forever?"

The Lord affirms that there is abundant forgiveness. Even so, every individual outside of Christ today is God's enemy. Once one learns the reality and depth of the life of sin—a life governed by self without God—one asks the same question, "Is there no hope for what I have done in rejecting God?" The good news is that there is the "wonderful grace of Jesus, greater than all my sin."

WHAT DO YOU THINK?

Was there a time when God restored you after you returned to him? What did the restoration involve?

III. UNFAILING WORD AFFIRMED (ISAIAH 55:8-11)

A. THOUGHTS AND WAYS (vv. 8, 9)

8, 9. "For my thoughts are not your thoughts,
    neither are your ways my ways,"
                declares the LORD.
"As the heavens are higher than the earth,
  so are my ways higher than your ways
  and my thoughts than your thoughts.

Clearly the Lord has resumed as speaker because it is the Lord's *thoughts* that are unsurpassed. That he is speaking to Zion is clear because the pronoun *your* in Hebrew is plural.

The fact that God's thoughts are so far beyond ours has at least two applications. First, this fact can give us hope when we see no way out of trouble. God can see a way out when we can't. Second, this fact should make us humble about our own ability to know. When we are "sure" that we know the motives of others who have hurt us, we ought to remember that only God truly knows the human heart (Jeremiah 17:9, 10).

WHAT DO YOU THINK?

What are some specific areas in which you have had to admit that God's thoughts and ways surpass your own? What happened when you finally made that admission?

PRAYER

Dear Father, We thank you for being absolutely trustworthy and effective. For all the times we still struggle with wanting to run our own lives apart from you, we ask your forgiveness. We, the most defiled, thank you for the relationship you have built with us through Christ, the Messiah, in whose name we pray, amen.

HIS THOUGHTS, AND OURS

Enrico Fermi (1901–1954) was an Italian immigrant and nuclear physicist who played an important role in building America's atomic bomb. His brilliance was evident early in his career. He received his PhD in 1922 at the age of 21. At his graduation ceremony he gave a lecture that put some of his professors to sleep; it was more intricate than they could follow.

He was present at the explosion of the first atomic bomb on July 16, 1945. With others, he was safely some distance away at the moment of explosion. Most of the witnesses were transfixed by the nature of the explosion itself. But Fermi was focused on determining the amount of power that the explosion released. Fermi dropped pieces of paper before, during, and after the passage of the blast wave. By measuring their displacement, he was able to estimate the strength of the blast.

We can see the grandeur of God's creation, and that is well and good as far as it goes (Psalm 19:1). Yet we can miss the power and force of his values if we're not careful. His thoughts and ways are indeed far beyond our own, and one of his highest values is the repentance of the sinner and the power of forgiveness. Though none of us saw the crucifixion and resurrection of Jesus, the immeasurable power of the cross still reaches us.

—J. B. N.

B. INTENT AND OUTCOME (vv. 10, 11)

10, 11. "As the rain and the snow
    come down from heaven,
and do not return to it
    without watering the earth
and making it bud and flourish,
    so that it yields seed for the sower and bread for the eater,
so is my word that goes out from my mouth:
    It will not return to me empty,
but will accomplish what I desire
    and achieve the purpose for which I sent it."

The Lord illustrates the certainty of his word by referring to *rain* and *snow . . . from heaven* in relationship to what gives life on *earth*. The phrase *do not return to it* brings out the point that the precipitation does not go back into heaven without having a useful effect.

Verse 11 is the lesson to be learned from the illustration. Precipitation from above corresponds to the Lord's Word *that goes out from* his *mouth*. He sends it down to earth through his prophets, but his word does not return to him without effect. Rather, it accomplishes what he intends.

WHAT DO YOU THINK?

What purposes of God's Word are being accomplished right now in your life? in your church?

CONCLUSION

I do not have a reputation in my family for always being able instinctively to find my way around while traveling. Since I know this, I (unlike many men) do not have any qualms about stopping to ask directions. However, some people are better at giving directions than others. Upon finishing the description, he or she may utter those often-heard words, "You can't miss it." Since on occasion I have indeed "missed it," those words do not offer me much comfort!

However, the Lord is saying to the exiles who will experience his punishment, "If you listen to what I say, if you give up trusting in your own ways, and if you seek me, then restoration will occur. Its scope will be beyond anything you can imagine. And this restoration is as certain as my word: you can't miss it."

His directions are clear: seek him. This always leads home. This was comfort to the faithful remnant. It is comfort to all who seek the Lord today.

THOUGHT TO REMEMBER

"How great is the love the Father has lavished on us" (1 John 3:1).

Discovery Learning

This page contains an alternative lesson plan emphasizing learning activities. Classes desiring such student involvement will find these suggestions helpful. The next page is a reproducible activity page to further enhance discovery learning.

LEARNING GOALS

After participating in this lesson, each student will be able to:

1. Tell what Isaiah says God expects of a holy people.

2. Compare the moral climate called forth in Isaiah 55 with the moral climate of his or her own society.

3. Create a prayer list of people who need to heed the invitation to accept Christ.

INTO THE LESSON

Because this week's lesson is a bold and gracious invitation from the Lord to Israel, send special "invitations" to your class members in advance. Inexpensive party invitations can usually be found at the dollar-or-less stores. Or you could recruit a computer-literate class member to design and send the invitations.

If mailing costs are prohibitive, have the invitations ready to be handed to each student upon arrival. On the invitation put the usual *when* and *where* information but incorporate key words such as "Eats!" "Delights!" and "Free Gifts!"

INTO THE WORD

Duplicate and distribute the following list of two-word expressions: *Big Thoughts; Caller Waiting; Exit Evil; Free Food; Heaven's Highway; Listen Up! National Race; People's Leader; Rat Race; Water Cycle; Word Works.* (These are to be related to vv. 8, 6, 7, 1, 9, 3, 5, 4, 2, 10, and 11, respectively, of Isaiah 55.)

Say, "Look at each of these two-word headings. Decide which verse from today's text can best be labeled with each. Put the verse number before each phrase." Give time for consideration and then come back to confirm the relationships. If a student has made connections other than those noted, let him or her explain the rationale.

Say, "Isaiah 55 may be considered a kind of evangelism study. It is one of God's great invitations to seek and find him." Divide your class into 3 groups of no more than 6 each. (If your class is larger than 18, duplicate the assignments.)

Say this to the group(s) you will call *Needs:* "Look at Isaiah 55:1-11 and make a list of basic human needs that you can identify from those verses." To the group(s) you will label *Provisions* say, "From Isaiah 55:1-11 make

a list of all the blessings God offers to the one who responds to him." For the group(s) you will call *Evangelism,* give this direction: "Look at Isaiah 55:1-11 and decide what that text offers to the one who would invite the unsaved to a meeting with God and his Son."

Allow about five minutes for deliberation. Then ask for a report from each group. Expect some of the following items to be included. *Needs* group: water; food; satisfying work; covenants—that is, agreements of various sorts; a leader and commander who knows the right way; mercy and forgiveness. *Provisions* group: delights for the soul as well as the body; a covenant with God; a witness to who God is; mercy; pardon; a predictable science; God's Word. *Evangelism* group: meaning for an otherwise dreary existence (purpose for being); God's Word as life for the soul; Jesus as our wise leader and commander; mercy and pardon readily available; possibility of a new direction in life.

INTO LIFE

Recruit a member of the class who enjoys computer work to produce for each class member a foldable sheet as a card. It will have a simple front, reading, "Come!" The inside right should also be simple, reading:

Dear _____,
    This is a simple invitation, sent by God himself. If you are feeling _____, *consider that Isaiah affirms* _____ *in Isaiah 55:* ____ . *God will welcome you to his celebration, and he will provide all the gifts! Hoping you can join us for the delights.*
        Signed, _____

Distribute these with the following directions: "Consider someone you know who needs to hear God's invitation. Write in his or her name, then identify the 'feeling' that may be keeping him or her from the Lord. Consider the elements introduced in our small group discussions and add a note of blessing that Isaiah affirms. You may not actually want to send this invitation. But use it anyway as a prayer and action stimulus to become God's ambassador to that person."

(Additional activities: use the Marvelous Invitation and Christ's Ambassador exercises from the Reproducible Page, as time allows.)

Marvelous Invitation

On numerous occasions, God graciously invites all to come to him for his blessing and grace. What is the basic joy in the following invitations? Why do people hesitate to respond today?

Isaiah 55:1, 2 _____

Matthew 11:28 _____

Luke 14:16, 17 _____

2 Corinthians 6:17, 18 _____

Revelation 18:4 _____

JOY!

Joy!

JOY!

Joy!

Christ's Ambassador

It is the high privilege of each Christian to be Christ's courier, the deliverer of his gracious invitation. To whom do you have opportunity to say "Come!" on his behalf? Today's text in Isaiah 55:1-11 has a treasure of verses for making God's invitation.

Is there someone you know who is struggling with the humdrum futility of his or her life? Which verse from today's text offers the most encouragement? Why?

Is there someone you know who considers himself or herself too great a sinner ever to be forgiven? Which verse from today's text can assure that person forgiveness is possible? Why?

Is there someone you know who thinks he or she has life all figured out and considers the idea of God to be irrelevant? What verses from today's text remind us of God's transcendence? Why?

Is there someone you know who comes from a non-Christian culture and knows little if anything of the Christ? What verse from today's text reveals that it is Jesus the Messiah who is God's designated Savior?

Is there someone you know who evidences some yearning for God's presence and whose heart appears fertile? Which verse from today's text can challenge that person to repentant obedience? Why?

COMMITTED TO GOD'S REQUIREMENTS

WHY TEACH THIS LESSON?

How often we fail to do what is in our own best interest! A doctor may prescribe a diet so we can have a healthy heart. But many things we like are not on that diet, and things we do not care for as much are the basics of the diet. Our desire to eat what we like then can take precedence over our following the doctor's orders.

Your students do the same thing in a spiritual sense (see Romans 7:19). The result is spiritual heart trouble. And when the spiritual heart is troubled and diseased, it becomes more and more difficult to make right decisions. It is important to heed the advice of our medical doctors to avoid health problems, and we need to listen to the words of our great physician and the prescriptions given in the Word of God to avoid spiritual sickness and divine disfavor. Today's lesson stresses this message—a message that is never obsolete.

INTRODUCTION

A. THE WALK OF HUMILITY

At his inauguration in 1977, incoming American President Jimmy Carter used the historic Bible that had been employed by George Washington at his own inauguration. Carter said, "Here before me is the Bible used in the inauguration of our first President, in 1789, and I have just taken the oath of office on the Bible my mother gave me a few years ago." Carter then read Micah 6:8, his key verse. Carter thus recognized that even the most powerful men on earth are called "to act justly and to love mercy and to walk humbly."

Yet humility, in particular, seems to be in scarce supply these days. We see a seemingly unlimited procession of people seeking to become famous celebrities. In the last century, a famous boxer was widely known for boasting, "I am the greatest!" More recently, we have seen the rise of so-called "reality" television, where ordinary people are thrust into a celebrity-type spotlight. In the 1960s, pop philosopher Andy Warhol predicted, "In the future, everyone will be famous for fifteen minutes." Warhol later reversed this line to say, "In fifteen minutes, everybody will be famous." The lists of famous celebrities seem to become increasingly crowded.

The Bible teaches us that "humility comes before honor" (Proverbs 15:33). The humbled/exalted paradox is that those who strive to be honored will not succeed in God's eyes, but those who serve humbly, without concern for applause, will be honored. Those seeking celebrity status should remember this warning: "God opposes the proud but gives grace to the humble" (James 4:6). Humility, then, is not an occasional choice. For the Christian it must be a walk, a lifestyle (compare Philippians 2:3).

DEVOTIONAL READING:
HEBREWS 12:6-12
BACKGROUND SCRIPTURE:
MICAH 2:1-4; 3:1-5, 8-12; 6:6-8
PRINTED TEXT:
MICAH 3:1-4; 6:6-8

Jul
1

LESSON AIMS

After participating in this lesson, each student will be able to:

1. Summarize Micah's rebuke of evil in his society and his call to do what God requires.

2. Compare and contrast what the Lord requires in Micah 6 with what the Lord requires in the new covenant.

3. State one specific way he or she can better "walk humbly with your God."

KEY VERSE

He has showed you, O man, what is good. And what does the LORD require of you? To act justly and to love mercy and to walk humbly with your God.
—Micah 6:8

LESSON 5 NOTES

As we seek to serve the Lord, we should begin by asking, "What does God expect?" Fortunately, we do not have to guess the answer to this question. One source of information for us is found in the writings of God's prophets. These men left a marvelous record of their messages: Bible texts that provide a clear picture of what God demands from his people.

B. LESSON BACKGROUND

Micah is one of the great eighth-century prophets of Israel. That was also the time frame of Isaiah, Hosea, and Amos. Micah 1:1 records that he prophesied during the reigns of Jotham, Ahaz, and Hezekiah, kings of the southern kingdom of Judah. However, this verse also tells us that his prophecies were for both Judah (with its capital city of Jerusalem) and the northern kingdom of Israel (with its capital in Samaria).

The reign of those three kings spanned the period of approximately 750–690 BC, roughly 60 years. This was a tumultuous time for the people of God. Micah lived through the destruction of the northern kingdom in 722 BC (2 Kings 18:9-11). About 20 years later, he was probably an eyewitness to a similar threat to Jerusalem in 701 BC. That time, however, God miraculously delivered Judah by destroying 185,000 members of the Assyrian army (2 Kings 19:35).

There are strong connections between Micah and Isaiah, indicating they may have been colleagues. For example, Isaiah 2:2-4 and Micah 4:1-3 are nearly identical texts. Both prophets share messages of the necessity for the people of God to repent and work for justice. Both preach the future hope of God's coming Messiah. We also know that the ministry of Micah influenced the later prophets of Judah (see Jeremiah 26:18, 19).

Micah's words are both forceful and eloquent. He was well aware of the empowerment of God's Spirit to give him his prophetic message (Micah 3:8). He also knew that his message was not well received by some, and that there were those who wanted to silence him (2:6, 7). He indicted Israel with God's accusation for failure to uphold the covenant of obedience and righteousness (6:1, 2). This accusation was not unique to Micah (see Jeremiah 25:31; Hosea 4:1; 12:2).

Micah's plea was that God's people must realize that if they did not seek justice in their society, then God would purge them of evil by allowing their destruction. While Christians are not citizens of Micah's Israel, that prophet's call for holiness and righteousness sounds a needed plea to the church today.

I. LOVING EVIL (MICAH 3:1-4)

The idea of *loving evil* seems detestable to most Christians. That idea is something that characterizes those "other people," the unbelievers. In our world, where sinfulness is not hidden but celebrated, we can find many examples of people who seem to seek wickedness passionately in every possible form.

Yet God, who knows our hearts, can see that this is sometimes true of all of us. For Micah, even the apparently respectable leaders of Israel had been judged by their actions and found to love evil more than good (compare Psalm 52:3). Micah points out two fundamental flaws in their thinking that have caused this.

A. MISTAKE #1: "GOD WON'T JUDGE" (vv. 1-3)
1. Then I said,
> "Listen, you leaders of Jacob,
> you rulers of the house of Israel.
> Should you not know justice,

HOW TO SAY IT

Assyrian. *Uh-SEAR-e-un.*

Byzantine. *BIH-zen-teen.*

Constantinople. *KAHN-stan-ten-oh-puhl.*

Hagia Sophia. *HAG-ee-uh So-FEE-uh.*

Hezekiah. *Hez-ih-KYE-uh.*

Hosea. *Ho-ZAY-uh.*

Istanbul. *IS-tun-bull.*

Jotham. *JO-thum.*

Leviticus. *Leh-VIT-ih-kus.*

Messiah. *Meh-SIGH-uh.*

Micah. *MY-kuh.*

Samaria. *Suh-MARE-ee-uh.*

Zechariah. *ZEK-uh-RYE-uh*

The British historian Lord Acton (1834–1902) commented, "Power tends to corrupt, and absolute power corrupts absolutely." History is full of examples of leaders who acted as if they were above the law rather than stewards of the law. Acton also said, "Remember, where you have a concentration of power in a few hands, all too frequently men with the mentality of gangsters get control."

It seems to be in this light that Micah thunders at the leaders of Judah and Israel the provocative question *Should you not know justice?* In other words, "Do you believe that you're above the law, that you can administer or withhold justice at your own whim?" Those who think they can administer justice this way are in for a shock. A time is coming when the wealthiest and most powerful people on earth will quiver in fear at the judgmental wrath of God (Revelation 6:15-17).

This admonition is not only for the rich and powerful, however. It is for the father who tyrannizes his family behind closed doors. It is for the boss who exploits his or her employees at the workplace. It is for the shoplifter who believes that petty theft can be done secretly and without consequence. It is for those of us who believe we can get away with private sins of lust or pride. God is the perfect judge, and no one escapes his all-seeing eye.

2, 3. *". . . you who hate good and love evil;*
who tear the skin from my people
and the flesh from their bones;
who eat my people's flesh,
strip off their skin
and break their bones in pieces;
who chop them up like meat for the pan,
like flesh for the pot?"

Micah employs some of the most violently graphic language of the Old Testament to drive home his point. God says that the leaders of Israel have exploited *my people.* These people are the very ones the leaders should have been protecting. Micah uses the horrific language of cannibalism, saying, in effect, "You have eaten my precious children." This does not refer to actual cannibalism, but to the relentless economic oppression of the poor people of Israel by the rulers. Those in power have manipulated the system to seize the property (and therefore the livelihood) of the lower classes (Micah 2:2). They have been consumed by greediness and wickedness (Micah 2:1).

CANNIBALISM

Most cultures regard cannibalism as repulsive. In spite of its hideous qualities, however, it has occurred repeatedly in history. Usually it occurs in situations where people are facing utter starvation, and it is a last resort to secure food.

One famous instance was the Donner Party, traveling to California in 1846. They were just a day late trying to cross the Sierra Mountains before snow blocked the passes. Only 1,000 feet from the top, a snowstorm caught the 81 travelers. In a desperate attempt, 15 people hiked out. They became lost. As some died of malnutrition, others butchered them for food (labeling the packages so no one would have to eat a relative). Survivors finally stumbled into civilization and relief parties went back to save the others. Cannibalism had occurred even in the main camp. Nearly half the people died (www.pbs.org).

Cannibalism is hard to conceive of, even in situations involving starvation. But Micah describes a situation in which the princes of Israel practiced economic cannibalism on their own people by choice, not by necessity. They had figuratively devoured their people. It is no wonder that Micah 3:4 says the Lord would hide his face from the perpetrators in their own time of need!   —J. B. N.

Visual for Lessons 4 & 5.
Keep this map of the Babylonian Empire posted for several lessons to help your students gain a geographical perspective.

DAILY BIBLE READINGS

Monday, June 25—Fear the Lord (Deuteronomy 10:12-22)

Tuesday, June 26—The Disciplined Life (Hebrews 12:6-12)

Wednesday, June 27—Human Plans and God's (Micah 2:1-5)

Thursday, June 28—Sins Denounced (Micah 3:1-7)

Friday, June 29—Micah Speaks Out (Micah 3:8-12)

Saturday, June 30—Promise of Peace (Micah 4:1-5)

Sunday, July 1—What Does God Require? (Micah 6:3-8)

B. MISTAKE #2: "GOD IGNORES MY EVIL" (v. 4)

4. Then they will cry out to the LORD,
*   but he will not answer them.*
* At that time he will hide his face from them*
*   because of the evil they have done.*

A difficult reality is that sometimes the consequences for sins are not immediately evident. Just because we are not incinerated by a lightning bolt every time we sin does not mean that God fails to notice or that God is indifferent.

A hard lesson that the people of Israel have to learn is that God is not endlessly forgiving. There comes a time when God acts with decisive justice. God offers salvation by grace through Jesus, yet a time is coming when God's wrath will be poured out on the disobedient (Ephesians 5:6).

Two centuries after Micah, the prophet Zechariah explains God's judgment in a similar way. He notes that God's prophets had called repeatedly for social justice but had been met by hard-heartedness. Eventually God responds this way: "When I called, they did not listen; so when they called, I would not listen" (Zechariah 7:13). God does not offer infinite opportunities to repent.

II. LOVING JUSTICE AND MERCY (MICAH 6:6-8)

To be sure, Micah has harsh words for those who have spurned God's standards, loving evil. But Micah balances this with encouragement for those seeking to live lives pleasing to God.

A. CORRECT ACTION #1: WORSHIP GOD (vv. 6, 7)

6a. With what shall I come before the LORD
*   and bow down before the exalted God?*

In examining our relationship with God, an important starting point is the issue of worship. The most foundational meaning of worship in the Old Testament is to *bow down before*. To do so is to acknowledge that God is great and worthy of honor and devotion (see Psalm 95:6).

Another key aspect of Old Testament worship is sacrifice. To sacrifice is to relinquish freely something of value back to God. Sacrifice for us today may be in the form of monetary offerings for the work of the church. Sacrifice in the Old Testament often takes the form of agricultural produce and livestock, things that can be used for food.

Any person's worship should include acts of sacrifice in order to be complete. Micah, however, drums a common beat of the prophets: that sacrifice without an attitude of submission to God is empty and worthless. God refuses to acknowledge such hollow acts (see Amos 5:22). The following verses expand on this.

6b, 7. Shall I come before him with burnt offerings,
*   with calves a year old?*
* Will the LORD be pleased with thousands of rams,*
*   with ten thousand rivers of oil?*
* Shall I offer my firstborn for my transgression,*
*   the fruit of my body for the sin of my soul?*

Micah checks off possible sacrifices in a list of accelerating value. He begins with simple *burnt offerings,* which could be as lowly as a small bird (see Genesis 8:20). This proceeds to a yearling calf, an animal of considerable value. Micah then moves to a kingly sacrifice, namely *thousands of rams* (see 1 Kings 8:63). He next mentions a sacrifice beyond the potential of even the wealthiest person: a myriad of flowing *rivers of* olive *oil*. This is an offering of unimaginable value.

WHAT DO YOU THINK?

What steps need to be taken to teach people that God has limits to his patience? Why is the church sometimes negligent in doing so?

WHAT DO YOU THINK?

Many attend church looking for "what the church can do for me." What steps can your church take to teach individuals about the importance and priority of worship?

Micah ends the list with an unspeakable offering: human sacrifice of a *first-born* child. This has dual significance for the Israelites of Micah's time. First, they are aware of God's testing of Abraham, who was commanded to offer his beloved son Isaac as a burnt offering (Genesis 22:2). The lesson of that story, however, is that while God has a right to demand the sacrifice of that which is most precious to us, he does not condone human sacrifice at our initiative. Second, Micah's imagery also reminds the Israelites of their pagan neighbors, who sacrificed children to false gods. This is abhorrent to the Lord (Leviticus 20:2; Jeremiah 7:31; 19:5; 32:35).

Micah leaves questions unanswered, but the expected response is clear. We cannot earn God's favor by our sacrifices, no matter how lavish they may be. Sacrifice can be empty or self-serving, and God does not desire such acts.

THE PRICE OF LOVE

What kind of gift does it take to demonstrate the value of love and devotion? Merchants want us to go overboard at Christmas. To convince a spouse of the depth of our love, we are encouraged to purchase expensive diamonds. Middle-aged husbands now receive advertising that tells them, "Now that the tight financial years of early marriage are past, purchase a ring that will tell her how much you really love her!"

The old Christmas carol *The Twelve Days of Christmas* also goes a bit overboard. "On the first day of Christmas, my true love gave to me a partridge in a pear tree," it says. And then come turtledoves, French hens, calling birds, etc. The list also becomes cumulative. That is, a partridge in a pear tree is given *each* of the 12 days, and all the other gifts also repeat on all later days. On the twelfth day there are 78 gifts given, for a grand total of 364. All to demonstrate true love!

Wouldn't one carefully chosen, thoughtful gift be more appropriate? Enough with all your birds and leapers! Rather than the quantity of sacrifices, God is more interested in the quality of love and devotion demonstrated in service.   —J. B. N.

B. CORRECT ACTION #2: OBEY GOD (v. 8)

8a. He has showed you, O man, what is good.

    And what does the LORD require of you?

Micah 6:8 is one of the most important verses in the Bible. It has been called the "key to the prophets." It is a concise summary of what God demands from his people. It is not a list of actions, but rather a trio of attitudes that will result in behavior that is pleasing to God. While this verse is addressed to the people of Israel, it still retains value for Christians who desire to live lives that are in accordance with God's will.

Micah is not teaching anything new to the people of Israel. He begins the verse by reminding them that they have been shown these things in the past. The requirements for goodness in the eyes of God can be boiled down to three things.

8b. But to act justly.

To act justly includes the concepts of justice in the society and righteousness in one's personal life. God's accusation against Israel is that the government of God's people is not just. Instead, it exploits and oppresses the poor and downtrodden for the advantage of the rich and powerful.

God wants a nation that flows with justice for all (Amos 5:24). The Lord has made it clear that sacrifice without justice is not what he wants (Proverbs 21:3). God wants leaders who will protect the most vulnerable members of their community, often symbolized by widows and orphans in the Old Testament (see Isaiah 1:17; compare James 1:27).

PRAYER

God of mercy, God of justice, we come to you in humility. May you help us have victory over pride. May you help us be merciful, just as you have been merciful to us. May you help us long for righteousness and justice according to your standards. We pray these things in the name of your Son, Jesus Christ, the righteous one, amen.

WHAT DO YOU THINK?

People see corrupt behavior from business or political leaders, yet may feel powerless to do anything. How can the church encourage Christians not to settle for the status quo?

Personal righteousness is also required. Righteousness is right actions, doing the right thing. The people of ancient Israel are to be guided by the Law of Moses, which clearly defines right behavior. As Christians we understand that we are righteous through our faith in Christ, not by keeping the law (Philippians 3:9). But this does not diminish God's expectation that we will continually strive for holiness in our lives, to live righteously (1 Timothy 6:11).

8c. And to love mercy.

The word translated *mercy* here may be the most significant doctrinal term in the Old Testament. It is sometimes translated *love* and is seen as a supreme characteristic of God. The love of God is to be valued more than life itself (Psalm 63:3). The love the Lord prevents us from being consumed (Lamentations 3:22).

On both the level of the society and on the personal level, the quest for justice must be tempered with mercy. When we seek righteous judgments, we must do so with the loving heart of the Father. As with justice, sacrifices and worship from those without mercy are not pleasing to God. Jesus was quick to quote Hosea 6:6 to his critics, reminding them that God desired mercy above sacrifice (see Matthew 9:13; 12:7).

8d. And to walk humbly with your God?

WHAT DO YOU THINK?

Suppose you were in charge of producing 3 videos, of 20 minutes each, designed to instruct the young people of your church how they can live out the three principles in Micah 6:8. What would you include in each video to illustrate how a Christian is to act justly, to love mercy, and to walk humbly with your God?

The third requirement is a necessary companion to the first two. God is not impressed by those who do acts of justice and mercy in order to call attention to themselves (compare Matthew 6:1-4). Humility demands that we behave in a godly manner because it is the right way to act, not because we will be rewarded for it. Virtue truly becomes its own reward. The humble person will do the right thing consistently, even when no one else is aware of his or her action.

The opposite of humility is pride. We are to clothe ourselves with humility, because "God opposes the proud but gives grace to the humble" (1 Peter 5:5). As a spirited stallion must be "broken" to be useful, so we must be broken and humble before God if he is to use us for his service (see Matthew 18:4). This brokenness and humility is our finest sacrifice to God (Psalm 51:17).

CONCLUSION

A. AN OUT-OF-BALANCE LIFE

One of the grandest church buildings in the world is the *Hagia Sophia* in Istanbul (ancient Constantinople). It was built by the Christian Emperor Justinian in the sixth century AD. Justinian was perhaps the greatest ruler of the Byzantine Empire, and the *Hagia Sophia* was his supreme accomplishment. Justinian established a court system that dispensed justice for centuries. He was merciful to his people and lavished his largesse upon them. Yet he wanted his *Hagia Sophia* to exceed the grandeur of the temple of Jerusalem. Upon seeing the finished building, it is said that Justinian exclaimed, "O Solomon, I have outdone thee!" Justinian loved justice and mercy, but he failed the last of Micah's three great standards: to walk humbly with his God.

WHAT DO YOU THINK?

What parallels, if any, are there between how the people responded to God in the text and how young people today respond to parental authority? If you see a problem, what solutions can you offer?

B. THE WELL-ROUNDED LIFE

The well-rounded life is measured by all three of Micah's cardinal virtues: *justice, mercy,* and *humility.* These three form an interlocking grid, and the absence of one will yield a life without proper balance. Studying Micah gives us an opportunity for self-evaluation. Do we seek justice and righteousness? Are there unrighteous elements in our lives with which we have become complacent? Do we really love being people of mercy? Have we become tired of kindness (2 Thessalonians 3:13)? How would we evaluate our personal humility?

THOUGHT TO REMEMBER

Practice God's requirements.

Discovery Learning

This page contains an alternative lesson plan emphasizing learning activities. Classes desiring such student involvement will find these suggestions helpful. The next page is a reproducible activity page to further enhance discovery learning.

LEARNING GOALS

After this lesson, each student will be able to:

1. Summarize Micah's rebuke of evil in his society and his call to do what God requires.

2. Compare and contrast what the Lord requires in Micah 6 with what the Lord requires in the new covenant.

3. State one specific way he or she can better "walk humbly with your God."

INTO THE LESSON

Pair off your students. Ask each pair to discuss these questions: (1) "What do people (both Christians and non-Christians) think God expects from them?" (2) "What does God actually require?" Allow your students several minutes to discuss the questions, then call for conclusions. Write their responses on the board.

After hearing from several volunteers, tell your class that today's lesson from the book of Micah explains the difference between what those in the prophet's day *thought* God expected of them and what God *actually* required. (Option: distribute copies of the What Does God Want? exercise from the Reproducible Page for students to work on as they arrive.)

INTO THE WORD

Divide your class into an even number of groups by combining student pairs from the previous exercise. Each group should have four to six students. Assign each group a number. The odd-numbered groups will answer questions one and three. The even-numbered groups will answer questions two and four.

Appoint a discussion leader for each group or let each choose its own leader. If you do not use the student books, you will need to copy and distribute the questions and instructions below.

Question #1: What angered God in Micah's day?

Read Micah 3:1-4. Compare what Micah says there with Micah 1:5-7; 2:1, 2; and 2 Kings 17:1-17. Of what sins were the people guilty? What happened to the people as a result? Why was God angry about these sins?

Question #2: What did God expect in Micah's day?

Read Micah 6:6-8 and compare it with Proverbs 21:3; Jeremiah 22:1-5; Hosea 6:6; and Amos 5:21-24. What did God expect? Why would God reject the Jews' sacrifi-

cial offerings if he commanded them to be made in the first place? (See Leviticus 26, especially v. 31.)

Allow the groups a few minutes, then discuss their findings. Especially discuss the meaning of the commands in Micah 6:8 to "act justly," "love mercy," and "walk humbly with your God." When you have finished this discussion, tell your groups to move on to questions three and four.

Question #3: How do Christians anger God today?

Read Matthew 25:14-30; 1 Corinthians 6; and Hebrews 10:26-31. Why are the sins mentioned here particularly offensive to God? How do they compare with the sins committed in Micah's day? What will happen to those who continue committing these sins?

Question #4: What does God expect of Christians?

Read Ephesians 5:1–6:9; Philippians 2:3-5; 1 Timothy 6:3-11; James 2:8-17; and 1 John 3:16-18. How does God expect Christians to behave today? Especially, how are we to treat one another? How does this compare with God's expectations for His people in Micah's day? What does it mean for a Christian today to act justly, love mercy, and walk humbly with God?

Allow the groups a few minutes to answer, then discuss their findings.

INTO LIFE

Display the following headings on the board: *Act Justly; Love Mercy; Walk Humbly with God.*

Ask each group to choose one of the categories for this last exercise. Make sure each category is chosen by at least one group. When each group has selected its category, group members should work together to write several introspective questions that will help an individual evaluate how well he or she is carrying out that command. For instance, a question for the category *Love Mercy* may be, "Do I make a regular effort to visit the sick, the elderly, and the poor?"

Instruct each group to write at least five questions. Next, ask for volunteers to suggest questions to the entire class. Write these on the board. Finally, tell your students to take a few minutes to ask themselves these questions and to look for areas in their lives that need improvement. They need not share their answers.

Close with a prayer for God to guide your students as they try to keep these commands.

What Does God Want?

Read Micah 3:1-4 and 6:6-8. Then fill in the blanks below with the missing words. Next, copy the highlighted letters to the line at the bottom to discover Micah's message to God's people.

1, 2. "You who hate ☐ _ _ _ and _ ☐ _ _ evil."

3. "Listen, you _ _ _ ☐ _ _ _."

4. "Should you not know _ _ ☐ _ _ _ _?"

5. "You ☐ _ _ _ _ _ of the house of Israel."

6. "Because of the ☐ _ _ _ they have done."

7. "What does the Lord _ _ ☐ _ _ _ _ of you?"

8. "Shall I come before him with _ ☐ _ _ _ _ _ _ _ _ _ _ _ _?"

9. "He will _ ☐ _ _ his face."

10. "Shall I offer my firstborn for my _ ☐ _ _ _ _ _ _ _ _ _ _ _?"

11. "With _ _ _ _ ☐ _ a year old?"

12. "To love ☐ _ _ _ _."

13. "Bow down before the ☐ _ _ _ _ _ _ God?"

14. "For the _ _ ☐ of my soul?"

15. "To act _ _ _ ☐ _ _."

16. "Shall I offer my _ _ _ ☐ _ _ _ _?"

Micah spoke of _ _ _ ' _ _ _ _ _ _ _ _ _ _ _ _ _ .

COMMITTED TO RIGHTEOUSNESS

LESSON 6

WHY TEACH THIS LESSON?

Things have a tendency to deteriorate. Our cars, houses, and clothes wear out. We also recognize this tendency with regard to our own bodies. We are also subject to spiritual deterioration as we live in a fallen world. God paid a large price (the death of his son) to renew and restore His people, but vigilance in prayer and Bible study on our part helps keep us from slipping away.

This lesson allows us to consider some ways in which we may be going through spiritual degeneration. As we study, let us rejoice in the fact that God is still in the business of restoring his people.

INTRODUCTION

A. MORAL CHOICES IN AN IMMORAL SOCIETY

A recent claim of some genetic researchers is that the DNA of men is programmed for infidelity. In other words, the males of the human species are not created in the image of God but are more like bread mold, which exists to spread its spores everywhere.

If this were true, then the Bible's teaching about confining sexual activity to marriage would seem to be fighting a losing battle against the irresistible forces of nature. While this may be welcome news to some in our society, it contradicts the picture of morality found in the Bible.

Is there such a thing as *biblical morality*? The answers given to this question range from *yes*, to *not really*, to *who cares*? Increasingly, there are large segments of the population that want to get away from *moral* versus *immoral* distinctions. They prefer to see things from an *amoral* perspective—a perspective that does not recognize any absolute standards of right and wrong. Under amorality, what may seem wrong to one person becomes enjoyable and right to another. This worldview is becoming more common, even within the church.

Yet the Christian who believes that the teachings of the Bible are from God will never be comfortable with attempts to paint morality a neutral gray. If we come from the perspective of biblical morality, then *amoral = immoral,* a violation of God's standards. We seek to live as God's people in a society that does not recognize God. We are moral people in an immoral world.

In the ancient world there were plenty of people who rejected God's standards, even within God's chosen people of Israel. God continually raised up prophets to proclaim his demands for justice and righteousness. The prophets' call for reform was accompanied by a dire warning: God would not allow wickedness to go unpunished forever. There would be a day when the righteous would be rewarded and the evil would be purged. Zephaniah was the ideal prophet for this message.

DEVOTIONAL READING:
PSALM 27:7-14

BACKGROUND SCRIPTURE:
ZEPHANIAH 3:1-13; 2 CHRONICLES 34:1-3

PRINTED TEXT:
ZEPHANIAH 3:1-9

Jul
8

LESSON AIMS

After participating in this lesson, each student will be able to:

1. List at least three sins that characterized the moral conditions of Josiah's Jerusalem.

2. Explain why God has a right to be angry at unholy behavior.

3. Praise God that he tempers his wrath with grace through Jesus Christ.

KEY VERSE

I have decided to assemble the nations, to gather the kingdoms and to pour out my wrath on them—all my fierce anger. The whole world will be consumed by the fire of my jealous anger.
—Zephaniah 3:8

B. LESSON BACKGROUND

King Josiah was the last righteous king to rule in Jerusalem before its destruction. He reigned from about 640 to 609 BC. The Bible teaches that "neither before nor after Josiah was there a king like him who turned to the Lord as he did—with all his heart" (2 Kings 23:25). Josiah came to the throne under very difficult circumstances. Manasseh, his grandfather, was king for 55 years and can be judged to be the most evil king in the history of Judah (see 2 Kings 21:9, 16; 24:3). Josiah's father, King Amon, continued in the evil ways of Manasseh. Amon reigned only two years before being killed in a palace coup (2 Kings 21:23). This brought Josiah to become king at age 8 (2 Kings 22:1).

Despite his heritage of evil and his tender age, Josiah eventually was responsible for many reforms in Judah. While Josiah was king, Hilkiah the high priest found the book of the law while making repairs in the temple. Josiah and his advisors used this book as the basis for reforms that purged Judah of its pagan practices and reinstituted the worship of God (see 2 Kings 23:24).

These reforms "didn't take," however. They only delayed the downward spiral of Judah. Josiah was killed in battle about 608 BC (2 Kings 23:29). His successors were not of his moral stature, and God allowed the Babylonians to dominate Judah. The cream of the crop of Hebrew young men (like Daniel) was carried into captivity. Eventually the city of Jerusalem was destroyed in 586 BC.

Zephaniah was one of the three great prophets of the last days of Jerusalem before its destruction. The other two, Habakkuk and Jeremiah, will be studied in the following lessons. Zephaniah preached the coming doom of Judah because of its deep sin. Although Zephaniah prophesied at the time of Josiah's godly reforms, he saw the coming demise of Judah after those reforms were rejected. But Zephaniah also gave a picture of God's future restoration.

Zephaniah was a spokesman for the concept of *the day of the Lord,* a future point in time when God would move powerfully to punish wickedness and redeem the righteous. *The day of the Lord* found fulfillment in the history of Judah with its exile and return but also looks forward to a future day of God's final judgment of all humanity.

I. GOD SEES MORAL FILTH (ZEPHANIAH 3:1-5)

Nations do not rise above the moral level set by their leaders. Under Manasseh, wickedness flourished. Unrighteousness was not confined to religious practices. It extended to business practices and to the integrity of public leaders. This was the moral situation that confronted the reformer king, namely Josiah. It is a situation into which God's prophet Zephaniah speaks.

A. POLLUTED, DISOBEDIENT CITY (vv. 1, 2)

1. *Woe to the city of oppressors,*
    rebellious and defiled!

A *woe* is the opposite of a blessing. As such, a woe is equivalent to a curse. Moses had promised that God would give blessings if the people were obedient and curses if they were disobedient (Deuteronomy 11:26-28). So the verse before us is not a blessing. Jerusalem is not the "holy city." Indeed, it is characterized by moral filth and by oppressing mistreatment of its citizens by the rulers.

2. *She obeys no one,*
    she accepts no correction.
  She does not trust in the LORD,
    she does not draw near to her God.

How can we speak so that both believers and nonbelievers can appreciate the contrast between the holiness of God and the awfulness of sin? Should we use different language to the two groups in this regard? Explain.

Zephaniah outlines four primary charges against Jerusalem: general disobedience, defiance in the face of *correction*, lack of *trust in the Lord*, and willful abandonment of relationship with *God*. All of these accusations hit home with the society fostered by King Manasseh; for half of a century, he had led Jerusalem away from the Lord.

The era of Manasseh had endured so long that the vast majority of citizens knew nothing else. How faith survived in persons like Jeremiah, Hilkiah, Josiah, and Zephaniah is a testimony to the providential power of God.

B. SELFISH, GREEDY RULERS (v. 3)

3. Her officials are roaring lions,
     her rulers are evening wolves,
     who leave nothing for the morning.

Zephaniah uses vivid metaphor to give a stark condemnation of the leaders of Judah. The government *officials are* like *roaring lions*, a picture of the wild beast hunting for prey that may be eaten. The *rulers*, those who should be stewards of the law, are like *wolves* after the kill. They don't even leave the bones of their victims uneaten.

God expects the leaders of the people to protect the innocent and preserve justice (see Isaiah 1:17). In God's plan people are not given authority in a government structure so that they may enrich themselves and increase their power. Yet the leaders of Zephaniah's Jerusalem are like wild, ferocious beasts. They terrify the citizens and are relentless in satisfying their own desires for wealth. The citizenry is not their field of duty but their hunting ground.

C. HAUGHTY, PROFANE PRIESTS & PROPHETS (v. 4)

4. Her prophets are arrogant;
     they are treacherous men.
   Her priests profane the sanctuary
     and do violence to the law.

After indicting the government leaders, Zephaniah turns his attention to the religious leaders, the *prophets* and *priests*. A prophet in the Old Testament is not just a person who gives accurate predictions of the future. Prophets are primarily tasked with demanding repentance from the people of God and calling out for justice and righteousness in the nation. Zephaniah is unconcerned as to whether or not the prophets of his day know the future. He condemns them for their reckless arrogance. These prophets have turned a blind eye and a deaf ear to the widespread sin of the city. They are in cahoots with those who profit from sins, and this has stilled their tongues from speaking right words.

The priests are responsible for the purity of Judah's religious practices, particularly in the Jerusalem temple. Yet they had stood silently (or even cooperated) when Manasseh had defiled the temple by building altars to pagan gods within its courts (2 Kings 21:4, 5). Zephaniah sees this as more than mere neglect. By allowing God's house to be spiritually polluted, the priests *do violence to the law.*

These priests had torn God's covenant book out of the heart of Israel and hidden it from the people. This is seen by the fact that during the reign of Josiah the high priest "found" the book of the law in the temple (2 Kings 22:3–23:3). This would be like someone "finding" a copy of the Constitution of the U.S. (or any other country) after 50 years of neglect. Zephaniah implies that the "losing" of the law was not an accident. It was planned deliberately. The only surprising detail is that it had not been destroyed altogether, to disappear without a trace.

WHAT DO YOU THINK?

How can leaders in the church stumble into following the bad example of the religious leaders described in our text? How do we guard against this?

D. RIGHTEOUS, UNFAILING JUDGE (v. 5)

5. *The LORD within her is righteous;*
  he does no wrong.
Morning by morning he dispenses his justice,
  and every new day he does not fail,
  yet the unrighteous know no shame.

In contrast to the wicked leaders, Zephaniah lifts up the perfect judge: the Lord God himself. The prophet points out important characteristics of God's judgments. They are untainted by sin, for God *does no wrong*. God never avoids making judgments. He does not decline to rule on the hard cases. Instead, he renders judgment in an unfailing, consistent manner.

These worthy characteristics of God the judge are compared with corrupt human judges in a simple statement: they *know no shame*. Shame is a powerful influence for social control. A shamed person has acted inappropriately and brought dishonor to himself or herself. Avoidance of public disgrace is a strong motivator. If, however, a person has become immune to feelings of shame, then outrageous behavior carries no social stigma. A judge with no shame has little reason to act with integrity and justice. Instead, favorable judgments are sold to the highest bidder. The immorality of judicial corruption becomes amoral and a matter of opportunity. God will not stand for this. Injustice is always injustice, no matter who the defendant is. Dishonesty from the bench of the judge is particularly grievous to the Lord.

II. GOD PUNISHES CORRUPTION (ZEPHANIAH 3:6, 7)

The focus now shifts to the future activity of God. At the time of Zephaniah, it may seem as if Josiah's reforms had put the nation back on track. Yet the prophet Jeremiah, Zephaniah's contemporary, revealed that the sins of Manasseh were so deep and pervasive that God had already made the decision to cleanse Judah through the exile to Babylon (see Jeremiah 15:4). The downfall of Jerusalem is coming. It is just a matter of time.

A. COMING DESTRUCTION (v. 6)

6. *"I have cut off nations;*
  their strongholds are demolished.
I have left their streets deserted,
  with no one passing through.
Their cities are destroyed;
  no one will be left—no one at all.

God first reminds the people that he has acted in the past to wipe out evil *nations*, including the northern kingdom of Israel. Such lands were depopulated, and their grand buildings became rubble. Today, the Near East is full of ruins of dead civilizations. Once thriving cities lie under layers of dirt and waste.

SCORCHED EARTH

Occasionally an invading army will follow a *scorched earth* policy, inflicting utter devastation. This is a policy that ancient Rome eventually followed in dealing with its major rival Carthage. These two rivals clashed in three conflicts known as the *Punic Wars*. The first war (264–241 BC) began as a squabble over Sicily, where both Rome and Carthage had colonies. The second war (218–202 BC) began in Spain, where both powers again had interests.

Despite the brilliant tactics of Hannibal, Carthage's general, the Romans ultimately prevailed in that second war. Yet Carthage eventually proved to be an eco-

"Morning by morning **he dispenses his justice.**"
—Zephaniah 3:5 (NIV)

Visual for Lesson 6. *Point to this visual as you ask, "How has God been merciful to you this morning?"*

nomic and military threat to Rome yet again. The Roman statesman Cato ended every speech in the Senate by declaring, "Carthage must be destroyed."

In the third war (149–146 BC), Rome attacked the city of Carthage directly. The army went from house to house, systematically slaughtering the citizens. The city was demolished, and salt was sown into the ground to render it infertile. Carthage became a desolate site.

The Punic Wars had not yet been fought when Zephaniah wrote. Yet that prophet was well aware of what God's plans of *scorched earth* would mean for various nations, particularly Judah. It is a sobering policy, indeed! Have you read Revelation 8:7 recently? —J. B. N.

B. PERSISTENT CORRUPTION (v. 7)

7. *"I said to the city,*
'Surely you will fear me
and accept correction!'
Then her dwelling would not be cut off,
nor all my punishments come upon her.
But they were still eager
to act corruptly in all they did.

God's frustration with his people is supremely evident here. No matter how dire the warnings or how persistent his prophets, Judah has continued to ignore God's pleadings. What must God do to get our attention? We are reminded of Jesus' parable of the wicked tenants (Mark 12:1-9). In this story, the owner is unable to get the rent payment from those who have leased his vineyard. Servants who are sent to collect are abused, even killed. In an act of utter exasperation, the owner sends his son, saying, "They will respect my son."

Yet they kill the son too, leading the vineyard owner to come and destroy them. This pattern is found elsewhere in the Bible and still has application today. Sometimes God uses extraordinary circumstances to wake us from our sinful daze. But there are those for whom no amount of prodding from the Lord will turn them back from their deserved destruction.

III. GOD RESTORES HIS PEOPLE (ZEPHANIAH 3:8, 9)

Zephaniah pictures God as the ultimate force behind the rise and fall of nations. Greek, Roman, British, Russian—history is littered with empires that have collapsed and disappeared, including the kingdom of Judah.

A. WAITING ON GOD'S WRATH (v. 8)

8. *"Therefore wait for me," declares the LORD,*
"for the day I will stand up to testify.
I have decided to assemble the nations,
to gather the kingdoms
and to pour out my wrath on them—
all my fierce anger.
The whole world will be consumed
by the fire of my jealous anger.

The picture of God's gathering *the nations* shows Zephaniah's understanding of God's mighty power. *The Lord* God is not just the God of Israel. He is the one God and the master of every human government.

God's motivation for national destruction is pictured here as red-hot jealousy. This is not the petty jealousy of a girlfriend who observes her boyfriend looking at another girl for a little too long. This is the righteous jealousy of the wrath of

HOW TO SAY IT

Amon. AY-mun.
Babylonians. Bab-ih-LOW-nee-unz.
Deuteronomy. Due-ter-AHN-uh-me.
Habakkuk. Huh-BACK-kuk.
Hilkiah. Hill-KYE-uh.
Josiah. Jo-SIGH-uh.
Judah. JOO-duh.
Manasseh. Muh-NASS-uh.
Punic. PYU-nik.
Zephaniah. Zef-uh-NYE-uh.

WHAT DO YOU THINK?

What descriptive models can we create to communicate an accurate picture of the awesome force of God's anger? Or should we just say what the Bible says and not be too "creative" in this regard?

WHAT DO YOU THINK?

The fulfillment of the prophecy in verse 9 has been explained in various ways. What safeguards can we put in place to keep the focus on winning the lost rather than fighting over interpretations of prophecies?

PRAYER

God of all nations, we pray for the day when our speech will become pure, and we will worship you with one voice. We pray this in the name of Jesus, our soon and coming king, amen.

THOUGHT TO REMEMBER

God is always righteous, whether in punishment or deliverance.

God. He is unwilling to share devotion with any man-made gods and false religions (Exodus 34:14). Why should he? There is no other God!

B. SERVING GOD IN UNITY (v. 9)

9. *"Then will I purify the lips of the peoples,*
that all of them may call on the name of the LORD
and serve him shoulder to shoulder."

From this litany of wrath and destruction emerges a bright ray of hope. Zephaniah looks forward to a restoration of the unity of humanity under God. He sees three specific elements.

First, to *purify the lips* is an image of atoning for sin (compare Isaiah 6:5-7) or purity of worship (Psalms 16:4; Hosea 2:17). Second, there will be a united effort to *call on the name of the Lord*. This is a way of referring to worship from the earliest days of humanity (Genesis 4:26). Unity of worship eliminates anyone calling upon a false god (see 1 Kings 18:24); this ties in to the purity of worship idea.

Third, humanity will *serve* God *shoulder to shoulder*. The idea of serve includes worship; numerous passages place the two concepts alongside one another as almost inseparable ideas (Daniel 3:28; Luke 4:8; etc.). True believers will serve and worship God in unity.

UNITY IN SERVICE

Thomas Campbell (1763–1854) had a burning desire for the union of all Christians under the simple authority of the New Testament. Born in northern Ireland, as a young man he joined a denomination that reflected many of the sectarian divisions then rife in the British Isles. Thomas Campbell became an Old Light, Anti-Burgher, Seceder Presbyterian, Protestant kind of a Christian. He immigrated to America in 1807, hoping to find an atmosphere that would foster unity.

Campbell was rebuffed by his denomination. So in 1809 he and some friends formed the Christian Association of Washington. Campbell wrote its constitution and bylaws, "Declaration and Address." In this document he laid out some general principles that would guide their activities. His first proposition was that "the church of Christ on earth is essentially, intentionally, and constitutionally one." All divisions, he contended, came either from neglecting part of God's Word or adding human teaching on top of Scripture. He believed that if everyone accepted the teachings of Scripture and followed the precedents of the New Testament church—no more and no less—then the church could have unity.

Today Campbell's spiritual descendants still try to follow his twin commitments to Christian unity and scriptural authority. The dream of Campbell is similar to the vision of Zephaniah. That prophet foresaw a time when the people would speak a pure language, turn to the Lord, and serve him in unity. It is an ideal that is yet to be realized.   —J. B. N.

CONCLUSION

The phrase *the day of the Lord* occurs several times in Zephaniah (see also Isaiah 2:12; Joel 2:31 [quoted in Acts 2:20]; etc.). Old Testament prophets foresaw this as a future day when God would intervene in history to punish evil and reward righteousness. This came about in an unexpected, preliminary way when Israel and Judah both suffered destruction at the hand of foreign invaders.

In the New Testament *the day of the Lord* is synonymous with Christ's second coming (1 Thessalonians 5:2). This too will be a pouring out of the wrath of God (see Revelation 6:17). The day of the Lord can be either terrifying or comforting, depending on one's relationship to God.

Discovery Learning

This page contains an alternative lesson plan emphasizing learning activities. Classes desiring such student involvement will find these suggestions helpful. The next page is a reproducible activity page to further enhance discovery learning.

LEARNING GOALS

After this lesson, each student will be able to:

1. List at least three sins that characterized the moral conditions of Josiah's Jerusalem.

2. Explain why God has a right to be angry at unholy behavior.

3. Praise God that he tempers his wrath with grace through Jesus Christ.

INTO THE LESSON

Below are several statements about morality from the pens of famous writers. Ask your students to critique the quotations.

1. "I know only that what is moral is what you feel good after and what is immoral is what you feel bad after" (Ernest Hemingway); *2.* "Morality is simply the attitude we adopt toward people whom we personally dislike" (Oscar Wilde); *3.* "Morality is the best of all devices for leading mankind by the nose" (Friedrich Nietzsche); *4.* "What is morality in any given time or place? It is what the majority then and there happen to like and immorality is what they dislike" (Alfred North Whitehead); *5.* "Morality is the theory that every human act must be either right or wrong, and that 99 percent of them are wrong" (H. L. Mencken).

When you finish your discussion, explain that today's lesson deals with upholding God's moral standards in an immoral society. (Option: distribute the Word Search puzzle from the Reproducible Page for your students to work on as they arrive.)

INTO THE WORD

Divide the class into pairs. Ask each to read Zephaniah 3:1-9 and answer these questions:

1. What does the word *woe* signify in verse 1? *2.* The people were guilty of what four sins, according to verse 2? *3.* What do the images of lions and wolves tell us about how the rulers treated their people? *4.* In what way could the Judean prophets be guilty of treachery? *5.* How did the priests profane the sanctuary and do violence to the law? (See 2 Kings 21:4, 5.) *6.* How did God dispense justice? How did the unjust respond? *7.* What nations had God destroyed before that time? (See Deuteronomy 3:1-11; Joshua 10; etc.) *8.* How had God warned Jerusalem concerning sin and impending destruction (v. 7)? How had the people responded? *9.* What warning did God give the nations? What promise did he make to the people? *10.* What is the contrast between purity of lips of verse 9 and the treachery of the false prophets in verse 4?

When your pairs have completed the exercise, discuss their answers. Also explain (from the lesson Conclusion) the concept of the "day of the Lord" in Zephaniah and the other prophets. Then ask your students to read 1 Thessalonians 4:13–5:15. Use these questions to discuss that passage. Answers are indicated in parentheses.

1. To what event does Paul link the day of the Lord? (the return of Christ) *2.* What will happen to those who are not ready for his return? (they will be destroyed; see Matthew 24:36-44; 25:31-46) *3.* How will Christians escape the wrath of God? (through the death of Christ; see also Romans 5:6-11) *4.* Knowing all this, how should Christians behave? (with self-control, living by faith, love and hope; we encourage one another)

INTO LIFE

Ask your students to return to the quotations from the Into the Lesson exercise. Below are summary statements of the quotes and a criticism of each based on today's lesson. Tell students to turn to their student books and do a three-way match: each author with a summary statement and a criticism. (If you don't use the student books, reproduce the text below as necessary.)

A. Morality is just the opinion of the majority. *B.* Morality is based on personal feelings. *C.* Morality is just a means of controlling others. *D.* Morality is just a theory that most human behavior is bad. *E.* Morality is a means to criticize people we dislike.

a. Biblical morality is about self-control, so that we are ready for Christ's return; it is not about controlling others. *b.* Christians are to use morality to encourage one another to be like Christ, not simply to condemn people. *c.* Only behavior that contradicts God's Word is evil. *d.* Morality is based on God's nature and his Word, not on human feelings. *e.* Morality is based on God's nature and his Word, not on majority opinion. (*Answers: 1Bd, 2Eb, 3Ca, 4Ae, 5Dc.*)

Discuss answers and relate them to question four of the 1 Thessalonians exercise.

Word Search

Read Zephaniah 3:1-9. All the words in this list are found in the Scripture passage from today's lesson. Look across, up, down, diagonally, and backwards, and draw a line around the words as you find them.

```
W O E E E L B M E S S A A A
S A N C T U A R Y F I R U P
T C A I I S I U F E A R E U
R C F T E E L I U U O S N
O E O S T R E E T S P G T I
N P R U I V I R S L S A S S
G T P J A E A S E E N N E H
H S E I I C O S T O O T I M
O F F I C I A L S I I U R E
L T R U S T U A T A L A P N
D E O B E Y S A W E I I O T
S E V E N I N G W O L V E S
```

accepts; arrogant; assemble; city; evening wolves; fear; justice; lions; nations; obeys; officials; peoples; priests; profane; punishments; purify; rulers; sanctuary; serve; streets; strongholds; testify; trust; wait; woe

COMMITTED TO HOPE

LESSON 7

WHY TEACH THIS LESSON?

An older lady in the church where I served as a young preacher did not like to hear anyone question God. She felt it was a slap in the face of God to do so. Yet at least some of your students are questioning God right now. They have questions as to why the jobs they invested so many years in were suddenly taken from them. They try to raise their children in the Lord and wonder why they stray.

They also wonder if it is wrong to question God about such things. Today's lesson will point them toward an answer.

INTRODUCTION

A. REFORMATION KEY

The great reformer Martin Luther (1483–1546) was of humble birth. His father, Hans, was a copper miner. Hans used his modest wealth to educate Martin, with plans for him to become a lawyer. So the son entered law school. But God dealt with him in mighty ways, and he left legal studies to take vows as a monk.

Luther progressed rapidly to ordination as a priest at age 23, to a doctor of theology degree at age 29, and to a teaching post at the University of Wittenberg that same year. He quickly became the most popular teacher at the university. His lectures on Psalms, Romans, and Hebrews brought standing-room-only crowds.

Yet Luther was not satisfied with this sparkling career. He had no peace in his soul. He was overwhelmed by his sense of sinfulness before a holy, righteous God. The then-current practice of penance did not relieve this feeling but only added to it. This young man, idolized by hundreds as a Bible expositor, was wracked by his own sense of inadequacy and sin.

The religious teachers of the Middle Ages instructed that people were bound to God by their love. This love must reveal itself in deeds of righteousness—"saving works of merit." For Luther such deeds were not a bad thing, but they did not relieve his feelings of personal sin.

Luther found his answer in Scripture. He discovered a verse from the ancient prophet Habakkuk that the apostle Paul used: the righteous person will live by faith (Habakkuk 2:4; Romans 1:17; Galatians 3:11). Luther thus discovered that salvation was founded on faith! This was the key that set in motion the reformation of the sixteenth century. No longer could the medieval church attempt to control salvation, allowing access because of sufficient good deeds. Luther may not have understood everything perfectly, but he broke the back of a doctrinal monopoly that had made salvation a tool of the church rather than a gift of God.

The Bible teaches that we cannot earn salvation, for it is a gift (Ephesians 2:8, 9). Salvation through faith (as opposed to works) was not invented by Luther; he found it in Paul's writings. But Paul did not coin the concept either; he found it in Habakkuk. This is not just a New Testament or an Old Testament concept. It is a Bible concept. This lesson will look at the roots of this way of understanding salvation by examining Habakkuk in its original context.

DEVOTIONAL READING:
PSALM 37:27-34

BACKGROUND SCRIPTURE:
HABAKKUK 2:1-20; 2 KINGS 23:35-37

PRINTED TEXT:
HABAKKUK 2:1-14

LESSON AIMS

After participating in this lesson, each student will be able to:

1. Name two challenges faced by Habakkuk in relaying God's coming judgment on the nation of Judah.

2. Explain how the knowledge of the glory of the Lord is a valuable hope.

3. Express his or her eternal hope through one act of kindness in the coming week.

Jul
15

KEY VERSE

The earth will be filled with the knowledge of the glory of the LORD, as the waters cover the sea.
—*Habakkuk 2:14*

B. LESSON BACKGROUND

There is no clear indication in the book of Habakkuk as to when that man of God served as a prophet. Outside the Bible there is a tradition that Habakkuk was a priest and prophet from the tribe of Levi. This tradition places him in Judah during the later career of Jeremiah and the early days of Daniel. This was a time when the Babylonians had begun to dominate Judah but had not yet destroyed Jerusalem and the temple. That destruction took place in 586 BC.

The message of Habakkuk fits very well into this period, approximately 600–590 BC. The ancient Jews held Habakkuk in high esteem. One of the most famous of the Dead Sea Scrolls is a commentary on the book of Habakkuk.

The form of the book is unusual among the prophets and more like the book of Job. The first two chapters are a dialogue between the prophet and the Lord. Much like Job, Habakkuk challenges God with some primary issues: Why do the righteous people of the world suffer? Why does God wait to punish evil? And how could God use an ungodly people like the Babylonians to punish Israel, his chosen people? The third and final chapter is a poetic prayer of praise and faith.

Habakkuk begins with the prophet's complaint to God: Why does lawlessness prevail (Habakkuk 1:2-4)? In the pagan world the answer to this question was easy: there are good gods and evil gods. But among the people of Israel, with their belief in one holy God, it was much more difficult. If there is one God—a good and holy God—then why is there still evil?

God's answer to Habakkuk is found in the next section (Habakkuk 1:5-11). God asserts that he is about to do something. He is about to bring the Chaldeans (another name for the Babylonians) to punish wayward Israel.

Habakkuk responds to this with amazement (1:12–2:1). How can a holy God use such evil people in this way? In other words, Habakkuk is saying that the Judeans might have been naughty, but that doesn't compare with the overwhelming evil of the Babylonians. This second question sets the stage for the second answer of God, which is where our lesson text begins.

I. WAITING FOR GOD'S ANSWER (HABAKKUK 2:1-3)

In the Old Testament, one of the answers to the problem of evil is that we must "wait for the Lord" (see Psalm 37:34). In chapter one, Habakkuk thinks he has asked God a very difficult question. He now waits for his answer.

A. HABAKKUK PREPARES TO HEAR (v. 1)

1. I will stand at my watch
    and station myself on the ramparts;
  I will look to see what he will say to me,
    and what answer I am to give to this complaint.

Habakkuk has gone to his watchtower to wait for the answer to his question, "God, how can you think of using the evil, violent Babylonians against your people?" Habakkuk expects that God should protect his nation from foreign threats, not support the aggressors. He admits his confusion and ponders what he should say to God when the answer comes.

It is common for us to have tough questions about God and faith. Many people have wished they could speak to God directly, to get simple, satisfying answers. It doesn't work that way, however. As Job said, "He is not a man like me that I might answer him, that we might confront each other in court" (Job 9:32). We should remember that God is under no obligation to answer us. He does not dance to our tune.

WHAT DO YOU THINK?

On a scale from one to ten, how would you rate yourself in the category of "waiting for the Lord" for a patient answer to the questions you have asked him? What steps can you take to improve your score?

Watchtowers, Then and Now

Watchtowers have played crucial roles in the history of defense and communication. Consider the Greek island of Chios (or Kios in Acts 20:15), in the eastern Aegean Sea. There a series of about 50 watchtowers, called *viglas*, were built around the perimeter of the entire island. From the top of each vigla, the watcher could see the next two viglas, one on each side. Any sighting of pirates or other enemies could be communicated quickly to the entire island (www.chiosonline.gr).

The southern coast of Spain was also once a prime target for pirates. During the Middle Ages, the Moors built a system of watchtowers. These towers could communicate with each other using smoke signals and fires. When the Christians conquered the territory, they kept the tower system and even strengthened it. The system worked well and could transmit news over large distances in a relatively short period of time. Watchtowers helped the populace avoid nasty surprises.

Habakkuk is not looking for an enemy attack while he is in his watchtower. Rather, he is alert for communication from the Lord. We would do well to make Habakkuk's choice our own. We can climb into our own, private watchtowers, meaning we make time for daily devotions when we're alone with God and his Word. This will make us more sensitive to his leading. This kind of a watchtower will give us the perspective to perceive his will more clearly. In a roundabout way, using our own watchtowers in this manner can keep us alert to attacks by Satan.   —J. B. N.

B. God Prepares to Respond (vv. 2, 3)

2, 3. Then the Lord replied:

"*Write down the revelation*
  and make it plain on tablets
  so that a herald may run with it.
For the revelation awaits an appointed time;
  it speaks of the end
  and will not prove false.
Though it linger, wait for it;
  it will certainly come and will not delay.

The Lord does indeed respond! But before the actual answer, God gives the prophet two instructions. First, he wants Habakkuk to *write* the answer in straightforward, unmistakable language. The image of a herald shows that the message must be shared with others. Second, God warns Habakkuk that he may need patience in order to see God's plan worked out. Even though there may be a delay, it will surely come, God says. As Paul would say, "This is a trustworthy saying" (see Titus 3:8). Our impatience does not require that God alter his plan.

II. HEARING GOD'S ANSWER (HABAKKUK 2:4-13)

The response of God is a comparison between two kinds of people. This is followed by three *woes* or curses against the proud person.

A. Pride and Faith (v. 4)

4a. "See, he is puffed up;
  his desires are not upright—

The Lord's answer is to contrast two human reactions to the dilemma. The first reaction is that of a person who *is puffed up*. This refers to the proud, self-sufficient person. His or her life is out of sync with the will of God.

4b. But the righteous will live by his faith—

The second reaction God describes is the kind he is seeking. The person with the outlook mentioned here does not trust in his or her own power. Instead, this

What Do You Think?

When we pray, we often have in mind the answer we want God to give us. Is that a good thing? Why, or why not? What guidelines will help us be ready for God's answer if it does not agree with our expectation?

WHAT DO YOU THINK?

What secrets (if that is the right term) need to be passed along to younger Christians about walking by faith versus trusting self to do it all?

person lives by an ongoing *faith* in God. Even in the face of trouble and seeming injustice, even in the shadow of looming national disaster, this person is unwavering in this regard. This is the person who surrenders the need to have all questions answered. This person falls back on the simple belief that God is in control and that God cares for him or her.

The effect of this answer is to rebuke Habakkuk and any who are like-minded. If we determine the questions that God must answer, then we have assumed the position of judge and inquisitor of God. God will not allow this. We are called to *live by . . . faith*, in full realization that we do not understand why everything happens. We take hope from our trust in God.

B. BEHAVIOR AND ATTITUDES (vv. 5, 6a)

5, 6a. *"Indeed, wine betrays him;*
    he is arrogant and never at rest.
Because he is as greedy as the grave
    and like death is never satisfied,
he gathers to himself all the nations
    and takes captive all the peoples.
"Will not all of them taunt him with ridicule and scorn. . . .

The language of this description is difficult to understand. But if we examine it carefully, we can identify five characteristics of the person who displeases God. First, this person is a drunkard. Second, this person is publicly proud. Third, he or she is restless.

WHAT DO YOU THINK?

How would you respond to someone who says that the use of wine (or any alcoholic beverage) could never become a problem in his or her life?

[Hint: make sure to consider texts such as Habakkuk 2:5, 15, 16; and 1 Timothy 5:23].

Fourth, this person's greed is as big *as the grave;* the person's greed *is never satisfied.* Fifth, this kind of person desires to dominate other *peoples* and *nations;* thus the greed is not just for material things but for power as well. All of this describes the leaders of Judah, who are deserving of condemnation.

C. THIEVERY AND WOE (v. 6b)

6b. *"Saying,*
    "'Woe to him who piles up stolen goods
    and makes himself wealthy by extortion!
    How long must this go on?'

The first woe describes a dishonest businessman. Stealing and *extortion* are his trademark actions.

ROBBER BARONS

The Robber Barons is the title of a 1934 book that examines the "captains of industry" of the late nineteenth century. These captains included Andrew Carnegie (steel), John D. Rockefeller (oil), Cornelius Vanderbilt (railways), as well as financiers such as Jay Gould and J. Pierpont Morgan. Their entrepreneurial methods were often questionable and sometimes downright illegal.

For example, Rockefeller made secret agreements with various railroad companies in order to create an oil monopoly. He and fellow refiners in the Standard Oil Trust had their freight rates sharply reduced while competing refiners saw their own freight rates increase dramatically. The railroads then kicked back to Standard Oil a large part of that increase. Within just a few months, many competitors yielded to Rockefeller and joined Standard Oil. He was then able to control the price for all oil sales throughout the United States.

Vanderbilt was able to consolidate several rail lines into one, also using dubious tactics. Once when questioned about the legality of his business methods, he responded, "What do I care about the law? Ain't I got the power?"

By squeezing out competitors, these aggressive business leaders were able to gouge the public without regard to ethics. They enriched themselves by taking advantage of powerless people. As Habakkuk phrases it, they were piling up stolen goods. But the Lord still watches, even in the twenty-first century AD.   —J. B. N.

D. REACTIONS AND CONSEQUENCES (vv. 7, 8)

7, 8. "Will not your debtors suddenly arise?
> *Will they not wake up and make you tremble?*
> *Then you will become their victim.*
> *Because you have plundered many nations,*
> *the peoples who are left will plunder you.*
> *For you have shed man's blood;*
> *you have destroyed lands and cities and everyone in them.*

God says that the problem will not continue for long. Eventually the victims will fight back, and the thief will become their *victim*. God promises that this person will get his or her just deserts. Those whom such a person has abused will eventually turn the tables and repay the scoundrel.

E. COVETOUSNESS AND WOE (vv. 9-11)

9. "Woe to him who builds his realm by unjust gain
> *to set his nest on high,*
> *to escape the clutches of ruin!*

The second woe is directed to the kind of person who seeks to remove himself or herself from the problems of society by setting a *nest* (home) *on high*. This person thus wants to live in the fortress enclave of wealth, untouched by the poor and needy of the community. Such an attitude begins with the sin of being covetous.

10. "You have plotted the ruin of many peoples,
> *shaming your own house and forfeiting your life.*

From the safety of a fortress-home, the greedy, covetous person continues to oppress the poor. In so doing, God says this person commits a serious sin. In other words, such a person truly sells his or her own soul. Therefore, that person's *life* is now forfeit.

11. "The stones of the wall will cry out,
> *and the beams of the woodwork will echo it.*

Habakkuk warns metaphorically that the components of this person's house will bring the accusation. This is because that lavish home has been built with ill-gotten wealth. Mighty *stone* walls are paid for by cheating the innocent. Massive ceiling *beams* are financed from the proceeds of criminal activity.

F. VIOLENCE AND WOE (v. 12, 13)

12. "Woe to him who builds a city with bloodshed
> *and establishes a town by crime!*

The third *woe* is a general condemnation against the violent, wicked person of power. *A town* built on *crime* and injustice cannot endure and will never be blessed by God.

13. "Has not the LORD Almighty determined
> *that the people's labor is only fuel for the fire,*
> *that the nations exhaust themselves for nothing?*

The exploitative, ruthless leaders have driven the workers of their land without rest. The great city they have built (namely, Jerusalem) is for *nothing*, because its

---

HOW TO SAY IT

Babylonians. Bab-ih-LOW-nee-unz.
Chaldeans. Kal-DEE-unz.
Chios. KI-ahs (I as in EYE).
Galatians. Guh-LAY-shunz.
Habakkuk. Huh-BACK-kuk.
Hebrews. HEE-brews.
Jerusalem. Juh-ROO-suh-lem.
Judah. JOO-duh.
Levi. LEE-vye.
Wittenberg. WIH-ten-berg or VIH-ten-berk.

DAILY BIBLE READINGS

Monday, July 9—The Lord Loves Justice (Psalm 37:27-34)
Tuesday, July 10—Judah Becomes Egypt's Vassal (2 Kings 23:31-37)
Wednesday, July 11—Habakkuk's Complaint (Habakkuk 1:12-17)
Thursday, July 12—The Lord Answers (Habakkuk 2:1-5)
Friday, July 13—Woes Reported (Habakkuk 2:6-14)
Saturday, July 14—The Lord Will Act (Habakkuk 2:15-20)
Sunday, July 15—The Lord Is Our Strength (Habakkuk 3:13-19)

PRAYER

God of Glory, may it be said of us as it was of King Hezekiah, that we "trusted in the Lord." Forgive us when we doubt. Strengthen us when we believe. We pray this in the name of Jesus Christ, your only Son, amen.

"The earth shall be filled with the knowledge of the glory of the LORD, as the waters cover the sea."
-Habakkuk 2:14

Visual for Lesson 7. *Point to this visual as you ask, "How has today's lesson increased your knowledge?"*

WHAT DO YOU THINK?

How does knowing that God's plan will ultimately be fulfilled help you deal with situations in life in which evil seems to be in control? How do you need to grow spiritually in this regard?

THOUGHT TO REMEMBER

Live by faith, especially in the midst of evil.

destruction is coming from the Babylonians. Thus *the people's labor is only fuel for the fire,* meaning it will be burned up and not endure. Even so, God hears the cries of his people, just as he heard their cries in Egypt as they labored to build the great cities for the pharaohs (see Exodus 3:7).

These series of woes explain God's anger toward Judah. His holy people have perverted God's gift of the land of Israel. Rather than use it for God's glory and for his service, they have allowed human greed and pride to reign supreme. God has been very patient with them, but his patience has run its course. Now the only hope for correction is destruction of Judah by the Babylonians. This will cleanse it of this pervasive sin.

III. HOPING FOR GOD'S GLORY (HABAKKUK 2:14)

Like many passages from the prophets, the predictions of doom and gloom are not the last word. Habakkuk ends this section with a word of hope, looking forward to a time when there will be universal acknowledgment of the Lord God.

14. *"For the earth will be filled with the knowledge of the glory of the LORD, as the waters cover the sea."*

Although often overlooked, this verse is one of the great texts of the Old Testament. It pictures in marvelous symbolic language a time when *the earth* will be flooded *with the knowledge of the glory of the Lord.* This spiritual deluge will engulf all people. There will be no holdouts who continue to deny the greatness and majesty of God.

A theme found throughout Scripture is the coming day of universal recognition of our glorious God. Isaiah saw a future time when all would come and see God's glory (Isaiah 66:18). Isaiah also looked forward to the day when every knee would bow to God and every tongue would acknowledge him (Isaiah 45:23). This scenario is repeated by Paul in Philippians 2:10, 11.

In the last chapter of his book, Habakkuk looks forward to a time when God's glory will cover the heavens and the earth will be filled with his praise (Habakkuk 3:3). This promise comforts the suffering saints of Habakkuk's day and gives hope to Christian believers today. Centuries later, the apostle Peter will offer similar hope when he writes that we "participate in the sufferings of Christ, so that [we] may be overjoyed when his glory is revealed" (1 Peter 4:13).

CONCLUSION

Habakkuk ends his book with a grim look at the bleakness of many people's lives. He knows there are times when "the fig tree does not bud and there are no grapes on the vines, . . . the olive crop fails and the fields produce no food, . . . there are no sheep in the pen and no cattle in the stalls" (Habakkuk 3:17). Even in these times, however, Habakkuk exclaims, "I will rejoice in the Lord, I will be joyful in God my Savior. The Sovereign Lord is my strength; he makes my feet like the feet of a deer, he enables me to go on the heights" (3:18, 19).

The life of faith means utter trust in God. It means that we serve him diligently. And, yes, it means that we work hard and enjoy life. But at the end of the day we continue in hope without fear, for we know that God controls the future, and we rest secure in him. This is what it means to live by faith.

Most of all, living by faith means that we trust in God for salvation. We do not fear judgment, for Jesus our Savior has prepared a place for us in Heaven (John 14:3). Martin Luther said that "the only saving faith is that which casts itself on God for life or death." May we have that faith!

Discovery Learning

This page contains an alternative lesson plan emphasizing learning activities. Classes desiring such student involvement will find these suggestions helpful. The next page is a reproducible activity page to further enhance discovery learning.

LEARNING GOALS

After this lesson, each student will be able to:

1. Name two challenges faced by Habakkuk in relaying God's coming judgment on the nation of Judah.

2. Explain how the knowledge of the glory of the Lord is a valuable hope.

3. Express his or her eternal hope through one act of kindness in the coming week.

INTO THE LESSON

Distribute copies of the survey below as your students enter the classroom (or direct them to this exercise in the student books). The instructions should read, "Rank-order the following tasks from most to least difficult, with 1 being the hardest. If you can think of a task more difficult than one of these, include it in your list."

___ *Notifying someone of a death in the family*
___ *Laying off an employee*
___ *Telling someone that she is terminally ill*
___ *Confessing to a loved one that you have broken a possession precious to that person*
___ *Admitting to your parents or spouse that you are in trouble with the law*
___ *Telling a child that his parents are divorcing*
___ *(your choice)* _____

After several minutes, ask volunteers to share their conclusions. What other difficult tasks did they list? What makes some tasks especially difficult? Ask your students what help or encouragement they would need to be able to fulfill such difficult responsibilities. Then inform the class that today's lesson explains how the prophet Habakkuk dealt with God's command to prophesy judgment and destruction upon Judah.

INTO THE WORD

Develop a brief lecture from the Lesson Background and the commentary on Habakkuk 2:1-3. Explain the difficulties Habakkuk faced in announcing God's coming judgment upon Judah.

When you have finished your mini-lecture, divide your class into groups of three or four students each. Give each group a copy of the following questions (or direct your students' attention to their student books, if using those, where they can find this exercise printed).

What Kind of Person Does God Want in a Crisis?
Read Habakkuk 2:4-14 to answer these questions: 1. What does Habakkuk mean in verse 4 when he says that a prideful person's desires are "not upright"? 2. What is the guiding principle in the life of a just, or righteous, person? 3. What are the sinful characteristics of a proud person (vv. 5, 6)? 4. What is significant about the term *woe* in verses 6, 9, and 12? 5. How does covetousness serve as a basis for other sins (v. 9)? 6. What are the crimes of the covetous person (vv. 9-11)? What will accuse such a person of his or her crimes? 7. Why is God angry with those who built Jerusalem (vv. 12, 13)? Why will their work be "for nothing"? 8. Despite the doom prophesied, what is the predicted outcome of God's judgment (v. 14)? Why should that information be important to the righteous person who tries to live by faith?

Call your groups back together and discuss their conclusions.

INTO LIFE

Use the illustration of Martin Luther and Habakkuk 2:4 ("The righteous will live by his faith") to introduce this portion of the lesson. Stress Luther's reliance on the Bible and its emphasis on faith (as contrasted with works) to receive God's gift of salvation. Remind your class that Luther was able to deal with a crisis in his spiritual life by drawing upon God's Word to change his attitudes about God, sin, and salvation.

Next, distribute the following open-ended statements (or direct attention to the student books, where they are reprinted). Ask each student to write at least one response to each statement. Encourage complete honesty, since no one else will see their work.

My Crisis of Faith
In order to respond to a crisis of faith, I predict that I would need to
    Change my attitude by . . .
    Remember these biblical truths:
    Avoid these sins and stumbling blocks:

After allowing several minutes, challenge your class to make these issues a matter of prayer this week. Close with the Committed to Hope antiphonal reading from the Reproducible Page.

Committed to Hope

Use the printed text below from Habakkuk 2:1-14 as the basis for an antiphonal reading. One individual or group should read the lines marked "A" and another individual or group should reply with the lines marked "B."

A: I will stand at my watch
B: And station myself on the ramparts;

A: I will look to see what he will say to me,
B: and what answer I am to give to this complaint.

A: Then the LORD replied:
B: "Write down the revelation

A: and make it plain on tablets
B: so that a herald may run with it.

A: For the revelation awaits an appointed time;
B: it speaks of the end and will not prove false.

A: Though it linger, wait for it;
B: it will certainly come and will not delay.

A: "See, he is puffed up;
B: his desires are not upright—

A: but the righteous will live by his faith—
B: indeed, wine betrays him;

A: he is arrogant and never at rest.
B: Because he is as greedy as the grave

A: and like death is never satisfied,
B: he gathers to himself all the nations

A: and takes captive all the peoples.
B: "Will not all of them taunt him with ridicule and scorn, saying,

A: 'Woe to him who piles up stolen goods
B: and makes himself wealthy by extortion! How long must this go on?'

A: Will not your debtors suddenly arise?
B: Will they not wake up and make you tremble?

A: Then you will become their victim.
B: Because you have plundered many nations,

A: the peoples who are left will plunder you.
B: For you have shed man's blood;

A: you have destroyed lands and cities and everyone in them.
B: "Woe to him who builds his realm by unjust gain

A: to set his nest on high,
B: to escape the clutches of ruin!

A: You have plotted the ruin of many peoples,
B: shaming your own house and forfeiting your life.

A: The stones of the wall will cry out,
B: and the beams of the woodwork will echo it.

A: "Woe to him who builds a city with bloodshed
B: and establishes a town by crime!

A: Has not the LORD Almighty determined
B: that the people's labor is only fuel for the fire,

A: that the nations exhaust themselves for nothing?
B: For the earth will be filled with the knowledge of the glory of the LORD, as the waters cover the sea."

COMMITTED TO ACCOUNTABILITY

WHY TEACH THIS LESSON?

What comes after Sunday morning worship is over and we've had our lunch? That warm, lazy Sunday afternoon, of course! The kitchen is clean, the newspaper is read, and there aren't any chores to do that can't wait until later. You feel like taking a nap, so you settle into your favorite chair or stretch out on the couch. Soon you are dozing. But the sleep is short as someone knocks on your door, the phone rings, the kids scream, or the dog jumps on you.

It's no fun to be distracted when we are comfortable. What is true with our physical comfort is also true with our spiritual comfort. But it is a dangerous thing to get lulled into a spiritual comfort zone. This lesson will be a sudden jolt, a mighty wake-up call from spiritual slumber. Consider how your students may have become comfortable in their spiritual walk and thus have failed to honor God truly. This lesson will help activate Ephesians 5:14 in your students' lives as it challenges them to "Wake up, O sleeper, rise from the dead, and Christ will shine on you."

INTRODUCTION

A. TRUSTING IN LIES

"If you tell a lie big enough and keep repeating it, people will eventually come to believe it." This was the strategy of Adolf Hitler's minister of propaganda, Joseph Goebbels. Goebbels and the Nazis perfected the modern art of misinformation, the concept of the *big lie*. Goebbels thought that the more outrageous the lie, the better, because the populace would think it was too extreme to be false.

As strange as that theory may seem to us, the Nazi propaganda machine successfully deceived the German people for over a decade. Yet the *big lie* technique did not originate with the Nazis. The history of human governments is littered with examples of lying kings and conquerors. Jeremiah the prophet was incensed by the ongoing deception of God's people by the leaders of Judah.

Jeremiah was particularly enraged by the deceptions of those who claimed to be speaking for God. He denounced this as villainy. As a true prophet of God, Jeremiah revealed God's displeasure: they "have spoken lies, which I did not tell them to do" (Jeremiah 29:23). Jeremiah also castigated the people who trusted "in deceptive words that are worthless" (7:8).

We as believers are called to be discerning of the truth. We have confidence that the Word of God is truth (John 17:17). Scripture is given to us as a measuring stick for all matters in life. Scripture is "the word of truth" (2 Timothy 2:15).

While some leaders in government are more truthful than others, history promises that the future holds more lying leaders. Today's *Honest Abe* may be

DEVOTIONAL READING:
2 CHRONICLES 7:11-16
BACKGROUND SCRIPTURE:
JEREMIAH 7; 2 KINGS 23:36, 37
PRINTED TEXT:
JEREMIAH 7:1-4, 8-15; 2 KINGS 23:36, 37

LESSON AIMS

After participating in this lesson, each student will be able to:

1. List at least five sins for which God held his people accountable.

2. List at least five modern behaviors that are parallel to the sins of the ancient Judeans.

3. Examine his or her life for signs of these sins and take measures to resist them.

Jul 22

KEY VERSES

Go now to the place in Shiloh where I first made a dwelling for my Name, and see what I did to it because of the wickedness of my people Israel. . . . I will thrust you from my presence, just as I did all your brothers.
—Jeremiah 7:12, 15

replaced by tomorrow's *Deceiver.* The unfailing Word of God stands above all of this. God is the God of truth (Deuteronomy 32:4). God's Word is not a mixture of truth, opinion, and falsehood. It is all truth, and it has the power to transform and change us. The more we study God's Word and incorporate its teachings into our lives, the less likely we are to trust in lies.

B. Lesson Background

The writings contained in the book of Jeremiah are drawn from his four-decade ministry as a prophet of God to the nation of Judah. The book opens with prophecies from the thirteenth year of Josiah's reign, approximately 627 BC (Jeremiah 1:2). The book closes with events surrounding the destruction of Jerusalem by the Babylonians in 586 BC (39:2). The book is somewhat unusual for the prophets, for it contains both *oracles* (the words of the prophet delivered to the people) and *narrative* (accounts of historical events during this period).

The book of Jeremiah bears testimony that that prophet suffered a great deal for his prophetic ministry. Although he was assured by God that he was chosen even before birth, he protested about his inadequacy (Jeremiah 1:5, 6). Later he complained that his prophecies had made him an object of derision in public (Jeremiah 20:7, 8).

Yet when Jeremiah tried to ignore God's prophetic voice in his life, it was as if his bones were on fire and he could not hold the words in (Jeremiah 20:9). This prophet's words caused him to be beaten and thrown into prison (Jeremiah 37:15). Later he was thrown into a dungeon-like cistern, where he wallowed in the smelly mire (Jeremiah 38:6).

Most of Jeremiah's words are sharp and condemning. This has caused him to be seen as the prophet of doom and gloom. Because of this, we have adopted the English word *jeremiad,* meaning an angry tirade. In English literature, a *Jeremiah* is symbolic of a person who is a persistent and vocal pessimist.

Yet Jeremiah also has a hopeful side. One of the most stirring passages in all the Old Testament is Jeremiah's vision of the new covenant. He foresaw this as a time when the law of God would be a matter of the heart, not just observance (Jeremiah 31:33), and a time when God would no longer remember the sin of the people (Jeremiah 31:34). Jeremiah's vision of fresh, new beginnings was adopted by the author of Hebrews to explain the new covenant that has been given to the church as the people of God (see Hebrews 8).

This week's lesson is drawn from one of the prophet's warnings against evil among the people of Judah. It is a biting condemnation of hypocrisy, particularly in worship.

I. FALSE SECURITY (JEREMIAH 7:1-4)

A. Hearing the True Word (vv. 1, 2)

1, 2. *This is the word that came to Jeremiah from the Lord:* "*Stand at the gate of the Lord's house and there proclaim this message:*

"'*Hear the word of the Lord, all you people of Judah who come through these gates to worship the Lord.*

Routines and habits provide a sense of security. We put out the trash on Wednesday, mow the grass on Friday, do laundry on Saturday, and go to church on Sunday. We work the same job and live in the same house for many years. What happens when the routine is disrupted—our trash day is changed to Monday, the washing machine breaks down, and we lose our job? Such changes can make us feel insecure.

How to Say It

Assyrians. Uh-SEAR-e-unz.

Baal. BAY-ul.

Babylonians. Bab-ih-LOW-nee-unz.

Canaanites. KAY-nun-ites.

Chaldeans. Kal-DEE-unz.

Diogenes of Sinope. Die-AH-jin-eez of Suh-NO-peh.

Ephraim. EE-fray-im.

Jehoiakim. Jeh-HOY-uh-kim.

jeremiad. jair-uh-MY-ud.

Josiah. Jo-SIGH-uh.

Manasseh. Muh-NASS-uh.

Nebuchadnezzar. NEB-yuh-kud-NEZ-er.

Pedaiah. Peh-DAY-yuh.

Philistines. Fuh-LISS-teens or FILL-us-teens.

Zebidah. Zee-BI-duh (I as in eye).

Jeremiah wants his people to know that routine does not equal a strong, secure relationship with God. We may appear religious because we do certain things on a regular basis, yet be far from the will of God. Our relationship may be empty and false. This is as true today as it was in Jeremiah's time.

God does not call Jeremiah to evangelize the pagan masses of the ancient world. His message is for the (supposed) people of God, the citizens of Jerusalem. His target audience is even more selective as shown by the location for preaching given to him: he is to stand at *the gate of the Lord's house,* meaning the main entry point of the temple in Jerusalem. Those he is to address are not coming for business, education, or meetings. They are coming *to worship* in the house of *the Lord.* They are following their routine, just as many attend church services each Sunday without much thought.

The gate is more than a doorway into the temple. It is an impressive structure that is more like a pass-through building than a simple wall opening. Gates in the ancient world can have rooms and open areas. They serve as gathering places. In the cities of ancient Israel, gates are places where judges dispense justice to the public (see Amos 5:15). Jeremiah's cry at the gate of the temple is to be a call for justice and righteousness and truth in worship.

B. REJECTING SOOTHING LIES (vv. 3, 4)

3. "'This is what the LORD Almighty, the God of Israel, says: Reform your ways and your actions, and I will let you live in this place.

Jeremiah's message is a warning with a promise: Quit sinning and *God* will *let you* continue to *live* in the land of Judah. Jeremiah is calling for a change in hearts and in practices. Empty ritual is not acceptable worship. Idolatrous practices are not tolerable for God (see Jeremiah 8:19).

Some of the hearers must wonder what is so wrong. Aren't they being faithful to worship at the house of the Lord? Aren't they wearing their best temple-go-to-meetin' clothes? Don't they bring their offerings? Don't they sing the temple praise songs? Haven't they repeated the proper prayers? Why is this prophet haranguing them?

4. "'Do not trust in deceptive words and say, "This is the temple of the LORD, the temple of the LORD, the temple of the LORD!"'"

Jeremiah's prophecy of doom for Judah is not new. It has been preached since the time of Isaiah. Yet through decades of national crisis and foreign threat, the southern kingdom of Judah has survived. *The temple* is some 300 years old by this time. It has survived threats from enemies such as the Assyrians, the Egyptians, and the Babylonians.

But that is exactly the point for Jeremiah: the presence of this house of worship has given the people a false sense of security! They believe that the temple is a sign of God's continued favor and protection. Jeremiah mocks the temple worshipers by repeating their falsely confident refrain, *This is the temple of the Lord, The temple of the Lord, The temple of the Lord.* Tradition, history, and edifices count for nothing when hearts are false.

II. DELUSIONAL DUPLICITY (JEREMIAH 7:8-15)

A. DOUBLE LIFE OF WORSHIP (vv. 8-10)

8. "'But look, you are trusting in deceptive words that are worthless.

Trusting in a lie does not make it the truth, for a lie will always be a lie. False security is just that: false. There is no value in accepting untruth, no matter how sincere and passionate the liar may be. Lies will always fail. They cannot protect us.

WHAT DO YOU THINK?

What are some innovations in the activities or schedules of your church that would be valuable in helping people hear God's messages?

WHAT DO YOU THINK?

What misconceptions, routines, slogans, and habits do people hold onto today that parallel the comfortable lies and behavior of the Jewish people in the text? How do today's lies hamper the effectiveness of the church? What do we do to expose those lies?

ACTIONS HAVE CONSEQUENCES

Visual for Lesson 8. *Use this visual to challenge your students to name actions for which they suffered immediate or delayed consequences.*

What Do You Think?

If God sent a specific message to Christians today, what list of sins do you think he would give to expose how people act one way in worship and another way the rest of the week?

[Hint: Put answers into two lists: sins of commission *and sins of* omission.]*

There is a story about Diogenes of Sinope, who comes along some 200 years after Jeremiah. The story pictures him as wandering around ancient Greece with a lantern in daylight, unsuccessfully searching for an honest man. Earlier in his book, Jeremiah also had searched Jerusalem for a person who was on the side of truth and justice (Jeremiah 5:1). God hoped for such a person, for this would be reason to spare Jerusalem. But Jeremiah's quest was as futile as that of Diogenes (compare Genesis 18:23-32). How sad it is when truth is seen as optional, and we find ourselves loving lies!

9, 10. "'Will you steal and murder, commit adultery and perjury, burn incense to Baal and follow other gods you have not known, and then come and stand before me in this house, which bears my Name, and say, "We are safe"—safe to do all these detestable things?

Jeremiah's complaint now gets very specific. He charges that the people of Judah have violated six of the Ten Commandments (Deuteronomy 5:7-21). They *steal* (Commandment Eight), *murder* (Commandment Six), and *commit adultery* (Commandment Seven). They have given false witness (Commandment Nine). They have worshiped *other gods* and made idols of them (Commandments One and Two).

Jeremiah warns that God knows of these abominations. God does not overlook them just because the people are going through the motions of worship at the temple. Most offensive to God is the mix of his worship with the worship of false gods like *Baal* of the Canaanites. This false worship is a sure way to bring about the wrath of the Lord (see Judges 2:13, 14).

PROBABILISM

A theory of moral theology known as *probabilism* came into being in the seventeenth century AD. The main idea is that if you can find a good ethical motive behind an action, even if it is highly improbable, then the action can be defended as allowable.

For example, if a merchant cannot sell his wine at a fair profit, he can add water to it and sell it as pure in order to make the profit. If servants are not being paid a proper wage by their master, they may take property from the master that will make up the difference. If necessity forces a person to take wood from someone else's pile, he is not obligated to restore it. If someone has committed a crime, he may swear in a loud voice, "I have not done this crime" and then in a subdued voice add, "today." Thus the total statement is true, and he is exonerated from falsehood.

The result of probabilism is to take moral laws and turn them inside out. Jeremiah condemned this kind of thinking centuries before Christ. This condemnation still stands.   —J. B. N.

B. DEN OF ROBBERS (v. 11)

11. "'Has this house, which bears my Name, become a den of robbers to you? But I have been watching! declares the LORD.

Jeremiah now brings a devastating charge against Judah: the hypocritical dishonesty of the leaders has found a home within the temple precincts. This has made the *house* of the Lord *a den of robbers.*

This charge likely has to do with the commerce going on in the temple courts, the location of a financial center for the nation. Rather than conduct business with integrity and truth, dealing is done with deception and greediness. This will also be a problem during the time of Jesus several centuries later. He will cleanse the temple of his day by running out the money changers and merchants (see Mark 11:15-17).

What Do You Think?

In what ways could God refer to today's church as a "den of robbers"? What can the church do to rectify this situation?

C. DISASTER OF SHILOH (vv. 12-15)

12. "'Go now to the place in Shiloh where I first made a dwelling for my Name, and see what I did to it because of the wickedness of my people Israel.

Shiloh was the original location in the promised land of the house of the Lord. This was the tabernacle transported by Israel through the wilderness. The tabernacle at Shiloh had become a more permanent structure than the tent of the exodus and was sometimes referred to as the temple (see 1 Samuel 1:9).

Although we do not have details, the Old Testament hints in several places that God allowed this former sanctuary to be destroyed, perhaps by the Philistines (see Psalm 78:60). The ruins of this temple are still around in Jeremiah's day. Those ruins should serve as a warning that building a house for God does not guarantee God's favor.

13. "'While you were doing all these things, declares the LORD, I spoke to you again and again, but you did not listen; I called you, but you did not answer.

Jeremiah's final accusation at this point is that the people of the temple repeatedly have turned a deaf ear to God's pleas for change. Although they are regular worshipers, they have forgotten the one whom they worship.

What we call "worship time" can easily become a noisy series of presentations designed to please the audience. We should remember that God is present at our worship efforts, and he may be speaking to us. By this we do not mean that we should expect an audible voice coming from Heaven. Rather, the idea is to expect our hearts to be touched through Scripture and prayer and praise. When God's Holy Spirit is prompting us to change our lives, to admit and abandon the love of sinful practices, then we should listen.

14, 15. "'Therefore, what I did to Shiloh I will now do to the house that bears my Name, the temple you trust in, the place I gave to you and your fathers. I will thrust you from my presence, just as I did all your brothers, the people of Ephraim.'"

History has a habit of repeating itself, even in tragic ways. Jeremiah reminds the hearers that God had thrown out *all* their *brothers, the people of Ephraim* (signifying the northern kingdom of Israel) on account of persistent sin and rebellion.

God also has abandoned an earlier temple of Israel, the sanctuary at *Shiloh.* God will do it again with the southern kingdom of Judah and the Jerusalem temple. And, let us be forewarned, God can do it with any church that tolerates and grows comfortable with a hypocritical lifestyle and empty, meaningless worship practices. The warnings in Revelation 2 and 3 are important to heed!

TRANQUILITY?

In Hebrew, the word *Shiloh* means "tranquility, rest." When the Israelites conquered the land of Canaan, they set up the tabernacle at Shiloh. This remained the seat of worship for some time. The tabernacle was still there in the early years of Samuel.

When the Philistines returned the Ark of the Covenant after its capture, it was not returned to Shiloh. Instead, it ultimately was sent to Jerusalem. The town of Shiloh began to decline; this continued into the days of Jeremiah. How interesting that a place named *tranquility* would come to represent desolation.

Because of its positive Old Testament connotations, many churches have been named *Shiloh.* One of the most interesting was a small country Methodist church in southern Tennessee near a spot on the Tennessee River called Pittsburgh Landing. A major battle of the American Civil War was fought there on April 6 and 7, 1862.

WHAT DO YOU THINK?

If you were asked to be a spiritual accountability partner by another Christian, what steps would you take to help your friend ensure that his or her worship does not become an empty ritual?

DAILY BIBLE READINGS

Monday, July 16—*Pay Greater Attention (Hebrews 2: 1-4)*

Tuesday, July 17—*Forgiveness Is Possible (2 Chronicles 7:11-16)*

Wednesday, July 18— *Choices of Consequences (1 Kings 9:1-9)*

Thursday, July 19—*Disaster Is Coming (Jeremiah 19:1-6)*

Friday, July 20—*Downfall Threatened (Jeremiah 26:1-6)*

Saturday, July 21—*Amend Your Ways (Jeremiah 7:1-7)*

Sunday, July 22—*Judgment of the Wicked (Jeremiah 7:8-15)*

Heavenly Father, God of ancient Israel and of the church, have patience with us. Please don't give up on reminding us of our hypocrisy and sin. Give us the spiritual strength to change and the joy that comes from serving you with clean hands and a pure heart. We pray this in the name of the one who never acted with hypocrisy, Jesus Christ your Son, amen.

Much of the battle swirled around the church building itself. Some 100,000 soldiers fought there, suffering over 23,000 casualties. How ironic that a place whose name means "tranquility" would be the scene of such horrible violence and death.

Yet that is a message of Jeremiah. God has been patient, but ultimately he will wreak vengeance upon the faithlessness of his people. Shiloh was desolate, and Jerusalem would be destroyed. Such is eventually the case with all who abandon God's paths to seek their own way.

        —J. B. N.

III. FAILED LEADERSHIP (2 KINGS 23:36, 37)

36, 37. Jehoiakim was twenty-five years old when he became king, and he reigned in Jerusalem eleven years. His mother's name was Zebidah daughter of Pedaiah; she was from Rumah. And he did evil in the eyes of the LORD, just as his fathers had done.

The historical record of the Old Testament shows that Judah did not heed Jeremiah's dire warnings. King *Jehoiakim* began to reign in 609 BC, and he was the son of the reformer King Josiah (Jeremiah 22:18). But the son did not continue his father's efforts to bring Israel back to an obedient relationship with the Lord. Instead, he chose the path of Manasseh and did *evil*. Jeremiah tells us that Jehoiakim went so far as to burn, out of contempt, a scroll of prophetic warnings (Jeremiah 36:22, 23, 28).

In 2 Kings 24:1-5 (which may have been written by Jeremiah) we learn that Jehoiakim arrogantly rebelled against Babylonian King Nebuchadnezzar. The result was disaster, for that king had been sent by God. Nebuchadnezzar looted the temple and physically humiliated Jehoiakim (2 Chronicles 36:6, 7). God's will, as proclaimed by Jeremiah, was accomplished. God's will shall always be accomplished!

CONCLUSION

We do not live in ancient Jerusalem. We do not worship at Solomon's temple. We need not fear Nebuchadnezzar and the Babylonian army. But Jeremiah's word should still be heard in our churches today. Are our efforts to worship God motivated by a true heart, or are they the empty acts of self-serving hypocrites?

As one who has ministered in many different churches for several decades, I have observed various hypocrites in action: the church staff member who complained about the miserly giving of the congregation, yet didn't give proportionately himself; the elder who griped about the rambunctious behavior of the youth group while having an affair with his secretary; the worship leader who focused the singing time on herself, then grumbled that the people weren't singing; the Sunday school teacher who carried the biggest Bible I've ever seen, yet was so dishonest in his business dealings that no one in the church would patronize his store; the committee member who had just paid cash for a new SUV, yet moaned when a missionary asked for funds to replace his 10-year-old van, which had in excess of 300,000 miles on it.

But I know the biggest hypocrite even more intimately. He is the one who wants Sunday worship only according to his tastes, not for God's glory. He is the one who gives far less than he could because he spends so much on his own whims. He is the one who looks down on those who don't know the Bible as well as he, but often turns a deaf ear to Scripture that confronts his life. That hypocrite is me.

Discovery Learning

This page contains an alternative lesson plan emphasizing learning activities. Classes desiring such student involvement will find these suggestions helpful. The next page is a reproducible activity page to further enhance discovery learning.

LEARNING GOALS

After participating in this lesson, each student will be able to:

1. List at least five sins for which God held his people accountable.

2. List at least five modern behaviors that are parallel to the sins of the ancient Judeans.

3. Examine his or her life for signs of these sins and take measures to resist them.

INTO THE LESSON

Say, "Sometimes we can get a false sense of security about our daily environment." To illustrate this point, ask your students to rank-order these creatures according to how many people they kill each year in the United States: bears; cougars; dogs; insects and spiders; sharks; and snakes. (This activity is also in the student book.) Answers are: 1. insects and spiders (50 to 150 deaths per year, not counting deaths from illnesses borne by mosquitoes); 2. dogs (about 15 deaths per year); 3. snakes (10 to 12); 4. sharks (2); 5. bears (fewer than 1); 6. cougars (fewer than 0.5).

After you have discussed their answers, say, "Sometimes the things we may fear the most, such as sharks and bears, are far less dangerous to us than things we take for granted, such as insects or dogs. Today's lesson deals with Judah's failure to realize the danger of their shallow religious routines."

INTO THE WORD

Deliver an introductory lecture from the Lesson Background to help your students understand Jeremiah's ministry. This will set the stage for the passages they will be studying. (Option: add or substitute the Interview with a Prophet exercise from the Reproducible Page.)

Next, distribute copies of the following true-false statements (or direct your students to their student books, where this quiz is also found). Tell your students to read Jeremiah 7:1-4, 8-15, and 2 Kings 23:36, 37 to find the answers to this quiz. (Answers are provided in parentheses, but don't distribute those.)

1. God told Jeremiah to preach in the gate of Solomon's temple in Jerusalem (*true, Jeremiah 7:1*); 2. God ordered the Jews to reform their ways (*true, v. 3*); 3. Jeremiah instructed the Jews to chant the phrase "the temple of the Lord" (*false, v. 4*); 4. Jeremiah accused the Jews of burning incense to the false god Dagon (*false, v. 9*); 5. God accused the Jews of making the temple a den of robbers (*true, v. 11*); 6. God said that he had made a dwelling for his name first at Shiloh (*true, v. 12*); 7. God warned Judah that he would destroy the temple, just as he had destroyed the tabernacle at Shiloh (*true, v. 14*); 8. God also warned that he would remove Judah from the land, just as he had removed Ephraim (*true, v. 15*); 9. Jehoiakim was 30 years old when he became king of Judah (*false, 2 Kings 23:36*); 10. Jehoiakim was a great religious reformer like his father, Josiah (*false, v. 37*).

When your students have completed the quiz, review the correct answers and discuss the meaning of the text. Use the following questions for discussion:

1. Why would Jeremiah stand in the gate of the temple to deliver his message? *2.* What offer did God make to the Jews if they changed their ways? *3.* How were the people given a false sense of security by the existence of the temple? *4.* Of what specific sins were the Jews guilty? *5.* How had the Jews made the temple a den of robbers? (Remember that Jesus leveled the same charge; Mark 11:15-17.) *6.* What punishment did God threaten against Judah? *7.* How would they know God's threat was genuine? *8.* Who was Jehoiakim? What happened to him?

INTO LIFE

Reproduce this chart to give to your students:

Judah's Sins	Our Sins
1. Trust in the temple	
2. Theft	
3. Murder	
4. Adultery	
5. False gods	

Ask your students to note one or two sins common today that are comparable to the sins of Judah. For example, they could list *tax fraud* in place of *theft* or *abortion* in place of *murder.*

Next, instruct your students to turn to 1 Corinthians 6:9-11 and 1 John 1:8–2:2 to see what God expects us to do about such sins today. Ask them to write a brief summary of God's instructions. Discuss the fact that God still offers forgiveness for people who return to him through Christ.

Interview with a Prophet

For this skit you will need two actors and a microphone. The script is based on Jeremiah 7:1-15.

REPORTER: *[holding microphone, as if speaking into a TV camera]* This is David Benjamin reporting from the front gate at Solomon's temple in downtown Jerusalem, where Jeremiah the prophet has been verbally abusing worshipers for several hours. Here he is now. Jeremiah, what are you carrying on about?

JEREMIAH: This word of the Lord came to me: "Stand at the gate of the Lord's house and there proclaim this message: 'Hear the word of the Lord, all you people of Judah who come through these gates to worship the Lord.'"

REPORTER: So you say the Lord told you to do this? What is his message?

JEREMIAH: This is what the Lord Almighty, the God of Israel, says: "Reform your ways and your actions."

REPORTER: Reform your ways? How can you say that to the most spiritual people in town as they come to the temple to worship? All the other prophets say this magnificent temple is proof of our godliness.

JEREMIAH: "Do not trust in deceptive words and say, 'This is the temple of the Lord, the temple of the Lord, the temple of the Lord!'"

REPORTER: So what exactly does God want us to do?

JEREMIAH: God says, "If you really change your ways and your actions and deal with each other justly, if you do not oppress the alien, the fatherless or the widow and do not shed innocent blood in this place, and if you do not follow other gods to your own harm, then I will let you live in this place, in the land I gave your forefathers for ever and ever."

REPORTER: Justice, aliens, fatherless, widows . . . OK, but Rabbi Rogerstein says we are God's chosen people and he likes us just the way we are. Why should we believe you and not him?

JEREMIAH: You are trusting deceptive words that are worthless. God says, "Will you steal and murder, commit adultery and perjury, burn incense to Baal and follow other gods you have not known, and then come and stand before me in this house, which bears my Name?"

REPORTER: Those are some pretty harsh words, Jeremiah. How do we know God really said them?

JEREMIAH: God says, "Go now to the place in Shiloh where I first made a dwelling for my Name, and see what I did to it because of the wickedness of my people Israel. I spoke to you again and again, but you did not listen; I called you, but you did not answer. Therefore, what I did to Shiloh I will now do to the house that bears my Name, the temple you trust in, the place I gave to you and your fathers. I will thrust you from my presence, just as I did all your brothers, the people of Ephraim."

REPORTER: So there you have it, folks. Jeremiah the prophet says that God will cast us out and destroy the temple, unless we repent. *[rolls his eyes in a "who is this nut?" facial expression]* From Solomon's temple—which is still standing, I might add—this is David Benjamin reporting for BAAL TV.

COMMITTED TO TRUSTING GOD

WHY TEACH THIS LESSON?

Waiting is not a popular thing. In a culture of broadband Internet connections, automatic teller machines, instant text messaging, microwave ovens, fast food, e-mail, and pay-at-the-pump gasoline, to wait on anything seems "so twentieth century." The old line, "God give me patience and give it to me *now*" is humorous because it reflects a mind-set that really does exist.

Scripture, though, challenges this kind of lifestyle, this desire for instant and sometimes continual gratification. God is not bound by time nor is he a servant to our schedules. Today's lesson will confront your students' "right now" mind-set with God's expectation that they are to wait on him. Life gets better when we do because we begin to look to God's strength instead of our own as we wait on his perfect timing. "Wait for the Lord; be strong and take heart and wait for the Lord" (Psalm 27:14).

INTRODUCTION

A. DESPERATE LIVING

I saw her again the other day. She was in the frozen-food section at the supermarket. This time she was tall and very thin. She had dark hair and a light complexion. At first I thought her face was dirty. Then I realized that even her heavy makeup could not hide the bruises. Her eyes were downcast, her expression blank.

But our eyes met for just an instant as our shopping carts passed, and I was stunned by her look of fear and pain. Who had beaten her? Boyfriend? Husband? Father? I realized that I had seen her too many times. Sometimes she had been short and blond. Other times her skin had been dark. She was the woman betrayed by a man who should have protected her, and she saw no way out of her wretched situation. She finished her shopping and returned to her world of horror.

Henry David Thoreau (1817–1862) wrote, "The mass of men lead lives of quiet desperation." This is still true. We drag ourselves through each day, overwhelmed by commitments, bills, and worries. We live vicariously through pop celebrities, sports heroes, or other media creations. When we are asked how we are doing, we automatically say, "Fine." But we aren't "fine." In our heart of hearts, many of us have given up hope and see nothing in the future but playing out a life of drudgery

This is not what God intends for us, though. God wants us to be people of hope, not fear. God created us to live with confident assurance, not daily desperation and aimless distraction. Today's lesson gives a clear view of the irrefutable fact that God intends the very best for his people. He asks that we trust him and obey him. He will give us full, rich lives.

DEVOTIONAL READING:
PSALM 145:13b-21
BACKGROUND SCRIPTURE:
JEREMIAH 28, 29
PRINTED TEXT:
JEREMIAH 29:1-14

LESSON AIMS

After participating in this lesson, each student will be able to:

1. Outline Jeremiah's letter to the captives.

2. Outline a letter that a modern Jeremiah could write to people of his own society.

3. Suggest one or two ways that he or she can seek the Lord more wholeheartedly on a daily basis.

Jul
29

KEY VERSE

"I know the plans I have for you," declares the LORD, "plans to prosper you and not to harm you, plans to give you hope and a future." —Jeremiah 29:11

LESSON 9 NOTES

B. LESSON BACKGROUND

It is difficult to imagine a more desperate time in history than the Jerusalem of Jeremiah's day. Religious and moral confusion reigned in the city and the surrounding countryside (Jeremiah 5:1; 11:13). The city was under constant danger from foreign invaders (1:15; 6:1). The threat of God's wrath was against the city (4:4); the Lord Almighty promised to lay the city in ruins (6:8; 9:11). Jeremiah constantly preached that the future for Jerusalem was dismal (see 13:16).

In spite of these dire warnings from Jeremiah and other prophets such as Zephaniah and Habakkuk, the leaders of the nation did not respond. Instead, they continued in ways of rank wickedness (see Jeremiah 22:17; 29:19). The few who understood the implications of Jeremiah's condemnation must have felt powerless, helpless, and without hope. National disaster would destroy them too even if, individually, they heeded Jeremiah's call to repent.

The Babylonians controlled Judah for many years before the destruction of Jerusalem in 586 BC. This control began about 605 BC, after the Babylonians defeated the Egyptians at the epic Battle of Carchemish (Jeremiah 46:2). After that, the Babylonians were the masters of the ancient world, including Jerusalem and Judah.

Three distinct groups of citizens from Judah were transported to Babylon (Jeremiah 52:28-30). Daniel was likely a member of the first group, taken about 605 BC. Ezekiel was a member of a group that was transported after the capture of Jerusalem in about 597 BC. The largest group was taken after Jerusalem's destruction in 586 BC. Jeremiah himself was not taken to Babylon but ended up in Egypt after the city was destroyed.

Jeremiah is often portrayed as a prophet of doom. Yet his book also offers hope for the future. Although Judah would be devastated, virtually ceasing to exist, God planned to gather a remnant of faithful people to rebuild the city (Jeremiah 23:3). This would be the cause of great rejoicing (31:7-14). This ray of hope shines brightly in Jeremiah 29, the focus of today's lesson.

I. COMMUNICATION IN CAPTIVITY (JEREMIAH 29:1-3)

In the tense periods between Nebuchadnezzar's initial deportation of hostages and exiles (605 BC), the capture of Jerusalem (597 BC), and the city's destruction (586 BC), Jeremiah works actively as a spokesman for God. In that role he interprets these judgmental events for the nation. His ministry even involves communication with the leaders in exile, those who had been transported to Babylon in 597 BC or earlier.

A. JUDAH IS UPROOTED (vv. 1, 2)

1. This is the text of the letter that the prophet Jeremiah sent from Jerusalem to the surviving elders among the exiles and to the priests, the prophets and all the other people Nebuchadnezzar had carried into exile from Jerusalem to Babylon.

If you were to travel straight across the desert from *Jerusalem* to ancient *Babylon*, the distance would be about 500 miles. But following the northern route, through the Babylonian administrative center of Riblah and down the Euphrates River valley, would make the distance more like 880 miles.

This is a well-traveled road in Jeremiah's day, and it takes six to eight weeks to make the journey. In the period between Jerusalem's capture and its destruction, those left in the city seem to communicate regularly with their exiled brothers and sisters in Babylon. Jeremiah's ability to send the exiles a *letter* is a confirmation of this.

DAILY BIBLE READINGS

Monday, July 23—The Goodness of the Lord (Psalm 145:13-21)

Tuesday, July 24—God Restores (Jeremiah 30:18-22)

Wednesday, July 25—Loved with an Everlasting Love (Jeremiah 31:1-9)

Thursday, July 26—Shepherd of the Flock (Jeremiah 31:10-14)

Friday, July 27—They Shall Be My People (Jeremiah 31:33-37)

Saturday, July 28—Jeremiah Writes the Exiles (Jeremiah 29:1-9)

Sunday, July 29—God's Good Plans (Jeremiah 29:10-14)

2. (*This was after King Jehoiachin and the queen mother, the court officials and the leaders of Judah and Jerusalem, the craftsmen and the artisans had gone into exile from Jerusalem.*)

Jehoiachin was the son of Jehoiakim. His surrender of Jerusalem in 597 BC allowed Nebuchadnezzar to sack the city and loot the temple (see 2 Kings 24:11-15). This verse thus dates the prophecy we are studying between 597 and 586 BC, during the reign of King Zedekiah in Jerusalem. Daniel and Ezekiel, who are in Babylon, are among the possible recipients of this letter. (See Daniel 9:2, which shows his acquaintance with the writings of Jeremiah.)

B. JUDAH IS NOT FORGOTTEN (v. 3)

3. *He entrusted the letter to Elasah son of Shaphan and to Gemariah son of Hilkiah, whom Zedekiah king of Judah sent to King Nebuchadnezzar in Babylon. It said:*

King *Zedekiah* uses two emissaries to communicate with his master, *King Nebuchadnezzar*. These men, *Elasah* and *Gemariah*, also serve the purpose of carrying Jeremiah's letter to the proper recipients in exile. The people in Jeremiah's target audience have been displaced. But he has not forgotten them.

II. WAITING IN CAPTIVITY (JEREMIAH 29:4-9)

The actual content of the letter begins with Jeremiah 29:4.

A. BUILD LIVES WHILE WAITING (vv. 4-6)

4. *This is what the LORD Almighty, the God of Israel, says to all those I carried into exile from Jerusalem to Babylon:*

The letter begins with two titles for God. First, he is *the Lord Almighty.* Older versions of the Bible translate this as *Lord of hosts,* meaning "master of the hosts of heavenly armies." It is a strong affirmation of the power of God.

Second, he is the *God of Israel.* The capture of Jerusalem and exile of its leaders do not mean that God has ceased to be Israel's God. He is still in control and has even caused the captivity according to his plan.

5, 6. *"Build houses and settle down; plant gardens and eat what they produce. Marry and have sons and daughters; find wives for your sons and give your daughters in marriage, so that they too may have sons and daughters. Increase in number there; do not decrease.*

Even after tragedy, life goes on. After disaster, you must pick up the pieces and keep living. God is telling Israel not to wait for some kind of quick solution and a return to Jerusalem. They need to understand that they are there for many years, so they should make the best of it. God still cares for them. His will is that their lives improve and that they have opportunities to flourish. He is still their God and wants to bless them.

TIMING

Timing is everything may be a bit of an overstatement but not by much! Often knowing *when* to do something is at least as important—if not more so—than knowing *how* to do it. During the American Civil War, Union General George B. McClellan was a genius when it came to organization and discipline but a failure at timing.

McClellan had overwhelming superiority during the Peninsular Campaign of 1862. But he was hesitant to attack. Ultimately, Confederate General Robert E. Lee took the initiative and forced McClellan out of Virginia. Later at Antietam, McClellan had a copy of Lee's battle plan. But still McClellan hesitated. He never

WHAT DO YOU THINK?

Name some individuals in your life who brought you the Word of God even though they seemed to have been working behind the scenes. In what ways are you doing the same for someone else?

WHAT DO YOU THINK?

What steps do you need to take so you can adjust your purposes to God's purposes in your current situation?

HOW TO SAY IT

Carchemish. KAR-key-mish.

Elasah. EL-ah-sah.

Euphrates. You-FRAY-teez.

Gemariah. Gem-uh-RYE-uh (G as in get).

Habakkuk. Huh-BACK-kuk.

Hilkiah. Hill-KYE-uh.

Jehoiachin. Jeh-HOY-uh-kin.

Jehoiakim. Jeh-HOY-uh-kim.

Shaphan. SHAY-fan.

Zedekiah. Zed-uh-KYE-uh.

Zephaniah. Zef-uh-NYE-uh.

threw all his forces into the battle. There is a time to be cautious, but there is also a time to attack. McClellan never seemed to know the difference.

When Grant faced Lee two years later, he knew it was time to attack. So he moved his army south. Even after the bloody battles of the Wilderness and Spotsylvania, Grant moved south. When it was time for movement, he moved. When it was time for trench warfare at Petersburg, he dug in. When the Confederate line cracked and Lee pulled out, Grant followed him and forced his surrender. Grant understood timing.

The Jews hungered for a return to Jerusalem, but Jeremiah knew that that was premature; return would occur decades later. Jeremiah was sensitive to God's timetable. Are we?   —J. B. N.

B. SEEK PEACE WHILE WAITING (v. 7)

7. *"Also, seek the peace and prosperity of the city to which I have carried you into exile. Pray to the LORD for it, because if it prospers, you too will prosper."*

Peace is a loaded term in the Old Testament. Coming from the word *shalom,* it means much more than simple absence of warfare. It has the added sense of prosperity and welfare. God's message for the exiles is that they should desire and *pray* for the peace and prosperity of their new community (Babylon), even though they have been brought there against their will. As Babylon prospers, so they will prosper. When Jeremiah writes, the prosperity of the exiled Jews is dependent upon the peace of this *city,* not the peace of Jerusalem.

C. REJECT DECEPTION WHILE WAITING (vv. 8, 9)

8. *Yes, this is what the LORD Almighty, the God of Israel, says: "Do not let the prophets and diviners among you deceive you. Do not listen to the dreams you encourage them to have.*

There are *prophets* among the exiles who are telling them that freedom is just around the corner. Their dreams and longings are focused on going home. The mighty God of Israel warns against this deception. This can be either self-deception (*the dreams you encourage them to have*) or an attempt to *deceive* the exiles by false prophecy.

9. *"They are prophesying lies to you in my name. I have not sent them," declares the LORD.*

The false prophet is a long-standing problem in the nation of Israel. Such people have contributed to circumstances leading to the capture of Jerusalem. The false prophets blamed the captivity in Babylon on the wrong reasons; they failed to pronounce that God was punishing Judah for its iniquity (Lamentations 2:14). Ezekiel, who prophesies in Babylon at about the same time Jeremiah is working in Jerusalem, sees the core problem when he says these prophets invoke the name of the Lord "when the Lord has not spoken" (Ezekiel 22:28).

A true prophet speaks for God, with God's authority. The nature of this position makes it easily susceptible to abuse and fakery. Even today, we should be careful whenever we encounter someone claiming to speak directly for God as a prophet. God has given us his Scripture to measure such words. The biblical pattern is that true prophets usually point out sin and call for repentance rather than tell people that prosperity is just around the corner (Jeremiah 6:13, 14).

WHAT DO YOU THINK?

How can your church help fortify Christians so they can discern between God's message and the messages of false teachers?

[Be sure to look at 2 Timothy 4:1-4!]

III. PROMISED FREEDOM FROM CAPTIVITY (JEREMIAH 29:10-14)

Having warned against the false prophets and having given strategies for the survival of the exile, Jeremiah now lays out a set of four promises from the Lord for the future of his people.

A. PROMISE OF RETURN (v. 10)

10. This is what the LORD says: "When seventy years are completed for Babylon, I will come to you and fulfill my gracious promise to bring you back to this place.

Jeremiah begins with a promise of return to Jerusalem. This is a classic good news/bad news message. The good news? The exile will not last forever. The bad news? Most adults hearing this will not live to see it, for it will be two or three generations down the road.

The prophecy of *seventy years* proves to be accurate. The first group of exiles (including Daniel) was taken to *Babylon* when Nebuchadnezzar became the king, about 605 BC. The Babylonian empire falls to King Cyrus of Persia in 538 BC. Cyrus serves as God's war club to break the power of the Babylonians (see Jeremiah 51:20). Cyrus then grants permission for the Jews to return to Jerusalem and rebuild the temple. That return begins in about 536 BC (see Daniel 9:2).

B. PROMISE OF PROSPERITY (v. 11)

11. "For I know the plans I have for you," declares the LORD, "plans to prosper you and not to harm you, plans to give you hope and a future.

God *plans* that the exiles will see *peace*, meaning future prosperity rather than new devastation. They will gain the *future* they *hope* for. This will be a return to the land of their inheritance (Judah), to their holy city (Jerusalem). There they will rebuild the house of the Lord (the temple). This is the second promise, the promise of future prosperity for Israel.

Although this promise was made to the exiles of ancient Judah, it still has application for us today. God's desire is that we prosper. Our Lord is not a vengeful, cruel God who delights in punishing us. He waits for our trust and obedience so that he may bless us with his bounty.

CAPTIVES

Captives. The word itself has a quite negative ring to it. The immediate word-picture is that of people confined and held against their will, probably herded off to some distant place they don't want to go.

History is filled with stories of captives. The Romans took many captives from their conquered lands, using their muscle power as the fuel to drive the empire. People from Africa were captured, sold into slavery, and transported to the New World. One of my ancestors was a 7-year-old running the streets of London in 1750. He woke up one morning on a ship bound for America. He had been kidnapped and was then sold as an indentured servant in colonial Virginia.

Many people are "captives" of their jobs, economically dependent on their employment but disliking every moment spent at work. We are captives of our culture, the values of our generation rather than those of previous or future generations. The fact is, we are all captives in one way or another. That's why the words of hope and comfort that Jeremiah speaks to those held captive centuries ago can apply to us today.   —J. B. N.

C. PROMISE OF ACCESSIBILITY (vv. 12-14a)

12-14a. "Then you will call upon me and come and pray to me, and I will listen to you. You will seek me and find me when you seek me with all your heart. I will be found by you," declares the LORD.

To *call upon* the Lord is Bible language for earnest prayer. It particularly refers to calling on God for assistance in the time of need. This practice began in the book of Genesis (Genesis 4:26). The psalmist taught that God was near to those who called upon him, but only if they did so in truth (Psalm 145:18). Another

WHAT DO YOU THINK?

How do you encourage those who have lost trust in God because God did not respond in the way they expected?

"I know the plans ...to prosper you ...plans to give you hope and a future."
—Jeremiah 29:11 (NIV)

Visual for Lesson 9. *Use this visual to introduce this question: "How do you think God is planning for you to prosper in His service?"*

principle taught in Psalms is that God turns a deaf ear to our pleas if we cherish sin in our hearts (Psalm 66:18).

After the time of Jeremiah, the prophet Zechariah will teach that God refused to hear the pleas of Israel during the Babylonian period because of their hard hearts (Zechariah 7:13). Israel's restoration needs to involve more than temple reconstruction. It needs to include a restored relationship with God, a time of renewed prayer and worship. This is the third promise, the promise of renewed accessibility to God in prayer (compare Zephaniah 3:9).

D. PROMISE OF RESTORATION (v. 14b)

14b. "*. . . and will bring you back from captivity. I will gather you from all the nations and places where I have banished you," declares the LORD, "and will bring you back to the place from which I carried you into exile.*"

God ends this section by reminding the exiles of his sovereignty. It was God who scattered the Israelites, first by the Assyrians and then by the Babylonians (see Jeremiah 50:17). It is only God, then, who can restore Israel (see 27:22). This is the fourth promise, a promise of restoration.

In the big picture of the Bible, Israel is to be restored for more than simply rebuilding the city of Jerusalem and its temple. Restored Israel is to be the nation that produces God's Messiah. This will bring "salvation to the ends of the earth" (Isaiah 49:6). The nation of Israel, whether in exile or restored, is not an end unto itself. It is intended by God to be the vehicle that allows for his Messiah to come and restore humanity to him. This is God's ultimate plan to give peace and well-being. The message of the New Testament is that we can be at peace with God through Jesus Christ (Romans 5:1).

CONCLUSION

Reading Jeremiah allows us to take "the long view." We can see beyond temporary adversity to a time of restoration and blessing. We can get through tragedy without doubting God's love for us. We can pray to God in our times of need, knowing that he is listening and gives us hope.

The horror of Jerusalem's destruction is almost incomprehensible to us today. The survivors of this catastrophe wept uncontrollably when they arrived in Babylon (Psalm 137:1). Most of us have faced personal tragedy that left us feeling the same way. Think of a time when you endured great pain and sorrow. Maybe some are in this state now, this week.

In this dark night of the soul, it is easy to think that we will never be happy again. This is particularly true when misfortunes come at us in waves. Will this never stop? Why is this happening to me? What did I do wrong?

We should be careful not to see every bad thing in our lives as God's punishment for sin. Bad things sometimes happen to good people because our world is full of sin, and this sin affects us directly and indirectly. We can, however, see that every tragedy will be followed eventually by God's blessings and peace. We are, after all, children of the light (1 Thessalonians 5:5).

Even after the horrific events of Jerusalem's destruction in 586 bc, Jeremiah saw hope in the future (see Lamentations 3:21-24; written by Jeremiah). His hope was based on eternal promises. First, God's compassion and mercy are inexhaustible; his fountain of blessings never runs dry. Second, God's faithfulness is great and continually renewed. We can depend on God, for he never betrays our trust. This is our antidote for the sickness of hopelessness. These promises are ours too.

Discovery Learning

This page contains an alternative lesson plan emphasizing learning activities. Classes desiring such student involvement will find these suggestions helpful. The next page is a reproducible activity page to further enhance discovery learning.

LEARNING GOALS

After this lesson, each student will be able to:

1. Outline Jeremiah's letter to the captives.

2. Outline a letter that a modern Jeremiah could write to people of his own society.

3. Suggest one or two ways that he or she can seek the Lord more wholeheartedly on a daily basis.

INTO THE LESSON

As your students arrive, give each one a copy of the following exercise. (It is also printed in the student book.) Ask your students to read the quotations and write either *agree* or *disagree* in response to each:

1. "A mind troubled by doubt cannot focus on the course to victory" (Arthur Golden). *2.* "He who despairs over an event is a coward, but he who holds hope for the human condition is a fool" (Albert Camus). *3.* "Worries go down better with soup than without" (Jewish proverb). *4.* "If you can solve your problem, then what is the need of worrying? If you cannot solve it, then what is the use of worrying?" (Shantideva). *5.* "Character cannot be developed in ease and quiet. Only through experience of trial and suffering can the soul be strengthened, ambition inspired, and success achieved" (Helen Keller). *6.* "Pain is inevitable; suffering is optional" (M. Kathleen Casey). *7.* "The mass of men lead lives of quiet desperation" (Henry David Thoreau).

Discuss your students' answers. Then tell your class that today's lesson will draw a clear, scriptural contrast between the daily desperation that many people endure and the hope and assurance that God intends for his people to enjoy. (Alternative: distribute the Hope in Time of Turmoil exercise from the Reproducible Page for students to work on as they arrive).

INTO THE WORD

Introduce this section with a brief lecture on the ministry of Jeremiah, using both the Lesson Background and the lesson commentary. Make sure you mention that although Jeremiah prophesied doom and destruction for Judah, he also foretold the reestablishment of the Jewish nation from the remnant that would survive.

Next, divide your class into pairs. Each pair will study Jeremiah 29:1-14 and create an outline of the passage, placing the phrases below into their proper location in the outline grid. (If you do not use the student books, you will need to reproduce both the grid and phrases.)

I. _____ (29:1-3)
  A. _____ (vv. 1, 2)
  B. _____ (v. 3)
II. _____ (29:4-9)
  A. _____ (vv. 4-6)
  B. _____ (v. 7)
  C. _____ (vv. 8, 9)
III. _____ (29:10-14)
  A. _____ (v. 10)
  B. _____ (v. 11)
  C. _____ (vv. 12-14a)
  D. _____ (v. 14b)

Phrases: *Build Lives While Waiting; Communication in Captivity; Judah Is Not Forgotten; Judah Is Uprooted; Promise of Accessibility; Promise of Prosperity; Promise of Restoration; Promise of Return; Promised Freedom from Captivity; Reject Deception While Waiting; Seek Peace While Waiting; Waiting in Captivity.*

When your students have finished their outlining, ask for volunteers to share answers. Write each line on the board as it is completed; resolve disagreements.

INTO LIFE

Ask your pairs from the previous exercise to outline a letter that a modern Jeremiah could write to people of our society. Each outline should include the following elements: a listing of and denunciation of the sins prevalent in modern society (see 1 Corinthians 6:9-11; Galatians 5:19-21); a warning of judgment from God because of those sins (Matthew 24:36-51; 2 Peter 3:3-13; Revelation 20:7-15); an offer of salvation (Acts 2:36-40; 3:17-26); and a promise of restoration to those who are faithful to God (Hebrews 10:23-31; Revelation 22:12-17).

When the pairs have completed their work, have each share the results. Challenge your students to identify privately any sins that are a continuing problem in their lives. Remind each one that he or she needs to confess those sins to God (1 John 1:7–2:2). Before the closing prayer, distribute copies of the My Search Strategy exercise from the Reproducible Page for students to use as a take-home activity.

Hope in Time of Turmoil

Read each statement below and circle the T or F, depending on whether the statement is true or false, according to Jeremiah 29:1-14.

T F 1. The Jews were exiled from Jerusalem to Babylon by Nebuchadnezzer.

T F 2. The king of Judah who was exiled at that time was Josiah.

T F 3. The king of Judah when Jeremiah wrote this letter was Zedekiah.

T F 4. God told the Jews in Babylon to build homes and plant gardens.

T F 5. Even in captivity, the Jews were promised peace and prosperity by God.

T F 6. God reassured the Jews that all their prophets were truthful and trustworthy.

T F 7. God promised the Jews that they would return from captivity after 50 years.

T F 8. God also promised that they would find him if they sought for God with all their hearts.

Answers: 1. True, v. 1; 2. False, v. 2; 3. True, v. 3; 4. True, v. 5; 5. True, v. 7; 6. False, vv. 8, 9; 7. False, v. 10; 8. True, v. 13.

My Search Strategy

Jeremiah 29:13 says, "You will seek me and find me when you seek me with all your heart." Outline a strategy for seeking God this week by completing the daily schedule below. For each day, indicate a Scripture passage you plan to read, concerns you need to pray about, and Christian service you plan to perform.

	Scripture Reading	Prayer Concerns	Acts of Service
Monday			
Tuesday			
Wednesday			
Thursday			
Friday			
Saturday			
Sunday			

COMMITTED TO HOPE EVEN IN PAIN

LESSON 10

WHY TEACH THIS LESSON?

Benjamin Franklin said, "Nothing in life is certain except death and taxes." Death and taxes may be universal realities, but suffering and pain are also part of our common experience. Some of your students have recently buried a parent or a child or a spouse. One student may have watched her husband walk out on their marriage recently. The fact that these students will be in class on Sunday demonstrates the faithfulness suggested by the lesson title. None of us escapes the wounds inflicted by our broken world; our response to that pain, though, is what shapes us.

The point of today's lesson is critical for those who have suffered, who are suffering, and who will someday suffer—meaning everyone! God is faithful. He is with us in pain, just as He is with us in health. Jesus was in all ways like us, subject to temptation, suffering, pain, loss, and humiliation. Our God knows what suffering is like, and today's lesson is one way he will help you gain a proper perspective on it.

INTRODUCTION

A. TRAGEDY THEOLOGY

The tsunami tragedy of December 26, 2004, resulted in massive loss of life. So did the earthquake on the Pakistan-India border of October 8, 2005. Many organizations and nations responded with immediate and continuing aid for the ones who survived but who had lost homes, possessions, and their livelihood.

Tragedies of such proportions affect everyone psychologically. The enduring question is *Why?* Accounts from those two tragedies tell of individuals or groups that were spared through various circumstances. Did that mean that God was with them more than he was with the ones who lost their lives?

God knows when tragedies occur, for he knows when even a sparrow falls to the ground (Matthew 10:29). The fact that death can come at any age or in any circumstance confirms that an individual must be prepared for that possibility at all times. Every day there are accidents and acts of terror. No one is guaranteed that he or she will be alive tomorrow.

Thousands around the world die each year because of the fact that they are Christians. They lose their lives simply because they give expression to their faith by assembling together, distributing literature, or even using charitable acts as methods of evangelism. In many parts of the world it is just expected that a Christian will suffer. Yet the ultimate purpose of life for the Christian is to die in Christ. Family members who survive have a loss, but they are blessed with expectation of reunion. They also have examples of how a Christian handles the trials of life. God is with his people in both life and death.

DEVOTIONAL READING:
PSALM 23

BACKGROUND SCRIPTURE:
2 KINGS 25:1-7; LAMENTATIONS 3:25-58

PRINTED TEXT:
2 KINGS 25:1, 2, 5-7; LAMENTATIONS 3:25-33, 55-58

LESSON AIMS

After participating in this lesson, each student will be able to:

1. Retell at least one expression of faith that resulted from the fall of Jerusalem.

2. Explain how experiences of deprivation and despair provide opportunities for strong expressions of hope.

3. Write a prayer to use for the next severe trial in his or her life.

Aug
5

KEY VERSE

It is good to wait quietly for the salvation of the LORD.
—Lamentations 3:26

B. LESSON BACKGROUND

Nebuchadnezzar became the king of Babylon when his father died in the summer of 605 BC. The Babylonians had just defeated the Egyptians, and to demonstrate that there was a new power in the region, Nebuchadnezzar took captives from Jerusalem. They included the prophet Daniel. Nebuchadnezzar allowed Jehoiakim to remain on the throne of David.

Nebuchadnezzar returned in the summer of 597 BC to put down a rebellion initiated by Jehoiakim. But Nebuchadnezzar found that Jehoiakim's son, Jehoiachin, had been reigning for three months. Nebuchadnezzar therefore took Jehoiachin and 10,000 others captive. He then placed Zedekiah (Jehoiakim's brother) on the throne (2 Kings 24:14-17). The prophet Ezekiel was among the captives taken to Babylon then.

Zedekiah, Judah's last king, was therefore a puppet king under Nebuchadnezzar. Zedekiah was not a good puppet, however. At the beginning of his reign he sponsored a gathering of messengers from other nations. They came to Jerusalem to plan rebellion (Jeremiah 27:1-3).

On that occasion Jeremiah was instructed by the Lord to put a yoke on his neck and to announce to the delegates that Nebuchadnezzar was God's servant, and that all the lands were given by God into Nebuchadnezzar's hand (27:4-6). To prophesy this submission did not seem very patriotic, but it was in the best interests of the nations involved. Would Jerusalem obey?

I. SIEGE OF JERUSALEM (2 KINGS 25:1, 2, 5-7)

King Zedekiah made a trip to Babylon in the fourth year of his reign (about 594 BC; Jeremiah 51:59). It is sometimes thought that he and others who plotted against Babylon were compelled to make this journey in order to give personal expressions of allegiance to Nebuchadnezzar.

A few years later, however, Zedekiah rebelled (2 Kings 24:20). Nebuchadnezzar then moved to subjugate the disloyal nations, and Judah was first on his list.

A. DATES DETERMINED (vv. 1, 2)

1, 2. So in the ninth year of Zedekiah's reign, on the tenth day of the tenth month, Nebuchadnezzar king of Babylon marched against Jerusalem with his whole army. He encamped outside the city and built siege works all around it. The city was kept under siege until the eleventh year of King Zedekiah.

The tenth month is in winter. This shows Nebuchadnezzar's determination as he begins the military blockade of Jerusalem. Polite warfare (if there is such a thing) in ancient times waits until spring and the dry season. To move an army and its equipment into position in the rainy, cold months of winter is a hardship.

The conditions inside Jerusalem are not pleasant during the long months of siege. There is the constant thought that the enemy outside is waiting for you to surrender or starve. In the meantime the Babylonians patiently work to break through the defenses. Undoubtedly, there is a lot of "foxhole faith" inside Jerusalem at this time.

Jeremiah's message is that the lives of the people and the city itself can be saved only by surrender (Jeremiah 38:17, 18). Some of the officials of the city attempt to have Jeremiah killed for discouraging the men of the city with these words. The food supply eventually becomes so critical that some women eat their children (Lamentations 2:20; 4:10). This time there is no miracle to save Jerusalem, unlike the threat by the Assyrians over 100 years prior (see 2 Kings 19:34, 35). In July of 586 BC, the Babylonians finally force their way into the city.

WHAT DO YOU THINK

What may be some reasons that God would allow an adversary to "besiege" your church today? What corrective action do you need to take?

WHAT DO YOU THINK

The old saying is, "There are no atheists in foxholes." How do some practice "foxhole faith" today? How do we avoid this?

B. DISASTERS DESCRIBED (vv. 5-7)

5, 6a. But the Babylonian army pursued the king and overtook him in the plains of Jericho. All his soldiers were separated from him and scattered, and he was captured.

Zedekiah and others attempt to flee from the wrath of the besieging *army*, but the tactic does not work. The Babylonians capture the fleeing *king* on *the plains of Jericho*. The *soldiers* who are pledged to defend the king abandon him. It is every man for himself!

6b. He was taken to the king of Babylon at Riblah, where sentence was pronounced on him.

Zedekiah is closely related to the three prior kings of Judah. But his royal pedigree is of no value. He is just a prisoner, walking many miles to the north to meet *the king of Babylon*, whom he has betrayed. Every step is difficult, and the anticipation of the outcome only increases the anxiety.

7. They killed the sons of Zedekiah before his eyes. Then they put out his eyes, bound him with bronze shackles and took him to Babylon.

The last thing that *Zedekiah* is allowed to see is the death of his *sons*. Then he is blinded, perhaps with hot coals. He will never rebel again. Several years earlier, Ezekiel had made an interesting prophecy about Zedekiah: he was to be brought *to Babylon*, but he was not to see it (Ezekiel 12:13). The judgment on him by Nebuchadnezzar fulfills the prophecy. Other leaders of Judah also experience death at Riblah (2 Kings 25:18-21; Jeremiah 39:6).

II. STATEMENTS OF JEREMIAH (LAMENTATIONS 3:25-33, 55-58)

Jeremiah is traditionally thought to be the author of the book of Lamentations. The theme of the book is the desolation that accompanies the destruction of Jerusalem. It has now been some 40 years since Jeremiah was called to prophesy. In one sense Jeremiah probably considers himself a failure. His nation is gone, and the majority in Judah did not heed his message. In God's sight, however, Jeremiah is a faithful prophet who preaches even when he does not wish to do so (Jeremiah 20:9). Future generations regard him highly. His is one of the names given to Jesus when he asked his disciples how others identified him (Matthew 16:13, 14).

The first four chapters of Lamentations are alphabetic acrostics: the 22 letters of the Hebrew alphabet are used consecutively to begin the verses. Here in chapter three there are three verses for each letter. In two places the letters are transposed, and no one knows why. Some think that this method of writing may increase the ability to remember or demonstrate the carefulness of the writer.

A. REMINDERS IN SUFFERING (vv. 25-27)

25. The LORD is good to those whose hope is in him,
    to the one who seeks him.

This verse and the two following not only begin with the same letter of the Hebrew alphabet, but in the Hebrew they also begin with the same word— *good*. Its position as first in the sentence indicates its importance.

First, Jeremiah reminds the reader that the Lord really is good to the ones who have hope or expectations concerning God's promises. God fulfills his word, whether it is the destruction of a sinful nation or the revival of a dead nation.

Notice that the triad of verses immediately before this one provides the background for one of the great hymns of the faith, namely, "Great Is Thy Faithfulness." Most who sing the words do not realize the depths of faith that Jeremiah

---

WHAT DO YOU THINK

How do you respond to someone who questions the goodness of God when he or she reads passages such as 2 Kings 25:7?

HOW TO SAY IT

Assyrians. Uh-SEAR-e-unz.
Babylonians. Bab-ih-LOW-nee-
    unz.
Chaldees. KAL-deez.
Jehoiachin. Jeh-HOY-uh-kin.
Jehoiakim. Jeh-HOY-uh-kim.
Micah. MY-kuh.
Nebuchadnezzar. NEB-yuh-kud-
    NEZ-er.
Riblah. RIB-luh.
tsunami. su-NAH-me.
Zedekiah. Zed-uh-KYE-uh.

was expressing when he wrote them. It is almost inconceivable that Jeremiah can say that God's mercies are new every morning (v. 23). The experiences of Jerusalem's siege are still vivid in his mind, but he can still see the blessings.

26. It is good to wait quietly for the salvation of the LORD.

The latter part of this verse is difficult for many. Today's generation wants immediate gratification. Action is thought to be much better than quietly waiting for anything. *To wait quietly* also means that complaining or murmuring is not present. *It is good* that faith and faithfulness combine to eliminate impatience with God's timetable concerning the fulfillments of his promises (see 2 Peter 3:4-9).

27. It is good for a man to bear the yoke
while he is young.

To bear the yoke is a figure of speech that means someone has been placed under a burden, similar to an animal that wears a yoke. It is a forced place of service. It indicates humiliation. The person who experiences tough times later in life is usually better able to accept them if they were also part of his or her earlier years. Pain and suffering are never desirable, but there may be valuable lessons for the ones who endure them.

The exhortations of this verse and the previous one add a different dimension to the laments. These are positive expressions, and they say much about handling the traumas of life.

GAIN FROM PAIN

Some parents try to bring up their children in a "risk-free" world. They try to protect them from all emotional pain or hardship. Yet going through emotional pain can have a positive result. The same is true physically. Exposure to certain less-severe viruses can build immunity against those that are even worse.

The discipline of children is an area in which some parents have abandoned the responsibility of administering healthy doses of pain or hardship. The TV show *Nanny 911* makes this all too clear: children run riot as parents attempt to be their buddies rather than their, well, parents. Scripture reminds us that tough discipline, though not pleasant at the moment, has ultimate value (Hebrews 12:11).

In our spiritual lives, times of pain and trial may have a good ultimate result if we will allow God to use them for that purpose. Paul reminds us that "our light and momentary troubles are achieving for us an eternal glory that far outweighs them all" (2 Corinthians 4:17). None of us would say, "Bring on the pain, let the bad times roll." Yet we do know that God can bring good out of our patient endurance in times of hardship and pain. The key is to allow him to do so. —A. E. A.

B. REACTIONS TO SUFFERING (vv. 28-30)

28. Let him sit alone in silence,
for the LORD has laid it on him.

Jeremiah's words in the next three verses seem to combine the thought of the previous verse (bearing a yoke) and the suffering that accompanied Jerusalem's siege and destruction. There is no question this time about the source of the sorrows. *The Lord* is the one who has placed the burden on his people.

One of the frequent questions in negative experiences is, "What did I do to deserve this?" In many cases the answer is that nothing was done; some things just happen. Sometimes there are accidents, and no one is to blame. For Judah, however, the causes are known. It is therefore simply better to maintain *silence*. Asking questions only intensifies the sense of guilt and loss.

God uses the Babylonians to punish Judah, and the Babylonians are certainly not considered more righteous than Judah. Would that be a good question to raise with God? The prophet Habakkuk addressed that same issue approximately 20 years before Jerusalem fell: How could God use such a sinful nation to punish Judah? God's response is one of the outstanding verses of the Bible. Regardless of what happens, the righteous will live by faith (Habakkuk 2:4; see also Romans 1:17; Galatians 3:11). God will also take care of the Babylonians (see Lesson 7).

29. Let him bury his face in the dust—
> **there may yet be hope.**

The figures of speech showing humiliation or abasement continue, and this one is distinctive. It is similar to "lick *dust*," as given in Micah 7:17. It is also reminiscent of a conqueror's putting his foot on the neck of the one conquered (Joshua 10:24). The one who is treated in this way, however, does not surrender *hope*. His or her spirit is not broken. Such a person anticipates that with God's help there will be better days ahead.

30. Let him offer his cheek to one who would strike him,
> **and let him be filled with disgrace.**

The mistreatment moves from humiliation to physical violence. It is possible to view this verse figuratively. If that is the case, then it is a recognition that God is behind the abasement that takes place. We recall that many who read these laments are righteous survivors of the catastrophe of 586 BC. For them, Jeremiah's words are spiritual encouragement. It is very difficult to accept punishment when you are innocent of wrongdoing, but sometimes it must be endured.

C. Reassurances in Suffering (vv. 31-33)

31. For men are not cast off
> **by the Lord forever.**

It is always easier to endure present suffering if one knows that it is only temporary. Here Jeremiah provides assurance that being *cast off* is not a permanent situation. Its real purpose is to purge and purify a sinful nation. Comparisons may be made to surgical procedures. These are painful for the present, but the promise of healing enables one to look past the pain and discomfort.

32. Though he brings grief, he will show compassion,
> **so great is his unfailing love.**

The strong medicine of discipline may not taste good, but it is good for the recipient. The *compassion* of God leads him to bring a restoration that is based on the qualities that a thoughtful person should expect God to have. God is holy, and sin must be punished; but he is also prompted by his abundant mercy to do what is best for those who serve him. After all, "God so loved the world," not just one person or nation.

33. For he does not willingly bring affliction
> **or grief to the children of men.**

The word *willingly* is interesting, for in the Hebrew it literally says "from his heart." This also says much about the character of our God. He is not a sadist who finds joy in torture. The writer of Hebrews expresses a parallel thought when he says, "The Lord disciplines those he loves, and he punishes everyone he accepts as a son" (Hebrews 12:6).

D. Responses by God (vv. 55-58)

55. I called on your name, O Lord,
> **from the depths of the pit.**

The verses immediately before this section show that Jeremiah is recalling the time when he personally was the object of violence. See Jeremiah 38:6-13.

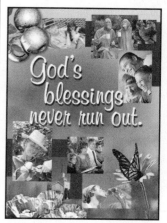

God's blessings never run out.

Visual for Lesson 10. *Use this montage to challenge your students to name an unending sequence of God's blessings.*

LOW COTTON

Being reared in an area where cotton was grown, I became familiar with the idea of someone being *in low cotton*. This spoke of the person who had to pick cotton in a field where the stalks were not very high, thus he or she had to stoop way over to pick the cotton. The reason for the low cotton was that the field was not producing well. But the cotton would grow higher in a good growing season, therefore the picker did not have to stoop so low. Thus to be *in high cotton* meant that times were good, but to be *in low cotton* meant times were tough.

We all go through tough times—times when it seems we are about as low as we can get. God's people are not exempt. Remember Daniel: he was in pretty low cotton when he was in the lion's den. Joseph was not much better off when he was cast into a pit by his brothers then sold into slavery.

But no matter how low we may go, the good news is we can never go so low that God cannot hear us or see us. We know we have victory through Jesus in the low times. The words of that great Easter hymn help us to recall this: "Low in the grave he lay, Jesus my Savior, waiting the coming day, Jesus my Lord. Up from the grave he arose!" Jesus knows what it means to be in low cotton, and he knows how to lift us out of that state.   —A. E. A.

56. You heard my plea: "Do not close your ears
    to my cry for relief."

This is Jeremiah's testimony: the Lord *heard* his prayer and his *cry* for help. The old saying, "Where there's life, there's hope!" comes to mind. Jeremiah is almost saying that since he is able to pray, then he is confident that he is heard.

57. You came near when I called you,
    and you said, "Do not fear."

Jeremiah recognizes answered prayer: *Do not fear.* The Christian today also has a blessed assurance in several ways. Centuries after Jeremiah, Jesus will promise to be with his followers to the end of the age (Matthew 28:20). Paul affirms that through Christ we conquer all things, no matter the peril (Romans 8:37-39). Look at those words again; they proclaim that there is hope even in pain.

58. O Lord, you took up my case;
    you redeemed my life.

The final response that is expressed by Jeremiah is the joy that the Lord has *redeemed* his *life*. The word *redeemed* is a special word for the Hebrew. It is the word for the relative who can avenge a death (Numbers 35:19), redeem a kinsman from slavery (Leviticus 25:47-49), retrieve a family inheritance that had been sold, or marry a widow of a close relative who has no sons. In this case it is Jeremiah's life that has been redeemed. This is a source of joy!

CONCLUSION

One preacher testifies that he often battled depression on Monday morning if things had not gone as desired on Sunday. The cure was simple: go to a local discount store! Merely being with people, many of whom he knew, would compel him to smile. Soon the depression would vanish. We are made for relationships!

To attempt to handle the trials of life alone is difficult for most people. One of the responsibilities of Christians is to help bear the burdens of others (Galatians 6:2). Even the apostle Paul expressed concern when he had to face his trials alone. When others deserted him, it was not pleasant (2 Timothy 4:16).

Some people will resist offers of help, but fellowship is important. If a person can conquer pride and actually ask for assistance, then everyone involved benefits. After all, it is not good for us to dwell alone!

Discovery Learning

This page contains an alternative lesson plan emphasizing learning activities. Classes desiring such student involvement will find these suggestions helpful. The next page is a reproducible activity page to further enhance discovery learning.

LEARNING GOALS

After participating in this lesson, each student will be able to:

1. Retell at least one expression of faith that resulted from the fall of Jerusalem.

2. Explain how experiences of deprivation and despair provide opportunities for strong expressions of hope.

3. Write a prayer to use for the next severe trial in his or her life.

INTO THE LESSON

As your students arrive, give each a copy of the following matching quiz. (The quiz is also printed in the student books.)

(In)Famous Disasters

___ 1. January 15, 588 BC   ___ 6. April 15, 1912
___ 2. August 24, AD 79   ___ 7. December 7, 1941
___ 3. November 1, 1755   ___ 8. September 11, 2001
___ 4. October 8, 1871   ___ 9. December 26, 2004
___ 5. May 31, 1889   ___ 10. August 30, 2005

A. Pearl Harbor attacked by military forces of Imperial Japan; B. the World Trade Center destroyed by terrorists; C. a tsunami hits Indonesia and 275,000 die; D. ancient Jerusalem is besieged by Babylonians; E. the Titanic sinks; F. Vesuvius erupts, destroying Pompeii, Italy; G. an earthquake, tsunami, and fires level Lisbon, Portugal, killing between 60,000 and 100,000; H. Hurricane Katrina floods New Orleans, Louisiana; I. the Great Chicago Fire destroys much of that city, leaving one-third of the inhabitants homeless; J. a flood in Johnstown, Pennsylvania, kills 2,200 people.

(*Answers: 1D, 2F, 3G, 4I, 5J, 6E, 7A, 8B, 9C, 10H*)

Correct quizzes together as a class. Then say, "Today's lesson deals with one of these infamous events: the siege of Jerusalem by the Babylonians and its aftermath." (You can also distribute the Cross Words for the Fall of Jerusalem exercise from the Reproducible Page for students to work on as they arrive.)

INTO THE WORD

To introduce your class to today's Bible texts, hand out copies of the quiz below (or direct your class to the student books, where the quiz also is found). Students may use their Bibles to find the answers in 2 Kings 25:1, 2, 5-7 and Lamentations 3:25-33, 55-58. Correct answers are indicated in parentheses.

Besieged by Babylon

1. Jerusalem was attacked in the ____ year of Zedekiah's reign. (*ninth*)

2. The Babylonians were led by King _____. (*Nebuchadnezzar*)

3. The Babylonians captured King Zedekiah in the plains of _____. (*Jericho*)

4. King Zedekiah was taken to Nebuchadnezzar at _____. (*Riblah*)

5. Zedekiah's ____ were put out. (*eyes*)

6. It is good to wait quietly for the ____ of the Lord. (*salvation*)

7. It is good to bear the _____ while young. (*yoke*)

8. Let the suffering man ____ alone in _____ and bury his face in the ____. (*sit, silence, dust*)

9. Let him offer his _____ to the one who would strike him. (*cheek*)

10. Men are not _____ off by the Lord forever. (*cast*)

11. Though he brings _____, he will show _____, so great is his _____ _____. (*grief, compassion, unfailing love*)

12. He does not willingly bring _____ or grief to the children of ____. (*affliction, men*)

13. Jeremiah called upon God from the depths of the _____. (*pit*)

14. God heard Jeremiah's _____. (*plea*)

15. Jeremiah requested that God not close his ears to Jeremiah's _____ for _____. (*cry, relief*)

16. God told Jeremiah, "Do not _____." (*fear*)

17. God redeemed Jeremiah's _____. (*life*)

When your students have completed their work, correct their quizzes together. This can be a small-group exercise. Use the answers as a springboard for your discussion of the lesson text.

INTO LIFE

Provide pencil and paper. Ask each student to use today's lesson as inspiration to write a brief statement or prayer of faith that he or she can share with others in a time of trial or despair. (This exercise is also printed in the student books.)

Cross Words for the Fall of Jerusalem

Read 2 Kings 25:1, 2, 5-7 and Lamentations 3:25-33, 55-58 to find the answers to this puzzle.

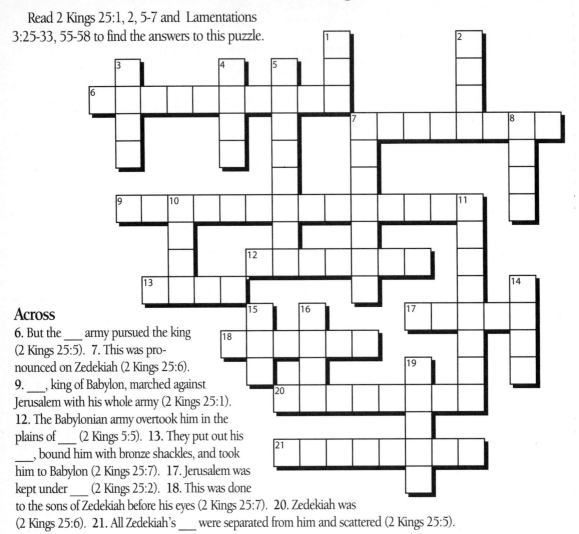

Across

6. But the ___ army pursued the king (2 Kings 25:5). **7.** This was pronounced on Zedekiah (2 Kings 25:6). **9.** ___, king of Babylon, marched against Jerusalem with his whole army (2 Kings 25:1). **12.** The Babylonian army overtook him in the plains of ___ (2 Kings 5:5). **13.** They put out his ___, bound him with bronze shackles, and took him to Babylon (2 Kings 25:7). **17.** Jerusalem was kept under ___ (2 Kings 25:2). **18.** This was done to the sons of Zedekiah before his eyes (2 Kings 25:7). **20.** Zedekiah was (2 Kings 25:6). **21.** All Zedekiah's ___ were separated from him and scattered (2 Kings 25:5).

Down

1. [The Lord] does not willingly bring affliction or grief to the children of ___ (Lamentations 3:33). **2.** It is good for a young man to bear the ___ when he is young (Lamentations 3:27). **3.** It is good to ___ quietly for the salvation of the Lord (Lamentations 3:26). **4.** The Lord is good to those whose ___ is in him (Lamentations 3:25). **5.** Let him be filled with ___ (Lamentations 3:30). **7.** Let [the yoked man] sit alone in ___, for the Lord has laid it on him (Lamentations 3:28). **8.** For men are not ___ off by the Lord forever (Lamentations 3:31). **10.** Let [the yoked man] ___ his face in the dust—there may yet be hope (Lamentations 3:29). **11.** O Lord, you took up my case; you ___ my life (Lamentations 3:58). **14.** You came ___ when I called you, and you said, "Do not fear" (Lamentations 3:57). **15.** I called on your name, O Lord, from the depths of the ___ (Lamentations 3:55) **16.** You heard my ___: "Do not close your ears to my cry for relief" (Lamentations 3:56) **19.** Though [the Lord] brings ___, he will show compassion, so great is his unfailing love (Lamentations 3:32).

COMMITTED TO TAKING RESPONSIBILITY

WHY TEACH THIS LESSON?

Despite God's grace, we continue to struggle with sin (compare Romans 7:14-25). For example, many are hooked on pornography. And before saying, "I would never," consider the plotlines and innuendos of today's afternoon soap operas and tonight's primetime lineup. The fantasies they inspire are no less lurid—or deceiving—than are those of airbrushed photos. Few (if any) are immune.

The starting point for repentance from this or any sin is four simple words: "It is my fault." Until we accept personal responsibility for our sins, we are just fooling ourselves. Today's lesson brings this truth back into focus.

INTRODUCTION

A. ALWAYS AN ALIBI

He was a very pleasant teenager. You could count on him to assist the elderly, to carry babies or diaper bags for young parents, or to do those extra tasks for teachers in the classrooms. His desire to please others and to be recognized by them did have one negative dimension: he sometimes followed troublemakers in their devious schemes in an attempt to please. When confronted with his wrong decisions, however, he always used the same alibi to explain his latest misdeed.

With tears—perhaps genuine tears—he would tell his story, and those who were in places of authority were ready to forgive him. His tale of suffering included the facts that his father had been killed in an accident when he was young, and he often had lived with his grandparents. This generation gap was just too big, and his life had been filled with woe. His grandparents just did not understand. They wanted to go to bed early, and he wanted to stay up late. They arose early in the morning, and he wanted to sleep until noon.

One day, however, he met a counselor who responded in a different way. After listening patiently, the counselor told the young man that if he was intelligent enough to blame his grandparents, then he was intelligent enough to accept the consequences for his actions. If he was not responsible for what he did, then there were institutions in the state where such people were sent.

This congenial young man had just encountered the doctrine of individual responsibility. He was learning that each person is responsible for what he or she does. As it says in Romans 14:12: "So then, each of us will give an account of himself to God." It is a lesson the ancient Judeans had to learn as well.

B. PROPHETS IN THE CONTEXT OF EXILE

Daniel, Jeremiah, and Ezekiel—each prophet had a definite place in God's plan for the final days and exile of the nation of Judah. Daniel's place of service was to the kings of Babylon, especially to King Nebuchadnezzar.

DEVOTIONAL READING:
PSALM 18:20-24
BACKGROUND SCRIPTURE:
EZEKIEL 18
PRINTED TEXT:
EZEKIEL 18:4, 20-23, 30-32

LESSON AIMS

After participating in this lesson, each student will be able to:

1. State the basic concepts of responsibility for Old Testament Israel as given by Ezekiel.

2. Compare and contrast Ezekiel 18:20 with Exodus 20:5; 34:7.

3. Eliminate one behavior in his or her life that profanes God's name.

Aug
12

KEY VERSE

I take no pleasure in the death of anyone, declares the Sovereign LORD. Repent and live!
—Ezekiel 18:32

LESSON 11 NOTES

Jeremiah's primary ministry was to the people in Judah and Jerusalem before the main exile began. In that role he offered hope in affirming that the Lord would bring his people back from Babylon after 70 years were completed (Jeremiah 29:10). That period is usually determined in one of two ways: it was approximately 70 years from the time that the first captives were taken (605 BC) until the time of the first return (538 BC); it was also about 70 years from the destruction of the temple (586 BC) to the dedication of the new temple some 20 years after the first wave of people returned from captivity (515 BC; Ezra 6:15).

Those in exile were given the prophet Ezekiel as a fellow captive. The exiles had attitudes that had to be corrected, and Ezekiel was the man to do it. We are fairly certain that Ezekiel was among the 10,000 captives taken from Judah and Jerusalem in 597 BC (2 Kings 24:14).

C. LESSON BACKGROUND

Like Jeremiah, Ezekiel was a priest (Jeremiah 1:1; Ezekiel 1:3). The first verse of Ezekiel's book is usually interpreted to mean that Ezekiel was 30 years old when he received a special revelation of God's glory. It was mid-summer of 593 BC, and Ezekiel had been a captive for about 4 years. Working the year 593 BC back to 605 BC means that Ezekiel was about 18 when he saw Daniel and his friends taken away by Nebuchadnezzar's army. Eight years later, Ezekiel himself was compelled to leave his home and his native land.

In his formative years, Ezekiel must have looked forward to reaching the age of 30. That's when he would qualify to function fully as one of the priests; the service of all priests and Levites began at that age (Numbers 4). The Lord had a ministry for Ezekiel starting at age 30, but it was not the one Ezekiel had anticipated. He was to be God's prophet in Babylonia, not a priest in Jerusalem.

One survey indicates that many people would not like to live next door to a conservative Christian. Ezekiel's neighbors may have thought about moving, for some of his actions were certainly strange. He spoke only when he had a message from God (Ezekiel 3:26, 27). The rest of the time he was silent and unable to give expression to the rebukes of his heart.

Ezekiel's strange actions and object-lesson sermons must have been the talk of the exilic community, and that is what God intended. Here are some examples. After Ezekiel's initial call, he played "toy soldier" with a tile or brick (Ezekiel 4:1, 2). He sketched an outline of the city of Jerusalem, and he portrayed the implements used in a siege against the city—that was not what the exiles wanted to happen to their beloved city! This was combined with his lying on one side or the other for over 14 months, and his occasional preaching against Jerusalem (Ezekiel 4:7).

During most of this time, Ezekiel's daily diet reflected the conditions of a city under siege: about eight ounces of bread from several grains (indicating the scarcity of food) and approximately two-thirds of a quart of water. These happened at the beginning of his prophetic ministry.

I. GOD'S PRINCIPLES (EZEKIEL 18:4, 20)

The lesson this week focuses on one aspect of Ezekiel's ministry: an attitude adjustment. It is a message that he gives after he completes a series of bizarre actions and before the next dated message of 591 BC (Ezekiel 20:1).

In the interval he declares that Jerusalem definitely will be destroyed (Ezekiel 14:12-23). The response of the people is normal: they look for someone to blame. The proverb that the people quote shifts the blame by stating that their fathers ate sour grapes, but it was the children's teeth that were set on edge (Ezekiel 18:2). The people in Judah, some 880 miles away, are using the same proverb to lament their own circumstances (Jeremiah 31:29, 30). It is a familiar expression that provides an alibi.

Ezekiel 18:1-3 indicates that God will not accept this alibi. Today many use alibis to blame society, parents, chromosomes, or overpowering compulsions for deviant behavior. The passage under consideration therefore flies directly against any culture that desires a no-fault society in which everyone is a victim and no one is to be blamed personally for anything. God is ready to pronounce profound truths that are ancient yet almost revolutionary in their implications.

A word of caution must also be sounded. While it is true that a person reaps what is sown (Galatians 6:7), this must not lead to a type of "retribution theology" that says that every tragedy in life is a direct, cause-and-effect payback for sin. The book of Job gives a rebuttal to applying the retribution concept universally. See also Luke 13:1-5.

A. ABSOLUTE #1: GOD IS SOVEREIGN (v. 4a)
4a. "For every living soul belongs to me, the father as well as the son—both alike belong to me.

The first absolute is that *every* person *belongs* to God. This is more than ownership; it is an expression of the sovereignty of God. He has the right and the power to work with both nations and individuals to accomplish his purposes.

A SENSE OF BELONGING
In a sitcom dialogue in 1984, comedian Bill Cosby reflected on the exasperations of fatherhood when he told his "son" on the show, "I am your father. I brought you into this world, and I can take you out." A son who receives this type of message from a father may not feel very wanted!

Our heavenly Father can say to us, "I brought you into this world." Psalm 139 reminds us that God was forming us even in our mother's womb. It is only because of the creative power of God that we exist. For those who have accepted Jesus, God has become Father in another sense: in our re-creation in Jesus Christ. God is both our creator for our physical birth and redeemer for our spiritual rebirth. He will also be with us when we leave this world. Revelation 2:10 exhorts us to be faithful, even to the point of death, and then we will receive the crown of life.

It is encouraging to realize that our Father in Heaven knows us personally, that he has created us and re-created us. And it is a source of hope to know that he will make us new again when we pass from this life. We anticipate the day when he will give us that new, glorified body in Heaven (2 Corinthians 5:4, 5). What can create any better sense of belonging than this?   —A. E. A.

B. ABSOLUTE #2: SIN BRINGS DEATH (vv. 4b, 20a)
4b. "The soul who sins is the one who will die."
20a. "The soul who sins is the one who will die.

The second absolute is that sin brings death. Ezekiel declares unequivocally that sin produces a punishment, and the punishment is death. This is true whether or not the individual acknowledges God. This same assertion is repeated in the New Testament in Romans 6:23. It is sad that so many live their lives in such a way that this absolute does not seem to be a controlling factor in what they do or say. There is a payday, and that is absolute truth.

The careful student will quickly observe that there are several verses between the two parallel statements. These verses contain three scenarios that represent

WHAT DO YOU THINK?

How does the knowledge that God owns your very being affect how you live? What changes do you need to make?

WHAT DO YOU THINK?

In what ways have you been guilty of circumventing or disavowing your personal sin? How have you made positive changes in this regard?

God's responses to three generations. The first (vv. 5-9) tells of an upright man who walks in righteousness, and the sentence is pronounced that he will live. The second setting is that of a son of the righteous man, and the son's life is full of wickedness. This time the judgment is that the son will surely die (vv. 10-13). The third illustration is of a righteous grandson who does all things well, and again it is stated that he will live. On each side of the three incidents, however, are the sobering words that death is the sentence for the sin.

C. ABSOLUTE #3: EACH IS RESPONSIBLE (v. 20b)

20b. The son will not share the guilt of the father, nor will the father share the guilt of the son. The righteousness of the righteous man will be credited to him, and the wickedness of the wicked will be charged against him.

The third absolute is that each individual's situation is his or her own. There is no generational transfer of either sin or *righteousness*. The consequences of just or unjust deeds may fall on others, but the *guilt* is nontransferable.

Those who are quoting the parable we see in Ezekiel 18:2 may be misusing Exodus 20:5 and its parallel in Deuteronomy 5:9. Those passages warn that God extends his punishment for a father's sin to the children down to "the third and fourth generation." But when harmonized with other Scripture, those passages simply indicate that God's wrath on the fathers is bound to have some indirect or collateral effect on their children.

II. GOD'S PROMISES (EZEKIEL 18:21-23, 30a)

Such sobering thoughts! What God desires is a response that will bring a person's life to where it should be.

A. GOD'S CONDITIONS (v. 21)

21. "But if a wicked man turns away from all the sins he has committed and keeps all my decrees and does what is just and right, he will surely live; he will not die.

The first two words of the verse show that God's promises are conditional. Two conditions are expressed: (1) the individual must turn from the present way of living, and (2) that person must begin doing *all* that God has prescribed. It is not just a matter of entering into a covenant relationship with God; it is also imperative that the terms of the covenant be kept. Jesus said the same thing in the Great Commission: Jesus' disciples are to be taught to obey everything that he has commanded (Matthew 28:20).

If a person does change *from all* the ways of wickedness, then the righteous should rejoice and provide encouragement. Sometimes it is tempting to want to get even, but forgiveness is to be extended instead. It is also true that the one who repents will do whatever he or she can to make restitution for wrongs.

B. GOD'S COMMITMENT (v. 22)

22. "None of the offenses he has committed will be remembered against him. Because of the righteous things he has done, he will live.

God promises to provide no reminders of sin. The person who has been forgiven probably remembers them all too well, and he or she does not need to be reminded. This is different from the individual who maintains a mental or written account of the shortcomings of someone else—in case he or she ever wants to use them in an attack. Love does not even think of such things (1 Corinthians 13:5). Such a list may be necessary when building a court case against someone, but the situation here is forgiveness, not litigation.

WHAT DO YOU THINK?

Though sin guilt is not passed from parent to child, the consequences may be. What are some ways that the consequences of one's sins may be visited upon another? Conversely, what are some ways that the consequences of one's holy actions may be a benefit to another?

WHAT DO YOU THINK?

God neither keeps a record of a Christian's sins nor remembers them. How do you use this fact to develop a godly nature?

C. GOD'S JOY (v. 23)

23. "Do I take any pleasure in the death of the wicked? declares the Sovereign LORD. Rather, am I not pleased when they turn from their ways and live?"

God does not find *pleasure* in giving sinners what they deserve. The implication is that he does find joy in forgiving so that *the wicked* may *live*. He is not willing that any should perish, but that all should repent and turn from their evil *ways* (2 Peter 3:9).

D. GOD'S JUDGMENT (v. 30a)

30a. "Therefore, O house of Israel, I will judge you, each one according to his ways, declares the Sovereign LORD.

God forgives all who repent. But here is the sobering reminder that *each* person will be judged *according to his ways*. It is not wise to try to take advantage of God's goodness. Peter warns that it is hard for the righteous to be saved (1 Peter 4:18). It has been stated that the gospel contains facts to be believed, commands to be obeyed, warnings to be heeded, and promises to be enjoyed. The words in the first part of this verse constitute a warning to be heeded.

TOUGH LOVE

Some organizations encourage parents to adopt a *tough love* policy in dealing with their children. The idea behind this is to take strong steps to counter aberrant behavior. There can be a need for this in marital relationships as well.

Dr. James Dobson says that one of the major culprits of relationship problems is disrespect of one person toward another. Whether it is a child's attitude toward a parent or one spouse toward the other, disrespect must be dealt with in a firm way. It can't be allowed to continue. It is not enjoyable or easy to practice tough love in this regard. But failure to do so will only make things worse—the cycle of bad behavior and disrespect will spiral downward, out of control.

God practices tough love with his children. The discipline he exerts (Hebrews 12:6-11) is not pleasurable at the time for either the giver or the receiver. But God knows it is a necessary part of the transformation of his children. Parents may say to their children when disciplining them, "This hurts me more than it hurts you." Children never quite understand that until they become the ones who have to discipline their own children.

We do well to remember this when God has to discipline us. He finds no pleasure in it. It even pains him to do so, but in the end it is for the best. It is tough redemptive love.   —A. E. A.

III. GOD'S PLEADINGS (EZEKIEL 18:30b-32)

God expects action and response. He is clear about what those should involve.

A. DECIDE ABOUT SIN (v. 30b)

30b. "Repent! Turn away from all your offenses; then sin will not be your downfall.

The apostle Peter makes a similar statement on the occasion of his healing the lame man in the temple. His message after the healing includes the challenge that his audience repent and turn to God so that their sins could be wiped out. Only then would times of refreshing come over them (Acts 3:19).

It is important to notice that God permits freedom of choice. That is one of the main thrusts of this lesson—that each person is to take responsibility for his or her own eternal destiny. That has ever been God's message. In the Garden of Eden it was by freewill choice that the first man and woman ate of the forbidden

---

HOW TO SAY IT

Babylon. BAB-uh-lun.
Babylonia. Bab-ih-LOW-nee-uh.
Corinthians. Ko-RIN-thee-unz
   (TH as in THIN).
Ezekiel. Ee-ZEEK-ee-ul or Ee-
   ZEEK-yul.
Ezra. EZ-ruh.
Jeremiah. Jair-uh-MY-uh.
Jerusalem. Juh-ROO-suh-lem.
Nebuchadnezzar. NEB-yuh-kud-
   NEZ-er.

WHAT DO YOU THINK?

Repentance leads to a restored relationship with God. What other benefits of repentance have you noticed in your life?

Visual for Lesson 11. *Point to this visual as you challenge your students to name a time when God granted them a new start after they repented.*

fruit. After Israel conquered Canaan, it was Joshua's challenge to the nation to "Choose for yourselves this day whom you will serve" (Joshua 24:15). The person who hears the conditions of the gospel (John 3:16; Acts 2:38; etc.) and does not respond cannot blame others. Each person must decide about sin.

B. DISCARD SIN (v. 31a)

31a. "Rid yourselves of all the offenses you have committed.

The discarding of sinful deeds must follow repentance from sin. No one can claim repentance of stealing a car if he or she continues to drive it without the rightful owner's consent!

C. DESIRE A NEW HEART (v. 31b)

31b. "And get a new heart and a new spirit. Why will you die, O house of Israel?

The sins to be discarded may include attitudes and language that are not pleasing to God. Such things are sometimes considered "little" sins, but the command to discard includes any sinful practice. Sin in any form is not acceptable.

The way to rid oneself of sin is to develop *a new heart* that will look on life with a new perspective. The writer of Hebrews affirms that without holiness no one will see God (Hebrews 12:14; compare Matthew 5:8). Therefore everything one does will be centered on the fact that God is holy. Having a new perspective means changing the way that a person thinks about life, and this is the new heart that God demands. It also involves the mind, for Jesus stated that the first commandment is to love God with all the heart, soul, and mind (Matthew 22:37).

D. DELIGHT IN LIFE (v. 32)

32. "For I take no pleasure in the death of anyone, declares the Sovereign LORD. Repent and live!"

Again we see that *God* has *no pleasure in the death of* any person (see v. 23). This is confirmed by what is called the Golden Text of the Bible, John 3:16. The verse states that God so loved that he gave his Son. The purposes are that mankind may believe and no one would have to perish. God desires that everyone choose to *live* for him.

The contrast in this verse is vivid: life or death. The challenge of the verse is the heart of the lesson: being committed to taking responsibility for one's spiritual destiny. It is a personal choice, and it cannot be delegated.

CONCLUSION

Today's lesson encourages everyone to accept responsibility for personal actions. Each should acknowledge that there are basic principles that God has set forth concerning the consequences of sin. We should be prepared, however, for a certain reaction from those confronted with their wrong deeds: anger.

This kind of anger often is directed toward the person who is trying to provide the correction. If a person is told that homosexuality is sin, one response is to point fingers at the messenger. Members of a congregation may be reminded that the ministries of the church need greater financial support; a person in the church who reacts with anger probably is guilty of inadequate giving. Yet anger does not bring about the righteous life that God desires (James 1:20). That principle is true for nations, churches, or individuals.

Sin—it produces many consequences in our lives. Yet God is willing to forgive. But before a person may be right *with* God he or she must repent and turn *to* God.

Discovery Learning

This page contains an alternative lesson plan emphasizing learning activities. Classes desiring such student involvement will find these suggestions helpful. The next page is a reproducible activity page to further enhance discovery learning.

LEARNING GOALS

After this lesson, each student will be able to:

1. State the basic concepts of responsibility for Old Testament Israel as given by Ezekiel.

2. Compare and contrast Ezekiel 18:20 with Exodus 20:5; 34:7.

3. Eliminate one behavior in his or her life that profanes God's name.

INTO THE LESSON

To begin class, share these creative excuses with your students, or substitute some that you have heard (or used!). (Examples are printed in the student books.)

I can't come in to work; it's Friday the thirteenth, and I'm really superstitious. I won't be in to work today because my dog has to have emergency cataract surgery. I didn't meet the deadline because I couldn't find matching socks. I'm locked in my car, and I have to go to the dealership so they can get me out. There was a bomb scare at my office building, and I couldn't call the personnel manager for my phone interview. I can't help it, officer; someone hypnotized me to park illegally.

Next, ask your students to share some excuses they have heard or used. After you have heard several examples, tell your students that today's lesson deals with taking responsibility for our behavior and not making excuses to God. (Option: distribute the God's Desire for Us exercise from the Reproducible Page for students to work on as they arrive.)

INTO THE WORD

Develop a mini-lecture from the Lesson Background to introduce today's text. After this introduction, divide your class into three small groups of three to five students each. For larger classes create additional groups in multiples of three. Each group will cover one section of the lesson text. Distribute the following instructions, along with pencil and paper (or direct attention to the student book). Allow several minutes for each group to complete its activity.

Group #1. Read Ezekiel 18:4, 20. Identify three absolute principles stated by God in these verses. For each principle write down at least one excuse that is invalidated by that principle.

Group #2. Read Ezekiel 18:20-23, 30a. Compare verse 20 with Exodus 34:6, 7. How can both passages be true? Identify three promises that God offers to the repentant sinner in Ezekiel 18:21-23, 30a. Also identify any conditions connected with those promises. What reason does God give for offering the promises?

Group #3. Read Ezekiel 18:30-32. List the steps God required for the ancient Israelite to move from spiritual death to life and to avoid God's judgment. Explain what was involved in each step and why it was essential.

When your groups have completed their work, discuss their findings. Be sure to address the implications for evangelism, missions, and preaching today.

INTO LIFE

Assign one of the following scenarios to each group from the previous exercise. Each team is to write a brief plan of action. The plans will use today's text to challenge the recipient(s) to take responsibility for personal actions and to allow God to renew a relationship with him.

Scenario #1. Kim and her two young children occasionally attend worship services at your church. She wants her boy and girl to have some religious training, since she never received any from her own parents. Kim has never been married but currently lives with her boyfriend. He is not the father of her children. She blames her parents for her situation because they showed her little affection as a child. What would you say to help her?

Scenario #2. Dave is despondent about his lifestyle. He has been in and out of treatment centers for alcohol abuse but can't kick the habit for good. Dave's friends and coworkers try to encourage him to stay sober but he blames them for his addiction because they drink socially. Now he's come to your church for help. What can you do for him?

Scenario #3. Bill and Stacy have a troubled marriage. They fight often and have separated on several occasions. They have no children. Stacy blames Bill for not wanting a family, for being gone from home too often, and for failing to meet her emotional needs. Bill blames Stacy for spending too much money so that he has to work a second job to pay the bills. How can you help this troubled couple?

God's Desire For Us

Fill in the missing words from Ezekiel 18:4, 20-23, 30-32. Then discover the message in the vertical boxes!

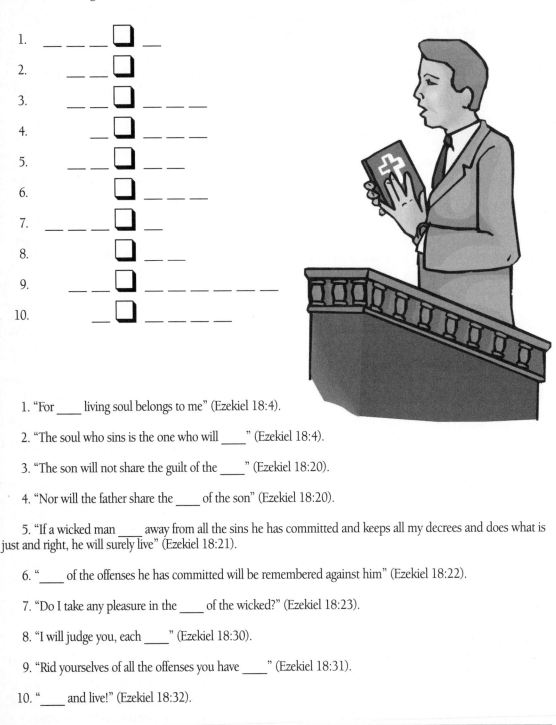

1. ___ ___ ___ □ ___

2. ___ ___ □

3. ___ ___ □ ___ ___

4. ___ □ ___ ___ ___

5. ___ ___ □ ___ ___

6. □ ___ ___ ___

7. ___ ___ ___ □ ___

8. □ ___ ___

9. ___ ___ □ ___ ___ ___ ___ ___

10. ___ □ ___ ___ ___

1. "For ____ living soul belongs to me" (Ezekiel 18:4).

2. "The soul who sins is the one who will ____" (Ezekiel 18:4).

3. "The son will not share the guilt of the ____" (Ezekiel 18:20).

4. "Nor will the father share the ____ of the son" (Ezekiel 18:20).

5. "If a wicked man ____ away from all the sins he has committed and keeps all my decrees and does what is just and right, he will surely live" (Ezekiel 18:21).

6. "____ of the offenses he has committed will be remembered against him" (Ezekiel 18:22).

7. "Do I take any pleasure in the ____ of the wicked?" (Ezekiel 18:23).

8. "I will judge you, each ____" (Ezekiel 18:30).

9. "Rid yourselves of all the offenses you have ____" (Ezekiel 18:31).

10. "____ and live!" (Ezekiel 18:32).

COMMITTED TO RETURNING TO GOD

WHY TEACH THIS LESSON?

Bryant was a junkie, a crack-head, committed wholeheartedly to one thing: getting high. Lisa fed her addiction to heroin by selling her body to men. Manuel was a gang leader with blood on his hands. What do they have in common? Christ's love touched them, transforming them, and they became committed to returning to God.

Your students may think, "I have done nothing like that! Why do I need to 'return' to God?" Because sin is sin. The "I deserve to relax" evening of drunkenness, the lustful gaze at a lingerie-clad woman, the uncontrolled rage at the children—in God's eyes, these are sins that call for repentance. The penalty for sin, any sin, is death (Romans 6:23; compare James 2:10).

The powerful message of today's lesson is that it is never too late. You are never too far. Your students can always return to God. Just as God remained faithful to Israel through years of disobedience and exile, he has never abandoned any of us. This lesson will help your students come near to God. When that happens, he will come near to them (James 4:8).

INTRODUCTION

A. TURNING TAKES EFFORT

At the time I learned to drive, one of the vehicles that my family owned was a 1957 Chevrolet. It had a gearshift on the steering column and no power steering. Needless to say, turning the wheel required what seemed at times to be a Herculean effort. Both hands were needed, yet there were times when one hand had to do because the other had to be free to shift gears.

What a far cry from the convenience of today's vehicles! Power steering now allows one to negotiate hairpin turns while sipping hot coffee or talking on a cell phone. (Some drivers, no doubt, could replace the *or* in the previous sentence with *and*!)

Today's text from the prophet Zechariah focuses on the idea of turning from sin to the Lord. That is often easier said than done. While we may intend to make such a turn, there may be a variety of factors (peer pressure, family members, pleasures of the world, intellectual doubts, etc.) that serve as unseen hands trying to steer us in the opposite direction.

For those who earnestly seek to turn to him, however, the Lord provides encouragement. Through his Word, his Spirit, and the support of those who have already learned how to negotiate the turn, he gives us the power steering needed to defeat the efforts of those who would keep us on the same dead-end road.

The words of today's text are still the Lord's promise: "Return to me . . . and I will return to you" (Zechariah 1:3).

DEVOTIONAL READING:
ISAIAH 12
BACKGROUND SCRIPTURE:
ZECHARIAH 1:1-6; 7:8-14; 8:16-23
PRINTED TEXT:
ZECHARIAH 1:1-6; 7:8-14

LESSON AIMS

After participating in this lesson, each student will be able to:

1. Cite at least one attitude and one behavior that the postexilic Judeans needed to eliminate from their lives in order to receive God's favor.

2. Name at least one attitude and one behavior that hinder people from having God's favor today.

3. Eliminate one attitude and one behavior that hinder his or her fellowship with God.

KEY VERSE

This is what the LORD Almighty says: "Return to me," declares the LORD Almighty, "and I will return to you," says the LORD Almighty.
—Zechariah 1:3

Aug
19

LESSON 12 NOTES

B. LESSON BACKGROUND

Zechariah was a postexilic prophet. This means he prophesied after the Babylonian exile had occurred and after God's people had been allowed to return home as a result of the decree of King Cyrus of Persia (2 Chronicles 36:22, 23). That journey home took place in the year 538 BC.

Those who returned to Judah were initially excited to be home—back in the land that God had promised would be the place where Abraham's descendants would live. One of the first orders of business was to rebuild the temple. This was an essential part of Cyrus's decree: "The Lord God, the God of heaven . . . has appointed me to build a temple for him at Jerusalem" (Ezra 1:2).

The work proceeded smoothly at first. Within two years of their arrival, the people had completed the foundation of the new structure. The Bible records the mixed emotions that were expressed at the dedication of the foundation. Many shouted with joy at this significant step; however, those who could remember the grandeur of Solomon's temple and who recognized that this new temple would in no way measure up to it began to weep (Ezra 3:12, 13).

Perhaps the disparity in response to the rebuilding began to dampen enthusiasm to complete the project. Ezra 4:1-5 notes the rise of opposition from without; because of this, "The work on the house of God in Jerusalem came to a standstill until the second year of the reign of Darius king of Persia" (Ezra 4:24). That was 520 BC. Thus from approximately 536 to 520 BC (16 years), the temple of the Lord lay unfinished—a sad witness to a discouraged people.

I. LORD'S CALL TO REPENTANCE (ZECHARIAH 1:1-6)

The Lord raised up two prophets, namely Haggai and Zechariah, in about 520 BC to awaken the people out of their apathy and spur them on to finish what they had begun. Both prophets are mentioned in Ezra 5:1. We see the impact of their ministries in Ezra 5:2: the leaders of God's people at this time (Zerubbabel and Jeshua, also called Joshua) "set to work to rebuild the house of God."

A. APPEAL BY WORDS (vv. 1-3)

1. In the eighth month of the second year of Darius, the word of the LORD came to the prophet Zechariah son of Berekiah, the son of Iddo.

The second year of Darius is also mentioned in Ezra 4:24. As noted previously, this is 520 BC. This particular Darius is Darius Hystaspes, who ruled the Persian Empire from 522 to 486 BC.

The phrases *in the eighth month . . . the word of the Lord came* are standard language in prophetic books. They indicate the source of the prophet's message. As 2 Peter 1:21 states, "Prophecy never had its origin in the will of man, but men spoke from God as they were carried along by the Holy Spirit."

2. "The LORD was very angry with your forefathers.

Many today are quick to describe God's love in glowing terms. At the same time, they are fearful of mentioning his wrath lest someone be offended. Not Zechariah! He wastes no time in getting right to the point: *The Lord was very angry with your forefathers.*

The people addressed by Zechariah are 66 years removed from the time when the Babylonian captivity took place in 586 BC. Some had experienced the devastation of the downfall of Jerusalem and the burning of the temple, but many had not. Yet God was displeased not only with that generation but with previous generations as well. Those generations had rejected his call to repentance as issued through his prophets.

God's anger is not something that erupts suddenly as a fit of rage. Rather, it is his holy hostility toward sin. He had warned his people repeatedly of this and of the bitter consequences they would face. But, as the succeeding verses of our text show, they refused to listen.

3. "Therefore tell the people: This is what the LORD Almighty says: 'Return to me,' declares the LORD Almighty, 'and I will return to you,' says the LORD Almighty.

The Lord's appeal to his people is remarkably simple: *Return to me, . . . and I will return to you.* James 4:8 issues a similar call: "Come near to God and he will come near to you." God's people had returned to the land some 18 years earlier, in 538 BC. But have they returned to the Lord? The Lord gives us the freedom of choice—a truth reflected in the various "whoever" and "anyone" passages of the Bible (John 3:16; Romans 10:11; Revelation 22:17).

B. APPEAL BY EXAMPLE (vv. 4-6a)

4. "Do not be like your forefathers, to whom the earlier prophets proclaimed: This is what the LORD Almighty says: 'Turn from your evil ways and your evil practices.' But they would not listen or pay attention to me, declares the LORD.

Zechariah's reference to *the earlier prophets* could include eighth-century BC prophets such as Amos, Hosea, and Micah. These men of God came from a variety of backgrounds, and God used a variety of circumstances to speak through them. All of them, however, conveyed essentially the same message, prefaced with the authoritative words *This is what the LORD Almighty says.* Sadly, the response to the prophets' appeals was also essentially the same: *They would not listen or pay attention.*

5. "Where are your forefathers now? And the prophets, do they live forever?

The answers to these questions are obvious. Both the *forefathers* and *the prophets* (that is, the audience and the messengers of the Lord who addressed them) are but a memory in Zechariah's day. They have passed from the scene of history. True, the prophets were holy men of God (2 Peter 1:21), but they were subject to death as is every human being (Hebrews 9:27).

6a. "But did not my words and my decrees, which I commanded my servants the prophets, overtake your forefathers?

Because the prophets spoke as servants of the Lord and proclaimed his *words* and his *decrees*, their message cannot die (and has not died to this day). The prophets' enemies may silence the messengers, but any effort to stifle or squelch their message is doomed to fail.

Zechariah asks, concerning the Lord's words and statutes, did they not *overtake your fathers?* The word *overtake* carries the sense of "catching up with" those who had neglected the message. The message held them accountable. A person can run from God's Word, but he or she cannot hide!

C. APPLICATION TO LIFE (v. 6b)

6b. "Then they repented and said, 'The LORD Almighty has done to us what our ways and practices deserve, just as he determined to do.'"

The word *they* in this verse gives us a slight challenge: to whom does it refer? The way that the NIV translators have chosen to punctuate this verse suggests that Zechariah is describing how the forefathers responded to the prophets' appeal. But different punctuation would suggest that Zechariah is recording his contemporaries' repentance before the Lord. Since Zechariah describes how the prophets' words "overtook" the people's fathers (first half of v. 6), it appears that this text relates the response of Zechariah's audience.

WHAT DO YOU THINK?

What are some specific things you need to do to conform your thoughts and actions to God's standards?

Some of these individuals, now listening to Zechariah, had witnessed the fall of Jerusalem. They recall the anguish of being forced to travel to a pagan land. They do not want to repeat the mistakes of the previous generation(s). They agree that they are "guilty as charged." They deserved the Lord's judgment.

The road to restoration lies in conforming our thinking and acting to God's standards, not in trying to create excuses for ourselves or lowering those standards. Like the prodigal son, we must determine to say to our Father, "I have sinned against heaven and against you" (Luke 15:18).

II. LORD'S CALL TO ACTION (ZECHARIAH 7:8-14)

According to Zechariah 7:1, the message in verses 8-14 comes to the prophet in the "fourth year of King Darius, . . . on the fourth day of the ninth month." This is a little over two years after the message that constitutes the first part of our printed text. This fourth year is thus 518 BC.

The seventh chapter begins by describing a delegation of men sent to ask the priests and the prophets about whether they should continue to "mourn and fast in the fifth month" as they had been doing "for so many years" (7:3).In verse 4, Zechariah notes, "Then the word of the Lord Almighty came to me." Though many priests and prophets are present at this time, only Zechariah is empowered to reply to the question they raise.

Because the temple in Jerusalem had been ravaged by the Babylonians in the fifth month of the nineteenth year of Nebuchadnezzar of Babylon (2 Kings 25:8, 9), some Jews had begun a fast in that month to commemorate the tragic event. According to Zechariah 7:5, that fast had been going on for nearly 70 years—in other words, ever since the city had fallen in 586 BC.

In response, Zechariah rebukes the people for their shallow acts of worship. They are shallow because those acts have not been accompanied by lives devoted to the principles that God wants to see demonstrated by his covenant people.

A. WHAT TO DO (vv. 8, 9)
8. And the word of the LORD came again to Zechariah.

According to verse 4, *the word of the Lord came . . . to Zechariah* earlier. A series of questions from the prophet in verses 5-7 follows. Perhaps Zechariah pauses to give the people time to reflect on those questions before speaking once again the Lord's message.

9. "This is what the LORD Almighty says: 'Administer true justice; show mercy and compassion to one another.

The commands given here are in keeping with the kind of conduct that the Lord has always required of his people. *Justice* may be considered to be treating people the way God would treat them. The ideals of *mercy and compassion* are an essential part of this.

B. WHAT NOT TO DO (v. 10)
10. "'Do not oppress the widow or the fatherless, the alien or the poor. In your hearts do not think evil of each other.'

This verse moves from the more abstract ideals of verse 9 to specific groups who need more than high ideals—they need to see the actions of flesh and blood put on those ideals! These groups include *the widow, the fatherless, the alien,* and *the poor.* The individuals in these groups are frequently taken advantage of because their circumstances leave them vulnerable. Churches today often have opportunities to exhibit the love of Jesus by initiating ministries to those who would

HOW TO SAY IT

Berekiah. Bair-uh-KYE-uh.

Cyrus. SIGH-russ.

Darius Hystaspes. Duh-RYE-us Hiss-TAS-pus.

Ezekiel. Ee-ZEEK-ee-ul or Ee-ZEEK-yul.

Haggai. HAG-eye or HAG-ay-eye.

Hosea. Ho-ZAY-uh.

Micah. MY-kuh.

Nebuchadnezzar. NEB-yuh-kud-NEZ-er.

Persia. PER-zhuh.

Zechariah. ZEK-uh-RYE-uh.

Zerubbabel. Zeh-RUB-uh-bul.

be considered, in Jesus' words, "the least of these" (Matthew 25:40, 45; see also James 1:27).

Notice that this verse also addresses our inner motives: *In your hearts do not think evil of each other.* Sometimes people view the Old Testament as concerned more with outward actions to the minimization of one's thoughts and motives. That is clearly not the case, as is apparent in the Tenth Commandment (covetousness). Also, we think of passages such as Proverbs 4:23: "Above all else, guard your heart, for it is the wellspring of life."

OF DOS AND DON'TS

As I write these words, we are just two weeks removed from Hurricane Katrina, which devastated the gulf coast of the United States in late August 2005. One area greatly affected was the city of New Orleans. Since that city is below sea level, levees had been built to protect it from flooding. But the levees failed, and most of the city was under water. Since New Orleans is noted for a party atmosphere and unholy events, there were some Christians quick to say that this was God's judgment on that city. They said that the city was suffering punishment for violating God's *don'ts.* But the number who said this was low in relation to the number of Christians who responded by providing various kinds of assistance to the evacuees.

Sometimes Christianity is known as a religion that focuses primarily on *don'ts.* The *don'ts* are indeed important—for example, the Ten Commandments are primarily worded that way. But the *dos* are important too!

The best way to counteract the charge of being primarily a religion of negative rules, a religion of *don'ts,* is to do positive things by showing mercy and compassion. Rick Rusaw and Eric Swanson have the right idea: "Externally focused churches have the advantage of deploying people into the community where they can be church to people through their love and service. Their light is not hidden under a bushel" (*The Externally Focused Church,* page 28).   —A. E. A.

C. PEOPLE'S DECISION (vv. 11, 12)

11. "But they refused to pay attention; stubbornly they turned their backs and stopped up their ears.

The *they* in this verse apparently refers to the former generations who were exposed to the pleas of the "earlier prophets" (7:7, 12), mentioned previously in Zechariah 1:4. What stubbornness the people had exhibited!

12. "They made their hearts as hard as flint and would not listen to the law or to the words that the LORD Almighty had sent by his Spirit through the earlier prophets. So the LORD Almighty was very angry.

Flint is an extremely *hard* material. Note the language used in Ezekiel 3:9, where God tells that prophet, "I will make your forehead like the hardest stone, harder than flint. Do not be afraid of them or terrified by them, though they are a rebellious house."

The *law* and the *prophets* are the two primary vehicles of revelation during the Old Testament period. The two terms came to be used in such a way as to designate the equivalent of the entire Old Testament (Luke 16:16; John 1:45; Romans 3:21). The influence of God's *Spirit* on the prophets is also noted (see also Nehemiah 9:30). The Lord's *angry* response to the people's stubbornness is the same as his response in Zechariah 1:2.

D. LORD'S DISCIPLINE (vv. 13, 14)

13. "'When I called, they did not listen; so when they called, I would not listen,' says the LORD Almighty.

WHAT DO YOU THINK?

The heart is considered the seat of the emotions. What steps have you taken to develop a proper heart for God and his kingdom? What steps do you yet need to take?

Visual for Lesson 12. *Use this visual as a discussion starter by asking, "What are some ways that people intentionally move away from God?"*

WHAT DO YOU THINK?

What modern applications can we see in Zechariah 7:12?

WHAT DO YOU THINK?

What are some modern examples of crying out to God as a last resort? Do you think God ever honors those cries? Why, or why not?

Earlier we read the Lord's invitation in Zechariah 1:3: "Return to me, . . . and I will return to you." The verse before us states the negative side of this truth: God will not respond if we repeatedly ignore his appeals or merely cry out to him only as a last resort.

14. *"'I scattered them with a whirlwind among all the nations, where they were strangers. The land was left so desolate behind them that no one would come or go. This is how they made the pleasant land desolate.'"*

This verse describes the consequences of the people's refusal to heed the Lord's message through his prophets. The impact on God's people was that they were *scattered . . . among all the nations.* As Adam and Eve had been evicted from their paradise in Eden, God's people were ousted from their home in fulfillment of his word—a warning issued since the time of Moses (Leviticus 26:27-35; Deuteronomy 28:36, 37).

The impact on *the land* is also noted. The land that had once flowed with milk and honey is here described as *desolate* and as a place where *no one would come or go.* In other words, normal activities could not be carried out because of the extent of the devastation. Tragic as these circumstances were, God's people had no one to blame but themselves. They—God's chosen people—were responsible for making the pleasant land desolate.

LOSING (THE) GROUND

Because of sin, the ancient Israelites ended up losing the very ground that God had given them, the promised land. Losing this ground in a physical sense was preceded by losing it spiritually. Instead of growing in obedience to God, the Israelites rebelled against his will. Instead of being a pure and holy people, they became defiled by the nations around them.

This is part of a disturbing pattern. The Roman Empire, for example, also "lost it all." A few reasons cited for the fall of this great empire include political corruption, urban decay, increased military spending at the expense of other vital needs, and a decline in morals. Rome's downfall seems to have been predicted in Daniel 2:33, 34.

It is easy to take pride in our own nation. But pride leads to a fall. We do well to remember that, "Righteousness exalts a nation, but sin is a disgrace to any people" (Proverbs 14:34). Failure to practice righteousness can still lead nations into "losing ground" physically. For the individual, failure to practice righteousness may also mean losing the promised land of Heaven.   —A. E. A.

PRAYER

Father, thank you for the opportunity to leave the life of sin and return to you. We are so unworthy of such an opportunity, yet in your grace you have opened up a way through your Son, Jesus. Help us to see that whatever we give up in the process of returning to you will be far, far outweighed by what you have in store for us. In Jesus' name, amen.

CONCLUSION

America's civil war ended in 1865. President Abraham Lincoln faced a particularly explosive issue: what was to be done with the southern states that had seceded from the Union to form the Confederacy? Some demanded a stiff punishment for what they considered treason against the United States. Lincoln, however, advocated a much more conciliatory policy. His eloquent response to the matter of how to treat the states in question was that it would be "as if they had never left."

Today's lesson has called attention to God's gracious invitation to forsake sinful ways and return to him. He has done all he can do to remove whatever obstacles exist. The most daunting obstacle, sin, has been addressed at the cross through God's provision of his Son, Jesus, as an atoning sacrifice. If we choose to accept that sacrifice and respond to the Father's invitation to come home, he will forgive us completely and make us new creatures.

It will indeed be as if we had never left.

THOUGHT TO REMEMBER

God is now—and always has been—ready for you to return.

Discovery Learning

This page contains an alternative lesson plan emphasizing learning activities. Classes desiring such student involvement will find these suggestions helpful. The next page is a reproducible activity page to further enhance discovery learning.

LEARNING GOALS

After this lesson, each student should be able to:

1. Cite at least one attitude and one behavior that the postexilic Judeans needed to eliminate from their lives in order to receive God's favor.

2. Name at least one attitude and one behavior that hinder people from having God's favor today.

3. Eliminate one attitude and one behavior that hinder his or her fellowship with God.

INTO THE LESSON

Give to each student a copy of the following Things to Eliminate quiz (or direct your students' attention to the quiz in the student book, if you're using those). Ask students to match the things they would eliminate with solutions.

1. To put out a fire, eliminate ___.
2. To avoid heartburn, eliminate ___.
3. To overcome insomnia, eliminate ___.
4. To avoid a broken leg, eliminate ___.
5. To avoid excessive debt, eliminate ___.
6. To avoid verbosity, eliminate ___.
7. To finish a task, eliminate ___.
8. To reduce the threat of heart disease, eliminate __.

A. nonessential words; B. oxygen; C. worries that fill your mind; D. spicy foods. E. credit cards; F. ice on the sidewalk; G. procrastination; H. smoking. (*Answers: 1B, 2D, 3C, 4F, 5E, 6A, 7G, 8H*)

Grade the quizzes together. Then tell your class that this lesson deals with eliminating barriers that keep us separated from God.

INTO THE WORD

Use the Lesson Background to introduce today's lesson text, then have two students read the text aloud. One will read Zechariah 1:1-6; the other will read Zechariah 7:8-14.

Next, divide your class into pairs. Half the pairs will study the text from Zechariah 1; the other half will study the text from Zechariah 7. Give each pair a copy of one set of instructions below (or tell them to turn to their student books, if you're using those, to find the exercise).

Exercise #1: The Lord's Call to Repentance. With your partner, reread Zechariah 1:1-6. Then answer the following questions: *1.* Why had God been displeased with their ancestors? *2.* What positive offer did God make to the Judeans of Zechariah's day, and how had the people responded to previous offers (see Ezekiel 18:21-23)? *3.* What two reasons did God give the Judeans for not imitating their ancestors but for obeying him?

Exercise #2: The Lord's Call to Action. With your partner, reread Zechariah 7:8-14. Then answer the following questions: *1.* What three things were the Judeans to do to demonstrate the sincerity of their repentance? *2.* What acts and attitudes were the Judeans to eliminate from their lives, and how were these related to the positive actions God commanded them to do? *3.* What was the reaction of the people to this call for repentance in times past, and what is significant about their rejection of both the law and the prophets? *4.* How did God respond to their hard hearts, and what lesson should the Judeans in Zechariah's day have learned from their history? *5.* What lesson should we learn from these events?

When your pairs complete their exercises, discuss their findings. Emphasize that God's call to repentance involves a call to action as well.

INTO LIFE

Join your pairs together to make groups of four. Instruct each group to read Ephesians 5 and brainstorm some common negative attitudes and behaviors that hinder people from experiencing the full joy of being a Christian. Give each group pencil and paper to record their results (or refer to this activity in the student books, if you're using those). When groups have had sufficient time to develop lists of negatives, ask volunteers to share their lists. Write examples on the board.

Next, ask your groups to brainstorm some scriptural attitudes and behaviors that are antidotes to these negatives, again referring to Ephesians 5 for ideas. When they have assembled lists, call for volunteers once more. List their solutions on the board, parallel to the negatives.

Challenge each student to find one (or more) negative attitude or behavior from the list that is a particular problem to him or her. Pray for your students to seek to eliminate those negatives by practicing the biblical positives you have discussed today. (Option: distribute copies of the Eliminate the Negative, Accentuate the Positive exercise from the Reproducible Page as take-home work.)

Eliminate the Negative,
Accentuate the Positive

From Galatians 5:19-23 and Colossians 3:5-10, 12-14, list in the left-hand column the negative attitudes and behaviors we should eliminate. Then list on the right the positive attitudes and behaviors we should accentuate. Where possible, draw a line between a negative and the positive that replaces it.

Negative Attitudes and Behaviors

_____

_____

_____

_____

_____

_____

_____

_____

Positive Attitudes and Behaviors

_____

_____

_____

_____

_____

_____

_____

_____

COMMITTED TO DOING RIGHT

WHY TEACH THIS LESSON?

We all live on a fallen and wounded planet. One result of the fall is an inherent unfairness to life. Your students have seen righteous and holy people suffer from cancer, fail in a business, or lose a child. They have also seen people who mocked God's name get rich and live full and healthy lives. No doubt many have wondered (though they may not admit it aloud) whether God is paying attention.

Some folks frame the matter very directly. In a world where innocent children get AIDS and hurricanes devastate cities, they assert, "If God is good, he cannot be all-powerful; if God is all-powerful, then he cannot be good." Your students may have heard that statement and struggled to respond. Today, Malachi will help your students frame a biblical response.

INTRODUCTION

A. "NOW GO DO THE RIGHT THING"

Laura Schlesinger's radio program has become one of the most well known and most listened to in the highly competitive world of talk radio. Her no-nonsense approach, characterized by a strong emphasis on Judeo-Christian values, has gained her a significant following. At the end of each hour of her broadcast, "Dr. Laura" concludes with this brief but compelling advice: "Now go do the right thing." Such counsel seems simple. Yet there is no question that if listeners really took it to heart and applied it to their circumstances, they would avoid numerous heartaches and tensions. Perhaps Dr. Laura would find herself with far fewer callers to deal with!

Today's lesson comes from Malachi, the last book in the Old Testament. Malachi, the last Old Testament prophet chronologically, is the final messenger of God to address God's people before the gap of 400 years until the New Testament era begins. As we will see today, the book of Malachi closes the Old Testament with an appeal from God that is appropriate for his people to hear, whether in an Old Testament or a New Testament setting. It may be summarized as, "Now go do the right thing."

B. LESSON BACKGROUND

Malachi's circumstances were somewhat different from those of the other prophets we have studied this quarter. Yet the basic thrust of what all these men of God had to say is the same: being part of God's covenant people means much more than basking in a special status. God expects a certain lifestyle of those who lay claim to that status. One of the primary tasks of God's prophets throughout the Old Testament was to call his people to account when they failed to carry out their sacred responsibility.

DEVOTIONAL READING:
PSALM 34:11-22
BACKGROUND SCRIPTURE:
MALACHI 2:17–4:3
PRINTED TEXT:
MALACHI 2:17–3:5; 4:1

LESSON AIMS

After participating in this lesson, each student will be able to:

1. Summarize what Malachi said in response to questions about God's justice.

2. List some ways that a lack of commitment to doing right wearies the Lord today.

3. Make a plan to resist one cultural trend that opposes God's expectations for justice.

KEY VERSES

"See, I will send my messenger, who will prepare the way before me." . . . But who can endure the day of his coming? Who can stand when he appears?—Malachi 3:1, 2

Aug
26

Not much is known about Malachi himself. One bit of information is his name. In Hebrew it means "my messenger"—a theme that will become crucial in today's text. We must examine information within the book itself to learn the time in the history of God's people when Malachi likely prophesied.

Such an investigation points to the time of Nehemiah as perhaps the best fit for Malachi's ministry. This is because many of the sins highlighted in the book of Malachi are the same sins that Nehemiah had to confront. These included indifference toward the kind of sacrifices required by the Lord (Nehemiah 10:37-39; Malachi 1:6-14), disregard for the Lord's teaching concerning marriage (Nehemiah 13:23-27; Malachi 2:14-16), and the bringing of tithes and offerings to support the Lord's work (Nehemiah 10:37-39; 13:10-13; Malachi 3:8-10). Furthermore, the mention of a governor in Malachi 1:8 fits well with Nehemiah's time, since he was recognized by that title (Nehemiah 5:14).

Nehemiah had traveled to Jerusalem in the twentieth year of Artaxerxes, king of Persia (445 BC). He went there primarily to spearhead efforts to rebuild the wall of the city (Nehemiah 2:1-11). This was approximately 100 years after the Jews had first returned from captivity in Babylon, and about 70 years after the second temple had been completed through the encouragement of the prophets Haggai and Zechariah. Today's Scripture from Malachi focuses on his challenges to God's people in his own day. But it also highlights a portion of his glimpse into the future and of what God planned to accomplish through a messenger far greater than Malachi—the Lord Jesus Christ.

I. PEOPLE'S COMPLAINT (MALACHI 2:17)

A. MALACHI ALLEGES (v. 17a)

17a. You have wearied the Lord with your words.

Much of Malachi is written as if *the Lord* is engaging his people in a dialogue. Malachi pictures the Lord as making a statement; then he pictures the people as challenging the statement. The Lord then responds to the challenge. In so doing he calls attention to an area of his people's relationship with him that they have neglected. Examples of these dialogues are found in Malachi 1:2, 6, 7; 2:13, 14; 3:7, 8, 13-15, as well as in the verses before us.

Here Malachi claims *you have wearied the Lord with your words*. One may ask how this can be true in light of Isaiah 40:28, which declares, "Do you not know? Have you not heard? The Lord . . . will not grow tired or weary, and his understanding no one can fathom." But there is no contradiction. The Lord does not grow weary in the sense of losing his power, strength, or majesty; he can become weary (meaning frustrated and disappointed) with the behavior of his people and their refusal to heed his call to change.

B. PEOPLE ASK (v. 17b)

17b. "How have we wearied him?" you ask.

One can understand why the people would want to know how they have *wearied* the Lord. Have they spoken blasphemous, angry, or lying words? Have they been "babbling like the pagans" (as Jesus would later call it in Matthew 6:7) in their prayers? Is God concerned because their lives are not consistent with their words? What's the deal?

C. MALACHI ANSWERS (v. 17c)

17c. By saying, "All who do evil are good in the eyes of the Lord, and he is pleased with them" or "Where is the God of justice?"

Here is the answer to the people's inquiry. The words that have wearied the Lord are words that have questioned his *justice*. It appears to the people that the Lord no longer cares whether *evil* is punished or *good* is rewarded. Earlier, the prophet Isaiah declared, "Woe to those who call evil good and good evil" (Isaiah 5:20). Has the Lord done the same? It seems so to Malachi's audience.

Why would God's people speak so critically of the Lord? At this point in Old Testament history, God's people have been back in the promised land for nearly 100 years. They know the words of the prophets who had spoken of a glorious new day for God's people. That day is to be ushered in by the coming of the Branch (Isaiah 4:2-6; 11:1-3; Jeremiah 23:5-8; 33:15, 16). They know of God's promise to "place over them one shepherd, my servant David, and he will tend them" (Ezekiel 34:23).

But where is this special person? When will he come and do all that the prophets had said he would do? God's people had finished the temple many decades previously. Hadn't a prophet declared that at that time the Lord would "fill this house with glory" and that "the glory of this present house will be greater than the glory of the former house" (Haggai 2:7, 9)? The people have done their part—why hasn't the Lord done his? Where is his glory?

II. LORD'S COMING (MALACHI 3:1-5; 4:1)

A. PREPARATION (v. 1a)

1a. "See, I will send my messenger, who will prepare the way before me.

The Lord proceeds to answer the challenge. He has not forgotten his promises. "Where is the God of justice?" He is coming, but he will not come without a *messenger* to *prepare the way before* him.

Earlier we noted that the name *Malachi* means "my messenger." Here the Lord promises another messenger. Malachi 4:5 describes him as "the prophet Elijah." The New Testament is clear that John the Baptist is the one who fulfills Malachi's prophecy in his role as the forerunner of Christ (Mark 1:1-4). Jesus equated John the Baptist's ministry with the promised coming of Elijah (Matthew 17:10-13).

THE ADVANCE TEAM

My wife and I were in Cincinnati, Ohio, in the 1980s when then-President Ronald Reagan was to visit the city for a speech. As we drove down the highway on which the presidential motorcade was to pass, we noticed police officers guarding the route. We drove downtown that evening to see if we could get a glimpse of the president. The streets were cleared of traffic and there were no parked cars along the path the motorcade was to follow. Barricades were up.

Arriving that evening at our friends' house, we greeted our hostess. She worked as a nurse at a hospital between the airport and downtown. She said she would not be coming home until the president's plane had cleared Cincinnati airspace.

All of these details were accomplished by an *advance team*. This team took great care and precaution to ensure that every eventuality was covered and that the president was kept safe for his entire visit. The team wanted nothing to impede the safe progress of the president in accomplishing his mission.

John the Baptist came as a kind of one-man advance team for the Messiah. He did all he could to prepare the way for Jesus. The church today plays the role of the advance team for the second coming of Christ. How are you preparing yourself and the world for his return?   —A. E. A.

B. PLACE (v. 1b)

1b. Then suddenly the Lord you are seeking will come to his temple.

WHAT DO YOU THINK?

We hope that there would be very few who would openly state that those who do evil are good in the sight of God! Yet may we unknowingly convey this false message in other ways? How do you guard yourself in this respect?

Visual for Lesson 13. *Point to this depiction of John the Baptist as you ask, "How will you be the Lord's messenger today?"*

As noted previously, part of the reason God's people question his whereabouts and his justice is the fact that the *temple* had been finished many decades previously. Perhaps they are expecting a display of glory similar to what occurred when the first temple was dedicated (1 Kings 8:10, 11). Thus far nothing at all like that has been witnessed with the second temple.

However, the glory of *the Lord* will, in time, fill this second temple. That is exactly what takes place when the Lord Jesus Christ enters there during his earthly ministry.

The word *suddenly* depicts how most people are caught off guard when he arrives because he comes in a manner that is unexpected. God's glory will enter the temple, but not in the dramatic way it had filled the tabernacle (Exodus 40:34, 35) or the first temple. Rather it will come about because "the Word became flesh and made his dwelling among us. We have seen his glory, the glory of the One and Only, who came from the Father, full of grace and truth" (John 1:14).

WHAT DO YOU THINK?

How will you use Malachi 3:1b to influence your behavior as you wait for the return of Christ?

C. PROGRAM (v. 1c)

1c. The messenger of the covenant, whom you desire, will come," says the LORD Almighty.

Malachi now declares the Lord to be another type of messenger—*the messenger of the covenant*. Thus one messenger (John the Baptist) will prepare the way for another messenger (Jesus), who will establish a new covenant.

Earlier, Malachi referred to two other covenants. One was "the covenant with Levi," involving the priests; in Malachi's day they have "turned from the way" (Malachi 2:8) and neglected their sacred duties. The other is "the covenant of our fathers" (2:10), which probably refers to the covenant God had established at Sinai. That covenant had been profaned (again, 2:10). Clearly there was a need for a new and better covenant. That is exactly what Jesus comes to establish (Jeremiah 31:31-34; compare Hebrews 8:8-12; 10:16, 17).

It may be with a tinge of sarcasm that Malachi describes the messenger of the covenant as one *whom you desire*. The people of Malachi's day act as if they desire the Lord to come and vindicate himself. But will they be ready to welcome him when he does? Sadly, most in Jesus' day were not (John 1:11).

D. PURPOSE (vv. 2, 3a)

2, 3a. But who can endure the day of his coming? Who can stand when he appears? For he will be like a refiner's fire or a launderer's soap. He will sit as a refiner and purifier of silver.

The two questions in this portion of our text are to be considered rhetorical; that is, they are asked not in order to produce an answer but to challenge people to think. Lest people become too complacent about the Lord's promised coming, they should realize that when he comes he will make some serious changes!

A *refiner's fire* is used to burn away impurities from precious metals such as *silver* (compare Isaiah 48:10; Zechariah 13:9). *A launderer's soap* (an alkaline lye) is used to cleanse, bleach, and sometimes dye cloth. Most likely the cleansing represented by these processes refers to a spiritual cleansing.

Thus it is easy to see why the question is raised as to who can *endure* or *stand* such treatment. The sins from which people need to be cleansed are too numerous to count. This messenger of the covenant comes to perform what in today's terms would be considered an extreme makeover—on the inside!

WHAT DO YOU THINK?

In what areas of your life has God had to apply his refining fire and purifying soap? How is your life better as a result? In what areas do you still need God's purification?

E. PRODUCT (vv. 3b, 4)

3b, 4. He will purify the Levites and refine them like gold and silver. Then the LORD will have men who will bring offerings in righteousness, and the offerings of Judah and Jerusalem will be acceptable to the LORD, as in days gone by, as in former years.

The Levites include the priests, who have already been called to account for having "violated the covenant with Levi" (Malachi 2:8). The priests have also been charged with offering blemished, unacceptable offerings to the Lord (1:6-10). All of this will change when the Lord's purifying work has been accomplished.

These verses describe another dimension of the consequences of Jesus' work as the "messenger of the [new] covenant" (Malachi 3:1). One of the most significant characteristics of the new covenant is that every Christian serves the Lord as a priest (1 Peter 2:9; Revelation 1:6). Priests offer sacrifices and good works. Similarly, every Christian is called to offer the sacrifice of praise and good works to God (Hebrews 13:15, 16).

The period described as *the days gone by* and *former years* may refer to any period in the history of God's people when there was a greater consistency between the sacrifices they offered and the lives they lived. This would have been true during the reigns of godly kings such as David, Hezekiah, and Josiah.

F. PUNISHMENT (3:5; 4:1)

5. "So I will come near to you for judgment. I will be quick to testify against sorcerers, adulterers and perjurers, against those who defraud laborers of their wages, who oppress the widows and the fatherless, and deprive aliens of justice, but do not fear me," says the LORD Almighty.

While some will choose to accept the refiner's cleansing fire, others will refuse to undergo the purifying process. Those who refuse will one day learn, to their ruination, that the fire of refinement can also become a fire of *judgment*.

Several of the sins mentioned in this verse bring to mind some of the Ten Commandments as listed in Deuteronomy 5. These include the actions of *adulterers* (Seventh Commandment), *perjurers* (Ninth Commandment), and *those who defraud laborers of their wages* (this amounts to stealing, a violation of the Eighth Commandment).

To engage in the practices of *sorcerers* could violate the First Commandment, which prohibits the worship of other gods. The neglect of *the widows, the fatherless,* and *aliens* is forbidden in Exodus 22:21, 22; Deuteronomy 24:17-22. All of these sins (indeed, any sin) can be traced to one root cause: they are the consequence of failing to *fear* the Lord.

Recall how our printed text began with Malachi alluding to the people's inquiry: "Where is the God of justice?" (Malachi 2:17). The verse before us gives the answer: he will come, and his judgment will be *quick* when he does come. Malachi's words are reminiscent of what Peter writes concerning Jesus' return in 2 Peter 3:9, 10.

MISTAKEN IDENTIFY

I was visiting a church one Sunday for the first time. In talking with the minister, he learned that I too was a preacher. But somewhere along the line he got my first name (Gene) confused with another man he knew (Gus). Gus and I have the same last name, although we are not related and have never met.

At the close of the service, the preacher called on me for the prayer. Before I prayed, he told the congregation about the family of Gus and how they had meant so much to his family through the years back in West Virginia. Many

WHAT DO YOU THINK?

Why do you think that many today do not fear the Lord? In what ways would your life change for the better if you had a greater fear of the Lord?

PRAYER

Father, forgive us when we fail to do right. Forgive us for those times when a Christian's influence was needed—yet we remained silent and inactive. May we follow the example of Jesus, "who went around doing good" (Acts 10:38). May our light shine in this sinful world. In Jesus' name, amen.

HOW TO SAY IT

Artaxerxes. Are-tuh-ZERK-seez.

Babylon. BAB-uh-lun.

Elijah. Ee-LYE-juh.

Ezekiel. Ee-ZEEK-ee-ul or Ee-ZEEK-yul.

Haggai. HAG-eye or HAG-ay-eye.

Hezekiah. Hez-ih-KYE-uh.

Malachi. MAL-uh-kye.

Nehemiah. NEE-huh-MY-uh.

Persia. PER-zhuh.

Sinai. SIGH-nye or SIGH-nay-eye.

Zechariah. ZEK-uh-RYE-uh.

THOUGHT TO REMEMBER

Right makes might—not just believing it, but doing it.

came to me after the service just thrilled at the great story the preacher had told about "my family."

This case of mistaken identity was hard to deal with given the situation. But there is another case of mistaken identity that is even worse. We see the fatherless and the widow, and we mistake them for the lazy who shouldn't eat (2 Thessalonians 3:10). Though we may smugly rejoice at the thought that swift judgment will be meted out on the sorcerers and the adulterers, we fail to see that the same judgment will be made against those who ignore innocent people who are in genuine need.

—A. E. A.

4:1. *"Surely the day is coming; it will burn like a furnace. All the arrogant and every evildoer will be stubble, and that day that is coming will set them on fire," says the LORD Almighty. "Not a root or a branch will be left to them."*

This verse also emphasizes the certainty of coming judgment. Both the attitudes of *the arrogant* and the actions of *every evildoer* are highlighted. Earlier prophets had used the terms *root* and *branch* as the basis for prophecies concerning the coming Messiah (Isaiah 4:2; 11:1; Jeremiah 23:5; 33:15). Now we see that this judgment pronounced by Malachi will be so complete as to leave *not a root or a branch*.

Thus we have seen today's text describe the impact of both the first and second comings of the messenger of the covenant—Jesus. With his first coming, he initiates a ministry of cleansing and purifying through his sacrificial death on the cross and his resurrection. That ministry continues through the testimony of faithful Christians who bear witness to what Jesus can do for others through the gospel message.

At his second coming, however, the refining ministry of Jesus will mean judgment on those who have not accepted for themselves his cleansing power. It is similar to saying that those who do not acknowledge Jesus as the "cornerstone" (1 Peter 2:6) will find him to be "stone that causes men to stumble and a rock that makes them fall" (1 Peter 2:8). The kind of rock and the kind of refiner that Jesus will be for us is up to us. Our choice!

CONCLUSION

The phrase "might makes right" is familiar. This reflects a belief that the strong or those in positions of authority generally gain the upper hand because of their ability to exercise sheer force. The supremacy they possess due to these factors gives them the power to determine what is "right" and to enforce their will on others.

The more biblical view (and the theme of today's study) is that "right makes might." When an individual is committed to doing right in the sight of the Lord, he or she gains a sense of accomplishment and purpose that not even the mightiest "might makes right" advocate can possess.

We began with a reference to Dr. Laura's oft-heard counsel, "Now go do the right thing." Consider how often Jesus gave essentially the same challenge. After telling the parable of the Good Samaritan, Jesus said, "Go and do likewise" (Luke 10:37). He told the disciples after washing their feet, "I have set you an example that you should do as I have done for you" (John 13:15).

Have you learned some important lessons from your studies this quarter? Sit down and make a list of the top ten lessons you have gleaned. With each one, list an action step that you can take in order to apply that particular insight. And then—"Go and do likewise."

Discovery Learning

This page contains an alternative lesson plan emphasizing learning activities. Classes desiring such student involvement will find these suggestions helpful. The next page is a reproducible activity page to further enhance discovery learning.

LEARNING GOALS

After this lesson, each student will be able to:

1. Summarize what Malachi said in response to questions about God's justice.

2. List some ways that a lack of commitment to doing right wearies the Lord today.

3. Make a plan to resist one cultural trend that opposes God's expectations for justice.

INTO THE LESSON

To open today's lesson, say, "In 1989, a researcher developed a model for robotic behavior. The author, Pattie Maes, says that for a robot the act of 'doing the right thing' should have the following characteristics:

1. It favors actions that are goal-oriented;

2. It favors actions relevant to the current situation;

3. It favors actions that contribute to the ongoing goal;

4. It looks ahead to avoid hazardous situations;

5. It never completely breaks down, even when certain parts fail;

6. It is reactive and fast."

Ask your students to imagine they are writing a manual for humans "to do the right thing." What characteristics would they specify for humans in this regard? Write ideas on the board. When you finish discussing this exercise, tell your students that today's lesson deals with God's explanation of how to do the right thing.

As an alternative, obtain a recording of Handel's *Messiah* and play one or two tracks based on today's text (Malachi 3:2, 3): "But Who May Abide the Day of His Coming?" and "And He Shall Purify." Then tell your class that today's lesson explains these words from Malachi.

INTO THE WORD

Use the Lesson Background and commentary on Malachi 2:17 to discuss the situation in Judah leading up to Malachi 3. Focus on the final question in verse 17: "Where is the God of justice?" Ask why students think that God would be weary of Judah's whining and how Malachi 3:1–4:1 is God's answer to the above question.

Next, divide your class into groups of three or four. Direct attention to the activity The Lord Has Come! in the student book. If you don't use the student book, provide paper and pencils; assign each team the follow-

ing passages: Malachi 3:1-5; 4:1; Mark 1:1-4; Luke 2:21-32, 41-47; John 1:14; 7:14, 33-41; Hebrews 8:8-10; 13:15, 16; 2 Peter 3:8-13; Revelation 20:7-15.

Instruct each group to paraphrase the Malachi passages, indicating how each verse is fulfilled in the New Testament. For example, Malachi 3:1a could be paraphrased, "See, I'm going to send John the Baptist to prepare the way for Jesus."

Tell your students that their paraphrases should answer the following questions: 1. Who prepared the way for the promised Messiah? 2. On what occasions did Jesus come to his temple? 3. What new covenant was brought by the Messiah? Why? 4. How were the people to be refined? 5. What will judgment be like for the wicked?

When your teams finish their studies, use the lesson commentary to evaluate the results.

INTO LIFE

Remind your students of their answers to the first exercise in today's lesson; then read the following hypothetical situations. Ask volunteers to suggest responses to each that reflect God's concern for doing the right thing.

Situation #1. A pro-abortion organization has opened a clinic in your area "to ensure the availability of safe, legal abortions to women who desire to make that choice." What can your congregation do to offer women an alternative consistent with God's Word? How will your response promote justice for pre-born children?

Situation #2. A local atheist has sued your school district to stop the daily recital of the Pledge of Allegiance on the ground that the phrase *under God* violates the First Amendment's separation of church and state. What can you do in response?

Situation #3. Your community newspaper has printed an editorial accusing a political candidate of being "too religious" because he has admitted that he consults the Bible when forming his position on moral and political issues. What would you say in a letter to the editor?

Situation #4. Use the skit from the Reproducible Page. What do you say to the business people portrayed?

After discussing their thoughts, encourage your students to act accordingly this coming week in response to other challenges to their faith.

The Business Meeting

For this skit you will need three chairs, arranged in a row at the front of the class, facing the back of the classroom. The scene opens with George, Bob, and Karen sitting together as if at a conference table.

GEORGE: Well, it looks like we are all here. Let's begin the meeting with prayer. Lord, help us to make good decisions about our business today, because a lot of shareholders are depending on us.

KAREN: Amen!

GEORGE: You know why I called this meeting. Sales of our tomato-turnip juice cocktail product are running 10% below projections. The president says we have to reverse that trend soon or close this plant. Ideas?

KAREN: Product Development has developed a new "lite" version of our juice. It will have half the calories because we will add more water. We can call it "new and improved" and charge the same as our regular juice. That should increase brand sales by 20% and profits by 26%.

BOB: Shouldn't we charge less since the product is watered down? That only seems fair to me.

GEORGE: Bob! What has gotten into you today? Have you seen the price of bottled water? Trust me, the public will pay full price for our new "lite" line—especially when they see the added health benefits.

BOB: What added health benefits? I thought the juice was supposed to be *very* healthy?

GEORGE: You know: less sugar, more water. I'm sure the lab boys will figure something out.

KAREN: Also, Human Resources recommends that we cut all production workers to 29 hours max per week. That way they are considered part-time, and we don't have to pay them benefits. The savings in health insurance alone will be substantial.

GEORGE: Great idea! Pass the word that we are cutting hours the first of next month.

BOB: Wait a minute, George. How can we do this to our employees? We don't pay them that much as it is. How will they make ends meet with less pay and no benefits?

GEORGE: Bob, it's perfectly legal. They'll get by. It's not like they can expect to retire on what we pay them anyway. Besides, it doesn't matter in the long run. We've already decided to close the plant next year.

BOB: What? When was this decision made? Why haven't we been told?

KAREN: We've been planning this, very quietly, for some time.

GEORGE: That's right. We're moving off shore to take advantage of the cheaper labor.

KAREN: You'd better pack your sunscreen and put your home up for sale now, Bob. I suspect that real estate prices here are going to drop a bit when the word gets out.

GEORGE: Well, that about wraps up this meeting. Bob, would you close with prayer?

What parts of this meeting would the Lord be pleased with? What parts would he be displeased with? Explain your reasons.